A Parish for the Federal City

Morris J. MacGregor

A Parish for the Federal City

St. Patrick's in Washington, 1794–1994

The Catholic University of America Press

Washington, D.C.

The paper used in this publication meets the
minimum requirements of American National Standards for Information Science—Permanence of Paper
for Printed Library materials.
ANSI Z39.48-1984

LIBRARY OF CONGRESS CATALOGING-IN-PUBLICATION ÐATA
MacGregor, Morris J., 1931–
    A parish for the federal city : St. Patrick's in Wash-
ington, 1794–1994 / by Morris J. MacGregor.
        p.   cm.
    Includes bibliographical references and index.
    1. St. Patrick's (Church : Washington, D.C.)—His-
tory.   2. Washington (D.C.)—Church history.
I. Title.
BX4603.W32M6   1994
282'.753—dc20
93–49694
ISBN 0-8132-0801-7   ISBN 0-8132-0802-5 (pbk.)

CONTENTS

ILLUSTRATIONS

The illustration on p. 43 is courtesy of the White House; that on p. 71, courtesy of the Historical Society of Washington; those on pp. 105, 106, and 205, courtesy of the Prints and Photographs Division, Library of Congress; those on pp. 307, 336, 359, and 394, courtesy of the *Catholic Standard.* All other illustrations used in this work are from the archives of St. Patrick's Church and Academy.

PREFACE

This volume recounts the history of St. Patrick's, a parish about to begin its third century of service to the people of Washington. Although St. Patrick's was the first Catholic church established in the new federal city, a number of Catholic institutions preceded it along the shores of the Potomac. Private and public chapels dotted the region in the late colonial period, followed in subsequent decades by congregations in nearby Montgomery County, Georgetown, and Alexandria. In 1789, eleven years before the arrival of the federal government, Georgetown College opened its doors on the palisades above the river. Yet St. Patrick's was altogether unique among these and later organizations because of its special relationship to the hierarchy and the nation's leaders, its leadership in diocesan affairs, and its contribution to the development of educational and charitable organizations in the capital. Throughout much of its history St. Patrick's could rightly claim that it stood at the hub of Catholic life in Washington.

No religious institution, especially one in the heart of the capital, could remain immune to forces shaping the nation and the American church. Certainly St. Patrick's history demonstrates how immigration, race relations, financial cycles, even the concept of universal education profoundly affect a congregation animated by the desire to serve God and neighbor in Washington. Similarly, most of the major issues that have affected development of the church in the United States, including questions of church-state relations, nativism and cultural isolation, evangelization, and ecumenism, all had a measurable impact on Washington's downtown parish. For two centuries St. Patrick's congregation routinely transcended parochial concerns to become involved in the broad issues of the day—a tendency, I believe, that justifies the extended discussion in what follows of the pressing concerns of the city, nation, and American church.

Despite my determination to discuss such issues in a way that emphasized the role of the people in the pews, available sources stubbornly thwarted such intentions and led to an administrative history written largely from the top down. Although historians have developed increasingly sophisticated techniques to measure public attitudes and their influence on the policies and practices of large organizations, histories of institutions like St. Patrick's still depend principally on written records. It is the nature of such sources to reflect primarily the thoughts and actions of prelates and pastors. This is not entirely unfortunate, since St. Patrick's has been blest with several remarkable leaders at once high-spirited, eloquent, and ambitious to spread the word, succor the needy, and elevate the people of the city. Moreover, to the author's good fortune, these strong and colorful personalities left a wealth of anecdotal material useful in illuminating the attitudes and goals of a vanished age. Even so, enough data survives to provide at least a glimpse of a congregation that from time to time cast off its habitual deference to express strongly held views or demand a hearing for its ideas.

Surprisingly, such an important religious institution has attracted little scholarly interest. A parish history by Milton Smith was published in 1904 (and slightly revised for a second edition in 1933). This work is invaluable for its wealth of factual information even if it remains stubbornly silent on motivation. Motivation, however, was a principal consideration in Father David H. Fosselman's 1952 doctoral dissertation on the adaption of the downtown parish to ecological change. My debt to this scholarly work is spelled out in the footnotes. These notes also indicate my debt to Brother Thomas W. Spalding, C.F.X., whose *Premier See* is rightfully considered the definitive history of the Baltimore archdiocese.

The hundreds of references in this manuscript notwithstanding, relatively few written records survive to relate the parish's long, rich history. With certain exceptions, the priests and people did not bother their bishop about many things; consequently, the important archival collections possess sparce information about St. Patrick's. Nor did the parish always take adequate measures to preserve documents relating to its heritage. This shortage of primary documentation has forced me to rely far more than I would like on newspaper accounts, secondary works, and, for the recent period, oral histories. Wherever possible, I have sought multiple sources to verify information in these accounts.

Such research has placed me in debt to many people. For their constant support and encouragement I would like to thank St. Patrick's pastor, Msgr. Donald S. Essex, and the president of the Paul VI Institute for the Arts, Msgr. Michael diTeccia Farina. They have been boon companions in this journey of ecclesiastical detection. Drawing upon his unique association with the parish and his own investigations into the history of Catholicism in early Washington, Msgr. Farina has been a particularly valuable consultant. Similarly, I thank three gifted laymen associated with the parish for sharing their specialized knowledge: Kenneth T. Pribanic, the author of the parish's guide to its furnishings and architecture; Jay R. Rader, the minister of music for St. Patrick's; and Dr. James F. Breen, an authority on local Catholic history.

Many people shared with me their recollections of St. Patrick's, and their contributions are set forth in the notes. Here I would like to give special thanks to Archbishop Philip M. Hannan; Msgrs. E. Robert Arthur and Thomas B. Dade; five principals of St. Patrick's Academy, all members of the Holy Cross Congregation: Sisters Miriam André Williams, Marie Julie Shea, Eleanor Anne McCabe, Jovanna Hanlon, and Mary Louise Full; and George G. Pavloff and Fathers David J. Conway and Donald P. Brice, associate pastors in recent decades. Others who deserve special mention include: Patricia Murray, an Academy alumna, Msgr. Edward B. Carley, an expert on old churches of the Eastern Shore, Elizabeth L. Sagle, for her help in interpreting nineteenth-century financial records, and Jennifer L. Altenhofel, who generously shared her findings on Irish immigrants in Washington.

Of the many archivists and librarians who smoothed my path and increased my understanding of St. Patrick's past, I must especially thank Father Paul K. Thomas, archivist of the Archdiocese of Baltimore, Rev. Mr. Bernard A. Bernier, who holds a similar post in Washington, Father John W. Bowen, S.S., director of the Sulpician Archives of Baltimore, Sister M. Campion Kuhn, archivist of the Sisters of the Holy Cross, Carl Roesch, archivist of the Diocese of Syracuse, Jon Reynolds and Anthony Zito, archivists of Georgetown and Catholic Universities respectively, and Sister Mary Nona McGreal, O.P., coordinator of Project Opus, a collaborative history of the Order of Preachers in the United States. Among librarians I gratefully note the special contribution and support of Carolyn Lee, director of Catholic University's Special Libraries. I also want to acknowledge the assistance of the staff of the Historical Society of Washington and the knowledgeable librarians in the D.C. Public Library's Washingtoniana Collection.

I was amazed at the ease with which men like Fathers Aldo P. Petrini and Joseph A. Ranieri translated Latin and Italian documents for me, a task made considerably more difficult by nineteenth-century handwriting and abbreviations. I gained important insights from the translations and textual criticisms of Propaganda Fide documents provided by my cousin, Professor Alexander P. MacGregor of the University of Illinois. His ability to analyze the intentions of prelates through their sometimes subtle choice of Latin phraseology is suggestive of further studies that could be undertaken.

Fresh from a long career in American military history, I needed the safety net of expert readers. I am grateful for the careful attention given the manuscript by Msgr. Robert O. McMain, the Washington archdiocesan historian, Brother Thomas Spalding of Spalding University, Sister Joan Bland, S.N.D.deN., of Trinity College, Nelson F. Rimensynder, authority on local history, Msgr. Robert F. Trisco, a member of Catholic University's faculty, and archivist Bernard Bernier. Any errors that remain in the text are mine; there would be far more without the help of these generous critics.

This book was ably edited by Susan Needham, whose insights very much helped to shape its final version. Anne Theilgard, of Kachergis Book Design, designed and typeset the book for the Catholic University of America Press, which generously agreed to set the notes at the bottom of the page. This placement necessitated the use of many abbreviations, which are defined at the head of the bibliography.

Finally, I want to thank two long-time friends. Father Paul F. Liston introduced me to the project, endured all my questions and doubts, and encouraged me to complete the task. He is a gifted stylist and grammarian, and it is to honor his constant exhortations concerning the misuse of conjunctions that the overused "but" never appears in this preface. John W. Elsberg, who is the chief editor of the U.S. Army's history program, is, as he would say, not of this flock. His knowledge of how large, disciplined institutions operate, however, has forced me to clarify many of my amorphous ideas about St. Patrick's and its long history.

Morris J. MacGregor
July 4, 1993

A Parish for the Federal City

CHAPTER I

An Old Religion in a New City

ON APRIL 14, 1794, Anthony Caffry, an Irish-born priest living in Washington, informed the Commissioners of the District of Columbia that "the increasing congregation of this city" lacked a place to worship. He wanted to meet with the commissioners to discuss acquiring land on which to build a church. Although unsold lots were plentiful and demand embarrassingly light, Caffry nevertheless took the time to explain in some detail why such an enterprise deserved the commissioners' support. Not only, he claimed, would it uplift the people at large by exposing them to the holy maxims of the gospel, but a church named in honor of St. Patrick would also make the city "exceedingly pleasing and familiar" to great numbers of his fellow countrymen.[1] In advancing these arguments, Caffry, who was undoubtedly seeking a well-situated site at a bargain price, revealed a canny understanding of his

1. Ltr., Caffry to The Honourable Commissioners, 14 Apr 1794, Letters Received, Records of the Commissioners of the District of Columbia, 1791–1802, vol. 1, ltr. 361, RG 42, NARA. Caffry's name has been spelled in various ways over the years. The priest himself consistently spelled it as rendered above.

I

audience. By 1794 the commissioners had come to recognize a settled and peaceful citizenry and a plentiful labor force as two of their most pressing concerns.

Caffry's reference to the city and its growing population was itself a subtle form of flattery. Even by the modest standards then prevailing, one would have been hard pressed to call Washington a growing city in the spring of 1794. In contrast to the bustling and independent ports of Georgetown and Alexandria (which, with Washington, formed the new District of Columbia) the community was largely moribund despite the commissioners' deadline to build a new capital by 1800. Most of its 450 citizens lived in rude dwellings grouped along a few primitive streets and pathways that cut across the hills and ridges rising above the confluence of the Potomac River and the Eastern Branch (later called the Anacostia). The main activity disturbing the prevailing rural calm centered around the rising outlines of what were to become two mighty and noble edifices, the President's House on a ridge overlooking the Potomac and the Capitol building, which was beginning to dominate Jenkins Hill, a mile to the east.

Father Caffry's request must have pleased the commissioners. The building of a church signified a gathering sense of community, reinforced expectations of more citizens and perhaps more skilled workers, and above all, implied that some people felt a sense of permanence in what was still an extremely tenuous enterprise. With the clock rapidly ticking toward their 1800 deadline, the harried administrators seized the new pastor's initiative as a step toward a permanent, viable community.

Creating a Federal City

The idea of building a capital from the ground up was unique to the United States, in part an expression of its continuing infatuation with the frontier and the pioneer spirit.[2] The creation of a federal enclave

2. Unless otherwise indicated, the following essay on the founding of Washington is based on Bob Arnebeck's *Through a Fiery Trial: Building Washington, 1790–1800* (Lanham, Md.: Madison Books, 1991), William Seale's *The President's House: A History* (Washington, D.C.: White House Historical Association, 1986), and James Sterling Young's *The Washington Community 1800–1828,* (New York: Columbia University Press, 1966). It also uses Constance McLaughlin Green's *Washington: A History of the Capital, 1800–1950* (Princeton: Princeton University Press, 1976 edition), and H. Paul Caemmerer, "Early Washington and Its Art," *Records of the Columbia Historical Society* (hereafter *RCHS*), vols. 48–49 (1946–47): 209–18.

independent of the states also had a practical purpose. Since 1774 the central government had dwelt like a poor stepchild in a number of different locales, frequently subject to the pressing parochial demands of its hosts. The final indignity occurred in 1783, when a group of Pennsylvania soldiers marched on Congress, then in session in Philadelphia, to demand back pay. Congress fled to Trenton and later to New York, but the memory of that incident prompted the Framers to insert a provision in the new Constitution for an independent seat of government under the exclusive legislative control of Congress.

A bill to create that permanent home was one of the new government's first items of business. Although the vote in 1790 promised to be close, a deal was finally struck, and Congress accepted an offer from Maryland and Virginia for a ten-mile-square site along the Potomac north of the Eastern Branch. The exact spot was to be chosen by President George Washington, who would supervise the erection of government buildings in time for occupancy in 1800. Except for the modest start-up money promised by Maryland and Virginia, the project was expected to pay for itself. This, and the closeness of the vote, produced a sense of impermanence about the enterprise that would continue to haunt Washington's inhabitants for more than a quarter century, coloring the progress of all the city's institutions, civic, commercial, and religious.

George Washington knew and loved the area well and chose quickly. The capital would not be the lively port of Georgetown, but instead a new Rome carved from the wilderness, a symbol of the new government itself. He sent his choice to Congress in January 1791, along with the request that the law be amended so that the district could include the eastern shore of the Eastern Branch with its southern tip extended to include his hometown, Alexandria. The federal city itself would include all the land between the rivers below a boundary road connecting the two, roughly along the path of today's Florida avenue.

This region might be described as a wilderness in the metaphoric sense, but in reality it had been settled for more than a century. Its sixteen landowners (proprietors) enjoyed their farms that rose to bluffs and plateaus providing fine views of the two rivers. The many acres of lowland seen along the Potomac today were mostly later additions, the result of ambitious land-filling operations of more recent times. The site Washington chose contained five thousand acres covered by great stands of oak and sycamore interspersed with cultivated, fenced fields and orchards. Its major watercourse, a tidal creek, flowed south and then west, with a wide estuary leading to the Potomac. The area was a remarkably healthy place, suffering none of the deadly fever epidemics of other eastern cities. The often-heard charge that Washington was built on a swamp was the latter-day invention of politicians desperate to explain away their failure to build the city expeditiously.

As required by law, the President appointed a three-man commission in 1791 to acquire land for the new city, sell property, and supervise the construction of the federal buildings. Included among its members was Daniel Carroll of Rock Creek, a wealthy Maryland landholder, signer of the Constitution, and brother of the first American Catholic bishop, John Carroll. While the President and his commissioners completed negotiations with the local owners for the purchase of their land, Major Pierre L'Enfant commenced planning the new Rome. One of that remarkable group of Frenchmen who fought with the Patriots during the Revolution, L'Enfant produced a masterpiece of civic design. It set out wide thoroughfares that connected all parts of the city, creating a series of awe-inspiring settings for its public edifices. Overlaid on a geometry of noble avenues, government buildings, and parks was a grid of narrower streets that centered on the Capitol and created the familiar quadrants. These streets were meant to provide for the residential and commercial needs of the community. L'Enfant intended both the Capitol and President's House to be major focal points from which Washington would radiate evenly. This hope was never completely realized, and the eastern part of the city never developed in ways comparable to the northwest, with lasting consequences for developing institutions, including the churches.[3]

Armed with the land and a site plan approved by Washington, the commissioners, working with Secretary of State Thomas Jefferson, named the city after the President, the district itself after Columbus, the avenues after the states, and the streets somewhat prosaically by number and letter. They transformed Jenkins Hill into Capitoline Hill and the meandering Goose Creek into the Tiber (thus endorsing the initiative of an earlier proprietor named Pope, who grandiosely called his plantation "Rome" and the creek "Tiber"). They also issued copies

3. This phenomenon has frequently been noted. See, for example, Wilhelmus B. Bryan, "Why the City Went Westward: A Discussion," *RCHS* 7 (1904): 107–45. For its effect on the development of the city's churches, see David H. Fosselman, "Transitions in the Development of a Downtown Parish: A Study of Adaptions to Ecological Change in St. Patrick's Parish, Washington, D.C.," (Ph.D. dissertation, The Catholic University of America, 1952), 90–94 and passim.

of the incomplete plan and nationally advertised and otherwise promoted the sale of government lots at an auction scheduled for October 1791.

The auction proved a fiasco. Only thirty-five of the government's ten thousand lots sold. There were some valid excuses—the weather was bad, L'Enfant's detailed design was never published, and the survey of lots by Andrew Ellicott and Benjamin Banneker had not progressed beyond a small area just north of the President's House—but, ominously, a second auction a year later similarly failed. Such serious problems strengthened the commissioners' resolve to oppose the irascible L'Enfant's grandiose plans. Finally even Washington, who agreed with L'Enfant that the new city needed a monumental character, had enough, and the Frenchman was dismissed. At Jefferson's suggestion, a competition was held for the design of the Capitol and President's House. The former was won by an amateur architect from Philadelphia, Dr. William Thornton; the latter, by an Irish immigrant, James Hoban.

Hoban arrived in Washington in September 1792 and lived there for his remaining thirty-nine years, an honored citizen and a leading member of St. Patrick's congregation. Trained in Dublin, he had been in America about seven years, most recently working in Charleston, South Carolina. He quickly found favor with the President, and his growing reputation as a practical and honest businessman and as a leader and go-getter led the commissioners to appoint him general supervisor of construction. By far his greatest challenge was to attract skilled workers to an area that lacked the basic necessities and any promise of future prosperity. At his urging, the commissioners finally began advertising for help across the United States and overseas. They also paid Georgetown shippers to provide passage for Irish immigrants, guaranteeing the newcomers employment and offering them advances of thirty shillings in return for a form of indentured service. Daniel Carroll himself had found a group of Irish workers for L'Enfant in 1791, and Hoban obtained bricklayers, sawyers, and masons from Ireland. In August 1792 he returned to Charleston to recruit workers, presumably some of his Irish compatriots.

Exact figures are unknown, but it is safe to assume that a significant number of the skilled workers on the federal buildings as well as the few private structures erected during the 1790s were Irish born. For example, although most of the stonecutters working on the President's House under the redoubtable master, Collen Williamson, were Scots, a rival group working on the Capitol under Cornelius McDermott

Roe, a business ally of Hoban, were mostly Irish. The brickmakers and masons were for the most part Americans from the middle states, but their numbers included many Irish in the gangs that produced each day's five thousand bricks. The carpenters and mechanics were predominantly Irish. Those Irish workers who came later in the decade would constitute a major part of the force that cleared the public lands and streets, worked on the new Rock Creek bridge, and dug local canals. Many of these immigrants, too, were skilled laborers reduced by economic necessity to menial jobs.[4]

The living conditions of even the skilled workers were extremely primitive. L'Enfant had constructed a series of small dwellings at the building sites similar to slave quarters on local plantations. He also erected a carpenter's shop or hall near the center of today's Lafayette Park. As the work progressed, more sheds and shanties were added to the area, competing for space with brickyards, kilns, sawmills, and storehouses. Eventually Hoban had to build tenement-like barracks where men lived three to a room. Those with families shared these same miserable conditions or made do with temporary shanties nearby.

The worker's day began at six o'clock and included a substantial free meal and, for some, a liquor ration to fight the heat. For recreation, the workers formed their own trade organizations. The Scottish stonecutters had their Masonic lodge, to which Hoban, the Irish Catholic, belonged. The brickmasons had their "gang" and the carpenters their "hall." Constables appointed by the commissioners imposed dire punishment in the form of whippings, brandings, and banishment on those who disturbed the peace, but they overlooked the heavy drinking and gambling that were the principal forms of recreation among the hard-working men. Definitely not tolerated were "riotous and disorderly" houses like the one opened by Mrs. Betsy Donahue, the wife of one of the carpenters.[5]

Civic demonstrations and entertainments were rare in those difficult times. An exception occurred when President Washington came to lay the cornerstone of the new Capitol in September 1793. These festivities were planned in part to stimulate interest in a third auction

4. Fosselman, "A Downtown Parish," 10. See also Jennifer L. Altenhofel, "The Irish Century: A Story of Irish Immigrants and the Irish Community in the District of Columbia, 1850–1950," a paper submitted to D.C. Community Humanities Council, 1992.

5. William Seale offers a comprehensive picture of the life of Washington workers during the 1790s. See *The President's House*, 64–68.

of city lots, but the results were even more disappointing than before. In disgust the commissioners turned to a group of supposedly well-financed syndicates and speculators including James Greenleaf, Thomas Law, Robert Morris, and Samuel Blodgett. Accepting the promise of immediate construction as down payment, the commissioners sold them choice land, which the speculators immediately began selling in competition with the government. Their activities left a trail of broken commitments and abandoned building projects that led the city for the rest of the decade on a roller coaster ride of real estate booms, bankruptcies, and broken promises.

The gloomy prognosis heard among congressional opponents of the capital's location was far from universal in the spring of 1794. Blodgett's grand hotel, designed by Hoban, was finally beginning to rise at Seventh and E Streets, and a number of houses, including Hoban's own residence, were planned for F Street near Fourteenth. Greenleaf built fourteen houses in southwest, including four that survive today as Wheat Row. He also began the "Six Buildings" at Twenty-Second and Pennsylvania Avenue, while nearby, General Walter Stewart started another series of residences known as the "Seven Buildings." An infirmary went up in Judiciary Square and a wharf on the Eastern Branch. Although generally lagging behind, the eastern part of the city likewise saw new residential construction with some mansions on Capitol Hill and more modest dwellings near the Eastern Branch.

Small wonder that Caffry decided the time was right to buy land and raise an outward symbol of God's blessing on this new enterprise.

The Catholic Church in the New Republic

The problems Caffry would encounter in organizing St. Patrick's prefigured the experience of other congregations throughout the United States. In almost every quarter, Catholics were regarded as aliens, part of a mysterious minority that their fellow citizens sometimes hated but generally tolerated in keeping with the new spirit of the Revolutionary era. American Catholics also puzzled church leaders in Rome, who were sometimes genuinely alarmed at what they considered radical ideas concerning personal freedom, religious tolerance, and church-state relations.[6]

6. Unless otherwise noted, this essay on the American church is based on Jay P. Dolan's *The American Catholic Experience: A History from Colonial Times to the Present* (New York: Doubleday, 1985); James S. Olson's *Catholic Immigrants in America*

Several salient features of the native church emerged even before Catholics arrived in British North America. The religious strife that racked Tudor England in the sixteenth century had reduced Catholics to a small, severely persecuted minority. Resigned to Protestant dominance and denied close ties with Rome, the survivors sought merely to live at peace with their neighbors and to enjoy the consolations of their religion in private. To a large extent these ambitions were realized in the seventeenth century, when, despite sporadic repressions, Catholics entered on a period of benign neglect, during which their numbers increased and they achieved a delicate balance: while demonstrating their loyalty to Crown and government, they remained faithful followers of the Pope in Rome. This society was dominated by the upper-class, landed gentry, and religion centered around their manors, where they increasingly assumed leadership over the local lay people and the priests who privately ministered to them. It was these lay leaders, members of a persecuted minority that had come to appreciate the advantages of religious toleration, who brought Catholicism to Maryland in 1634.

Maryland was not designed primarily as a refuge for persecuted Catholics, but, like neighboring Virginia, was first and foremost a commercial enterprise founded for profit. Its proprietors, the Calvert family, were prominent Catholics who also enjoyed royal patronage. Cecil Calvert, the second Lord Baltimore, hoped to attract colonists from among his co-religionists, but most of them were optimistic about their future in England under the Stuarts and shunned the rigors of settlement in the New World. He was forced instead to recruit settlers from among the Protestant majority. When the *Ark* and the *Dove* set sail, their passenger lists included sixteen gentlemen, mostly Catholics, along with scores of artisans, laborers, and servants, mostly Protestants.

To ease the concerns of this Protestant majority and at the same time reassure the Catholics, Lord Baltimore sought to make religion a private affair without special governmental consideration. This sentiment was formally endorsed by the Maryland assembly in 1639, when it guaranteed all rights and liberties to "Holy churches within this

(Chicago: Nelson-Hall, 1987); and Thomas W. Spalding, *The Premier See: A History of the Archdiocese of Baltimore, 1789–1989* (Baltimore: The Johns Hopkins University Press, 1989). Also consulted were John Gilmary Shea's *The History of the Catholic Church in the United States,* vol. 2 (Akron, OH: McBride, 1886) and Peter A. Guilday's, *The Life and Times of John Carroll: Archbishop of Baltimore, 1735–1815* (New York: Encyclopedia Press, 1922).

province," but the attempt to keep religion out of politics failed. The Calverts lost control of the colony during the English civil war, which broke out in 1642, and for several years government in Maryland ceased to exist. The Catholic settlers were persecuted by their Puritan neighbors, their leaders and priests returned to England in chains. Later restored to power, Calvert and his assembly sought again in 1649 to defuse the religious debate by promulgating an "Act Concerning Religion."

This act of toleration, a major milestone in the struggle for religious freedom in America, was actually a last pragmatic effort by the Proprietor to solve a basic American problem—to achieve peace and harmony in a commonweal divided by conflicting religious loyalties. Limited in application—the law, for example, offered no safeguards for non-Christians—the measure nevertheless presented a practical, and for its time, unique prescription for religious peace when it guaranteed that none in the Province should "from henceforth bee any waies troubled, Molested or discountenanced for or in respect of his or her religion nor in the free exercise thereof."[7]

Such measures failed to save the New World haven for Catholics. The ascension of William and Mary to the throne in 1689 swept the Calverts from power and turned Maryland into a Crown colony. The era of toleration ended abruptly when the new assembly declared the Church of England the official religion of Maryland and instituted a series of penal laws that extinguished the civil rights of the Catholic minority. During the next thirty years measures were passed that systematically barred Catholics from the legal and teaching professions, imposed crippling taxes and restricted their rights of inheritance, denied them the right to hold public office, and as a final insult, disenfranchised them. The new laws also banned priests from saying Mass publicly and ended their successful proselytizing by outlawing their baptizing any but children of Catholic parents.

The upper house of the assembly, always more sympathetic to the Catholic gentry, worked to soften the lower house's most stringent measures. Some of the harshest forms of persecution were gradually ameliorated after 1720, but the Crown colony never restored full civil rights to Catholics during the colonial period and actually reinforced some of its strictest penal codes at mid-century, when doubts rose about Catholic loyalty during the colonial wars. No Catholic escaped

7. Reprinted in Henry Steele Commager, *The Documents of American History* (New York: Appleton Century Crofts, 1968), 31.

persecution under the Crown laws, but the social and economic advantages enjoyed by the gentry isolated most of the colony's three thousand Catholics from some of the harshest consequences. Despite legal restrictions, they continued to enjoy the consolations of their religion in the privacy of their domestic chapels. As a distinct social group, they married into each other's families, sent their sons abroad for education, imported their comforts and libraries, and pursued the usual recreations of the eighteenth-century landed class.

Later immigration not only dramatically increased the proportion of Catholics in Maryland by the end of the colonial period, but also introduced a new Catholic social class of small landowners, tenant farmers, and common laborers. Religious persecution mutually endured bound these new colonists to the old aristocracy in what became a tight-knit community. Together they attended religious services and encouraged vocations among their children. Together they sought toleration and the opportunity to live in peace as part of the larger, non-Catholic society. Just as the English Catholics had done in earlier times, Maryland Catholics in the decades before the Revolution evolved a distinctive religious outlook that would have a direct bearing on the congregations forming in Washington and elsewhere at the end of the century.

Since the foundation of the colony, Catholics had been ministered to by priests of the Society of Jesus. These Jesuits had braved high mortality rates, relentless repression, and incredible physical hardship to carry out their priestly duties. They were frustrated by the Proprietor's refusal, in the name of separation of church and state, to grant them special status. Bereft of subsidies, they were forced to support themselves while administering the sacraments and evangelizing both the Indians and their Protestant neighbors. Thus they established a network of farms, becoming in time among the greatest landowners in the colony. For 150 years, Catholicism in Maryland was supported by the profits from these commercial enterprises.

Maryland was a rural society, and the Catholic minority lived on widely scattered estates and farms, where distance and legal restrictions precluded the development of religious administration along the European model. Except in the early decades, when Protestants and Catholics might have shared the chapel in the capital at St. Mary's City, the village church with its resident priest was unknown in Maryland. Only those colonists living near one of the chapels erected by the Jesuits on their farms enjoyed a semblance of religious community. Most were forced to wait for infrequent visits by priests, some of whom, at considerable personal peril, rode regular circuits across the colony, preaching and administering the sacraments to neighboring families at the local estates and manor houses.

Despite the cohesion developed by the persecuted minority, Catholicism remained largely a private affair, one that emphasized personal devotion and prayer in the absence of frequent sacramental life and public ritual. This emphasis on interior piety started to give way at the end of the colonial period as Catholics, ignoring the prohibition against public worship, began to form congregations or primitive parishes around the Jesuit chapels. Suddenly, after 1763, in the wake of the French and Indian War, registers, account books, and the rest of parish paraphernalia appeared. Also coming into vogue were popular communal devotions such as those to the Sacred Heart of Jesus and the Blessed Sacrament.

Such changes would prove important in the evolution of Catholic worship in future decades, but in most essentials the position of American Catholics as a persecuted and isolated minority remained in 1770 as it had for generations. Change, when it did come in the next decade, would be sudden and total and would arise from forces that evolved within the secular community.

The American Revolution reflected a fundamental shift in the way people viewed government. Although imperfectly realized, most conspicuously in the case of slavery, the ideals of liberty, equality, and freedom of the individual animated the Patriot cause. This emerging respect for the individual was a gift of the Enlightenment philosophers and brought with it a new respect for freedom of conscience and religious toleration that would be enshrined in the United States Constitution. As members of a persecuted minority, Catholics were among the first to profit from this philosophical and political change.

There was a practical aspect to the sudden change in the status of Catholics. Pragmatic American leaders had come to understand the wisdom in Lord Baltimore's conclusion that religious toleration was the only solution to religious plurality. In their attempt to forge a new nation out of such disparate colonies, the leaders of the Continental Congress adamantly opposed "every thing like vexation on the score of Religion."[8] Although the 25,000 Catholics accounted for just one percent of the total population of the thirteen colonies, their concen-

8. John Carroll, "The Establishment of the Catholic Religion in the United States," trans. Charles C. Pise, repr. in Thomas O. Hanley, ed., *The John Carroll Papers* (hereafter *JCP*) (Notre Dame: University of Notre Dame Press, 1976), 1:408.

tration in Maryland and Pennsylvania made them critical to the future
in those key areas. Further, Congress was hoping to forge a partnership with England's enemy, Catholic France, and even entertained
hopes of alliance with French Catholics in Canada. Obviously the new
nation's treatment of its Catholic minority would influence the course
of these diplomatic efforts.

Catholics also contributed to the spread of religious toleration by
their actions during the Revolution. Throughout the colonies the people were choosing sides between the Patriots and the Loyalists. The
choice posed a special dilemma for American Catholics. Confronted
on one hand by anti-Catholic sentiment among their colonial neighbors and on the other by continuing repression by the British government, they cast their lot with the Patriots. Led by the nationally
prominent Charles Carroll of Carrollton, most Catholics in Maryland
joined the great majority of their co-religionists in Pennsylvania in
fighting for political freedom. Carroll represented Maryland in the
Continental Congress, where he signed the Declaration of Independence. He was later elected to the Maryland assembly that adopted
the state's constitution that abolished the religious penal codes. His
fellow Catholics quickly took advantage of their new freedom. In
great numbers they joined the local Committees of Safety that organized the Patriot cause in the states, ran for and frequently served in
public office, and fought under General Washington in the Continental Army.[9]

The sense that Catholics had become partners in a great national
cause not only won them acceptance by the Protestant majority, but
also helped break down the feelings of isolation that tend to haunt all
segregated minorities. All this was later deftly alluded to when President Washington told Catholic leaders, "Your fellow-citizens will not
forget the patriotic part which you took in the accomplishment of
their Revolution and the establishment of their government." He
went on to predict that the new government would guarantee equal
protection under the law.[10]

The spirit of liberty that animated the new nation's fundamental
laws could not but have had some effect on the ways American
Catholics thought about the organization of their own church. That

9. Charles H. Metzger, *Catholics and the American Revolution* (Chicago: Loyola University Press, 1962), esp. 273–79.

10. Ltr., George Washington to the Roman Catholics in the United States of America, 12 Mar 1790, repr. in John Tracy Ellis, ed., *Documents of American Catholic History*
(Milwaukee: Bruce Publishing, 1956), 176.

organization had lately come under intense scrutiny. In 1773, Pope Clement XIV, responding to problems in Europe, suppressed the Society of Jesus, leaving the American clergy dispirited and leaderless, their relations with Rome reduced to a vague and politically unacceptable tie through the Pope's vicar apostolic in London. Although the ex-Jesuits continued to minister in their local missions, the church in America clearly stood at a crossroads.

Into that crossroads strode the commanding figure of John Carroll, the father of the American hierarchy. It is difficult to ignore the striking parallel between Carroll and the Founding Fathers, particularly General Washington. Like Washington, Carroll readily embraced the Revolution and the spirit of freedom and individualism that animated it. He organized the government of the American church, deftly guiding it through the formative period of its history. He carefully fostered the Americanization of Catholic immigrants, whose millions in the next century would change the face of their adopted land and the American church. He constantly preached to his co-religionists in Europe the salutary effects of religious toleration, separation of church and state, and cooperation with non-Catholics. Under his leadership, the American church began to develop those singular characteristics that would in later times come to enrich the universal church's understanding of religious liberty.

Carroll, like many sons of the Maryland gentry, was educated at St. Omer's in French Flanders. From there he joined the Jesuit order. The suppression of the Society prompted the deeply troubled priest to come home. Using his mother's plantation near Rock Creek at Forest Glen, Maryland, as a base of operations, he ministered to Catholics in a far-flung mission that included parts of northern Virginia in an area centering on the homes of his Brent in-laws, later leading members of St. Patrick's congregation. Like other members of his family, Carroll played an active role in the Revolution. When the Continental Congress launched an abortive attempt to enlist the support of French Canadians, it asked Father Carroll to participate. The leader of the mission was Benjamin Franklin, and the friendship that developed during the trip between the old philosopher and the young priest would have lasting consequences on the future of the American church.

It was obvious that the church was in desperate need of organization. In 1783 Carroll arranged a meeting at which the former Jesuits discussed his ideas for a constitution of the American clergy and the disposition of the Jesuit properties. The group also petitioned the

Pope to appoint a superior for the American church, explaining that the war just concluded made it impossible to accept direction from abroad. Carroll was even more blunt when he reported on Catholic attitudes. He warned Rome that, while Catholics readily accepted the Pope's spiritual authority, they would never accept a vicar who represented the Congregation of the Propagation of the Faith (Propaganda), the arm of the Holy See charged with administering missions worldwide. If there was to be a bishop at the head of an independent diocese, let him be an American, preferably one elected by the American clergy.[11] Propaganda officials never gave up the idea of a vicar apostolic for the American church, but faced with an adamant American clergy, Rome temporized, agreeing to appoint an American superior. After further consultation that included conversations with the persuasive Benjamin Franklin, the Holy See named Carroll to the post in June 1784.

Although Carroll's powers were temporary and restricted, he never hesitated. He began by summing up for Propaganda, an audience largely ignorant of American political and social realities, the state of the church in the new Republic. He counted nearly 16,000 Catholics in Maryland, including 3,000 slaves; 7,000 in Pennsylvania; 1,500 in New York, 200 in Virginia, along with uncounted thousands living without any contact with priests, especially in the new regions of the trans-Appalachian west. Fewer than thirty priests were available to serve this population; although this was a burden on everyone, he argued that it was preferable to the wholesale employment of "incautious and imprudent priests."

He also assessed for Rome the piety of the American Catholics. He reported them assiduous enough in the exercise of religion, but missing that ardor that came from frequent reception of the sacraments and hearing the word preached. This he laid not only to the shortage of priests but also to the scattered nature of the congregations and the vast distances involved. He particularly noted a lack of fervor among the slaves, who were afforded little opportunity to receive religious instruction, and above all among the newly arriving immigrants, who, for the most part, he claimed, failed the essentials of religious duty.[12]

Carroll took seriously his obligation to educate his Roman superiors in the new spirit that had developed in the American church out of

11. Ltr., Carroll to Charles Plowden, 27 Feb 85, *JCP* 1:166–67.

12. Carroll, "Report for the Eminent Cardinal Antonelli Concerning the State of Religion in the United States of America," 1 Mar 1785, repr. in Ellis, *American Church Documents*, 151–54.

the decades of repression and the new way of looking at church-state relations, religious pluralism, and accommodation. He warned that toleration was still a new concept and might not survive if Rome failed to adapt, adding that a church dependent on foreign officials would be unacceptable to "our jealous government."[13] Far from something to fear, he saw this new freedom and toleration opening a great future for the church. Yet he kept returning to the same point: to prosper, the American church must emphasize its independent American spirit and shed any hint of foreignness. If the severe shortage of priests dictated the acceptance of foreign clergy, they must be sensitive to this attitude.

In the long run, Carroll believed, the American church needed to develop a strong, native clergy imbued with the American way of looking at things. Very early on he started planning for an American seminary and an academy to train Catholic clerics and laymen, plans that would soon see the foundation of St. Mary's Seminary and Georgetown College. Meanwhile, Carroll looked with a conciliatory spirit at the possibility of educating young Catholics at Washington College in Chestertown, Maryland (where he was a trustee), and at St. John's in Annapolis. He hoped to see Catholic teachers appointed at both schools.[14]

Carroll's position as superior of the American mission left him without adequate authority to deal with pressing problems concerning religious discipline and control of church property. In 1788, he and representatives of the clergy asked Pope Pius VI to create a diocese co-extensive with the boundaries of the United States and, at least initially, to allow the American priests to elect their own bishop. The Pope agreed, and after Baltimore, the most populous community in the most Catholic state, was chosen as his cathedral city, Carroll was overwhelmingly elected by his American colleagues.

During his first years as bishop, Carroll established a series of precedents that would affect the church for generations. He convened a synod of the clergy that established norms for the administration of the sacraments and set a new system for church finances, including a decree on voluntary contributions. In keeping with his support for church-state separation, Carroll rejected any proposal for state subsidy in his first pastoral letter. For the first time, native Catholics and new

13. Ltrs., Carroll to Giuseppe Doria-Pamphili (papal nuncio at Paris), 26 Nov 1784, and to Charles Plowden, 27 Feb 1785 (source of quote), both in JCP 1:152–53 and 166–67.

14. Ltrs., Carroll to Joseph Edenshink, Apr–Jun 1785, and to Charles Plowden, 24 Feb 1790, both in JCP 1:185–86 and 430–31.

immigrants alike were told they must support the church. To that end, the synod had ordered a collection taken up at each mass by trustees appointed by the pastor, the money to be divided in three equal parts: for the support of the pastor, for the upkeep of the church, and for the relief of the poor.

The word *pastor* was not accidental, for Carroll clearly intended from the start that in place of the old circuit-riding missionaries of colonial times, the American church would establish permanent parishes in fixed geographical areas. These parishes would have resident pastors financially supported by their congregations. As the Catholic population grew, congregations would be subdivided and more pastors appointed. Although several generations would pass before this system could be enacted in rural areas, parishes with fixed boundaries and regularly assigned clergy quickly began to spring up in the cities.

While concentrating on pressing ecclesiastical matters, Carroll continued to foster friendly relations with non-Catholics. Such associations came easy to the new bishop, whose family background led to a comfortable familiarity with many of the nation's leaders. He was well acquainted with President Washington and was once a guest at Mount Vernon. He used these friendships to advance Catholic claims for equality. In an address of homage after Washington's inauguration, Carroll and a group of prominent laymen reminded the general of the sacrifices made by Catholics during the Revolution and of the fact that their rights were still restricted in some states.[15] Probably the best example of the bishop's openness and tolerance is found in his prayer for civil authorities. The first synod decreed that this plea for divine protection be read in all churches following the gospel on Sundays. Still recited today on great national occasions, Carroll's words reveal how closely intertwined were his piety and patriotism and how great was his affection for his fellow citizens.[16]

Catholic Washington, 1794

Carroll's carefully argued beliefs did not fully reflect the religious and political thinking of all the clergy and laity, although they faith-

15. "An Address from the Roman Catholics of America to George Washington, Esq. President of the United States, 1790," copy in *JCP* 1:409–11.

16. Reprinted in Ellis, *American Church Documents,* 178–79. A copy of the prayer in Carroll's hand is preserved in the library at The Catholic University of America.

fully mirrored the attitudes of those Catholics who had lived for generations on land that was to become the new federal city. Many of these families could trace their history to the early days of the Maryland colony, and six of them were among the sixteen proprietors in the capital. Duddington and Cern Abbey manors, the seventeenth-century estates owned by branches of the Young and Carroll families, included a major part of the acreage transferred to the government. In addition to these families, a significant number of wealthy Catholics soon bought or inherited land in the city, including Dominic Lynch, John Nicholson, and Comfort Sands. Other major landholders living in the region and closely related to the proprietors through marriage and business were the Digges, Queens, Darnalls, Brents, Fenwicks, and Matthews. All would figure in the early history of the church in Washington.[17]

These families were the most prominent members of the Catholic community in the Washington area, but by 1794 they no longer constituted the majority. The number of immigrant artisans and laborers, principally Irish but including at least some Germans and Italians, had steadily increased as work progressed on various federal and private projects. Like the Maryland Catholics, the new Irish immigrants had been a persecuted minority, but the suppression in Ireland was far more savage, the British seemingly intent on obliterating the Irish language and culture. In contrast to the Maryland Catholics, who supported the concept of religious toleration that had evolved in their midst and stood ready to enter the American mainstream, the Irish newcomers hated the British and remained deeply suspicious of anything Protestant. These eighteenth-century immigrants, victims of intense poverty and illiteracy, had suffered for generations from a scarcity of priests, and they were consequently largely unschooled in church doctrine and irregular in their observance of religious duties.

African-Americans formed another significant element in this Catholic community. Although population figures for eighteenth-century Washington are somewhat speculative, it is certain that the District of Columbia counted 4,027 black residents in 1800, including 746

17. John Beverley Riggs, "Certain Early Maryland Landowners in the Vicinity of Washington," *RCHS* 48–49 (1946–47): 249–62, and Margaret B. Downing, "Development of the Catholic Church in the District of Columbia from Colonial Times until the Present," *RCHS* 15 (1912): 23–53. See also an address given by Msgr. Cornelius Thomas and reprinted as "St. Patrick's Church, Washington, Celebrates Its 125th Anniversary," Baltimore *Catholic Review*, 3 May 1919.

(139 freedmen and 607 slaves) in the city of Washington itself.[18] A significant number of these slaves were the property of the Catholic proprietors. Notley Young owned 265 slaves, who in 1791 lived scattered across his estate in southwest Washington. Daniel Carroll and his mother at nearby Rock Creek owned 91 slaves between them, and Ignatius Fenwick and William and Abraham Young all owned and employed slaves on their lands in the eastern part of the city. It was common for slaves in the colonial period to share the religion of their masters, and it is reasonably certain that a sizable portion of Washington's black population in 1794 was Catholic.

For many decades the wealthy Catholic families in the Washington area had observed the usual Maryland practice of acting as host for visiting priests and putting their private chapels at the disposal of local Catholics, white and black. Although Mass was probably celebrated in the Washington region during much of the seventeenth century, the first of record was said by Father Thomas Digges in the 1760s at the home of his Young relatives in their mansion on the banks of the Potomac near what is now Maine Avenue.[19]

The Washington region was one of the first to respond to Bishop Carroll's effort to make the parish the focus of church organization.[20] Carroll himself had built the first quasi-parish church, at Forest Glen, in 1775. Historically significant on two counts, St. John the Evangelist was the first church established by the secular clergy in the thirteen colonies and, after St. Peter's, Baltimore, the first erected by a congregation that supported a resident pastor. St. John's was followed by Holy Trinity in Georgetown. Built on donated land, Holy Trinity was organized in 1792 by the Jesuit fathers and opened for worship two years later under its first pastor, Francis Neale. Until that time the congregation held services in the nearby chapel of Georgetown College. The congregation of St. Patrick's, now seeking land from the District Commissioners, would be the second parish in the District and the first in Washington City.[21]

More than in the case of St. John's or Holy Trinity, St. Patrick's was

18. Letitia W. Brown, "Residence Patterns of Negroes in the District of Columbia, 1800–1860," *RCHS* 69–70 (1969–70): 67–68.

19. For a description of the Young chapel, see Sister M. Xavier Maloney, "The Catholic Church in the District of Columbia (Earlier Period: 1790–1866)" (Master's thesis, The Catholic University of America, 1938), 7–8. See also description of early Washington Catholics in the *Evening Express,* 8 Aug 1867.

20. The word *parish* will be used in the following chapters, although until the 1830s the words *congregation* and *mission* were more commonly employed.

21. St. Mary's of Alexandria, then in the District of Columbia, must be counted

clearly a response by ecclesiastical authorities to fundamental social and economic changes taking place in the region. The transition from chapel to parish paralleled the change occurring in Washington from the old Maryland plantation society to an urban-based economy and the inevitable concentration of a large, heterogeneous population promised by such an economy. It did not promise to be an easy transition. In a period of sustained underemployment and general economic hardship, the new congregation of St. Patrick's faced the task of bridging both the geographical distances and great social gulf that separated the well-established gentry and their servants in their mansions and plantations from the rude tenements and dilapidated homes of the immigrant workers. Even more daunting, the parish must weld a Christian community out of groups with different views on religious obligation, church discipline, and relations with the larger American society. Sometime in late 1793 Bishop Carroll presented this challenge to Father Caffry.

The traditional assumption is that James Hoban, the supervisor immediately responsible for the discipline and welfare of the workers, petitioned Carroll for a parish that would accommodate the newcomers. Caffry arrived in Washington sometime between September 1792, when Hoban took up residence, and January 1794, when Carroll reported the Irish priest "now settled and provided for."[22] By the latter date, Carroll had assigned the new parish to Caffry, approved naming St. Patrick as its patron, and set its boundaries to coincide with the "precincts" of the city.[23]

Caffry was about thirty-four years old when he became St. Patrick's pastor.[24] Born near Newport, County Mayo, he received the habit of the Order of Preachers for the nearby Convent of Burrishoole and en-

among the District's first churches. Records suggest that a congregation was formed in Alexandria as early as 1792, although its first pastor, John Thayer, was not assigned until 1794. On the founding of Holy Trinity, see William Warner, "For Town and Nation: Holy Trinity of Georgetown," *Woodstock Report,* and Wilhelmus Bogart Bryan, *A History of the National Capital,* 2 vols. (New York: Macmillan, 1914), 1:84–86.

22. Ltr., Carroll to John Thayer, 13 Jan 94, *JCP* 2:109.

23. No record survives of the initial boundaries of the parish. The reference to its "precincts" is found in ltr., Bp. Leonard Neale to Carroll, 27 Jan 1804, 5-P-5, Carroll Papers, AAB.

24. Details of Caffry's early life are from H. Fenning, "The Irish Dominican Province," *Archivum Fratrum Praedicatorum* (1986): 294–95; Padraig O Morain, *Annala Beaga Pharaiste Bhuireis Umhaill (A Short Account of the History of Burrishoole Parish)* (Mayo: Padraig O Morain), 39–42; ltrs., C. Kearns, O.P., to Msgr. Philip M. Hannan, 22 Sep 1953, SPA; and L. Taheney, O.P., to Reginald Coffey, O.P., 27 May and 7 Jun 1950, in Coffey's "Notes on Anthony Caffry" file, St. Joseph Province Archives, Providence

tered the novitiate at Athenry, where he remained until 1778. Caffry took pride in his educational achievements and always included the familiar "D.D." in his signature denoting the coveted degree in divinity he had earned at the Sorbonne in Paris after his ordination. He also reportedly pursued further theological studies in Portugal, being in Abercia as late as 1792. The date of Caffry's arrival in the United States and the sponsor for his travel remain tantalizing mysteries—the likelihood of any previous connection with Hoban appears remote.[25] Suffice it that Hoban and Caffry recognized each other as aliens in a strange land, and that the popular Washingtonian provided the often-beleaguered cleric friendship and support during his years in America.[26]

On April 19, 1794, Caffry consummated his real estate deal with the commissioners. For a modest down payment and the bargain price of forty pounds each (approximately $900 at today's values), he purchased lots five and six on F Street, Northwest, between Ninth and Tenth Streets in square 376.[27] Caffry was obviously pleased with the reasonable price and the fact that the lots were situated almost equidistant between the Capitol and President's House in a neighborhood already showing signs of becoming a desirable and fashionable location. He returned to the commissioners two months later to add to the congregation's holdings by purchasing for sixty pounds the adjacent lot seven. It is unlikely that Caffry overlooked the small print in the deeds ominously warning that the sale was subject to "the usual terms of payment" and to conditions concerning the manner of buildings and improvements declared by the President. As in so many human enterprises, this small print was destined to exert much influence on the course of St. Patrick's progress in the next few years.

College, R.I. See also H. Fenning, *The Undoing of the Friars of Ireland* (Louvain, Belgium: University of Louvain, 1972), 293, 298.

25. Hoban was born and raised in County Kilkenny in southeast Ireland, at a considerable distance from Caffry's convent in the far northwest. Although the men were of a similar age, Hoban spent only six of his adult years as a student and craftsman in Dublin before immigrating to Philadelphia at the age of twenty-seven in 1785. It seems unlikely that Caffry, occupied as a theological student in Burrishoole and abroad, could have become an intimate of Hoban during those early years.

26. See, for example, ltr., Rev. James Griffin to Carroll, 8 Sep 1804, SpA-G-1, Carroll Papers, AAB, and "Diary of Mrs. William Thornton," *RCHS* 10 (1907): 136.

27. To clarify the church's finances over the years, equivalent values in 1992 dollars will be mentioned parenthetically throughout this volume. These translations are based on a formula developed by the U.S. Bureau of Labor Statistics and published in its annual *Handbook of Labor Statistics*.

CHAPTER 2

A Time of Testing

THE SMALL Catholic community in Washington faced an unusual challenge when it set about organizing a permanent parish in 1794. As the first congregation formed in the new city, St. Patrick's predated most of those ecclesiastical and civic organizations that traditionally support such an enterprise. Later parishes would enjoy a safety net in the form of planned communities, the orderly acquisition of appropriate sites, and even, in some cases, sufficient funds to cover property purchases.[1] In the case of St. Patrick's, both the bishop and the commissioners appeared largely unconcerned with the practical problems facing the small group of Catholic immigrants and local landowners, focusing more on their own desire to establish a church at the new political center of the nation.

For his part, Bishop Carroll contented himself with establishing the "precincts" of the parish and appointing a pastor to carry out the task of organization. Conspicuously absent was any personal effort to induce his well-off relatives and acquaintances to provide financial support or meld together the distinct social groups in the new congregation into an effective unit. On his frequent vacations in the city, he stayed with the Youngs and in the early years did not visit the congregation or generally involve himself

1. Fosselman, "A Downtown Parish," 5 and 244.

in its affairs.[2] He did not select the site for the parish; that choice was made by the District of Columbia commissioners when they offered the property on F Street at a substantial discount. No doubt they considered their act both a benefit to religion and a stimulus to development of a settled population, but in any case their selection did not take into account the needs of the widely scattered Catholic citizens.

Concern about these needs was left to the new pastor. In the end, success would depend on the financial ingenuity and social adaptability of Anthony Caffry, himself a recent immigrant largely unfamiliar with the economic and social realities of the new city and the new republic. To him and his successor fell the task of pulling together the diverse elements of the small congregation to face the sacrifices involved in forming a parish and building a church.

The First Church

A debt totalling approximately $280, payable in three yearly installments, appears relatively modest even by 1790 standards, but it must have seemed truly formidable to Caffry. He was in a position to understand the dire financial straits faced by many of his parishioners, who, far from supporting a new parish, were more likely to turn to him for aid. Many were indentured workers whose hope for a secure future depended largely on the commercial development that President Washington and others confidently expected would accompany the government building program. Their hopes were dashed when the bustling metropolis failed to materialize. Jobs continued to depend on the slender resources of the commissioners and their off-again on-again building program as the economy further contracted when the schemes of the great land speculators collapsed in 1797. The signs of prosperity and settlement that had heartened the commissioners in early 1794 rapidly disappeared as one small business after another opened to great fanfare and then quickly folded. Even the substantial houses completed that year near Greenleaf Point at the confluence of the two rivers were left vacant or occupied by squatters. By the end of the decade the commissioners would report just 363 dwellings in the city, many of them dreary huts thrown up for workers who lived in direst poverty.[3]

2. Ltrs., Carroll to William Strickland, 4 Aug 1804, and to Charles Plowden, 10 Jan 1808, *JCP* 2:445–46 and 3:35–37.

3. Rpt. of Commissioners, *American State Papers*, Misc. Ser. 1, 256–67. For more on

With poverty and misery came social disorder. Especially hard hit were the new immigrants, as Benjamin Latrobe, the famous architect and builder, noted in his journal:

The city abounds in cases of extreme poverty and distress. . . . Workmen who are ruined in circumstances and health are to be found in extreme indigence scattered in wretched huts over waste which the *law* calls the American metropolis. . . . Distress and want of employment has made many of them sots. Few have saved their capital. Most of them hate, calumniate, or envy each other, for they are all fighting for the scanty means of support which the city affords.[4]

This description fit some families at St. Patrick's, and the parish's own financial plight was closely linked to this continuing poverty. In December 1794 it became clear that the congregation would be unable to meet its debt and would be forced to give up its property. Bishop Carroll intervened. Applying to the commissioners for an extension, he described the parishioners as mostly "tradesmen and labourers, struggling under the difficulties incident to new settlers," who were "not yet" able to raise the money for the first payment. Borrowing the theme that Caffry successfully used earlier, Carroll reminded the commissioners that these poor Catholics understood that a church was a public manifestation of settlement and an encouragement to immigration. Although building must await suitable funds, Catholics too were anxious to promote the city's growth.[5] The commissioners readily agreed to the extension.

In his desperation Caffry solicited funds from a variety of sources. He even received a substantial donation from the great real estate speculators James Greenleaf and Robert Morris. Although Morris, the financier of the Revolution and signer of the Constitution, eventually lost his fortune and was condemned to debtor's prison, he scrupulously fulfilled his pledge to the church.[6] No doubt the pressing needs of impoverished parishioners competed for these and other donations,

financial problems during the 1790s, see Young, *The Washington Community*, 23–24. See also Arnebeck, *Through a Fiery Trial*, especially chaps. 49 through 53.

4. Benjamin H. Latrobe, *The Journal of Latrobe, Being the Notes and Sketches of an Architect, Naturalist and Traveler in the United States from 1796 to 1820* (New York: Appleton, 1905), 131–32. Latrobe's observation is dated 12 August 1806.

5. Ltr., John Carroll to D.C. Commissioners, 14 Dec 1794, Carroll Letterbook, Carroll Papers, AAB.

6. Ltrs., Caffry to Morris, 1 Sep 74, reprinted in Allen C. Clark, *Greenleaf and Law in the Federal City* (Washington: F. N. Roberts, 1901), 93; and Morris to Caffry, 14 Nov 96, Morris Papers, Library of Congress (hereafter LC).

and in January 1798 a part of the debt was still outstanding. At that time the city clerk announced that the congregation's lots were to be sold at auction unless full payment was made by the fourth Monday of the month.[7]

This public notice of foreclosure marked the lowpoint in the financial history of St. Patrick's parish. It also underscored the problems Caffry must have encountered in his effort to integrate the various social elements into a unified congregation. Even if, as Carroll had reminded the commissioners, most of the congregation were struggling tradesmen and laborers, there were certainly notable exceptions. And even if the local recession had begun to affect the fortunes of these wealthy landowners, it certainly did not leave them unable to meet the church's modest debt. After all, it was members of this local gentry who, in similar financial times a decade later, quickly pledged a thousand dollars and a full city block for a proposed church near the Eastern Branch.[8] It appears that Washington's premier families, content with their private chapels and visiting priests and reluctant to associate with the less fortunate newcomers, shunned St. Patrick's. Caffry's inability to induce these native Catholics to associate with the more numerous immigrants in a united congregation must count as the major failure of his pastorate, although the blame probably rests more fairly on the great landowners and their bishop.

The foreclosure notice introduces another puzzling note. In September 1796, in the midst of the financial crisis, Caffry purchased the adjacent lot number 4 on F Street from proprietor David Burns for sixty pounds. He always treated this land as his private property: it was not included in the deed that conveyed St. Patrick's property to the bishop at Caffry's departure in 1804; in fact, it remained Caffry's until, shortly before his death in 1811, he sold it to James Hoban.[9] Such purchases were not uncommon. Everyone, it would seem, was buying and selling land in those speculative times. Vows of personal poverty were loosely observed by missionary friars in the eighteenth century, and it is known that Caffry had his own personal resources. Although historian Peter Guilday and others have suggested that Caffry bought the lot to provide a convenient site for a future home for himself, an

7. Washington *Gazette,* 13 Jan 1798.

8. "Catholics living near the Eastern Branch, Subscribers list, 1806," 11-H-5, Carroll Papers, AAB.

9. Caffry's purchase of lot 4 is recorded in D.C. Land Records, *liber* B-2-B, folio 397, 9 Sep 1796; his sale of the property to Hoban in *liber* A.A.26, folio 235, 5 Jun 1811; both in Office of the Recorder of Deeds.

obligation he preferred not to pass on to his strapped congregation, the purchase could also be interpreted as a sign of the estrangement that was developing between the pastor and some members of his congregation.[10]

The foreclosure announcement must have spurred contributions from well-to-do Catholics or prompted Caffry to use some of his own money (which he later reported expending at St. Patrick's). On February 28, 1798, the commissioners acknowledged payment in full for the three lots, opening the way for building.[11]

The exact date of the first church on F Street is unknown. The city generally required full payment before building could begin, but this rule was frequently ignored by the commissioners. With volunteer labor available and materials cheap or readily obtained, the congregation might well have overcome Carroll's insistence on waiting. Supporting the argument for an early date is the 1796 notice in the Washington *Gazette* of a marriage performed by Caffry, "Rector of St. Patrick's Church."[12] On the other hand, the paper might well have been referring to a congregation and not a building, for by 1796 St. Patrick's congregation had become a fixture in Washington. According to a near-contemporaneous account, Catholics had been gathering in Father Caffry's rooms on the second floor of a brick house on the corner of 10th and E Streets since 1793.[13] Whatever the exact building date, the increasing number of notices in the press and other contemporary accounts make it likely that the congregation was worshiping in a small chapel on F Street by 1798.[14]

10. Charles H. Wentz, ed., *Inventory of Records of St. Patrick's Church and School* (Washington, D.C.: Library of Congress, 1941), 11. Msgr. Peter Guilday prepared the historical commentary in this useful work. See also ltr., Sister M. Nona MacGreal, O.P., to author, 31 Oct 1991, SPA.

11. Caffry later reported spending $200 on the church. See ltr., Caffry to Carroll, 26 Feb 1811, 2-F-1, Carroll Papers, AAB. The deed for St. Patrick's original holdings is recorded in D.C. Land Records, *liber* B.2, folios 478 and 479, Office of the Recorder of Deeds (copy in 11-A.E-2, Carroll Papers, AAB).

12. Washington *Gazette*, 2–5 Nov. 1796.

13. William Clarke, S.J., the source of the story about St. Patrick's temporary location, was the pastor of St. Aloysius's Church during the Civil War. He was born in St. Patrick's parish in the early years of the nineteenth century and was educated at the Washington Seminary next door. His account is frequently cited. See, for example, Edwin M. Williams, "The Roman Catholic Church in the District of Columbia—Its Institutional History," in *Washington Past and Present: A History*, John Claggett Procter, ed. (New York: Lewis History, 1930), 2:789; and Virginia Frye, "St. Patrick's—First Catholic Church of the Federal City," *RCHS* 23 (1920): 31.

14. Msgr. Guilday (in Wentz's *Inventory*), citing Christian Hines, *Early Recollections*

A description of this chapel, most of which could be tucked under the choir loft of today's church, has come down from two members of the original congregation.[15] They remembered a simple rectangular building, "little better than a barn," made of wood (probably over a brick foundation) with a white-washed exterior. The chapel's unadorned interior included behind the altar a story-and-a-half addition that served as a temporary accommodation for the pastor. Such a "small and mean frame building," as it was characterized by Washington socialite Margaret Bayard Smith, was in all essentials typical of the chapels built during late colonial times around southern Maryland and the Eastern Shore.[16] The outline of this standard design with sleeping quarters for a priest can be seen today in a particularly elaborate form in the recently restored St. Francis Xavier Church in Newtowne, Maryland. Unlike the Newtowne church, St. Patrick's contained no pews or other furnishings. Parishioners were expected to bring their own chairs or stand during services.

It is unlikely that Caffry lived for long in the cramped quarters behind the altar. This space was hardly adequate for an active pastor with obligations to manage an expanding congregation, and almost certainly within a few years he had a small rectory with an attached stable under the same roof constructed northwest of the chapel.[17]

Despite the gloomy economic picture, there were some signs of quickening in the city by the time St. Patrick's congregation erected

---

of Washington City (Washington, D.C., 1866; repr. Junior League of Washington, 1981) and Bryan's *History,* accepted the 1796 date. The generally reliable Hines uses the church as a landmark in his description of Washington in 1798. Further evidence can be adduced from an advertisement run by James Dermot in early 1799 for the sale of land "directly opposite the Roman Catholic Chapel." See *Centinel of Liberty and Georgetown Advertiser,* 5 Apr 1799.

15. Their recollections were printed in an article by the Washington Correspondent ("Juvenels") of the *Catholic Mirror,* 8 Feb 1851. The description of the chapel corresponds with the brief description supplied by Hines in *Early Recollections of Washington City,* 30.

16. Smith described the building as it looked in November 1800. See Gaillard Hunt, ed., *The First Forty Years of Washington Society, In the Family Letters of Margaret Bayard Smith* (New York: Frederick Ungar, 1906), 16. For a description of eighteenth-century Maryland churches, see interview, author with Msgr. Edward B. Carley, 22 Jan 1992, SPA. Carley is a noted student of eighteenth-century church architecture and has restored one of the Eastern Shore churches.

17. The rectory is mentioned in the *Catholic Mirror* article (8 Feb 1851) cited above, and in a reminiscence by C. V. Callan printed in Martin I. J. Griffin, "St. Patrick's Church, Washington," *American Catholic Historical Researches,* n.s. 1 (1905), 65. It does not appear in the Hines account, indicating that it was built after 1800.

its little frame chapel. In particular, F Street was gradually assuming an urban character. While half the city still lay under forest cover, and isolated fields of used land and scrub pine continued to separate the little neighborhoods, settled commercial activities were beginning to appear. By the last years of the decade, the commissioners had finally cleared most of the streets of tree stumps and undergrowth and clamped down on those proprietors and new owners who insisted on sowing crops on the roadways and unoccupied lots.[18] From the heights of Capitol Hill a visitor could now trace the course of the major streets and avenues by the clearings through the woods.

Actually F Street, although still little more than a dirt trail alternately muddy or dusty, enjoyed a decided advantage over Pennsylvania Avenue, vaunted as the city's major thoroughfare. The commissioners had ignored their surveyors' warnings and balked at assuming responsibility for the expensive work connected with the proper grading and drainage of streets and squares, and as a result much of the Avenue was frequently under water when nearby Tiber Creek was at high tide. No wonder that F Street, commanding the high ridge above, found itself serving as the main link between the population centers around the President's House and the Capitol.[19] In fact, by the end of the century substantial homes had begun to appear between Thirteenth and Fifteenth Streets, and increasingly modest residences, often with shops or other commercial ventures sharing the same lot, were spreading eastward.

When the first worshipers emerged from their little chapel they found themselves on land considerably elevated above the ungraded street. Their view to the south was unbroken to the Tiber except for a half dozen houses scattered between Ninth and Tenth Streets. Behind them, north of G Street, stood a lone farmhouse, part of the extensive holdings of proprietor David Burns, and then nothing but a few shanties dotting the fields of corn and grass that stretched to the city boundary.[20] To the east, F Street rose abruptly to high ground along

18. For an eyewitness description of Washington before 1800, see George Watterson's letter to the editor of the *National Intelligencer*, 26 Aug 1847.

19. Caemmerer, "Early Washington and Its Art," *RCHS* 218. See also Arnebeck's *Through A Fiery Trial*, 226–27, 231–32, and 573, for discussion of Pennsylvania Avenue and drainage problems.

20. Unless otherwise indicated, the following description of Washington in 1800 is based on Hines, *Early Recollections;* Jane W. Gemmill, *Notes on Washington, or Six Years at the National Capital* (Washington: Brentano Bros., 1883); and a series of articles on the origin and history of F Street, N.W., by the "Rambler" in the *Star*, 27 Jan 1916, and 3 and 14 Feb 1918.

Ninth Street, the future site of the Patent Office, while to the southeast, beyond Eighth Street, stood Blodgett's Hotel, the city's largest private building.

St. Patrick's itself sat in Square 376 on lots that ran for 170 feet along F Street beginning some 75 feet east of Tenth. The square had been part of a large farm called Beall's Levels that ran from the boundary of Daniel Carroll's property at First Street to Nineteenth Street and included what would become the center of Washington. Originally deeded in 1703 to Ninian Beall, a Scottish immigrant, the land was inherited by David Burns, who eventually divided ownership of the twenty-two lots in the square with the commissioners. As late as 1800 St Patrick's shared the square with one small house located on Tenth Street near the site of the present church. This building was owned by one Daniel Caffray. Although this Caffray was unrelated to the pastor, the uncanny coincidence of names has caused historians and city officials considerable confusion over the years.[21]

The city surveyors provided a vivid description of the area in 1818.[22] They found that the squares bounded by Ninth and Tenth and D and G Streets actually formed a series of valleys, the most noteworthy feature of which was the major watercourse that flowed through square 376. Rising from springs near Fourteenth Street at Massachusetts Avenue, the stream ran across what is now Franklin Park and then south and east beyond lot 5 against the high ground along Ninth Street. Where it crossed F Street on its way to the Tiber, its ravine was fourteen feet deep. This allowed a considerable body of water to run through the neighborhood, especially after storms, and was the source of Father Caffry's boast that he could cast his fishing line from his own property. In time a sidewalk and carriageway would be thrown across the ravine to gain passage for F Street traffic, but the barrier remained uncovered for several decades until a distinguished citizen fell into the stream while returning home after a late night on the town.[23]

21. The confusion extended to the city clerk who in 1804 filed the deed conveying Anthony Caffry's lots to Bishop Carroll under Daniel Caffray's name. See D.C. Land Records, *liber* L-11, folio 176, Office of the Recorder of Deeds. Father Fenning and others sought to explain the odd coincidence by suggesting that Daniel might have been Father Caffry's baptismal name or, conversely, his name in the Dominicans, but Daniel Caffray was assuredly a different person, an unlettered man who witnessed a land sale with an "x." Msgr. Guilday explored all these possibilities and concluded, "It is chance identity of name, not identity of person." See Wentz's *Inventory*, 11.

22. Report of D.C. Surveyor published in the Washington *Gazette*, 27 Apr 1818.

23. Of the many descriptions of the watercourses in early Washington, see espe-

Square 376 also boasted one of Washington's famous freshwater springs. Located near Ninth and F Streets and variously known as Caffry's or St. Patrick's spring, it pumped two barrels of excellent water a minute, enough to supply the needs of the neighborhood for many years. Until it was covered over by the city in 1809 and its output piped to residences as far away as Twelfth and Pennsylvania Avenue, the spring was the site of neighborhood gatherings where residents came to socialize and play games in good weather.[24]

A Change in Leadership

It would be difficult to imagine two more contrasting figures than the patrician bishop of Baltimore and the fiery Irish pastor of St. Patrick's. Carroll was a member of the American ruling class, an intimate of the founders of the new republic; he shared much of their enthusiasm for religious toleration and separation of church and state. His direction of the church and his many irenic acts demonstrated his hope that Catholics would take advantage of the fundamental changes in American society and participate fully in national life. To this end, he constantly sought to soft-pedal the "foreignness" of the Catholic church. Caffry, on the other hand, was an exile who had witnessed first-hand the results of brutal discrimination. There is no evidence to suggest that he deviated greatly from the strong disinclination of most Irish immigrants to accommodate themselves to the Protestant majority.[25] The need to assimilate or to mask the uniqueness of his religious practices was not among his interests.

Carroll would not have counted the learned Caffry among the "missionary adventurers" (his term for some immigrant priests then beginning to wander across the American landscape, offering spiritual support to the new immigrants while sowing seeds of dissension). On at least one occasion, the bishop was prepared to appoint Caffry to the delicate task of serving on an ecclesiastical court. Yet, even if Caffry was one of Carroll's "worthy & able men" among the Irish clergy, he also clearly fell into the group Carroll described as having excited prej-

---

cially James F. Duhamel, "Tiber Creek," *RCHS* 28 (1926): 203–25; Bryan's *History*, 1:304 and 560–61; and the *Star*, 3 Feb 1918.

24. St. Patrick's spring has been described in many sources. See especially, John Claggett Proctor, "Springs and Pumps Once Furnished City Water," published in the *Star*, 10 Mar 1935; and Bryan, *History*, 1:562–63.

25. Olson, *Catholic Immigrants in America*, 7, 11–13.

udices against themselves "very difficult to be removed."[26] As documented in the few letters surviving Caffry's pastorship, the often-troubled priest was never loath to stand up forcibly against anyone—including his bishop—whom he considered challenging his pastoral prerogatives.

The first of these outbursts occurred when Carroll, believing that the D.C. commissioners wanted him listed as trustee of the church property, allowed his name to be put on the title. In fact Carroll never wanted to own church property and was quite comfortable with the use of lay trustees. He obviously considered his name on the deed a mere technicality and expressed surprise when Caffry complained, beating a hasty retreat in the face of the priest's continued "uneasiness." He agreed to having Caffry's name substituted for his, but he wanted it expressed that the property so granted by this title was for the use of the congregation and of the pastor "who remains subject to ecclesiastical jurisdiction of the bishop."[27] In the end, Caffry's name appeared on the title without any reference to the bishop's authority.

The complaints continued from an obviously depressed pastor. In August 1800 he planned a vacation to southern Maryland where, he told Carroll, he hoped to obtain a servant, because he simply could not live alone. In a burst of frustration he confessed, "If I can crawl thro existence this year, I never shall, I hope, afterwards drag the chains of wretchedness in this territory." Ill and unable to bear the weather, he frankly warned the bishop that he might not last the winter in this city he had come to dislike. Adding to his depression were the continuing conflicts within the congregation. He complained about the "tide of coalition," which was against him, and appealed to Carroll's innate sense of justice to "dispose of the controversies." Carroll had decided other cases in his favor in the past, but Caffry obviously wasn't sure how the latest controversies would be settled. As if to nudge the scales of justice a little in his favor, he reminded Carroll how he had exposed his life to great danger in order to save the bishop's during the yellow fever times in Baltimore.[28]

The poverty haunting so many in his congregation, another cause

26. Carroll discussed the missionary adventurers in his letter to Francis Beeston, 22 Mar 1788, *JCP* 1:262; he writes about Caffry and the other Irish priests in letters to Denis Cahill, 11 Jun 1786, *JCP* 2:183–84 and to Charles Plowden, 12 Mar 1802, *JCP* 2:382–83.

27. Ltr., Carroll to Anthony Caffrey [sic], 15 Jul 1794, *JCP* 2:122–23.

28. Ltr., Caffry to Carroll, 29 Aug 1800, 8-AC-3, Carroll Papers, AAB.

of the pastor's depression, had not been relieved by the arrival of the federal government. Jobs, especially those in the building trades, remained scarce and housing for all the newcomers inadequate. Competition for the available housing drove up prices and in 1800 provoked the carpenters working on the President's House to revolt. When the commissioners, anticipating President John Adams's arrival, ordered the jumble of shanties around the still-unfinished mansion cleared away, the desperate Irishmen, worried about the welfare of their families, threatened to quit.[29] The commissioners backed down, but later Hoban bought many of the shanties and had them hauled away to be rented as dwellings elsewhere. Making all this hardship more difficult to bear was the continuing uncertainty over the city's future. It was a vicious circle. Uncertainty about the government's commitment to Washington prolonged the city's financial distress, which in turn strengthened the determination of the city's foes to continue their fight to move the capital.

Although a pastor had no control over the city's financial health, he could be expected to address the other great challenge facing his parish: a congregation divided not only by economic and social outlook but by dissimilar attitudes toward religious practices and discipline. Caffry's solution to the discord was to bar those who disagreed with him from the church, an act that marked the culmination of the growing antagonism toward the fiery pastor among a substantial number of the city's Catholics. Continuing dissension between the local gentry and the pastor must share the blame with the city's financial plight for the parish's problems. Perhaps as a result of these persistent troubles, the early history of St. Patrick's shows none of that attention to charitable and educational matters that gave so much distinction to its later years.

Caffry's inability to unite his congregation during the years of extreme hardship was real enough, but some of his threats about leaving must be discounted, because he remained in the job for four more years. By 1804, however, it had become impossible to ignore the controversy that continued to swirl about Caffry, especially when Bishop Leonard Neale became involved. Neale had been designated Carroll's coadjutor in 1795 and, before becoming archbishop in 1815, lived quietly near the Georgetown convent of the Visitation Sisters, a group he had long sponsored. Often in poor health, he assisted Carroll with his

29. For the text of the workers' letter to the commissioners, see Abby G. Baker, "The Erection of the White House," RCHS 16 (1913): 146–47.

episcopal duties, mostly in the southern part of the diocese. By 1804 he had had enough of the Irish pastor across Rock Creek.

The argument was one close to any pastor's heart: territorial jurisdiction. Caffry insisted that the whole city belonged to St. Patrick's. Neale warned the archbishop that if the "precincts" Carroll assigned Caffry included the whole city "the difficulty would be enormous." By implication, Caffry was claiming control of the chapels still operating in Washington and perhaps even of Holy Trinity in Georgetown and St. Mary's in Alexandria, although that would mean Caffry was claiming jurisdiction over the whole District of Columbia, an amazing assertion even for him. At any rate things had come to such a state, Neale reported that Caffry read something sinister into every proposed solution and had resorted to barring "many living near St. Patrick's" from entering the church. Neale wanted Carroll to end the disagreement, "which is continually sounding in every ear."[30]

As if angering the coadjutor were not enough, Caffry also managed to elevate a petty argument with one of his fellow priests into a series of formal charges brought before the archbishop. He accused James Griffin, the pastor of St. Mary's, Alexandria, of assault, robbery, and the misappropriation of stole fees, those donations traditionally given at baptisms, weddings, and other church ceremonies.[31] These charges were still being investigated when Caffry left Washington.

The circumstances of Caffry's departure in September 1804 can only be surmised. He was certainly the center of controversy, but there is no evidence that he was driven out. In fact, Caffry remained in the country, spending at least the greater part of a year serving as an assistant at St. Peter's Church in New York. He always retained the affection of Archbishop Carroll, who in 1811 lamented the death of his "good-hearted friend, Dr. Caffrey." For his part, Caffry spoke of Carroll with fondness and always remembered him "in the pride of my heart as my bishop."[32] Before leaving Baltimore, Caffry received from the archbishop $80 of the $200 he had personally spent while at St. Patrick's.

Surprisingly, Archbishop Carroll did not turn to a veteran pastor to put the struggling church on its feet, but selected instead a young American whose experience until then had centered on the class-

30. Ltr., Neale to Carroll, 27 Jan 1804, 5-P-5, Carroll Papers, AAB.

31. Ltr., Griffin to Carroll, 8 Sep 1804, SpA-G-1, Carroll Papers, AAB.

32. Ltrs., John Troy, Abp. of Dublin, to Carroll, 2 Nov 1811, 8-N-7, and Caffry to Carroll, 26 Feb 1811, 2-F-1, both in Carroll Papers, AAB; and Carroll to Troy, 16 Jan 1812, JCP 3:171–72.

rooms of Georgetown College. In William Matthews, St. Patrick's acquired a priest who would dominate Catholic life in Washington for a half century. He was born in 1770 into the landed gentry of southern Maryland.[33] His father, a descendant of the early English settlers, owned properties in Charles County derived from a seventeenth-century grant from the Lord Proprietor. His mother was a Neale, an old English Catholic family that gave many sons and daughters to the service of the American church. (Bishop Neale was Matthews's uncle.) The widespread intermarriage among Catholics in colonial Maryland meant that the young priest was also closely related to many of the leading Catholic families of the day, including the Carrolls, Youngs, and Taneys.

Matthews was a son of the Revolution. As a young boy he watched British Redcoats loot and burn his family's plantation near Port Tobacco. Perhaps it was this formative experience that inspired his ardent patriotism. Throughout his long life he remained manifestly proud of the nation's struggle for independence and dedicated to the ideals enshrined in its Declaration of Independence and Constitution. Even in later decades, when fervor for the Revolution had dimmed, Matthews continued to express publicly his admiration and affection for the early patriots and, long after it ceased to be fashionable, to recite Carroll's prayer for civil authorities at his masses. That this patriotism had a slightly anti-British tinge must have endeared him to many of his Irish-born parishioners.

Like many children of his class, Matthews was educated at St. Omer's. He came home in 1794 to become a teacher of rhetoric at Georgetown, thus beginning a long association with that institution and the Jesuits. It was during this period that the young professor personally welcomed George Washington, an old family friend, to the college when the President dropped by for a surprise visit in 1797. In later years Matthews would regale audiences with an account of the conversation as he guided his hero around the campus.[34]

33. Unless where otherwise noted, this sketch of Matthews' early life is based on Joseph T. Durkin, *William Matthews: Priest and Citizen* (New York: Benziger Brothers, 1963), 3–16, and "Gonzaga College," *Woodstock Letters*, vol. 19 (1890), 3–22.

34. The date of Matthews's return is variously given, but John Carroll dates it to 14 November 1794. See his letter to Charles Plowden, 15 Nov 1794, *JCP* 2:131. The story about George Washington appears in many accounts. See, for example, Rev. Charles Stonestreet's letter quoted in Michael J. Riorden, *Cathedral Records of Baltimore* (Baltimore, 1906), 50. See also "Gonzaga College," *Woodstock Letters*, 11–12; and John M. Daley, *Georgetown University: Origin and Early Years* (Washington, D.C.: Georgetown University Press, 1957), 95.

WILLIAM MATTHEWS

In 1797 Matthews decided to become a priest and entered St. Mary's Seminary in Baltimore. Following Carroll's custom of using his seminarians as part-time teachers at Georgetown, Matthews divided his theological training between the Sulpicians at St. Mary's and the former Jesuits at Georgetown. In March 1800 he became the first American ordained to the priesthood in the United States. He remained at Georgetown for four more years, teaching English and being "greatly useful," as the St. Mary's account put it, to Bishop Neale, probably performing occasional pastoral duties in southern Maryland.[35]

Matthews arrived at St. Patrick's in 1804 and was on hand to receive the deed to the parish property from Father Caffry in September. Caffry turned over the St. Patrick's lots, "including the improvements advantages commodities and appurtenances thereunto belonging," to the archbishop "for the use of the congregation worshiping in the place called St. Patrick's Church."[36] The particular wording of this deed would cause legal problems in later years when St. Patrick's considered other uses for the property on F Street.

Matthew's arrival produced a measurable change in the congregations attitude. Although Robert Plunkett, the president of Georgetown College, would later assert that after Caffry's departure "the Irish abandoned the sacraments or frequented them in the city of Georgetown," his claim flies in the face of Bishop Carroll's boasting to Bishop Neale in 1805 that "all had been united" at St. Patrick's under the new pastor.[37] As a close neighbor for over six years, Matthews was no doubt well acquainted with the situation at St. Patrick's, and in a few short months he made amazing progress in bringing harmony to the little congregation. As amply demonstrated in succeeding years, his sympathetic yet no-nonsense approach to the city's newcomers and his extraordinary interest in the welfare of the poor won the immediate affection and trust of many of the Irish parishioners. For the

35. "Nom des Seminarists du Seminaire de Baltimore," vol. 1, SAB, and ltr., Leonard Neale to Father Stone, 19 Oct 1801 (4-T-1), Maryland provincial archives, GUA.

36. D.C. Land Records, liber L-11, folio 176, 10 Sep 1804, Office of the Recorder of Deeds. The deed was misfiled under the name Daniel Caffray. The exact date of Matthews's arrival at St. Patrick's is uncertain, but Fosselman ("A Downtown Parish," 22–23) and others put it at 31 Jul 1804. Msgr. Guilday argues convincingly (Wentz's Inventory, 11) that the marginal notation on the 4 September 1804 document that conveyed the deed indicates that Matthews had certainly assumed the pastorship by that date.

37. Ltrs., Robert Plunkett to Carroll, 10 Apr 1807, 6-V-10, Carroll Papers, AAB, and Carroll to Leonard Neale, 25 Oct 1805, JCP 2:495.

older Catholic families, Matthews's arrival meant literally that a relative was now in charge.

As implied in his letter to Neale, Carroll faced stiff competition for the young priest's services. Even after becoming pastor, Matthews remained a member of the Georgetown faculty and for a number of years entertained thoughts of becoming a Jesuit. He was a member of the Corporation of the Roman Catholic Clergy of Maryland, the group of priests, mostly former Jesuits, that managed the properties owned by the order before its dissolution in 1773. In 1806, the year after the restoration of the Society of Jesus in the United States, he accepted the post of vice-president of the college, and in 1808 became its sixth president. During his short presidency the school consolidated its financial position and launched an ambitious building program. He was forced to resign the position because others considered "being a missionary in Washington," meaning pastor of St. Patrick's, incompatible with the job of president. But Matthews continued to serve on the board of directors until 1815, providing Carroll with first-hand reports on affairs at the school and news about members of the recently restored order.[38]

In his fifth year as pastor of St. Patrick's and his second as president of Georgetown, Matthews became a Jesuit novice. His biographer explains this seemingly puzzling move as an obliging response to an unwritten rule that the president of the college be a member of the order, but there must have been more at stake. On this and at least one other occasion Matthews showed a genuine interest in becoming a Jesuit, and his failure to remain in the order in 1809 was only in part his own decision.[39] The likelihood of the pastor's leaving was certainly real enough to Carroll. Explaining that Matthews might be wanted elsewhere, "as will probably be the case," he offered the parish to Si-

38. R. Emmett Curran, *The Bicentennial History of Georgetown University*, vol. 1: *From Academy to University 1789–1889* (Washington, D.C.: Georgetown University Press, 1993), 62–63. Daley, *Georgetown University*, 154–55, and Coleman Nevils, *Miniatures of Georgetown, 1634 to 1934 Tercentennial Causeries* (Washington, D.C.: Georgetown University Press, 1935), 125–26. The quotation is from a letter by John Grassi reproduced in Thomas Hughes, *History of the Society of Jesus in North America: Colonial and Federal,* 4 vols. (London: Longmans, Green, 1907–17) *Documents* 1:830. For examples of Matthews's reports to Carroll on Jesuit affairs, see ltrs., Matthews to Carroll, 14 Nov 1809, 5–I–13, Carroll Papers, AAB; and Carroll to Enoch Fenwick, 28 May 1813 and 1 Jun 1815, *JCP* 3:224 and 336.

39. "Gonzaga College," *Woodstock Letters,* 12; Somehow Matthews antagonized his Jesuit superiors. See ltr., Benedict Fenwick to John Grassi, 20 Feb 1815, quoted in Hughes, *Documents* 1:881.

mon Felix Gallagher, the gifted Irish preacher and controversial pastor in Charleston, South Carolina.[40] In fact, until 1809 Matthews was scarcely more than a part-time pastor and resident on F Street.

Even with his energies only partially focused on St. Patrick's Matthews proved a formidable administrator. Supported by a newly united congregation, he developed plans for the financing and construction of a permanent church. Building began in 1807, with frequent halts until funds were sufficient to justify further activity. Obviously Matthews's appearance at St. Patrick's loosened some purses in the congregation, for the new building was financed on a pay-as-you go basis, using parish fund raisers that featured appearances by popular guest preachers. For example, the parish celebrated St. Patrick's Day in 1809 with Mass and "a discourse in honor of the Saint" delivered by a noted orator, to be followed, the *National Intelligencer* announced, by a collection to help defray completion of the new church.[41] There is no evidence that the building involved the parish in any debt or that Matthews used his own personal fortune to keep construction going.

According to an oral tradition going back to the days of Father Matthews, the new church was the work of architect James Hoban, still a parishioner and F Street neighbor.[42] Although the substantial brick building dedicated on July 2, 1809, was some ninety feet in length, it was actually little more than a simple rectangular space, constituting only the first section of what was planned as a church in the "gothic motif." It ran parallel to F Street on lots six and seven with its main entrance facing west toward Tenth Street. The sole exterior decoration consisted of a series of slender lancet-sashed windows running along the nave, the west portal doors denoted by another pair of these windows rising above them to within a few feet of the steeply pitched roof. Inside, a series of galleries ran around the walls of what

40. Ltr., Carroll to Gallagher, 30 May 1809, folios 147rv and 148v, *Congressi*, sec. 5, Archives of the Propaganda Fide (hereafter APF). Although by then on friendly terms with Gallagher, Carroll obviously wanted to keep the troublemaker closer to Baltimore. No record survives of Gallagher's reaction to the offer.

41. *National Intelligencer*, 15 Mar 1809. The visiting preacher was merely identified as a "Rev. Gentleman lately from New York."

42. Interview, author with Msgr. E. Robert Arthur, 25 Jun 1991. Arthur was an assistant at St. Patrick's in the late 1930s when he heard the story from his pastor, Msgr. Cornelius F. Thomas, who in turn had learned it from Jacob Walter when Thomas was serving as assistant at St. Patrick's in the 1880s. Walter, who had been pastor of the church since 1860, was a close witness of the parish's affairs back to the later years of the Matthews's era.

remained essentially a large, unfinished room.[43] Until James Barry, the wealthy Baltimore Catholic who had recently come to live in southeast Washington, donated pews to the church in 1810, parishioners brought their own seats.

The dedication of the new church was the first recorded grand occasion in the parish's history. Archbishop Carroll officiated and delivered the "discourse" marking the event. Mass was sung by the coadjutor, Bishop Neale, who in the style of the day was usually referred to in the press and church records by his Roman title, the Bishop of Gortyna. In the congregation that flocked to witness this rare piece of religious theater were people of note in the early history of the city, including the mayor, Robert Brent, and the future mayor, Thomas Carberry, along with members of the Ennis, Young, Clarke, Sims, Mattingly, Ward, Masi, Whelan, Dyer, Callan, Claggett, Mohun, Carroll, Manning, Noyes, and Orme families.[44] Consistent with Matthews's style of raising money, the announcement of the ceremony contained the now-familiar notice that a collection would be taken up during the service to help defray the cost of the church and its furnishings.[45]

Following a custom common in village parishes and in keeping with the largely rural character of Washington in 1800, St. Patrick's had buried its dead in the grounds surrounding the little chapel on F Street.[46] This practice continued after the construction of the new church, and in time a picturesque graveyard ran along both sides of the building. With the extension of the parish's holdings in square 376 during the next few years, the size of its graveyard increased; burial plots extended north of the church to a receiving vault constructed on G Street near the later site of St. Patrick's Academy. Although more graves would be added from time to time, notably in the case of Father Matthews's interment in 1854, most of the dead after 1810 were buried in a new cemetery donated by Notley Young's daughter, Ann Casanave. In a carefully worded deed that later became the subject of legal dispute, Casanave conveyed to the church two and one-half acres in Washington County (that part of the District outside the northern

43. James M. Goode, *Capital Losses* (Washington, D.C.: Smithsonian Press, 1979), 194–95.

44. Milton Smith, *History of St. Patrick's Church Washington, D.C.* (Washington: Privately published, 1933), 13.

45. *National Intelligencer*, 30 Jun 1809. See also same paper, 14 Mar and 22 and 29 Nov 1810.

46. For an early description of a funeral conducted by Father Caffry, see *National Intelligencer*, 14 Sep 1803.

boundary of the original city, beyond today's Florida Avenue) between First and Third Streets, N.W. She specified that the land was to be used for "no other intent or purpose" than a graveyard for the Catholics of Washington.[47]

The advent of the new cemetery and dismantling of the original church gave the parish some breathing room, but it was obvious that more space would soon be needed. Plans for a major expansion of the new church and replacement of Father Caffry's little house were quickly initiated. Unlike many contemporaries, Matthews never questioned the government's commitment to the city, and he recognized the development potential of F Street. Stately homes of distinguished citizens, including Secretary of State James Madison, were going up nearby, and the next few years would witness a rapid growth all along F Street, an interesting mix of substantial residences, important commercial firms, boarding houses, and small hotels. Combining his basic faith in Washington's future with a shrewd mastery of business affairs and the personal resources to back his judgment, Matthews set out to provide for his parish's financial future.

In his real estate ventures Matthews sidestepped the lengthy negotiations with bishop and congregation that usually accompanied such transactions. To avoid the inevitable delays associated with parish fund raisings, he used his own assets to purchase, at opportune times over the next three years, all the lots in the western half of the square.[48] As further evidence of his financial acumen or perhaps just plain good luck, Matthews removed his money from the Bank of Columbia, the favorite repository for the wealth of the area's leading citizens, and

47. D.C. Land Records, *liber* T.19, folio 233, 3 May 1808, Office of the Recorder of Deeds. For further description of the cemetery, see *Star*, 14 Apr 1888, and *Catholic Mirror*, 6 Dec 1879.

48. Matthews's purchases included: in September 1811, lots 13–15 on G Street from John and Marcia Van Ness (the daughter of David Burnes) for $1,000; in October 1811, lot 10 on Tenth Street from Henry Pratt for $248.17; in April 1813, lot 12 on the corner of Tenth and G from John Cox for $154; in March 1814, lots 8 and 9 on Tenth Street from Walter Hellon (including the equity of Daniel Caffray); in April 1814, lot 11 on Tenth Street from James Dunlop for $250. When added to the original St. Patrick's property, these purchases totaled 245 frontage feet on F Street, 257.9 feet on Tenth, and 237 feet on G. In later years, the city changed the lot numbers, and St. Patrick's holdings were renumbered as lots 36 to 46 and 59 to 62 inclusive. The present church stands on lot 59; the rectory on lot 60, and the school on lots 61 and 62. All these transactions have been summarized in Wentz, *Inventory*, 11–12. The deeds are recorded in D.C. Land Records in *liber* 27, folios 130 and 282; *liber* A.E. 30, folio 258; *liber* 32, folio 148; and *liber* A.G. 32, folio 227; all in the Office of the Recorder of Deeds.

made his real estate investments before that well-known institution collapsed.[49] In these and later investments made for the parish and the church in the city, Matthews prefigured the best of those "brick and mortar" pastors who would build the American church.

The City and Its People, 1800–1820

Although poverty and its attendant miseries continued to stalk Washington's laboring classes, signs of a modest economic upturn began to appear in the early years of the new century.[50] The arrival of the federal government in 1800 meant that more than three hundred employees of the executive departments and their families, court officials, and members of the diplomatic corps were now added to the city's full-time residents. The government would remain small for many years, but even in those decades and especially following the decision to rebuild after the British invasion in 1814, it began that inexorable growth associated with all bureaucracies.

The introduction of this new group of permanent residents also meant the presence of a steadily employed consumer class and a healthy demand for a wide variety of goods and services. Finally a real chance existed for the hard-working shopkeeper, blacksmith, cabinet maker, or apothecary, to mention just a few of the scores of occupations upon which urban society depended, to make a go of it. The periodic sessions of Congress also created a demand for hotels, boarding houses, restaurants, and taverns, all sources of livelihood for increasing numbers of entrepreneurs and laborers. Competition from Alexandria and Georgetown, continuing concern over the government's commitment to the area, and the failure of the real estate speculators all inhibited the development of basic industry, but the people kept coming nevertheless. By 1820 the population of Washington City stood at 13,117, representing a fourfold increase in two decades.

People began to enjoy a bit of spare time. In addition to hunting along the reaches of the Tiber and fishing for herring in Rock Creek, all classes frequented the horse races. The annual Jockey Club meets

49. The bank lost half its specie in 1819 and was finally forced to close in 1826, taking with it many Washington fortunes.

50. Unless otherwise noted, this section is based on Green's *Washington*; Bryan's *A History of the National Capital*, vol. 1; Hunt, ed., *Forty Years of Washington Society*; Hines, *Early Recollections*; and David B. Warden, *A Chronological and Statistical Description of the District of Columbia, the Seat of the General Government to the United States* (Paris: Smith, 1816).

were the most popular amusement in town, and even before 1800 the city boasted two tracks, one near Foggy Bottom, the other above Franklin Square, not far from St. Patrick's. All forms of gambling, particularly cock-fighting, were popular among the city's workers, while dancing assemblies, magic shows, and music halls provided more genteel amusement. In 1800 a theater opened in Blodgett's Hotel, although performances tended more toward tight-rope walkers, performing animals, and ethnic dancers rather than the dramas and oratory of later years. At the far end of the social scale, high society sponsored balls and banquets and entertained the rich and famous, whose carriages could often be seen navigating the perilous ruts and puddles in front of homes along F and other streets near the White House, as the President's home was beginning to be called.

Visitors commented on the extreme hospitality of the residents. A casual introduction would immediately be followed by invitations to dinners, teas, and balls. Also noted was how Washingtonians united simplicity with refinement of manners. Here the brilliant Thomas Jefferson led the way, welcoming distinguished guests to the White House in his homespuns and bedroom slippers. One proper visitor complained that in the boarding houses residents would remove their coats in summer and their shoes to warm their feet by the fire in winter, "customs," he sniffed, "which the climate only can excuse."[51] The use of umbrellas, even by those riding horses, was universal in all seasons. Horseback was the standard mode of transportation between the city's scattered neighborhoods. Father Matthews, dressed in the garb of a city gentleman (both Maryland and Virginia law forbade clerical dress in public except during sacred services), was frequently seen riding about on business and visiting his parishioners.

President Jefferson's love of art and music introduced a significant group of newcomers to the city with close ties to St. Patrick's. To complete the intricate stone carvings and other works of art planned for the Capitol, Jefferson arranged in 1805 for the hiring of a group of Italian artists led by Giuseppe and Carlo Franzoni and Giovanni Andrei from Carrara. Although illness and homesickness took their toll, the group remained long enough to fashion the city's earliest examples of noteworthy art and enriched its culture. Some, including both Franzonis and Andrei, remained lifelong parishioners of St. Patrick's.

The artists' arrival coincided with the appearance of a group of Italian musicians who would also leave their mark on the city and on St.

51. Warden, *A Chronological and Statistical Description*, 183.

Patrick's. Jefferson himself was an able violinist, and he arranged for the Marine Corps to recruit musicians from Sicily, where a U.S. naval squadron was based during the war against the Barbary pirates. When the men arrived, some with their families, they quickly learned "Hail Columbia" along with the rest of the standard American repertoire and were soon performing at public gatherings throughout the city. Victims of military red tape and government economies, most of the Italians did not last long in Marine uniform, although some would eventually complete long careers in the band. Others became successful American entrepreneurs and teachers. Most notably, Lewis Carusi opened his saloon, which, at Eleventh and Pennsylvania Avenue, would become a center of Washington social life and the site of civic meetings, graduations, and other grand events.[52]

Statistics on nationality and religion in this period are scarce and highly questionable, but it is certain that the Irish dominated the ranks of the newcomers, prompting one respected witness to note in 1816 that "nearly half of the population of Washington is of Irish origin."[53] The Irish supplied most of the drayers, who moved the city's goods, as well as a significant number of the town's blacksmiths, tavern keepers, grocers, skilled laborers, and boardinghouse proprietors. Architect Hoban was probably the best known of the small group of Irish-born in the city's professional class, which included several prominent teachers and government clerks. The great majority of the Irish, however, toiled as unskilled laborers, often in temporary jobs at low wages. As late as 1816 these immigrants, many of them unable to speak English, had displaced the area's free blacks in the most dangerous jobs and arduous domestic positions. This was the group that dug the canal to connect the Tiber and the Eastern Branch, worked on the bridges that spanned the city's waterways, and completed and repaired the streets. Later, crews of Irish workers macadamized Pennsylvania Avenue and built the city's first water works. Many Irish were also employed at the Navy Yard after the War of 1812, when Congress

52. Elsie K. Kirk, *Music at the White House: A History of the American Spirit* (Urbana: University of Illinois Press, 1986), 25–31.

53. Warden, *A Chronological and Statistical Description,* 27. On the Irish in Washington, see Jennifer L. Altenhofel, "Irish Women in Antebellum Washington: Their Lives and Labor," a paper prepared for the American University Research Seminar, May 1992, which is the basis for the following paragraphs. Matthew E. Hickey's "Irish Catholics in Washington up to 1860," (Master's thesis, The Catholic University of America, 1933), despite dubious research techniques, also contains some useful information on immigrant occupations.

JAMES HOBAN

authorized construction of fifty gunboats and a ship-of-the-line. A sub-stantial number of these immigrant laborers were women, members of impoverished family groups as well as an ever-increasing number of single women. They were quickly enlisted into domestic service, a field they came to monopolize.

The Irish ensured that St. Patrick's Day was a notable annual occa-sion. Numerous accounts mention the parades and Irish bands and the wearing of the green that enlivened the city each spring. More than one visitor commented on a signboard on Pennsylvania Avenue that advertised "Peter Rodgers, saddler, from the green fields of Erin and tyranny to the green streets of Washington and liberty."[54]

54. The sign continued: "See Copenhagen; view the seas, 'tis all blockade—'tis all a blaze. The seas shall be free—Yankee Doodle keep it up." Rodgers was a seventy-year old native of Cork. See Warden, *A Chronological and Statistical Description*, 27–28. See also Newman F. McGirr, "The Irish in the Early Days of the District," *RCHS* 48–49 (1946–1947): 93–94.

As if to underscore this patriotic sentiment, Irish workers formed the city's first volunteer militia unit. Hoban organized the Washington Artillery in October 1796. Its founding members, all apparently Irish born, were well armed and, most importantly, were predominantly veterans of the strict militia organizations of their native land, thus explaining the unit's expertise and military air. The Washington Artillery mustered regularly at the racecourse at Twenty-third and K Streets and was frequently called on to participate in local civic ceremonies. Hoban remained captain until the congressionally mandated militia reorganization of 1802, when the unit was assigned to the First Legion of the Columbian Brigade. As late as the Battle of Bladensburg in 1814, where the Washington Artillery fought in support of the Baltimore Volunteer Regiment and was one of the few units to make a good account of itself, the majority of its members came from among the city's Irish.[55]

Such activities say something about the motives and spirit of the newcomers, some of whom were beginning to rise through hard work and perseverance into the city's emerging middle class. Unfortunately, most newcomers, including a substantial proportion of St. Patrick's congregation, continued in desperate straits. At the extreme were those that Margaret Bayard Smith found huddled in "wretched cabins" without furniture of any kind, malnourished and exposed to all sorts of illness and disease. One group of immigrant parishioners, perhaps marginally better off, lived in a row of shanties that lined E and F Streets five blocks to the east of the church.

Responding to the pressing needs of these newcomers, James Hoban and some of the better-off immigrants organized the Society of the Sons of Erin in 1802. Members collected money and distributed food and clothing and sought jobs for the unemployed. Its efforts were matched by those of the Female Union Benevolent Society, but obviously the need was too great for private charity. Those left without work when the government building programs periodically ceased operation were forced on the dole. Almost half the city government's expenses in those decades went to relief of the poor, far surpassing the percentage allocated for such things in New York and elsewhere.

The continuing poverty of the laboring class was just one of the challenges that faced the city. Despite brave demands that it be

55. Martin K. Gordon, "The Militia of the District of Columbia, 1790–1815" (Ph.D. dissertation, George Washington University, 1975), 20–21, and 34–46; and Frederick P. Todd, "The Militia and Volunteers of the District of Columbia 1783–1820," *RCHS* 50 (1948–50): 410–11 and 433.

granted territorial status with federal representation, Washington remained a poor stepchild of the federal government. Constantly threatened by congressional critics who schemed to give the troublesome place back to Maryland and Virginia, the city fathers settled for a municipal corporation similar to the governments in Georgetown and Alexandria. The 1802 congressional charter provided for a city council elected by white male taxpayers in the city's four separate wards and a mayor, at first appointed by the President, but in later years elected by the council. Several prominent members of St. Patrick's parish served in the new city government, including Robert Brent, the mayor until 1812, and Hoban, who remained on the city council for a record thirty years.

Congress had Washington over a barrel. In addition to relief of the poor, the city bore the expense of maintaining streets, building bridges, and providing the usual municipal services concerning health, protection, and welfare. Except for approving Jefferson's request for $3,000 to repair Pennsylvania Avenue and plant trees along its length, the legislators refused to provide for the city's infrastructure. Taxpayer complaints merely emboldened those in Congress who were pushing for a return to Philadelphia. The Federal government paid no tax for its own buildings, forcing the city to assess all private property at high rates. Limited in this effort, the council imposed licensing fees on everything from stores and taverns to carriages and pets and asked citizens to subscribe to public improvements. In response, Hoban and some of his neighbors banded together to form the "F Street Inhabitants and Proprietors Association," which imposed assessments on its members to pay for wooden sidewalks and street improvements.[56] Washington was simply ill-equipped to provide minimal services. Within two years of its incorporation, the city was forced to borrow money, slipping into a pattern of municipal poverty that lasted, with brief exceptions, throughout the century.

Washington's problems were only compounded when Congress declared war on England in June 1812. Easy accessibility to the British fleet left the capital painfully vulnerable to attack. Citizens panicked in 1813 when Admiral George Cockburn's ships sailed up the Potomac to within sixty miles of the city. The enemy's temporary withdrawal allowed the people to resume their somnambulant ways, but they were rudely awakened in August 1814 by news that a force of 4,500

56. Nelson Rimensnyder, "White House Bicentennial Renews Interest in Civic Life of James Hoban, Architect," *The American Foundation for Irish Heritage,* vol. 1, no. 3 (Fall 1992).

Redcoats under General Robert Ross had landed at Benedict, Maryland, and was headed their way.

While the local militia along with a group of naval gunners and a few scattered Regulars assembled under the inept command of Brigadier General William Winder at the northeast boundary of the District, the government and most of the city's prominent citizens hastily packed and fled. The skilled veterans of the Napoleonic wars quickly overwhelmed the Americans on August 24 in a humiliating and semi-comic rout that became known as the "Bladensburg Races." Unopposed, the British marched down Maryland Avenue to the Capitol where, eager to avenge the recent destruction of Toronto by American units and understandably angered by foolhardy snipers, they set fire to the Capitol and several nearby buildings. Later that evening, their route illuminated by the rising flames, the British commanders marched with a small contingent up Pennsylvania Avenue, within two blocks of St. Patrick's where a group of anxious parishioners had gathered to wait out the night with their pastor.[57]

After a late supper the British set fire to the White House, but a violent thunderstorm doused the flames before they could spread to other buildings. The only other major loss on the 24th occurred when, under orders, its American commandant set the Navy Yard ablaze. The next day the British continued their carefully circumscribed destruction, burning the War and Treasury buildings near Fifteenth Street and the bridge across the Potomac before withdrawing, as suddenly as they came, in the wake of a furious hurricane that assailed friend and foe alike.

When asked why he had not joined the many who fled the city, Father Matthews was widely quoted as replying: "Why should I? I have more business here now than ever before."[58] The destruction of public buildings so near St. Patrick's and the undoubted presence of Matthews and a group of parishioners at the church throughout the occupation gave rise to several colorful anecdotes illustrative of the character of the popular pastor but impossible to document. Supposedly, before the night's storm relieved the danger, the doughty priest repeatedly climbed a steep ladder to toss buckets of water on flying sparks

57. Walter Lord, *The Dawn's Early Light* (New York: W. W. Norton, 1972) is a standard modern account of the British in Washington. George R. Gleig's *The Campaigns of the British Army at Washington and New Orleans* (Totowa, N.J.: Howman and Littlefield, 1972, repr. of 1847 ed.) recounts the event through the eyes of a British soldier.

58. This version of the familiar quotation is taken from Lord's *The Dawn's Early Light*, 171.

and cinders that threatened the church's wooden roof. Eyewitness accounts by two leading citizens lend some credence to this story, but the height of the building, the distance to the conflagration, and the remoteness of the water supply make their report dubious.

Matthews was also represented as having successfully petitioned General Ross to spare several private dwellings, but that such a conversation ever took place is extremely unlikely, given British intentions and Ross's movements in Washington. Another tale concerned the reported appearance of several British soldiers in St. Patrick's on the morning of August 25th. They supposedly attended mass in silence and then, still without a word, followed the pastor to his rectory. Concluding that his arrest was imminent, Matthews was surprised when the soldiers merely asked him to hear their confessions. Almost as though the story had been crafted for its punchy conclusion, the reporter added that Matthews readily forgave the Redcoats, "even though he was a great patriot."[59]

The haunting picture of the Capitol and White House in flames naturally frightened the citizens of Washington, but of far greater danger to their well-being and that of the struggling congregation at St. Patrick's was the fact that the British invasion seriously revived efforts in Congress to abandon the city. Throughout much of September the House met in the crowded confines of the Post Office building to debate the issue. Although the southern faction held firm, New England representatives were ready to leave, and only after three anxious months of discussion did Congress finally agree to rebuild on the Potomac. Seasoned veterans of the fight to retain the capital in Washington knew that, until the buildings were restored and the legislators accommodated, the threat to move would persist. A group including Daniel Carroll of Duddington and Thomas Law hastily built the "Brick Capitol," where Congress met in tolerable comfort while Benjamin Latrobe restored the Capitol. Hoban rebuilt the White House, a job completed in three years. More than one commentator noted the contrast between the feisty Irish artisans who did much of the original work in the 1790s with the docile, largely illiterate crew assembled for the job a generation later.[60]

During this restoration Washingtonians experienced another brief

59. The stories about Matthews on the roof and talking to Ross are repeated in several sources. See, for example, Durkin, *William Matthews*, 16, and the *Catholic Mirror*, 23 Apr 1865 (which may have been Durkin's source). The confession story is from *The Republican*, 26 Oct 1884, a rare copy of this newspaper in the Toner Collection, LC.

60. Seale, *The President's House*, 142.

period of prosperity. By 1817 new businesses and residences were springing up at a satisfying rate. Pennsylvania Avenue between the Capitol and White House had finally become the city's business center. Central Market between Seventh and Ninth Streets was the first of a large group of stores, hotels, newspapers, and other businesses to open along the Avenue near St. Patrick's. The canal across town (although of limited use because of silting problems) and new bridges and local packet boat routes rapidly improved transportation around the District. Federal spending associated with the rebuilding program and activity at the restored Navy Yard immunized Washington from the worst of the depression that visited the country at the end of the decade. Also significant for the future was the appearance of a number of private businesses associated with government activities such as land claims, patents, and pensions that promised employment for a new working class.

Challenges to a Growing Institution

During this period of peace and prosperity, St. Patrick's congregation set out to complete its church. The increased population in the northwest section and steady salaries justified borrowing the necessary funds, and in 1816 the building was completed as planned by adding a pair of wings flanking a central altar area, itself an extension of the old nave. Completed in the form of a T-shaped cross measuring 120 feet in length and 85 feet across at the transept, the building was large enough to seat 800. The gothic revival style of the exterior was further emphasized by continuing the lancet-style windows in the addition and arranging them in triangular fashion around the transept doors. The transepts themselves were surmounted by prominent, steeply pitched cornices, and all three entrances were dominated by large crosses. A flight of stairs led to the main entrance, some fifteen feet above the roadway.[61]

The simplicity of the design precluded a bell tower. Bells were not only a source of pride but a practical necessity in parishes where people often travelled great distances and lacked timepieces. For years the congregation was called to Mass by the sound of an old-fashioned hand bell rung by the pastor from his front steps. There was much demand for a proper bell to grace the new church. Eventually Matthews

61. James M. Goode, *Capital Losses*, 195, offers the most complete description of the second church, but his history of St. Patrick's early years contains several errors.

ST. PATRICK'S CHURCH, 1809–1870

purchased an old Spanish bell from a local Protestant church and mounted it on a halter in a nearby open shed. It proved a poor bargain. Not long after its purchase it cracked, and its peculiar sound became a continuing source of amusement to the congregation until it was finally discarded during the Civil War. Furnishing of the building was completed with the addition of a pipe organ, the first in the city, a pulpit carved from a single piece of mahogany, the gift of Emperor Dom Pedro I of Brazil, and a large renaissance painting, a gift of Charles X of France.[62]

Shortly after completing the addition, Matthews sent Archbishop Ambrose Maréchal, who had succeeded Neale in December 1817, a report on the financial condition of St. Patrick's. This preserved document provides a rare glimpse of parish revenues in those early years. The church's debt totalled $2,900. Its income averaged in excess of $400 a quarter "when regularly paid." The greater part of this sum went toward paying the debt, which at the current rate of reduction

62. For a full description of these articles, see chapter 14. The bell was purchased from the Rev. John C. Smith, pastor of the Fourth Presbyterian Church, about 1841, when his church was undergoing remodeling. See Anna H. Dorsey, "Recollections of Old St. Patrick's Church," *Sunday Morning Chronicle,* Sep 1873, and *The Evening Express,* 8 Aug 1867.

would be liquidated in three years. Matthews denigrated the Sunday offering—"the casual" as he called it—as insignificant. Although the first diocesan synod had decreed that the Sunday offering would be the major source of parish income, Matthews dismissed it as "a mere trifle," adding that pew rent (referring to the practice of selling and renting seating space to the church's parishioners) was his major source of support.[63]

With the church completed and full payment of the debt in sight, Matthews began thinking about a new rectory. The question was linked to the need for an assistant, as he admitted to Maréchal. He could use the help, but even if a priest were available, Caffry's little house was insufficient for one, let alone two residents. In 1817 he decided the question could be postponed. Washington was so healthy, he claimed in one of his frequent compliments to the city, that he had had only five sick calls in the last seven months, and he could handle the rest of the parish's affairs if he could get help from the nearby Jesuits on Sundays.

But Matthews's light-hearted treatment of the matter could not mask the genuine need for a second priest. In addition to the full religious schedule (two Sunday masses with confessions, vespers, weekday mass, and Sacred Heart devotions as well as funerals, weddings, and periodic masses at some of the city's chapels), Matthews had by now become heavily burdened with diocesan and civic affairs. He sought to postpone the inevitable by striking an agreement with the Jesuits for regular assistance, but, finally exasperated by these faltering negotiations, he decided in 1822 to build a rectory "large enough for one or two assistants" and to ask Maréchal for permanent help.[64] There is no record of the parish's borrowing money for this project, nor of any of the usual fund-raising events. Given Matthews's irritation with his Jesuit neighbors and the speed in which the rectory was built, it is entirely possible that he paid for it himself.

The rectory, described as a comfortable southern home, stood on Tenth Street just above the F Street corner. The windows of its parlor were shaded from the west sun by a row of Osage orange trees planted by the pastor. This room was large enough to serve as a reception area for those parishioners who habitually gathered there for a so-

---

63. Ltr., Matthews to Maréchal, 27 Sep 1817, 19-A-6, Maréchal Papers, AAB.

64. Ltr., Matthews to Maréchal, 27 Sep 1817, 19-A-6, Maréchal Papers, AAB; Maréchal, Draft "Notes on the General's Report (on temporalities and jurisdictions)" for the Propaganda Fide, Mar-May 1822, reprinted in Hughes, Documents 1:455–59. St. Patrick's relations with the Jesuits are discussed in chapter 3, below.

cial hour after Sunday vespers. When the church was being repaired, Matthews celebrated Mass in the parlor, using its antique sideboard as an altar. The rectory yard was carefully fenced. Matthews was an avid gardener, and for years he grew vegetables for the rectory, supplying the poor and selling the surplus at bargain rates to his parishioners. Eyewitnesses recalled the sturdy pastor, sporting his old wide-brimmed straw hat, reminding visitors to shut the gate to keep stray animals from invading his precious rows of beans.[65]

Shortly after the rectory was completed, St. Patrick's welcomed its first assistant priest, Stephen Dubuisson. The recently ordained Jesuit was a native of Hispaniola and a veteran of Napoleon's army who had served on the Emperor's staff before immigrating to America. He remained at St. Patrick's three years before becoming president of Georgetown College. The urbane priest was a popular figure in Washington, particularly revered by the congregation for his extraordinary piety and beautiful singing voice. His arrival coincided with the beginning of that rich devotional life that would become a hallmark of St. Patrick's Church. In earlier decades the lack of discretionary time among parishioners struggling to make ends meet and the difficulty in travelling to the church had reduced attendance, while the lack of proper ecclesiastical facilities precluded some of the more elaborate rituals of the Roman rite. With these difficulties largely overcome, the new church with its "grand orgue" as the congregation proudly called it, allowed full play to those ceremonies and rites that characterized the Tridentine tradition. Archbishop Maréchal's confirmation of three hundred parishioners in 1818 was an example of this new liturgical splendor at St. Patrick's. Now public devotions stood at the center of parish life, largely replacing the private prayer, meditation, and other forms of personal piety that had figured so prominently in earlier times.

In contrast to his new assistant, who was noted for his fine tenor voice and oratorical skills, Matthews was remembered far and wide as one who never sang High Mass and always read sermons without gesture from prepared texts. In an age when Americans showed an unbe-

65. The location of the rectory is described in Wentz, ed., *Records of St. Patrick's Church and School*, 16. Stories about Matthews and his garden are repeated in Anna M. Dorsey, "Recollections of Old St. Patrick's Church," and Virginia K. Frye, "St Patrick's—First Catholic Church of the Federal City," 36–37. Although both accounts contain much valuable detail supported by the primary sources, they also repeat stories that are probably apocryphal. For example, Frye's assertion that the rectory was located on G Street is contradicted by various documents and news accounts from the 1850s.

lievable appetite for eloquent preaching, as Maréchal reported to Propaganda, Matthews made do with a barrel full of sermons, which he would read successively to the congregation. Once delivered, a sermon was relegated to a second barrel, which when filled would be turned over, and beginning with the sermon on top, the pastor would repeat the process.[66] Although he was no orator, Matthews had the wit to provide his sermon-loving congregation with their fill. The leading preachers of the day, prelates and priests from across the country, spoke frequently from St. Patrick's pulpit. Particularly noteworthy in those early years was the Christmas Day 1825 sermon of Bishop John England of Charleston. This memorable oration was a rebuttal to John Quincy Adams's well-known anti-Catholic prejudices and became the talk of Washington, leading to the bishop's address before Congress two weeks later.[67]

Although Maréchal was enthusiastic about the growth of popular devotions in his diocese, the only one evident at St. Patrick's was that sponsored by the Confraternity of the Sacred Heart. This ancient devotion, especially fostered by the Jesuits, had received a new emphasis from the visions of St. Margaret Mary Alacoque in seventeenth-century France. It particularly appealed to Matthews, who served as unofficial coordinator of the confraternity in the Baltimore archdiocese. He distributed to interested pastors printed certificates on which the names of individual members in each congregation could be inscribed. He maintained a correspondence with moderators throughout the diocese, encouraging them to keep careful records and instruct their congregations in the duties and privileges of confraternity members.[68]

The quiet progression of sacramental and devotional life in the parish was abruptly shattered in early 1824 by reports of a miracle in-

66. Reports on Matthews's habit of reading sermons and his aversion to singing are repeated in numerous sources. See The Republican, 26 Oct 1884, copy in Toner Collection, LC, and "Gonzaga College," Woodstock Letters, 17. Maréchal's comment on the American Catholic's love of sermons was made in his "Report to Propaganda," 16 Oct 1818, reproduced in Philip Gleason, ed., Documentary Reports on Early American Catholicism (New York: Arno Press, 1978), 214–15.

67. Peter Guilday, The Life and Times of John England (New York: The America Press, 1927), 2:48–53. For an account of England's appearance at the Capitol, see ltr., England to William Gaston, 29 Jan 1826, reproduced in Ellis, American Church Documents, 234–36.

68. Documents on this subject have been preserved. See, for example, ltr., Matthews to Rev. Dr. Daniphoux, 3 Aug 1833, SAB.

volving one of the city's most prominent families and St. Patrick's assistant pastor. For some time Mrs. Ann Mattingly, the widowed sister of Mayor Thomas Carberry, had been seriously ill, and in February a team of three doctors declared her breast cancer at terminal stage. Father Dubuisson was a devout student of miraculous cures, and he and his colleague, the noted Jesuit educator Anthony Kohlmann, had been following reports of cures effected through the prayers of Prince Alexander Hohenlohe, a priest in Bamberg, Germany. Dubuisson petitioned the prince to intercede on behalf of the dying woman and several other of Washington's sickest people.

At the German's instruction, the group in Washington began a novena to the Holy Name of Jesus on March first, the prayers to be recited at sunrise to synchronize intercessions from both sides of the Atlantic. The petitions culminated with the reception of Holy Communion at 3 A.M. on March 10, again timed to coincide with Hohenlohe's schedule. Mrs. Mattingly, completely immobilized and in great pain, had great difficulty in swallowing the host, but immediately afterward experienced a total recovery and personally greeted Father Matthews at the door when he called some hours later.

Both archbishop and pastor piously accepted the miraculous nature of the cure, but both were concerned with the unbridled enthusiasm of Dubuisson and Kohlmann and the effect of their exaggerated stories. Matthews worried about the crowds that were expected to assemble around the homes of the other petitioners, hoping to witness another miracle on the tenth of April. He criticized Kohlmann's "zeal and credulity" and admitted to the archbishop that exhorting such excited priests to moderation had proved useless. Matthews issued a public statement in an attempt to end speculation, but thanks to Dubuisson and Kohlmann, news of the cure was widely publicized throughout the United States, and the Carberry house, on the site of today's headquarters of the Daughters of the American Revolution, became known as the "miracle house."[69]

Like Matthews, Maréchal treated the cure with great reverence, but he warned Matthews that the pious could overdo such things and

69. Ltrs., Matthews to Maréchal, 27 and 31 Mar 1824, 19 and 21-B-17, Maréchal Papers, AAB. For a description of the miracle house, see Goode, *Capital Losses*, 21–22. For a modern, comprehensive account of the miracle, see Robert Emmett Curran, S.J., "'The Finger of God Is Here': The Advent of the Miraculous in the Nineteenth-Century American Catholic Community," *Catholic Historical Review* 73 (Jan 1987): 41–61.

passed on all kinds of precautions and instructions. Matthews confessed to the archbishop that Kohlmann "had caused me to laugh more during a few days than I have done for a year," but he also ruefully observed that the miracle had "caused a great deal of trouble— happy thing they do not occur often—Divine Providence in its infinite wisdom regulates their occurrence." He dutifully collected and published all the facts in the form of a series of affidavits from those most closely involved (Mayor Carberry's affidavit was sworn to before Chief Justice John Marshall).

Although Maréchal never submitted the case to Rome for official judgment, the Holy See was kept informed. Final word on the matter came from the combative Bishop England, who offered a spirited defense of Father Hohenlohe in response to criticism from Protestant extremists. After examining all the evidence, that popular scholar concluded, "What then was the restoration of Mrs. Mattingly, if not a miracle?"[70]

The Mattingly miracle occurred at a time of strong growth in the American church. Since 1776 the number of Catholics had risen from 25,000 to 60,000, and St. Patrick's, one of the first parishes in the nation, was now but one of more than 100 congregations. Even if such numbers appear modest when compared with those swollen by the great wave of immigration about to begin, they nevertheless reveal a secure and confident community of Christians. The church was prospering in the benign climate of religious liberty guaranteed in the Bill of Rights, gaining acceptance and even, Archbishop Maréchal reported to Rome, "a certain amount of veneration" from non-Catholics.[71] Mirroring this general situation, St. Patrick's had successfully met the challenges of its formative years. Along with the city, it too was enjoying the "era of good feelings" that had engulfed the nation. In 1820 Matthews could report "a very respectable number" in at-

70. Quoted in Smith's *History of St. Patrick's,* 18. The Mattingly miracle is well documented. See William Matthews, *A Collection of Affidavits and Certificates, Relative to the Wonderful Cure of Mrs. Ann Mattingly* (Washington: James Wilson, 1824), which later, at Pope Leo XII's request, was translated into Italian. See also ltrs., Matthews to Maréchal, 10 and 19 Mar 1824; and Maréchal to Matthews, 12 Mar 1824, 21-Q-1, Maréchal letterbook. All in Maréchal Papers, AAB. On Dubuisson's interest in miracles, see material in Maryland provincial archives, 14-H, 2.2, GUA. The Mattingly case was reported to Rome by Bishop Francis P. Kenrick. See his letter to Propaganda Fide, 6 Aug 24, *Congressi,* sec. 8, APF. On Mrs. Mattingly's later life, see *Catholic Standard,* 26 Feb 1965.

71. Ambroise Maréchal, "Report to Propaganda," 16 Oct 1818.

tendance at both Sunday masses with up to forty communicants on average in a time when reception of the Holy Eucharist was infrequent.[72] These numbers grew steadily in succeeding years.

Pronouncing a sort of valedictory on the congregation's first three decades, Father Matthews summarized the state of the parish for the archbishop at the end of 1822: "It will doubtless afford great consolation to your paternal heart," he told Maréchal, "to hear that the mercy of God has continued to manifest itself in this portion of it, in a singular manner by an almost daily increase in our number, piety & fervour; all things proceeding in perfect harmony & fraternal charity."[73]

72. Ltr., Matthews to Maréchal, 4 May 1820, 19-A-10, Maréchal Papers, AAB.
73. Ltr., Matthews to Maréchal, 28 Nov 1822, 19-B-13, Maréchal Papers, AAB.

CHAPTER 3

Mater Ecclesiarum

LONG AFTER it had ceased to be the only parish in the city, St. Patrick's continued to play a unique role in local ecclesiastical affairs. Such distinction might seem appropriate for the city's mother church, but in fact this special status survived well into the twentieth century. As late as 1931 an astute commentator compared St. Patrick's relationship with the local Catholic community to that of a cathedral in other dioceses.[1] This continued leadership and influence cannot be explained by the usual hallmarks. In terms of size of congregation, wealth and prominence of members, and even importance of its downtown neighborhood, St. Patrick's pre-eminence did not long survive the Civil War. More likely, the parish's continued centrality in church affairs derived from the habit of leadership it developed during the formative years of Washington's history.

After 1820 St. Patrick's repeatedly transcended traditional parish responsibilities to shoulder projects truly diocesan in scope. It created new parishes and organized city-wide institutions for the care and education of Washington's children; Father Matthews and leading members of the congregation served effectively in important munic-

1. Louis G. Weitzman, *One Hundred Years of Catholic Charities in the District of Columbia* (Washington: The Catholic University, 1931), 5.

ipal projects; and the energetic pastor also represented the American hierarchy in church-state negotiations and even administered the church in Philadelphia when that diocese was in turmoil.

That it was organized first may justify the title mother church, but St. Patrick's special distinction actually derived from this larger role in diocesan affairs, a role reinforced by pastors and congregation in later generations. Successive archbishops would regard the church as their headquarters in the capital, and into recent times it seemed entirely unremarkable for Washingtonians to refer familiarly to St. Patrick's as their "other" parish, a feeling attested by the thousands of non-parishioners who regularly passed through its doors. These Catholics might not have been aware that St. Patrick's was the city's oldest church, but they all seemed to recognize its special status.[2] This reputation began in the decades between 1820 and 1850, when the congregation was playing a crucial role in establishing Catholicism in Washington.

Daughter Parishes

St. Patrick's changed as a result of the city's growing size and prosperity following the War of 1812. That growth brought new responsibilities to a far from affluent congregation. Less than twenty-five years after Archbishop Carroll defined the parish and drew its boundaries, some of its members were calling for the organization of a second parish. Even before the size of the Catholic population and its material resources made another church practical, consideration of distance made division irresistible. The title mother church may be an honorific, but in a literal sense St. Patrick's can claim three ecclesiastical daughters: St. Peter's, St. Matthew's, and Immaculate Conception. The first two, organized in the early years of the city's history, presented special challenges to St. Patrick's that involved the congregation in diocesan business.

Abbé Jose Correa da Serra, the Portuguese minister and only diplomat in holy orders, tactfully called the Washington of 1817 "a city of magnificent distances." Although new bridges and steadily improving streets had by then increased access to the far reaches of town, Correa knew that the city's residents still dwelt in a series of widely separated neighborhoods. Actually, the early growth of Washington and its

2. Archbishop Philip M. Hannan and Msgr. E. Robert Arthur, both careful students of the archdiocese's history, commented on the hold St. Patrick's has exercised on the loyalty and affection of the area's Catholics into recent times. See their interviews with author, SPA.

churches deviated markedly from the regular American pattern. In place of uniform expansion outward from a central area, the capital followed, albeit imperfectly, a unique bi-polar pattern devised by its designer. To its great good fortune St. Patrick's stood central to the focal points established by L'Enfant, and it benefitted from the city's early and continued growth in the area between the White House and the Capitol along Pennsylvania Avenue and the F Street corridor.

In a modest way those parishioners who lived east of the Capitol had also found their numbers increasing after the war, because of renewed activity associated with rearmament programs at the Navy Yard and the rebuilding of the burned-out Capitol. More so than those who were flocking into the already-populous areas north and west of the White House, however, these parishioners experienced severe hardship in traveling to F Street to fulfill their religious obligations. The rude roadways that connected them with St. Patrick's were still often impassable. In the development of a second parish for the city, the emphasis would be less on population pressure and more on those magnificent distances.

Physical isolation also strengthened the strong sectional rivalry between the two areas of the city and defeated L'Enfant's plan for complementary communities radiating from the White House and Capitol. The lag in population in the eastern wards (four and six) only increased inequality in economic strength and political power. Some 70 percent of the city's residents lived in its first three wards (the area north of E Street and west of First Street west). Since these wards also paid roughly 70 percent of the taxes, which the law required to be spent in the same ward in which they were collected, the eastern and southern wards also lagged behind in city services and government-related business. Ecclesial matters reflected a similar inequality. St. Patrick's, which stood in the exact center of populous Ward Two, tended to look to its own neighborhood and westward for economic support and participation in major projects, leaving the eastern section of the parish isolated and somewhat neglected.[3]

The parish had never commanded attendance by all these parishioners. Those at great distances were welcomed instead in the private chapels, such as those of Notley Young and Daniel Carroll, that still dotted the landscape. More recently, Ann Young Casanave built a chapel in her mansion on Delaware Avenue at the edge of Capitol

3. Green, *Washington*, 1:91–92. For an analysis of the impact of the city's geography on its churches, see Fosselman, "A Downtown Parish," 44–46 and 90–94.

Hill, where Catholics in her neighborhood (which in those days was considered an excessive distance from St. Patrick's) would gather for Mass. Well into the new century some freestanding chapels were regularly used by large congregations and even from time to time enjoyed a resident priest. Such places of worship included those beyond the city's boundaries, like the one sponsored by Nicholas Queen in what is now St. Francis de Sales parish, and John Boone's chapel at a distance in Prince George's County.

The most noteworthy of these chapels was built by James Barry in 1805 at Half and P Streets, Southwest, near Buzzard's Point. Known as St. Mary's, the Barry chapel served in effect as a mission of St. Patrick's where Father Matthews or visiting priests would periodically celebrate Mass for the convenience of local parishioners. Archbishop Carroll clarified the chapel's position when he set up guidelines for one such visiting priest. Mass must include religious instruction in the form of a homily and catechism classes for the children. Accurate records must be kept and inscribed in St. Patrick's register, and while the visitor might arrange with Matthews on a division of stole fees, no parishioner could withhold support from the parish in favor of the chapel.[4]

If Washington had followed the usual pattern of population growth, St. Mary's would soon have evolved into an independent parish. But the southern section lagged behind other areas, and by 1820 the place was abandoned. Barry and his children were buried in the chapel, later to become no more than a romantic ruin whose falling walls and empty vault attracted sightseers in the post–Civil War era. Eventually its cornerstone was placed in the wall of St. Dominic, which by mid-century had become the center of Catholic life on the Island, as the area between the Tiber and the Potomac was called.[5]

Nothing had come of the scheme advanced in 1801 to build a grand church on South Capitol Street, even after Daniel Carroll of Duddington donated a city square to the project. Nor had the more modest proposal in 1806 to build a small church for Catholics living in southeast Washington succeeded, despite a subscription of two thousand

4. Ltrs., Rev. Notley Young to Carroll, 17 Nov 1806, 8-R-2; and Carroll to Young, 10 Dec 1806, Carroll Letterbook, vol. 1, p. 77. Both in Carroll Papers, AAB. See also ltr., Carroll to Leonard Neale, 26 Jan 1807, *JCP* 3:6–7.

5. The story of the Barry chapel has intrigued Washington's antiquarians and early church historians. See, for example, Allen C. Clark, "Captain James Barry," *RCHS* 42–43 (1943), and Margaret Brent Downing, "James and Joanna Gould Barry," *RCHS* 15 (1921).

dollars and a city square pledged for the enterprise.[6] By 1819 parishioners east of the Capitol decided to press the cause again, and with Matthews's "full approbation" Barry broached the matter with Archbishop Maréchal, citing transportation problems and the lack of assistants at St. Patrick's as reasons for a new church. Perhaps exaggerating a bit, he told Maréchal that St. Patrick's—which could jam sixteen hundred people into its two Sunday masses— "will not contain one half the congregation," compelling one quarter of the parishioners to stand outdoors during each mass.[7] Barry wanted Maréchal to approve a drive at St. Patrick's to see what funds could be raised among the city's Catholics. To stimulate contributions, Daniel Carroll offered to donate another group of lots for a building on Second Street near the Capitol.

When Maréchal asked for Matthews's views, the pastor replied that he had participated in the original discussions about a new church, going so far as to explore various ways to raise the money. The always financially shrewd pastor had even asked one wealthy parishioner to build the church at his own expense, promising a fair return on the investment from future pew rents. When this proposal failed, Matthews reported, he had agreed to launch a fund drive in the parish, but only if Maréchal approved. Matthews made it clear that he was not so much concerned with winning approval for a second parish or promoting any specific financial scheme as with ensuring that such an enterprise would be under strict clerical control and that Washington would remain free from any taint of trusteeism.[8]

Trusteeism was one of the great issues in the early American church. It grew where local legal custom dictated that ownership of church property be vested in a committee composed of congregation members. This so-called board of trustees, not the bishop, was recognized by the local government as owner, with all the legal power such status entailed. In those places where the bishop held legal title—as in the case of St. Patrick's after Caffry signed the property over to Archbishop Carroll in 1804—that church official controlled the parish and its pastor. Where trustees controlled the property—as in hundreds of other parishes throughout the country—the congregation was

6. "Catholics Living Near the Eastern Branch, Subscribers List, 1806," 11-H-5, Carroll Papers, AAB. The idea of a national cathedral in southeast Washington is discussed in chapter 5, below.

7. Ltr., Barry to Maréchal, 25 Apr 1820, 13-I-4, Maréchal Papers, AAB.

8. Ltr., Matthews to Maréchal, 4 May 1820, 19-A-10, Maréchal Papers, AAB.

empowered by civil law to reject pastors appointed by the bishop or protect renegade pastors from the bishop's discipline—in Maréchal's words, "to raise the flag of rebellion against the bishop."[9]

The trustee controversy has undergone considerable reinterpretation in recent years by historians. They now tend to downplay its danger to the church, viewing it as part of a natural progression in the development of immigrant congregations in the context of the American legal system. While sometimes the cause of public controversy, trustee control also provided a means of venting hostilities during a period of dynamic growth, thereby avoiding schism. In most parishes that employed them, trustees worked in effective partnership with the hierarchy. Indeed the vast majority of Catholic congregations (numbering 230 in 1830 and 1,712 parishes by 1854) worked harmoniously under the bishop, whether they were managed by pastors or by lay trustees. The serious disputes that became the focus of so much concern occurred in about a dozen parishes, principally Philadelphia, Norfolk, and Charleston.[10]

Matthews was not one to underestimate the seriousness of these notorious parish fights and was determined to squelch anything that smacked of trusteeism in Washington. He assured Maréchal that laymen involved in the project regularly reported to him, such was the "anxious solicitude of the good people here that the harmony of the Church may not be interrupted or its discipline infringed." Though some few "Catholics in name" had demanded an "Independent church, trustees, etc." (Matthews made no distinction in such terms), they would never prevail. He had every right to be confident. Daniel Carroll had accepted his advice and promised to deed the site to the archbishop "in trust and no other way." Furthermore, nothing was being done without the key players asking assurance at every step that it met with the archbishop's approval. As for the ringleader of those who had called for trustees and public meetings, Matthews reported that he was a Freemason and only included on the building committee because of his influence over the city's mechanics. Matthews added cryptically, "Another will be put in his place."[11] To Matthews's credit, he managed to retain firm control for the archbishop through-

9. Maréchal, "Report to Propaganda," 16 Oct 1818.

10. The trustee controversy and the extensive literature on the subject has been examined in Patrick W. Carey, *People, Priests, and Prelates: Ecclesiastical Democracy and the Tensions of Trusteeism* (Notre Dame: University of Notre Dame Press, 1987).

11. Ltr., Matthews to Maréchal, 4 May 1820, 19-A-10, Maréchal Papers, AAB.

out the negotiations for the new parish without damaging the laity's enthusiasm. He constantly praised the people for their zeal and urged them to collect the money as quickly as possible.

At the same time, Matthews, who was still trying to pay off the debt on the addition to St. Patrick's, was less than sanguine about raising money for a new church from the same source. His fear seemed well founded, as contributions trickled in slowly. By February 1821 the new church was under roof, but at the cost of increasing St. Patrick's debt by $2,700. With work at a standstill, Matthews passed on to Maréchal without comment Daniel Carroll's proposal to turn the church over to the Jesuits at Georgetown, whose carpenters could quickly finish the building. Nothing came of this idea. Maréchal was involved in a major fight with the Society, and the Jesuits could not spare a priest to man the new parish. Besides, if the Jesuits were going to acquire a parish in the city, they wanted St. Patrick's itself.[12]

The church, a modest frame structure, was eventually finished and formally dedicated to St. Peter in October 1821. The archbishop drew the boundary lines that gave the new parish jurisdiction over the city east of the Tiber and appointed James F. Lucas its first pastor. Because the new parish started off with a significant debt, the building committee, with Matthews as its adviser, remained in existence to manage the church's financal obligations. Such an arrangement only invited trouble, and almost immediately the new pastor, who, as pastor of a church in Norfolk, Virginia, had only recently been involved in a major trustee fight, became the center of a controversy that would last until his departure nine years later. Beginning with an argument over the pace of debt liquidation versus the financial needs of the pastor, the dismal fight dragged on, the ill-suited Lucas accusing the committee and Matthews of the sin of trusteeism.

Actually, the intemperate pastor had a point. For all Matthews's fulminating against trustees, his committee's control of St. Peter's finances clearly resembled that of the typical trustee arrangement. But if Matthews acted somewhat imperiously with the hapless Lucas, he acted prudently. Title to the property rested safely with the bishop, and contrary to the pastor's charge, the committee accepted the archbishop's instructions at every turn, thereby sparing the diocese the turmoil and embarrassment of a public dispute. It was enough that during St. Peter's ill-starred infancy the church in Washington ex-

12. Ltr., Matthews to Maréchal, 2 Feb 1821, 19-A-11, Maréchal Papers, AAB; Anthony Kohlmann, "A Note," 12 Jul 1820, reproduced in Hughes's *Documents* 1:561.

pended an enormous amount of energy better spent elsewhere in the vineyard.

The conflict surrounding the formation of St. Peter's obviously taught Matthews a lesson, one he applied when establishing the city's third parish sixteen years later. By that time, steady growth in the western portion of the city had not only replaced all the parishioners lost when St. Peter's took everyone east of the Tiber, but led to calls for yet another parish. To support the undertaking, Matthews advanced a different scheme for raising the money. In April 1837 the *National Intelligencer* announced that St. Patrick's would open a subscription drive, with monthly collections continuing until sufficient money was on hand to start a new church.[13] Less than a year later parishioners had donated a sufficient amount to purchase a site at the northeast corner of Fifteenth and H Streets. At the archbishop's request the congregation met twice to discuss the finances of the new parish. The city was divided into eight sectors and each was assigned a crew of collectors, with others designated to solicit contributions throughout Georgetown and Alexandria and from the President, government agencies, and diplomatic corps. "Every citizen of the District," the *National Intelligencer* warned, "would be called on by the collectors."[14] This carefully organized and well-publicized collection, aided by the advent of economic good times in Washington and a $10,000 donation from Matthews himself, produced the needed funds.

The ceremony in September 1838 surrounding the laying of the cornerstone at St. Matthew's (a name chosen as a compliment to St. Patrick's pastor) was the most impressive religious event in the city to date. A local reporter provided a breathless description of the procession led by the Marine band and including Archbishop Samuel Eccleston "in full pontificals" that marched up Pennsylvania Avenue from St. Patrick's. He also commented on the litanies and chants "beautifully intoned" by St. Patrick's choir despite the inclement weather.[15] The church was completed in 1840 and shortly thereafter the committee of St. Patrick's laymen delegated to supervise its erection paid off the debt and turned over the balance of $30.29 to the new pastor.[16] The new foundation required another adjustment in parish boundaries. As

13. *National Intelligencer*, 29 Apr 1837.

14. *National Intelligencer*, 18 Jul 1838.

15. *National Intelligencer*, 24 Sep 1838. Eccleston had become the fifth archbishop of Baltimore in 1834.

16. Helene, Estelle, and Imogene Philibert, *Saint Matthew's of Washington, 1840–1940* (Baltimore: A. Hoen, 1940), 24.

confirmed by the archbishop in 1852, St. Patrick's precincts, which until recently were coequal with the city limits, now covered the blocks
between Third and Thirteenth Streets and from the Washington canal
(today's Constitution Avenue) on the south to the city line on the
north.

Having cooperated in the establishment of two other churches and
seen a major reduction in size and population, St. Patrick's congregation understandably looked askance on a proposal for yet another
church within its boundaries, this one for the city's German Catholics.
The phenomenon of churches organized on the basis of nationality
rather than geography arose during the great wave of immigration before the Civil War. Responding to demands that linguistic and cultural
differences be accommodated in separate congregations, and anxious
to preserve the faith against threats of widespread schism if such demands were ignored, the hierarchy agreed to exceptions to the rule
that parishes be attended by all within their precincts. Such an exception had seemed unnecessary in early Washington where, aside from a
significant number of black communicants, the Catholic population
was remarkably homogeneous. With no ethnically defined neighborhoods, the city had easily absorbed the relatively small numbers of immigrants into the general population. Early lists of St. Patrick's parishioners hint at a broad diversity of national origins.[17] German, Italian,
and French families, like the English and Irish, were among the first
settlers in the new capital. These residents, well represented among
the parish's second generation, had no need of or special interest in
belonging to separate language congregations.

By 1829, however, construction of the Chesapeake and Ohio canal
and other major government projects suddenly brought Washington a
burst of new immigrants. This group, which, like that of the previous
generation, was dominated by the Irish, also included a number of
German artisans and their families. It was these newcomers, estimated
at about two hundred Catholics in all, who objected to being included
in what they called "Irish" parishes and who pressed for the city's first
German parish.[18] By 1840 they were gathering for Mass with sermons
in German in a small basement chapel in the new St. Matthew's whenever a visiting German cleric was available. Matthias Alig, a Redemp-

17. See, for example, a list of St. Patrick's families prepared by Stephen Dubuisson
(circa 1830), Maryland provincial archives, 15-C-l, GUA.

18. Charles L. Boehmer, *History of St. Mary's Church of the Mother of God, Washington, D.C.* (Washington: 1946), 13–18. See also Sister M. Xavier Maloney, "The Catholic
Church in the District of Columbia (Earlier Period: 1790–1866)," 48.

torist priest recently arrived in the Baltimore archdiocese, was such a visitor in late 1845. He subsequently canvassed the widely scattered German residents to gauge interest and potential financial support for a separate church.

The meager response seemed to doom hopes for a German parish until a wealthy non-Catholic intervened. John P. Van Ness, a congressman from New York and husband of Washington heiress Marcia Burns, offered the group a lot at Fifth and G Streets, provided a church be built within the year. Alig used his own funds to finance the church dedicated to St. Mary, Mother of God, and in October 1846 Washington witnessed another Catholic spectacular, as the archbishop, preceded by the city's German band and a long parade of citizens, processed from St. Matthew's down Pennsylvania Avenue to lay the cornerstone of the new church.[19]

Notably absent from the festivities and the list of contributors to the building fund were the pastor and congregation of St. Patrick's. Perhaps feelings were running high. Matthews knew that under church law, attendance at St. Mary's was supposedly restricted to German-speaking Catholics, but such a stipulation was not likely to survive the assimilation of the new immigrants. The lure of the territorial parish rested on the habit of most Catholics to frequent a church that was convenient. The location of St. Mary's was related solely to Van Ness's generosity and not to any concentration of German residents, and the presence of two churches within five blocks of each other was sure to stimulate future rivalry with St. Mary's openly appealing to nearby St. Patrick's parishioners. The astute pastor kept his counsel, probably realizing that objection was fruitless since Archbishop Eccleston, fearful of a repetition of the schisms occurring in other American cities and supportive of the new immigrant groups, approved the project. Anyway, such concerns must have seemed of minor importance in view of the rapid growth of Catholic population before the Civil War. Disputes over national parishes were something for the future.

The Care and Education of Catholic Children

If the development of new parishes attested to the central role of St. Patrick's in diocesan affairs, the parish's work on behalf of Washington's children explains the major influence exercised by a small and far

19. A detailed description of the ceremony and its participants is contained in Philibert, *Saint Matthew's of Washington,* 27.

from economically secure minority on the early development of the city's educational and social institutions. In an age when formal schooling was still considered the prerogative of the wealthy, William Matthews constantly preached the importance of universal education in a democracy. His words found ready acceptance among all elements of his financially and socially diverse parish. Free schools fulfilled the church's obligation to assimilate the immigrant and provide concrete, long-range assistance to its poorest members. The organization of private academies, on the other hand, addressed a pressing need of the growing Catholic middle class. Under Matthews's guidance the congregation expended much of its resources on the establishment and support of schools that, on the eve of the Civil War, were teaching almost half the city's students.

Strictly speaking, the three major educational institutions organized during Matthews's pastorate, along with a fourth that opened shortly after his death, were not parochial schools—each was controlled by an independent board of trustees, was operated by a religious order, and included pupils of all faiths drawn from all parts of the city. Such distinctions tend to blur, however, since for much of the time the schools were largely dependent on the parish for direction and support, and St. Patrick's schools, which would educate thousands of children in the next 150 years, rightly trace their roots to these early foundations.

Actually the first to benefit from Father Matthews's interest in education were the city's nascent public schools. In 1804 the city council set up a school system and agreed to appropriate $1,500 annually for their maintenance, the money derived from a special tax on slaves and pets and a license fee on carriages, hacks, liquor, and amusements. Congress added some support by authorizing a series of lotteries to underwrite the schools, but until 1860, when a tax was assessed on all private property for the purpose, public support of the schools was erratic and inadequate, and the struggling system depended more on tuition and private donations. The schools were opened to all white children (no provision was made for black students until 1862), but they were intended mainly to educate the city's poor, especially the new immigrants, and those who could were expected to pay tuition. Unfortunately, most of those who could afford to contribute shunned what were universally considered pauper schools in favor of the city's private academies. Consequently the public schools chronically suffered a lack of support.

To run the schools the council appointed a board of trustees, whose thirteen members were elected by the council and the private donors. President Jefferson was the first honorary president of the board; Father Matthews was elected to the body in 1813. Most trustees showed little interest in their job, and in one fourteen-year period more than half the board's meetings had to be canceled for lack of a quorum. In contrast, Matthews never missed a meeting. He remained on the school board for a record thirty-one years, a forceful and hard-working advocate of public education.[20]

Matthews spent countless hours on committees that supervised teachers, raised money and built schools, and petitioned Congress and the council in an unending battle for funds. Fellow trustees quickly came to depend on his fund-raising ability and frequently asked him to organize drives for the purchase and maintenance of school houses. Among the busy pastor's most time-consuming chores was his work on a three-man subcommittee that supervised Washington's Lancasterian school.[21] A pedagogic innovation introduced to America in 1806, the Lancasterian schools made a virtue of necessity by using the older, brighter students to instruct their classmates. Such "modern" techniques called for close supervision, and Matthews was actively involved in the school's administration, overseeing discipline and testing student progress. The Lancasterian school, like the other public schools, was non-sectarian but was expected to teach morality and religion. Revealing a strong ecumenical bent, Matthews was a forceful advocate of religious instruction in the public school curriculum, even as he insisted that such instruction not be controlled by any particular religious denomination.

Father Matthews's long service on the school board was important for several reasons. Washington benefitted from his outspoken complaints about the wretched state of public education and his constant goading of a reluctant city council to allocate the tax revenues collected for the schools. The church gained from the respect and affection such effective public service won for a leader of the Catholic minority in an age when anti-Catholic bigotry was on the rise in Washington and other cities. Finally, Matthews's service provided him with valuable experience in the organization and development of schools, experience that would stand Catholic Washington in good stead.

20. Durkin, *William Matthews*, 57–81. See also J. Ormond Wilson, "Eighty Years of the Public Schools of Washington 1805 to 1885," *RCHS* 1 (1895): 119–20.

21. See description in the *National Intelligencer*, 15 Aug 1814.

St. Patrick's first foray into Catholic education, a school for boys operated by the Jesuit fathers, developed out Matthews's early failure to procure an assistant. The shortage of diocesan priests made it unlikely that the parish could expect help from that quarter, so the pastor turned instead to his former colleagues at Georgetown. Aware that the Jesuits wanted to establish a novitiate away from the secular distractions of the college, he offered them a building site on F Street in exchange for the assistance of the novitiate's priest-directors with his parish duties. A deal was struck, and in June 1815 Matthews deeded to Georgetown's former president, Father Francis Neale, the lot adjoining St. Patrick's, land Matthews had recently purchased from James Hoban, who in turn had bought it from Anthony Caffry. Taking advantage of a recent bequest and a further contribution from Matthews, the Jesuits purchased lot 3 on F Street, as well as the two lots directly behind on G, and laid plans for a large, three-story building.[22]

Matthews might have thought he was engaged in a straightforward exchange—valuable property and a gift of money for long-term priestly assistance—but the Jesuits had other goals in mind. Ever since the restoration of their order, they had been seeking to regain control over not only their old settlements around Maryland but also a significant number of new missions, including St. Patrick's. Although Archbishop Carroll had welcomed the building of a novitiate on F Street and the promised help for Matthews and although he was willing to honor most of the society's claims, he was adamantly opposed to making St. Patrick's a Jesuit foundation. "You cannot however expect," he told John Grassi, the Jesuit superior, "that I am either willing or able to place the Church of Washington under the government of the Society." He was, he claimed, thinking about the welfare of the Jesuits. "I would not prepare the seeds of so much enmity, reproach, & disquietude for the Society, as would be produced by placing that city entirely under its pastoral care; nor control; nor would my regulation be regarded by my Successors."[23] But here Carroll was wrong, for his

22. The purchase of the Jesuit property in square 376 is detailed in Wentz, *Inventory*, 13. The sales of lot 4 are recorded in D.C. Land Records: *liber* B-2-L, fol. 397, 9 Sep 1796; *liber* A.A. 26, fol. 235, 1 Mar 1811 (recorded 5 Jun 1811); *liber* A.C. 28, fol. 19, 1 Jun 1811 (recorded 15 Jun 1811); and *liber* A.I. 34, fol. 290, 13 Jul 1815; all in Office of the Recorder of Deeds. It is of some interest that Hoban paid Caffry five pounds sterling for the land, which he resold to Matthews ninety days later for the considerably higher price of $500. Matthews sold the lot to the Jesuits for $1.00. On the controversy between Matthews and the Jesuits and the foundation of the Washington Catholic Seminary, see Fosselman, "A Downtown Parish," 51–66.

23. Ltr., Carroll to Grassi, 31 Mar 1815, *JCP* 3:331–32.

successor, Leonard Neale, was a staunch supporter of Jesuit claims, and one of his first deeds as ordinary was to sign an agreement with Grassi that, among other things, placed St. Patrick's under the Society of Jesus.

Unfortunately for Jesuit ambitions, Neale died before the transaction could be carried out. His successor, the French Sulpician Maréchal, who immediately became embroiled in a heated battle with the Society over jurisdiction in the diocese, proceeded to dismantle the Neale-Grassi agreement, nullifying its provisions and refusing to grant faculties to the Jesuits except in those places where he wished to send them.[24] Undaunted by Maréchal's intervention, the Jesuits continued their campaign to gain control of St. Patrick's. As one of the fathers reported to Grassi, by occupying the house on F Street "they may occasionally help Mr. Matthews and secure that house and mission for the Society."[25]

Father Matthews's initial reaction to the conflict swirling around his church is unclear. Maréchal, not the most impartial witness, reported that the pastor, "in other respects very intelligent," had accepted the Jesuit offers at face value and reacted angrily when the attempted take-over was revealed to him. Given Matthews's close connection with the Jesuits, such surprise seems unlikely, and in fact before Neale's death Matthews had served on a committee that examined the effect of the Neale-Grassi agreement and concluded that it was legal and binding.[26] This conclusion might have been Matthews's pragmatic response to a *fait accompli*, because once Neale's successor rescued St. Patrick's for the archdiocese, Matthews turned against his old colleagues. He refused their assistance when it was finally offered, and, according to Maréchal, destroyed a will made out in their favor, making heated charges against his old colleagues that, according to Maréchal, "did not spare the not very honorable epithets."[27]

It was at this point that the frustrated pastor decided to build a large

24. The Neale-Grassi Concordat, 3 April 1816, is reproduced in Hughes's *Documents* 1:952–53. For Maréchal's reaction, see his "Notes on the General's Report." Also see Sister M. Bernetta Brislen, "The Episcopacy of Leonard Neale, Second Archbishop of Baltimore," *Historical Records and Studies* 34 (1945): 56; and Spalding, *Premier See*, 77 and 90–91.

25. Ltr., Peter Kenney to Grassi, 31 May 20, quoted in "Our Scholasticate—An Account of its Growth and History to the Opening of Woodstock, 1805–1869," *Woodstock Letters*, 32 (1903), 208–9.

26. "The Concordat in Operation," 16 Oct 1816, reproduced in Hughes's *Documents*, 1:954.

27. "Notes on the General's Report," reproduced in Hughes, *Documents*, 1:456.

rectory and again ask the archbishop for an assistant. When Maréchal ordered Stephen Dubuisson, S.J., to serve under him, the canny Matthews was reluctant to pay his salary, since he considered his recent donation of valuable land to the Jesuits sufficient compensation. Feelings would run high for years, providing the essential context for the changing fortunes of the Jesuit school that would soon prosper largely because of St. Patrick's help.

In 1817, the Jesuits, rebuffed in their attempt to gain control of St. Patrick's and concluding that the bustle of F Street made it an inappropriate site for a novitiate, leased their new building to George Ironsides for a private boy's school. The Washington Literary Institute proved an instant success among parents reluctant to send their sons to public schools. Listing both Matthews and the Georgetown staff as references, Ironsides enrolled many of the sons of Washington's best-known families during his three-year stay on F Street.[28]

The Jesuits would remember Ironsides's success when they repossessed the building in 1820 and converted it into a house of studies for their philosophy and theology students. To make the place self-supporting, the superior, Father Anthony Kohlmann, opened a day school using his scholastics as faculty. The Washington Catholic Seminary (today's Gonzaga College High School) proved a stunning success. Beginning with about eighty pupils in 1821, it more than doubled in the next six years, exceeding the total enrollment of the city's public schools. The increase eventually justified closing the house of studies and transforming the whole building into a school offering "the complete number of classes usual in a Jesuit College." Spanning elementary through what today would be called the junior college level, the school was attended by boys of all faiths and quickly gained special éclat in Washington society among parents vying to win a place for their children in its classes.[29]

Kohlmann's maneuver obviously frustrated Matthews, but actually neither party got what it bargained for. Matthews had wanted a church full of assistants, the Jesuits, a parish in the city. What they ended up with was a flourishing school, an institution whose continued existence would depend on the good will and sacrifice of both parties.

28. *National Intelligencer*, 24 Jun 1817.

29. The early history of Gonzaga is well covered in Durkin, *William Matthews*, chap. 5. See also "Gonzaga Days." The popular school was costly for its time; an ad announcing tuition fees of $50 per annum ($525 in 1992 values) payable quarterly in advance appeared in the *National Intelligencer*, 2 Aug 21.

WASHINGTON SEMINARY (GONZAGA COLLEGE), *with St. Patrick's Church at left*
and the tracks of the Metropolitan Street Railway in foreground

Although many of the pupils were St. Patrick's parishioners, the
pastor at first kept the popular school at arm's length, fulminating
over what he perceived as a last-ditch attempt to take over his church.
In August 1823 he warned Maréchal that the Jesuits were trying to get
their newly ordained assigned to the city, and he hoped they would
not be authorized "to interfere in this Congregation, where their services are not necessary." He took it upon himself to tell the Jesuit superiors "very candidly" that if more assistants were needed at St.
Patrick's they would not be Jesuits. The next year he was still fretting,
this time that the Jesuits might try to use Dubuisson's anticipated departure to insert a successor who would be on the spot "& thus worm
himself in the Congn. & make himself necessary." Matthews promised
Maréchal that he would find a new assistant "from a distance."[30]

30. Ltrs., Matthews to Maréchal, 22 Aug 1823, 19-B-14, and 27 Mar 1824, 19-B-17. Both
in Maréchal Papers, AAB.

It was clear that Matthews would never again be able to work closely with Kohlmann, who in his view had taken the property and run. Yet the school obviously filled a pressing need of Washington Catholics, and even while the jurisdictional differences continued, Matthews found himself becoming involved in its affairs. After Kohlmann's departure in 1825 Matthews marched with the students in the city's first Fourth of July parade and later that year led the seminary contingent in a parade honoring the Marquis de Lafayette and joined in the noisy welcome for the old Revolutionary War hero when he visited the school. Such association quickly evolved into active participation in the school's management and direction when a financial crisis developed. For some time the Jesuits had been under pressure from their father general in Rome to observe a rule that prohibited charging tuition at Jesuit institutions (tuition at Georgetown, considered payment for room and board, was exempted from this stricture). To no avail they pointed out that the lack of state support precluded free education in America. Nor could they adequately explain how middle-class Americans regarded free schools with disdain and took pride in paying for their children's education. Clearly, if the order's rule was upheld, the school must close.

In an effort to avert this calamity, St. Patrick's pastor entered a conspiracy with his old enemies. To forestall the ax, Matthews, a secular clergyman, assumed the office of president of Washington Seminary and in that capacity set rates, collected tuition, and used those funds to pay the Jesuit teachers and maintain their building. The Jesuits, as before, provided the teachers and ran the school. This unique money-laundering scheme lasted for several years before the father general finally ordered the Jesuits out. During this period the school continued to fulfill an important mission, educating many of the city's Catholic youth along with many of its most prominent non-Catholics and thereby creating much good will and understanding for the church in the capital. Its exhibitions, semi-annual events staged at Carusi's Saloon and elsewhere at which the students performed classical dramas and competed in oratorical contests often in the presence of the archbishop, became highlights of the Washington social season.[31] Attesting to the local significance of the institution, the 1827 commencement

31. An indication of this good will can be found in the writings of the acerbic Anne Royall, who once described the school as "next to Yale College, the most flourishing and best conducted seminary in the United States." See her *Black Book* (Washington, 1828), 116. The semi-annual exhibitions are summarized in Records of the Washington

ceremony found Father Matthews, President of the Washington Seminary, sharing the stage with John Quincy Adams, President of the United States.

The closing of Washington Seminary was just as much a blow to St. Patrick's as to the local Jesuits. Although he harshly criticized the school's principal, Jeremiah Keily, for quitting the order and opening a rump school on Capitol Hill, Matthews was by now a firm supporter of the school and looked to the speedy lifting of the prohibition by the father general.[32] He quietly set out to keep a remnant of the school alive, financially supporting and otherwise organizing the use of the building by a succession of schoolmasters, both lay and clerical, including several of St. Patrick's assistant pastors, who for the greater part of the next fifteen years managed to keep a classical school in operation. He also used his influence in Rome and elsewhere to get the father general's order rescinded.

By 1841 the Jesuits had despaired of ever reopening the school. The heirs of the priest to whom Matthews had originally deeded the land sold it back to Matthews for a consideration of $10,000, specifying that it was to be used as a Catholic orphanage. When the Jesuit ban against operating a tuition school was finally lifted seven years later, however, Matthews quickly deeded the property back to the President of Georgetown (consideration: $1 to Matthews; $499 to the orphanage). The first student exhibition in the re-opened school, held on two consecutive nights in July 1849 at Carusi's Saloon, was "crowded to overflowing with the elite of Washington, the President of the United States [Zachary Taylor] amongst their number."[33] Within two years the school could boast an enrollment of 525, and in 1858 President James Buchanan signed the document that incorporated Gonzaga College as a degree-granting institution. It remains today one of the city's premier schools.

Even as this fruitful collaboration between the parish and the Jesuits was being renewed, the old conflict over jurisdiction continued. As

---

Seminary, Maryland provincial archives, Box 20, GUA. One exhibit was described in detail in the *Catholic Mirror*, 23 Feb 1850.

32. Ltrs., Matthews to Maréchal, 25 Sep and 2 Oct 1827, 19-B-20 and 21. Both in Maréchal Papers, AAB. See also ltr., Matthews to Louis Deluol (rector of St. Mary's Seminary), 2 Oct 1827, RG 24, SAB.

33. Matthews' $10,000 purchase is recorded in D.C. Land Records, *liber* W.B. 85, fol. 363, 19 Oct 1841, Office of the Recorder of Deeds; its resale to the Jesuits in *liber* W.B. 144, fol. 13, 2 Jul 1848, same source. The quotation is from the *United States Catholic Magazine* 8 (1849): 478.

early as 1847 Father Matthews warned Archbishop Eccleston that, once assured regaining their school on F Street, the Jesuits would again push for control of St. Patrick's. Matthews's solution: set the Jesuits up on the other side of the Tiber. When Eccleston hesitated, Matthews carefully marshalled the arguments for a Jesuit church in a growing area well removed from St. Patrick's. Finally in 1855 Eccleston's successor gave the Jesuits permission to build St. Aloysius on North Capitol Street.[34] Much later Gonzaga moved to the same area.

As in the case of the Washington Seminary, St. Patrick's second educational venture, a free school for girls, occurred in a roundabout way. Father Matthews was concerned with the plight of children neglected or abandoned in a city that still numbered many dreadfully poor residents in its population. He had been a faithful contributor to the local orphan asylum since its opening in 1815, but the training provided in that institution was indifferent and religious instruction for Catholic children non-existent.[35] The solution was a Catholic orphanage where impoverished girls could be sheltered and educated under church auspices. Such an arrangement was of paramount importance to the increasing number of struggling Catholic immigrants who viewed such an institution as a temporary home for their children while they found work and established themselves in the community. In fact few of the children were orphans in the literal sense, and the stay for any individual child in the orphanage typically lasted from just a few months to four years.

Matthews made clear that the primary purpose of a combined orphanage and school was to shelter the needy while providing Christian training and a practical education that prepared children for life as useful citizens.[36] The parish responded to this idea generously, and in July 1825 Matthews could report to Mother Rose White, superior of the Sisters of Charity, the American order founded by St. Elizabeth Seton, that a sum of $400 annually had been subscribed for the establishment of a branch of her society in Washington.[37] As a consequence, three sisters arrived in October and were installed in a small house

34. Ltrs., Matthews to Eccleston, 1 and 6 Mar 1847, 25-L-6 and 7. Both in Eccleston Papers, AAB.

35. In 1828, for example, St. Patrick's donated $150 to the city orphanage. See Green's *Washington* 1:71.

36. Altenhofel, "Irish Women in Antebellum Washington," 26–30.

37. Ltr., Matthews to Mother Rose White, 15 Jul 1825, reprinted in Sister Serena Branson, "Two Child-Care Institutions Administered by the Sisters of Charity in the District of Columbia," (Master of Social Work thesis, The Catholic University of

owned by Matthews near Fourteenth and F Streets. There they commenced operations as the Female Free School and Orphan Asylum,
beginning an association with St. Patrick's and the girls of Washington
that would continue into recent decades.

As their first order of business the pastor and sisters drew up articles
of agreement which enumerated a four-fold mission for the institution. First was the care of orphans, instructing them in Christian piety,
"all the necessary branches of English education," and instilling in
them vocational skills useful in the home and marketplace. (Because
infant care would have consumed the sisters' complete attention, it
was stipulated that only orphans over the age of three would be admitted.) The sisters also agreed to conduct a school, visit the sick and
poor of the parish, and teach catechism. The orphans would attend
the school, which would also be opened to the public free of charge. It
was assumed that the pupils would include children whose parents
could not afford one of the city's private academies as well as those
whose parents contributed to the orphanage. Reflecting trends in the
public schools, the school would employ, at least to some extent, the
Lancaster system, older pupils participating in the instruction of
younger. Matthews's admiration for the sisters did not move him to
relinquish personal control of the enterprise. The sisters would manage the institution, but he would provide all necessary support and
"have total control of admissions to the asylum and day school."

Although the free school was discussed in some detail in the agreement and afforded premier place in the institution's original name, it
seems unlikely that the parties involved gave it much notice at first.
After all, free public schooling was readily available for the city's less
affluent, schooling that, under the watchful eye of Father Matthews
and the other trustees, inculcated in its students basic Christian principles. Nor was it likely that a free school under Catholic auspices
would particularly appeal to the Catholic middle class, which shared
the popular prejudice against pauper schools. The presence of just
three sisters and one small dwelling implied that no full-scale educational establishment was anticipated, at least for a good while. Contrary to expectations, however, St. Patrick's, which had assumed responsibility to nurture the orphan, soon found itself with a popular
girl's school on its hands. From the beginning the day students greatly

America, 1948). Unless otherwise indicated, the following account of St. Vincent's orphanage and school are taken from the Branson work and from Durkin's *William
Matthews,* chap. 6.

outnumbered the orphans. When Bishop England preached at the church on New Year's Day, 1826, for the benefit of the sisters, an announcement in the *Intelligencer* boasted that the new institution already had 105 girls enrolled in its school in addition to its first six orphans. This imbalance continued in succeeding years; in 1839, for example, the total included 50 orphans and 150 day students.[38]

With private donations mounting at a satisfactory rate, including a significant contribution from Mayor Carberry in the wake of the miraculous cure of his sister, Mrs. Mattingly, the orphanage abandoned the house on F Street in 1828 in favor of a new building situated on lots purchased by Father Matthews on the southwest corner of Tenth and G Streets. Two years later the pastor could report that the examination of the orphans and students had "surpassed our most flattering anticipations" and that all debts were paid with a tidy surplus in the bank.[39]

The enterprise was put on solid legal footing in February 1831 when Congress granted a charter that incorporated St. Vincent's Orphan Asylum and placed the orphanage, open to both sexes,[40] under the ownership and direction of a board of trustees who shared their responsibilities with a board of nine female managers elected from among the contributors. These women, who would come to include some of the city's most prominent matrons, served as general supervisors of the sisters, solicited contributions, and performed many of the necessary social services, including examining the facilities and students, judging applications for admittance, and deciding which orphans could be placed in foster homes. They even exercised their right to examine the institution's books, although this caused considerable tension between them and the nuns. After what a later history called some "tactful maneuvering" by the superior, that privilege was quietly discontinued.[41] The initiatives undertaken by the managers demonstrate the easy association of the laity with Matthews in local church

38. Weitzman, *One Hundred Years of Catholic Charities*, 23. The announcement of the New Year's collection appeared in the *National Intelligencer*, 31 Dec 1825.

39. Ltr., Matthews to Mother Augustine, 6 Jul 1830, reprinted in Branson, "Two Child-Care Institutions," 17. The school was located on lots 7 and 8 in square 346, purchased from John McLeod on 4 Oct 1827 on a 99-year lease (see D.C. Land Records, *liber* W.B. 22, fols. 238–40). The lease was later conveyed to the Board of Trustees (see *liber* W.B. 85, 5 Nov 41).

40. A male branch was opened in October 1843, but the sisters abandoned the experiment in 1846.

41. Branson, "Two Child-Care Institutions," 21.

affairs; the considerable powers reserved to the president of the trustees, an office he held until his death, also indicates that this firm opponent of trusteeism was not about to relinquish control of any parish function to others.

Continual growth demanded a continual flow of contributions, which came from a wide variety of sources. In addition to the money collected from parishioners, Congress agreed in 1832 to divide some government-owned land in the District valued at $20,000 between St. Vincent's and the city orphanage. In the depressed real estate market, however, St. Vincent's was unable to sell many of its seventy gift lots, and Congress was forced to come to its rescue by remitting tax payments and exempting the land-poor institution from future property taxes.[42]

Probably the most noteworthy contribution came from President Andrew Jackson, who ordered that a Numidian lion, a gift to the White House from the King of Morocco, be sold and the proceeds divided between the two orphanages. When St. Vincent's portion was not forthcoming, the pastor protested to his friend in the White House, who was widely quoted as saying, "Are not the Catholics to have their lion's share?" When told by an official that St. Vincent's did not need the money, Jackson replied, "They do need it and they shall have it."[43]

The success of the day school in particular put a premium on space in the crowded orphanage. At times Father Matthews even co-opted the recently closed Washington Seminary building as a temporary annex, but with the boy's school scheduled to reopen in 1848, a new home for the girls became necessary.[44] A year later a new four-story edifice was begun on the site of the old building, again under the supervision of trustee Thomas Carberry. Constructed at the considerable cost of $18,000, the new St. Vincent's was fully paid for before its opening by contributions, including a $1,200 gift that represented half the proceeds from President Zachary Taylor's inaugural ball in March 1849.

42. The lots were recorded in D.C. Land Records *liber* W.B. 44, fols. 210–214, 22 Dec 1832. For a list of lots and their locations throughout the city, see Smith, *History of St. Patrick's*, 23–24.

43. Jackson's comment, partially quoted here, was first printed in *The Evening Express* on 8 August 1867. Convincing corroboration for the incident was provided by Margaret Bayard Smith. See Hunt, ed., *Forty Years of Washington Society*, 367.

44. Ltr., Matthews to Peter Schreiber, 19 Oct 1831, RG 26, SAB. Matthews also used the occasion to inform Schreiber that he had been appointed one of the trustees.

The exemplary care the sisters gave the orphans was widely celebrated, but even they could not ameliorate all the sad features of nineteenth-century orphanages. The children were still subjected to an unenviable amount of regimentation. Their subsequent treatment at the
hands of foster parents was often harsh and a constant concern to the
sisters. Adding to the dreariness, they wore identical dresses and were
regularly paraded about and extolled for their unending expressions of
gratitude.[45] The plight of the orphans no doubt moved the hearts of
Washington's charitable citizens and accounted for all the publicity
and contributions, but the fact is that until the eve of the Civil War, St.
Vincent's rarely housed more than fifty orphans, while its school
numbered three hundred day students, thus providing an important
and enduring educational service to St. Patrick's parish and Catholics
of the city.

The third educational institution established by St. Patrick's began
unambiguously enough as a school, but unlike the others, its purpose,
preparing young women from Washington's emerging upper classes
for their role in society, limited its clientele. Nor, given the restricted
academic content of its classes, was St. Joseph's School for Young
Ladies—to use its original name—a female equivalent of the Washington Seminary. The disparity reflected prevailing nineteenth-century
attitudes, which sought to educate young girls, as one historian put it,
"for a useful (and decorative) place" in society.[46] However restrictive an
education based on such principles might be, it could not be attained
in the city's public schools or in St. Vincent's free school. Furthermore, the long-standing prejudice of the affluent against the free or
public schools had obviously not been overcome by the practice at St.
Vincent's of collecting tuition in the form of donations from those
who could afford it.

The model for such a female academy was the successful school run
by the Sisters of the Visitation in Georgetown, but that group was
forced to reject Father Matthews's appeal for help because of a shortage of teachers. In 1846 he turned again to the Sisters of Charity, who

45. For an example of the children's publicized expressions of gratitude, see the
1827 "Address of the Orphans to Their Benefactors," a twenty-line poem with strong
Dickensian overtones quoted in Branson, "Two Child-Care Institutions," 16. For an
example of a frank and extremely laudatory appraisal of the care provided the orphans
by the Sisters of Charity, see critic Anne Royall's observations in her newspaper, The
Huntress, 31 Aug 1839.

46. Durkin, Father Matthews, 119. This brief account of the Visitation Academy is
drawn from the Durkin work and Fosselman's "A Downtown Parish," 84–88.

responded by sending seven sisters to begin a school for "the daughters of the elite of Washington" in a house owned by St. Patrick's near Seventh and E Streets.[47] This arrangement, which attracted an initial enrollment of one hundred day students, proved short-lived. In 1850 as part of a realignment of their basic mission, the Sisters of Charity gave up their tuition academies, and a second appeal to the Visitation sisters, this time backed by a request from the archbishop, resulted in that order's agreeing to take over the school, renamed the Convent and Academy of the Visitation.

In 1851 the school moved for a brief stay to a remodeled boarding house at Ninth and F Streets before the sisters purchased a mansion built for the French minister (along with the two adjoining houses at a later date) on the northwest corner of Tenth and G Streets. There in a tranquil spot girded by extensive gardens and high brick walls in the heart of a bustling city, the sisters taught those skills expected in a lady of the day. At the same time, in what must be regarded as forward thinking, their students received at least some grounding in the liberal arts and sciences.

Unlike St. Vincent's, Visitation was completely independent. No board of trustees audited its finances or examined its students. Nevertheless the purchase of the new buildings overwhelmed its resources, and the sisters found themselves unable to meet the initial note for $3,000. Their pleas for help were rejected by an irascible Father Matthews, who had obviously not learned in his long years of business to tolerate financial independence in less-experienced colleagues (in purchasing the splendid mansion on G Street the sisters had turned down Matthews's offer of a less pretentious residence). Even the pleas of Mother Juliana Matthews, his niece, failed to move him, and the anxious nuns started a novena to the Virgin. Shortly after telling them they did not deserve his help and should close the school, the elderly Matthews appeared at their door with a gift of $10,000, enough to cancel all their debts. His gruff reply to their thanks: "Don't thank me. Thank the Blessed Virgin. She made me do it."[48]

Such incidents underscore the problem of assessing accurately the

47. Quotation from *The Catholic Almanac* (Baltimore: Fielding Lucas, Jr., 1848), 99. See also "Gonzaga College," 16–17.

48. This quotation is reproduced in Durkin's *William Matthews*, 123, and is derived from material in the Visitation archives. The story, perfectly in keeping with Matthews's gruff but generous personality, is corroborated in "Gonzaga College," 17. The $10,000 gift is confirmed by Archbishop Francis P. Kenrick in a letter to his friend Bishop Michael O'Connor of Pittsburgh, 2 Oct 1852, *Congressi*, sec. 16, APF.

influence of St. Patrick's congregation, in distinction to that its pastor, on the development of educational institutions serving the whole city. Attendance at the three schools offers some evidence of popular support, but the congregation's much stronger support for St. Vincent's (and in later decades for St. Joseph's orphanage and school for boys) suggests an interest more narrowly focused on the needs of the poor and the immigrants. There was no extraordinary effort on their part, even by the wealthy, to rescue Gonzaga when the Jesuits were forced to leave, nor did they appear deeply concerned with the financial problems at the Visitation academy. In contrast, Matthews exhibited an abiding belief in the importance of education for all classes of citizens in a democracy and the willingness to support that belief with forceful leadership and his own money. From the beginning his educational interests appear universal; it would be some decades before the majority of the congregation came to embrace this all-encompassing vision.

A Diocesan Leader

From the beginning Matthews's dealings with his ordinaries demonstrated St. Patrick's special place in diocesan affairs. Like his first bishop, Matthews was a child of the old Anglo-Catholic church in America. While at St. Patrick's he strongly supported John Carroll's efforts to organize and govern the church in the new nation in a way that emphasized the best in the republican tradition. As was vividly demonstrated in his first months at St. Patrick's, Matthews was an ecclesiastical statesman in the Carroll mold, able to reconcile the often-divergent attitudes of the old society with those of recent Catholic immigrants and to lead a united effort to improve the moral and physical well-being of the new capital. Both men championed the American idea of religious liberty and saw a bright future for the church under the Constitution. Matthews's biographer tells of the many meetings between the two when Matthews's inexhaustible fund of political and economic knowledge, much of it first-hand and based on his close association with the federalist leaders, energized Carroll's plans for church growth and development.[49] Politically conservative, Matthews sympathized with the archbishop's innate suspicion of those immi-

49. Durkin, *William Matthews*, chap 3. Unless otherwise noted, this essay on Matthews's relationships with church and state leaders is based on Durkin's carefully researched monograph.

grant priests who sought to agitate the Catholic newcomers, and he tried to convince Carroll, who remained sympathetic with the trustee system of church management, that, unless firmly under the control of loyal pastors as in the case of St. Vincent's, trustees were unwitting tools of troublesome, undisciplined clergymen.[50]

The record has little to say about Matthews's relations with the second archbishop, although Leonard Neale was a frequent visitor at St. Patrick's during his brief reign. Toward the third archbishop, Ambrose Maréchal, Matthews was invariably respectful, but he was not loath to press a point in plain language. Concerning his effort to import valuable altar furnishings duty free for Maréchal in 1820, for example, he warned his superior not to expect miracles. He was working through his friend, Secretary of the Treasury William H. Crawford, and even after the Comptroller had promised to make the most liberal interpretation of the laws, Matthews was skeptical of winning a favorable decision.[51] He was far more blunt when he learned that Maréchal had granted the ex-Jesuit Keily faculties in Washington. He told the archbishop that Keily was not wanted at St. Patrick's and that Maréchal's kindness to the "renegade" was being falsely interpreted as approval of his "criminal disobedience to his lawful superior."[52]

Despite such bluntness on Matthews's part, Maréchal should have had no doubt as to the Washington pastor's loyalty. Matthews had strongly supported the beleaguered archbishop when Propaganda, in response to the petitions of rebellious trustees and troublesome priests in Charleston and Norfolk and without consulting the American hierarchy, created the dioceses of Richmond and Charleston and appointed Irish prelates to run them. Matthews could hardly contain himself. He was convinced that the Pope had been deceived in these "high-handed and indecorous proceedings" by political intriguers who seemed unaware that church law required a bishop's consent before his diocese could be divided. He reminded Maréchal, who had fought

50. On Matthews's opposition to trustees, see Fosselman, "A Downtown Parish," 99–100. His irritation with Irish clergy appears frequently in his correspondence. See, for example, his letter to Anthony Kohlmann, 26 Feb 1829, *Congressi*, sec. 10, APF, in which he comments that Conwell is "acting like an Irishman generally does—that is, he does the thing first and then asks permission to do it."

51. He was right. Maréchal was forced to pay the duty in the end. See ltrs., Matthews to Maréchal, 15 and 20 Apr 1820, 19-A-8 and 9, Maréchal Papers, AAB.

52. Ltr., Matthews to Maréchal, 2 Oct 1827, 19-B-21, Maréchal Papers, AAB. In the end Maréchal did not accept Keily, who went on to be an active clergyman in Philadelphia.

so valiantly in the past, that the new bishops could not assume office until Maréchal agreed, and he told his superior that he planned to send a remonstrance to the Pope, signed by the clergy of the diocese, "expressing the deep regret & astonishment of the American Clergy at the imperious proceedings of the Propaganda."[53] When Maréchal failed to respond to this offer to continue the fight against the Roman bureaucrats, Matthews on his own discussed the matter with his friend the French minister to Washington, who agreed to ask French authorities in Rome to take an interest in American church affairs. Concerned that the archbishop's mail was being examined by unfriendly forces in Rome, he also arranged for correspondence to the Pope and other officials to travel in the minister's diplomatic pouch and be delivered by French authorities.

Nor did he hesitate to tell Maréchal that the archbishop had made a poor bargain over the division of church property with the Jesuits and had shortchanged the rights of the secular clergy. He also charged that Roger Brooke Taney, the future Chief Justice and St. Patrick's parishioner who had advised the archbishop in the matter, lacked all the facts. Although he softened the scolding somewhat by admitting that neither Maréchal nor the Pope was fully informed, he also added that the affair might end in court.[54] While these contentions unfolded, Matthews kept up a steady drumfire of advice, suggesting assignments for specific priests, admonishing Maréchal for neglecting St. Patrick's on his visits to Washington, and interpreting for his French-born superior the subtle shifts in the political landscape from his vantage point as a Washington insider.

Matthews's handling of the incipient trustee problem at St. Peter's and his adamant defense of Maréchal in the Norfolk trustee case made him a likely candidate for an assignment as a diocesan administrator. For some time the elderly bishop of Philadelphia, Henry Conwell, had been engaged in a running battle with the trustees of St. Mary's Church in that city. Even after Rome condemned the rebels, Conwell sought to compromise with them, in effect offering them a veto over clerical appointments. Compounding his problems, the aging Irish prelate was locked in a nasty dispute with two Irish Dominicans, William Harold, his vicar general, and John Ryan. These ambitious adventurers were looking for special preferment, and their struggle with Conwell resulted in their faculties being lifted by the beleaguered

---

53. Ltr., Matthews to Maréchal, 7 Feb 1821, 19-B-12, Maréchal Papers, AAB.
54. Ltr., Matthews to Maréchal, 1 Feb 1825, 19-B-19, Maréchal Papers, AAB.

bishop. Finally an exasperated Propaganda stepped in, ordering Conwell to Rome to explain the situation and arranging with the Dominican superior to transfer Harold and Ryan to Cincinnati. Asked to administer the troubled diocese in Conwell's absence, an ailing Maréchal instead nominated Matthews for the job. On February 26, 1828, Pope Leo XII named Matthews administrator of Philadelphia.[55]

Neither St. Patrick's congregation nor its pastor relished this significant assignment, which was widely assumed to be the first step toward Matthews's appointment as bishop and coadjutor. Carberry spoke of the parish's "great consternation" and discussed schemes to thwart the pastor's permanent transfer to Philadelphia.[56] Probably the clearest manifestation of this opposition occurred in 1829 as Matthews was about to leave St. Patrick's for a stay in Philadelphia. Upon hearing the news, a group of parishioners surrounded his carriage and refused to let it move until he promised to return in a few days.

For his part, Matthews made it obvious from his infrequent trips to Philadelphia that he had little taste for the job— "condemned to Philadelphia," he once called it. He was strongly criticized by Archbishop James Whitfield, Maréchal's successor, for his delinquency. Sometimes Matthews offered excuses for the briefness of his stays in Pennsylvania; usually he ignored his superiors' admonitions and did what he could to end the strife in Philadelphia from the quiet of his rectory on Tenth Street. Such seeming neglect was fatal to any clerical ambition, but Matthews was obviously indifferent to promotion. Commenting on a persistent rumor that he was to be made Marechal's successor, he had once confided wistfully to Father Kohlmann that if such a burden was unavoidable, it was at least preferable to being sent to rule in the city of brotherly love.[57]

The situation was hopelessly stalemated by the administrator's lack of clear authority. Some of the frustrated troublemakers complained

55. *Decreti Della S. Congregazione*, 1828, vol. 309, fol. 214, 9 Feb 28, and *Brevi*, vol. 3, fols. 372–73, 26 Feb 28. Both in APF. Maréchal's nomination of Matthews is made in ltr., Maréchal to Propaganda, 3 Feb 28, *Congressi*, sec. 6, fols. 686–88, APF. See also ltr., Kohlmann to Propaganda, 1 and 3 Feb 28, fols. 690–91, same file. Matthews's role in the Philadelphia controversy, which is merely sketched here, deserves a full study in itself.

56. Ltr., Carberry to Dubuisson, 16 May 28, reprinted in "Gonzaga Days," 175–77.

57. Ltrs., Matthews to Kohlmann, 11 Jul 28, *Congressi*, sec. 6, fol. 729 and 26 Feb 1829, same file, sec. 10, fols. 74–75. Both in APF. On Whitfield's dissatisfaction with Matthews's performance, see ltr., Whitfield to Propaganda, 24 Oct 1829, *Scritture Originali Riferite Nelle Cong. Generali* 1829, vol. 945, fols. 116–17, APF.

about Matthews's efforts at reconciliation to the absent and increasingly jealous Conwell while Harold and Ryan appealed their banishment to the American government on the grounds that no foreign power (the Pope) had the right to interfere with the freedom of American citizens. The pot continued to boil, and Matthews, considered more or less a powerless outsider by the antagonists, could do little to bring lasting peace to the diocese. The obvious solution, as Matthews pointed out to Propaganda officials, was to appoint a coadjutor who, armed with full episcopal power, could deal forcibly with the malcontents. He recommended the tough and brilliant Francis Patrick Kenrick for the task. Coincidentally, Archbishop Whitfield also recommended Kenrick.[58]

Meanwhile Matthews was not idle. He sought constantly and deferentially to assuage Conwell's suspicions of his changes in Philadelphia. He arranged for Daniel Brent, the first clerk at the State Department, to forward the Harold-Ryan appeal to the American minister to France with the suggestion that the charges be discussed with the papal nuncio in Paris, knowing full well that that able cleric would explain the facts satisfactorily and thereby end the government's interest in the affair. At the same time he used his close friendship with Henry Clay, the American secretary of state, to further defuse the situation. He pointed out to Clay that these priests were tied by their oaths to the Pope, who was merely exercising his spiritual authority as he did "in every region of the known world whether the government thereof be Despotic, Regal, or Democratic." He reminded Clay that the separation of church and state worked two ways. Harold and Ryan had no more right to appeal the Pope's spiritual order to the American government than did the Pope to solicit the President's temporal assistance in removing the two from Philadelphia. He concluded with an example of the rhetoric the old Whig pastor was wont to use:

When they [Harold and Ryan] talked to Government about 'undefined menaces'—about their fears and apprehensions, you [Clay] would have said to them, Gentlemen, define your fears, tell us what you are afraid of, before we can espouse your cause—If they dreaded the thunders of the Vatican you would have replied to them, we cannot still *that* thunder, we cannot avert *that* thunderbolt in its fleet career. If they dreaded the Pope's *posse comitatus,* you have made them this consoling answer O! Gentlemen

58. Ltrs., Matthews to Cardinal Cappellari, 27 Nov 29, and to Kohlmann, same date, both in *Congressi,* sec. 10, fols. 247 and 239, APF.

dispel your fears, lay aside your apprehensions, we will spread the national Agis over you.[59]

These maneuvers successfully frustrated Harold and Ryan's efforts to involve the government in their case, and by August 1829 a weary Matthews could report to Rome that the two had finally quit Philadelphia and that a reasonable calm prevailed in the trustee situation.[60] But that did not end his problems. As apostolic administrator he participated in the First Provincial Council in Baltimore in October, where the trustee question was addressed and where the bishops petitioned Rome to allow Conwell to return but with all his episcopal powers entrusted to a coadjutor. By this time Matthews had clearly had enough. Anticipating further criticism for his refusal to stay away from St. Patrick's for any length of time, he blamed his abrupt departure from the council on the need to post a letter to Rome in the Department of State mail pouch and asked to be released from the assignment. He endorsed the council's recommendation to appoint the no-nonsense Kenrick as Conwell's coadjutor.[61]

His wish to be free of Philadelphia was granted in March 1830. Looking back on the painful ordeal three months later, Matthews declared himself tolerably satisfied with his efforts. "Everything continues tranquil in Phila.," he told Kohlmann. He had been especially busy in his last months as administrator. With Harold and Ryan out of the way he had decided to neutralize the power of the trustees at the problem parishes by building two new churches nearby. He had also actively recruited for German pastors who would remain loyal to the bishop and predicted that "the coast is clear" for Kenrick, whose only difficulty would be to shirk the advice of certain priests. In a rare burst of self-congratulation he concluded, "I have labored hard to restore faith in Phila.—& Almighty God has blessed my endeavors."[62] A more ambitious cleric could have made much of such an opportunity, but Matthews appeared genuinely reluctant to leave his church and congregation in Washington. As one prelate advised Propaganda, Matthews clearly deserved a miter, but since he refused to leave Washington, Rome should make that city a diocese for him.[63]

59. Ltrs., Matthews to Clay, 10 and 11 Oct 1828 (the latter is the source of the quote). Copies in *Congressi*, sec. 6, fols. 724–25, APF.

60. Ltr., Matthews to Propaganda, 27 Aug 1829, *Congressi*, sec. 10, fol. 163, APF.

61. Ltr., Matthews to Whitfield, Nov 1829, 23A-I-4, Whitfield Papers, AAB. The work of the provincial council is discussed in Spalding, *Premier See*, chap. 5.

62. Ltr., Matthews to Kohlmann, 14 Jun 1830, *Congressi*, sec. 10, fol. 390, APF.

63. Ltrs., Frederick Rese (vicar-general of Cincinnati and later bishop of Detroit) to

This comment by Frederick Rese was just one of several recommendations concerning the advancement of St. Patrick's pastor. It was an era, it seemed, when everyone had an opinion on who should fill the increasing number of episcopal positions in the growing American church, and everyone, cleric and lay, felt free to express these opinions to officials in Rome. In a happier day Bishop Conwell had included Matthews in his official list of nominees. So did Bishop Edward Fenwick of Cincinnati, who reported to Propaganda the high regard government officials, diplomats, and congressmen had for Matthews, who possessed, in his opinion, "all those necessary qualities to sustain the dignity of bishop." He wanted Matthews to be consecrated as Maréchal's coadjutor, a view he repeated in 1823 during an audience with the Pope. This initiative earned him a tart rejoinder from Propaganda: the matter would be dealt with "if and when" the archbishop of Baltimore asked for a coadjutor.[64]

Although Maréchal constantly relied on Matthews's support and held him in high regard, he may have distrusted the Washington pastor's naivete in the diocese's battle with the Jesuits. When he finally asked for a coadjutor, he turned instead to another Sulpician student, the English-born James Whitfield. The fourth archbishop and the pastor of St. Patrick's had an uneasy relationship. Whitfield complained to Propaganda about Matthews's work in Philadelphia, and in 1831 he warned his agent in Rome, Nicholas Wiseman, that Charles Constantine Pise, a priest then serving at the Baltimore cathedral but soon to be an assistant at St. Patrick's, was in Europe and might come to Rome to engage in "schemes" on behalf of Matthews, who "wants to be made bishop of Washington." Whitfield admitted that this suspicion might be unfounded, but since Pise could expect nothing from him and much from Matthews, the archbishop was taking precautions. He wanted Wiseman to be on guard for any "plots" on their part. He only hoped that Propaganda would not fall for any such scheme to reduce the size and importance of the premier see in such a fashion.[65]

Propaganda, n.d. (ca. 1827), *Congressi*, sec. 9, fols. 642–43, and n.d., *Acta.* (1827), vol. 190, fol. 542. Both in APF.

64. Ltrs., unsigned (presumably Fenwick or Bishop Benedict Flaget writing for Fenwick) to Propaganda, n.d., *Congressi*, sec. 8, fol. 399, and Fenwick to Propaganda, 8 Nov 1823, *Udienze* (1823), vol. 61, fols. 268 and 270 (the Vatican's "if and when" response is appended to this document at fols. 270 and 271). See also, ltr., Conwell to Propaganda, 20 Jul 1825, *Cong. generalii*, vol. 938, fols. 95–96. All in APF.

65. Ltr., Whitfield to Wiseman, 17 Oct 1831, *Congressi*, Baltimore Papers, no. 123, APF.

No evidence can be found to support this extraordinary accusation, but at least Whitfield must have been aware that Matthews was extremely critical of his administration. In 1828 Matthews had commented on Whitfield's continuing feud with the Jesuits, adding that "he is at least equally as hostile to the Jesuits, as was the late Abp— Rome must necessarily admonish him to lay aside his animosity to the Society the hope, the *only* hope of religion in this Country." He also strongly disapproved of what he considered his superior's indifference toward Mount St. Mary's College.[66]

In retrospect it appears odd that Whitfield and Matthews should have so often been at loggerheads. Both represented the old Anglo-Catholic strain in the American church personified by John Carroll. Both, as was often the case in those trained by the French Sulpicians, seemed uncomfortable with the new, assertive immigrant clergy, particularly Irish priests as typified by Bishop John England of Charleston, who had begun to make their presence felt in church government. In particular England's "acrimonious expressions" in favor of the Irish trustees was disturbing to Matthews in Philadelphia.[67] On another level, both Whitfield and Matthews were conservative men of wealth and practical businessmen who shared many political and social opinions. There is no evidence of an open break between the two, and in fact the St. Patrick's pastor continued to exercise some influence over church government in Washington. After considerable lobbying, for example, he succeeded in having a former assistant, Peter Schreiber, transferred from what Matthews considered an inappropriate assignment in Richmond to the pastorship of St. Peter's. He accompanied Whitfield to St. Peter's in March 1832 to announce the forthcoming change to what must have been a startled pastor.[68] He also routinely selected his own assistants at St. Patrick's. Nevertheless, until Samuel Eccleston, the young convert and another Sulpician student, became archbishop in 1834, St. Patrick's ties to the archbishop remained strained.

Matthews seemed anxious to get off on the right foot with Eccleston. Effusive in his congratulations on the occasion of the new bish-

66. Ltr., Matthews to Kohlmann, 2 Jul 28, *Congressi*, sec. 6, fols. 722–23, APF.

67. Matthews expressed himself to his superiors on the immigrant clergy on a number of occasions. This quote is from ltr., Matthews to Maréchal, 1 Feb 1825, 19-B-19, Maréchal Papers, AAB.

68. Ltr., Matthews to Shreiber, 30 Mar 1832, RG 26, SAB. Matthews sent the letter to Shreiber in Richmond, playfully addressing it to the "Rector of St. Peter's Church, Capitol Hill," thus breaking the news to his old friend.

op's consecration and aware that he would soon be in Washington for confirmation at St. Matthew's, he asked Eccleston to "stop at St. Patrick's first just as Carroll always did."[69] He also gave Eccleston a tangible sign of his support, one that directly affected St. Patrick's. As early as 1825 Matthews had recommended to Maréchal that he acquire the status of a corporation sole, a legal device that would allow the archbishop to accept title to church property in the diocese in perpetuity and thus invest ownership in himself and his successors without danger of legal alienation. Matthews also realized that this arrangement would finally end the trustee system and was an important and necessary legal step for the church in the United States. He wanted Maréchal to consult with Justice Taney, who could advise him on securing a private bill in the Maryland assembly that could serve as a model for the other bishops, but Maréchal hesitated, and the subject was dropped until the Provincial Council met in 1829.[70] As a member of the council Matthews participated in the discussion on property rights and trusteeism and supported its decree that called for church property to be vested in the bishops. In 1833 the Maryland assembly enacted legislation providing for such transfers to the bishop in his capacity as corporation sole.[71]

Although Matthews was one of the instigators of the idea, and the transfer of church property began in the diocese at Eccleston's insistence in the 1840s, nothing was done about St. Patrick's property that remained in Matthews's hands. The Caffry deed, executed in 1804, gave the original three lots to the archbishop of Baltimore. Presumably this title passed on to Carroll's successors according to terms of his will, but Neale's agreement to turn over St. Patrick's to the Jesuits and the continuing attempts by members of that order to assert their claims certainly muddied the legal waters. In any event, Matthews, in his seventy-fourth year, deeded all his holdings in square 376 to the archbishop. (On the same date in February 1843, Eccleston gave Matthews use of the property and income therefrom for the remainder of his life.) Matthews had already transferred title of St. Vincent's property to its trustees after ensuring that the pastor of St. Patrick's would remain president of those trustees.[72]

69. Ltr., Matthews to Eccleston, 31 Oct 1834, 25-L-5, Eccleston File, AAB. The evidence suggests that Matthews overstated the case about the frequency of Carroll's visits to St. Patrick's.

70. Ltr, Matthews to Maréchal, 1 Feb 1825, 19-B-19, Maréchal Papers, AAB.

71. Spalding, *Premier See,* 116–17 and 141.

72. D.C. Land Records, *liber* W.B. 97, fols. 171–72, 13 Feb 1843, Office of the Recorder

Throughout these decades of intense activity, rumors continued to circulate about the imminent creation of a separate diocese in Washington.[73] Although a century premature, the talk persisted for years, in great part because of the obvious vitality of the church in Washington, a vitality that had been fostered and guided by the hard work and sacrifice of St. Patrick's congregation and its pastor. In many important areas and with considerable self-confidence, that congregation continued to treat the whole city as its parish.

---

of Deeds. Matthews transferred St. Vincent's property to the trustees on 5 November 1841 for the price of $5. See *liber* W.B. 85, fol. 365, 5 Nov 41, same file and source. Archbishop Carroll's will, in which he gives all church property held in his name to his designated successor, Leonard Neale, is reprinted in *JCP* 3:370–71.

73. For the extent of these rumors and Matthews's reaction, see his ltr. to Kohlmann, 14 Jun 1830, *Congressi,* sec. 10, fol. 390, APF.

CHAPTER 4

The Church and the City, 1830-1855

THE HISTORY OF ST. PATRICK'S, indeed the history of Catholicism in Washington during the first half of the nineteenth century, was dominated by the figure of William Matthews. A remarkable leader in an era of remarkable growth and change in the American church, he was respected by prelates and politicians alike and loved by his congregation. Those in office appreciated his blunt and pragmatic approach to problems affecting church and state. The network of personal friendships Matthews enjoyed with many national leaders led to St. Patrick's playing an important role in acquainting federal officials with the Catholic church and its needs. The pastor's fellow citizens, seeing through his gruff aristocratic demeanor, were entranced by his fabled generosity and simple republican ways. In a private communication Mayor Thomas Carberry listed his "amiable" pastor's qualities: "his prudence and good sense, the systematic management of his flock, his conciliatory deportment toward all, and his kind and generous heart." Trying to explain "the love we have for him," Carberry concluded simply that Father Matthews "has raised us up as his children."[1] Such sentiments from a

1. Ltr., Carberry to Dubuisson, 16 May 1828, reprinted in "Gonzaga College," 175–77.

savvy and most unsentimental man of the world suggests that the often-used encomium "patriarch of Washington" was not an inappropriate description for St. Patrick's second pastor.

Principally through the work of this priest, his assistants, and the leaders of the congregation, St. Patrick's played a significant role in the life of the city in the decades before the Civil War. Although that congregation continued to increase in size even after the formation of three new parishes in the city, Washington itself remained a small, southern community. Despite the growing strength and importance of the federal government and the ambitions of its founders, the capital could boast merely 18,000 residents in 1830, a figure that would increase by only 4,400 in the decade that followed. It remained much the same unsophisticated place where President John Quincy Adams used to walk unnoticed down to the Potomac every morning in good weather and, hanging his clothes from a tree, take his daily swim. It was also a community where its few wealthy citizens, along with its political and diplomatic transients, an emerging middle class of merchants and clerks, and a growing population of free blacks and immigrant newcomers lived in relative harmony, the sick and needy tended by their neighbors, all bolstered by an abiding faith in communal progress.

In such small-town intimacy the Catholic minority came to be known and respected by its Protestant neighbors. This familiarity and acceptance accounted for Washington's comparative serenity at a time when the country was beginning to undergo its first nativist-inspired disturbances. While opposition to the foreign born in general and Catholics in particular was fomenting mob attacks on churches and convents from Massachusetts to Maryland, Washington's bigots contented themselves mostly with empty bombast, and even that did not last long. In general Washington's Catholics lived in peace with their neighbors. Such comity can be traced at least in part to the fact that Catholic leaders, especially William Matthews and prominent laymen at St. Patrick's, were closely involved in city and national affairs and widely admired for their contribution to the community.

Catholics and Their Civic Responsibilities

These civic contributions took many forms. Father Matthews's role in the establishment of the city's public schools was matched by his involvement in the foundation of the public library. Again motivated by his belief in the need for an educated and socially stable citizenry, he co-founded the Washington Library Company in 1811 and served as its president from 1821 until 1834. In its first years the library relied on an association of sponsors, which explains why, in 1822, President Matthews went to the White House to enlist President Monroe as its first subscriber.[2] The library lacked a permanent home, and in 1827 Matthews again visited the White House, this time to seek President Adams's help in obtaining a free site for a building. Although sympathetic, Adams claimed he lacked the legal power to dispose of government land.[3] When Congress refused the library board's request to hold a lottery to raise the money, Matthews arranged instead to purchase the Masonic lodge on Eleventh Street and convert it into a library, with the provision that the Masons could continue holding their meetings in the building. Before leaving office Matthews could count more than six thousand books in a collection that included the valuable private library assembled by the famous archivist and publisher Peter Force and purchased with funds loaned for that purpose by St. Patrick's pastor. Ironically, the public library's only real competitor during these years was a small circulation library organized by the Charitable Society of St. Patrick's, which depended entirely on private donations and collections taken up for that purpose during church services.[4]

More immediately noticeable by the public at large was the dedicated work performed by Catholic religious and charitable societies, especially during the cholera epidemic in 1832. The disease caused 459 deaths in less than eight weeks. It struck particularly hard among the city's poor, whose numbers had increased in recent times with the arrival of new immigrants drawn to the area by the promise of jobs on the canals, roads, and water works. These laborers, mostly Irish and German/Swiss immigrants, were subject to unrelenting toil outdoors, and they and their families were unfamiliar with Washington's summers and the practical precautions adopted by residents to counter illness. The epidemic was exacerbated by years of neglect of the city's drainage problems and increasingly swampy conditions around the Washington canal. Though a singular occurrence, it was

2. For a comprehensive account of Matthews's association with the D.C. Library, see Durkin, *William Matthews*, chap. 2. These paragraphs are based on that source and on an article by Francis deSales Ryan in the *Catholic Standard*, 30 Mar 1962.

3. Charles Francis Adams, ed., *Memoirs of John Quincy Adams Comprising Portions of his Diary from 1795 to 1848* (Freeport, NY: Books for Libraries Press, 1969), 7:283.

4. See, for example, notice in the *National Intelligencer*, 15 Mar 1823, of a collection to be taken up at St. Patrick's for its circulating library.

enough to shatter Washington's reputation as a disease-free community.[5]

With public assistance at a minimum and hospital facilities, except the poorhouse infirmary, non-existent, the care of the cholera sufferers fell to their neighbors. The Sisters of Charity from St. Vincent's as well as the priests and parishioners of St. Patrick's and St. Peter's performed the heroic work of tending to the victims. Lest this charity be overlooked, citizens were forcibly reminded by that caustic critic and freethinker, Anne Royall, who had only praise for the Catholics of Washington and their relief efforts. Her popular weekly paper, *Paul Pry*, offered a pointed picture of this service:

In this city the Catholic ladies are out from morning till night hunting up the poor and distressed. They do not visit the wealthy, but visit the poor hovels from street to street. The Catholic Priests, Rev. Matthews and [James] Hoerner [of St. Peter's] take not rest, going continually from house to house, and to the Hospitals, comforting the afflicted and relieving their distress. . . . Laterally, however, there is a society of ladies formed in this place, of all sects, who are now engaged in this human business, and are said to be attentive in visiting the poor, and collecting relief. We have seen none, however, but the Unitarians, and Catholics, most of the others, though their names are on the paper, have left the city.[6]

Although the new immigrants and their families received much care from members of St. Patrick's congregation, only a few lived in the immediate neighborhood. By the mid-1830s both F and G Streets had become a placid site of unpretentious private homes, boarding houses, small businesses, and the growing collection of church institutions centered on St. Patrick's. Both ends of the street were in the process of major additions, the monumental Treasury Department building going up at Fifteenth Street and the beautiful new Patent Office at Ninth. Nearby the Post Office found a permanent home at Eighth Street. Although the F Street area was more developed than most other sections, the city in general lagged behind many others in

5. For a vivid description of the course of the disease through the poor neighborhoods of the city, see Hunt, *Forty Years of Washington Society*, 335–38.

6. *Paul Pry*, 22 Sep 1832 as quoted in Fosselman, "A Downtown Parish," 114. Although an accurate reporter, Anne Royall was not entirely an unbiased one. She considered Father Matthews her closest friend and confidant. For a study of this fascinating and witty woman (once charged in the circuit court of the District of Columbia as a "common scold" for the views expressed in her newspapers), see Sarah H. Porter, *The Life and Times of Anne Royall* (Cedar Rapids, Iowa: The Torch Press Book Shop, 1909).

urban amenities. It lacked organized police and fire-fighting forces. Street lighting was still in the future, and sewerage was becoming a major problem in a city without the money or the political will to do anything about it. Support for the city's poor, old, and ill, as evidenced in the epidemic, remained meager, a problem aggravated by Congress's continued refusal to pay its fair share of municipal expenses.

Nevertheless, enough improvement had been promised lately to stimulate a strain of local boosterism. Thomas Carberry proudly linked the city's progress to that of the country at large when he remarked, "We are marching onward to our destined greatness as a nation."[7] Carberry was referring in particular to the announcement that a railway link to Baltimore would soon be opened. By far his greatest news, however, and indeed the most important local project of the Jacksonian era, concerned the new Chesapeake and Ohio Canal.

Money for the grand project, which was expected to fulfill George Washington's dream of connecting the capital to the vast reaches of the old Northwest, had been pledged by local jurisdictions with congressional backing. Work began in earnest in 1828, when approximately one thousand Irish laborers were recruited under contract to join local laborers in constructing the engineering marvel. Like all good Whigs, Father Matthews was a strong supporter of such internal improvements and their financing through a partnership between local and national government and private business. Symbolizing this support, he joined a group of city leaders and Archbishop Whitfield on a well-publicized trip in 1831 through the finished portions of the lower canal. The colorful news account of the barge ride not only underscored the ease and utility of the route, but predicted a glowing financial future for Washington.[8]

In fact the never-completed canal system brought very little new commerce to the city, which would pay a high price in the form of formidable taxes for the debt it incurred during its construction. There was an even higher price to pay during the next decade, when Alexandria, desperate for relief from the crippling economic burden it had incurred in projects associated with the canal and angered by congres-

7. Ltr., Carberry to Dubuisson, 16 May 1828, reprinted in "Gonzaga College," 175–77. Green's *Washington* 1: chaps. 4–6, still contain the best description of Washington in the 1830s and 1840s. See also essay by "The Rambler," *Star*, 18 Mar 1918.

8. *National Intelligencer*, 4 Aug 1831. Matthews subsequently took several restful trips on the canal. See ltr., Matthews to Rev. Peter Schreiber, 19 Oct 1831, RG 26, SAB. Construction of the canal and the financial consequences of the venture are detailed in Green's *Washington*, 1: chap 4.

sional neglect, petitioned for retrocession to Virginia. In a move engineered by slave interests both in Richmond and on Capitol Hill, Alexandria and all the District south of the river were returned to Virginia in 1846, reducing the federal enclave by a third.

As to be expected in the capital in an age of strong partisanship, members of St. Patrick's congregation held widely differing political views. In common with many of the old Maryland gentry, its pastor was a staunch Whig (that party having succeeded the Federalists as the voice of the Eastern property and mercantile class), and his personal friendship with Henry Clay, the great Whig leader, was well known. James Hoban and Thomas Carberry, on the other hand, considered themselves the political representatives of the common man. When Hoban ran for office under that banner shortly before his death in 1831, he had to suffer the embarrassment of watching his pastor ostentatiously vote against him. Carberry fared better. Although he won the race for mayor as the "poor man's" candidate and managed to rescind temporarily the property qualification for voting, he remained one of Matthews's close friends and collaborators. The eminent lawyer and future chief justice of the United States Roger Brooke Taney was also a St. Patrick's parishioner who strongly supported the Democratic party then coalescing around President Andrew Jackson. United by the complex personal relationships that governed Catholic Maryland society, Matthews and Taney's warm friendship endured despite the pastor's obvious discomfort with Taney's political philosophy.

Stories of these political friendships abound, but two must suffice here.[9] Father Matthews was once invited to the White House to baptize the newborn son of the French minister to Washington and Mme Pigeot, his American wife. The couple had asked President Jackson to serve as honorary godfather, and their child was to bear the famous hero's name. When, according to the ritual, Matthews asked the child, "Andrew Jackson, dost thou renounce Satan?" a startled President responded, "I do, sir." "And all his works?" Matthews continued without pause. "Most undoubtedly, I do, sir," came the testy reply from the President, who, lest anybody further question his sincerity, empha-

9. It is easy to agree with Matthews's biographer that if all the stories of the pastor's dealings with the politically famous were true, the man would have had no time to perform his priestly duties. The following anecdotes were considered authentic by Durkin and were accepted by Fosselman; the author of "Gonzaga College"; Anna Dorsey, in her "Recollections of Old St. Patrick's Church"; and the near-contemporaneous account in the *Evening Express*, 8 Aug 1867.

sized his response with a sharp tap of his cane. On another day, while visiting Father Matthews at his rectory, Henry Clay in company with Matthews's brother-in-law, William Merrick, a senator from Maryland and important Whig leader, noticed an engraving of General Jackson gracing the wall of the pastor's sitting room. Believing the President's countenance bore a somewhat penitential look, Clay playfully asked the pastor would he consider giving absolution to the great Democrat? "Yes," replied Matthews, "I would give absolution to anyone who repents." Immediately grasping the wisdom in this ambiguous reply, Clay added about Jackson, "That he will never do."

The record also provides some indication of the attitude of St. Patrick's pastor and congregation toward emancipation, which first became a topic of national concern during the Jacksonian era. Washington had 5,400 black residents in 1830, slightly more than 57 percent of them free men and women. (By 1840 the number of free African-Americans would rise to 4,800, more than 73 percent of the city's black population.) Both the free blacks and the diminishing number of slaves (the latter mostly employed as house servants or hired out as waiters or other menials in Washington's service industry) escaped the worst abuses of racial discrimination. All, however, found their freedom severely curtailed by a series of restrictive ordinances which the city had enacted to discourage immigration of free blacks. These so-called Black Codes required black residents to carry papers certifying their free status, imposed strict curfews, curtailed black businesses, required black families to post bonds, and generally compelled them to observe all sorts of restrictions that underscored the African-American's place as a second-class citizen.[10]

Actually black immigration to the generally less hostile capital accounted for only part of the growing number of free blacks in Washington. Many were former slaves who had been manumitted as the need for slaves and the popularity of that peculiar institution ebbed in the city. Another large group had purchased their own freedom and that of their families through a system that allowed ambitious slaves to earn money for extra work. Nevertheless, fear of insurrection after the Nat Turner Rebellion in 1831 fueled anti-black sentiment and led to violence four years later. Gangs of white men, mostly young, uneducated, and unemployed, reacting to an attempted murder by a black

10. Constance M. Green, *The Secret City: A History of Race Relations in the Nation's Capital* (Princeton, N.J.: Princeton University Press, 1967), chaps. 2 and 3, and her more comprehensive *Washington,* are the basis of the following paragraphs.

man, roamed the streets for several days, destroying black property and schools. Authorities responded by organizing military units composed of locally stationed soldiers and government clerks. This militia patrolled the streets and quelled what became known as the Snow Riot before it escalated into bloodshed. Although local black residents would continue to suffer unjust restrictions and general discrimination, the antebellum period saw no further outbreaks.

With the possible exception of New Orleans, Washington offered its free blacks greater opportunity than any other American city. Paradoxically in an era of black codes and slave trade, Washington was free of the patterns of segregation that would later come to stain the city. Before the great influx of ex-slaves during the Civil War, black residents owned or rented homes and operated businesses in all parts of town. Significant numbers lived and owned stores and restaurants within the boundaries of St. Patrick's, and the Catholics among them were members of the congregation.[11] Recreating a picture of daily mass at the church in 1856, reporter Lorenzo Johnson wrote: "Here may be seen genteel persons kneeling at the side of the day-laborer, who might have been born in other lands, and at the same time with persons of color, as if to say 'In the presence of God all distinctions are forgotten.'"[12]

The presence of African-Americans in Washington's Catholic parishes might be expected in 1850, but it could not be taken for granted, for by then many of the free blacks, including the Catholics, were abandoning the churches of their former masters and were establishing their own. The loyalty of Washington's black Catholics appears exceptional and was attributed by one federal official to the effort at St. Patrick's and other Catholic churches to make them feel accepted. Reviewing the pre-Civil War period, he singled out the attitude of Father Matthews, who "recognized the poorest and most benighted Negro of his parish as inferior to none in all the privileges and duties of the church." Cases of priests acting otherwise were, he claimed, rare, and he went on to describe the Catholic pastors as "friends of the poor, showing no distinction on account of color."[13]

11. Brown, "Residence Patterns of Negroes in the District of Columbia, 1800–1860," 74–77.

12. Lorenzo D. Johnson, *The Churches and Pastors of Washington, D.C.* (New York: Dodd, 1857), 45. This volume is a collection of Johnson's articles that first appeared on the front page of the *National Intelligencer* during 1856.

13. U.S. Office of Education, *Special Report of the Commissioner of Education on the Condition and Improvement of Public Schools in the District of Columbia* (Washington:

But here a qualification must be made. St. Patrick's congregation, dominated by a non-slave holding, middle-class constituency, exhibited a markedly progressive policy toward both bonded and free blacks before the Civil War. Characterizing this outlook, Chief Justice Taney was quoted as saying: "Thank God that at least in one place all men are equal, in the church of God. I do not consider it any degradation to kneel side by side with a negro in the house of our Heavenly Father."[14] In Taney's time, parish services were fully integrated; free pews were available for African-Americans; and the church had no special gallery or area reserved for blacks as did Holy Trinity, St. Peter's, and most of the Catholic churches in surrounding Maryland and Virginia. Segregated seating in these other parishes derived from the social attitudes of their congregations still strongly influenced by their southern and colonial heritage. It also reflected the influence of the Irish newcomers, many of whom were hostile to free blacks, their major competitors for low-paying jobs as laborers and domestic servants. As historian Albert Foley pointed out, the frequently quoted praise for the racial practices of Washington's Catholics in the pre-Civil War era was based almost exclusively on observations made at St. Patrick's, where there were relatively fewer recent immigrants.[15]

Reports of Father Matthews's zealous attention to the spiritual care of black Catholics, his personal generosity toward impoverished freedmen, and his efforts to purchase the freedom of individual slaves are numerous and convincing. There is no reason to doubt, for example, that he intervened in the case of a slave who, with her two children, was being transported through the neighborhood on the way to the auction block. Answering her call for help, Matthews purchased the family's freedom on the spot and went on to hire the woman as cook for St. Patrick's rectory and support her children. Nor is there any sign of a change in racial policy at St. Patrick's after the Nat Turner uprising, when most Protestant churches began to bar black Christians or strictly segregate them. Although there is no evidence that the schools and orphanage associated with St. Patrick's ever admitted a black child before the Civil War, black children attended its Sunday school, where they received religious instruction. Finally, that blacks felt welcome at

---

GPO, 1871), 218. See also, John T. Gillard, *The Catholic Church and the Negro* (Baltimore, 1928), 28–29.

14. Quoted in ltr., Rev. Jacob Walter to editor, *Century Magazine* 4 (May-Oct 1893): 958.

15. Albert Foley, "The Catholic Church and the Washington Negro," (Ph.D. dissertation, University of North Carolina, 1950), 55–56 and 130–32.

St. Patrick's might be inferred from the number of black adult converts registered during the pre-Civil War years.[16]

Washington became a center of abolitionist activity during the Jacksonian period, and although Matthews's biographer probably overstated the case when he called St. Patrick's pastor "a fierce opponent of slavery," evidence from congressional sources suggests that Matthews and his congregation were among those opposed to slavery and the slave trade in Washington.[17] Despite the small number of slaves in the city, the District retained a large and lucrative slave trade which enjoyed the protection of federal law. The notorious slave pens and auction block on the Island in southwest became a regular target of abolitionists, who bombarded Congress with memorials demanding an end to the odious business. As might be expected, most of these hundreds of petitions came from northern communities, but one, submitted to Congress in March 1828, originated in Washington and was signed by more than 1,000 citizens of Washington and Alexandria. It called on Congress to end the slave trade and abolish runaway slave laws in the District, ban the importation of slaves into Washington, and, significantly, gradually emancipate all slaves born in the city after July 4, 1828. Included among the signers were William Matthews, James Hoban, Thomas Carberry, and many of those whose names appeared on the roster of parishioners drawn up by Father Dubuisson in 1830.[18]

Support in the parish for such a forthright memorial is somewhat surprising, given the general antipathy felt by most Catholics toward the largely Protestant abolitionist movement colored even then with anti-foreign bias. Neither Matthews's name nor that of any of these

16. Exact figures are unavailable because baptismal records did not always include reference to race. Durkin (46) mentions "the considerable number of baptisms of slaves and freed black persons." In particular he points to the conversion of older blacks (126). The story of the St. Patrick's cook is repeated in a number of sources. For a colorful account, see Smith's *History of St. Patrick's*, 28–29. On the integration of the Sunday school, see Gillard, *The Catholic Church and the Negro*, 29. Both Green (*The Secret City*, 52) and Foley ("The Catholic Church and the Washington Negro," 55–56 and 130–33) compare the treatment of blacks by the various denominations in Washington.

17. See Durkin's article in the *Catholic Standard*, 10 May 1979, with its additional and likewise unsupported claim that Matthews frequently purchased and manumitted slave families.

18. Twenty-third Congress, second session, "Memorial of Inhabitants of the District of Columbia, Praying for the gradual abolition of slavery in the District of Columbia," 24 Mar 1828, House of Representatives, doc. no. 140.

same parishioners appeared on subsequent petitions circulated in the city by famed abolitionist Benjamin Lundy (including one in 1830 with 3,000 local signatures). Perhaps, like some other Washingtonians, parishioners considered the earlier petition sufficient or preferred its more circumspect language to what they later considered the radical rhetoric of William Lloyd Garrison and his abolitionist allies. In fact the slavery debate in the city became so upsetting by 1835 that most citizens supported a gag rule whereby Congress barred anti-slavery petitions.[19]

Such a stance was not particularly surprising in the wake of the Nat Turner Rebellion and the Snow Riot. Fear of black uprisings weakened local support for emancipation, and even in Quaker and Unitarian congregations, where sentiment against slavery as an institution ran especially high, congregations were divided over the need for government intervention. St. Patrick's pastor was a scion of an old Maryland family, member of a society whose concept of Christian duty required care for the physical and spiritual needs of their bondsmen, but did not question the morality of slavery. Archbishop Carroll himself owned a slave, whom he manumitted at his death. Matthews would no doubt approve Carroll's remark to one of his priests who had asked to be released from his assignment because of the treatment of slaves in Prince George's County. "I am as far, as you," the bishop told the man in refusing his request in 1794, "from being easy in my mind at many things I see, and know, relating to the treatment & manners of the Negroes. I do the best I can to correct the evils I see; and then recur to those principles, which, I suppose, influenced the many eminent & holy missioners in S. America & Asia, where slavery equally exists."[20]

Given the imperfect understanding of racial justice that prevailed among most Christians in those decades, the fact that St. Patrick's pastor and congregation supported the gradual emancipation of local slaves seems worthy of note. The picture of integrated church services, based on parish records and the eye-witness account of Lorenzo Johnson, meant that parishioners afforded their black neighbors a

19. Merton L. Billon, *Benjamin Lundy and the Struggle for Negro Freedom* (Urbana: University of Illinois Press, 1966), 122–24. The 1830 Lundy petition, with its many rolls of signatures, is on file in RG 233, NARA. On anti-abolitionist sentiment among the Irish Catholics, see Gilbert Osofsky, "Abolitionists, Irish Immigrants, and the Dilemma of Romantic Nationalism," *American Historical Review* 80 (Oct 1975): 889–912.

20. Ltr., Carroll to John Thayer, 15 Jul 1794, *JCP* 2:123. Carroll's servant was mentioned in Carroll's will. See *JCP* 3:370–71.

measure of respect as equals before the altar. In so doing they wrote one of the brighter pages in the parish's history.

Concerning its relations with other Christian bodies St. Patrick's parish exhibited a surprisingly modern attitude. In the spirit of John Carroll, it welcomed the opportunities opened to the Catholic minority in a religiously plural society. Its pastor showed none of the self-conscious aloofness of some of the immigrant priests toward non-Catholics, but worked with ease and understanding with his Protestant neighbors. Just as he had demonstrated no special concern about the teaching of nondenominational religious principles in the public schools, he also made sure that all those Catholic institutions under his influence imposed no religious bars. Consequently, leading non-Catholic citizens were educated in the city's Catholic schools, thus increasing interdenominational understanding and good will. Several historians have commented on the fact that Matthews personally provided financial assistance to needy Protestant clergymen and worked with them on projects of mutual concern.[21] One such ecumenical project addressed the plight of the Mormons following their savage expulsion from Nauvoo, Illinois. In October 1847 Washington's clergy, including Matthews and the pastors of St. Peter's and St. Matthew's, met at the E Street Baptist Church, where they addressed an open letter to "every benevolent and Christian mind" in Washington, appealing for support for the Mormon oppressed. They also organized a committee to collect and distribute the charity.[22]

The Capital in 1850

The city to which Matthews and his fellow clergymen appealed in 1847 differed considerably from the town that had welcomed Andy Jackson eighteen years before. It was still small and sleepy compared with the great metropolises rising to the northeast. It was still the butt of jokes by the tourists—on his visit in 1842, for example, Charles Dickens had called it a "City of Magnificent Intentions" with "broad avenues that begin in nothing and lead nowhere" wanting "only homes, roads, and inhabitants."[23] Only three streets were opened all the way to the city boundary. The rest stopped at M Street, beyond

21. See, for example, Eleanore C. Sullivan, *Georgetown Visitation Since 1799* (Baltimore: French-Bray, 1975), 92, and Durkin, *William Matthews*, 45.

22. Allen C. Clar, "Colonel William Winston Seaton and His Friends," *RCHS* 29–30 (1928): 58–59.

23. Charles Dickens, *American Notes* (New York: St. Martin's Press, 1985), 106. These

which all was scrub growth relieved now and then by a corn field or market garden. But with nearly forty thousand residents and increasing numbers of congressmen bringing their families to live, even if only temporarily, new businesses and stimulating social events had begun to enliven the city's central wards. After Congress rescued the local government in 1832 by paying off its debt on the C&O Canal, Washington temporarily achieved a semblance of fiscal stability.

Despite many earnest studies and proposed solutions, Congress and the local government never seemed able to arrive at an equitable division of financial responsibility for city services. Nevertheless, as the years passed the federal government slowly began spending more money in town. For example, it provided for a primitive police force, an "auxiliary guard" it was called, to quell local lawlessness, principally caused by the young hooligans who now manned the city's rival amateur fire companies. Congress also increased its support of medical care and housing for the immigrant poor and voted funds for a new Washington Infirmary and the National Medical College, which trained physicians and cared for poor patients. Yet even in 1850 the average citizen continued to assume that charity was an individual rather than a government obligation. With ethnic organizations and church groups leading the way, and with considerable involvement by the city's various benevolent societies, private donations secured food and shelter for many of the destitute, especially those foreign immigrants ineligible for admission to the city almshouse.

On the whole Washington had begun to assume a more enlightened air by the 1850s. A new city charter reduced the fearful number of crimes that demanded the death penalty, and Congress abolished the law requiring imprisonment for debt. A better but still-problematical tax system was instituted to support an enlarged public school system. By mid-century the city's early predictions of an urban renaissance had begun to be fulfilled. The National Observatory opened in 1844, and three years later the Smithsonian Castle rose on the Mall, beginning a fruitful partnership between government and academy. Carusi's Saloon sponsored frequent concerts of serious music, and the National Theater, opened in 1831, presented plays featuring the leading actors of the day. Local residents also liked to attend the Marine Band concerts on the south lawn of the White House on Saturday after-

---

paragraphs on Washington in the 1840s and 1850s are based on Green's *Washington;* Sarah Veddes, *Reminiscences of the District of Columbia or Washington City Seventy-Nine Years Ago* (St. Louis: A. R. Fleming, 1909) and "How the City Looked," *Star,* 14 Apr 1888.

noons or at the Capitol on Wednesdays (the workday for most government employees ended at three in the afternoon). The city now boasted some fine promenades, especially through the well-landscaped grounds of the Capitol, with its gravel walks and fountains, and along Pennsylvania Avenue between Fifteenth Street and the Capitol. Finally, after considerable argument and a last-minute gift of land from Congress, the Washington Monument Society on July 4, 1848, laid the cornerstone for its mighty memorial on the Mall that would come to symbolize the nation's respect for the father of the country and founder of the city.

These decades of growth and progress were also a time of misgivings for Washingtonians, who were beginning to worry about the future of the Union. Washington was a southern town, but even if its residents tended to share many customs and attitudes with the southern states, its fate was closely tied to the well-being of the federal government. Fearful that the government would disappear if the nation divided over slavery, local leaders began to see slavery as a threat to the city's future. Anti-slavery sentiment had advanced to the point in 1849 where a shrewd freshman congressman from Illinois named Abraham Lincoln could propose abolition of slavery in the federal city. Washington's leading citizens no longer protested when abolitionist petitions attacking slavery in the city once again flooded Congress. None objected when, as part of the great compromise in 1850 to preserve the union, the government abolished the slave trade in the capital. With considerable relief, residents saw the slave pens and auction houses south of the Smithsonian building abandoned.

The Patriarch of Washington

St. Patrick's parish also participated in the growth and prosperity of the 1840s and 1850s. Its boundaries encompassed most of Wards Two and Three, the city's most populous, and along with Ward One, richest neighborhood. When, at the invitation of Archbishop Kenrick, Dominican priests established St. Dominic Church in southwest in 1852, they relieved St. Patrick's of any residual responsibilities for that area of the city. Economically and socially, the parish was beginning to assume the profile it would retain for the next eighty years—middle class professionals, storekeepers and tradesmen, mechanics, government clerks and office workers.[24] Some of the city's newest and poor-

24. Hickey, "Irish Catholics in Washington Up to 1860," 32–41 with tables, provides a occupational survey of some of the residents of Wards Two and Three.

est residents, the laborers imported to work on the roads and canals, lived in Bricktown, a neighborhood in the northern reaches of the parish along Seventh Street, but most dwelt outside the parish in southeast, in the area south of Rock Creek known as Foggy Bottom, and especially in Swampoodle, the name given to the region along North Capitol Street.

It is difficult to judge the exact size of the congregation in this period. Matthews estimated the number of Catholics in the District of Columbia at 12,000 in 1830; Archbishop Whitfield offered a more conservative figure of 10,000 in 1832. Although these estimates included the parishes in Alexandria and Georgetown, they were almost surely inflated. The *Catholic Mirror,* the unofficial diocesan newspaper published in Baltimore, estimated the Catholic population of Washington City in 1850 at seven to eight thousand, 20 percent of the city's total. This appears reasonable, given later, reliable figures. Considering the population of Wards Two and Three in 1850, it also seems reasonable to assume that St. Patrick's still commanded the lion's share of the Catholic total with perhaps as many as thirty-five hundred parishioners. Lending credence to such estimates, the *Mirror* reported in 1851 on the "vast crowds" at all the church's masses on both Sundays and weekdays, noting that they were far larger than those in any of the city's other Catholic churches and equal to any church in the diocese.[25]

Obviously such crowds sorely taxed the church's facilities, and since the assignment of Father Dubuisson as its first assistant priest in 1822, St. Patrick's had come to depend on a whole series of curates to help the aging pastor. Although successive archbishops tried to provide diocesan priests, they had few to spare, and the resourceful Matthews often managed to recruit helpers from other sources. Despite the pastor's battles with members of the Society of Jesus and his earlier vow to reject aid from that quarter, a number of Jesuits, mostly teachers connected with the neighboring Washington Seminary, assisted in the parish throughout the period. In addition the parish served as host for several temporary residents who in return helped on a part-time basis.

The earliest and most noteworthy of these guests was Gabriel Richard, the vicar general of Detroit and representative of the Michigan Territory in the House of Representatives. Father Richard was

25. *Catholic Mirror* 6 Jul 1850 and 8 Feb 1851. Whitfield's estimate was included in his report to the Propagation of the Faith Society in France. See Whitfield to M. le Redacteur des Annales, 16 Feb 1832, *Annales* 5 (1831–32): 714–23. Matthews's figure was reported to Anthony Kohlmann in a letter dated 14 Jun 30, *Congressi,* sec. 10, fol. 390, APF.

THE PATRIARCH OF WASHINGTON. *An 1841 lithograph by*
Charles Fenderich

among that group of Sulpicians, including Ambroise Maréchal and
François Matignon, who left revolutionary France in 1792 to teach at
St. Mary's Seminary. With little need for a mathematics professor, Carroll soon reassigned Richard to the vast Illinois territory, where he
ministered to the Indians and French Canadians. In 1798 he transferred
to Detroit with responsibility for all the missions in Wisconsin and
Michigan. Here Richard's extraordinary activities included co-found-
ing the University of Michigan and running the first printing press
west of the Alleghenies. His popular newspaper, the *Michigan Essay or
Impartial Observer*, proved not at all impartial. Its fiery attacks on the
British caused the priest's imprisonment when the Redcoats captured
Detroit during the War of 1812.

Elected to the Eighteenth Congress in 1822, Richard lived at St.
Patrick's, where he devoted much time to parish duties. A contempo-

rary account describes the colorful Frenchman walking down a Washington street:

. . . his low-crowned, broad-brimmed hat was thrown back on the crown of his head, and a pair of large goggles sat enthroned on the uppermost of an expansive, bulging forehead. He had on the nicest-fitting and best-polished shoes man could ever wear, with silver buckles, but no stockings. He was tapping a fine gold snuff-box and appeared in the act of offering a pinch to a friend. . . .[26]

Watching Richard study public issues late into the night, Father Matthews concluded that a congressman was "a complete slave." He was amazed, he told Archbishop Maréchal, that despite so much hard work the Michigan priest was anxious to win a second term.[27] Richard was not re-elected, however, thanks in great part to the opposition of church trustees in Detroit.

St. Patrick's also enjoyed the temporary labors of Father Timolean (Jean) Figeac, who served as assistant during the extremely busy time before the opening of St. Matthew's somewhat relieved the strain on the F Street facilities. Described by Matthews as "a little French priest who speaks very little English, yet sings well," Figeac must have filled a noticeable void in the sacramental life of a parish whose tone-deaf pastor preferred to avoid high masses. That Matthews was aware of his deficiency in this area can be deduced from his playful note to Father George Fenwick, one of the local Jesuits who often helped at St. Patrick's: "Are we to have the pleasure to hear you sing Mass tomorrow? Or are we to expect another?"[28]

Probably the most noteworthy assistant at St. Patrick's before the Civil War was the Annapolis-born Charles Constantine Pise. Roman trained, he gained early fame as a teacher and as editor of *The Metropolitan,* the nation's first Catholic literary magazine. He was also the author of the popular poem "The American Flag," which he wrote in response to nativist charges against Catholic patriotism. The priest's

26. Nicholas M. Williams, "Rev. Gabriel Richard, V.G., a Recollection of Forty-seven Years Ago," *The Catholic Family Almanac, 1871.* Williams, a member of St. Patrick's congregation, was introduced to Richard by Father Matthews in 1824. He frequently served the priest's daily mass on F Street.

27. Ltr., Matthews to Maréchal, 1 Feb 1825, 19-B-19, Maréchal Papers, AAB. For a modern account of Richard's career in America, see Frank Woodford and Albert Hyma, *Gabriel Richard: Frontier Ambassador* (Detroit: Wayne State University Press, 1958).

28. Matthews's description of Figeac is found in a letter to Peter Schreiber, 19 Oct 1831, RG 26, SAB. His note to Fenwick, dated 13 May 1837, is in the Maryland province archives (56 S-I-W4), GUA.

close friendship with Father Matthews and his free-wheeling association with various Roman authorities led to Archbishop Whitfield's
suspicion that Pise was part of a conspiracy to make Washington a
separate diocese. Yet this concern did not stop Whitfield from assigning the dynamic Pise to St. Patrick's in 1832. It may, however, have convinced Pise that his future best lay elsewhere. A year later he accepted
an invitation from the bishop of New York to work in that diocese,
where he spent years founding churches, preaching, and writing
scholarly histories.

The Fulton Sheen of his day, Pise attracted many Washingtonians to
the church during his brief stay in the city, prompting socialite Margaret Bayard Smith's wry comment, "Mr. Pise is carrying all before
him." After listing some of his prominent converts, Smith concluded
of Pise that "his zeal, his eloquence, and his personal beauty combine
to give him an influence no priest has before had amongst us." As a token of that popularity, his friend Henry Clay arranged for Pise's election as chaplain of the U.S. Senate in 1832, the only Catholic priest so
honored. Mrs. Smith, a fair but not particularly sympathetic critic,
quoted a Mississippi senator to the effect that Pise's election was an attempt by the Senate to demonstrate the government's universal toleration. Yet even Smith had to admit that when the learned and extremely popular preacher was scheduled to speak, St. Patrick's was
filled with crowds so large that people packed the aisles.[29]

Pise's preaching may have been extraordinary, but in fact many of
the assistants who served during Matthews's long pastorate were
noted for their eloquence and their ability to attract converts in a period when, even in Washington, anti-Catholic sentiment had become
respectable. The parish registers attest to the important and fruitful
work of men like Henry Myers, Peter Schreiber (later the pastor of St.
Peter's), the brothers John Philip and James Donelan, who both went
on to become pastors of St. Matthew's, Thomas P. Foley (later bishop
of Chicago), and Matthews's last assistant and eventual successor,
Timothy Joseph O'Toole. Described by Archbishop Kenrick as one
"who has learning, a good mind and piety," O'Toole came well recommended, as a recent Irish immigrant trained at Maynooth College, the
famous Irish seminary.[30]

29. Hunt, ed., *Forty Years of Washington Society,* 340. Summaries of Pise's interesting
career were carried in the *Catholic Mirror,* 4 Mar 1905, and in the *Catholic Standard,* 31
Mar 1961.

30. Ltr., Francis P. Kenrick to Peter R. Kenrick, 12 May 1854, reproduced in *Kenrick-
Frenaye Correspondence, 1839–1852* (Philadelphia: Wickersham, 1920), 370.

These men participated in a busy round of ecclesiastical duties, not unlike their successors a century later. In the decade before the Civil War the crowds at the church necessitated three Sunday masses, including an elaborately sung mass featuring one of the city's most noted choirs, a ceremony sensibly suspended during Washington's torrid summers. In addition to daily masses, Sunday vespers, administering the sacraments (for example, 266 baptisms in 1834 and 290 in 1856, with marriages running at a rate of about 90 per year), and officiating at popular devotions, the priests were involved in supervising catechism classes, instructing converts, and visiting the sick at the local infirmary. In 1854 the *Catholic Mirror* reported that despite the strong nativist rhetoric which had stirred anti-Catholic sentiment in some parts of the city, the church was constantly crowded and the parish flourishing.[31]

Although William Matthews, even in extreme old age, was not about to surrender his spiritual and material stewardship, the parishioners themselves appeared to play an increasingly significant role in some of the organizations in what had become a large urban parish. Lay teachers staffed the parish's Sunday school with its carefully structured catechetical program. They also organized programs for the care of the needy. The most important of these groups was the Charitable Society of St. Patrick's. Typical of the locally funded, small-scale charities that operated throughout the diocese before systematically organized, city-wide efforts were established during the Civil War, the St. Patrick's society was formed by women of the parish in 1823, the first Catholic group of this kind in the city. Anticipating the simple organization of the later-formed altar societies, the women arbitrarily divided the parish into districts, assigning to each a chairwoman and committee responsible for collecting goods and money and distributing them to the poor of that district. Along with two similar but smaller groups with more specialized missions—the Indigent and Sick Society and a local branch of the Young Catholic Friends Society—the Charitable Society constituted one of city's major private relief groups until it was superseded in 1860s by the St. Vincent de Paul Society and diocesan efforts that began to organize Catholic charity along inter-parish lines.[32]

---

31. *Catholic Mirror*, 2 Dec 1854. The statistics are derived from parish registers and a letter, O'Toole to Kenrick, 27 Jan 1857, 31-V-6, Kenrick Papers, AAB.

32. Both Weitzman, *One Hundred Years of Catholic Charities*, 129, and John O'Grady, *Catholic Charities in the United States* (Washington: National Conference of Catholic

Members of the congregation were also responsible for the formation of the St. Patrick's Total Abstinence Society in 1840, the first such Catholic group in the United States. Responding in later years to the special needs of the immigrants and the enthusiastic leadership of several eloquent priests, the Catholic temperance movement would take on the appearance of a holy crusade against alcohol. When George Savage and like-minded instructors in the Sunday school decided to lead the fight at St. Patrick's in 1840, however, the necessity for this rigor was only beginning to be felt. On Independence Day fifty parishioners took the pledge in the presence of Father Matthews and a sizable congregation.[33]

Parallel to this growth in social groups was the proliferation of popular devotions. There was nothing new in organized public veneration of the Sacred Heart at St. Patrick's, but now special emphasis was also being given to public devotions to the Blessed Sacrament, stations of the cross, the rosary, and novenas to the Holy Name of Jesus, the Blessed Virgin, and other saints. In earlier decades these exercises of piety had been clearly subordinated to the twin staples of the American Catholic tradition: the sacraments and private prayer. Influenced by the newcomers and the priests who accompanied them during the great wave of Catholic migration after 1830, parishes throughout the country began to emphasize the congregation's public and extra-sacramental prayer life. In stark contrast to the Bible-centered services of their Protestant neighbors, the warmth and emotional immediacy of communal prayers especially appealed to the newcomers. Their enthusiasm spread, and in succeeding decades what historians call "devotional Catholicism" would come to dominate the prayer life of the whole American church.[34] These devotions were supported by an outpouring of prayer books and other printed materials in the decades before the Civil War. Popular publications guided the faithful through the prayers and ceremonies, which were invariably in English and in-

Charities, 1930), 318, point to the Charitable Society as the beginning of Catholic relief services in the District.

33. Spalding, *Premier See*, 144; and "Gonzaga College," 20.

34. Both Dolan's *The American Catholic Experience*, 210–13, and Spalding's *Premier See*, 144–45, discuss the cause and growth of popular devotions. See also Ann Taves, *The Household of Faith: Roman Catholic Devotions in Mid-Nineteenth Century America* (Notre Dame: University of Notre Dame Press, 1986) and Michael J. McNally, "A Pecular Institution: A History of Catholic Parish Life in the Southeast (1850–1980)", in Jay Dolan, ed., *The American Catholic Parish: A History from 1850 to the Present* (New York: Paulist Press, 1987), 1:117–234.

volved the congregation to a greater extent in the ritual. This sense of individual participation was not so evident to many in the Mass. Moreover, in contrast to the private orisons found in the prayer books of earlier times, the social nature of these public devotions imparted a sense of community among those who were essentially strangers in the growing anonymity of a large city parish. Always the dominating devotion was the Sodality of the Blessed Virgin Mary. Organized in separate groups for men, women, and children, the sodality at St. Patrick's, as indeed in most churches, counted almost every member of the congregation in its bands, and its weekly devotions vied with Sunday Mass for the most participants.

If such devotions distinguished the Catholic church from other denominations, the sudden popularity of the parish mission during the same period clearly echoed the revivals so important to many elements in American Protestantism. These missions, usually lasting a week with separate sessions for men and women, involved a series of sermons or exhortations on various aspects of Christian ethics and personal morality with special emphasis on penance and renewed attention to the Eucharist. Certain religious orders, particularly the Redemptorists and Jesuits in the earlier decades, specialized in conducting such missions, and St. Patrick's, like most churches, usually scheduled at least one each year. They attracted massive crowds, so much so that in later years one was canceled because the pastor could not guarantee that the floor of the old church would support the throng. The retreat given by two Jesuit fathers at St. Patrick's in April 1852, for example, lasted one week with some three thousand parishioners attending its sessions, going to confession, and receiving Holy Communion.[35]

Father Matthews's appearance at the parish mission in 1852 prompted the *Catholic Mirror* to conclude that the spiritual success of the affair had imparted new strength and vigor to "the aged pastor" whose youthful zeal kept him busy hearing confessions from morning till night. In fact at eighty-two Matthews had begun to curtail his activities. He still celebrated Mass early each morning, but he gave up preaching completely.[36] His well-recorded visit to the nearby Visitation school in 1853 to present the startled sisters with a large check was one

35. Fosselman, "A Downtown Parish," 133. On the mission movement in Catholic parishes, see Jay P. Dolan, *Catholic Revivalism: The American Experience, 1830–1900* (Notre Dame: University of Notre Dame Press, 1978), especially 15–29.

36. *Catholic Mirror*, 6 May 1852 and 22 Oct 1853.

of his rare ventures outside the rectory garden; even that was on the arm of a friend. Clearly the pastorate was nearing its end, a knowledge, it seemed, that only increased the public's expressions of affection for so singular a citizen.

His last public appearance on record was at the celebration of the parish's patronal feast in 1854. One city paper used the occasion to offer a tribute to the pastor and the city's Irish:

We attended the celebration of mass at St. Patrick's Church on this great festival day of the Irish. When Father Matthews, the beloved pastor of this church, walked up the aisle, his venerable form decorated with a badge upon the borders of which the shamrock was embroidered, our heart was filled with a strange emotion. It was tied with a green ribbon, and we thought it emblematic of his love, which is ever found green and fresh, [as it is] in the hearts of the sons of the Emerald Isle for their native land.[37]

On Sunday evening, April 30, church bells tolled the news to the city of the old pastor's death. What followed was an unprecedented outpouring of tribute for a spiritual leader, fully chronicled in the secular press in both Washington and Baltimore. The *Baltimore Sun* reported on the throngs of people "of all denominations and all classes" that filled the church neighborhood for two days. The Circuit Court adjourned to permit its judges and lawyers to attend the funeral, which saw extraordinary crowds of citizens follow the procession that wended its way up Pennsylvania Avenue before returning for the burial next to the church Matthews built.

The *National Intelligencer* commented on "the high estimation which not the people of his own flock and denomination only, but of all names and parties amongst us, have formed of this excellent man." As might be expected, much of the editorial comment focused on the priest's benevolence, but the editors also noted his strong individuality which led to forthright opinions on all subjects, all presented with fearless conviction. These candid expressions of his personal beliefs were never held against him. On the contrary, as the *Star* noted:

He was a man without guile, and though enthusiastic to impetuosity in his temperament, was literally without an enemy. It is a remarkable fact, that though such were his labors, walks and character, no one was even known to say aught against him, even when sectarian jealousies ran highest, causing both Catholic and Protestant religious teachers to be invidiously criticized. Washington will hardly look upon his like again.[38]

37. Washington *Weekly Metropolitan*, 25 Mar 1854.
38. *Star*, 1 May 1854. The quotation from the *National Intelligencer* is dated 5 May

Such immunity from criticism was especially remarkable in an age when sectarian strife was beginning to assume political force in the city. Matthews was widely recognized for his legendary charities and concern for the welfare of the community. That this concern transcended the interests of the Catholic minority was universally admired and won for St. Patrick's pastor the esteem of all citizens, a measure of acceptance rarely accorded a Catholic leader in nineteenth-century America. Although difficult to measure, it seems clear that some of this respect and affection transformed itself into a general tolerance for the Catholic religion in Washington. It certainly explains in part the city's civility during the wave of anti-Catholicism that was whirling through the country.

This transfer of goodwill was especially remarkable because Matthews was by then one of a very small minority within a minority. He was a product of the old Catholic aristocracy of Maryland who had survived to see the Church transformed by newcomers. Throughout the decades of growth and change in Washington he remained true to the principles extolled by the nation's founders. Throughout his long career he preached in word and deed the importance of patriotism, tolerance, and the obligations of citizenship. In religious matters he closely resembled his spiritual father, John Carroll, combining a simple and sincere faith with a practical approach to the material world in which that faith must operate and spread. Small wonder that the congregation reveled in the widely circulated anecdotes that illustrated how Matthews's spiritual and pragmatic sides were sometimes revealed in humorous exchanges.

One incident, frequently retold, concerned a time when Matthews was visited by a group of his old Charles County neighbors, who asked him to pray for much-needed rain. Striding to the rectory window, the pastor looked at the weather vane atop the steeple of the Ninth Street Baptist Church (the later site of Ford's theater) and responded: "Pray for rain? It's no use to pray for rain when the wind's northwest." Other stories highlighted the generous man's notorious frugality. When parishioners complained that the church stove was rarely lighted and thus Mass was often a freezing experience, he told them: "What do you want with a fire? Let your faith keep you warm."

1854. See also the Baltimore *Sun*, 3 May 1854; Washington *News*, 3 May 1854; and *Weekly Metropolitan*, 6 May 1854. Bulletins on Father Matthews's last illness appeared regularly in the daily press. See, for example, the *Star*, 28 Apr to 3 May 1854 and the *Sun*, 30 Apr to 8 May 1854.

The congregation also admired the pastor's simple republican ways. While reading in his parlor on an extremely cold day, Matthews was interrupted by a parishioner anxious to introduce him to his distinguished companion, the minister of the Russian Tsar. Matthews looked up from his book and responded abruptly: "Come in, Russian Minister, shut the door," thus demonstrating to the delight of the many who heard the story the popular conviction that a Maryland gentlemen was at any time the equal of a European aristocrat.[39]

It was St. Patrick's great good fortune to be led through its formative years by a man who combined a keen sense of civic responsibility with strong and simple faith. The institutions he fostered and the principles of religion and patriotism he preached through the years created a community of faith, informing three separate generations of parishioners in their responsibilities as Catholics and as citizens. His death marked the end of a unique period in the long history of St. Patrick's, a source of special pride for later generations of Washington Catholics. The rapid growth of the congregation, the proliferation of Catholic institutions, and the crowds that thronged the church, including many converts, all attest to the vitality of a pastor and congregation who looked outward, associating with their fellow citizens with an openness, lively concern, and self-confidence that belied their minority status.

Recent historians have labelled this openness and self-confidence the "Maryland tradition." They are referring to the development of a distinct American Catholic attitude that evolved during the decades of persecution in colonial times and the era of tolerance and acceptance of the ideals of the enlightenment, ideals reflected in the Declaration of Independence and Bill of Rights. No doubt too much can be made of such distinctions and the invidious comparisons with the later period of strong immigrant influence, but it is obvious that under the leadership of the likes of John Carroll, Ambrose Maréchal, William Matthews, and leading laymen of those first generations, St. Patrick's congregation triumphed over its minority status and participated openly and freely in all aspects of citizenship.

All this would change in subsequent decades when the parish, echo-

39. These three examples of Matthews's remarks first appeared in print in an article in the *Evening Express*, 8 August 1867. See also "Recollections of Thomas Callan," Baltimore *Catholic Review*, 21 Jun 1919. It is tempting to repeat more Matthews anecdotes, many of which were used by Father Durkin in his *William Matthews* to illustrate Matthews's principles and method of operation.

ing a trend running through the American church, would adopt habits of introspection that emphasized to a far greater extent its differences with its neighbors. Armed with a love for church and city learned from its patriarch and so far immune from the anti-Catholic prejudice gaining strength elsewhere, the congregation never betrayed such attitudes during Matthews's time. It is interesting to note, however, that the city-wide mourning of Father Matthews's death that involved people of all faiths was one of the last ecumenical events to occur in Washington in the nineteenth century.

CHAPTER 5

Newcomers

THE DECADE preceding the Civil War proved a momentous one for the Catholic church in America. A generation
of unprecedented growth, principally through immigration from Ireland and Germany, produced a startling transformation. The small religious minority of 1820, relatively
homogeneous in social and economic background and
dominated by an Anglo-American elite, was by 1850 the
largest religious body in the United States, with 1.6 million
members, a number that would double in the next ten
years.[1]

Such dynamic growth strained the attitude of respect
and tolerance that American Catholics had enjoyed since
the days of the Revolution. Competing with the immigrants for jobs, associating the newcomers with increases
in poverty, crime, and disease, and fearing the spread of
"popery," some elements in the non-Catholic majority
were galvanized into an anti-foreign, anti-Catholic crusade. In the vanguard was the American Protestant Associ-

---

1. It is difficult to supply exact figures for the Catholic population,
which would total an estimated 3.1 million by 1860. Figures cited are
from Gerald Shaughnessy's *Has the Immigrant Kept the Faith: A Study of
Immigration and Catholic Growth in the United States, 1790–1920* (New
York: Macmillan, 1925), 145.

ation, a national organization of clergymen that viewed growing Catholic strength as a threat to Protestant liberties. Inflamed rhetoric and calumnious rumors led to mob attacks on Catholic convents and churches and to deadly religious riots in the streets of several eastern cities; in the 1850s the offensive continued with the organization of a national political party, the Know-Nothings, expressly dedicated to restricting immigration and curtailing Catholic rights and influence.

Although this specially virulent anti-Catholicism proved short-lived, it nevertheless had a significant influence on the evolution of the American church. It reinforced the inclination of many of the newcomers, particularly the Irish, to isolate themselves from their Protestant neighbors and to develop a separate society complete in itself. In contrast to attitudes in earlier decades, this desire "to be in the world but not of the world" increasingly centered all interests on the parish.[2] In time, many of the social, educational, and even to some extent economic institutions that regularly affect people's lives would be found duplicated in parish organizations.

Lacking basic industries and possessed of a plentiful supply of free black labor, Washington never experienced a flow of immigrants comparable to that in the great urban centers of the north and west. Even in the wake of the immigration prompted by the building of the C&O canal, the 1850 census listed fewer than 5,000 foreign born in the District of Columbia (9.5 percent of the population). In the next decade that number rose to 12,484, nearly 17 percent of the total. Half of the city's foreign born in 1860, some 6,070 residents, were from Ireland, the large majority, presumably, Catholic.[3]

Many of the foreign born had been residents of the city for years and were thoroughly assimilated. The small number of recent immigrants failed to ignite much local opposition, and thanks to the cordial relations existing between local Catholic leaders, especially Father Matthews, and the non-Catholic majority, the city remained generally serene. But if Washington's Catholics escaped much of the bigotry directed at their co-religionists elsewhere, they were not immune to the changes in outlook that had begun to affect the American church in

2. Quoted in Olson, *Catholic Immigrants in America,* 22. For an extended discussion of the influence of nativism on the American church, see Olson's work, and Dolan's *The American Catholic Experience,* chaps. 6 and 7.

3. Statistics used in this chapter are based on figures compiled by Jennifer Altenhofel in support of her ongoing study of Irish immigration to Washington, copy in SPA.

reaction to nativist intolerance. These changes were already to some extent noticeable at St. Patrick's by the end of the 1850s and in many respects could be said to have first crystallized during the pastorate of the parish's immigrant rector, Timothy O'Toole.

The Know-Nothings in Washington

Washington's nativist-inspired outburst against immigrants and Catholics, a pale imitation of those occurring elsewhere, can be precisely dated to 1854, when a Vatican official, Archbishop Gaetano Bedini, visited the city as part of a national fact-finding tour for the Pope. Before that date, events that frequently led to violence elsewhere were quietly defused in the capital. Where, for example, rumors of nuns leaving convents in the 1830s prompted riots and the burning of convents in Massachusetts and elsewhere, a similar situation in Washington prompted intense speculation but no anti-Catholic demonstration. News that Sister Gertrude, for eleven years the superior of the Visitation Convent, had abruptly left religious life in 1831 and taken up employment as a private teacher caused a sensation in local society, but Father Matthews readily gave out reports that stopped the ensuing rumors. In words that dispelled the mystique that seemed to surround convents, he explained that she "took French leave, and decamped," because a new mother superior had been assigned. Rather than suffer a reduction in status, she decided on a change in career.[4]

Far from fearing the power of the American Protestant Association, Washington Catholics ridiculed its local efforts. When an association representative spoke in a local church in 1844 on "the Responsibilities of Protestants, in view of the present State of Romanism in this Country," a letter to the editor of the Catholic Herald from "Verus Americanus" reported on the inept presentation, the meager audience, and the tawdry emphasis on relieving the congregation of its cash. The critic went on to object to the notice given the scurrilous talk in the National Intelligencer while reminding his readers that Catholics and Protestants had fought side by side during the Revolution. He urged them to reunite against such rabble rousers.[5]

4. Matthews spoke of this incident on several occasions. The quotation is from his letter to Peter Schreiber, 19 Oct 1831, RG 26, SAB. The story appears in several histories of old Washington. See especially Benjamin Poore, Pereley's Reminiscences of Sixty Years in the National Metropolis (Philadelphia: Hubbard Bros., 1886), 1:161.

5. Catholic Herald, vol. 12, no. 25 (20 Jun 1844), 198.

This atmosphere of gentlemanly debate over anti-Catholicism in the capital abruptly changed in 1854. Bedini's initial visit the previous July had been cordial enough, with a stream of Washington's clergy and distinguished citizens visiting the Pope's representative at the National Hotel.[6] Following his official meeting with President Franklin Pierce, he took up residence at Georgetown College, where he interviewed collegians both there and at the nearby Visitation school, marvelling at the presence of so many Protestant students at both institutions. As he crisscrossed the country in succeeding months, however, Bedini became the excuse for a series of increasingly violent demonstrations. The Pope and his representative were burned in effigy in a number of major cities. Feeling ran so high that the archbishop of New York warned Catholics in his state to protect their property and churches if public authorities failed to act.

Objections to Bedini's presence originated primarily in a small, vocal body of anti-clerical revolutionaries, particularly German and Italian exiles, who had recently fled Europe. But if these elements led the charge, the nativist crusaders happily reaped the harvest of riots and demonstrations that ensued. The riot during Bedini's visit to Cincinnati particularly shocked the nation and roused criticism in the foreign press, which lamented the government's handling of the violence directed against the Italian prelate.

Bedini's second visit to Washington, in January 1854, at the end of his national tour, allowed the *Star* to note that he was treated "with every mark of politeness and respect." His stay featured much flowery oratory in Congress, receptions sponsored by the diplomatic corps, and a vigorous defense of the archbishop in the *National Intelligencer*. It also gave local bigots an excuse to demonstrate. They hanged the archbishop in effigy at the corner of Seventh and Pennsylvania Avenue.[7] This act seemed to spur local nativists on. On the night of March 5, nine men sneaked onto the Washington Monument grounds, locked up the watchman, and made off with a block of marble, a gift of Pius IX to the people of the United States. This ancient stone, part of the Temple of Concord in Rome, was one of many received from states and societies throughout the world to decorate the

6. James F. Connelly, "The Visit of Archbishop Gaetano Bedini to the United States of America (June 1853–February 1854)," (Doctoral dissertation, Pontifical Gregorian University, 1960), 17. Connelly's comprehensive summary of the Bedini mission is the source of the following paragraphs.

7. *Star,* 23 and 30 Jan 1854. The lengthy defense of Bedini's career as a Vatican diplomat appeared in the *National Intelligencer* on 14 Jan 1854.

interior walls of the monument then rising on the Mall. The robbers subsequently hauled the heavy relic to the nearby Washington canal and, rowing out into the Potomac, unceremoniously dumped the symbol of papal generosity and respect for the country's first President into the channel.[8]

The vandalism was promptly condemned by responsible authorities— "a deed of barbarism," the *National Intelligencer* branded it. The perpetrators were never caught, but in this case it seemed clear that the act could be traced directly to the fulminations of a radical Protestant clergyman. Just two years before, a Baltimore minister had delivered an inflammatory address that called on his audience to resist "desecration of the Monument, by placing the Pope's stone or any other Foreign material" in its walls. He added a new twist to the old fears: the inscription carved on the Pope's gift, "Rome to America," was "predictive," he warned. Soon Americans will hear that the Pope must flee Rome for his safety, and then "he may modestly erect his heaven-on-earth throne in Father Mathew's [sic] Cathedral in Washington, nearby the base of the Monument." Although the idea of the Pope ensconced under the decaying roof of old St. Patrick's might have given its congregation a laugh, the sermon was printed and thousands of copies distributed throughout the region, adding to the growing atmosphere of suspicion and hate.[9]

Opposition to foreigners and Catholics eventually led to establishment of the American, or Know-Nothing, party.[10] Part of a nationally organized secret society (hence the Know-Nothing label), the party's leaders especially railed against the danger of papal interference through the growing power of the American bishops and the crime and corruption stemming from lax immigration and naturalization laws. One particular point of contention was recent Catholic opposi-

8. *National Intelligencer,* 8 Mar 1854, and *Star,* same date. The *Star* also reported the confession of one of the participants in considerable detail on 29 September 1893.

9. John F. Weishampel, *The Pope's Stratagem: 'Rome to America'* (Baltimore: 1852). Weishampel went on to charge that the pastor had collected money throughout the United States for the purchase of a lot "at tremendous price" in Washington, the site of a great cathedral for the Pope's use. Subsequent sections of the sermon make it clear that the learned bigot was confusing William Matthews with the peripatetic temperance crusader, Theobald Mathew.

10. Ray Allen Billington, *The Protestant Crusade, 1800–1860: A Study of the Origins of American Nativism* (New York: Macmillan, 1938), especially chaps. 12 and 13, is the source for the following paragraphs. See also Paul Barry's "The Know-Nothing Party in the District of Columbia" (Master's thesis, The Catholic University of America, 1933).

tion to public schools on the grounds that these institutions insisted on using Protestant-oriented texts and Bible translations. Under the banner of "Americans should rule America" the Know-Nothings raised the anti-foreign, anti-Catholic issue to the national level, electing governors in one-quarter of the states by 1855, as well as five senators and forty-three representatives to Congress. In nearby Maryland they eventually won control of the state assembly, the major cities, and finally the governor's office.

The Know-Nothings captured Washington's city government in 1854, electing John T. Tower mayor. In analyzing the election the *Star* admitted that the main issues were hostility to the Catholic church and the civil rights granted foreigners. It also made a further distinction: American-born supporters of the new party said they were voting against the lax immigration laws; the non-Catholic newcomers considered their vote one against the Catholic church.[11] The party's success seemed to incite the extremists to further acts of rowdyism and rioting. Know-Nothing supporters, especially those in the street gangs like Washington's "Chunkers" and Baltimore's "Rip Raps," roamed the neighborhoods, destroying property and setting upon terrified immigrants. Even St. Patrick's cemetery did not escape desecration—the rowdies left many of its tombstones in ruins.[12] At times the Catholics struck back. When, for example, the Montgomery Guards, a local paramilitary society composed largely of Catholic youths, learned that Know-Nothing gangs were planning to disrupt their annual drill scheduled to take place in Arlington shortly after the affair at the Washington Monument, they prepared themselves for battle and thoroughly drubbed the surprised attackers.[13]

Things did not go well for the local nativists. Washington's Catholics retained the respect and sympathy of many of their fellow citizens, while the inept administration encountered considerable opposition. In September, for example, three thousand Washingtonians met at Carusi's saloon to condemn the Know-Nothing program, and the *Star* ran articles reminding its readers of the contributions of Catholic priests and sisters to community charities. In response to the continuing trouble, President Pierce blocked the appointment of some Know-Nothing nominees to city posts, and Congress killed several vital bills initiated by the city government. In 1856 the party was swept out of office. When, the following year, Know-Nothing stalwarts abetted by

11. *Star,* 6 Jun 1854.
12. Hickey, "Irish Catholics in the District of Columbia," 73.
13. *Catholic Mirror,* 16 Aug 1890.

a gang of "Plug Uglies" from Baltimore, announced that they would demonstrate at the voting sites, President James Buchanan sent in a Marine unit to maintain order. The demonstrators commandeered a canon and threatened voters at the Northern Liberties Market, whereupon the Marines opened fire, killing several protestors. Only with the arrival of a company of federal artillery from Baltimore was order finally restored.

Although popular attention focused on the anti-foreign and anti-Catholic aspects of the city's brief infatuation with organized nativists, students of Washington's government have since concluded that the popular vote won by the Know-Nothings was based more on class issues than on deep-seated prejudice. Washington in the 1850s was extremely class conscious, and the relaxation of voting-eligibility rules (now any white adult male, resident in the city one year, could participate in local elections) had produced a strong reaction against the propertied class. The more-numerous laborers generally supported the Know-Nothings, not because of the party's religious attitudes, but because it was anti-establishment.[14] Their revolt proved short-lived, and they soon returned to their traditional political moorings. Once seen as the national possible successor to the Whigs, the Know-Nothings rapidly declined when the great sectional fight over slavery reached the critical stage. Although Washington would continue to witness sporadic outbursts of anti-Catholic and anti-foreign protest, the emphasis was always on the latter.

The country's native-born Catholics, still dominated by the old Anglo-French-Irish elite, might have been angered by religious bigotry, but they looked to political compromise to solve such controversies as religion in the public schools. They also believed that greater assimilation into the American mainstream was the best path to take at a time when Protestantism was losing its strong theological content. For years the old Catholics had tended to ignore the newcomers and their many problems, but the overwhelming size of the post-famine Irish immigration, special needs of the new Catholics, and growing stridency of the nativists who insisted on coupling the newcomers and the native Catholics now made that impossible. Increasingly during the 1850s the old and new Catholic Americans began to unite as a matter of necessity.

The immigrants had their own ideas about how the church should

14. This is a major conclusion of Barry's thesis, "The Know-Nothing Party in the District of Columbia." The point is also made in Green, *Washington,* 1:208.

react to the nativists. Irish and Germans were the principal targets of the Know-Nothings, and the Irish especially reacted with a defensiveness that long survived any blatant anti-Irish prejudices. They considered the Know-Nothings an extension of the Anglo-Protestant elite that had restricted their religious liberty and livelihood in the old country. They almost seemed to exult in the attacks. As the *Catholic Mirror's* Washington correspondent put it, "We all live upon persecution and we are now well supplied with food."[15] They considered the efforts of the native-born Catholics to assimilate useless and even dangerous. Instead they sought protection in an insulated, church-centered society that provided a sure sense of community. In the next decades these views would strongly influence the church that the immigrants came to dominate through sheer numbers and steadfast loyalty. Through them nativism, although short-lived, would profoundly influence the future development of parish institutions.[16]

St. Patrick's and the New Immigrants

St. Patrick's could never be classified among that large group of parishes across America that came to be dominated by the new immigrants in the 1840s and 1850s. Nevertheless, the parish did not remain immune to the changes that began in the American church in those decades. Irish immigrants, predominantly Catholic and from the poorer classes, were by far the major foreign element in Washington, and St. Patrick's received at least a small share of the newcomers.[17] Equally significant, the parish's new pastor, himself a recent immigrant, shared many of the enthusiasms and fears, the "us against them" attitude ascribed by the native Catholics to the newcomers.

Nowhere is the contrast between the older American Catholics and the new immigrants more noticeable than in the ongoing and deteriorating relations between Father O'Toole and his superior, Archbishop Kenrick. The dignified Kenrick was himself a native of Ireland, but Ro-

15. *Catholic Mirror*, 2 Dec 1854.

16. Both Olson's *Catholic Immigrants in America*, 8 and 31–42, and Spalding's *Premier See*, 130–35, discuss the influence of nativist prejudice on attitudes in the Catholic community.

17. According to the 1860 census, Wards Two and Three, the great part of which were co-terminous with St. Patrick's boundaries, contained 1,434 Irish-born residents. Not all were Catholics; some, of course, had been citizens for decades. By way of contrast, the same census counted 2,410 Irish-born in the sparsely populated Ward Four (the area around North Capitol Street known as Swampoodle).

man trained and long resident in the United States. A brilliant scholar and linguist, he seemed more comfortable in the company of the intellectual and socially prominent than among the numerous new immigrants. A man of prudent if unassertive leadership, Kenrick enjoyed close and easy relations with many of his non-Catholic contemporaries, entertaining them and conducting prayer services in their homes and encouraging and aiding many prominent converts. Although he instituted the popular Forty-Hours devotion in the diocese in 1858, he opposed many of the new, idiosyncratic devotions and liturgies favored by some of the faithful— "devotional trash" he called them. In this and many other ways he sought to make the church more understandable to its sons and daughters and more accessible to their non-Catholic neighbors.[18]

Father O'Toole had been in America less than four years when he was appointed pastor of St. Patrick's.[19] A warm, forceful preacher and a cleric of boundless energy and enthusiasm, the young priest was popular with his congregation and the archbishop, who described him as one with "learning, a good mind and piety."[20] Nevertheless he remained extremely suspicious of both non-Catholics and some of the native Catholics, both priests and laity, and jealous of his prerogatives as pastor of so prominent a parish. Unfortunately, his grasp of financial and legal matters was no match for the scope of his lofty ambitions for St. Patrick's, and consequently his brief administration was one of perpetual trial for himself, his fellow priests, and his archbishop.

O'Toole was never hesitant to share his many scruples and anxieties with his superior. His lengthy, quite hurried and often undated communiqués to Kenrick reveal the scope of his concerns. "Please answer quickly by telegram," he once wrote the archbishop. Could he bury an unbaptized baby in St. Patrick's graveyard? Father Matthews had done so before, O'Toole explained, "but I do not feel so authorized."

18. Both John P. Marschall's "Francis Patrick Kenrick, 1851–1863: The Baltimore Years," (Doctoral dissertation, The Catholic University of America, 1965), 160–77, and Spalding's *Premier See*, 177–78, offer concise sketches of Kenrick's character and interests.

19. The date of his arrival in the United States is unknown. O'Toole, a native of Galway, entered Maynooth Seminary in 1843 and was ordained in 1850 or 1851 for the diocese of Tuam. He was in residence at St. Patrick's by 1852. See Msgr. P. J. Hamell, "Maynooth Students and Ordination Index, 1795–1895," encl. to ltr., Rev. Dermot Farrell to author, 8 Jul 1992, SPA.

20. Ltr., Kenrick to Bp. Peter Richard Kenrick, 12 May 1854, reproduced in *The Kenrick-Frenaye Correspondence*, 370.

The family was a noted one, he warned, and they might well go to a Protestant cemetery if refused. On another occasion he pressed the archbishop for instructions in a case involving a Catholic who desired burial in a Protestant graveyard. Although the 1853 diocesan synod had barred priests from officiating in non-Catholic graveyards, O'Toole explored all contingencies in great detail. How he should consecrate the ground was but one of his weighty concerns.

Bothered by relations with the non-Catholic majority, he passed on to Kenrick what he described as a big problem: may a Catholic teacher recite the Protestant version of the Bible to children in a public school class? This query must not have seemed quite so urgent, because Kenrick was merely asked to reply "by return mail." On yet another occasion O'Toole warned Kenrick about a man selling fake altar wine in the diocese. In a letter of numbing length he described the fraud and warned of complications because of the archbishop's previous dealings with the man. In addition O'Toole now demanded a letter "vindicating the justice" of his recent hiring of the man's brother.[21]

Local sentiment for replacing the city's poorly situated and neglected Catholic cemeteries prompted Father O'Toole to organize the effort that ended with the establishment of Mt. Olivet.[22] In June 1855 he reported to the archbishop that he had met with the city's priests to discuss their financial options in the matter. One possibility under consideration was to incorporate and sell stock in the enterprise, but O'Toole was especially anxious to learn Kenrick's opinion of his own plan, which entailed the joint purchase of land, the debt to be retired through the sale of lots and the use of all burial fees collected in the city's parishes. Once the cemetery was paid for, parishes could treat any burial fees it collected as part of its regular revenue.[23]

Considerable discussion of the various proposals ensued, with O'Toole reporting on those that he believed dangerous. He was concerned, for example, about those priests who advocated leaving the cemetery in the hands of the laity and so treated Kenrick to a little lecture on the dangers of trusteeism. Almost two years would pass be-

21. These four letters from O'Toole to Kenrick, all undated (31-U-2; 31-U-10; 31-U-11; and 31-U-6) are taken from the dozens contained in the Kenrick Papers, AAB. O'Toole would often return to a problem several times. See, for example, his follow-up on the infant burial case in his letter to Kenrick, 14 May 1856, 31-V-4, same file.

22. *Catholic Mirror*, 2 Dec 1854. Old cemeteries have proved of perennial interest to local journalists and historians. See for example detailed articles in the *Star*, 14 Apr 1888, and *Catholic Mirror*, 6 Dec 1876.

23. Ltr., O'Toole to Kenrick, 19 Jun 1855, 31-V-3, Kenrick Papers, AAB.

fore O'Toole could report that the pastors had agreed to take out a joint note to purchase the "Fenwick Farm," a forty-acre site on Bladensburg Road. The land would cost $9,000 (it cost $10,000 in the end) with "a few thousand" extra allotted for initial improvements. O'Toole promised to inform Kenrick when all had been arranged.[24] This kind of procedure, informing the archbishop after the fact and thereby precluding his exercising control over legal or financial transactions, particularly irritated Kenrick in his many discussions with St. Patrick's pastor. And as might be expected, O'Toole was soon back, this time reporting his concern lest the management of the institution arouse jealousy among the city's pastors. Those priests together formed Mt. Olivet's board of trustees, and he wanted the presidency of the board to rotate among them, or better yet, have the archbishop serve as president of the cemetery.[25] How the dignified Kenrick reacted to this latest alarm and demand for his personal intervention went unrecorded.

Again in 1858 O'Toole thought it necessary to consult Kenrick on the fact that the U.S. Senate had invited Washington's clergy, including its Catholic priests, to take turns offering an opening prayer at its sessions. O'Toole's proposal that his fellow priests meet to discuss a common procedure "to secure the mark of unity" was met with indifference on their part. He was concerned, he told Kenrick, that they would not all start and end their prayers with the sign of the cross. He was also anxious to know how they should vest themselves for the occasion. Despite his treatment at the hands of his fellow priests, he considered it his duty to make these suggestions, which he proceeded to elaborate on for many pages.[26]

Many entries in Kenrick's letterbook contain notices beginning "scripsi ad O'Toole" or "resp. O'Toole," but the more the archbishop wrote and responded, the more the harried pastor communicated. Matters would take a more serious turn at the end of the decade, but even from the first months of O'Toole's pastorate, his anxiety about the little things clearly exasperated the sternly intellectual bishop and complicated their relationship. This uneasiness was especially unfortu-

24. Ltr., O'Toole to Kenrick, 27 Apr 57, 31-V-7. For O'Toole's views on the dangers of lay trustees at Mt. Olivet's, see his ltr. to Kenrick, 14 May 1856, 31-V-4, both in Kenrick Papers, AAB.

25. Ltr., O'Toole to Kenrick, 20 Dec 1858, 31-W-5, Kenrick Papers, AAB.

26. Ltr., O'Toole to Kenrick, 17 Dec 1858, 31-W-4. For Kenrick's reluctant approval, including instructions for priests to be robed in cassock and surplice, see *Litterarum Register*, 18 Dec 1858, both in Kenrick Papers, AAB.

nate because in many ways Father O'Toole shared his predecessor's ability to unite the various factions of his congregation. He was a popular leader who, despite his suspicions, won the cooperation of the old Catholic families and the newcomers in promoting several projects that transcended parish boundaries and had special importance and meaning for the newcomers. In fact, O'Toole reserved his greatest enthusiasm, and most effective performance, for these causes and for the enhancement of charities aimed at bettering the condition of the destitute.

Much to the consternation of the archbishop, some of O'Toole's charities were little more than spontaneous acts with no effort made to maintain the accurate records by then demanded of diocesan administrators. During his first year as pastor, such "promiscuous charities," as O'Toole called them in his accounts, added up to more than ten percent of the parish's operating expenses.[27] Later he showed better sense by turning the management of parish charities over to others. In 1855 he organized the parish's Indigent and Sick Society. This group supplemented the work of the Charitable Society run by the women of the congregation by concentrating exclusively on short-term relief for the immigrant poor. Many parishioners joined in collecting money, which they distributed in the form of food, fuel, and rent to the needy. Eventually the successful organization would be absorbed by the St. Vincent de Paul Society conference formed at St. Patrick's during the Civil War.

O'Toole also strongly encouraged the work of the Young Catholic Friends Society. Founded by a group of businessmen in Baltimore in 1842 for the distribution of clothing to destitute children, the organization quickly evolved into a broad-ranging charitable effort with affiliates throughout the country. Its Washington chapter was organized at St. Patrick's around 1855, where it dedicated itself to relief of the "helpless poor," focusing on the Irish famine victims. The society played a significant role in the founding of the new St. Joseph's orphanage, an institution that would remain its special cause into the twentieth century.[28]

O'Toole's first city-wide project was the long-delayed boys' orphan-

27. "Accounts of St. Patrick's Church, May 1854–November 1855," AAB.

28. The Young Catholic Friends Society was first listed at St. Patrick's in the *Catholic Directory* for 1856; the Sick and Indigent Society in 1857. The part such groups played in relief of the immigrant is discussed in Spalding's *Premier See*, 143–44 (source of the quote). The part played by the Young Catholic Friends in the founding of St. Joseph's is noted in the *Catholic Mirror*, 2 Dec 1854.

age. The need for an institution comparable to St. Vincent's was obvious and now especially pressing because of the increase in immigrant poor and the nativist influence on the city orphanage, yet efforts to open one had been frustrated by difficulty in procuring a staff and raising adequate funds. Father Matthews was unable to find another religious group to take the place of the Sisters of Charity who in 1846 had been forced by their order's new constitution to close the male branch of St. Vincent's opened just three years before.[29] Money was also a problem. In vain the trustees of St. Vincent's addressed an open letter to Washingtonians outlining the pitiful condition of many of the city's male orphans. In one of his last acts, Matthews added a provision to his will bequeathing some $3,000 to St. Vincent's trustees for the foundation of a male counterpart of the orphanage.[30]

As the new president of St. Vincent's board of trustees, O'Toole did not wait long to act on this generous bequest. In October 1854 he gathered together a group of philanthropists headed by former mayor Thomas Carberry. This meeting led to the incorporation of St. Joseph's Male Orphan Asylum and, subsequently, to its recognition by Congress in a charter granted in February 1855. Staffing the new institution proved to be a time-consuming task. Archbishop Kenrick particularly desired that a male religious order be employed, but both the Christian Brothers, who had been caring for a few orphans in their St. Matthew's Institute, as well as the Holy Cross Brothers declined the invitation. After casting about for more than a year, O'Toole finally turned to the Holy Cross Sisters of St. Mary's, Indiana. With Kenrick's approval, he entered an agreement in August 1856 that placed the orphanage "together with the school attached thereto" in the care of the sisters, initially three in number, who would be paid $60 a year along with travel expenses and all receipts from the school.[31]

29. Joseph C. Eckert, *Souvenir Book of the One Hundredth Anniversary St. Joseph's Home and School* (Washington, 1955), 63. See also Weitzman, *One Hundred Years of Charity,* 21–23 and 32. The short-lived male asylum, which was located at Tenth and G Streets, had a staff of three sisters under Sister Bibiana O'Mealy. Like St. Vincent's it also sponsored a day school. It was included in the list of St. Patrick's institutions in the 1844 edition of the *Catholic Directory.*

30. Father Matthews's gift, with its prerequisite that the orphanage be started within five years of his death, was well publicized. See, for example, *Catholic Mirror,* 2 Dec 1854. The open letter to the city is quoted in Durkin's *William Matthew,* 117–18.

31. At the discretion of the board, an increase in salary could be substituted for the school receipts. See "Agreement between Trustees of St. Joseph's Male Orphan Asylum and the Sisters of the Holy Cross, 29 Aug 1856," St. Mary's Archives, Notre Dame, Indiana. The agreement is discussed in Eckert's *Saint Joseph's Home and School,* 6. See

With the Matthews legacy as a base, supplemented by funds donated by the parish's organized charities, the trustees collected enough money to rent a building at the southwest corner of Thirteenth and H Streets. Although they had agreed to furnish the building, it was not ready for the sisters, who upon their arrival moved in with the Visitation sisters at Tenth and G. Finally, years after Father Matthews had first conceived the idea, St. Joseph's opened its doors in September 1856, thus beginning the parish's association with the Holy Cross congregation that would endure for more than a century.[32] Unlike St. Vincent's, which remained largely self-sustaining throughout its history, St. Joseph's relied on the charitable efforts of its board of lady managers. Over the years these women, who despite their title had little control over operation of the orphanage, sponsored countless fund raising events like the parish "hop" in 1858 that realized $417 for the building fund. These events, along with the sums raised by the Young Catholic Friends, remained the institution's major source of support for decades.

Almost immediately the Thirteenth Street location proved too small, necessitating a move in May 1859 to larger quarters near Twelfth and G Streets and again the next year into the old Darius Claggett residence on the southwest corner of Tenth and F. Purchased by the trustees for $12,000, this large home, increasingly crowded and almost immediately inadequate to the task, would continue to house the orphanage and school throughout the Civil War.

As in the case of St. Vincent's a generation earlier, the orphans received the lion's share of attention both in the press and in the parish's charity. The students in the attached school, however, quickly outstripped them in numbers. For several decades the school averaged 180 pupils, the orphans usually less than half that number. This ratio would continue through the rest of the century because, while the need for a suitable shelter for Catholic orphans was undeniable, de-

---

also Sister M. Campion Kuhn's "The Sisters Go East—and Stay," paper prepared for the Congregation of the Sisters of the Holy Cross Annual Historical Conference, March 1983, 1–4. The following paragraphs are based on these surveys.

32. Sources disagree over the year of opening. Guilday (in Wentz's *Inventory*) and Weitzman (in *One Hundred Years of Charity*) claim the school started in 1855. The *Catholic Dictionary* lists the orphanage in its 1856 edition, which usually reflects activities in the previous year. Insisting on the 1856 opening, Eckert (*St. Joseph's Home and School,* 67) points to the title page of the institution's register book! Further supporting the 1856 date was the fact that Kenrick did not approve the employment of the Holy Cross sisters until 27 August 1856 (see *Litterarum* Register, 108, Kenrick Papers, AAB).

mand for a Catholic school for boys of modest means was overwhelming at a time when prejudice against public education, especially among the immigrants, remained strong. Prejudice might also explain O'Toole's decision in 1857 to start a small parochial school for boys at St. Patrick's similar to those at Holy Trinity and St. Matthew's. He built an addition to his rectory to serve as classrooms, asking each family to contribute a dollar to the enterprise. Apparently little came of the effort. Most parish children continued to receive their elementary educations at St. Vincent's and St. Joseph's.[33]

Like many Irish reformers, O'Toole considered the threat of demon rum as great a danger as poverty and ignorance. Some of his most effective work in the parish was done on behalf of its temperance crusade. Early Washingtonians were a hard-drinking lot; as far back as 1830 the city could boast five hundred grog shops and taverns, one for every eighty inhabitants. Politicians frequently gave voice to the popular belief that drinking was the cause of most poverty and misery. While this charge managed to divert blame for the city's social ills from the government's economic blunders, it did nothing to lower the consumption of liquor, and temperance, perforce, became a major goal of local reformers. By 1835 they had registered a few victories; Congress, for example, banned the sale of intoxicants in the Capitol. When further pleas for reform were ignored, the reformers changed their tactics, abandoning the goal of moderation in favor of total abstinence and taking to preaching about the curse on street corners and in the market place.[34]

The first Catholic temperance society in the United States, the one organized at St. Patrick's by laymen led by George Savage, also saw the fight against liquor in apocalyptic terms. Their pledge before Father Matthews in 1840 went beyond temperance to an abstinence total and permanent. Such austerity attracted converts throughout the city, and within two years of its founding the society could count some two thousand members. These efforts seemed to make a difference. In 1842 the National Intelligencer reported a singular victory for the temperance cause when "for the first time in this city" Ireland's exiled

33. O'Toole's plan for a school is discussed in his letter to Kenrick, 26 Nov 1856, 31-V-5, Kenrick Papers, AAB. Although Msgr. Guilday apparently agreed that the school did in fact open (see Wentz's Inventory), no record survives of teachers hired or pupils enrolled.

34. The subject of temperance in the capital needs further study. These paragraphs are based primarily on Bryan's History of the Capital, 2:345–401, and Green's Washington, 1:134 and 218.

sons celebrated St. Patrick's Day "free from the influence of intoxicating beverage—ardent spirits—the excessive indulgence in which has been properly denounced as the 'National Vice.'"[35]

Although long concerned about intemperance, the hierarchy did little more than rail against it. Archbishop Maréchal, for example, complained in his report to Propaganda in 1818 that the Irish workers "consider drunkenness only a slight imperfection" and that many otherwise exceptionally able Irish priests were addicted.[36] Several priests also pressed the temperance cause, and the bishops spoke out on the subject after the meeting of the Fourth Provincial Council in 1840, but most of the earlier reformers were laymen such as George Savage. The reluctance of church leaders to become closely involved flowed from their concern that the major national temperance groups were the special preserve of the notably anti-Catholic, evangelical clergy. Wary of this influence and perhaps a little put off by the ardency of some of the adherents, the bishops retreated somewhat in their next council in 1843, explaining that an abstinence pledge was not binding in conscience. Kenrick, still bishop of Philadelphia, agreed with this declaration, telling his friend the Irish bishop Paul Cullen that "if not checked and regulated," the temperance movement would degenerate into "fanaticism, and a cold water regimen would be the *unum necessarium* and *summum bonum.*" He preferred that the bishops grant indulgences to those who joined the temperance societies rather than try to enforce pledges.[37]

Kenrick was not personally opposed to moderate drinking and remained at odds with Father Theobald Mathew, the famous apostle of temperance, because Kenrick steadfastly refused to declare breaking the pledge a sin.[38] Nevertheless the American Catholic temperance movement had come alive in the wake of Mathew's tour of the country in 1849. Despite some controversy with the abolitionists, the Irish-

35. *National Intelligencer,* 23 Mar 1842.

36. "Archbishop Maréchal's Report to Propaganda," October 16, 1818, reprinted in Gleason, ed., *Documentary Reports on Early American Catholicism,* 211.

37. Ltr., Kenrick to Cullen, 23 Nov 1843, American Papers, 1823–1849, no. 88, Irish College, Rome, APF. For a discussion of the changing attitudes of the American bishops on the subject, see Spalding, *Premier See,* 144–45.

38. Marschall, "Francis Patrick Kenrick," 53–58, discusses Kenrick's position on temperance. On the Mathew crusade, see Sister Joan Bland's *Hibernian Crusade: The Story of the Catholic Total Abstinence Union of America* (Washington: The Catholic University of America Press, 1951), 21–42.

man's crusade was headline news and a remarkable inter-faith event. While in Washington he was invited to address both houses of Congress and dined at the White House with President Zachary Taylor, a strong sympathizer. His major work centered on visits to individual parishes, where he organized and encouraged parish temperance societies and persuaded people to take the pledge of total abstinence.

If the politicians were wrong in claiming drink caused poverty, they were accurate in implying that those hardest hit by alcoholism were the city's laborers. Ever since the days spent building the White House, the poor Irish immigrants had been among the special victims of the disease. Somehow nativist propaganda had succeeded in associating the worst of the plague with the new immigrants, particularly the Catholic Irish. Actually demon rum was no respector of race or creed, and partly in an attempt to attack the false linkage between Catholics and drunkenness, priests like O'Toole became forceful leaders in what had been before a predominantly lay crusade. O'Toole himself had taken the pledge from Theobald Mathew and as pastor quickly became a "bold, fearless, and vigorous champion" of temperance, "untiring in his efforts to banish the demon of strong drink from every Catholic household in the city."[39] As president of the St. Patrick's Total Abstinence Society he did much to strengthen and enlarge the influence of that organization, preaching the temperance cause all over Washington and appearing at temperance rallies and civil events that extolled total abstinence. Symbolizing his devotion to the cause and the parish's love of theater, he led a phalanx of seven hundred "stalwart teetotalers" as they marched to St. Patrick's to open a festival celebrating the great saint's feast in March 1858.[40]

A Grand Church for Washington

Despite Know-Nothing agitation in the city and the immediate challenge of integrating immigrant newcomers into the congregation, St. Patrick's was a crowded and flourishing place of worship in the 1850s. One eyewitness expressed surprise at finding the 6 a.m. week-

39. Taken from O'Toole's obituary, written by a member of the St. Patrick's Total Abstinence Society, in the *Catholic Mirror*, 24 Mar 1888. The association of the temperance movement with the Irish immigrants is explored in Olson's *Catholic Immigrants in America*, 33–43.

40. *Catholic Mirror*, 24 Mar 1858.

day mass in 1856 a standing-room-only affair, necessitating an immediate second mass to provide for the overflow. Later that year O'Toole reported that a mission conducted by the Redemptorist fathers netted thirty-one hundred attendees and was the occasion for many city residents, "after years spent afar-off riotously," to return to the sacraments. Some 290 baptisms were registered in the church in 1856. O'Toole was especially pleased with the number of converts, most, he noted, from the city's "humble classes."[41]

These and similar signs of spiritual vitality revived plans for a new and "grand" church as it was often described at St. Patrick's. Such a building would not only realize the old dream of a national cathedral in the capital, but also demonstrate to the Know-Nothings the growing strength of the church in America. Although Father O'Toole was certainly not immune to the "let's show the Protestants what we can do" allure of the enterprise, it was obviously not his primary motive. As he would make clear on numerous occasions in the months to come, he looked on the building of a new church as a chance to pull native Catholics and newcomers together in a great common effort.

The idea of a grand religious edifice in the capital, symbolizing the church's support of the government and fulfilling its desire for a national memorial, was almost as old as the city itself. Even while the American clergy was discussing the formation of a separate American hierarchy, proprietor Daniel Carroll of Duddington offered his relative Bishop John Carroll a site on Capitol Hill for a national cathedral. And even after Baltimore was designated the seat of the diocese and plans for a cathedral commenced, the idea of some kind of national church in Washington continued to be seriously discussed.

In 1801 a committee of Catholic residents petitioned President Jefferson concerning a site for such a church. In reply the D.C. Commissioners professed themselves "fully impressed with the real utility of such establishments, & would be glad to facilitate their rise in every convenient part of the city." At first Carroll seemed anxious to begin. He personally preferred James Hoban's design for a building that could be raised in stages, with a first section costing $2,000, and he was ready to tell the commissioners that Catholics would need a two hundred-square-foot lot, a size that must have somewhat dampened local

41. Ltrs., O'Toole to Kenrick, 26 Nov 1856, 31-V-5 and 27 Jan 1857, 31-V-6, both in Kenrick Papers, AAB. The eyewitness was Lorenzo Johnson, reporting in the *National Intelligencer*, 29 Apr 1856. The crowded church was noted in the *Catholic Mirror*, 2 Dec 1854.

ambitions.[42] Plans were quickly revised when Daniel Carroll renewed his offer of land, this time promising a whole city square just twelve blocks from the new Capitol. Although the bishop was circumspect in describing the timetable—the building would not start until Catholics were "more numerous than at present"—he announced that they would eventually produce a church that would be "ornamental to the city" and large enough to accommodate them all.[43] Building such an ornament would remain beyond the ability of the hard-pressed local Catholic community, and so the land, known locally as the cathedral lot, was left vacant for over a century until it became the site of St. Vincent de Paul Church.[44]

Although adamantly opposed to a separate Washington diocese, Archbishop Whitfield was enthusiastic about building a great church in the city and in 1832 made a pitch to European benefactors for funds. St. Patrick's, he reported, was small and shabby, and its later additions "made it a building of unmatched pieces, unworthy of the capital of the United States and in no way suitable to the majesty of divine services in a city where several public edifices and private homes are remarkable for their elegance and beauty." Convinced that the magnificent cathedral in Baltimore designed by Benjamin Latrobe was winning respect for Catholicism from Protestants "who flocked to it in crowds," he looked to a similar effect in Washington.[45]

St. Patrick's parishioners were painfully aware of the dilapidated condition of their church, which had been built in haste with great economies on poorly drained land. Although still afforded pride of place, given its age, central location, and prominent congregation, St. Patrick's was physically inferior to the city's new parishes, especially after St. Matthew's opened its doors. The congregation had always wanted a grand church, and it was determined to combine the obvious need for new quarters with the long-standing vision of a great na-

42. Ltr., John Carroll to James Barry, 16 Sep 1801, *JCP* 2:363; and ltr., D.C. Commissioners to Bishop Carroll, et al., 10 Sep 1801, 11-H-4, Carroll Papers, AAB. Daniel Carroll's offer of land is related in Philibert's *Saint Matthew's of Washington*, 114–15.

43. Ltr., Carroll to D.C. Commissioners, 26 Sep 1801, 9-T-4, and *Litterarum* Register, both in Carroll Papers, AAB.

44. Ltr., Jacob Walter to John Gilmary Shea, 23 Apr 1888, reproduced in *American Catholic Historical Researches*, new vol. 1 (1905), 65. A remark by the local Jesuit superior, John Grassi, in 1818 that the foundations for such a cathedral had been laid (Bryan, *History of the Capital*, 1:602) must be discounted.

45. Ltr., Whitfield to M. de Redacteur des Annales, 16 Feb 1832, *Annales* 5 (1831–32): 718–19.

tional memorial now reintroduced by Whitfield. The parish's ambition would encounter many serious obstacles, not only because of their unrealistic financial projections in a period of frequent economic depressions, but more importantly, because of the steadfast resistance of Father Matthews, who refused to replace the aging facility he had erected years before.

Matthews's objection was probably more economic than sentimental. Only after a subscription drive he authorized in 1837 failed to produce the necessary funds for a new building did he turn against the project.[46] Despite these financial realities, the congregation continued to hope, and during the next twenty-five years Washingtonians were periodically treated to diverting reports on the new and mighty St. Patrick's that was about to rise on the site of the old. In 1846 the *National Intelligencer* described plans for a church "of magnificent dimensions, something after the manner of the most extensive Cathedrals in Europe." Its cost was estimated at $75,000, which would be collected from Catholics across the country. Scoffers were quick to point out that such a sum would hardly buy one window for a mighty cathedral and speculated that the planner must have had a toy model of a European cathedral in mind or at most a truly miniature edition.[47]

Five years later the *Catholic Mirror* reported a "magnificent Cathedral" intended for St. Patrick's, costing "say a million of dollars." In keeping with the city's public buildings, it would be of stone or marble "in the richest style of architecture" on a scale in which the "imposing ceremonies of the Catholic service might be performed with all their pomp and solemnity." The formidable difficulty in collecting such a sum in a parish that could not raise the modest amounts needed for a boy's orphanage failed to faze the dreamers. "Every Catholic in the U.S. will contribute," the local reporter predicted, and congregations and societies around the country "will vie with each other in their contributions." Even large sums could be expected from Europe and the Protestants of Washington.[48]

Clearly such journalistic speculation was based on the enthusiasm of a handful of local boosters, including the *Mirror's* reporter, himself a parishioner at St. Patrick's. Each successive scheme went the way of its predecessor, leaving the press to lament from time to time about the continuing deterioration of the church, which reporters liked to point

46. *National Intelligencer*, 29 Apr 1837.
47. *National Intelligencer* 26 Jan and 9 Feb 1846.
48. *Catholic Mirror*, 22 Feb 1851.

out was by no means weatherproof and even "antediluvian in its style and appearance." One correspondent went so far as to argue for a church not only "worthy of the seat of government" and in keeping with the social standing of the F Street neighborhood but also "characteristic of the Almighty Founder of our Holy Religion."[49]

Father Matthews's priorities were obviously different from the priorities of those who were pushing for a "metropolitan" church on the site of St. Patrick's which they predicted would be "an ornament to the city and the pride of every Catholic." Public appeals to his sympathy for the need of an edifice that might take its place among the many "fine and capacious buildings" being erected by the Protestants had failed to move him. Small wonder that just two weeks after his death, the *Baltimore Sun* reported that attention would now turn in earnest to the erection of "a magnificent church edifice."[50]

When Archbishop Kenrick appointed O'Toole to succeed Matthews, he did not discuss ongoing plans to make Washington a separate diocese within the Baltimore province (the United States now had six archbishops, each overseeing a separate province with subordinate suffragan dioceses). The proposal for a new episcopal see and its corollary—designation of St. Patrick's as the cathedral parish—quickly became enmeshed in larger considerations of church politics. In effect, the future of the parish became a hostage to the American hierarchy's struggle for greater independence. As early as 1830 Father Matthews had reported on widespread expectations for a diocese in the District of Columbia, pushed by the diplomatic corps and necessitated by the dynamic growth of the church in the region.[51] In 1852 speculation took a more serious turn when Archbishop Kenrick confided to his brother, the bishop of St. Louis, that Washington should be elevated to a episcopal see "so as not to leave the seat of government without due prominence."[52]

As might be expected, Kenrick had more than one motive for overriding the opposition of his predecessor, James Whitfield, to separating Washington from Baltimore. Soon after becoming archbishop,

49. *Catholic Mirror*, 15 Nov 1851.

50. *Baltimore Sun*, 8 May 1854. For an example of how proponents combined their arguments for a roomier church and the need to outshine the Protestants, see *Catholic Mirror*, 11 Jun 1853.

51. Ltr., Matthews to Kohlmann, 14 Jun 1830, *Congressi*, sec. 10, fol. 390, APF.

52. Ltr., Francis P. Kenrick to Peter R. Kenrick, 4 Jan 1852, quoted in John P. Marschall, "Francis Patrick Kenrick," 122. See Marschall's work, especially chap. 4, on the proposed new diocese and the fight over a papal nuncio.

Kenrick was visited by the local Jesuit superior, who acquainted the new archbishop with the provisions of the Neale-Grassi agreement and, as a result, won Kenrick's agreement to transfer St. Patrick's to the Society after Matthews's death. But that was before Kenrick learned the full history of the dispute and the fact that, in an effort to "guard against" just such a contingency, Matthews had transferred the property to Kenrick's predecessor. Once so informed, Kenrick was determined to block transfer to the Jesuits, but for some reason he confessed himself at a loss as to how he could "defeat" their effort. In fact his solution to the problem was anything but decisive. He pushed for a suffragan diocese in Washington and told the Jesuits that St. Patrick's and all Matthews's holdings— "everything pertaining to the building of a Cathedral church"—would be turned over to the new bishop, not the Jesuits, who might use old St. Patrick's as a chapel only after a separate cathedral church had been erected.[53]

It was not his intention to demand the establishment of a new bishopric immediately, he told his friend and agent in Rome, Bishop Michael O'Connor, although he believed that the Sacred Congregation should be ready to act because of Matthews's extreme old age. Meanwhile, he did not oppose a request from the bishop of Richmond that, in view of its recent retrocession to Virginia, Alexandria be transferred to the Richmond diocese (thus reducing the size and strength of any new Washington diocese). Nevertheless, despite arguments advanced against it, he remained adamant that Washington should have its own bishop.[54] His solution, he predicted, would end all Jesuit "pretensions" concerning the parish's future.

Kenrick was mistaken, for, unknown to him, the matter was already being discussed in Rome. For some reason the bishop of Chicago, the former Jesuit James O. Van de Velde, had tired of his burden in Illinois and proposed to Pope Pius IX that instead he be made what he called vicar apostolic of Georgetown, with episcopal jurisdiction over Washington. He admitted that such an appointment would allow him to resume his position in the Jesuit order and, with Washington removed from Baltimore's control, might induce Matthews to change his will and leave St. Patrick's property to the new vicariate. To cinch this au-

53. Ltr., Kenrick to Michael O'Connor, 12 Jul 1852, *Congressi*, sec. 16, fols. 146–47, APF. Kenrick's discussions with the Jesuits are summarized in his *Acta Episcopalia*, 3 May 1852 and 17 Feb 1853, Kenrick Papers, AAB.

54. Ltr., Kenrick to O'Connor, 13 Jul 1852, *Congressi*, sec. 16, fols. 144–45, APF. See also *Litterarum* Register, 12 Jul 1852, Kenrick Papers, AAB.

dacious request he dangled before Roman authorities the idea that after his own death, they might appoint an archbishop to Washington who could serve as a papal nuncio to the U.S. government.[55]

The question of a nuncio went to the heart of the matter, raising anew the argument over the American church's relations with the Vatican. Pointing to the recent establishment of a primate in Ireland, the American bishops had been pushing for a primate for the United States as well. They had formally proposed such a title during the Seventh Provincial Council in 1849, only to have Rome defer a decision, and, three years later, reject outright a decree issued by the First Plenary Council of the American bishops designating Baltimore a primatial see. Rome's rejection was actually a reaction to what it perceived as a dangerous spirit of independence in the American hierarchy. Bedeviled by a growing tendency toward separation of church and state in countries that had previously accorded special status to the church, Rome responded with a renewed effort to discourage administrative autonomy in national hierarchies.

The Pope and his advisors had come to regard the request for a primate, who would represent the nation's bishops with one voice in their dealings with Rome, as indicative of this growing administrative independence. Far preferable in the eyes of the Vatican was the appointment of a nuncio, who would represent the Pope to the individual bishops as well as to the national government. Hence Van de Velde's proposal for a separate Washington vicariate and the possibility of wresting control of St. Patrick's property from the archbishop of Baltimore was made considerably more palatable by the suggestion that in time such a bishop could also serve as nuncio. As might be expected, where the bishops' demand for a primate raised suspicions and apprehension in Rome, Van de Velde's proposal was carefully entertained.

Aware of Roman concerns, Kenrick sought to scuttle Van de Veldes's plan by ignoring its wider implications, concentrating his opposition on the proposal for a vicar apostolic in Washington. He condemned the idea, explaining that the capital rated a "proper bishop so that the divine worship might be carried out with elegance." Such a post required the appointment of an "outstanding American," one with the eloquence to stir audiences at great national gatherings. No

55. Ltr., Van de Velde to Pope Pius IX, 19 Aug 1852, quoted in Marschall, "Francis Patrick Kenrick," 123–24. At the time of Van de Velde's letter the United States had a minister to the Papal States.

doubt with an eye on the prevailing winds, he prudently agreed to postpone his suggestion for a separate diocese until such a paragon became available.[56] Unfortunately, Kenrick's arguments in favor of a separate diocese and a regularly appointed bishop in Washington could likewise be used to support the arguments for the appointment of a nuncio. In the end a compromise was arrived at—the proposal to make Washington a diocese was rejected, Van de Velde's idea of a vicar was also forgotten, and the Pope granted "prerogative of place" to the Baltimore archdiocese in the American church. Nevertheless, the idea of a nuncio to the United States was not abandoned. When Archbishop Bedini came to investigate conditions in Catholic America in 1853 he recommended establishment of a nunciate and offered to explore the idea with both secular and religious authorities.

Although Rome twice rejected proposals from Baltimore that Washington be made a separate diocese, the discussions eventually became common knowledge and fired many local imaginations—none more so than that of Timothy O'Toole. Grandiose plans for a great edifice that would honor God, the American church, and the national capital would continue to be bruited about long after any practical discussion of a separate diocese had ceased. For years such dreams would animate discussions of the parish's future and compete with any practical consideration of its pressing material needs. In July 1854 O'Toole announced intentions "to commence the new Cathedral of the Metropolis" early the next spring. The *Star* went on to report that the new pastor anticipated building the largest church in the city, a task, it estimated, that would require four years to complete.[57]

Washingtonians might well have greeted this latest announcement with some cynicism, and indeed plans for a new church continued to languish while the parish concentrated on starting the boys' orphanage and school, enlarging the rectory, and providing emergency help for impoverished newcomers. What finally energized the organizers was the threat of competition from the Jesuits. In 1855 Archbishop Kenrick gave the Jesuit Fathers permission to build a church in Washington "beyond the Tiber" as Father Matthews had long before recommended. O'Toole thought it unlikely that Catholic Washington could support two building projects simultaneously. In May 1856 he warned Kenrick that such news might be all the "good, native

56. Ltr., Kenrick to Cardinal Fransoni, 4 Oct 1852, quoted in Marschall, "Francis Patrick Kenrick," 124.

57. *Star*, 21 Jul 1854.

Catholics" needed to cancel their support because some influential segments of the congregation "don't require much of an excuse to keep aloof now from their Irish pastor or priests."[58] Meanwhile O'Toole wanted Kenrick to register the deeds to St. Patrick's property in the local courts, in part to support the parish's petition concerning ownership of the alley that appeared in the original survey of Square 376. If this strip of land in the center of the square remained city property, O'Toole feared, that fact could be used by the Jesuits to frustrate plans for a new St. Patrick's. He also pressed Kenrick for the assignment of a second assistant to work exclusively on the building project, discussing at length the merits of several candidates.[59]

Whether Kenrick was much impressed with the threat of Jesuit competition or O'Toole's perceived problems with his American congregation, he took his time granting approval for the project. It wasn't until September that he finally agreed to the concept of a new church.[60] Another eight months would elapse before representatives of the congregation met to launch the project. O'Toole wanted Kenrick present or a letter to read at the meeting conveying the archbishop's encouragement and approval. He got neither, so, O'Toole confessed, he had "in general terms implied, rather than roundly expressed" the archbishop's approbation and outlined for the assembled congregation what he assumed would be the archbishop's minimal approval in the way of fund raising—a general appeal throughout the diocese. O'Toole attributed Kenrick's silence to his desire to appear even-handed in regard to the two building projects. He assured Kenrick that the Jesuits would be willing to postpone their drive until 1858, but they believed themselves under pressure from Baltimore to begin immediately. (In fact the Jesuits would begin their church in 1857. St. Aloysius, a magnificent brick structure on North Capitol Street in the area known as Swampoodle just three blocks east of St. Patrick's boundary, was completed in record time and dedicated in October 1859).

Whatever had aroused O'Toole's fears about the congregation's reluctance to work with its Irish-born pastor disappeared in the general euphoria bathing that first gathering in May 1857. O'Toole characterized those who immediately subscribed to the building fund as "men of mark and character, business men & good—whose names are bet-

58. Ltr., O'Toole to Kenrick, 14 May 1856, 31-V-4, Kenrick Papers, AAB.
59. Ltrs., O'Toole to Kenrick, 14 May 1856, 31-V-4, and 26 Nov 1856, 31-V-5, both in Kenrick Papers, AAB.
60. *Litterarum* Register, 25 Sep 1856, Kenrick Papers, AAB.

ter than ten times the sum they have given." These worthies proceeded to form committees, organize subscriber lists, and pass resolutions later distributed to the press. The latter expressed the congregation's determination to erect a church "becoming the perpetual historic grandeur of our holy faith, its steady, dignified progress in this free land, while, at the same time, in keeping with the well-sustained efforts of the whole country to adorn our Federal Metropolis." The resolutions also signified the committee's approval of a preliminary design for a large edifice in the High Gothic style prepared by the Baltimore architect, Louis L. Long, and charged him with developing a cost estimate.[61]

Typical of the pastor's unbridled enthusiasm, his prolix style, and his persistent blindness to the concerns of his superior, his report concluded with a dream sequence:

So, Most Rev & dear Archbishop, we are afloat, & you would call me a dreamer if I told you a very peculiar dream I had last night. I am afraid I am always too bold with your Grace—but I have often said you know best how much I am concerned, & how much I should be strengthened by your Grace's support—Is it too much to beg of you by a line or two to the Mirror to congratulate our parishioners & city on their good spirit, their liberality, & the (to say the least) fair hopes that spring for our first step—O! what a fine *roll of the log* that would be—[62]

No such felicitations were forthcoming, and in fact when Kenrick did approve the committee's work three days later, he felt compelled to warn: "but not at such an expense." Before he would agree to lay a cornerstone, the parish must reconsider its plan and obtain a fair estimate of costs. Meanwhile, the parish was not to sign any contracts "until the whole is fully understood and arranged."[63] By that time Kenrick must have had some inkling of just how grand a church was being planned. The design called for a building 240 feet long, 130 feet wide at the west front, and 210 feet at the transept, with a 312 foot central tower and octagon towers in the transepts reaching 215 feet. All this, including auxiliary towers, oratorios, chapels, and separate rec-

---

61. At that time Long was also designing St. Mary's, the gothic church erected by the Redemptorists in Annapolis between 1858 and 1860.

62. Ltr., O'Toole to Kenrick, 10 May 1857, 31-V-8, Kenrick Papers, AAB. The committee's resolutions were printed in the *Catholic Mirror* on 23 May 1857. For O'Toole's request for a letter from Kenrick for the congregation, see ltr., O'Toole to Kenrick, 27 Apr 57, 31-V-7, same file.

63. *Litterarum* Register, 13 May 1857, Kenrick Papers, AAB.

tory, would be covered in stone and adorned with rich stained glass. The *Catholic Mirror* quoted "the enterprising authorities of the new church," who admitted that Germany has its Cologne, France its Notre Dame, and England its York Minster, "but none a church which for richness, considering the size, that will compare with that of St. Patrick's, if properly constructed from the designs."[64]

Kenrick's growing doubts could not dampen O'Toole's irrepressible optimism. He had made no commitments, he assured his superior on May 20, and he promised to do nothing that would "involve this property or my own name—without seeing clearly the way to get through." He had re-examined all the committee's transactions and found nothing to fear. But nothing that Kenrick heard during his Trinity Sunday visit to the parish quelled his belief that the congregation's plans were too grandiose and its means too slender. It would be difficult for the ordinary reader to mistake his blunt warning to O'Toole: "Serious difficulties hang over you."[65]

Such bluntness only spurred O'Toole on to an even lengthier explanation of the parish's financial plans and a not-so-subtle exhortation that the prudent archbishop show more faith in the mighty endeavor. The parish planned to spend no more than $250,000, O'Toole argued, and its ability to raise that amount was beyond doubt. Always providing what he called conservative estimates, he canvassed the various sources of funding. Washington Catholics would subscribe $30,000 initially and possibly $50,000 ultimately (676 people had already pledged $20,000). The building committee had started a separate subscription drive committing signers to five cents a week for five years. Women and children would help in this drive, which, O'Toole estimated, would yield another $65,000. The city's laborers seasonally employed on local public works would give $5 a year and, along with similar funds collected from the female servants in the city, could be counted on for $45,000 over the next five years.

O'Toole was particularly enthusiastic about these last two groups. He had personally canvassed them, he told Kenrick, and in his mind their pledge "is as sure as an order on the bank of the Metropolis." He knew these people who were, he explained, "in the full flush of doing something grand for the church." Such a sum would not seriously inconvenience them because they all wanted to make a "Catholic

---

64. *Catholic Mirror*, 30 May 1857.

65. *Litterarum* Register, 29 May 1857, 123; and ltr., O'Toole to Kenrick, 20 May 1857, 31-V-9, both in Kenrick Papers, AAB.

demonstration and do not relish it the less for its being in some way an Irish demonstration too."

All this solicitation would leave the committee $100,000 short of its goal, a deficit O'Toole expected to offset by a collection outside the diocese. Dismissing the archbishop's flat ban on such efforts ("I know you will blame me for disagreeing with you altogether on this point"), he reminded Kenrick that "the whole Union looks to Washington as its center. . . . The whole people look for the day when they may give something toward a grand Church in Washington."

After boasting some about his willingness to apply "exertion, system, and unflagging energy" to this holy work, he warned Kenrick of where his refusal to approve the parish's plans might lead. It would injure the pastor in the eyes of the city and cause more dissatisfaction "on account of my being an Irish priest." He went on to paint a picture of a parish on the verge of open dissension. "Some will say if they had a priest according to their own heart, it would succeed. Others may say, if they had a bishop of their own land, it would be successful." The numerous critics who were whispering in the archbishop's ear false estimates about costs, O'Toole charged, merely used such arguments to mask their opposition to any project run by a foreigner. He was clearly worried about what he called the "spirit of nativism" in the church itself and considered the building project a wonderful means of counteracting this growing evil when

a body of native gentlemen combine with a foreign priest to effect a work that they all think will be to the honor of religion & of the Church; after the gravest consideration they all believe that between us just as we are, we have the very elements of success. I myself to rally our Irish Catholics to the good cause, & to gratify them, to whom so seldom a pleasure is allowed in such things, by seeing me an Irish priest striving for the success; we have also those gentlemen to satisfy the Americans, as such, & to obtain their aid, etc. To be engaged together, even if success were delayed, will prove how we can work together—to be severed now, will be to confirm bad impressions, that we cannot work in harmony.[66]

O'Toole's lengthy plea failed to move a resolute Kenrick, who had far more to fear from an unrealistic financial plan than from any possible anti-Irish sentiment in Washington. He announced that the new church could not exceed $100,000 in cost (nearly 1.5 million today), a decision he firmly repeated when the building committee visited him

66. Ltr., O'Toole to Kenrick, n.d. (circa 21 Jun 1857), 31-V-12, Kenrick Papers, AAB.

in June.[67] Discussions would continue intermittently during the next two years, but little money was collected, and the project received no further notice in the press. The crowning blow came in late 1859 when the architect threatened to sue the parish for $1,000 for services rendered. Father O'Toole explained that when the architect submitted detailed plans with an estimated price tag of $374,000, the parish had dropped the project. He asked for the archbishop's guidance, but for himself, he concluded, he would let the thing go to court since "all agreed" the claim was insupportable.[68]

With estimated costs rising and the archbishop resisting all outside sources of income, even the most optimistic parishioner must have come to realize that, for the foreseeable future, a grand Gothic cathedral at such enormous cost was out of the question.

Removal of a Beloved Pastor

Financing the new church was just one of the sources of tension between the pastor and archbishop, who were often at loggerheads. Early on, O'Toole had argued over the choice of assistants for St. Patrick's, showing a ready inclination to criticize Kenrick's selections. He did not want Father Richard Hardy as an assistant, he told his superior in 1856, because he found it impossible to get along with the man's friends, the prominent Sims family. "They are abominably *native,*" O'Toole charged. They had often referred to St. Patrick's and its pastor "in a most unbecoming way." As for Hardy, O'Toole believed he differed with the man in spirit and sentiment, and he wanted to avoid confrontation.[69]

This suspicion of native-born Americans runs through much of O'Toole's correspondence. Relations with his assistant, the Baltimore native Francis E. Boyle, deteriorated to the point that the eloquent and charismatic Boyle requested a transfer. With Know-Nothing agitation persisting in the city, Kenrick was anxious to see Boyle's extremely cordial and effective associations with non-Catholic Washingtonians continue, so in October 1858 he arranged for a simple exchange of assistants between St. Patrick's and St. Matthew's. O'Toole still objected. If St. Matthew's pastor, himself an American, had diffi-

67. *Litterarum* Register, 26 Jun 1857, Kenrick Papers, AAB.
68. Ltr., O'Toole to Kenrick, 13 Jan 1860, 31-W-9, Kenrick Papers, AAB.
69. Ltr., O'Toole to Kenrick, n.d. (circa 1856), 31-U-1, Kenrick Papers, AAB. Hardy had been serving at Boone's Chapel in Prince George's County in recent years.

culty with the American Father Edmund Q. S. Waldron, O'Toole opposed his transfer to St. Patrick's, where "we have quite enough" difficulty with native clergy. O'Toole clearly was eager to see Boyle leave— "his has not been the needed, full measure of co-operation with me"—but not at the price of taking on Waldron.[70]

Another occasion found St. Patrick's pastor close to outright insubordination concerning a pipe organ. The parish purchased a new organ in 1858 to replace its old Episcopal hand-me-down. To finance the handsome new instrument O'Toole had signed two notes; with one due in mid-May and no funds available to cover it, he decided to sponsor a performance featuring the "much improved" choir and new organ, hoping thereby to induce parishioners to contribute the balance. Church concerts for a fee were strictly forbidden in the diocese, and when reminded of that fact, O'Toole told Kenrick, "it must appear to you as if I were intent on cross purposes." He claimed that his plan differed little from what was common practice in other churches where "something extra is promised by the choir, and priests use it as an influence to bring many to church." To "avoid the difficulty, and yet obtain the result," he proposed to call the event a lecture on sacred music during which the choir would perform two or three compositions. Demonstrating again that he never knew just when to stop, O'Toole added that he had never contemplated a concert and trusted that Kenrick would not so construe this lecture. Besides, he had already sold one thousand tickets, so the parish would be in "inexplicable confusion" if forced to cancel.[71]

An exasperated Kenrick responded immediately: the pastor would suffer suspension of his faculties "*ipso facto*" if the event were held at St. Patrick's.[72] Eventually the concert, without benefit of the new organ, was held in the Smithsonian's new building on the Mall.

The following February found an already-irritated archbishop forced to intervene again, this time in reaction to a story in the press concerning an altercation between Father O'Toole and local medical students. The *Star* reported that, after visiting the sick at the Washington Infirmary, St. Patrick's pastor had mounted his steed only to be

70. Ltrs., O'Toole to Kenrick, 28 Oct 1858, 31-W-2, and 24 Sep 1859, 31-W-8, both in Kenrick Papers, AAB. The popular O'Boyle, who would later become the pastor of St. Peter's and St. Matthew's, could claim a certain historical distinction as the last clergyman to open a session of the Senate in its old chambers in the Capitol.

71. Ltr., O'Toole to Kenrick, 12 May 1858, 31-W-1; and Kenrick, *Litterarum* Register, 11 May 1858, both in Kenrick Papers, AAB.

72. *Litterarum* Register, 14 May 1858, Kenrick Papers, AAB.

greeted by what he construed as disrespectful remarks about his horsemanship from a group of students. He immediately dismounted and threatened "to handle without gloves individually or collectively any of his critics." When O'Toole failed to respond to Kenrick's queries about the incident, the archbishop promptly barred him from visiting the infirmary. O'Toole's rejoinder, at once obsequious and critical, thanked Kenrick for explaining the ban, looked forward with gratitude to the day it would be lifted, and added, "I must in candor say I feel the interdict very keenly as a very severe sentence without a hearing."[73]

These contretemps were all peripheral to O'Toole's major disagreement with the archbishop over parish finances. Although the subject was discussed as far back as in John Carroll's synod in 1791, the system of self-supporting parishes remained a constant problem. By Kenrick's time, poor accounting had emerged as a major impediment to sound financing. His first synod in 1853 required not only that clerical salaries be determined in consultation with the archbishop but that accurate financial reports be submitted annually by each parish. O'Toole fought the former and was notoriously delinquent in the latter, and in the end his financial derelictions, manifestly trivial but irritatingly persistent, led to his dismissal.

O'Toole took exception to the diocesan pay scale that set his annual salary at $800 and that of his assistant at $600. Although he collected $200 from Father Boyle for board, he was liable for all rectory expenses, which, he reported, amounted to some $1,500 annually. But what O'Toole considered essential, others saw as luxuries. Father Boyle was particularly incensed by the heavy financial burden imposed by the cost of what he considered excessive numbers of servants and other expenses incurred by the pastor.[74] O'Toole ignored these complaints, explaining that the shortfall should be covered by applying the pastor's share of the stole fees to the house expenses. That, however, would leave O'Toole just $117 annually, an impossible situation, he claimed, given calls on his charity, support for his family, and personal needs, which, he pointed out, would probably be supplied gratis if he were not Irish. His solution, in disregard of diocesan guidance, was to credit himself with a $400 salary after payment of all expenses. He laid this all out at incredible length for Kenrick in January

73. Ltr., O'Toole to Kenrick, 23 Feb 1859, 31-W-6, Kenrick Papers, AAB. See also *Star*, 7 Feb 1859. For a colorful account of the incident (and the source of the first quote), see "Recollections of Thomas Callan," Baltimore *Catholic Review*, 21 Jun 1919.

74. Ltr., O'Boyle to Kenrick, 28 Jan 1860, Kenrick Papers, AAB.

1857, justifying his arrangement and warning the archbishop that, if denied the money, he would be forced to close his purse to all appeals for charity, thus earning a reputation for avarice and causing scandal. Concerning the latter, O'Toole again reminded Kenrick that he was the only foreign-born priest in Washington and consequently suffered much from the nativism of both priests and people.[75]

Despite the special pleading, Kenrick simply insisted that St. Patrick's observe diocesan guidelines, but by summer's end he had had enough. He ordered O'Toole to appear at the chancery for an ecclesiastical trial. Only at the last moment did he relent, forgiving O'Toole and allowing him to remain in Washington.[76] The repentant pastor apparently learned little from this close call, because within months he was back apologizing for his delinquent accounts, some a year overdue, and offering lengthy legalistic arguments for his unique allocations for salaries and other expenses.[77]

When a weary Kenrick again rejected O'Toole's arguments for receiving subsidies greater than other pastors, O'Toole stepped up his pleas. He claimed that the archbishop had not ruled on what he called the essential justice of the case, and until he did, O'Toole would continue his special allocation of parish funds. He was ready to be judged, he said. He had queried several of his fellow priests on the subject and concluded that, though there might be some *"apparent peculiarity"* in his case, there was "substantially no *real* peculiarity" when compared with others. "I am satisfied," he concluded, "that substantially it is entirely true to say—that there is not even anything peculiar in my position as far as our revenues are concerned—Indeed, Most Rev. Archbishop, I will thank you to say a word definitely on this matter."[78]

Kenrick did as he was asked. As a result of this appeal, which also included the unwelcome news that architect Long was about to sue the parish, he ordered O'Toole to stand trial in February 1860. A formal hearing was dispensed with, as it turned out, and the pastor was relieved of his position as of April 8, Easter Sunday.[79] A chastened

75. Ltr., O'Toole to Kenrick, 27 Jan 1857, 31-V-6, Kenrick Papers, AAB.

76. *Litterarum* Register, 31 Jul, 21 Sep, and 17 Oct 1857, Kenrick Papers, AAB.

77. Ltr., O'Toole to Kenrick, 11 Nov 1859. For O'Toole's reaction to Kenrick's forgiveness, see ltr., O'Toole to Kenrick, 22 Oct 1857, 31-V-10. For examples of postponed accounts, see ltrs., O'Toole to Kenrick, n.d. (circa Oct 1858); 31 Dec 1857, 31-V-11; and 23 Feb 1859, 31-W-6. All in Kenrick Papers, AAB.

78. Ltr., O'Toole to Kenrick, 13 Jan 1860, 31-W-9, Kenrick Papers, AAB.

79. Ltrs., O'Toole to Kenrick, 11 Feb (31-W-11); 11 Feb (31-W-12); and 20 Feb 1960 (31-W-13). All in Kenrick Papers, AAB.

O'Toole apologized to Kenrick, to the parishioners, and to Archbishop John Hughes of New York (to whom he later appealed for a parish post) for his errors, but this time the archbishop's decision stood.[80]

To judge by the record, O'Toole was manifestly unsuited for the daily management of a large urban parish. Probably his greatest mistake was his continued misreading of the congregation's attitude toward him, a mistake that he seemed to sense only during his emotional farewell. Even discounting the hyperbole common in nineteenth-century news accounts, it would be difficult to dismiss the evident depth of affection for the man manifested by the congregation at his farewell appearance. The *Star* reporter noted the "simultaneous expressions of grief" that sprang from every part of the packed church. The pastor was forced to pause because "none seem able to restrain their feelings." After referring to "past relations which we have sustained," he promised that as long as God spared him "I shall cherish the memory of my relations with you with the greatest pleasure, for they have indeed been happy." And these feelings seemed genuinely reciprocated by the congregation. Their expressions of regret at his leaving exceeded anything required by politeness, a reaction duplicated by spokesmen for the city's non-Catholics and especially by his co-workers in Washington's various abstinence societies.[81]

In a special way Father O'Toole could be counted as a victim of the Know-Nothings, which peaked in Washington during the 1850s. A warm and generous man who moved people with his eloquence and brought them together with his enthusiastic support for popular causes, O'Toole shared with many intelligent and prominent immigrants a special sensitivity to the prejudices of both the nativists and some Catholics toward newcomers. O'Toole especially seemed to exaggerate the strength of the anti-Irish criticism, certainly that coming

80. O'Toole's application to Hughes was supported by Kenrick, but it is questionable that he ever served in New York. In December 1865 O'Toole was readmitted to the Baltimore archdiocese by Kenrick's successor, who assigned him as assistant to the president of Mount St. Mary's. See ltr., Hughes to Kenrick, 3 May 1860, 29-J-5; and *Litterarum* Register, 5 May 1860; both in Kenrick Papers, AAB. See also "Baltimore Journal of Martin John Spalding," 16 Dec 1865, Spalding Papers, AAB. O'Toole eventually served at Sacred Heart Church in Weir, Massachusetts. He died at the home of his sister in Brooklyn, New York, in 1888. His funeral was witnessed by a great crowd in the new St. Patrick's. He was buried in Mt. Olivet, the cemetery he had founded thirty years before.

81. *Star,* 9 and 16 Apr 1860.

from the "native" Catholics as he often called them. Even if he had not exaggerated the slights, he certainly misjudged the danger they posed to the church and the need to adjust both church policies and parish activities in reaction to them. His constant anxiety cast him in the role of an alarmist and troublesome interventionist to the consternation of his bishop and fellow pastors.

To a great extent his reaction to nativism, which was never particularly virulent or lasting in the capital, mirrored a tendency among the new Catholic residents in particular, but to some extent among all Catholics, to isolate themselves from the society around them. Born in response to attacks on the city's new Catholic residents, this tendency toward a church-oriented society would strengthen during the great civil war that was about to begin.

CHAPTER 6

St. Patrick's in the Civil War Era

HARDLY A Washington household was left untouched by
the Civil War that began in 1861. One of the seminal events
in American history, the war and the era of reconstruction
that followed brought lasting change not only to the city
but also to its oldest Catholic church. While many of the
interests and concerns that had animated St. Patrick's during the preceding decades continued to absorb the energies of its priests and people, living as they did at the hub
of a mighty war machine led to a host of new demands
on their charity and an ever-greater need for expanding
Catholic facilities in the city. Ironically, an era that marked
the beginning of Washington's rise to international prominence also brought changes to the center city that, to the
discerning, foretold a different future for Washington's
premier parish.

A Capital at War

These conclusions would have seemed fanciful to the
average parishioner in late 1860. The electoral victory of
Abraham Lincoln and a Republican party vowing to curtail

the spread of slavery in the new states of the West was considered a final challenge to those leaning toward secession.[1] Local residents, deeply concerned by the rush to war, nevertheless generally supported the Union. The native-born majority, although closely tied to nearby Maryland and Virginia and opposed to coercion of the southern states, clearly understood that the future of the city depended on its continued role as capital of the Union. The new immigrants, especially the many Irish-born, although generally suspicious of the Republican party, which included many of their erstwhile Know-Nothing enemies, and hostile to the newly freed slaves, whom they saw as competition for scarce employment, nevertheless had little desire for secession.

Despite general support for the Union, rumors about an armed uprising in Washington persisted during the months before Lincoln's inauguration. To counter such talk and supply Washington with a modicum of safety, a group of prominent citizens, many opposed to Lincoln's election but all eager to support the Constitution, raised thirty-three companies of volunteer infantry and two troops of cavalry in early 1861. Included in this local defense force along with the government clerks and aged veterans were a large number of Irish and German laborers, part of the latest wave of immigration to the capital. Residents began to breathe easier when they saw more than a thousand of these hastily trained and equipped men parade on Washington's birthday, even though there was probably little such a force could achieve in any real emergency.

Local mobilization began in earnest after the fall of Fort Sumter in April 1861. Units of the D.C. militia were mustered into federal service; within a month more than 3,500 residents were under arms. By the following January, Washington had answered Lincoln's call for volunteers by fielding two infantry regiments and a cavalry regiment, along with several cavalry companies assigned to units in Maryland and Pennsylvania. Most of these volunteers were veterans of pre-war service in local militia units, which were often organized around nationalist clubs such as those sponsored by the city's Irish and German residents. Other units were organized by groups of men from similar occupations, such as one formed by Italian stone masons working on the Capitol.

1. The following paragraphs on wartime Washington are based on Green's *Washington*, 1: chaps. 9–11, and Margaret Leech's *Reveille in Washington* (New York: Harper, 1941), a classic account of daily life in the federal government and city during the war.

Because these unseasoned troops would be of little value if invasion threatened, the government rushed in regiments of volunteers from northern states, some 35,000 in number, and erected a string of forts around the city. Meanwhile, most of the city's militia units were assigned to garrison duty in the vicinity, guarding federal property and army depots in Alexandria and other nearby areas known to be sympathetic to the Confederate cause. Until the last months of the conflict, the capital was never entirely free from fear of invasion. Probably the most anxious moment for local residents occurred during the summer of 1864 when General Jubal Early's veterans marched down the Seventh Street Road (now Georgia Avenue) and laid siege to Fort Stevens (adjacent to Nativity Church). His advance was halted only when the War Department called in a force of Union regulars from the battle zone.

When Congress passed the nation's first compulsory draft law in 1863, the District's quota was set at 3,863 men (out of a pool of 19,000 eligible citizens). The law allowed the provost marshal to accept volunteers in place of those whose numbers were picked in the draft, so it was usual for local governments or well-to-do draftees to pay men, often from among the city's poor immigrants, to fill the quota. The city council voted $50,000 as bonuses, and when the price for substitutes escalated, asked for volunteers from among the black residents. Despite considerable opposition, a number of black companies were raised and trained locally. In all, the District provided 13,265 white and 3,269 black soldiers, volunteers or draftees, to the Union army.[2] It is also estimated that six hundred Washington residents joined the Confederate army.

No accurate record survives of the number of St. Patrick's parishioners who served in uniform. The church's death records and anecdotal evidence compiled by local historian John V. Hinkel, however, suggest that a significant number fought with the Union forces and at least one for the Confederacy.[3] The undisputed presence of so many Irish laborers in Washington's units supports the probability of such parish participation.

Given its proximity to a major theater of operations, Washington

2. *War of the Rebellion: Compilation of Official Records of Union and Confederate Armies* (hereafter *OR*), ser. 3, vol. 4, p. 1269. On the induction of Washingtonians, see Fred A. Shannon, *The Organization and Administration of the Union Army, 1861–1865* (Cleveland: Arthur Clarke, 1928), 1:28–31.

3. John V. Hinkel, "St. Patrick's: Mother Church of Washington," *RCHS* 57–58 (1960): 39.

was frequently reminded of the grimness of modern warfare. After the Union defeat at Bull Run in July 1861, thousands of wounded and panic-stricken survivors flooded the city. During the next year, military hospitals sprang up all over town to care for sick and wounded soldiers, and many churches and public buildings were pressed into service. Holy Trinity in Georgetown was converted into a hospital. St. Aloysius escaped a similar fate when the congregation erected a large, barracks-like hospital at First and K Streets in seven days. St. Patrick's was prepared to offer the government the use of St. Joseph's orphanage as a hospital in place of the church, but was never called on to do so.[4] The government, aided by religious groups and other private Washington charities, cared for as many as 50,000 soldier-patients at a time in the city, both the wounded and those many who had fallen victim to disease. Local cemeteries received a share of the military dead.

War traditionally produces an upsurge in trade and manufacture, but if the Civil War brought a business boom to the capital, it proved of little lasting benefit to most local residents. Hoteliers, restauranteurs, wholesalers, and other tradesmen catering to the war machine prospered, while most citizens suffered severely from the resulting inflation. Residents on fixed salaries—clerks, teachers, small tradesmen, and even members of Washington's old genteel families—saw the cost of food and housing rise precipitously as the value of their money melted away. Meanwhile the city's laborers continued to face periods of extreme want, especially during the seasonal lay-offs at large government projects such as completing the Capitol and bringing the aqueduct into town. The hardship, which seemed to spare none, likewise placed an unprecedented demand on the resources of local charities.

Of special concern to Washingtonians was the continuing cloud of suspicion that hung over the city. Ironically, most of those who actively supported secession had left town or been arrested in the early months of the war, and by 1863 the great majority of those remaining were loyal Unionists. Nevertheless, throughout the war Washingtonians found their loyalty questioned and their personal freedoms threatened. The federal government imposed a loyalty oath on its own em-

4. Ltr., Bernardine Wiget to Angelo Paresce, 15 Sep 1862, quoted in George M. Anderson, "Bernardine Wiget, S.J., and the St. Aloysius Civil War Hospital in Washington, D.C.," *Catholic Historical Review* 76, no. 4 (Oct 1990), 758. Father Anderson's article also provides a detailed description of one of the major military hospitals in Washington.

ployees as well as certain city officials, school teachers included, and toward the end of the war openly discussed imposing similar measures on residents at large. The provost marshal arrested Mayor James Berret when he refused to take the loyalty oath. He also created a metropolitan police force, one controlled by federal, not city, authorities.

Although Washingtonians resented this usurpation of their traditional freedoms, all recognized the urgent need for more adequate police protection. Even so, the new police force, augmented by provost marshal troops, was unable to control the motley of volunteer soldiers whose enlistments had expired, soldiers on leave, and thousands of camp followers, confidence men, and criminals who flocked to the capital in pursuit of easy money and fun. Wartime Washington became a mecca for crime, delinquency, and all sorts of vice with criminals routinely rounded up, convicted, and imprisoned. In addition to these unworthies, the city was also host to thousands of honest civilians seeking employment and more than 40,000 contraband, the name given those slaves newly freed by Union troops. Without financial support, these refugees had fled to Washington seeking federal assistance.

Its primitive municipal facilities overwhelmed by a huge wartime population, an underfinanced city government faced insurmountable problems with refuse, sewage, and even a shortage of drinking water. Despite the work of the Army's new Sanitary Corps, a smallpox epidemic hit Washington in 1862, and this and other illnesses soon posed more danger than any possible Confederate invasion. To supplement the overtaxed civilian medical facilities, the federal government set aside one of its large military hospitals and contracted with private health-care institutions, such as the infirmary operated by the Sisters of Charity (afterwards named Providence Hospital), to provide shelter for the civilian sick.[5] Only the opening in 1864 of the new Washington aqueduct, whose construction was pressed in spite of enemy troops nearby, averted calamity.

Little noted during the war but of special significance to the city's future was the wartime change in white Washington's attitude toward black residents. In April 1862 the federal government emancipated the

5. The Sisters of Charity had operated the City Infirmary and Dispensary since the 1840s. The long-time director of the institution, Dr. Thomas Miller, was a member of St. Patrick's parish. It was his family that arranged for the purchase of the church's first pipe organ after the War of 1812.

District's remaining thirty-one hundred slaves, and shortly thereafter the Black Codes, which for fifty years had restricted the personal freedom of the city's African-Americans, were repealed.[6] These moves allowed enterprising black residents to engage in new businesses and otherwise seek employment in a war-stimulated market. They also provided similar opportunities for Washington's newly freed slaves, although many in this group chose to remain in the employ of their former masters. These changes proceeded smoothly and promised a continuation of the generally cordial if not mutually advantageous relations that existed under the old order.

All this, however, was before the great influx of contrabands who, supported by private charity and the government dole, took up permanent residence in federal camps and crowded shanty towns around the District. As the war progressed the presence of these many thousands of often-disorderly newcomers hardened the racial attitudes of the whites, who seemed unable to differentiate their educated and hard-working black neighbors from the new proletariat. Adopting attitudes of racism familiar in later days, they demanded segregated facilities and bitterly resented government efforts to use city revenues for financial assistance and educational opportunities for the freedmen. That local Catholic opinion shared these sentiments can be deduced from later articles in the *Catholic Mirror,* which complained that the government's promotion of the freedmen had pushed many local Irish workers out of their jobs. The paper also condemned the mayor's efforts after the war to integrate the public schools and bitterly criticized attempts to enfranchise black residents.[7]

The District of Columbia's clearly perceived population trends seemed at the base of this resentment. The number of foreign-born residents, the object of Know-Nothing agitation in the previous decade, had peaked in 1860 when 12,484 immigrants accounted for some 16.5 percent of the population. Although the number of immigrants would continue to grow in subsequent years, their percentage of the population would drop significantly. Among these foreign born, the 1870 census counted 8,218 Irish, the high point of Irish immigration, which would decrease steadily after that date. The number of black residents, on the other hand, rose spectacularly during the war decade, from 14,000 to 43,422, a third of the city's population. These

6. The number given is for the entire District of Columbia. Slaves left in Washington city totaled less than eighteen hundred by 1862.

7. *Catholic Mirror,* 16 Apr, 20 Nov, and 4 Dec 1870.

figures only partially reflected the District's unprecedented growth during the Civil War era. The 1870 census listed 115,446 residents, a 42 percent increase during the decade.[8]

Statistics on the city's Catholic population are less reliable, but Archbishop Kenrick put it at 20,000 in 1862. Based on parish estimates, the *Catholic Mirror's* Washington correspondent reported a total of 30,000 Catholics in 1870, nearly 26 percent of all residents. The newspaper's population breakdown by parish in 1870, obviously rounded off, showed St. Patrick's in a three-way tie for third place, marking the slow beginning of the shift away from the center city that would continue for a century.[9]

The great increase in population during the war had done little to alter the general appearance of the city, which remained unkempt and unfinished. One English visitor described the contents of a typical street in wartime Washington: "one marble temple or public office, a dozen good houses of brick, and a dozen of wood, and fill in with sheds and fields."[10] Indeed, some neighborhoods were graced by beautiful public buildings like the magnificent new Patent Office at Ninth and F Streets and the newly completed city hall in Judiciary Square, but many residential areas continued to be marred by hundreds of empty lots overgrown with weeds and strewn with rubbish. Even the new Mall, which ended just beyond the half-finished Washington Monument in an evil-smelling tidal marsh, sported ugly lumber and coal yards. The old Washington canal that ran along the path of today's Constitution Avenue was now little more than an open sewer. Save for a few paved avenues, all was dust and mud. In many blocks, the alleys were rapidly filling with the crowded shanties and tenements of the freedmen.

The F Street area around St. Patrick's fared a little better. It was described by one eyewitness as "just a pleasant and beautiful village street, somewhat sleepy withal, with comfortable homes, surrounded

8. Note that these figures are for the District of Columbia, which included the now-sizeable populations of Georgetown and the region north of Florida Avenue.

9. *Catholic Mirror*, 19 Nov 1870. St. Peter's and St. Aloysius, with 4,000 parishioners each, led the *Mirror's* list. St. Patrick's tied with St. Dominic and St. Matthew's with 3,500; with slightly lesser numbers given for Immaculate Conception, St. Stephen's, St. Martin de Porres (today's St. Augustine's), St. Mary's, and St. Joseph's. Archbishop Kenrick's estimate is found in his "Relation Status Ecclesiae Baltimorensis 1862," 32B-V-10, Kenrick Papers, AAB.

10. Henry Latham, *Black and White, a Journal of a Three Months' Tour in the United States,* quoted in Green's *Washington,* 1:238.

in many cases by considerable grounds and protected by high board fences."[11] St. Patrick's shared the block with the Model House, described as "a tavern of the old wholesome Maryland sort—very big and substantial," which stood at the Ninth Street corner. Next to it and immediately west of the square's still partially uncovered waterway stood the Masonic Temple. It was built over the old St. Patrick's spring, whose pump on the sidewalk continued to draw people from all over the neighborhood for its exceptionally pure water. Beyond the temple stood Gonzaga College, whose playground was a gathering place for neighborhood children, and then the extensive grounds of St. Patrick's itself, elevated six to eight feet above the street grade. Most of this ground would be enclosed by an imposing brick wall and fence in 1866. Before then, the bank facing the street was so sheer that, especially after heavy rain, the edge of some of the coffins buried in the old graveyard might be seen poking out of the eroding ground.

On the south side of F Street at Ninth stood the neighborhood's other public tavern, the Herndon House (soon to become the St. Cloud Hotel). Except for one large vacant lot, the rest of the block was filled with private residences, some with substantial yards. In fact, the immediate neighborhood around the church consisted for the most part of private homes alongside the orphanages and schools associated with St. Patrick's. The few commercial establishments along F Street and Ninth and Eleventh Streets were usually on the street level of what otherwise remained private residences. The major exception to this neat village-like ambiance was the largely unimproved square north of G Street between Ninth and Tenth with its deep ravine abutting the grim, spooky Van Ness mausoleum, the bane of Washington's superstitious and the joy of its old romantics.

F Street itself, like the great majority of Washington's thoroughfares, remained unpaved, its clay surface often the victim of wet weather with carts and carriages stuck to their axles. Small wonder that when once offered a lift in a neighbor's carriage, St. Patrick's pastor, without breaking his rapid pace, answered, "No, I thank you, but I am in a hurry today." So bad had conditions become toward the end of the war that the *National Intelligencer* temporarily abandoned its analysis of weighty world events to complain specifically about conditions on F Street between St. Patrick's and Eleventh Street. The paper

11. Joseph T. Kelly, "Memories of a Lifetime in Washington," *RCHS* 31–32 (1930): 124. The following description of F Street is based on Kelly's work and on Henry E. Davis's "Ninth and F Streets and Thereabout," *RCHS* 5 (1902): 238–58; and Virginia Frye's "St. Patrick's, First Catholic Church of the Federal City," *RCHS* 23 (1920): 26–51.

reported that six coaches had shipwrecked in the mud on one day, including one carrying the chief of a foreign legation who, in full diplomatic regalia, was carried to safety on the back of a strong passerby.[12] Especially trying for the carriages, but loved by young sledders in winter, was the steep rise in F Street beginning just east of Gonzaga.

The street appeared largely divorced from the mighty events of the day. Neighbors were aware of the unusual bustle at the nearby temporary hospitals, where thousands of war wounded were being tended, and they periodically watched units of blue-clad soldiers march past the church on their way to or from the railroad station at the foot of Capitol Hill. Yet the only event in the vicinity that local historians saw fit to record was the hanging of the city's largest outsized banner over the intersection at Ninth and F Streets urging support for the Lincoln-Johnson ticket in 1864.

The war brought few changes to the neighborhood, although private construction was stimulated enough that by 1865 local boosters could point to several substantial new buildings. F Street had even received a few outdoor lights from the new Washington Gas Light company before the city, short of funds, postponed the project until after the war. Even this modest beginning lent some distinction in a city where only Pennsylvania Avenue was fully lighted; elsewhere citizens depended on hand-held lanterns. By war's end the city had also begun grading the streets and its residential squares properly, a move particularly important to the F Street area with its watercourses. Largely unnoticed, the war marked the area's apogee as a residential neighborhood. Those small businesses that had begun to radiate out from the streets surrounding the Patent Office were harbingers of the neighborhood's future as Washington's premier commercial district.

One portent of this change was the laying of horsecar tracks on F Street in 1864. The city already had one line between the Navy Yard and Rock Creek, and now a larger, locally financed venture, the Metropolitan Street Railway, began service along the length of F Street to the railroad station. The company got off to a rocky start when it laid its rails directly on the street's surface with a plank roadway set in between for the horses. Trying to avoid the rails, heavy vehicles immediately began cutting away the clay edging along the tracks. This caused the rails to bow and resulted in frequent derailments and overturned cars. It was not unusual to find a streetcar perched on the sidewalk in front of St. Patrick's.

12. *National Intelligencer,* 6 Mar 1865.

Such accidents proved only temporary inconveniences. Like its namesake a century later, the Metropolitan would quickly expand throughout the District to open whole new areas for development by promising a dependable and speedy means of getting to work. The coming of the streetcars began the movement of Washingtonians out of the center city that continued into recent times. It also meant that farsighted investors could begin to plan a central business district where merchants and other businesses, eager to cater to Washington's increased population, would bring department stores and professional offices, now commonplace in New York and elsewhere, to what had been until the war a sleepy southern village.

An Energized Parish

Like most Washingtonians, members of St. Patrick's congregation appreciated the importance of the Union to the community's future, though many members remained sympathetic to southern aspirations and generally opposed the extreme demands of the so-called radical Republicans and abolitionists. Some families had relatives fighting for the Confederate cause and retained close personal ties to communities in Virginia and Maryland's southern counties. The diary of John Abell Morgan, a Jesuit scholastic who lived in Washington during part of the war, provides a fascinating glimpse into the thinking of local Catholic supporters of the South. Although Morgan witnessed the war from a safe vantage point, some local Catholics donned the gray of the Confederacy. One member of St. Patrick's parish served as an officer in Mosby's Rangers, the famed irregular force led by Confederate General John S. Mosby.[13]

Although St. Patrick's pastor did not trumpet the information, his Maryland background left him with strong sympathies for the South's cause. One priest visiting from New York in 1866 described Father Jacob Ambrose Walter as "hasty but kind, and outspoken; quite opposed to the negroes, and to Yankees." During that same year Walter received a letter from "your friend, Jefferson Davis," who thanked the pastor for some unspecified kindness during the Confederate president's incarceration.[14] Walter's largely unrecorded sympathies were

13. George M. Anderson, "The Civil War Diary of John Abell Morgan, S.J.: A Jesuit Scholastic of the Maryland Province," *Records of the American Catholic Historical Society of Philadelphia* 101 (Fall 1990): 33–54. The Confederate officer was identified in Hinkel's "St. Patrick's: Mother Church of Washington," 39.

14. Ltr., Davis to Walter, 30 Oct 1866, Original in St. Patrick's archives. The 1866

probably never as extreme as those exhibited by pewholders in the Baltimore cathedral, who, when Carroll's prayer for civil authority was read after the fall of Fort Sumter, either stalked out or otherwise showed their disapproval.[15] In fact, American Catholics received mixed signals from their bishops concerning the war, and their attitudes toward slavery and secession tended to be sectional, not religious. Archbishop Kenrick, for example, encouraged the integration of black Catholics in local parishes. Although pronouncing slavery theologically acceptable, he considered it far from ideal and called on Catholics to obey the law of the land.[16]

Yet what could such an exhortation achieve during a civil war? Some of Kenrick's fellow bishops were ardent Unionists, while others strongly opposed the government and were loyal to the Confederacy. Bishop William H. Elder of Natchez was arrested and Patrick N. Lynch of Charleston temporarily exiled on charges of disloyalty. The inflammatory denunciations of Union policies in the *Catholic Mirror* led to the imprisonment in Fort McHenry of the editors of that quasi-official diocesan paper on charges of possessing secessionist literature.

Divisions in the hierarchy and debates in the Catholic press only increased suspicions about Catholic loyalty among some of the Radicals who, while retaining their Know-Nothing heritage, were coming to dominate the federal government. Washington's Catholics operated under a double burden—they were residents of a city whose loyalty was constantly being questioned, and they were members of a religious group some of whose leaders were suspect. The evidence suggests that, however mixed its sympathies might have been, St. Patrick's priests and congregation strictly heeded Archbishop Kenrick's guidance: "Be cautious not to take sides in the politics which divide the country, but pray for peace and respect the constituted authorities."[17] One witness commented that while other pulpits in town resounded with appeals for one side or the other, St. Patrick's parishioners were exhorted to consider the "God of peace and love" and to pray for the public good.[18] The scanty records indicate that through-

characterization of Walter is from the "Diary of the Reverend Richard L. Burtsell, 24 Jan 1866," quoted in Fosselman, "A Downtown Parish," 159.

15. Spalding's *Premier See,* 175–77 and 180–1, surveys the American church's attitude toward the war and is the basis for these paragraphs.

16. On Kenrick's views on slavery and his strong criticism of the Dred Scott decision, see Marschall, "Patrick Francis Kenrick," 320–35 and 340–345.

17. Quoted in Spalding, *Premier See,* 176.

18. Joseph M. Walter, ed., *A Memorial Tribute to Rev. J. A. Walter, Late Pastor of St. Patrick's Church, Washington, D.C.* (Washington: Stormont and Jackson, 1895), 18.

out the war the congregation abstained from political discussion and adhered to its time-tested interests, succoring the needy and providing for the growth of the church in Washington.

To carry out these commonplace but essential responsibilities, the parish had found the perfect leader in Jacob Walter. Although only thirty-two years old when he became pastor on Easter Monday, 1860, he already clearly exhibited an extraordinarily shrewd business acumen so obviously missing at St. Patrick's in its recent past. Walter was a Baltimore native who had spent some years in his father's jewelry business before entering the seminary. Later, as the builder of two churches in northern Maryland, he demonstrated a strong strain of fiscal conservatism and an almost pathological fear of indebtedness.[19] His lasting renown would rest on a lifelong passion for private and organized charity. This trait was widely recognized. His longtime superior, Cardinal James Gibbons, who certainly had his disagreements with St. Patrick's pastor, nevertheless extolled Walter both in speeches and in print as a model of Christian charity. In later years this personal charity and concern for the welfare of the individual parishioners would also win the congregation's affection and loyalty, but Walter's impetuosity, sometimes brutal candor, and frank aversion to any form of pretense made for a rather rocky debut on F Street. It would take some time for people, used to Timothy O'Toole's warm loquaciousness, to appreciate the value of the blunt little priest who told them in no uncertain terms that their schemes for a grand cathedral were unrealistic and that unless they curtailed their ambitions they would wait another fifty years for a new church.[20]

Walter's impatience was understandable. His quick assessment of the parish's financial position revealed the extent of his predecessor's unrealistic assumptions and poor bookkeeping. Far from ready to launch an expensive building project, the parish was in debt, its rectory and church in the early stages of collapse, St. Joseph's orphanage, a special parish responsibility, overcrowded, and parish charities ill-organized to meet the demands of a city at war.[21] Walter concluded

19. After graduating from St. Mary's College in 1844, Walter joined his father's firm, only to return to St. Mary's as a seminarian in 1851. He was ordained in 1854.

20. This brief assessment of Walter's personality is based on his nephew Joseph Walter's useful compilation of biographical materials and testimonials of contemporaries (*A Memorial Tribute*) and Patrick Henry Ahern, *The Life of John Keane: Educator and Archbishop, 1839–1918* (Milwaukee: Bruce Publishing, 1955), 17–34.

21. Walter outlined the parish's financial situation in a letter to Kenrick, 18 Oct 1861, Kenrick Papers, AAB. See also Walter's *A Memorial Tribute*, 14.

JACOB A. WALTER. *Portrait by Matthew Brady, circa 1861*

that the church should get emergency repairs, enough to keep it us-
able until a realistic decision could be reached about a new building;
similarly, St. Joseph's would have to struggle on in its F Street building
until after the war. The rectory was another matter, because sometime in 1861 Archbishop Kenrick, probably recalling his own uncomfortable visits in Father Matthews's drafty house at Tenth and F
Streets, ordered the parish to build a new pastoral residence. Among
other pressing matters that could not be postponed were reorganization of parish charities, settlement of a legacy left to St. Joseph's, and,
later in the war, some kind of accommodation for the swelling num-

ber of Catholics who lived in the northern reaches of the parish. With just six dollars in the parish till and the city in the midst of an epic war, Walter and the congregation set off to provide new help for the poor and the newcomers.

Until the archdiocese became actively involved in the direction of Catholic charities sometime after the Civil War, individual parishes in Washington were left to collect alms and dispense money and goods to the poor as they saw fit. Much useful work was done under this informal procedure, but rivalry among the various fund-raising groups led to duplication of effort and frustrated a coordinated attack on city-wide concerns. A beginning was made on the parish level in 1857 when Father Charles I. White organized the city's first conference of the Society of St. Vincent de Paul at St. Matthew's. Recruiting most of his members from the Young Catholic Friends Society, White organized the conference so that funds might be collected and goods and services distributed in an efficient and systematic manner by the various parish groups. Although the St. Vincent de Paul Society left much to be desired in those early days—with no female members, for example, the parish conferences largely ignored the special needs of the female destitute, while proselytism, rather than charity, seemed to absorb a major part of the society's energies—subsequent reforms rapidly transformed it into an effective system of local charity.[22]

Although St. Patrick's charitable organizations had been providing substantial relief for the sick and poor for decades, Father Walter realized that the parish lacked the necessary organization to meet the demands of a war-torn society. Following St. Matthew's example, he petitioned the superior council of the St. Vincent de Paul Society in New York for permission to begin a conference at St. Patrick's. Permission was forthcoming in March 1861. As president of the boards of trustees of both orphanages, Walter was particularly concerned with devising ways to organize city-wide charities, and he saw in the St. Vincent de Paul Society, which was rapidly springing up in every parish, a vehicle for such needs. In 1861 he formed a Particular Council of the St. Vincent de Paul Society for the District of Columbia to serve as an umbrella organization for the separate parish conferences and a clearing house for city-wide charities. Although Archbishop Martin J.

22. Daniel T. McColgan, *A Century of Charity; The First One Hundred Years of St. Vincent de Paul in the United States* (Milwaukee: Bruce Publishing, 1951), 1:212–15. The society was listed as the Confraternity of Brothers of St. Vincent de Paul in the 1860 edition of the Catholic Directory.

Spalding, Kenrick's successor, would seek to distinguish between local (parish) and general charity collections and demand that the latter receive his prior approval and be equitably organized with due publicity, there was in fact no such diocesan appeal until 1885. The work continued in the main to be done by the St. Vincent de Paul Particular Council, which served as a model for the later-organized Catholic Charities. Walter remained closely associated with the group until his death, regularly attending meetings of both the parish conference and the particular council, a sparkplug for its important work.[23]

The war severely tested St. Patrick's charitable resources. With the sisters from St. Vincent's and St. Joseph's in the lead, parishioners assisted the wounded in the nearby military hospitals. In 1862 the parish opened what was then called a bread line for the indigent. This effort earned their pastor a rebuke from the always-exacting Archbishop Kenrick, who told him that it was inappropriate for a parish to distribute meat on days of abstinence.[24] Both orphanages temporarily sheltered children whose fathers were off in military service. Typifying the spontaneous acts of charity that still prevailed in an age when churches were only beginning to systematize their charitable efforts, parishioners repeated the story of their absent-minded pastor's reaction to a poor man's appeal for clothes. Remembering that he owned two overcoats—one somewhat the worse for wear, the other a recent gift from a parishioner and suitable for appearance at public meetings—Walter reached into his wardrobe, grabbed a coat, and put it on the freezing stranger. Only later, when dressing for an important appointment, did he discover that the beggar had his new worsted, leaving Walter to face his very proper company in the old threadbare.

Walter, though a paragon of charity, had a passion for fiscal regularity. His fear of debt was legendary; his insistence that the parish undertake building projects that were both practical and simple and that stayed within its means became the guiding spirit in the parish's multiple endeavors during the next thirty years. Walter's tightwad proclivities were sorely tried in 1861, when Archbishop Kenrick told the new pastor to build a parish house, one that was to be the "residence of the future bishop of Washington." Unlike his predecessor, Walter always

23. Weitzman, *One Hundred Years of Charity*, 5–13. Walter's association with the St. Vincent de Paul Society is detailed in Ahern's *John Keane*, 22. Archbishop Spalding's decree on general charities was announced in a Circular to the Clergy, reproduced in *Catholic Mirror*, 17 Sep 1864.

24. Kenrick, *Litterarum* Register, 10 Feb 1862, Kenrick Papers, AAB.

accepted his superior's directives without question, but building an episcopal residence must have seemed a great burden to a pastor with a crumbling church and many demands on parish resources.

Surviving financial statements provide a glimpse into Walter's management techniques. He began by paying an architect $25 to design a brick mansion in the southern federal style to be situated on the southeast corner of Tenth and G Streets (the site of today's rectory). The house included a separate suite suitable for a bishop as well as rooms for a pastor, several assistants and visitors, along with public reception rooms, kitchens, servant quarters, and a yard large enough for Father Walter's peach tree and roses. Its cost was estimated in excess of $10,000 (equal to $155,000 today).[25] Walter proceeded to raise the necessary amount, along with the money needed for emergency repairs to the church's decaying roof, in a way that avoided saddling the parish with long-term debt. A special subscription fund netted only $281, but through constant exhortation, pew rents and Sunday collections rose to $5,000 in 1864, an almost 50 percent increase in two years and more than $2,000 over current expenses. Walter also took advantage of nineteenth-century Washington's love of church fairs to raise $3,000 at one sponsored by the parish in 1863. For the rest he borrowed $2,200 from the church building fund unspent from O'Toole's time and an equal amount in the form of personal loans from wealthy parishioners. These efforts paid off. In less than two years after breaking ground, the final $300 payment was made on the loans, and the new parish home stood free and clear.

Although the rectory would witness many important events during its forty-two year life, perhaps none earned as much comment as an incident that occurred in 1864. Father Walter was awakened one cold winter night by a loud pounding on the door. Looking out a window he saw two small children, who pleaded with him to come tend their dying father. Obtaining the address, Walter proceeded to dress and took off for a distant tenement where he found an old man, obviously near death. Walter identified himself as a priest, but the man, all alone, denied sending for him. When Walter described the two children who had fetched him, the startled man thanked God and re-

---

25. Exact cost is unknown because of incomplete financial statements. The approximate cost has been extrapolated from expenditures in fiscal years 1862, 1864, and 1865. See St. Patrick's financial statements, various years, SPA. Description of rectory is from Virginia K. Frye, "St. Patrick's—First Catholic Church of the Federal City," 44, and Walter, *A Memorial Tribute*, 29, 36, and 79.

sponded, "I wanted a priest, but had no one to send. They must have been my children who died years ago."[26]

It seems likely that part of the money raised for the new rectory was eventually used as seed money for a temporary church constructed in the northern region of the parish in 1864. For the third time in fifty years, St. Patrick's congregation was called on to sponsor a daughter parish, this time in the fast-growing residential area along Seventh Street north of Massachusetts Avenue known as "Northern Liberties" or "Bricktown." The recent spurt of immigration had caused a rapid growth in the number of Catholics in northwest Washington. In 1854 the archbishop had approved Father Matthews's plan to raise funds for a church in the northern part of the parish, but the pastor's death and the subsequent drive to rebuild St. Patrick's itself caused the project to be dropped. A decade later Archbishop Spalding resurrected the idea when he asked both St. Patrick's and St. Matthew's to build and finance auxiliary churches, so-called chapels-of-ease, within their respective boundaries. All this was part of the new archbishop's plan for the development of parishes necessitated by Catholic growth but halted by the war. He wanted settled parishes to buy land and erect buildings that would temporarily serve as a combined church and school in fast-growing areas while real estate and building costs were still affordable, leaving to a later date the funding of a permanent church by the new congregation.[27]

With Spalding's approval Walter purchased property on N Street, at that time a dirt road in an area dominated by small frame houses, deserted clay pits, and brick works. There on October 30, 1864, St. Patrick's pastor laid the cornerstone of Immaculate Conception church and school, named in honor of the recently proclaimed dogma. By the time the new church was dedicated the following July, St. Patrick's congregation had already raised half of its $16,000 cost. A month later Father Walter reported that the new congregation was large enough to require two Sunday masses, and so he was planning to build a gallery in the church to accommodate the crowds. Although the ever-prudent pastor was reluctant to let the new parish go before it had proved self-sustaining, he warned Spalding that he needed more help

26. The incident is related in several sources. See, for example, Smith's *History of St. Patrick's*, 43–44.

27. Baltimore Journal of Martin John Spalding, 20 Dec 1864, 8–9, Spalding Papers, AAB. See also Fosselman, "A Downtown Parish," 123–26, and Spalding, *Premier See*, 180.

to serve what had already become a second major congregation. Meanwhile he had also purchased a home for the Sisters of Charity who were to teach in the new parish school.[28]

Spalding approved the real estate transactions and additional building, he informed Walter, so long as St. Patrick's would arrange for the speedy payment of the purchases, "for which, of course, I will not be responsible."[29] Immaculate Conception became an independent parish in September 1866, with Father Patrick F. McCarthy, who had served as Walter's assistant since 1863, appointed its first pastor.

The promptness with which St. Patrick's responded to the archbishop's request for help in forming a new parish seemed to underscore the reluctance of St. Matthew's pastor to undertake a similar assignment in the area west of Washington Circle. Father White was convinced that no new parish was needed in his area and argued the point at length with the archbishop. Father Walter made no secret of his reaction to these arguments, which at this distance do smack of a self-serving attempt to reduce competition and preserve support of a socially prominent congregation. White in turn complained to Spalding about what he called Walter's interference in the business of other parishes, interference which, if left unchecked, he claimed, would prove "very injurious to the rights of other clergymen and detrimental to the interest of religion in this city." Walter's age and experience in Washington, White contended, scarcely authorized him to affect a superiority of judgment; he passed on the unanimous conclusion of four city pastors: Walter's "meddlesome disposition, his imprudent talk among the laity, his palpable selfishness and petty ambition, have rendered him obnoxious, not only to many of the clergy of this city, but to a large portion of the laity even of his own congregation."[30]

Spalding wisely brushed aside such fulminations, and White quickly agreed to build St. Stephen's church in the same manner that St. Patrick's had sponsored Immaculate Conception. But White's outburst, surely an overwrought expression of his impatience with his

---

28. Ltrs., Walter to Spalding, 14 Jun 1865, 36-K-6; 15 Aug 1865, 36-K-9; and 8 Sep 1865, 36-K-10. See also Baltimore Journal of Martin John Spalding, 7 Sep and 21 Sep 1864 and 2 Jul 1865. All in Spalding Papers, AAB. A brief, modern account of the formation of Immaculate Conception parish appeared in the *Catholic Standard*, 29 May 1964.

29. Ltr., Spalding to Walter, 19 Aug 1865, "Copies of Letters, January 1, 1865-October, 1869," Spalding Papers, AAB.

30. Ltr., White to Spalding, 11 Oct 1864, 36-O-5. Even after a mild rebuff from Spalding, White repeated the charges in a second letter, 16 Oct 1864, 36-O-6. Both in Spalding Papers, AAB.

young colleague, is strangely echoed even by Walter's warmest admirers, when in later years they went to great pains to explain the young man's often tactless ways. Certainly Spalding himself would experience a somewhat similar reaction when this "honestest of men" continued to air his opinions in public in the wake of the President's assassination a year later.[31]

Death of a President

Although Washingtonians had greeted Abraham Lincoln with considerable misgiving in 1861, his vision for the postwar Union offered them a ray of hope. Small wonder that after enduring the restrictions of an increasingly vindictive Congress, they warmly welcomed the President's promise in his second inaugural address to bind up the nation's wounds "with malice toward none; with charity for all." With Lee's surrender at Appomattox on April 7, 1865, the local community looked forward to a speedy end to the bloodshed. Yet the euphoria evaporated instantly on Good Friday night, when the news spread that Lincoln had been shot. Many St. Patrick's parishioners joined their pastor in the crowd that kept vigil across from Ford's Theater, just a block from the church, as the President lay dying.

Archbishop Spalding promptly condemned the crime as an atrocious deed "hitherto, happily, unparalleled in our history," but he did not call for any concerted Catholic reaction, adding that he considered silence "perhaps the best and most appropriate expression for a sorrow too great for utterance." In the poisoned atmosphere that surrounded Lincoln's death, such silence could be interpreted another way. The fact that a few of those implicated in the assassination plot were Catholics was seized by some in the Know-Nothing wing of the Republican party, who began a campaign in the press to implicate all Catholics in southern Maryland in the conspiracy. The Army's inspector general, James A. Hardie, himself a Catholic and frequent advisor to the Baltimore archbishop, warned Spalding that the church should associate itself with the Union's grief in some demonstrable way or

31. Baltimore Journal of Martin John Spalding, 21 Oct 1864, Spalding Papers, AAB. Both Joseph M. Walter and Archbishop John J. Keane (in *A Memorial Tribute*) refer repeatedly to Walter's bluntness and impolitic rhetoric, especially in his earlier years. Archbishop Hannan recently speculated on how Walter's forthright expression might have clouded his relations with his superiors in Baltimore. See interview with author, SPA. The "honestest of men" remark was attributed to Archbishop Peter Kenrick of St. Louis by Bishop William Elder in Walter, *A Memorial Tribute*, 84.

risk courting a recurrence of the anti-Catholic riots and disorders of earlier times. He recommended that churches be draped in black and the clergy and people participate in the national period of mourning. Hardie was particularly worried about the conduct of such well-known critics of the administration as the pastor of St. Matthew's, whom he particularly wanted enjoined to participate.[32]

Spalding heeded the warning. Priests and seminarians from the diocese were in the cortège that accompanied Lincoln's coffin as it moved through Baltimore on its way to Illinois, and Catholic churches throughout the diocese, suitably draped in black crepe, joined in the national day of mourning on June 1 by tolling their bells for a half-hour and singing a high Mass for the repose of the fallen leader. Spalding also designated St. Matthew's as the site for a Mass of Thanksgiving and special prayers for the nation marking the end of the war.[33]

It was in this heightened atmosphere of suspicion and reprisal that Father Walter gained national prominence, when he stubbornly insisted on the innocence of a member of his congregation implicated in the conspiracy to assassinate the President.[34] Walter was unacquainted with Mary Eugenia Surratt, a well-educated woman from a moderately well-to-do southern Maryland family, who came upon poor times during her widowhood. Her boardinghouse, described by President Andrew Johnson as "the nest in which the egg was hatched," was located at 541 H Street, NW. Like many parishioners in that area, Mrs. Surratt preferred to attend nearby St. Aloysius, whose pastor, Father Bernardine Wiget, was a family friend. Nevertheless, while incarcerated in the old Carroll prison on Capitol Hill before her military trial, she asked St. Patrick's pastor to visit her. At the time authorities denied the request.

Walter did not protest. He was representing the archbishop in negotiations with Attorney General James Speed over the return of Bishop Lynch, and, convinced that Surratt was innocent, looked for her release any day.[35] It was not until July 6, after her conviction, that he de-

32. Ltr., Hardie to Spalding, 16 Apr 1865, 34-D-10. Spalding's condemnation of the murder is contained in a special circular addressed to the clergy and people of the archdiocese, 15 Apr 1865, 39B-A2. Both in Spalding Papers, AAB.

33. *Catholic Mirror*, 20 May 1865; and Philibert, *St. Matthew's of Washington*, 94. See also, Spalding, *Premier See*, 181.

34. For a summary of the charges and findings of the military court, see War Department General Court-Martial Orders No. 356, 5 Jul 1865, *OR*, ser. 2, vol. 8, 696–700.

35. Lynch was forced to remain abroad for some further months, but Walter's negotiations with Speed and Secretary of State William H. Seward eventually led to

EXECUTION OF MARY SURRATT, *with Father Walter at left*

manded permission from the War Department to see the prisoner. To the Army orderly who delivered the necessary pass, Walter remarked that he had read the trial record and concluded that "there was not evidence enough to hang a cat." Further, he was unable to accept the proposition that a "Catholic woman would go to Communion on Holy Thursday and be guilty of murder on Good Friday."[36]

When these comments were relayed to General Hardie, that thoroughly concerned individual hurried to St. Patrick's to caution the agitated priest about using inflammatory language in a time of "public

Lynch's return. See ltrs., Walter to Spalding 9 and 26 Jun 65, 36-K-5 and 36-K-7, Spalding Papers, AAB.

36. Jacob A. Walter, "The Surratt Case. A True Statement of Facts Concerning this Notable Case," *United States Catholic Historical Magazine* 3 (Dec 1890): 353–61, is the source for this and the following Walter quotations. The role of St. Patrick's pastor in the case is detailed in Guy W. Moore, *The Case of Mrs. Surratt: Her Controversial Trial and Execution for Conspiracy in the Lincoln Assassination* (Norman: University of Oklahoma Press, 1954).

excitement" and demand Walter's silence as a condition for visiting the condemned. For his pains Hardie received a good tongue lashing which was later widely quoted in the press:

You wish me to promise that I shall say nothing in regard to the innocence of Mrs. Surratt. Do you know the relation existing between a pastor and his flock? I will defend the character of the poorest woman in my parish at the risk of my life. Thank God I do not know what fear is, I fear neither man nor devil, but God alone. You wish to seal my lips; I wish you to understand that I was born a freeman and will die one. I know where all this comes from, it comes from your Secretary of War [Stanton], whom a Congressman in my breakfast room two weeks ago called a brute. Of course I cannot let Mrs. Surratt die without the sacraments, so if I must say yes, I say yes.

Walter sought an interview with President Andrew Johnson. Accompanied by Surratt's young daughter, he went to the White House only to be turned away at the President's door. The next day he attended the prisoner and stood with her on the scaffold to the end. He also recorded her last moments:

"Father I wish to say something." "Well what is it my child?" "That I am innocent," were her exact words. My reply was "you may say so if you wish, but it will do no good." These words were uttered whilst she stood on the verge of eternity, and were the last confession of an innocent woman.

The summary judgment of the military commission that tried the accused and the lack of response to its recommendation for leniency in the case of Mary Surratt prompted the inevitable reaction from the enemies of the vindictive Secretary of War, Edwin M. Stanton. The role played by Father Walter in the drama was fully aired in the national press; he himself repeated for a reporter his heated rejoinder to Hardie quoted above. In the ensuing public debate, a thoroughly-aroused Hardie lashed out at Walter, accusing him of imprudent conduct and lacking the proper disposition to attend a condemned prisoner. Secretary Stanton was sufficiently concerned to send General Winfield S. Hancock to Baltimore to ask Spalding to intervene.[37]

Spalding was convinced that any attempt to debate the innocence of Mrs. Surratt was inexpedient "in the present agitated state of the public mind." He promptly warned Walter that further discussion "can do no possible good and may do harm." He begged his subordinate to leave Hardie's remarks unanswered and "to caution your friends not

37. Benjamin P. Thomas and Harold M. Hyman, *Stanton: The Life and Times of Lincoln's Secretary of War* (New York: Knopf, 1962), 433.

to bring your name before the public *in any way.*" Walter agreed, although, he replied, "You require of me a very painful duty, not to assert the innocence of one who is considered here even by Protestants as a kind of martyr." Even then the feisty pastor could not resist a parting shot at Hardie who, he charged, should stop interfering in church affairs. Catholics could take care of themselves, he claimed, without the help of "a weak timorous man" who feared the Secretary of War "as no *man* should fear a fellow creature." Hardie hastily presented his side of the matter to Spalding, justifying himself as only striving to induce "discreet behavior where circumspection and prudence were especially called for."[38]

Mary Surratt was at rest in Mt. Olivet, but public debate over her trial left the archbishop of Baltimore wrestling with the age-old problem of reconciling principle with expediency. Spalding, mindful of the continuing negotiations with the government over amnesty for the bishop of Charleston and deeply concerned over the fate of Catholics in the vanquished South, was obviously anxious to get this unexpected confrontation with the administration behind him. Walter, with the clear eye of the crusader and fearing "neither man nor devil but God alone," remained oblivious to such considerations. That Spalding was at least aware of the dilemma could be inferred from his final response to Hardie. Although he called the general a staunch friend of the church, he admonished him for his heated castigation of Walter, who, Spalding said, also acted for what he believed the best. Nevertheless, the prelate admitted, he had cautioned the pastor to remain silent.[39] Walter maintained that Spalding had requested, not ordered, his silence, yet he faithfully complied for a quarter century until just before his death, when he published a full account of his view of the case.

Reconstruction

The surrender of the Confederate armies ushered in an exciting period of change in the nation's capital, when Washington first began to assume the appearance and social patterns familiar to today's residents. Beginning in May 1865, the victorious Union troops paraded in

38. Ltrs., Spalding to John Timon, 21 Jul 1865, and to Walter, same date, Spalding Letterbook; Walter to Spalding, 22 Jul 1865, 36-K-8; Hardie to Spalding, 22 Jul 1865, 34-D-14, all in Spalding Papers, AAB.

39. Ltr., Spalding to Hardie, 23 Jul 1865, Spalding Letterbook, Spalding Papers, AAB.

seemingly endless ranks up Pennsylvania Avenue on their way home. Washington's own veterans returned, and, taking advantage of President Johnson's liberal reconstruction policies, so too did the city's Confederate supporters. The local military hospitals, filled all spring with the wounded and dying, rapidly emptied. Despite an initial period of business downturn, the local economy, stimulated by the organization of new governmental departments and activities and a population that continued to grow, quickly revived. New housing and commercial buildings began to spring up all over town, and the once sparsely settled blocks along Massachusetts Avenue beyond Thirteenth Street quickly became Washington's newest fashionable address.

St. Patrick's congregation shared the general euphoria and pent-up energy that seemed to embrace the city. Interest turned again to the long-delayed "metropolitan cathedral," which, in addition to meeting the need for new accommodations, would also satisfy the yearning for some outward expression of the parish's position as the city's oldest Catholic community. In common with congregations throughout the country, they wanted to produce some tangible sign of the power and permanence of their religion in America. For some years they had been forced to stand by as the new St. Aloysius across the Tiber with its breathtaking church interior and renowned choir, garnered the city's attention. They were also aware of the equally imposing St. Dominic Church rising on the Island and no doubt knew of the developing plans for a second German parish (St. Joseph's on Capitol Hill) that was expected to resemble an old-world cathedral.[40] Even their fiscally conservative pastor seemed ready to abandon his usual careful ways when in early 1866 he razed the old rectory near the corner of Tenth and F and otherwise cleared the ground west of the church for new construction.

Walter was clearly following what he believed was the late Archbishop Kenrick's intention to build a church in size and splendor appropriate for a cathedral. The description of the church announced in the press in 1867 also indicated that there had been only a slight modification in the design for the grand church developed by Father O'Toole and his building committee a decade earlier. Again as in 1857,

40. The Jesuit fathers founded the city's second national church on Capitol Hill in 1868. Their elaborate plans were scaled down in the economic hard times after Father Wiget's death. In 1886 St. Joseph's, by then under the care of diocesan clergy, was converted into a regular territorial parish.

the new structure was to be located on F Street just west of the present building, extending back across the square toward the new rectory. Furthermore, it was to be in a style appropriate "for the future cathedral of Washington."[41]

Of all those involved, Walter must have been the most concerned about the formidable task at hand. Beyond a small building fund accumulated from the pledges subscribed in O'Toole's time, the parish had no money to support so costly a project. Moreover, the congregation was facing an uncertain future. With the formation of the new Immaculate Conception parish, St. Patrick's had finally assumed its definitive and considerably reduced territorial limits (about 110 square blocks from the south side of L Street to the Mall and from the west side of Third Street to the east side of Thirteenth Street). Although this area covered one of the city's most populous neighborhoods, the growth of business in the region forcast a different future. The loss of the fast-growing northern sections of the parish, the habit of many neighborhood residents to frequent nearby St. Aloysius and other churches, and the increased competition for donations for diocesan and city-wide causes meant that sources of support formerly counted on by those planning a cathedral-like structure had evaporated.

Walter began his quest for new revenues by trying to capitalize on the church's central location. In June 1866 he laid the cornerstone for a spacious brick auditorium named in honor of the first archbishop. Offering the city's many religious and social organizations a much-needed place for their meetings and entertainments, the 800-seat Carroll Hall was expected to produce a steady income that might be applied to the building program. The hall quickly fulfilled its promise as a center for Washington's scholarly and social gatherings. Included in the list of prominent speakers who graced its stage over the years were well-known authors like Charles Dickens, Gilbert Keith Chesterton, and Hilaire Belloc. Dickens's four appearances in February 1868 proved to be one of Washington's grand occasions. With considerable grumbling about the price of tickets ($3.00), Washington society, led by President Johnson and Chief Justice Samuel Chase, struggled through the mire on G Street to hear the popular novelist read from his works. Long forgotten were the author's acerbic description of the city made during his earlier visit, although Dickens continued to show some of his old testiness when he sarcastically commented on the inadequate lighting during his first lecture. His manager paid $250 in

41. *Catholic Mirror*, 16 Mar 1867.

rent for the four evenings, while the parish spent $15 for special car-
pentry for an occasion that must have produced the building's most
profitable week.[42]

Although Carroll Hall proved popular, it was never a great revenue
producer. Costing $33,000, some of which was presumably borrowed
from the parish's modest building fund, the auditorium failed to realize a profit for many years. In place of a source of support for the new
church, Walter found himself burdened with yet another debt. His error came from overestimating the willingness of local Catholic organizations to pay. While all admitted Carroll Hall was a convenient and
useful building, most groups expected it to be made available gratis. If
denied such hospitality, they were willing to settle for less convenient
but free accommodation elsewhere. Ironically, the hall proved in the
end to be one of the pastor's best ventures. Its basement rooms provided meeting space for the increasingly important Sunday school and
the many other societies associated with the parish, while its auditorium served as a setting for conventions and other ecclesiastical meetings noteworthy in the development of American Catholicism. For
more than thirty years Carroll Hall remained the center of parish life,
for a large part of that time serving as its sanctuary when the old
church on F Street was forced to close. Walter would live to see his decision to build fully justified.

Despite what must have been growing apprehension on the part of
one with such an inordinate fear of debt, Walter went ahead and obtained Spalding's permission to begin church construction. In March
1867 the local press reported on elaborate plans for the cornerstone
laying on St. Patrick's Day, which was to include a parade featuring
the Marine Corps band and various Catholic marching societies
capped by imposing ceremonies celebrated by the archbishop. The
Catholic Mirror added that although all loved and cherished the old
church, they were ready to see it torn down and replaced by the new
cathedral.[43] Again, they were doomed to disappointment. In what

42. *Star*, 4 Feb 1868. The Dickens lectures were exhaustively covered by the local
press. For a summary of their remarks, see John Claggett Proctor, "Visits of Dickens
to National Capital," *Star*, 3 Jun 1934. The visit was also covered in detail in Raymund
Fitzsimons, *Garish Lights The Public Reading Tours of Charles Dickens*, (Philadelphia: J. B.
Lippincott, 1970), and in K. J. Fielding, ed., *The Speeches of Charles Dickens* (Oxford:
Clarendon Press, 1960), 375–76. The *Catholic Mirror* complained about the cost of the
lectures in its 8 Feb 1868 edition.

43. *Catholic Mirror*, 2 Feb and 16 Mar 1867. See also *Star*, 16 Mar 1867. Apparently the
scheduled ceremony was purely symbolic, somewhat akin to today's turning the first

would later be interpreted by some as an act of God, a record-breaking winter storm on March 17 brought the city to a standstill and
forced cancellation of the event.

The *Catholic Mirror* announced that the ceremony would be rescheduled for "next Sunday or whenever convenient," but as weeks
stretched into months with no further news, it became obvious
that the storm had given everyone involved time for sober second
thoughts. In fact, all public discussion of a new church abruptly
ceased. When two months later the paper complimented Walter on
transforming the area around Carroll Hall "from one of the city's
wildernesses of brambles, heaps of earth and refuse matter, rarely tra-
versed by civilized man" into an "urban aspect, befitting the neighborhood," it made no mention of a new church.[44] Everyone seemed to
have entered a conspiracy of silence, with no recorded reaction to the
cancellation in either Baltimore or Washington. Actually, worry about
the debt on Carroll Hall and the parish's financial overcommitment
had became too much for the hard-working pastor. Walter's health began to deteriorate rapidly. Warned by his doctor that his lung condition posed a clear danger, he agreed to endure the standard treatment
prescribed for so many nerve-wracked nineteenth-century patients: a
strenuous European tour. Expenses for the trip were assumed by
some of the parishioners, who were beginning to understand that
Walter's chronic personal poverty was further evidence of his remarkable charity.[45]

Beset by financial worries, Father Walter nevertheless had ample
reason to rejoice as he set off for Rome in December 1867. Signs of renewed vitality abounded in the parish. Much of the new enthusiasm
could be traced to the efforts of John J. Keane, the dynamic young assistant the pastor was leaving in charge. Before going on to a distinguished if sometimes troubled career as the bishop of Richmond, first

spadeful of dirt. There is no evidence that the foundation work preceding the actual
setting of a cornerstone was ever undertaken in 1867.

44. The appearance of the property was discussed several times in the *Catholic Mirror* (see, for example, 16 Mar 1867). The quote is from the issue of 4 May 1867 and accompanied a discussion of a fair being held to help defray the cost of Carroll Hall. The
Mirror's only mention of the new church was its notice on 23 March 1867 that the cornerstone laying would soon be rescheduled.

45. Walter spent most of his trip in Rome in the company of Archbishop Peter Kenrick of St. Louis and other American clergymen. At one point dangerously ill with an
inflammation of the lungs, he quickly recovered his health. His activities are chronicled in a informative series of letters to Spalding, various dates, 36K-11-14, Spalding Papers, AAB. See also, John J. Keane's comments in Walter, *A Memorial Tribute*, 73–75.

rector of the Catholic University of America, and archbishop of
Dubuque, Keane served for a dozen years at St. Patrick's. His gift for
organization and charismatic preaching profoundly influenced the development of many of the parish's and the nation's most important religious institutions. The pastor and assistant made an effective team.
Keane's gentle charm and self-effacing mien did much to soften Walter's blunt impatience. That Walter fully understood the role each was
to play was apparent when he told his talented assistant early on, "I'll
rub the cat up the back, and you'll sleek it down." Walter seemed to
relish his reputation as a curmudgeon, but was finding it increasingly
difficult to carry off. As Keane later noted, the parish had come to realize that none could be more "touchingly tender" than Walter when
circumstances warranted.[46]

Two immediate concerns faced the Walter-Keane team in the immediate postwar period: how to direct the parish's response to recently enunciated diocesan polices concerning parochial schools and
the apostolate for the newly freed slaves.

Reflecting his strong support for the concerns of the immigrant
church, Archbishop Spalding had made the development of parochial
education a primary focus of his episcopacy. Through his efforts, the
Second Plenary Council in 1866 had emphasized the indispensability
of parochial schools, and at his direction every urban parish in the diocese was asked to support one. St. Patrick's involvement in Catholic
education predated the archbishop's request by many decades, but, as
already noted, this support did not extend to the establishment of a
parochial school in the strict sense of the term. Father O'Toole's small
elementary school for boys, if in fact it ever opened, certainly struggled through the war with few pupils and little notice. Finally in 1866
the Christian Brothers accepted Father Walter's invitation to staff a
school at St. Patrick's that would combine free (parochial) classes with
an academy that charged tuition. The parish built a small, joint residence and school house on G Street behind the new rectory and organized additional classroom space in the basement of Carroll Hall.

Walter's motives for starting the new school remain unclear. Proximity to Gonzaga, Washington Visitation, and the successful schools
operated by St. Vincent and St. Joseph orphanages placed it in direct
competition with those institutions. Meanwhile, the Christian Brothers were finding the primitive educational conditions difficult to endure. Their cramped space was scarcely enhanced by the constant din

46. Keane as quoted in Walter, *A Memorial Tribute*, 71–72.

emanating from the parish's popular new auditorium, dismissed in their diary as a "music hall." They were also disappointed that Walter had failed to fulfill his promise to build a suitable school and furnish their new home. In 1868 they decamped for the more salubrious surroundings of St. Matthews.[47] The school continued with lay teachers, but eventually Walter, unable to attract another teaching order and worried by mounting parish debt, closed it, leaving the larger question of an appropriate parochial education at St. Patrick's hanging fire. Most of the parish's children continued to be educated at St. Vincent's and St. Joseph's or at one of the city's private Catholic schools. Increasingly, if inaccurately, the schools attached to the orphanages were referred to as St. Patrick's parochial schools.[48]

Recent diocesan directives also altered the settled pattern of race relations at St. Patrick's. At Archbishop Spalding's insistence, the American bishops at the Second Plenary Council had finally discussed methods for the evangelization and Christian education of the African-Americans. Some bishops were concerned that separate churches and special ministries devoted exclusively to the welfare of black Catholics would only perpetuate the division between the races already evident in the church. Others argued that black Catholics, strongly objecting to the discrimination they endured in many churches, had made clear their preference for separate churches. Still others, reflecting the indifference or prejudices of many northern Catholics, overwhelmed by the demands the immigrant newcomers had made on their scarce manpower and money, and anxious not to disturb the status quo, objected to any special ministry. Although in the end the council came out in favor of separate black churches, it also concluded that questions of race were best left to individual provinces to decide. Meanwhile, black Catholics were reacting with their feet, leaving the church in increasing numbers. It has been estimated that about one third of the nation's black Catholics, 50,000 people, left the church in the fifteen years after the Civil War.[49]

47. Bro. Joseph Grabenstein, F.S.C., "Called to the Capital," *St. John's Quarterly* (Spring 1984): 7–8. The brothers had operated an academy at St. Matthew's between 1851 and 1855, returning to St. Matthew's Institute in 1868. They would move again in 1890 to Vermont Avenue, where they opened the renowned St. John's High School. See O. B. Corrigan, *The Catholic Schools of the Archdiocese of Baltimore: A Study in Diocesan History* (Baltimore, 1924), 70.

48. For the evolution of St. Patrick's schools, see chapter 13 below.

49. Statistics on black Catholics and a careful survey of the bishop's discussions at the Council are discussed in Edward J. Misch, "The American Bishops and the Negro

In view of the dynamic growth of all-black congregations in the various Protestant denominations and the opposition of black Catholics to the enforced segregation in many churches, Spalding decided "as a matter of necessity for the preservation of the freedman's faith" to establish all-black parishes in the Baltimore archdiocese. Like the various national churches built for immigrants, these would transcend regular parish lines. Lest his decision be interpreted as capitulation to pastors and congregations eager to exclude black Catholics, Spalding reiterated the requirement of canon law that pastors must minister to all within their parish boundaries. At the time he appointed a pastor for Washington's first black congregation, he specified that while the new parish was being organized for their convenience, blacks remained "free to go to any priest or church they may prefer, and the priest called on should hear them." Although he dropped the idea of a special diocesan office devoted to black Catholics, Spalding asked Propaganda officials to help him obtain missionary priests to serve the black community.[50]

The establishment of a separate black church was already well underway in Washington. Beginning in 1862, Father White had sponsored separate services and a school for black parishioners at St. Matthew's. In 1864 the parish obtained President Lincoln's permission to hold a Fourth of July festival on the White House grounds to raise money for a chapel in honor of Blessed Martin de Porres. The entertainment, which President and Mrs. Lincoln attended, netted $1,200 and led to construction of a two-story combined church and school on Fifteenth between L and M Streets.[51] Although free to attend any church, black parishioners from the tier of five northwest parishes were expected to use the new black parish. (Those in southeast would continue to attend segregated services at St. Peter's until the organiza-

---

from the Civil War to the Third Plenary Council of Baltimore (1865–1884)," (Doctoral dissertation, Pontifical Gregorian University, 1968) and Stephen J. Ochs, *Desegregating the Altar: The Josephites and the Struggle for Black Priests, 1871–1960* (Baton Rouge: Louisiana State University Press, 1990), 9, 38–44.

50. Spalding's directive was published in a ltr., Vicar-General Thomas Foley to Felix Barotti, 22 Aug 1868, quoted in Foley, "The Catholic Church and the Washington Negro," 60. The first of these missionaries, Barotti was assigned to Blessed Martin de Porres in 1868. Practically all priests associated with black parishes in the nineteenth century were foreign missionaries. See John P. Kirrane, "The Establishment of Negro Parishes and the Coming of the Josephites, 1863–1871" (Master's thesis, The Catholic University of America, 1932), 37.

51. Kirrane's "The Establishment of Negro Parishes," 17–18, provides a detailed account of the White House fund raising event.

tion of the all-black St. Cyprian's in 1894.) By 1870 Blessed Martin de Porres had registered 2,000 black parishioners gathered from all over northwest Washington; in 1874 it was established as a separate (non-territorial) parish under the patronage of St. Augustine. To the consternation of some nearby pastors, St. Augustine's began to attract many white worshipers because of its convenient location, magnificant choir, and special mass schedule (featuring very late and early masses for the convenience of black workers).[52] In later years prominent pewholders at St. Augustine's included Chief Justice of the United States Edward D. White.

The *Catholic Mirror* liked to boast that every Washington parish counted "large numbers of devout colored Catholics" in its congregation. In fact most of those parishioners were rigidly segregated, as indicated by the galleries reserved for blacks at St. Aloysius, Holy Trinity, and St. Peter's. In contrast to this "minimum participation," to use the sociologist's jargon, St. Patrick's integrated services, a rarity in the city's churches of all denominations in the post–Civil War era, represented "medium participation" of blacks.[53] That is, while attendance at all liturgical functions was totally integrated, blacks did not participate in any of the parish's socio-religious organizations, including its schools and orphanages. Despite the lure of St. Augustine's, African-Americans continued to attend services on F Street, although in diminished numbers. Further indication that some blacks felt welcome at St. Patrick's could be read into the number of black converts baptized at the church in the post-Civil War period. The funeral of one black parishioner, "Good Robert" Herbert, noted for his faithful attendance at daily mass, was reported in the *Catholic Mirror* in 1881.[54]

The newspaper was probably accurate when it reported that the majority of black Catholics preferred going to St. Augustine's "which is distinctly their own." But some pastors used this preference as an excuse to divest themselves of any responsibility for black Catholics in their parishes, routinely referring requests for assistance to St. Augustine's and refusing to let funds collected for their St. Vincent de

52. Jane W. Gemmill, *Notes on Washington, or Six Years at the National Capital* (Washington: Brentano Bros, 1883), 108–9. The change in name from Blessed Martin to St. Augustine was based on a canon law that required persons honored in the name of a church (in distinction to a chapel) to have achieved sainthood.

53. Foley's "The Catholic Church and the Washington Negro," 129–56, provides a useful sociological analysis of race relations in Washington's Catholic churches. The quote from the *Catholic Mirror* appeared on 10 Apr 1870.

54. *Catholic Mirror*, 4 Jun 1881.

Paul Society be used for indigent blacks. The situation worked such a hardship on the slender resources of St. Augustine's that its pastor, Father Felix Barotti, finally asked the archbishop to intervene.[55] There is no evidence that St. Patrick's ever tried to foist its charitable obligations off on others, and in fact Barotti considered Father Walter "his most trusty helper and friend" because of the financial and other support he received from St. Patrick's.[56]

Despite the loss in worshipers to St. Augustine's, Immaculate Conception, and nearby St. Aloysius, St. Patrick's remained a vital and popular place in the postwar era. Increasingly referred to as the "venerable old church," it continued to host great crowds. Some twelve hundred people reportedly received communion at one mass on Christmas Day in 1870, a number that, if accurate, surely must have overwhelmed the capacity of the building. This event marked the end of a decade in which special religious occasions, such as Forty-Hours devotion, Holy Week services, and ceremonies featuring visiting prelates routinely attracted overflow congregations. Especially noteworthy during the later 1860s was the annual parade and celebration marking St. Patrick's Day that always drew great crowds to the church from all parts of the city, including distinguished representatives of the federal and city governments anxious to pay tribute to the Irish.[57]

Reports from that era ascribed the crowds primarily to the zeal of the pastor and his very popular assistant as well as to the sudden jump in the size of the city's Catholic population, including the sharp increase in the number of adult converts. Frequent reference was also made to the large numbers of non-Catholics who habitually attended Catholic services. Washington's flirtation with nativism, it would seem, was over. No doubt to the surprise of plain-spoken pastors like Jacob Walter, the presence of so many members of the diplomatic community in their congregations had made churches like St. Matthew's and St. Patrick's fashionable in the eyes of Washington society. But reporters were also quick to point out that most non-Catholics were attracted to the church for more edifying reasons:

55. Foley, "The Catholic Church and the Washington Negro," 61. The article about black preferences in churches appeared in the *Catholic Mirror* on 28 Jul 1883.

56. So reported by Keane in Walter, *A Memorial Tribute*, 83.

57. The *Catholic Mirror*'s weekly column devoted to church news in Washington is a rich source for parish activities during this period, frequently reporting estimates of attendance and descriptions of special ceremonies. See, for example, editions of 28 Mar 1863, 5 Jan 1867, 28 Mar and 18 Apr 1868, and 1 Jan and 9 Apr 1870.

good preaching, a beautiful and timeless ritual that contrasted with the aridity elsewhere, and the devotion of the clergy.

One such non-Catholic visitor was President Andrew Johnson, who occasionally attended mass at St. Patrick's. Enmeshed in the impeachment proceedings that dominated the national news in 1868, Johnson was particularly attracted by the preaching of Father Bernard McGuire who, the President observed, avoided politics to concentrate instead on the fundamental Christian virtues.[58] Returning from mass in March 1868, Johnson told his secretary how impressed he was by Father McGuire's references to the constant war between the rich and poor and viewed his own situation in similar terms. "I don't know anything more depressing," he told Colonel W. C. Moore, "than for a man to labor for the people and not be understood. It is enough to sour his very soul." The President was impressed to see poor old ladies "in calico and poke bonnet" seated among the city's fashionable families. Such intermingling was rare in Washington's churches, he believed, and it strongly echoed his own devotion to the principles of universal democracy.[59]

The signs of St. Patrick's spiritual vitality must have heartened the ailing Father Walter as he set sail for Rome in December 1867. At the same time he could be excused for any lingering anxiety. Replacing the old church could not be long postponed, although with a reduced congregation, local resources were obviously insufficient to undertake the kind of church envisioned by many parishioners. Plans for a grand edifice must be reconsidered. Of even greater concern to the foresighted pastor was a question that he had just begun to pose to himself: considering demographic changes in the neighborhood, did it make sense at all to erect a new church on F Street? These were, he must have realized, explosive thoughts sure to create turmoil for his congregation in the months ahead.

58. Bernard McGuire was the president of Georgetown College, one in the long line of Jesuits who assisted at St. Patrick's especially, as in this case, during the absence of the pastor overseas. On McGuire's work at St. Patrick's, see Father Owen Campion's article in *Our Sunday Visitor*, 18 Oct 1987.

59. Quoted in "Notes of Colonel W. G. Moore, Private Secretary to President Johnson, 1866–1868," 29 Mar 1868, reprinted in the *American Historical Review* 19 (Oct 1913): 99. See also Robert Winston, *Andrew Johnson: Plebeian and Patriot* (New York: Barnes and Noble, 1928), 475–76. Johnson's interest in the Catholic church extended to his attendance at the closing session of the Second Plenary Council in Baltimore on 21 Oct 1866.

CHAPTER 7

Building A Mighty
Temple

ST. PATRICK'S congregation treated its pastor to a rous-
ing welcome on his first night home from Europe in June
1868. Once again in good health and now showing a hint
of the stoutness that would mark his figure in later life,
Walter tearfully responded to the cheers, speeches, and
songs, assuring his audience that "this evening adds years
to my life."[1] Yet even as he replied to the well wishers, Walter must have been of two minds about the future. On the
one hand there was much to satisfy any pastor. The parish
had survived the tensions of wartime Washington united
and respected and in just five years had built a substantial
rectory, sponsored a new church and school for Immaculate Conception, and raised Carroll Hall. With old anxieties tempered by the knowledge that the parish's minor
indebtedness was manageable within current resources,
Walter could pursue his primary interest, the inauguration
of new city-wide charities, especially ones to alleviate the
distress of the city's elderly poor and orphans.

On the other hand, Walter faced the daunting task of

1. John Keane left a vivid description of the welcoming party in Walter, *A Memorial Tribute*, 75.

building a new church. Even if his stern sense of duty had somehow allowed him to postpone consideration of this onerous and potentially divisive obligation, the physical condition of old St. Patrick's would not. Answering an inquiry from Archbishop Spalding in August 1869, Walter reported that the building was so dilapidated that, after testing the strength of the floors, the Redemptorist fathers had refused to conduct a parish retreat. In some places the flooring was less than a quarter inch thick, and Walter assumed the joists were also in an advanced state of decay. Moreover, the galleries had partially given way during Christmas Mass, so that the flooring in the children's gallery was now being supported by a temporary wooden beam. Walter ascribed the building's problems to age, yet a church just fifty years old, even one constructed in haste and subject to the wear and tear of great crowds, should have been in better condition. Modern experts suggest that a more likely culprit was the poor drainage and underwater streams that remain even today a hazard to building in square 376. At any rate, the condition of the building was public knowledge, and some parishioners refused to enter the church when crowded. Walter considered it imprudent to continue holding services there much longer.[2] Clearly the decision could not be postponed; new accommodations must be found.

A Controversial Decision

Deciding on what and where to build engaged the congregation's energies for many months and provided what sociologist David Fosselman called a clear illustration of the role of sentiment as a determinent in the life of an ecclesiastical institution. Certainly when it came to the parish's fiscal responsibilities and his duties as pastor, Father Walter could never be accused of sentimentality. He had obviously thought long and hard about the new church and concluded, as he bluntly told the archbishop, that it would be impossible to build based solely on contributions raised in Washington. He had personally conducted two subscription drives that netted only about $10,000, which, he cautioned, did not represent cash in hand, but merely promises of future contributions. Even if this amount were collected, he pointed out, it would not pay for the building's foundations. His inescapable

2. Ltr., Walter to Spalding, 28 Aug 1869, 38-P-1, Spalding Papers, AAB. This lengthy letter is the basis for this and succeeding paragraphs. On the cause of the church's decay, see the author's interview with Kenneth Pribanic, copy in SPA.

conclusion: a new church was possible only if the parish sold some of its property.

Walter offered Spalding two options. The first, clearly an opening gambit, called for selling the property fronting on F Street—a transaction Walter estimated would fetch $150,000—and using that money to erect a new church on Tenth Street next to the rectory. What he really wanted was to sell all the church's holdings in square 376 and relocate to the residential center of the parish several blocks to the north and east. The very conditions that made F Street property so valuable, he argued, also made it undesirable as a site for a church. Exaggerating a bit to make his point, he classified F Street as a business region, adding that just one square south (E Street between Ninth and Tenth) now had "stores, market house, lumber yards, saw-mills, and houses of ill-fame. Until Spalding decided on the location, Walter recommended that the parish tear down the old church and refit Carroll Hall, which, with the addition of pews and a small sacristy, would be sufficient for current needs.

Walter's radical proposals about location of the new church probably struck Spalding as just one more example of the pastor's impulsiveness. He could not make a decision, he told Walter, until he had what he called "definite facts and opinions based on facts." He wanted the matter thoroughly discussed by the parishioners, and he told Walter to secure their vote on the following questions: (1) Is it expedient to tear the old church down, sell the F Street lots, and relocate on Tenth Street?; and (2) If the decision is made to destroy the old church, should the property in square 376 be sold and a new site sought, and, if so, where and at what cost?[3] Walter dutifully invited sixty-five "principal members" of the congregation to meet at Carroll Hall on September 5 to consider the archbishop's questions. With the pastor as chairman, Father Keane served as recording secretary. His record of this and a subsequent meeting a week later provides a glimpse of individual members laymen at stage center in the drama.[4]

The general discussion that followed the pastor's summary of his

3. Ltr, Spalding to Walter, 28 Aug 1869, Spalding Letterbook, Spalding Papers, AAB.

4. Keane's notes are preserved in "Minutes of the Meeting of the Principal Members of St. Patrick's Congregation," 5 Sep 69, 38-P-2, Spalding Papers, AAB. The *National Republican*, 13 Sep 1869, provided a lengthy account of both meetings and included an especially detailed summary of the second meeting held on 12 September. Keane included the newspaper account along with his own minutes in his report to the archbishop. The following paragraphs are based on these documents.

views indicated that, despite their reputations as successful men of the world, these parishioners were prone to vote with their hearts. One group championed Walter's proposal to build on Tenth Street, but, in deference to the parish's historic association with the F Street site and apparently in total disregard for the fiscal implications of their stand, demanded that at least some part of the original property on F Street be used for the new church. Others, betraying their strong allegience to the old idea of a great metropolitan cathedral, argued that only the sale of all the parish's downtown property could support the congregation's determination to build such a church. They pictured the Tenth Street site as a dark, narrow place that would soon be squeezed between the rectory on one side and stores on the other. They rejected it as an inadequate setting for the magnificent architecture they envisioned.

The latter arguments carried the day. By a vote of twenty-two to thirteen the group recommended vacating square 376 altogether. Before Father Walter could enjoy his victory, however, the opposition won a week's postponement before final consideration of the issue. In the interim, each side gathered reinforcements so that on the following Sunday more than one hundred men assembled in Carroll Hall to renew the debate.

The traditionalists, led by William H. Ward, opened the discussion. Ward, who had served as executor of Father Matthews's will, seemed to enjoy being cast in the role of defender of the old pastor's policies. He rejected Walter's claim that commercial establishments were driving the parishioners northward away from the church. Ignoring the heart of the pastor's argument, he asserted that no house in the parish was devoted exclusively to business and predicted that a careful survey would show a majority of the people in the area still lived south of F Street. The innovators, to coin a name for those pushing for a new church in a new neighborhood, countered by pointing out that people in the northern reaches of the parish felt so isolated from St. Patrick's that they had taken to attending other churches. They also produced a building contractor who testified that the Tenth Street site was so narrow that any church raised there would be devoid of light and air.

The traditionalists offered a counterproposal. They wanted to repair the old church, replacing its floors and adding masonry supports to assure its solidity, and then to remodel the building in the Gothic style. They estimated that for no more than $10,000 the parish could remodel the present structure so that it would accommodate fourteen hundred worshipers, sufficient space for any foreseeable needs, and, with suitable landscaping of the grounds, provide a convenient and beautiful place of worship. Reflecting the sentiments of this group, Ward asserted that he would never consent to selling even one inch of the property. He reminded the audience that Father Matthews had desired and the people expected that a magnificent church would one day be erected on the present site through contributions from Catholics all over the nation. Since Archbishop Spalding had rejected that idea, the parishioners should accept remodeling as a means of holding on to the property until the original plan could be reconsidered.

The motion was rejected by a vote of twenty-three to eighteen, although the potency of this appeal to tradition can be deduced from the fact that some families with deep roots in the parish, names like Ellis, Masi, Callan, Galt, and Bogus, supported the motion. While supporters of the status quo failed to carry the meeting, they were able to defeat the next motion—to sell the F Street lots and build around the corner on Tenth Street—by a vote of twenty-six to six. By then positions had hardened. Before considering the final motion—to sell all the land in square 376 and move elsewhere—the traditionalists demanded that the question be submitted in writing to the individual pewholders. In answer to the argument that those who had failed to attend either meeting were obviously not interested and therefore undeserving of consideration, they pointed out that technicalities in Caffry's deed would require court supervision of any sale and that the courts would demand just such a survey. William Ward again appealed to the sentiments of the group, reiterating his hope that the property could be retained until a national drive for a "splendid" church could be held. When reminded by Father Walter that the archbishop had rejected such a scheme, Ward shocked the gathering by replying that he hoped the archbishop "will change his mind, or have a successor."

The next vote, on the sale of the entire property, saw those wanting to leave square 376 losing to the traditionalists eighteen to twenty. The committee had rejected all three motions, a state of affairs that prompted Father Walter to remark:

Well, gentlemen, if these views are to be acted upon, good bye to the idea of a new church, for at least fifty years to come. The people of this parish have already been talking about it for about that length of time, and will be likely to spend as much longer in considering it.

Walter's frustrated reaction to enfolding events found a sympathetic audience in at least one member of the opposition. Thomas Sullivan announced that he was changing his vote against relocation. He was now convinced, he said, that without selling all its holdings, the parish would never get a new church. Declaring the old church "an eye-sore to the city and a disgrace to the people of the parish," he accused the long-time parishioners, "men who ought naturally to be relied upon for the furtherance of this so-long-desired object," of blindly support- ing the status quo. When interrupted by Seraphim Masi, who sug- gested that Sullivan should go elsewhere if the old church displeased him, Sullivan brushed aside what he called "the old-fogy conservatism manifested by the 'oldest inhabitants' of the parish" and said he was voting for "real progress" and a "fitting church." Sullivan's change of heart resulted in a tie vote in regard to leaving square 376 altogether.

Cooler heads finally prevailed, and the meeting adjourned with the understanding that the archbishop would be informed of the parish's deeply divided views. Father Keane summarized these for Spalding: all opposed to selling the church's property saw repair of the old church as the only solution; all who wanted a new church immediately saw the sale of the property as the only solution. Conspicuously absent from his summary was any mention of the alternative proposal to build on Tenth Street. Keane concluded his lengthy summary with the pious but certainly wry comment that all anxiously awaited Spalding's decision.

This attempt at extending the democratic process to ecclesiastical affairs produced very little light but much heat and ended badly for the archbishop. With lines now firmly drawn between the opposing sides and tempers considerably frayed, any decision on his part was guaranteed to offend half the parish. Apparently unsure of how to pro- ceed, Spalding actually contradicted himself several times. At first he ignored the advice of the pastor and his allies and came down firmly on the side of tradition. Because he feared that selling the site of the old church would create an outcry "injurious to the undertaking & to Religion," he directed that the new building be raised on the corner of Tenth and F Streets, extending no more than sixty feet along its F Street front. The remaining 185 feet along F could be sold later to fin- ish the church and pay off the debt, but he wanted to keep this possi- bility secret because its premature disclosure could "create excite- ment" and depress contributions.[5]

5. Ltr., Spalding to Walter, 22 Sep 1869, Spalding Letterbook, Spalding Papers, AAB.

Two weeks later he reversed himself. "After mature reflection," he decided that the new church should be situated on the exact site of the old, that is, halfway down F Street. Presumably the rest of the property could be considered available for future sale. This time Spalding provided some consolation for a frustrated pastor by raising the cost ceiling on the project to a more practical $150,000. On the other hand, in a paragraph meant to end the decades-long discussion about a great metropolitan church supported by a national subscription drive, he added:

The Congregation should understand that, like all others in the country, they must rely *upon themselves* to build their Church, which is to progress only in proportion to the means available. While so many hundreds of Catholic congregations in the country, including several in Washington, have built their own churches, it would be a shame for old St. Patrick's to go begging through the country, at the imminent risk of receiving more reproaches than contributions. Let them, then, be independent, ingenious, & build such a church as will accommodate their children & be a credit to them.[6]

In the tumultuous decade ahead Walter would repeatedly refer to this letter, which he considered an episcopal prohibition against indebtedness. Yet one less dedicated to fiscal conservatism might readily interpret Spalding's "in proportion to the means available" as considerably less than a total ban on church debt. After all, Spalding himself had mentioned selling property at a later date to pay off the debt, and several other congregations in Washington were in the midst of ambitious building programs which left them with sizable debts that did not incur any special notice from Baltimore. More likely, Spalding was trying to curb the parish's old ambition for erecting some kind of monumental edifice and persuade them to settle for a more modest parish church. Walter preferred to use the archbishop's words to support his determination to proceed on a pay-as-you go basis. He would endure much complaint and criticism over the years as construction of the much-desired church repeatedly ground to a halt for lack of funds. On each occasion he would refer to his directive "in writing" that forbade borrowing.

In the months that followed, this self-imposed pay-as-you-go policy ruled at St. Patrick's. Although the *Mirror* announced in June 1870 that "active measures are in contemplation" for a handsome and commodious new church, in fact it would be more than two years before

6. Ltr., Spalding to Walter, 7 Oct 1869, Spalding Letterbook, Spalding Papers, AAB.

building would even begin.[7] Meanwhile Walter set about transforming Carroll Hall into a temporary church as the modest funds subscribed for the new building trickled in. A sacristy was built onto the rear of the hall and 178 pews installed (twenty more than were contained in the old church). As customary, these were rented to parishioners at rates ranging from five to fifty dollars per year. Indicative of changes in diocesan discipline since Kenrick's time, the parish announced that a grand concert would be staged in the newly furnished temporary church to help defray the expenses of the renovation.

The last Mass in the old church was celebrated at the end of June 1870. By then those who had opposed the change had been fully informed about the dangerous condition of the old building, and, as the *Mirror* noted, now saw the wisdom of averting a possible calamity. Everyone was talking about the recent disaster that occurred when a church collapsed in Richmond, probably aware that St. Patrick's itself had recently suffered a brief but dangerous fire.[8]

The remodeled Carroll Hall proved sufficient to accommodate the crowds who came to hear Father Keane's discourse on the newly proclaimed doctrine of papal infallability in the wake of the First Vatican Council in September 1870. As a temporary church, however, it did not take part in the city-wide demonstration that welcomed the archbishop back from Rome in November. Catholic churches were illuminated for that occasion, and 30,000 people, including President Ulysses S. Grant, welcomed Spalding and paraded in protest of the Italian army's seizure of Rome. To Spalding's gratification, members of the vast gathering all signed a document protesting the action that left the Pope a virtual prisoner in the Vatican.[9] The archbishop as usual stayed at St. Patrick's during this visit. It seems likely that during his leisure hours he discussed plans for the new church with the pastor and inspected the site for himself. At any rate, at about this time he once again changed his mind and ordered that the new church be located next to the rectory on Tenth Street.

It also appears that shortly after Spalding's visit, Walter commissioned Laurence J. O'Connor to design the new church. O'Connor was a professional architect who had studied in Europe, where he had

7. *Catholic Mirror,* 18 Jun 1870.

8. In a dramatic moment during Holy Thursday services, Walter rescued the host and sacred vessels before the men in the congregation managed to douse the flames. See *Catholic Mirror,* 23 Apr and 2 Jul 1870.

9. Baltimore Journal of Martin John Spalding, p. 54, Spalding Papers, AAB. See also *Catholic Mirror,* 3 Dec 1870, *Star,* 25 Nov 1870, and Spalding, *Premier See,* 204.

been a pupil of the noted English architect Augustus Pugin, the father of the Gothic revival movement and designer of the remodeled Parliament buildings in London. O'Connor spent the early part of his career in pre–Civil War Washington, where he lived and worked at his home and office at 236 I Street, N.W., and no doubt made himself known to St. Patrick's pastor and parishioners. By the time he started work on the new church, he was established in New York, where during a four-year period in the early 1870s he designed four noteworthy Catholic edifices. Constructed of different materials and varying in many external features, the four churches remain even today splendid examples of the Victorian Gothic revival that dominated church architecture in the United States for more than a century.[10]

Building the new church on any part of square 376 required clearing away the old building and the graveyard that surrounded it. The exhumations associated with the latter precipated a ceremony that obviously appealed to a congregation with strong attachments to parish traditions. Father Matthews's coffin was dug up and opened on Halloween to reveal a remarkedly preserved body that Walter placed in a new coffin and installed on a catafalque before the altar in Carroll Hall. On All Souls Day a special mass was celebrated before "a surging mass of people" who had hoped (in vain) for a last glimpse of the beloved old patriarch.[11]

After the remains of the early parishioners were reinterred in Mt. Olivet, the church they had built was razed. Some effort was made to assuage the feelings of the older members of the congregation. Descriptions of the new church always included the highly dubious claim that "all the material in the old church will be used" in the concrete foundations of the new. Walter subsequently faced considerable opposition when he sent the bricks, windows, and other parts of the exterior walls still considered useful to Father Barotti for the new St. Au-

10. In addition to St. Patrick's his churches include: St. Agnes, New York City; Assumption, Morristown, New Jersey; and St. Mary's (now the cathedral), Syracuse, New York. Despite his accomplishments, O'Connor remains an obscure figure. He worked in Baltimore during the Civil War and came recommended by Archbishop Kenrick and other religious and business leaders. He soon moved to New York, where he remained active until 1899. The above information is based on city directories, a newspaper advertisement (*Catholic Mirror*, 29 Sep 1860), and the records and correspondence from the archives of Assumption Church and St. Mary's cathedral, the latter material provided by Mary Jo Allen, a member of the cathedral restoration committee, and Carl Roesch, the archivist of the Diocese of Syracuse.

11. Anna H. Dorsey, "Recollections of Old St. Patrick's Church," *Sunday Morning Chronicle*, Sep 1873, and *Catholic Mirror*, 11 Nov 1871. The parish later commissioned the

gustine's then abuilding.[12] Later commenting on the influence of the traditionalists in the congregation during this admittedly traumatic period, Walter remembered that some parishioners wanted the old bricks bonded into large blocks and put in the new building; others demanded that the new church be made entirely from parts of the old. With a trace of his old testiness, Walter told them that, considering the strength of their veneration for the old building, they would be better off if they simply preserved the whole thing in alcohol.[13]

In December 1871, the pastor announced that construction would commence in the spring, using the occasion to kick off yet another fund drive. The highlight of this effort was a week-long fair at the Odd Fellows Hall. Despite an appeal to "every true hearted Catholic in Washington who feels pride in the history of the old parish" and the gaudy presence of the Knights of St. Patrick's and the Governor's Mounted Guard in full uniform, the fair netted a disappointing $4,000. The *Mirror* blamed the poor showing on the weather and competition from the circus. It also warned its readers that the sum collected amounted to scarcely one-fiftieth of the total needed for the new church and encouraged their further generosity.[14]

Archbishop Spalding's death in February 1872 led to a further delay in the cornerstone-laying ceremony, but by then Walter considered funds sufficient to commence putting in the foundations. Following O'Connor's concept, the contractor set the supports for a structure 169 feet in length (exceeding the 150 foot maximum set by Spalding in 1869) with a width of 75 feet on the west front (Tenth Street) and 86 feet at the transepts. The foundations were deep enough to support a planned two-hundred foot high central steeple and spire on the west front with smaller turrets at the outer edges. In its detailed, page-one description of the new building, the *Star* reviewed the debate over the location of the new church and concluded that the site chosen would allow the congregation to avoid the noise of vehicles on busy F Street's stone paving.[15]

---

impressive monument that now stands over Matthews's grave in Mt. Olivet. See *Catholic Mirror*, 2 Aug 1878.

12. St. Patrick's donated ten thousand bricks along with a large amount of loaned materials which St. Augustine's was expected to repay upon demand. In 1881 Walter cancelled the debt. See ltr., Walter to Gibbons, 27 Aug 1881, 76-W-1, Gibbons Papers, AAB.

13. From interview with Walter quoted in the *National Republican*, 26 Oct 1884, copy in the Toner Collection, LC.

14. *Catholic Mirror*, 22 Apr 1872. See also, same source, 9 Dec 1871 and 6 Apr 1872.

15. *Star*, 18 Nov 1871.

Such consolations failed to still the opposition, and soon after Spalding's successor, James Roosevelt Bayley, was installed as the eighth archbishop, it launched one last effort to locate the new church on or near the site of the old. Once again William Ward served as spokesman. Charging that Walter had timed the construction of the new foundations to preclude the new bishop's participation in the decision, Ward rehashed all the old arguments and asked Bayley to review the matter. He dwelt at length on the rumored sale of the F Street property, which, he warned, would place any church on Tenth Street "virtually in the back-yards of business houses." Ward and his allies charged that the new church would only add to the hardship of an already over-burdened parish and blamed what they called the pastor's high-handed insistence on a new building for the loss of parishioners and the indifference of the congregation to the frequent fairs, subscription drives, and sermons appealing for contributions.[16]

Bayley was not about to become involved in the protracted controversy. His predecessor approved the move to Tenth Street, and, he told the petitioners, "I cannot and will not interfere." Bayley's response, followed by his participation in the cornerstone laying on November 3, 1872, merely made official what was already obvious.[17] The massive foundations for the new church were in the ground, and the debate was over. The lengthy argument concerning the size and site of the new St. Patrick's had ended in compromise, which, like most such solutions, left many expectations unfulfilled. The limits imposed on size and cost and Spalding's rejection of a move away from square 376 stilled forever the old dream of a great national church. The decision to build on Tenth Street also ended the dream of the traditionalists to memorialize the exact site of the "cradle of Catholicity" in Washington.[18]

Although their enthusiasm was muted, many parishioners had by 1872 come to see some validity in the Tenth Street compromise. The street still retained a quiet, dignified air, and the new church would have a pleasant prospect across to the handsome buildings of St. Vincent's and well-tended residences with their beautiful gardens. The fu-

16. Ltr., Ward to Bayley, 15 Oct 1872, 43A-Q-8, Bayley Papers, AAB.

17. Episcopal Diary of Archbishop Bayley, 3 Nov 1872. The quote is from a note attached to ltr., Ward to Bayley, 15 Oct 1872, 43A-Q-8; both in Bayley Papers, AAB.

18. The expression "cradle of Catholicity" originated with Archbishop Bayley. See Sister M. Hildegarde Yeager, "The Life of James Roosevelt Bayley, First Bishop of Newark and Eighth Archbishop of Baltimore, 1814–1877" (Ph.D. dissertation, The Catholic University of America, 1947), 353.

ture of the F Street lots that would abut the building on the south was uncertain, but many who lacked Father Walter's foresight were free to imagine that section of the property remaining indefinitely a handsome, manicured lawn. In short, in common with most groups, a growing majority in the congregation judged only current conditions and took little thought for the changes occuring in the city's ecology. The archbishop's decision won general acceptance because, though the site he chose was not particularly convenient, the neighborhood appeared stable.

Curiously, only the pastor who had authored the Tenth Street compromise and his allies who had wanted to leave the area altogether seemed to grasp the fact that a radical transformation was soon in store for the neighborhood. They understood, even if the majority of their fellow-parishioners did not, that the decision to remain in Square 376 dictated a different future for the parish. It remained to be seen whether this future would threaten the very existence of the parish or if somehow St. Patrick's could accommodate to the changes and harness the new realities in its interest.

A Decade of Depression

The new archbishop put a serious damper on the long-awaited cornerstone festivities in advance of his arrival in Washington. James Roosevelt Bayley, convert, nephew of St. Elizabeth Seton, and son of wealthy American aristocrats, was embarrassed by the noisy public displays put on by the rapidly proliferating Catholic societies and so enjoyed by the immigrant church. He went so far as to express the hope that parades on St. Patrick's Day would be abolished! Even before such an abomination was expressed, however, he warned Father Walter on the eve of his first official visit that, while everything should be "bright and grand in and about the church itself," he wanted no parades and no "noise of drums and trumpets and crowds in the streets."[19]

It was Walter's unenviable job to tell the representatives of the various local Hibernian branches, along with some fifteen temperance, benevolent, and beneficial societies (both white and black branches), including the Spalding Temperance Guards, Knights of St. Peter, Blessed Martin's Education Society, St. Benedict's Society (Colored), St. Joseph's Beneficial Society, and St. Matthew's Catholic Association,

19. Ltr., Bayley to Walter, n.d., quoted in *Catholic Mirror*, 2 Nov 1872.

that a solemn procession with no music was to replace the planned parade. Bayley expressed himself satisfied with the admirable sermons and crowds at the ceremony, but the *Mirror* probably more accurately reflected the reaction of the congregation when it noted that the affair "lacked the enthusiasm that drum and fife would have imparted."[20]

It would take more than the enthusium occasioned by drums and fifes to solve the project's money problems. Laying the foundations had absorbed all the funds collected to date, and Walter had found it necessary to suspend all building in mid-August. Warning that the pastor understood a pay-as-you-go policy to mean absolutely no indebtedness, the *Mirror* quoted Walter: "If the people want a new church, they will have to supply the funds as the work progresses." He hoped that money collected during the winter would allow resumption of building in the spring, "if not, it will stand as is."[21] Walter's first financial report after laying the cornerstone was discouraging. The 1872 campaign represented the third attempt in twenty-five years to build a new church, he told Bayley, and so far subscriptions amounted to just $1,796, the greater part of which was a single legacy. The $4,000 netted at the well-advertised fair was less than half of what was anticipated, and a week-long festival had brought in little more than $300. The parish received some $300 from the sale of lumber from the old church and just a little more than that from the collection taken up at the cornerstone laying. Walter had just received from the parish temperance society the proceeds of their festival—a total of $30.89. These dismal figures proved to Walter "how utterly impossible for me it is to rely on the contributions of these people." If it were not for the F Street property held in reserve, he would never, he asserted, have agreed "to lay a stone upon stone."[22]

Actually, thinking that sale of the F Street property could bail the parish out of its financial woes or that renewed appeals for contributions would add significant amounts to the building fund was especially inappropriate after September 1873, when a panic in the nation's banking system ushered in a profound economic depression that brought business to a halt in Washington as elsewhere. As the number of unemployed grew, more pressing demands on parish charity brought contributions to the building fund to a halt. The purposeful

20. *Catholic Mirror*, 9 Nov 1872. For the participating societies and a summary of the day's activities, see Smith's *History of St. Patrick's*, 48–49. Bayley's reaction to the event was recorded in his Episcopal Diary, p. 2, AAB. See also Spalding, *Premier See*, 219.

21. *Catholic Mirror*, 3 Aug 1872.

22. Annual Reports of Churches, St. Patrick's, Washington, 1872, AAB.

activity of the previous summer quickly faded into memory, when, except for a few brief spurts of activity, construction ceased altogether. Carpenters erected a high board fence around the building site. For more than a decade this green wall would serve to shield the bare, weather-beaten foundations and partially raised walls of the new building from public view, just as it came to symbolize to the public the parish's failure to achieve its long-cherished dream.

The fortunes of St. Patrick's church have always been closely linked to those of the city it served, but perhaps never more so than during the 1870s. That decade proved to be one of considerable turmoil and change in Washington, one that saw the capital physically transformed, its government radically reorganized, and most of its citizens financially strapped.[23] The Civil War and the period of reconstruction that followed had added greatly to the power and size of the federal government. It had also stimulated a strong demand for public improvements and urban conveniences considered commensurate with the new image of Washington as the capital of an emerging world power. Once again, frustrated federal officials began to question the ability of local authorities to cope with the challenge and, when the long-overdue renewal of the city charter was discussed in Congress, took the occasion to re-introduce the possibility of moving the capital. Congressmen from all parts of the republic found themselves in rare agreement when they complained about the city's filthy, unpaved streets where animals ran wild, its open sewers, the multitude of its homeless and destitute beggars, and the rise in crime and municipal debt. As usual they lambasted the local government for failures for which, as the city's largest landowner, they shared the blame.

Although it meant surrendering a major portion of the home rule they had enjoyed for decades, most voters joined in the public celebration when Congress passed the District Territorial Act in 1871. The law abolished the old municipal government and finally brought Washington, Georgetown, and the County (those rapidly growing sections of the district north of the old city boundary) under a single territorial form of government. Control of the new territory fell to a presidentially-appointed governor and council, while local voters elected a lower house of the legislature and a non-voting representative in Congress. Washingtonians apparently considered loss of home rule a small price to pay for ending the threat of transferring the government else-

23. Green's *Washington*, 1:339–400 and 2:2–12, offers a comprehensive account of the momentous changes in Washington during the 1870s.

where, eliminating the costly duplication of municipal services, and ensuring that the city would be controlled by prominent men rather than what they called a rag-tag band of carpetbaggers. Race also played a part. Most white residents were willing to surrender local control to the national government rather than share it with their black neighbors.

Largely ignored in the general euphoria was the potential for fiscal chaos inherent in the new municipal orgnization. Although Congress had pledged to contribute to necessary public improvements, federal property remained tax exempt and the costly civil works projects were controlled by a federally-appointed board of public works, whose ability to incur debt and assess taxes on property owners went largely unsupervised. In the end it was the unbridled extravagance of this board, personified by its director, the single-minded visionary and swashbuckling gambler Alexander "Boss" Shepherd, that bankrupted the city and financially stunned many of its citizens even as it transformed Washington into the beautiful, nationally acclaimed capital envisioned by L'Enfant eighty years before.

Boss Shepherd was a native Washingtonian determined to realize L'Enfant's plan overnight while providing residents with those urban amenities necessary in any modern capital. He found it easy to cajole the government into approving the necessary bond issues and to tax property owners for one-third of the cost associated with neighborhood improvements. The results were spectacular. In less than three years Shepherd graded three hundred miles of streets, leveling hills and filling in depressions so that the visual aspects planned by L'Enfant might be realized. He brought water mains to all parts of the city, installed a sewerage system that included the costly task of covering over Tiber Creek and filling in the old Washington Canal near the Mall. Streets in the center city and avenues out to the District lines were paved, 128 miles of sidewalk built, city lighting installed throughout the residential areas, and 60,000 trees planted. Parks and circles were landscaped with trees, fountains, and statuary. Although much remained to be done (some of the new wood paving began to deteriorate before the job was completed and some remote parts of town were left largely unimproved), the boundless energy of Boss Shepherd had produced a general transformation that pleased everyone.

Then the bills came due. Despite special assessments on property owners, confiscating tax increases, and government-approved bonds that tripled early debt estimates, the city went bankrupt in 1873, forcing the federal government to step in. It abolished the territorial government—and Shepherd's base of power—and instituted emergency measures to ease the crisis. Unfortunately, Washington's fiscal disaster coincided with the onset of one of the nation's severest depressions. While the continued flow of federal salaries in the region and the government's payment of back wages to those working on the public improvment projects staved off the worst initially, by 1874 local workers' wages were down to a dollar a day. The Navy Yard and other major employers had laid off most of their workers, and the number of federal clerks had shrunk. Soon Washington was sharing with the rest of the nation the brunt of hard times. The relief rolls grew as did the incidents of public begging and homelessness. Much of middle class Washington was left in desperate straits. Everywhere there was unemployment, depression, and despair.

The failure of the territorial government stemming from the unchecked extravagances of the Shepherd regime convinced Congress that its close control of city affairs was warranted. In the Organic Act of 1878 it established a commission form of government, which invested all power (except a separately-appointed judiciary) in a three-man commission appointed by the President, including two civilians and an officer from the U.S. Army Corps of Engineers. This commission reported yearly to the appropriate congressional committees, which approved the city budget and otherwise controlled all District affairs. In exchange for a system of taxation without representation, the city won the federal government's pledge to underwrite one-half its annual budget. A chastened electorate accepted the new regime without complaint, and the commissioners, possessed of autocratic powers over the fortunes of all residents, would continue to run the city for nearly a century. Meanwhile in Congress, the long-held impression that local citizens were a fiscally irresponsible lot incapable of controlling their own destinies gained strength.

Many residents survived the last years of the long depression on local charity, government relief, and a trickle of public works projects. Only at the end of the 1870s did business start to revive and real estate begin a modest boom. The upswing was clearly visible on F Street. Between the Treasury and Judiciary Square the street had become an almost unbroken row of office buildings and stores interspersed with livery stables. Still, the north-south numbered streets in the neighborhood retained their residential character. Imposing Victorian dwellings along Sixth Street still represented one of the city's most fashionable neighborhoods, rivaling the emerging prestige of Connecticut Avenue. Father Walter's concern over the evolving character of F

Street could no longer be dismissed, but for a while at least the parish would hold its own against the changes.

Financing the New Church

Although William Ward and his allies claimed that the congregation's failure to raise money for the new church was the result of a general opposition to the Tenth Street site, it is more likely that the parishioners, along with most of their neighbors, were suffering from the squeeze of rising taxes imposed by an extravagant city government and the unemployment and lowered wages caused by the national depression. Moreover, many worthy charities were competing for support as the parish's various organizations struggled to alleviate the suffering of those worst hit by the depression.[24] Whatever the exact cause, one failure followed upon another as successive appeals for contributions to the building fund went largely ignored.

Building drives, including a homey strawberry festival in 1873, Father Keane's popular illustrated lecture series on his European trip, and even a grand parish fair in early 1875, netted very little cash. After more than two years of appeals, only some $20,000 was collected, enough to raise the outer walls twenty feet, but with nothing left over to pay for most of ten granite columns, a major architectual focus of the new church and its most costly feature. Imported from Aberdeen, Scotland, these imposing granite shafts, rising out of huge stone bases, were designed to support the gothic vaults of the ceiling. Despite repeated assurances in the press in early 1875 that the roof would be in place "next year," Father Walter was forced to report in December that until another $50,000 was collected, all work must cease.[25]

Walter's announcement generated yet another flurry of effort. The congregation divided the parish into districts and assigned collectors to receive subscribers' monthly payments to yet another building fund. It also sponsored another parish fair, in anticipation of which Father Keane ruefully noted that "not a stone had been added to the new church building for the past eighteen months."[26] These parish fairs were elaborate productions featuring the sale of all sorts of goods

24. The work of St. Patrick's charitable organizations during this period will be discussed in the next chapter.

25. Collecting for the new church was carefully followed in the *Catholic Mirror*. See, for example, 24 May and 8 Nov 1783; 6 Feb, 27 Mar, and 24 Apr 1875. For Walter's announcement see same source, 4 Dec 1875.

26. Quoted in the *Catholic Mirror*, 9 Dec 1876.

and services, together with dances, musicales, and games of chance (the ubiquitous "wheel of fortune"). Usually lasting two weeks in rented quarters like the nearby Masonic Temple, they often even boasted publication of a daily newpaper, which contained scores of advertisements, letters, and reports on a variety of religious and historical subjects, along with pertinent information concerning what was being sold at the various booths. The papers, written in a lively style and featuring articles on the day-to-day success of the event and news about the participants, were not at times above a genteel sort of social blackmail. It was not unusual, when the fair was poorly attended, to find its journal publishing stern editorials on the duties of the rich and warnings that the paper was about to publish the names of prominent parishioners who failed to attend the festivities.[27]

Unfortunately such efforts generated little money. The press reported that the 1875 fair was lightly attended "owing to the hard times and extremely cold weather," and in the wake of the 1876 social, Walter reported that total parish receipts had actually declined a thousand dollars over the previous year. As if to underscore the lack of progress, Walter had the parish bell, rescued from the old church and lately ensconced on the rectory lawn, placed on the partially raised northwest wall of the new church. There it would remain for more than six years, another reminder of the unfulfilled dream, calling people to Mass in Carroll Hall and signaling national events, such as the assassination of President James A. Garfield in 1881.

As years passed, cynicism over the project grew. In May 1878 the *Mirror* reported that St. Patrick's (as it now routinely called Carroll Hall) was about to undergo extensive remodeling with the addition of new frescoes and doorways and a refurbishing of its pews. Such activity, the paper added, "seems to indicate something more than the *temporary* occupation of the building as a church for the Catholics of that parish."[28] Walter quickly denied that what he called necessary renovations implied an indefinite residency in the hall. He took the occasion to provide the public with a complete history of the property dispute and to defend his proposal to relocate out of square 376.

27. These fair journals, containing articles by John Keane, Maurice F. Egan, the associate editor of *Freeman's Journal,* and such prominent Washingtonians as Madclaine Dahlgren, Dr. Thomas E. McArdle, and Maj. Edmond Mallett, provide a special insight into the interests and aspirations of Washington Catholics in the late nineteenth century. A collection of these journals is on file in the Rare Books and Special Collections, CUA Library.

28. *Catholic Mirror,* 11 (source of quotation) and 25 May 1878.

For nine years Walter had followed Archbishop Spalding's admonition to avoid discussing property sales lest such talk inhibit donations, but with donations at an all-time low, he decided that it was appropriate to raise the subject. In what sounded like the opening round in a fight to sell the hallowed F Street lots, he recalled that some years before, the church was forced to reject an offer of $175,000 from New York business interests because of the opposition of older members of the congregation "who at their stage of life would have been more spiritually benefitted by thinking of other things." In the current depression no such profitable offers were being made, but serving notice on the sentimental, and with perhaps a sidelong glance at his superior in Baltimore, Walter added that, "contrary to general opinion," the property could be sold at any time thought proper.[29] That time was obviously not yet at hand, and the dreary business of trying to raise money dragged on, a source of profound discouragement to the parish and the cause of considerable irritation to the pastor.

Through most of this period Walter's pessimism about the parish's future was tempered by the genial personality of his able assistant, John Keane. A close personal friendship had grown up between the always sunny, resourceful Keane and the short-tempered Walter, so it came as an especially hard blow to the latter when in June 1878 the Pope chose Keane to be the fifth bishop of Richmond. In the aftermath of that move the parish increasingly came to feel the sting of its pastor's anxiety. Walter was convinced that, despite the depression, the people could do more to support the church. Long before news of Keane's selection was known, he had warned the parish that, unless the many vacant pews were rented and the overdue payments on the rest were quickly forthcoming, he would tell the archbishop that St. Patrick's was incapable of supporting two priests and so his popular assistant would have to go. When this threat proved unavailing, he announced that unrented pews would henceforth remain locked during Sunday mass, deeming the move "imperative" if the parish was going to continue to support two priests.[30]

Only after Keane's departure, an incident entirely unsought and greatly lamented by Walter, did he carry out his threat. He bluntly informed the new archbishop, James Gibbons, that the parish could no longer afford two priests and that Keane's successor, Ludovic A. Mor-

29. Walter's comments were delivered from the pulpit on Sunday, 19 May 1878, and reported extensively in the *Catholic Mirror* on 25 May 1878.

30. These threats were fully aired in the pages of the *Catholic Mirror*. See for example 25 Aug and 29 Dec 1877.

gan, for whom Walter had nothing but praise, should be reassigned elsewhere. Gibbons was so astonished that he asked Walter straight out if he had some other motive for this "extraordinary request." For his pains Gibbons received a touch of that old asperity only too familiar to his predecessors:

I have no other motive than the statement that I have made. If I have any fault it is my frankness. I have always acted thus with your predecessors & I hope that you will allow me the same privilege. . . . If I had any other motive no matter what that might be you would be the first to know it. This has always been my character & I hope to maintain the same till I die.

Walter went on to paint a picture of a parish in grave trouble. He estimated that only fifteen hundred people, less than half those on the parish roles, attended St. Patrick's regularly, while the majority favored St. Aloysius and other nearby parishes. The neighborhood was rapidly becoming a business district, prompting many of the more affluent parishioners to move to better locations. Meanwhile, Catholic laborers had been driven away after losing out to the neighborhood's growing black population in the fierce competition for scarce jobs. He blamed it all on Spalding's refusal to move the church to the eastern part of the parish. He had begun the new building under protest, he claimed, and every day matters were growing worse. With two-thirds of his pews either vacant or nonpaying, he was concerned about notes coming due.[31]

Despite Walter's protestations, Gibbons was right to question the pastor about his motives. No one familiar with parish budgets would believe that eliminating the position of assistant pastor was an effective cost-cutting measure, nor would it in any way address those problems associated with a changing neighborhood so clearly outlined by Walter. It seems likely that in making the request Walter was trying to dramatize problems in central Washington and to explain St. Patrick's lack of progress vis-à-vis neighboring parishes. And just in case the new archbishop turned out to have any tendencies toward loose spending, the exhange let Walter renew his always adamant stand against indebtedness, a position he strongly reasserted in a postscript: "P.S. I do not wish to be in the same condition as some other parishes [which] are heavily in debt."[32]

31. Walter's report on conditions at St. Patrick's was contained in two letters to Gibbons, 23 Oct 1878, 74-B-3, and 25 Oct 1878, 74-B-5 (source of quotations), both in Gibbons Papers, AAB.

32. Ltr., Walter to Gibbons, 23 Oct 1878, 74-B-3, Gibbons Papers, AAB.

Walter's insistence on a pay-as-you-go approach was strongly at odds with the build-now-pay-later philosophy of the pastors at neighboring churches like St. Aloysius and St. Dominic. Yet this extraordinary fear of debt aside, Walter had shown himself far ahead of his contemporaries in his understanding of the inevitable transitions in the development of a modern city. Long before it had become a standard technique of urban sociologists, Walter had accurately plotted the progressive changes that were to occur in the F Street area over the next generations. In view of the later history of the parish, his insistence on limiting expenditures to resources on hand, in the face of strong pressure to act otherwise, stands out as a remarkably prudent and brave position to take during Washington's Gilded Age.

Gibbons diplomatically allowed the matter to drop. There was no further discussion about the lack of financial progress, and Father Morgan remained at his post. Nevertheless, adjusting to St. Patrick's new and largely peripheral position in the scheme of things in Catholic Washington proved a hard pill to swallow. As recently as 1872 the patronal feast on March 17th was observed by the city's parading societies, who, joined by a Baltimore contingent led by the Ft. McHenry band, marched to St. Patrick's Church. There they attended Mass and began a day-long celebration capped by an evening of festivities at the Odd Fellows Hall that included John Keane's popular lecture on "Ireland's Past, and Its Bearing on Her Future."[33] By 1879 the bands and crowds had gone elsewhere. With only one hundred in attendance at Carroll Hall on St. Patrick's Day, Walter watched the pastors of St. Aloysius, St. Dominic, and St. Matthew's combine forces for a grand celebration on the Island. Walter could hardly contain himself. He had been "grossly insulted," he told Gibbons. The parishioners were also indignant at the conduct of the local clergy, he claimed, and many of the various marching societies already regretted their part in the affair. St. Patrick's had been ignored during the last five years, and "if this matter is not settled so that I can have the feast of my Church without the interference of others I ask my removal." Denying the obvious, he assured the archbishop that these remarks had been made "in all calmness and under no excitement."[34]

Once again it was the parish's inability to finish the new church that was at the heart of the pastor's frustration. The St. Patrick's Day parade at St. Dominic Church was just the latest in a string of events

33. Ahern, *Life of John J. Keane*, 26.
34. Ltr., Walter to Gibbons, 18 Mar 1879, 74-L-5, Gibbons Papers, AAB.

where the city's newer churches captured the attention of the press and the area's Catholics. Particularly galling to the pastor was the way in which the protracted construction was draining the parish's energies and pocketbook while many important charities—always the center of his interests—were left wanting. In his frustration he continued to dun the congregation for extra support, especially on the subject of pew rents.

Although since John Carroll's time the bishops had stressed the importance of the offertory collection as the basic source of pastoral support, the practice of paying for seating space, brought to America by German and other northern European immigrants, remained the principal source of parish funds.[35] Fees were charged for seating at the principal mass on Sunday and at special occasions. Almost always, pews were sold to the highest bidder at prices that varied according to the distance from the altar. Even purchased pews were subject to an annual rental fee. The bishops were concerned because of the obvious discrimination involved, and during both the Second and Third Plenary Councils they warned against the practice. Yet it was hard to wean pastors away from this one sure means of support.

In December 1877 Walter had announced that unrented pews would be locked during the principal mass and the public forbidden their use. Apparently some parishioners saw a way around this prohibition, and during 1878 Walter watched attendance shrink at the 11 o'clock mass in favor of the 9 o'clock or so-called children's mass, when pews were free. Noting that the sermon at the principal mass was geared to the needs of the adult congregation and pointing to the number of vacant pews, which he said the parishioners had a duty to rent, he warned that, unless there was a marked change in accordance with his desires, he would bar adults from the 9 o'clock mass and thus force them "to hear the word of God" at the later mass. True to his word, Walter later refused admittance to the children's mass to all adults who did not pay a ten-cent entrance fee. But here the pastor was on shaky ground. The *Mirror* speculated on the obvious fact that his get-tough policy would merely drive more people to other churches. More important, entrance fees had been forbidden by Rome (and would be condemned by the Third Plenary Council in the next decade), although they

35. Michael N. Kremer, "Church Support in the United States" (Dissertation in Canon Law, The Catholic University of America, 1930), 32, 73–77. Kremer presents a comprehensive summary of the various methods of revenue raising in the American church, including the somewhat arcane evolution from pew purchase to seat rent.

would linger on in isolated parishes for many years. In April 1879 Walter reversed himself, adding that he was doing so because many were unable to pay and as a consequence were missing mass. He only hoped, he added, that this reversal would not be construed as cancelling any parishioner's obligation to contribute liberally to the box (offertory) collection.[36]

Strangely enough, the more he scolded them, the more the congregation seemed to understand his concerns and to approve his cautious approach to the expensive project. In a show of affection reminiscent of their impromptu welcome home a decade before, parishioners celebrated Walter's silver anniversary as a priest in September 1879 with a surprise party. A throng of well-wishers presented him with a basket of silver dollars, and in a moment of high emotion, an obviously moved pastor demonstrated once again what was obvious to everyone—that his stern, authoritarian manner masked a truly warm and generous heart. Coming from someone else, his response to their greetings might have sounded stilted or pompous, but from this often-spikey and undoubtedly brave little man it carried the impress of sincerity. He began by asking for their prayers, continuing, as the *Mirror* later reported:

we are all human, he said, and he needed prayers on account of being a pastor more than anyone else. He might have offended some of his parishioners at times, and if he had, he asked pardon of them all. Few people understood the relations existing between a pastor and his people. A true pastor would, if necessary, lay down his life for them. If God should spare him he would willingly be with them twenty-five years longer, and try to do better than before.[37]

The occasion might also be said to have marked the end of the dreary years of fiscal hardship. Washington was finally starting to emerge from the doldrums as salaries slowly began to increase and jobs became more plentiful. With confidence in the financial future of the city restored, men of business also resumed their interest in the long-term commercial possibilities of F Street.

In the ensuing months the parish took the first moves toward exploiting the commercial value of its property. It began in early 1880 by dividing its F street holdings into eleven building lots, each 80 feet deep with a 22-foot front. It had the lots graded and otherwise made

36. The incident was fully aired in the *Catholic Mirror*. See articles on 29 Dec 1877, 28 Sep and 9 Nov 1878, and 12 Apr 1879.

37. *Catholic Mirror*, 27 Sep 1879.

LOOKING WEST FROM NINTH AND F STREETS. *A 1900 view of St. Patrick's leased property (upper right).*

suitable for business use, leasing the first three for twenty-five years at the rate of $300 annually for the first ten years and $400 annually thereafter. At the end of the lease, the land and all improvments were to revert to the church. Apparently the possibility of selling the property outright was not considered at first, although the Jesuits adopted that approach in 1881 in regard to the Washington Seminary building. After Gonzaga moved to its new building behind St. Aloysius church, the old F Street edifice was used for a variety of purposes, lastly as the home of Georgetown University's law school. Now, redolent with memories of Father Matthews and the first great experiment in Catholic education in Washington, it was razed to make way for a group of handsome new stores "suitable to the surroundings," as the *Mirror* put it, to help pay off part of St. Aloysius's $100,000 debt.[38]

One consideration favoring the immediate sale was the fact that subdivision of the F Street property had again placed the valuable as-

38. *Catholic Mirror,* 22 Oct 1881.

set on the city's tax roles. Between 1874, when the city began taxing church property, and 1879, when Congress repealed the practice in the case of land used for religious purposes, St. Patrick's had faced a hefty annual bill for property valued at more than $179,000, an expense that would continue on that portion of the parish property to be leased.[39] In June 1881 Walter sent the commissioners a plat of the proposed subdivision for recordation with the object of separating taxable from nontaxable parts of St. Patrick's holdings. To keep his options open, however, he also arranged a so-called friendly suit in the Supreme Court of the District of Columbia in which Archbishop Gibbons, as Caffry's heir, was named complainant and four parishioners defendants. The court decided that the sale of the Caffry legacy best fit the purposes expressed in the original deed, and that Gibbons was free to sell or otherwise dispose of the property.[40]

Although the suit cleared up the legal ambiguity in Caffry's legacy, Walter was convinced that the property would continue to rise in value, and he rejected the idea of immediate sale. In 1882 he leased the rest of the lots under terms that called on lessees to assume responsibility for erecting buildings. During the year, they obtained city permits for the construction of 34-foot high brick offices and stores, each costing $4,000.[41] In what he called an "Easter offering," Walter announced in April 1882 the final lease agreements, which meant liquidation of the parish's current debt. Although the exact amount of the initial payments to the church are unknown, all annual payments during the first four years totalled only $3,300, which gives some indication of the size of what Walter seemed to consider a burdensome debt. Lest the congregation expect some immediate change in the status of the uncompleted building, Walter added that "the new church stands there unfinished, and it will stand there forever before I will go one cent in debt for its completion or for any other purpose."[42]

39. St. Patrick's had inadvertently failed to pay the taxes for 1878 and 1879, and it took a special act of Congress to relieve it of the interest, penalties, and costs associated with the unpaid taxes. See HR 1136, 49th Cong. first session, "St. Patrick's Church in the District of Columbia," 17 Mar 1886. The issue of taxing church property was a lively one in the District. See, for example, *Star*, 5 Nov 1873.

40. Supreme Court of the District of Columbia, Doc. No. 7576, filed 23 Feb 1881, copy in SPA. See also *Catholic Mirror*, 18 Jun 1881.

41. D.C. Building Permits, NARA. See, for example, permits 986 and 1049, 1882, obtained by F. W. Howard, owner, and Charles Martin, builder, for lots 7 and 8, square 376.

42. Quoted in the *Catholic Mirror*, 15 Apr 1882.

A Long-Awaited Dedication

Evidence of the parish's renewed financial security and brightened prospects for finally completing the building did not prepare the congregation for the news in November 1882 that Father Walter was to be transferred to Immaculate Conception. Whatever Gibbons's motives for such an abrupt change, the archbishop could scarcely have been prepared for the spontaneous reaction of St. Patrick's parishioners.[43] Galvanized by the news, more than three hundred of them met in Carroll Hall after Sunday mass on November 12 and drew up a petition for Walter's retention. They also appointed a committee of eight men headed by Seraphim Masi and George Bogus to wait on Gibbons in Baltimore the following day to present their views and deliver the petition which, with its double column of signatures, measured eleven feet in length. Exhibiting the sure social instincts and diplomatic grace that always characterized this pre-eminent member of the hierarchy, Gibbons interrupted the group's presentation and offered to return with them by train to Washington. There they confronted the surprised pastor in his living room. After a brief private conversation with Walter, Gibbons brought him back into the parlor and presented him to the group as their "past, present and future pastor."[44]

If any believed such an outpouring of support would soften their pastor's stern fiscal resolve, they were mistaken. In March 1883 he announced that building would recommence, but only if the money were available. He promised to canvass each family in the parish personally and urged the older members to subscribe the price of individual columns and windows as a practical way to memorialize their family's historic connection with the parish. At his direction the architect substantially reduced costs by eliminating the massive steeple and spire. He initially decided to forgo the elegant Potomac bluestone and sandstone trim (the expensive product of Ohio's Berea quarry)

43. The *National Republican,* 13 Nov 1882, attributed Walter's transfer to Immaculate Conception's need for a man with special fiscal and executive ability. The *Post,* on the other hand, referred to "some hasty decision or other" as a contributing factor to the change. On Walter's reputation with the archbishops, see author's interview with Archbishop Phillip Hannan, SPA. The priest scheduled to succeed Walter was Jeremiah O'Sullivan, pastor of St. Peter's and later bishop of Mobile. See *Catholic Mirror,* 20 Jun 1885.

44. Ltr., Masi, et al., to Gibbons, 12 Nov 1882, 76-V-14, Gibbons Papers, AAB. *Catholic Mirror,* 18 Nov 1882 and 20 Jun 1885. Walter, *A Memorial Tribute,* 27–29, contains a comprehensive account of this incident.

planned for the exterior, but competitive bidding proved more favorable than expected, and the builders were allowed to continue with the costly material. In late April the pastor signed contracts for the completion of the walls and roof. At that time he was able to publish a reliable estimate of total remaining costs (exclusive of furnishings): $115,000.

Such a sum must have appeared less frightening in the more prosperous 1880s, and indeed within eighteen months the parish had amassed almost two-thirds of the total. Much of this came from stepped-up contributions, including a successful drive for the individual purchase of the costly columns ($800 to $1,000 each) and most of the windows ($250 and $1,000 each). Another $30,000 was obtained in the form of a start-up loan secured by the F Street lots whose income was directly applied to the principal and interest of this mortgage. Various estimates of the total cost place it at $167,000—roughly equal to $2.3 million dollars today. So successful was the money-raising effort that, when what was claimed to be one of the largest churches south of New York opened its doors in 1884, the parish owed less than $40,000.[45]

Beginning in April 1883 progress was rapid and uninterrupted. Frequent notices in the press kept the city fully informed. By November the slate roof was in place, the twin turrets completed and roofed over, and the parish bell installed in the north tower. Not all the work was understood or appreciated by a congregation largely unfamiliar with the finer points of the gothic style. The intricately carved and functional gargoyles that peered out from either side of the turrets, for example, were a special source of puzzlement. The *Mirror* reported the firm put-down one critic received at the hands of an elderly Irish immigrant who, while admitting her ignorance of medieval bestiary, closed the discussion in no uncertain terms by declaring, "If Father Walter ordered them put on you may be sure they ought to be on."[46]

Walter awarded general responsibility for construction to three contractors: B. Hanrahan of Baltimore supervised the stonework exterior; John Stack of Baltimore the interior; and Edward J. Hannan of Washington the heating and plumbing. While the exterior was finally

45. Although no official records survive, information about plans and contracts was regularly aired in the press. See, for example, *Catholic Mirror*, 10 Mar, 28 Apr, 19 May, 20 Oct 1883, *Star*, 23 Jun 1883, and *Post*, 30 Mar 1884. Father Walter's nephew claimed that $127,000 was spent to finish the church (see *A Memorable Tribute*, 27). Other sources estimated the cost of earlier work on foundations and walls at $40,000.

46. Quoted in the *Catholic Mirror*, 25 Aug 1883.

completed by the addition of a simple flight of concrete steps rising from Tenth Street, the plasterers and carpenters attacked the extensive task of finishing the interior. Of oak and polished ash, the vestibule and pews were also elaborately carved, with special divisions in the pews designed to carry the forced air heat from the basement. Brass rods also projected from the pews and walls to hold the brackets and chandeliers for gas light. The prominent bases for these instruments would remain attached to the pews for a century, relics of an illumination system that lasted for little more than a decade.[47] Craftsmen worked throughout the summer and fall of 1884, carving the sandstone capitals atop the great pink granite columns, installing the tinted glass windows, including the sixteen-foot west rose window, and carving the decorations in the groined arches of the ceilings of both the church and the baptistry that projected from the northwest side of the building.

In keeping with Walter's fiscal policies, the church was left uncompleted at its dedication. Expensive proposals for painting and gilting the walls and ceilings, adding a marble floor in the sanctuary, and installing gothic altars would await consideration when funds were available. Meanwhile, the simple marble altar, a major link to the old church, was brought over from Carroll Hall. It was nearly overwhelmed in the vast new sanctuary where it and the old carved wood pulpit comprised the major furnishings. The parish organ, purchased in the midst of so much controversy in 1858, was once more dismantled and reassembled in the new gallery loft, where for the first time its full potential could be heard.

The public got its first glimpse of the interior in early October, when the choir performed a sacred concert for the benefit of the building fund. The press was unanimous in its praise of the building's beauty, their accounts dwelling particularly on the overwhelming effect on visitors as they passed through the tinted glass doors of the vestibule to confront the full length of the nave and the great height of the gothic ceiling. Their enthusiastic reaction indicated that, by making the massive columns and their surmounting arches the focal point of the interior, O'Connor had achieved his desired effect.

When Archbishop Bayley's attendance at the Third Plenary Council forced postponement of the formal dedication, Walter decided not to

47. The interior of the church was minutely described in a series of articles in 1884 appearing in the *Post* and the *National Republican,* assembled in the Toner Collection, LC.

wait to begin using the new building. On November 2, 1884, Father Cornelius F. Thomas, the young assistant pastor, celebrated the first Mass in the new church.[48] In his sermon Father Walter admitted that conditions in the old church had been so bad that he had at first regretted accepting the assignment to St. Patrick's. Now willing to make light of the years of turmoil, Walter wryly thanked everyone for their patient support. Referring to those who had complained about the lengthy delay, he added that if he had built as quickly as they had wished, the resulting debt would have put him in his grave.[49]

The new church was solemnly dedicated on December 28th. A winter storm caused some last minute changes. The archbishop, decked out in a brilliant cloth-of-gold cope and miter and carring his crozier, circled the building along a pathway hastily dug out of the snow. After the outer walls were appropriately blessed and the prayers and litanies chanted, Father Walter celebrated solemn high Mass and John Keane, now bishop of Richmond, preached, congratulating his old friends on providing the Lord "a mighty temple worthy of His majesty."[50]

The pastor and congregation were right to be pleased. They had endured the long struggle and built an imposing new edifice that regained for the old mother church the prestige lost in recent years to the newer and larger parishes. Yet in the last analysis, it was not so much their efforts as it was Father Matthews's foresight that had made it all possible. His name was much evoked during the dedication, and with good reason. Without the financial backing insured by the property he had purchased during Washington's infancy, it seems unlikely that a church, even in the scaled-back size finally decided upon, would ever have been built.

Although unnoted in the general euphoria of the occasion, the problems outlined by Father Walter six years before had only worsened. The congregation continued to dwindle as more people deserted central Washington for quiet and affordable residential areas farther out. Viewed in this light, the decision to build a substantial parish church in square 376, was probably a mistake. At the same time, Walter's alternative, to build a church a few blocks to the northeast,

---

48. Accounts differ on the date. The usually reliable Smith in his *History of St. Patrick's Church*, 50, cites 2 November, as do several other sources. The *National Republican* (26 Oct 1884), on the other hand, places it on 26 October.

49. Quoted in the *National Republican*, 26 Oct 1884.

50. A comprehensive account of the ceremony with quotations from Keane and Gibbons appeared in the *Post*, 29 Dec 1884. The event was also described in Smith's *History of St. Patrick's Church*, 50–51.

would have been at best a short-term palliative. Perhaps in the long run the sentimentalists who fought for the old dream of a grand national shrine in the center of Washington were on the right track. At any rate, thanks to Walter's careful stewardship, the parish faced its uncertain future practically debt free. For the moment all could rejoice in the beauty and grandeur of the new church. It would be left to Walter's successors and later generations of parishioners to confront the new challenge.

CHAPTER 8

A Parish Profile,
1870-1900

THE PROTRACTED effort to build a new church tends to overshadow the vital and absorbing activities that marked day-to-day life at St. Patrick's during the last decades of the nineteenth century. The picture drawn in the press of a pastor and congregation struggling to finance their grand project was inaccurate to the extent that it distorted the parish's clearly established priorities. To judge by sums expended and work performed, primary interest remained focused, as it had before the Civil War, on matters of charity, education, and devotional life.

Such emphasis might seem especially appropriate in the financially depressed decade that followed war, but not so the subtle transformation in perspective that accompanied it. In place of the confident, outward-looking approach to the city that prevailed in William Matthews's day, the parish began to develop a largely self-absorbed interest in parochial concerns. Echoing a trend evident throughout the American church, St. Patrick's adopted a habit of introspection that emphasized to a far greater extent than ever before how it differed from its neighbors. Often defensive and belligerent at the same time, this new spirit would become more pronounced in the first decades of the century about to begin.

The ghetto church is commonly associated with the great wave of mid-century immigrants and their wary reaction to the nativists, but this generalization has to be qualified in the case of St. Patrick's. The number of Catholic immigrants in Washington, mainly Irish, actually declined rapidly after the Civil War, and most foreign-born lived outside St. Patrick's boundaries, principally in the neighborhood around St. Aloysius, on the Georgetown waterfront, and especially in later decades in Foggy Bottom beyond St. Stephen's. The great majority of St. Patrick's parishioners, on the other hand, were American-born and represented the wide-ranging political, economic, and social interests of middle-class Washington. To all outward appearances they had no particular tie to the immigrants, beyond the faith they shared and the obligations owed under Christian charity. Often overlooked, however, was the strong sense of ethnic community that developed after the war, particularly among the second and third generation Irish-Americans.[1] Although never personally affected by the Know-Nothing attacks, these native-born Catholics nevertheless increasingly came to consider the persecution a shared experience and, as a consequence, found themselves more inclined to look for social fulfillment in the exclusive company of their co-religionists.

It was these long-time residents who introduced the attitudes of the ghetto church to St. Patrick's and who influenced the inward direction of parish interests. The erection of an imposing church might symbolize the permanence and pre-eminence of their often-derided religion, even as it allowed them to feel a certain sense of parochial superiority over other, upstart parishes. But these motives clearly took second place among those who now looked to the parish community to fulfill their social needs. As important as were the charitable and educational ends that motivated them, the myriad of societies, church festivals, fairs, picnics, parades, excursions, balls, and lectures added to the growing sense of Catholic community and provided a safe, comfortable center for social intercourse that sustained Catholics well into recent decades.

The complementary talents of Jacob Walter and John Keane channeled the energies released by this new sense of community. The for-

1. Altenhofel, "The Irish Century," 10–11. See also Kathryn Schneider Smith, Port Town to Urban Neighborhood: The Georgetown Waterfront of Washington, D.C., 1880–1920 (Dubuque: Kendall/Hunt, 1989).

mer's altogether extraordinary interest in welfare projects—and especially his work on behalf of the poor and neglected—together with the
latter's dynamic leadership in self-help societies and enriched devotional life lent St. Patrick's a leadership in these areas despite the
growing importance of neighboring parishes. Nor would Keane's influence cease with his transfer to Richmond. In later years he was a
frequent guest at St. Patrick's, and during the early days of his tenure
as first rector of The Catholic University of America he once again
resided on Tenth Street, continuing to influence parish organizations.

Widows and Orphans

The first to benefit from this increased charitable activity after the
Civil War were the orphans at St. Joseph's. Father O'Toole and the
rest of the board of trustees had opposed building the much-needed
new orphanage for boys on land donated in 1857 by local Catholic
philanthropist Ambrose Lynch. They believed its remote location,
near St. Aloysius Church across the Tiber, would discourage visitors,
especially the society matrons whom they sought as patrons. They assumed that they had Archbishop Kenrick's approval for an arrangement with the Jesuits: in return for the Lynch property, which the Jesuits wanted for their new Gonzaga, the orphanage would receive the
old Washington Seminary building on F Street. What they had not
counted on was the archbishop's puritanical reluctance to having sisters control a male orphanage, especially one located next to a
church. In protracted negotiations rich with potential for comedy,
these Victorian gentlemen sought to reassure their fastidious superior
that the arrangement merely pertained to a home for the youngest
boys and that brothers would soon be obtained to care for the older
orphans in a separate institution; that it was appropriate and even customary for sisters to live next to parish churches; and that the board in
no way meant to insult or be discourteous to "your grace."[2] They
failed. Kenrick would agree to the deal only if the Holy Cross brothers

2. O'Toole was usually the author of these lengthy reports. See, for example,
O'Toole to Kenrick, 19 Apr 1859, 31-W-7; 24 Sep 59, 31-W-8; and n.d., 31-V-7. All in Kenrick Papers, AAB. Although Kenrick had agreed to the employment of Holy Cross sisters, subsequent discussion revealed him increasingly anxious to replace the sisters
with Holy Cross brothers. See, for example, Kenrick's prohibition against the nuns,
but not the brothers, operating an orphanage next to the new Gonzaga College, in *Litterarum* Register, 12 Apr 1858, Kenrick Papers, AAB. For his final decision, see same
source, 26 Sep 1859.

were employed to run the orphanage. Thus St. Joseph's struggled through the war in its overcrowded home at Tenth and F Streets. In the end the board sold the land to the Mercy sisters for the paltry sum of $17,000, which it applied toward the purchase of the old Washington City Orphan Asylum on H between Ninth and Tenth Streets.[3] This fine brick building, with several later additions and renovations, would remain the boys' home for sixty years.

Although the day school provided a small but steady source of income for the orphanage, the cost of the new building percipitated a financial crisis. A worried Father Walter had agreed with the laymen on the board to borrow for the new building, only to see many of the institution's wealthy benefactors disappear after the panic of 1873. While curtailing donations, the ensuing depression increased the number of indigent children and forced the sisters to beg for food and clothing. The asylum's colorful donkey cart, driven by one of the sisters and several of her charges on its daily quest for donated food at the old Central Market, became a familiar sight to a generation of Washingtonians. Even after the board managed to pay off the debt during the more prosperous 1880s, it lacked a steady source of income to operate the orphanage. Tuition collected in the day school provided some support, and in 1885 Walter organized an annual city-wide collection for charities of concern to all Catholic parishes, which included St. Joseph's as one of its principal recipients. Nevertheless, the amounts thus collected proved insignificant; even the congressional payment of $2,000 annually that began in 1893 abruptly ceased three years later when Congress, under pressure, abolished donations to sectarian institutions. Reporting to a congressional committee in 1896, the principal of St. Joseph's explained that the $7,201 in public moneys received by the institution since its founding forty-six years before meant that Congress had provided the princely sum of $2.40 per boy per year. Yet during that time the orphanage had remained a public institution that

3. With Lynch's permission the board had already traded the land for a plot to the west. The Sisters of Mercy eventually founded a short-lived girl's academy on the site. Later sold to the Jesuits, their building became the part of the Gonzaga complex known as Kohlmann Hall. Gonzaga moved from F Street to its present location in 1871. The complicated story of the Lynch legacy is well documented in the Spalding Papers, AAB, with additional material in the archives of St. Aloysius Church and Gonzaga College. See for example ltrs., Walter to Spalding, 12 Sep 1864, 36-K-2; and 6 Oct 1864, 36-K-3, both in Spalding Papers, AAB; see also Margaret Mary duFief's "A History of St. Aloysius Parish, Washington, D.C., 1859–1909" (Master's thesis, Georgetown University, 1960), 84–86, and Sketch of Gonzaga College from Its Foundation in 1821 till the Celebration of the Diamond Jubilee in 1896 (Washington, 1897), 84–87.

enrolled boys irrespective of creed, mostly from St. Ann's infant home.[4] Until the advent of an organized Catholic Charities and the Community Chest in later decades, St. Patrick's remained the principal sponsor of the orphanage. In good times and bad the parish's resources were tapped to support an institution popularly considered part of the parish family.

The principal vehicle of this support was the annual Pound Party and Supper. Sponsored by the Catholic Knights of America, the party was a highlight of the local Catholic social season. The original idea of charging a pound of donated food for admission soon gave way to the sale of tickets for an evening of dancing, entertainment, and dinner. The crowds were so large that the sponsors were forced to hold the affair in Convention Hall at Fifth and L Streets, then the largest auditorium in the city.[5] In August 1889 Father Walter organized a fair for the benefit of Catholic orphans. Held at the cavernous New York Avenue Rink, the benefit realized a substantial amount and provided Cardinal Gibbons an audience for one of his amusing portraits of St. Patrick's peripatetic pastor. Commenting on the fast gait Walter habitually adopted while out and about "doing good," Gibbons remarked that he had been told, "If a stranger should see a gentleman hurrying along the street with head erect and coat tails flying, he might be sure it was Father Walter."[6]

In addition to their well-publicized attendance at the annual pound parties, St. Patrick's parishioners also showed up in droves for the innumerable minstrel shows, amateur theatricals, and lectures given for the benefit of the orphans throughout these decades. Father Walter likewise sponsored parish picnics and day excursions down the Potomac for the orphans and their sponsors. Thus in the days before radio and television, St. Joseph's became not only the reason for many charitable events, but the excuse for much of the congregation's entertainment.

Nor were the girls neglected. Thanks to a generous bequest from

4. Ltr., Sister Euphrasia to chairman, House Committee on Appropriations, 25 Feb 1896, reproduced in *Church News*, 7 Mar 1896. Federal subsidies are discussed in Weitzman's *One Hundred Years of Charity*, 7–9, and Eckert's *St. Joseph's Home and School*, 9–10.

5. For a description of one of these popular parties, see *Catholic Mirror*, 28 Oct and 2 Dec 1888. The Catholic Knights of America is a fraternal insurance society founded in 1877. In later years it shared sponsorship of the parties with the Knights of Columbus and the Ancient Order of Hibernians. Fund raising for St. Joseph's is described in Kuhn's "The Sisters Go East—And Stay," 4, 6.

6. Quoted in Smith's *History of St. Patrick's Church*, 62.

Father Matthews, St. Vincent's had considerably enlarged its facility in 1857 with the addition of a large school on G Street. Its population of 115 orphans and 300 day students remained at that level in subsequent decades, and with its well-appointed buildings debt free and its school a steady source of income, the institution was able to endure the depression decade far better than its impoverished male counterpart. Still, St. Vincent's had a problem. Accustomed to discharging their orphans at age fourteen and sometimes earlier to the care of foster families, the Sisters of Charity were dismayed to find some children cruelly overworked and even physically abused. Sister Blanche Rooney, who like Father Walter possessed what observers euphemistically called "a warmth of nature" that often expressed itself in a "hot and holy indignation," acted decisively. She decided to keep the girls in her charge until they reached their majority, organizing a new department in the asylum for their care and training. Called St. Rose's School of Industry (later incorporated by Congress under a separate charter as St. Rose's Industrial School), it was designed to train girls in domestic economy, plain and fancy sewing, dressmaking, and practical household management. With laudable ambition, the school opened in 1868 in a fourth-floor room with three teenage girls and one sewing machine.[7]

The need for separate quarters soon became apparent. In an act of piety widely understood in those times, Sister Blanche buried a medal at a spot near Twentieth and G Streets which she considered suitable for the new school. In 1871 the wealthy Washington jeweler William Galt offered that very lot to the sisters on condition that St. Vincent's donate $500 in the next two years to the city's other Catholic orphanages. He soon canceled this unusual condition, donating the $500 himself and giving the promised lot and an adjacent one to St. Rose's. When a crusty old bachelor, a non-Catholic, refused to sell a third lot for the project, the formidable Sister Blanche promptly appointed him to her board of administrators and shortly thereafter accepted his gift for the needed addition. Thanks to these and other generous donors, the school opened in its new building in March 1872.

From the first, St. Rose's proved self-supporting. The work of its young dressmakers was much admired among Washington's matrons, and it was not unusual to see a White House carriage parked in front of the school while the President's wife attended a fitting. Many a

7. Branson, "Two Child-Care Institutions," 27–40, and Smith, *History of St. Patrick's Church,* 52–53, are the principal sources for the following paragraphs. The description of Sister Blanche's temperament is from Smith, 53.

wedding dress worn at St. Patrick's was made by the skilled young seamstresses. Although such work received the most publicity, those trained in the domestic skills were also appreciated. One reporter claimed that the society women waited in line to hire the graduates.[8] Although no longer residents in the parish, St. Rose's pupils regularly joined in the many social events St. Patrick's sponsored for orphans. It can only be hoped that the picnics, excursions, and other entertainments somehow softened the drabness of what, despite the sisters' best intentions, remained a highly regimented nineteenth-century orphanage, where students routinely formed in ranks to march to church or exercise.

The orphanages were but one of the parish's wide-ranging charitable interests in the postwar period. For some time Father Walter had been concerned with the treatment of the city's indigent old folks. He invited the Little Sisters of the Poor to open a home in Washington. These French nuns, famous for their special mission to the elderly, already had foundations in nine American cities, but Walter correctly surmised that the added prestige gained from operating in the nation's capital would spark their interest.[9] With Archbishop Spalding's permission and the support of the parish's St. Vincent de Paul Society, six sisters made the long trip from Paris in February 1871 to take up residence with their first four clients in the building next to Carroll Hall recently vacated by the Christian Brothers and now refurbished and decorated for its new mission.[10]

Public begging is an intrinsic part of this group's mission, but the sight of the nuns with their wooden bowls approaching strangers or carrying donated supplies of firewood on their shoulders proved, in the words of a report to the order's Mother General, "an incomprehensible mystery for the Americans."[11] It also quickly attracted a loyal band of supporters, both Catholic and non-Catholic, who responded

8. *New Century,* 19 Oct 1901.

9. Several commentators make this point, most explicitly Weitzman in his *One Hundred Years of Catholic Charities,* 78. Such a foundation might have served the group's renown in France, but hardly in the United States, where Washington was still considered socially beyond the pale.

10. Little has been written about the sisters in Washington. This account is based on "Histoire de notre Maison de Washington Commencée en Février 1871, sous le patronage de St. Joseph," a chronicle in the archives of the Little Sisters of the Poor, Washington, DC., and Weitzman, *One Hundred Years of Catholic Charities,* 77–83. See also Walter, *A Memorial Tribute,* 331–32.

11. Ltr., Sr. Marie de la Conception to the Mother General, 5 Feb 1871, reproduced in "Histoire de notre Maison," 9–12.

when Walter helped the sisters move into a new building on H Street, N.E., in 1873. The debt for the land and original home, some $30,100, was discharged in less than two years—a staggering achievement, considering the city's severe financial problems and the many worthy causes competing for the little money available. Through the intercession of influential patrons, the Little Sisters also received an additional $25,000 from Congress in 1874, enough for the first substantial addition to their new home. In less than a decade the sisters had more than 150 elderly in their care.[12]

Although the Little Sisters had moved outside St. Patrick's boundaries, Father Walter encouraged parishioners to maintain their special relationship with the home. The parish's St. Vincent de Paul conference remained a principal sponsor of an institution that lacked any formal city-wide or diocesan support. Like the various affairs for the orphans, the benefits held for the home, especially the annual dinner on the Feast of St. Joseph given for the old people by Washington's social elite, featured well-publicized appearances by members of the diplomatic corps and emptied many well-lined pockets in the good cause. The spectacle of the usually austere pastor decked out in a long linen apron and wielding an oversized serving spoon while waiting table at these events became a familiar part of parish lore.[13]

Walter was the driving force behind St. Patrick's strong commitment to charitable causes, and the parish's St. Vincent de Paul conference was the vehicle he used to collect and disperse the funds. Matured into an efficient social welfare agency during the hard times of the 1870s, the group supervised parish collections for the local needy as well as figured prominently in the support of larger, city-wide institutions. Most of the charities that transcended parish boundaries were left to the Society's particular council. Father Walter remained the spiritual director of the city-wide organization until his death, presiding over its business meetings in Carroll Hall and attending its monthly mass at St. Patrick's.[14] In a no nonsense age, the spiritual ben-

---

12. *Catholic Directory, 1883.* In 1881 the sisters built a small frame house on an adjoining lot for elderly African-Americans in a city that had by then fully succumbed to the rule of Jim Crow. See "Histoire de notre Maison," 38. For some years Father White had sponsored an old-age home for black Catholics near St. Matthew's, but that residence had closed after his death in 1878.

13. See, for example, *Catholic Mirror,* 24 Mar 1889 and 25 Mar 1893.

14. These meetings at which city-wide concerns were discussed were regularly reported in the religious press. See, for example, *Church News,* 27 Oct 1889, 16 Feb 1890, 22 Feb and 13 Dec 1891.

efits associated with the St. Vincent de Paul Society were explicitly tied to the member's material obligations. To earn the indulgences promised those who attended the society's monthly mass, for example, members were also required to attend the general business meeting that same day. Being an officer in the local conference was considered a social distinction, and the names of those elected were regularly featured in the newspapers.

In 1875 Walter organized a women's auxiliary, the Ladies of Charity of St. Vincent de Paul of Washington, to assist the city-wide particular council. (In time this city-wide organization was augmented by separate chapters established at the parish level.) Imitating the foundation in Paris, the women initially played no part in the distribution of charity, which was controlled by the presidents (male) of the local parish conferences. They were at first discouraged from soliciting money, which was still considered men's work, and limited themselves to collecting, repairing, and storing used clothing or visiting poor women and children. But these restrictions did not long survive, as the women rapidly expanded the mission of their association to assume leadership in many local charities.[15] Within a few years they were collecting and distributing money and goods and, in a move that prefigured the social workers of later decades, investigating individual cases to define individual needs. They visited jails and hospitals and in general carried on a wide range of social welfare services. Their annual reports, reproduced in the diocesan press, presented a picture of their growing responsibilities. In 1899, for example, the St. Patrick's Ladies of Charity reported visiting twelve hundred families and providing food, clothes, and fuel for a significant number. They also placed poor children in local orphanages; arranged for the care of troubled girls at the House of the Good Shepherd and the placement of boys in the U.S. Marine Corps; and induced lapsed Catholics to return to the sacraments and have their children baptized—all this while regularly visiting eleven local institutions and distributing thousands of garments and some $1,650 in cash.[16] To support their work, the women sponsored many of the parish's major socials. Their week-long fair in

15. John O'Grady, *Catholic Charities in the United States: History and Problems* (Washington: National Conference of Catholic Charities, 1930), 319. The limited role of the Ladies of Charity is outlined in Weitzman, *One Hundred Years of Catholic Charity,* 138–39, and McColgan, *Century of Charity* 2:224–26. The women's auxiliary was the second organized in the United States, in the wake of the group begun in St. Louis in 1858.

16. *Church News,* 1 May 1887, 10 Jun and 28 Oct 1899, and 5 Jan 1890.

October 1899, for example, drew thousands and featured, in addition to the regular events usual at such extravaganzas, concerts by the U.S. Marine Band and a raffle whose grand prizes included a piano and a portrait of a popular assistant pastor.

There is no indication that a parish society ever offered the pastor's picture as a prize, even though Walter's concern for the needy and spirit of poverty drew universal praise. Local historian Margaret Downing described his work with the St. Vincent de Paul Society as part of his "almost divine compassion for the poor."[17] As Cardinal Gibbons put it shortly after Walter's death:

Whilst he was Rector of St. Patrick's Church, large sums of money fell into his hands; but none of it clung to them. It was distributed among the orphans, or secretly dispensed to the poor, and especially to genteel, but indigent applicants for office in the [federal] Departments, who daily called on him. Profuse in his hospitality to visiting clergy, his own private apartment was more destitute of ornaments and comforts than that of a seminarian.[18]

Walter's charity might have been unlimited, but his patience was not. That his picture was never offered as a prize might relate to the fact that even in later years he did not hesitate to chastise those he considered in error. One such victim was the socially august ladies of the Tabernacle Society. Organized by Father Keane in 1876 at the suggestion of Fannie Whelan, the society sewed altar linens and made vestments for poor churches across the country. For a time some of the glittering names in Washington society (Mrs. Edward White, wife of the Chief Justice of the Supreme Court was a long-time president) put in long hours each week, their time carefully calibrated to register the plenary indulgences that were their due, in rooms provided by the parish in the well-worn building that had served in turn the Christian Brothers and the Little Sisters of the Poor.

Unfortunately, in the years after Father Keane's departure the women lost sight of the fact that St. Patrick's, and not the night school, which had by then become the principal occupant of the building, was their landlord. They began to complain publicly about what they concluded was indifference on the part of the local clergy. Father Walter set the record straight in no uncertain terms. In a blistering letter that found its way into the archbishop's archives, he pointed out that he was their landlord and was far from indifferent to their work.

17. Dowling, "The Development of the Catholic Church in the District of Columbia from Colonial Times Until the Present," 47.

18. James Gibbons, *Ambassador of Christ* (Baltimore: John Murphy, 1896), 122–23.

"Your conduct, at least that of some of your members towards me," he concluded, "has been unladylike, unchristian, and most certainly *uncatholic*. How you can continue to occupy these rooms after such conduct surpasses my comprehension. Yours truly."[19] The Tabernacle Society decided to move elsewhere. Until their worthy work was taken over by the Sisters of the Perpetual Adoration some years later, they remained under the more soothing sponsorship of the priests of St. Matthew's.

Walter was more pleasantly disposed toward the parish's Sunday school teachers. For many years these lay men and women, carefully trained by the assistant pastors, conducted classes in the basement of Carroll Hall that all the children in the parish, including those studying at St. Vincent's and St. Joseph's, were expected to attend. The teachers were a popular bunch, and their frequent fundraisers for the school, which ranged from tea parties to comic operas, realized considerable sums. In February 1888, for example, they sponsored a stereopticon show of the sights of Europe that attracted a crowd of five hundred people to Carroll Hall.[20]

On Self-Help and Mutual Benefit

Adult education and self-improvement programs were especially welcome among second-generation Americans in the late nineteenth century. Institutions like the Chautauqua Assembly and the YMCA became familiar to all, and in fact almost every city and social group began to organize literary societies to provide, as the Catholic sponsors of one such group put it, "intelligent recreation . . . and aid toward employment when necessary."[21] The most prominent and long-lasting Catholic self-improvement society in Washington was the Carroll Institute, founded at St. Patrick's in 1873.

The Carroll Institute grew out of the Young Catholic Friend's Society. Even this highly dedicated charitable organization was not im-

19. Ltr., Walter to Members of the Tabernacle Society, 15 Feb 1881, 75-Q-5, Gibbons Papers, AAB. The work of the society is outlined in Smith, *History of St. Patrick's Church,* 57–58, and articles in the *Church News,* 6 Nov 1887, 9 Feb 1890, and 7 Mar 1896.

20. See, for example, descriptions of Sunday School money-raising events in the *Church News,* 19 Feb, 6 May, and 2 and 16 Dec 1888. Periodically the Sunday school staff was augmented by seminarians studying at various religious houses associated with Catholic University.

21. Quoted in Spalding, *Premier See,* 219. Spalding provides a useful guide to the diocesan literary, temperance, and beneficial societies in chapter 9 of his work.

mune to the siren call of mental uplift and self-improvement, and soon after the Civil War lectures and adult education courses for the edification of its members became a regular feature of its meetings. In 1873 a group of its leaders, including Major Edmund Mallet, John Carroll Brent, and John Bingham, all members of St. Patrick's parish, decided to form a separate Carroll Literary Association aimed at "natural improvement and social intercourse, dissemination of Catholic literature and furtherance of Christian education."[22] Fully in support of such laudable aims, Father Walter pledged an annual donation of $50 to the group and provided them a home in the old schoolhouse on G Street. Renamed the Carroll Institute, the group opened for business with a library formed around the St. Vincent de Paul Society's collection of books and seven hundred volumes donated by the Masi family. It also provided separate rooms reserved for reading, study, and board games.

National prominence would rest in part on the institute's successful effort to distribute thousands of books and magazines to American soldiers and sailors and the role of its leaders, especially Father Keane, in creating a national union of such organizations. The group's local reputation, however, developed from its free night school for working youth, which opened in 1874, and its many recreational activities, especially its sports program, that made it a magnet for young Catholic men. The school was restricted to workers unable to attend day classes or to afford private education. In addition to basic academic studies, it offered courses in mechanical drawing, accounting, and other vocational subjects.

The institute rapidly outgrew its quarters on G Street. In 1884 its 215 members organized a subscription drive to purchase and remodel a public school at Sixth and F Streets, which in turn was sold at considerable profit just six years later, permitting the purchase of a well-designed building near Tenth and New York Avenue. Now equipped with a large gymnasium, classrooms, a 3,000-volume library, and an elegant hall, the institute quickly surpassed Carroll Hall as the social center of Catholic Washington. For several generations its headquarters would regularly entertain the likes of Cardinal Gibbons and other

22. Quoted in the *Star*, 1 Jun 1889. While the institute lacks a proper history, it has been the subject of several comprehensive articles, including retrospective pieces in the *Star*, 18 Jul 1903, and one in the *Church News*, 27 Jul 1890. Several issues of *The Carroll Institute Gazette*, the organization's informative journal, are among the holdings of the CUA library. Spalding's *Premier See*, 248–50, discusses the role of these literary societies. The following paragraphs are based on these sources.

visiting luminaries of church and state. Its fairs ranked among the city's most elaborate; its *Gazette* the most literate; its dramas, concerts, and minstrel shows, the most entertaining; and its sports teams the most victorious. In 1893 the society broke new ground "to keep abreast of the times," by opening its well-appointed gym to day sessions for women athletes. To judge by the press, St. Patrick's parish never tired of boasting of its role in the successful organization's formation or abandoned its proprietary interest in the institute's activities.

Somewhere in all this success the institute began to lose sight of its literary and educational mission. During its first decade it had managed to maintain a precarious balance between the not-always-compatible goals of wholesome recreation and adult education, the major interest of its younger members being more social than cultural. In 1893 the *Church News* complained that the secular press always emphasized the institute's sport's program at the expense of its classrooms, but by then the night school had only twenty-five pupils from five of the city's parishes and would soon cease operations. Some tried to put a good face on it by pointing to the discipline learned through physical culture and the fact that the library still hosted literary readings. By 1902, however, the *New Century* was tacitly admitting that the institute had become a social fraternity and sports club.[23] As with most Catholic organizations in the city, the enduring attraction of the Carroll Institute was the opportunity it provided members for enjoying a richer, varied social life. The parties and dances, picnics and river excursions, the excitement of its grand national conventions, and above all the evenings filled with lively discussion and debate constituted the major reason for joining.

The drift from early goals was not necessarily to be lamented. With basic education now more readily available, the need for free night classes in a city with few immigrants had abated, but the need for wholesome entertainment had not. Bishop Keane alluded to this evolution when he addressed the delegates of the Catholic Young Men's National Union during their convention in Carroll Hall in 1890. "You are banded together in your own various societies for social entertainment," he noted, "and to give to young men in the various localities of the country opportunities for good recreation, without any badness or

---

23. *Church News*, 7 Jan 1893 and *New Century*, 15 and 22 Feb 1902. The *Church News* is a particularly good source of information about the institute, between 1889 and 1895 featuring regular reports on its activities.

danger in it."[24] Nor did Keane and other bishops overlook the fact that the Carroll Institute and like societies were useful in disseminating their teachings on church solidarity within a predominantly Protestant culture, pressing their growing emphasis on patriotism, and offering an attractive alternative to the secret societies and labor organizations that so many of them feared. Such wholesome outlets for youthful interests were also welcomed in a puritanical age when other pulpits were routinely used to remind Catholics that waltzes, polkas, and other fashionable dances were banned, drama suspect, and variety theater condemned.

Literary societies and sports clubs never equalled in popularity the parish's temperance society, which, thanks to Keane and a small group of dedicated laymen, emerged after the Civil as the major focus of the parish's reform impulse. St. Patrick's had organized the first Catholic temperance society in the nation, and George Savage was revered throughout the country as the father of the Catholic total abstinence movement. Yet total abstinence was not generally supported by Catholics. The old American aristocracy, the German immigrants, and especially the Irish workers showed little enthusiasm for the cause. As one scholar shrewdly noted, the movement represented a quest for middle-class respectability that appealed chiefly to white-collar Catholics and never gained the influence that prohibition won in the Protestant churches.[25]

Little of this indifference was evident at St. Patrick's after John Keane became president of the St. Patrick's Total Abstinence Society. His passionate interest in the cause led him to lecture constantly on the evils of drink and the need for a crusade. He was one of the organizers of the national union of Catholic temperance societies in 1872, and long after his years at St. Patrick's he continued to participate in the parish's temperance work, coming back frequently to encourage members and win new converts to the cause.

As in the case of other groups, the social activities associated with the temperance crusade filled a need in the lives of parishioners. They provided many a hard-working clerk and small businessman, who had little time or money for more formal amusement, with an opportunity to recreate with his Catholic neighbors. Whatever their motives, parishioners joined in ever-increasing numbers during the 1880s and

24. Quoted in *Proceedings of Sixteenth Annual Convention, Catholic Young Men's National Union*, 7–8 Oct 1890, copy in CUA library.

25. Olson, *Catholic Immigrants in America*, 43–44.

1890s. The parish also formed a women's branch, which organized a full spate of social and literary events promoting temperance, as well as a cadet branch in which teenagers took the pledge. It was not uncommon to find boys taking the pledge at their confirmation, but here some of the more zealous members found ground to criticize their archbishop. Gibbons strongly supported abstinence among minors and approved temporary pledge-taking among the young, but he was opposed to any young person taking some form of permanent vow, and he joined with the majority of his fellow bishops in refusing to declare breaking the temperance pledge by Catholics a matter for confession. At a later date Gibbons sounded almost antagonistic to the crusaders. "The Catholic Church is not fanatical on the subject of temperance," he would tell an audience at St. Patrick's in 1909. "Men have first one fad and then another in this country, and seem to think that the fate of the nation depends on their success."[26]

The temperance society, with its ladies auxiliary, gathered every Sunday evening in Carroll Hall and, after a business meeting that usually included a few new members taking the pledge, enjoyed dramatic and musical entertainments. At times the parish choir would perform; one memorable evening a packed house heard Professor A. J. Keenan give his dramatic reading of "Uncle Sam's Pledge to His Dying Mother" and "The Angel's Visit to a Bar-Room." The group usually concluded with a hymn-singing session. Later the society rented rooms in the Riggs Fire Insurance Building on F Street so that young men might enjoy reading papers and magazines or playing billiards free from unwholesome influences.[27]

The St. Patrick's group always counted members from all over town, and in an effort to underscore this city-wide mission it changed its name in 1889 to the Father Mathew Total Abstinence Society. Under that title it organized a grand reception for Bishops Ireland and Keane and other important temperance orators at the New York Avenue Rink in 1889 that began with a monster parade from the Ebbitt House led by the 3d U.S. Artillery band. The society also helped spearhead formation of the Catholic Total Abstinence Union, a national organization of parish temperance groups, and it hosted several of their

26. Quoted in *New Century,* 23 Oct 1909. For a discussion of church attitudes toward the Catholic temperance movement, see Bland, *Hibernian Crusade,* esp. chaps. 6–8.

27. The Washington Catholic temperance movement lacks a history but enjoyed wide notice in the press. See, for example, articles in the *Church News,* 13 Apr 1890, 10 Apr and 17 Sep 1892, and the *Catholic Mirror,* 18 Sep 1886 and 23 Feb 1889.

conventions in Washington. Such receptions became commonplace, and the dynamic parish society continued well into the new century as an influential force in the American church.[28] Whether it ever had much effect on the consumption of the devil's brew in Washington is open to debate; that it was a major element in the close-knit society of St. Patrick's is beyond dispute.

The beneficial societies and Catholic knighthoods that flourished during the 1870s and 1880s were further components of this network of self-help organizations figuring prominently in the social life of the parish. Ostensibly efforts to assist the immigrant to find employment and otherwise acclimate to the American scene, the first beneficial societies actually amounted to little more than mutual insurance organizations providing modest relief for sick members or their widows and orphans. Most were organized around individual parishes. Typically, members of a local organization paid a substantial initiation fee, then continued their support with a small sum contributed monthly in the form of dues and a separate monthly donation for each widow of a society member. With its business affairs settled, the meeting turned to the main event of the evening, an entertainment, sometimes a musicale, often a popular lecture or debate on some special phase of Irish history or some topic of special interest to new Americans.

In time the poorly financed local beneficial societies gave way to nationally organized groups that could offer dependable insurance rivaling national firms. The Catholic Benevolent Legion, one of the largest of these national organizations, formed two councils in Washington, one started at St. Patrick's in 1883. The similarly influential Catholic Knights of America also formed several branches in Washington with many St. Patrick's men counted among the 224 members of its Carroll Branch. True to their mission, these fraternal insurance societies also supported spiritual and cultural activities and sent money to the foreign missions. The *Catholic Mirror* strongly endorsed them while chiding the rest of the city's clergy for not joining with the pastors of St. Patrick's and St. Matthew's in boosting this lay effort.[29] Walter, always a strong supporter of sound conservative business arrangements, was

28. These national conventions were major church events in Washington. See *Church News*, 27 Dec 1891 and 3 and 10 Jan 1892. The elaborate opening of the twenty-first general convention at St. Patrick's in 1891, for example, is described in Smith, *History of St. Patrick's*, 64, and Bland, *Hibernian Crusade*, 163–64.

29. *Catholic Mirror*, 18 Sep 1886. These paragraphs are based on the information in the many articles in the *Mirror* in the 1880s concerning these beneficial societies and knighthoods and Spalding's *Premier See*, 215–19 and 245–50.

a charter member of the St. Patrick's branch of the legion, faithfully attended its monthly meetings in Carroll Hall, and purchased a $2,000 insurance policy that named the two orphanages and the Little Sisters of the Poor as beneficiaries.

The Catholic knighthoods that began to proliferate during this same period featured many similar beneficial services, but with the added attraction of providing Americans the excuse to don fancy uniforms and participate in the camaraderie of military formations. Many church-related parades and ceremonies were visibly enriched by the colorful presence and military discipline of the Emmitt Guards, the Knights of St. Columbkille, the Knights of St. Joseph, and the Knights of St. Bernard. The city's black parish and German churches also sponsored Catholic knighthoods, but the Knights of St. Patrick was among the most venerable, with a unit organized at St. Patrick's church in 1871. The stated aim of this group was to honor the Irish saint, maintain the spirit of Irish nationalism among Irish immigrants, support their widows, and encourage their literary association.

The knighthoods also had a national union. Adopting the impressive title of the Roman Catholic Union of the Knights of St. John, the national organization held its 1889 convention at St. Patrick's, where the members listened to an address by their national chaplain, Cardinal Gibbons.[30]

The meetings of the various knighthoods were filled with discussions of coming parades and ceremonies. Practice drills followed, with much attention paid by senior members to the spit and polish condition of swords, badges, and other military accoutrements. These were the organizations so sorely disappointed when Archbishop Bayley banned music at the cornerstone laying of the new church in 1872. Their feelings must have been assuaged when several months later a great crowd watched their units, bedecked with elaborate flags and banners, accompanied by five bands (including those of the U.S. Marine Corps, Naval Academy, and Fifth Maryland Infantry) march the length of Pennsylvania Avenue on St. Patrick's Day. President Ulysses S. Grant reviewed the parade, described by the *Catholic Mirror* as the "longest and finest procession of Irish-American societies ever witnessed in this city." With a bow to the many temperance groups involved, the reporter also commented on the sobriety of the occasion, in which "uninterrupted order and harmony prevailed throughout."[31]

30. *Church News*, 30 Jun 1889. Gibbons was elevated to the College of Cardinals by Pope Leo XIII in May 1886.

31. *Catholic Mirror*, 22 Mar 1873.

It was only in the last years of the century that the Knights of Columbus and the Ancient Order of Hibernians began to attract the
large numbers of members that would make them the most popular
Catholic fraternal societies. Originating in New Haven, Connecticut,
in 1882, the Knights eschewed parish affiliation, but it was the men of
St. Patrick's who introduced the group to the capital and organized
the first local group, Washington Council 224, in April 1897. Many St.
Patrick's parishioners were also included in a second council named in
honor of Bishop Keane a year later. In addition to offering attractive
insurance benefits, the Knights featured degrees of membership with
an emphasis on ceremony and sociability that were hallmarks of the
mainstream fraternal organizations then inaccessible to Catholic men.
With its skillful combination of ardent patriotism and religious devotion winning the support of the clergy, the Knights soon had thousands of members in the Baltimore diocese as well. Their headquarters north of St. Patrick's on Tenth Street became a familiar landmark
to generations of Washingtonians. It was a common occurrence for
the Knights to march in procession to St. Patrick's to attend Sunday
evening vespers in a body.[32]

The Hibernians trace their organization in the United States to
1836, although their influence in early decades was somewhat curtailed by the debate over secret societies. With the active support of
powerful sponsors like Cardinal Gibbons, however, the Hibernians
later emerged as one of the largest Catholic social societies, dedicated
to the acclimation of the immigrant and furtherance of human rights
both in the United States and in Ireland. At St. Patrick's the Hibernians have always been closely associated with the elaborate commemoration of the parish's patronal feast.

Beneficial societies organized by and for Catholic women did not
appear in significant numbers in the archdiocese until the turn of the
century. The first in Washignton was the Father Walter chapter of
the Catholic Women's Benevolent Legion, formed in 1898. This group
remained entirely separate from the similar, all-male Catholic Benevolent Legion. In contrast, the D.C. chapter of the Catholic Knights of
America voted to admit women in 1899, the first chapter of that national group to do so. Although the temperance society associated
with St. Patrick's had long boasted a women's auxiliary, it was not
until 1898 that another Catholic male society in Washington, the Car-

32. See, for example, description of one such parade from Carroll Hall to the
church in the *New Century*, 26 Sep 1908.

roll Institute, followed suit. Soon after, both the Hibernians and the Knights of St. John also formed auxiliaries for women.

Influence of the New Church on Parish Life

Opening the new church in 1884 restored to St Patrick's pride of place in Catholic Washington. Its priests and people innocently reveled in the stream of august visitors and the constant flurry of activity as St. Patrick's became the setting for national and international religious events. If such a revival failed to banish the pastor's fear that the parish was losing ground to the advance of commercialism, it did seem somehow to fulfill the old dream of a grand national cathedral in the center of Washington. The national events that began to take place in the church soon after its opening were conscientiously reported in the Catholic press. The *Church News* kept a running list of the members of the hierarchy and distinguished Catholic orators and scholars who followed one another in rapid succession in the new sanctuary. During several long stretches Cardinal Gibbons was a weekly visitor, either in connection with his role as local ordinary, as a leader in the organization of the new national university, or in his dealings with the government.

The new church also spurred a renewed interest in the parish's traditional devotional groups. The sodality, especially during the period when assistant pastor Joseph F. McGee was in charge, experienced a dramatic growth in membership.[33] Its Wednesday night meetings became a popular social event, a week night out for many parishioners. The League of the Sacred Heart, formally established in the parish in January 1888 when the Apostleship of Prayer was aggregated to a new international organization, enrolled hundreds of members in just a few months. Its promoters, "installed with edifying ceremony," rapidly formed bands of new members. With 72 such promoters and 2,000 associates in 1895, the league had just about realized its intention of enrolling every adult in the parish.[34] The parish also formed a perpetual adoration society, the People's Eucharistic League of St. Patrick's, in the 1890s. Specially recruiting members from among the city's clerks and businessmen, the league was organized into about

33. In January 1887 the popular McGee was assigned to St. Patrick's, where he served until his appointment as first pastor of Sacred Heart in 1899.

34. *Church News*, 8 Apr and 10 Jun (source of quote) 1888. See also, same source, 14 Dec 1895.

ST. PATRICK'S CHURCH CIRCA 1900 *with partial view of the old rectory at left*

one hundred bands of twelve persons each who promised to spend a half-hour each week before the Blessed Sacrament.[35]

The large church lent a special dignity to elaborate religious rites and processions, which became even more frequent and elaborate toward the end of the century. One such impressive event was the solemn Mass of thanksgiving sung in July 1898 to mark the American victory in the war with Spain. The parish also offered prayers for American servicemen as directed by Cardinal Gibbons in response to a presidential request. (In a separate ceremony at Arlington Cemetery, Father McGee officiated at the burial of 252 American soldiers, many of them Catholics.)[36] The May procession, which now ended with Benediction in the new church, finally came into its own; processions marking the feast of Corpus Christi and the parish's annual observance of Forty Hours drew large crowds. Yet all this paled in comparison to the annual spectacle mounted on St. Patrick's Day. Once more

35. *Church News*, 14 and 21 Jun 1899.
36. *Church News*, 9 Jul 1898 and 8 Apr and 6 May 1899. The text of Gibbons's request is quoted in Philibert, *Saint Matthew's*, 94–95.

the parish was firmly in control of the city's observance, and its celebration always featured several members of the hierarchy, most often
led by the apostolic delegate. All joined in a grand procession into
church where some renowned orator delivered a sermon during
solemn high Mass, demonstrating to a city-wide audience the grandeur and theater of the Roman rite.[37]

New parish organizations were formed to support this increased
ceremonial life. In addition to the upgraded choir, the congregation
also supported a master of ceremonies who drilled the ranks of altar
boys and directed traffic in the crowded sanctuary during the many
ceremonies involving the hierarchy. The ladies of the Sanctuary Society held sway over the sometimes costly decorations, the flowers,
flags, and bunting needed on a regular basis. In 1891 the church hired
Patrick Vaughan, formerly the principal of Immaculate Conception's
boys school, as the new, full-time sexton with increased responsibility
and staff to maintain the church.

The juxtaposition of the stately new church and the convenient
meeting facilities at Carroll Hall, along with the presence of the many
tourist attractions in the nation's capital, lured many national Catholic
societies to St. Patrick's. Beginning in 1886 with the fourth general assembly of the Society of St. Vincent de Paul, the church routinely
played host to conventioneers.[38] Certainly the grandest of all these
events in the waning years of the century was the solemn opening and
closing of the First National Eucharistic Congress in October 1895.
The church, extensively redecorated and lighted by electric lamps,
witnessed one of the great Catholic gatherings of the nineteenth century. Probably more than any other single occasion, the Congress signified the special place St. Patrick's was coming to assume in the
American church.

That church had undergone considerable transformation in the decades since the Civil War. In the twenty years after 1870 the number of
American Catholics doubled to stand at nine million, including two

37. The *Church News*, far more than its predecessor, the *Catholic Mirror*, was interested in the everyday activities of individual parishes and Catholic organizations. A
perusal of this weekly's local events section in the period between 1887 and 1894 provides an altogether unique picture of Washington parish life.

38. A partial list, in addition to the St. Vincent de Paul Society, includes: the Nine-
teenth Annual Convention of the Irish Catholic Benevolent Union, 1887; the Eleventh
Annual Convention of the Knights of St. John, 1889; the Sixteenth and Twenty-fourth
Annual Conventions of the Catholic Young Men's National Union, 1890 and 1898; the
Twenty-first General Convention of the Catholic Total Abstinence Union of America,
1891; and the First Eucharistic Congress of the United States, 1895.

million immigrants and 155,000 converts. It would double again during the next twenty years, the single greatest period of growth in the church's history.[39] Such growth posed tremendous problems for Catholic leaders as they struggled to assimilate the newcomers. Although all these millions shared the same rich deposit of faith, their faith expressed itself in a myriad of languages and customs that all demanded expression. A way had to be devised to channel these demands without losing thousands of Catholics to religious indifference or radical causes. At the same time church leaders had to address the lingering antagonism and suspicion of the Roman traditionalists toward America's support for separation of church and state. Since the days of John Carroll the Americans had sought without success to demonstrate to skeptical leaders in Rome the advantages of democratic government, just as they had chafed at Rome's efforts to impose old disciplines on the problems of a dynamic and growing church.

How best to solve the problems that beset a fast-growing church naturally produced differences of opinion in the hierarchy. While it would be inaccurate to portray a church divided, it was true that leaders like Keane, Ireland, and Denis O'Connell, the rector of the American College in Rome, urged a more progressive approach to church government, while Archbishop Michael A. Corrigan of New York, Bishop Bernard J. McQuaid of Rochester, and their friends in the Propaganda demanded a more traditional approach. Towering over them all was Cardinal Gibbons, who generally, though sometimes reluctantly and often unsuccessfully, aided the Keane-Ireland faction. If such cosmic concerns seemed remote from the day-to-day life of a single American parish—albeit a singularly prominent one in the nation's capital—they nevertheless gave additional meaning to some of the events that occurred at St. Patrick's in the last years of the old century just as they surely animated the parish's new mission in the triumphant decades to come.

It is unlikely that the congregation at large was particularly well informed about disputes over such issues as the appointment of an apostolic delegate or the nature of a national university, although the *Catholic Mirror* and *Church News* were remarkably informative about current issues.[40] Whatever the issue, the parishioners remained staunchly loyal to Keane, who with good reason they always considered one of

39. Shaughnessy, *Has the Immigrant Kept the Faith,* 153, 166, and 182.

40. See, for example, extensive coverage and analysis of the controversial appointment of Archbishop Francesco Satolli as first apostolic delegate, *Church News,* 3 Dec 1892, 21 and 28 Jan, 4 Feb, and 1 Jul 1893.

their own, and to John Ireland, the charismatic church leader, as they sought to demonstrate to Europeans the advantages of the American governmental system to the progress of religion. In fact, Ireland's widely quoted sermon, "The New Age," which summarized these ideas, was delivered before a sympathetic audience at St. Patrick's in 1897.[41]

The priests and parishioners of St. Patrick's strongly supported John Keane's work as first rector of the Catholic University of America. A subject of considerable dissension in the hierarchy, including disagreement over its location, the new school was constantly included among the parish's leading charities, and members of the congregation eagerly responded to the cardinal's invitation to be represented at the cornerstone-laying ceremony in 1888. Father Walter, who had his old friend Keane living at St. Patrick's once again, was an enthusiastic contributor to the new school, and his name led the list of those subscribing to the university's divinity fund. And when Keane finally lost the fight and was dismissed as rector, the parish sponsored a glittering banquet for him at the Shoreham Hotel.[42] Interestingly enough, when Thomas O'Gorman, professor of church history at the university, was consecrated bishop of Sioux Falls, the ceremony at St. Patrick's featured appearances by the leading representatives of the progressives, including Keane and Ireland, the latter being O'Gorman's principal patron and promoter. Archbishop Francesco Satolli, the apostolic delegate, presided at the consecration.[43] It should be noted that Satolli, who in later years became a firm opponent of Keane and Ireland and the so-called Americanist school, was always given a warm welcome during his frequent appearances at the church, where the people were obviously pleased to play host to the Pope's personal representative.

An important demonstration of the progressive support within the church for the American experiment was the archdiocese's celebration in 1892 of the four-hundredth anniversary of Columbus's landfall in the new world. As directed by Gibbons, every church in the diocese celebrated the discovery with a special Mass and sermon and other appropriate festivities. The "gentlemen of St. Patrick's parish" met earlier in the month with their pastor to plan the parish's role in a torch-

41. Spalding, *Premier See*, 267.

42. Walter, *A Memorial Tribute*, 83. See also *Catholic Mirror*, 13 May 1888 and *Church News*, 21 Aug and 16 Oct 1897.

43. Marvin R. O'Connell, *John Ireland and the American Catholic Church* (St. Paul: Minnesota Historical Society Press, 1988), 418–21.

light procession scheduled for October 12, an occasion that must have put the Catholic knighthoods and marching societies in seventh heaven. The parade, dubbed the greatest outdoor event in the history of Catholic Washington, featured thousands of marchers bearing lanterns and flaming torches, richly caparisoned horses pulling carriages and floats, a 2,000-pound bell, six bands, and five bugle corps. The long route of march carried them past specially illuminated buildings and ended at Gonzaga field, where fireworks and cannon salutes concluded the night. St. Patrick's special distinction: each marcher carried a red, white, and blue umbrella with a lighted torch atop. Although the president of the Carroll Institute served as grand marshal, it was Walter who was responsible for ensuring that every parish in the city was included. The *Church News* claimed the enormous turnout showed what citizens could do when the occasion demanded.[44] Left unsaid was what the parade really demonstrated: In celebrating Columbus's achievement, Catholic Washington was also publicly demonstrating its faith in the principles of the American government that guaranteed religious freedom.

As an exhausted Walter put it a week after the Columbus extravaganza, "We are getting over the Columbus fever and waiting to catch the centennial one."[45] He was referring to the fact that the one hundredth anniversary of the founding of the parish was fast approaching. Even then the figure of Anthony Caffry was somewhat mysterious, and Walter wanted his former assistant, Father Thomas, to search the chancery records for information about the first pastor. The church's centennial was celebrated with due honors on St. Patrick's Day, 1894, but public notice of the event seemed largely subordinated to the usual accounts of the Irish feast. The centennial celebration, which occurred just three weeks before Walter's sudden death, was the last public ceremony he was to superintend.

Change of Leaders, Change of Policy

During the last decade of his life, Walter directed the expenditure of thousands of dollars in the parish's many educational and charitable enterprises. He also managed to wipe out all but $3,000 of the building debt. Decorating the church in a style appropriate to its position in the

44. *Church News*, 8, 15, 22, and 29 Oct 1892. Both the *Post*, 22 Oct 1892, and *Star*, same date, provided detailed coverage of the event.

45. Ltr., Walter to Cornelius Thomas, 2 Nov 1892, Gibbons Papers, AAB.

city obviously ranked a distant third in his priorities. Major parish fundraisers, like the 1888 parish fair that collected a record-breaking $5,000, were used to pay off the debt; much-desired improvements to the church's interior would depend on individual gifts or go undone.

Pride in the new building prompted an outpouring of gifts as various individuals and parish groups, more financially secure in the post-depression 1880s and 1890s, donated a few specific furnishings. The sodality contributed the gothic altar for the Blessed Virgin's chapel; a "charitable gentleman," the altar for the Sacred Heart chapel; and a group of fourteen donors contributed $100 each for stations of the cross made in Munich. Bishop Keane gave his old church a portable pulpit, and the noted philanthropist, Annie Orme Barbour, an acoustical shell, a necessity in a large church in the days before electric amplification. Several statues were also installed in that period, including a colorful one of the parish's patron saint holding a model of the church in his hand, the gift, as the paper put it, "of one of Father Walter's Protestant friends."[46]

A practical addition to the church during this period—granite steps with rails and coping for the main entrance—was also the most expensive. The women of the parish had collected part of the necessary $2,000, but the deteriorating condition of the entrance had induced the pastor to take a hand in the collection. The *Catholic Mirror* warned that Walter was going to canvass his wealthy parishioners for contributions, and since "in his vocabulary there is no such word as fail, and since he will no doubt succeed," the paper advised its readers to accept the inevitable and send in their money to save Walter's time and shoe leather.[47] These donations were certainly welcome, but they left unfinished the most obvious and costly items, the so-called grand altar, the marble altar rail, and the frescoing. Cost of the altar alone was estimated at more than $10,000. On numerous occasions Walter made clear that such costly items would not be considered until the money was in the bank. In fact, none would be purchased during his lifetime.

The reason for Walter's insistence on a debt-free parish was not difficult to understand. By the time the new church opened its doors in 1884, the relentless advance of commercialism into what just a decade before was still a largely residential neighborhood was obvious to all. Seventh, Ninth, and F Streets were now all thriving business ar-

46. These few additions to the church were described in great detail in the pages of the *Church News*. See, for example, editions for 20 Jan 1889, 30 Mar, 20 Apr, and 22 Jun 1890. For further detail on church furnishings, see chapter 14 below.

47. *Catholic Mirror*, 12 Mar 1887.

eas with continuous blocks of retail firms and offices. The exodus of local residents had accelerated, with the region's wealthiest families leading the way. Increasingly, the fine old homes on Sixth Street and the northern section of the parish along K Street and Massachusetts Avenue were being vacated by families moving to new neighborhoods developing north of Florida Avenue. The buildings were being converted into multiple-family rental units or commercial establishments. Further complicating St. Patrick's problem was the continual lure of neighboring parishes that were located near the parish's major concentration of residences. For that reason Father Walter complained bitterly when plans were announced in 1888 for construction of a new St. Mary's on Fifth Street. Arguing that there was no further need for any such national parish "since there will not be 20 German families after 10 or 20 years in Washington City," Walter urged Gibbons to veto the plan, warning that if the church was built "there will be no need of two priests at St. Patrick's."[48]

Despite the undeniable popularity of the new church, the changing nature of the neighborhood and competition from nearby parishes were making a difference. Less than a year after the new building was consecrated, Walter warned Gibbons that he was canceling the second daily mass since "were it not for the Sisters of Charity [at St. Vincent's] and the Holy Cross [at St. Joseph's] no one would hardly be left to hear Mass." Three years later the trend was unmistakable. "The parish is losing ground every year," he told Gibbons. "The people are all moving out on account of business occupying all the houses. St. Patrick's is fast becoming the 'Church of Strangers.'" The loss in church revenue followed population trends. Pew rents, which brought in some $4,300 in 1886, experienced a steady decline during the next ten years; the Sunday collection dropped from $2,400 in 1885 to $1,600 in 1895. By 1888 one-half of the church's 168 pews were going unrented.[49] A further sign of decline: where once St. Patrick's had ranked only behind the Baltimore cathedral in donations to diocesan collections, it now usually ran well behind St. Aloysius, St. Dominic, and St. Matthew's.[50]

48. *Notitiae,* Churches of Washington, St. Patrick's 1888, AAB. Fosselman ("A Downtown Parish," 196–210) analyzes the parish's loss of population and wealth in the 1880s and 1890s.

49. *Notitiae,* Churches of Washington, St. Patrick's 1885 and 1888, as quoted in Fosselman, "A Downtown Parish," 199 and 201.

50. The *Catholic Mirror* and *Church News* frequently published lists of donations by parish. See, for example, *Church News,* 9 Mar 1890.

Walter's only solution to the problem was retrenchment and self-denial. It would remain for a new generation of leaders to reassess the problem and devise new methods for dealing with what Walter called a "church of strangers." Meanwhile, he concluded his long years in Washington involved in things much closer to his heart. Cardinal Gibbons left a humorous word portrait of the still-busy Walter in his last years:

If you should spend a few days in Washington, you will not fail to observe the rapidity of the motion of the lips of Father Walter, which, I think, move more rapidly than those of any congressman in our city, and which would be a terror to the reporters if they were required to record what he had to say. You would also not fail to observe the rapidity of the motion of his feet, which would put to shame any professional walker. But, gentlemen, I will say for your information, that, if you put your ear to his heart, you will find that it beats still more rapidly in this and in every other good cause for the advancement of liberty.[51]

Gibbons too, it appeared, had come to love and admire his often outspoken but generous subordinate. After the Third Plenary Council called for the designation of irremovable rectors, Walter was one of the three (the only Washington pastor) so honored by Gibbons in 1887.[52]

Another bout of poor health, this time a persistent sore throat, forced Walter to take another vacation, again paid for by a congregation that received bulletins on the patient's condition as he made a whirlwind tour to Lourdes and the British Isles. He was back in four weeks, apparently restored to his old self. He kidded the parishioners about how he was finally relieved of the persistent salty taste that had been his most annoying symptom. The doctors told him he was suffering from pynosis, Walter explained, but none could tell him what it meant nor could he find it in any dictionary. He decided to overlook it for the present but to have placed on his tombstone: "He died of pynosis."[53]

---

51. Remarks of Cardinal Gibbons before the Catholic Young Men's National Union, recorded in *Proceedings of Sixteenth Annual Convention, Catholic Young Men's National Union, of the United States,* 7–8 Oct 1890, 12.

52. *Catholic Mirror,* 10 Sep 1887. The other two were Fathers William T. Gaitley and Edmund Didier, long-time pastors in Baltimore. The subject of irremovable rectors was discussed at the tenth and last diocesan synod, see Spalding, *Premier See,* 251–52.

53. *Catholic News,* 11 Jul 1891. Walter's illness and trip were well covered in the Catholic press. See, for example, the *Catholic News,* 30 Sep, 7 and 28 Oct 1888, and the *Catholic Mirror,* 29 Sep, 6 Oct, and 17 Nov 1888.

Walter had hurried back, he said, because there was still so much work to do. He had been instrumental in establishing a House of the Good Shepherd in Washington and was anxious to watch over its care of delinquent girls. He had also become treasurer of the Bureau of Catholic Indian Missions, a time-consuming and difficult task as that new organization tried to set guidelines for the missionary associations, collect money nationwide, and establish mission schools.[54] Closer to home, Walter led the fight against the rule that barred religious instruction at the District's reform school. After prolonged negotiations, men of the parish's St. Vincent de Paul Society were permitted to visit the school weekly, teaching catechism and leading prayer services for young Catholic inmates.[55] In 1890 Cardinal Gibbons made further use of Walter's financial expertise by asking him to help select sites for new churches in Washington. His committee arranged for the purchase of two lots on Eleventh Street, Northeast, for Holy Name parish, and St. Patrick's played host to its first pastor until his new quarters were completed. At Gibbons's request Walter also selected and purchased the land for St. Teresa's Church in Anacostia.

He remained busy and useful to the end. In June 1893 he was on hand to administer the last rites to the dying when the floor of Ford's Theater (then an office building) collapsed. In July he treated the orphans and sisters of the city to a river excursion to Marshall Hall, one of those small generosities, the *Church News* stated without exaggeration, "that fill many hearts with admiration." In September he received a medal from the Don Bosco Society, acknowledging his aid for the homeless—denizens of the city's almshouse, jail, and reform school. In reporting the award, the *Church News* noted that, like Bosco, Walter had begun his own singular life of charity by helping one orphan boy. Now, the paper commented, his help was extended to thousands and limited only by his means.[56] His sudden death on April 5, 1894, led to great public obsequies that included a funeral procession

54. *Catholic Mirror*, 30 Jul 1887. The Bureau was established in 1874 at the request of the bishops with Native Americans in their care. It had a lay commissioner, who was charged with advancing Indian rights before the federal government and operated under a director general appointed by the archbishop of Baltimore. Walter served as treasurer until his death in 1894.

55. *Catholic Mirror*, 20 Feb 1886 and 6 Jul 1889. For more on the need for such negotiations, see same source, 2 Jun, 11 and 18 Aug 1883.

56. *Church News*, 3 Sep 1893. Some events during Walter's final months were discussed in the same source, 9 Jun and 16 Jul 1893.

stretching from the gates of Mt. Olivet to St. Patrick's Church. Many noble orations extolled the life and work of St. Patrick's fourth pastor. None, however, better defined the man's character nor explained the wellsprings of his congregation's affection than the verse from the Fortieth Psalm carved into his tombstone: "Blessed is he that understandeth concerning the needy and the poor; the Lord will deliver him in the evil day."[57]

In choosing John Gloyd as the new pastor and assigning St. Patrick's a second assistant priest in the person of the noted orator Denis J. Stafford, Cardinal Gibbons signified a willingness to defy the implications of the shrinking congregation. The grand new church in the center of the nation's capital had proved a suitable and popular site for major religious ceremonies, and it was clear that Gibbons wanted somehow to find a way to reverse the trend in local attendance and the drop in parish support. Gloyd, a native of Gaithersburg, Maryland, had most recently spent five years as pastor of St. Stephen's, where he enjoyed a considerable reputation for parish building and sound fiscal management.[58] His appointment, and the addition of the charismatic and nationally prominent Stafford to the staff, gave some indication of how Gibbons expected the reversal to occur. Meanwhile, St. Mary's would get its new church just five blocks away, and St. Aloysius would continue to attract St. Patrick's parishioners. In a very real sense, Gibbons was challenging the new pastor to create and maintain a dynamic new center for Catholic Washington in an environment that some skeptical observers had decided was due for a long slide into irrelevance.

Gloyd's solution to the parish's problems quickly became apparent. He would complete the church without delay and use its magnificence to instill a new sense of pride, attract greater attendance, and increase local support. When asked later how he could achieve all this without incessant appeals for money, he told the press that, while he would be grateful for any offers of help, he would not be soliciting funds. He had the cardinal's permission to borrow, and he would leave

57. Walter, *A Memorial Tribute*, 59–69. Walter's death and funeral were fully covered in the secular and religious press. See, for example, *Star*, 6 Apr 1894, *Church News*, 14 April and 15 Sep 1894. The *Post*, 10 Apr 1894, gave a long description of the funeral. In addition to the large monument over his grave in Mt. Olivet, Walter was also commemorated by an elaborately carved memorial tablet in the church.

58. For an outside assessment of Gloyd's abilities that dwells on his fiscal acumen, see *Star*, 3 May 1894.

the meeting of these new obligations up to the congregation and its "sense of honor, religious zeal, and appreciation of the work."[59]

He began with a well-publicized flurry of activity. Within weeks of his arrival the rectory was completely renovated. In less than a year contracts had been let for frescoing the interior of the church, building the grand altar, enlarging the sacristy, replacing the gas lighting with electric fixtures, and installing a new pipe organ, probably the city's largest (the old one was dismantled and once again installed in Carroll Hall). The sanctuary was being tiled with a center stone brought from St. Peter's in Rome by a "lady of the city"; a sanctuary lamp, whose finely decorated panels and lights veiled by red glass cost more than $1,000, was installed. Reflecting the wonder people still held for electricity, reporters frequently commented on the "numberless electric lamps hidden away in the carvings of the ceiling and capitals" ready to burst forth in light "at the command given by pressing a single button." Plans were also afoot to build a marble and onyx altar railing with wrought metal gates.[60]

The new additions were scheduled to be installed in time for the Eucharistic Congress, but the altar was not yet in place when Satolli and Gibbons, enthroned on matching seats on opposite sides of a dramatically illuminated sanctuary, presided over the opening ceremonies in October 1895. The altar was finally blessed in April 1896. A 25-foot addition to the sacristy, a new altar rail, and installation of carved oak cathedral stalls in the sanctuary followed in rapid succession. Each new addition was accompanied by press notice that it ranked as "one of the biggest in the city" or among "the most elaborate in the nation." Such hyperbolic appeals to parish pride aside, Gloyd had successfully completed the grand design of the church in just a few years, a task his predecessor predicted would take a generation to achieve. In recognition of such efforts, a grateful cardinal bestowed on Gloyd the title irremovable rector of "this important parish" in 1896.[61]

Gibbons was correct in referring to St. Patrick's as an important parish. Against considerable odds it had constructed an edifice that stood at the center of Catholic ceremonial life in the capital. More im-

59. Quoted in Church News, 12 Oct 1895.

60. All these changes were carefully recorded by the Catholic press. See the Church News, 9 and 16 Jun 1894, 9 Feb, 20 and 27 Apr, and 11 May 1895, 21 Mar 1896, and New Century, 5 Mar 1898, and 9 Jun and 14 Jul 1900. Comments on the lighting are from articles in the Church News, 17 Aug and 28 Sep 1895.

61. Ltr., Gibbons to Gloyd, 1 May 1896, 93-G-1, Gibbons Papers, AAB.

portant, an energetic and generous congregation had maintained its effective role as a leader of the city's charitable life, shouldering responsibilities considerably beyond what should be expected of a parish that had begun to dwindle in population and economic resources. In doing so the congregation had also developed a rich social life, a Catholic fellowship (to borrow a word so often used by their Protestant neighbors) that bound them to the parish and to each other. It would remain for Gloyd and his successors to bend the congregation's pride in their mighty temple and their loyalty to the parish into an effective weapon to fight the inevitable problems that were sure to come with the church's changing environment.

CHAPTER 9

A Church Triumphant

THE TWENTIETH CENTURY opened to find St. Patrick's approaching the zenith of its fame and influence in the American church and the federal city. By any standard of measurement the church far exceeded the role usually assumed by a parish in that period, even one historically or architecturally significant. In the solemnity and opulence of its religious ceremonies, the variety and effectiveness of its parish organizations, and even the renown and authority of its pastors, St. Patrick's had come to fulfill the hope expressed by John Carroll and others more than a century before that Catholics might possess a grand national church in Washington.

As Father Gloyd had predicted, the congregation responded to this renown with renewed generosity and unparalleled participation in parish affairs. Alluding to the increased activity, parishioners playfully took to calling the old brick rectory on Tenth Street the "red house" in contrast to the White House just six blocks to the west.[1] Still, increased activity would not in itself solve the problem so starkly outlined by Father Walter in his last years. St. Patrick's boundaries now embraced much of "downtown,"

1. Abbé Felix Klein, *In the Land of the Strenuous Life* (Chicago: A. C. McClurg, 1905), 264.

to use a term just then coming into vogue. The half-empty church and unrented pews of recent years were a natural result of changing residential patterns and a haunting reminder that whatever the parish's future, it must be accomplished with fewer members, and a reduced base of financial support.

The renaissance that occurred early in the new century was largely the work of two men, Denis Stafford and William Russell, dynamic leaders and nationally prominent priests who served in turn as pastors between 1901 and 1917. Their solution to the challenge facing St. Patrick's was straightforward enough: ignore shrinking parish rolls and increase both attendance and support by attracting persons living outside its boundaries, those whom sociologists call externs or extra-territorials. Retain the loyalty and support of this larger group by involving them in a series of revitalized devotional and social programs. Nothing was guaranteed in this approach; success depended ultimately on the convenience of an increasingly mobile urban population, the continued interest of second- and third-generation American Catholics in the old-world religious splendor that had so moved their parents, and, finally, the desire of a transient congregation to participate in the work of a church closely involved in the life of the inner city.

It would be a mistake to underestimate the difficulties these men faced. Dependent as they were on outside support, they must accurately gauge the nature of that support and ensure that St. Patrick's continued to reflect the interests and aspirations of Catholic Washington. These interests had been changing. The old antagonism between the early Anglo-Catholic leaders and the later, more numerous and mostly Irish immigrants had long faded. Unlike the church in communities where immigration from eastern and southern Europe was beginning to pose severe problems, Washington Catholics were becoming a largely homogeneous, upwardly mobile group that eagerly embraced the American traditions, interests, and ideals expounded by leaders like Theodore Roosevelt. At the same time, in common with their co-religionists across the country, local Catholics were also under attack from a new generation of nativists, groups like the Evangelical Alliance, the formidable American Protective Association, and, later, the Ku Klux Klan, which fanned the flames of bigotry by stressing Catholicism's foreignness and questioning Catholic loyalty. Such attacks served to remind Catholics of the differences that still separated them from the American mainstream and consequently caused them, even as they fought for acceptance, to cling to the safety and comfort of their Catholic ghetto.

Pastors had to take this ambivalence into account, appealing to sentiments to join the American mainstream by underscoring Catholic patriotism while emphasizing traditional Catholic interests and loyalty to Catholic organizations. Deftness of the kind shown by the universally respected Cardinal Gibbons was required; it remained to be seen how men like Stafford and Russell, the most visible leaders in the local Catholic community, would meet the challenge.

The Gift of Oratory

Actually Father Gloyd deserves credit for beginning the reversal in the parish's fortunes with his headlong drive to complete the interior of the church and thereby attract Catholics from all over the city to attend St. Patrick's regularly. Yet within less than three years of his arrival, the popular priest began to suffer from the health problems that led to his death in 1901. Increasingly the direction and execution of the parish's new programs were left to his assistant, Denis Stafford.

Stafford must be counted among the most celebrated churchmen in the history of the city. A well-educated man with an earned doctorate from Georgetown University, he was abundantly endowed with what historian John Tracy Ellis called the high social graces. Dr. Stafford, as he was habitually addressed, counted among his friends leaders of church and state, including President Theodore Roosevelt.[2] He retained as well a large and loyal following among Catholics of all classes. The wellspring of this popularity was his unparalleled achievement as an orator. Stafford's reputation preceded him to St. Patrick's, where his first sermon, given before a packed congregation, was fully reported and analyzed in the press.[3] From that date, it was enough to announce his appearance in any pulpit or theater to assure a standing-room-only audience.

Even into recent times Americans have reserved a special adulation for their great orators, and St. Patrick's was fortunate to number among its priests and visitors some of the most notable speakers pro-

2. Ellis, *Gibbons*, 2:481. Stafford was the subject of countless newspaper articles (see, for example, *Catholic Mirror*, 12 May 1894 and *New Century*, 11 Jan 1908) and more extended treatment in Smith's *History of St. Patrick's Church*, 78–89, and Fosselman's "A Downtown Parish," 212–23.

3. *Catholic Mirror*, 19 May 1894.

duced in the American church. Early assistants Stephen Dubuisson and Constintine Pise were famous for their winning eloquence; Timothy O'Toole was counted among the city's most gifted speakers. Excerpts from one of O'Toole's sermons, an extemporaneous discourse on the light of faith prompted by a church suddenly plunged into darkness when a winter wind extinguished the lights during Mass, have survived.[4] In it the reader sees how the poetry produced by his considerable imagination was carefully disciplined by a classical rhetoric, a skill especially treasured by nineteenth-century audiences.

In John Keane the parish enjoyed sermons and lectures from a man nationally recognized for his oratorical skills. Many of his words survive, and one can only marvel at the power and logic, if not the Victorian excesses, of even his most spontaneously offered remarks. For example, pressed suddenly to address a convention of young Catholic men, he used their presence at St. Patrick's to underscore the importance of patriotism: "Love of God and the love of country, two loves which together form the virtue of charity, meet in our hearts as Catholics and citizens, and blend to form and make our character."[5] Keane's speeches must be counted as one of the reasons for the growth and vitality of parish organizations in the later nineteenth century.

St. Patrick's provided the setting for famous orations by bishops like England and Ireland. Within living memory, Ignatius Smith thrilled St. Patrick's audiences and standing-room-only crowds gathered to hear Fulton J. Sheen, who was a frequent guest and whose gift was admired by millions of Americans. Yet even in such eloquent company, Denis Stafford was altogether exceptional. For years the papers kept a running record of his appearances before hundreds of audiences, appearances that fell into several general categories. First were his frequent speeches at public gatherings and college exercises. Generally on patriotic and civic topics, these talks were ecumenical in content (many were delivered under Protestant auspices) and skillfully explored the underlying theological basis of the liberties guaranteed by the Constitution.

Stafford's dramatic readings, especially those from Shakespeare's tragedies, probably won him his greatest fame. These performances, given throughout the eastern United States, always before capacity au-

4. *Catholic Mirror,* 7 Jan 1860.
5. Quoted in *Proceedings of the Sixteenth Annual Convention of the Catholic Young Men's National Union,* 17.

DENIS J. STAFFORD

diences, earned considerable sums for various charities.⁶ In 1898 he turned down an offer of $40,000 (equivalent to some $620,000 today) plus a third of the profits to present a season of dramatic readings on Broadway. Commenting on the offer, the Baltimore *American* touched on Stafford's "remarkable intonation and modulation of voice, perfection of gesture and great power of expression." The New York *Sun* called him "one of the greatest living masters of expression." Discussing a series of sixty-five performances of Shakespeare's tragic heroes that netted more than $1,800 each, the Washington *Times* concluded that neither the celebrated actor Henry Irving nor the grand opera could draw such audiences. In 1908 the *Star* summed up his local fame: "The most remarkable feature is the fact that in this city, where he has been preaching for nearly 20 years, he always commanded the largest and most representative audience ever gathered to pay tribute to a lecturer."⁷

And then there were the sermons. For every time and season, it seemed, Stafford was ready with homilies inspiring, passionate, and even shattering. Reports circulated in the city of overwrought parishioners fleeing the church in tears, unable to contain their emotions during one of his moving homilies.⁸

All this posed a dilemma for Cardinal Gibbons when Father Gloyd died in 1901. Stafford's ever-growing popularity in the city made him the logical successor, but, considering his youth and recent incardination in the diocese (although born in Washington, Stafford was ordained and had served until recently in the Cleveland diocese), such an early promotion would mark a sharp break with tradition. Meanwhile, Gibbons was being overwhelmed with an extraordinary number of petitions on Stafford's behalf from many sources, including civil and national leaders of all faiths. All dwelt on his eloquence, ecumenicism, patriotism, and ability to fight prejudice. One noted civic leader, who had refused to sign the petitions because she was not a Catholic, had initially considered Stafford "pompous because of his eloquence

6. Stafford's performances were frequently subject to press notice that rarely failed to provide details on the purpose of the show, size of the audience, and gate receipts. In some years Stafford delivered monthly and even weekly lectures at the National and Lafayette theaters and at Metzerott Hall. See, for example, *Church News,* 3 Feb and 3 Nov 1900 and *New Century,* 22 Feb 1902.

7. Press reaction was collected and printed in Smith, *History of St. Patrick's Church,* 80–85 and Fosselman, "A Downtown Parish," 213. See also, *Star,* 3 Jan 1908.

8. Archbishop Hannan, a Washington native, repeated the testimony of several witnesses to Stafford's performances in his interview with author.

and . . . flattered by women admirers." Nevertheless, Charlotte Smith had changed her opinion, she told Gibbons, because Stafford "has the eloquence that draws, is humble as a priest, and above all, is charitable and good to the poor. Protestants as well as Catholics hope that he will be retained as pastor."[9] Always sensitive to popular appeals, Gibbons broke with tradition and summoned Stafford to an examination of pastoral candidates. Soon thereafter he installed the young administrator as sixth pastor of St. Patrick's.

Stafford had a noted advantage over his immediate predecessors in that he could initiate a number of expensive parish programs with solid financial backing. The power of his oratory and the effect of the beautiful church interior, finally completed according to the design of its gifted architect, had together prompted a dramatic reversal in parish fortunes. Despite a parish population that had averaged less than 3,000 people since the opening of the new church in 1884 and in 1901 totalled only 1,800 within its territorial limits, the church was filled to the doors every Sunday. The reason, of course, was the attendance of regular visitors from other parishes. Although church law required Catholics to support their pastor and recognized his exclusive right to officiate on certain occasions, it also recognized individual preference and geographical convenience and thus sanctioned attendance at any church. In 1901 Stafford could report "the number of people in the parish," by which he meant residents and externs, at 2,500. By 1905 the number had grown to 4,000–4,500, indicating that by that date 60 percent of the regular attendees at the church came from outside the territorial limits of the parish.[10]

As to be expected, this influx had a dramatic effect on the church's financial position. The pews, which remained half-rented in Walter's last days, were now leased to generous externs. In 1908 the list of pewholders contained the names of 100 people living within the parish boundaries along with 167 from other parts of the city. Sunday collections also continued to rise even as the number of residents dropped. When the leases on the F Street property expired in 1907, the parish was able to take advantage of the growing popularity of the local business district to raise the rates appreciably.[11]

9. Ltr., Charlotte Smith to Gibbons, 6 Apr 1901, 98-T-12, Gibbons Papers, AAB.

10. Figures in this and the following paragraphs are from Notitae, St. Patrick's Washington, various dates, AAB. Their significance is analyzed in Fosselman's "A Downtown Parish," 221–22.

11. Total parish receipts, exclusive of money borrowed by Gloyd to decorate the church in 1895 and by Stafford to build the new rectory and school in 1904, averaged

Business in the Red House

Its newfound financial security provided the parish with the means to launch an ambitious building program in 1904, the catalyst being the recent closing of St. Vincent's orphanage and school. The continued influx of business establishments into the area had caused the trustees (who, under the presidency of the pastor of St. Patrick's, retained control of the institution) to begin searching for a more congenial location even as it raised the value of their property. They had sold two lots facing Eleventh Street in 1896, but retained the main buildings until 1899, when department store magnates Woodward and Lothrop offered the unprecedented sum of $450,000 for the remaining land. It is interesting to note that both Gloyd and Stafford, along with their fellow trustees were well aware of the purpose to which the merchant buyers meant to put the land directly across the street from the church.

When the orphanage moved to "Edgewood," the Kate Chase Sprague estate in northeast Washington, in December 1900, the parish resorted to several stop-gap measures for the female students, including recruiting the Holy Cross sisters to open the short-lived St. Vincent's Academy. Meanwhile, despite the parish's declining population, Stafford made clear his determination to sponsor a parochial school in keeping with the exhortations of the hierarchy and the renewed prominence of the parish.[12] Accustomed to thinking on a large scale, he planned to raze Carroll Hall and the adjoining schoolhouse and in their place erect a building large enough to house four hundred pupils and a spacious auditorium. At the same time, to complete the parish facilities, he proposed to replace the rectory with a modern residence that would meet the needs of an expanding staff and important ecclesiastical guests. While at it he decided to finish the exterior of the church by constructing either twin octagon towers with lofty spires on the west front or the 300-foot central tower called for in O'Connor's original plan.

Carroll Hall and the rectory were substantial buildings not yet fifty years old. Frequent references to their antiquity must be taken as part of Stafford's campaign to win the cardinal and parishioners over to his

---

$15,000 annually between 1885 and 1905. There followed a steady increase to an average of $73,000 in 1916–1917. Meanwhile the congregation continued to shrink, standing at 2,500 people (both residents and externs) by 1917. See statistical record file, SPA.

12. For a history of St. Patrick's Academy, see below, chapter 13.

proposal, when all that was absolutely required was an enlarged schoolhouse. Like Gloyd before them, both Stafford and his successor appreciated the importance of parish image in attracting visitors. At the same time it must be said that Stafford and Russell were part of what historian Spalding described as a general trend among the clergy of that time to live better than their congregations. The pastor's $1,000 yearly salary (assistants received $600) was in addition to room, board, and other benefits, thus providing considerably more discretionary funds than the typical parish family, whose annual income totalled little more than $600.[13] Such an observation does not detract from the well-documented generosity of both men or impugn their motives when it came to the vast amounts expended at St. Patrick's for valuable and beautiful things. It does, though, illustrate how men used to associating with the city's affluent in luxurious surroundings and to receiving handsome compensation for their labors came to consider such expenditures appropriate and even necessary.

There was little doubt that Stafford wanted the best. To harmonize with the church, the new buildings were designed in the English gothic style using the same expensive blue gneiss stone and Ohio limestone trim. Although he went so far as to hire a firm of architects to prepare sketches of a completed church exterior, cooler heads prevailed and costly plans for one or more towers were quietly dropped.[14] Cardinal Gibbons, agreeing to the rest of the building program, signed a series of promissory notes totalling $150,000 that used the F Street properties as collateral. The total cost of the buildings was $140,480 (equivalent to more than $2.1 million today) exclusive of fees for architects and lawyers.[15]

In contrast to earlier times when a lack of consensus on where to build and difficulty in obtaining funds caused incessant delays, the new rectory and school rose almost overnight. Stafford planned the

13. Spalding, *Premier See*, 271–72.

14. Plans for a tower (costing more than a million dollars in today's values) were mentioned in Klein's *In the Land of the Strenuous Life*, 255–56, and were still being discussed as late as 1907. The architects hired for the task were William Franklin Wagner and Haswell R. Williams. An artist's rendition of the proposed tower was printed in *The Patrician* (Dec 1909), 2.

15. The loan, which was extended in 1913 to cover an addition to the school, was discharged in October 1919. See Deed of Release, recorded 10 Dec 1919, *liber* 6402, fol. 161, and annex, dated 14 Jun 1928, copies with annotations by Msgr. Cornelius Thomas in SPA. A breakdown of construction costs was prepared by John S. Larcombe, the building contractor, and submitted on 23 Dec 1904. Copy in SPA.

dedication ceremony to coincide with what he declared was the parish's 110th anniversary. Actually the date chosen for the week-long gala had no discernible connection with the parish's foundation; more to the point, it fit in with Teddy Roosevelt's busy schedule. For what he would later call the "proudest day in the history of St. Patrick's," Stafford had achieved a considerable social coup: the appearance of the President of the United States at the opening of a parish school and rectory.[16]

Roosevelt spoke on November 21, the first day of the dedication. Standing on the balcony of the new rectory with Cardinal Gibbons and other dignitaries of church and state, he addressed a throng estimated at twenty to thirty thousand on the parish's distinguished service to the city and the duties of its citizens, ending with one of his familiar exhortations on the importance of manliness and moral courage. Cardinal Gibbons and the president of the D.C. Commissioners, Henry B. F. Macfarland, also spoke, but the oratorical fireworks were saved for later in the week. Stafford joined with Bishops Keane, Ireland, and John Lancaster Spalding in a series of sermons and lectures in the church and new hall on Catholic education, recent developments in church-state relations, and the role of St. Patrick's in the history of the American church.[17]

If a presidential appearance and Stafford's frequent patriotic addresses delivered before all sorts of audiences around the city were used to push Washington's Catholics into the social mainstream, the unabashed splendor and variety of religious services at St. Patrick's could be viewed as a response to the yearnings of those still dwelling in a religious ghetto. Catholics who thrilled to the beauty and pageantry of the sacred rites filled the church. An estimated fifteen thousand visited the elaborately decorated sanctuary on Holy Thursday in 1907. People solaced by the popular devotions regularly sponsored by the parish flocked to services, often with their non-Catholic neighbors in tow. The press frequently noted the "crowds" of non-Catholics at St. Patrick's, especially during the annual Lenten services that featured weekly lectures by the pastor.[18] Nor did it fail to com-

16. Stafford mentioned this "proudest day" on several occasions. See, for example, *Star*, 14 Jan 1907.

17. Speeches by Roosevelt and Gibbons were reproduced in the *Catholic Mirror*, 26 Nov 1904. For a program of the week's events, as well as an exhaustive front-page account of the first day's ceremony, see the *Star*, 21 Nov 1904.

18. See, for example, *New Century*, various issues, 1902, especially 22 Feb, and *Star*, 4 Mar 1907.

A SPEECH FROM ST. PATRICK'S BALCONY. *President Theodore Roosevelt at the 1904 dedication with a seated Cardinal Gibbons*

ment on the pageantry. Reporting on the celebration of Corpus Christi in 1907 with, as was frequently the case, the apostolic delegate presiding in pontifical robes, the *New Century* editorialized: "The ceremonies at St. Patrick's were august and impressive to a degree only possible in a parish where tradition of pomp in church ceremonies is in the air."

To enhance these frequent religious events, Stafford reorganized the choir around a cadre of professional musicians and inducted a battalion of well-trained acolytes.[19] He also obtained the services of Holy Cross priests and seminarians at Catholic University. These clerics

19. For a description of the music program under Stafford and Russell, see chapter 14, below.

would continue to supply the parish with extra confessors, preachers, and ministers for more than half a century. Rarely a week passed without some noteworthy event taking place in the church. Christmas, Holy Week, and St. Patrick's Day were in a class by themselves. Whether for a special appearance by one of the Pope's colorfully costumed Noble Guards, the presence of royal visitors at solemn high Mass, or the frequent gatherings of the Perpetual Adoration Society with the main altar resplendent with colored lights and banks of flowers, St. Patrick's would be filled with those drawn by the moving pageantry.[20]

Even these ceremonies paled in comparison to the reception tendered the archbishop each January. Evolving from a special New Year's Eve Mass of thanksgiving first held at St. Patrick's in 1895, this annual reception for Cardinal Gibbons came closest to fulfilling Stafford's dual ambition of pushing the church into the American mainstream and appealing to his co-religionists' traditional love of pomp. The celebration centered around a Mass presided over by Gibbons and the apostolic delegate, usually in the presence of other members of the hierarchy. It began with a procession of church dignitaries and ministers accompanied by a guard of honor drafted from the parish's various organizations and the city's marching societies. After Mass the cardinal received his many Washington friends, including representatives of the government and diplomatic corps, and shook hands with individuals in the large congregation (a reported 2,500 people jammed into the church and rectory in 1899). The long line of well-wishers patiently worked its way through the front door of the rectory, past the cardinal, and then managed to exit through the back.[21]

Encouraged by the parish's enthusiasm, Stafford succeeded in making the reception, dubbed "Cardinal's Day," an annual event on the second Sunday of January. The parish pulled out all the stops in 1907 for this "homage to the Prince of the Church," transforming St. Patrick's into a riot of scarlet lights, ribbons, and flowers. When the long line of greeters finally passed through the rectory, Stafford entertained at a luncheon where the cardinal, Vice President Charles W. Fairbanks, Justice Edward White, and others spoke. For over a decade

20. *New Century*, various issues, 1905–1907. See, for example, 25 May 1907. Stafford organized the Perpetual Adoration Society in 1895. By the end of the century it had become one of the parish's most popular devotions. See *Church News*, 3 Feb and 23 Dec 1899.

21. Descriptions of some of these early receptions survive. See, for example, *Church News*, 4 Jan 1900, *New Century*, 11 Jan 1902 and *Star*, 22 Jan 1906.

the ceremony would be repeated, always attracting large crowds, a varied roster of celebrities, always with full notice in the press.[22] Amid descriptions of the pomp and circumstance, the press also managed to underscore the special message of the occasion: Gibbons was being honored by his distinguished guests for his clearly articulated Americanism. In fact religious freedom was the recurring theme of the annual celebration. Both the cardinal and guest speakers paid tribute to the Bill of Rights, which, they agreed, had produced a system of laws mutually beneficial to church and state. Gibbons put it succinctly in 1910 when he reminded his Cardinal's Day audience that "every Catholic who loves his church must love the government under which it is prospering."[23]

Despite the pace imposed by a heavy speaking schedule and church ceremonies, Stafford found time for other projects, using his growing prestige to represent the diocese in matters great and small. He was regularly deputized by the cardinal to arrange his White House visits and perform delicate diplomatic missions. In 1905, for example, he reported to Gibbons that, as instructed, he had appealed to the President concerning the church's interests in Paris, and Roosevelt had ordered the secretary of state to do everything he could to see things settled as the cardinal wished.[24] Stafford also found time for diocesan minutiae. In 1906 he represented Gibbons at the dedication of a church at what was then North Chesapeake Beach, Maryland, built by members of St. Patrick's congregation in that popular vacation resort. The donors wanted the new church named in honor of St. Anthony, Stafford told the chancellor, while he preferred to use one of the sacred mysteries, like Nativity or Epiphany, "of which fine names the Episcopalians are always getting the monopoly."[25] The parishioners won that debate, but closer to home Stafford had his way when he named the popular needlework school he established for young girls of the city St. Zita's Sewing Class.[26]

22. New Century, 19 Jan 1907 and Star, 14 Jan 1907. For subsequent celebrations, see, for example, Star, 10 Jan 1910, 10 Jan 1916, and 14 Jan 1918 and Baltimore Catholic Review, 8 and 15 Jan 1916.

23. Quoted in the Star, 19 Jan 1910. On Gibbons's Americanism, see Ellis, Gibbons, 2:1–80, and Spalding, Premier See, 234.

24. Ltrs., Stafford to Gibbons, 29 Jun 1904, 101-K-8; to Msgr. Patrick Gavan, 10 Jan 1905, 102-J-2; and Gavan to Stafford, 12 Jun 1905, 102-J-4. All in Gibbons Papers, AAB.

25. Ltr., Stafford to Gavan, 10 Apr 1906, 103-H-7, Gibbons Papers, AAB.

26. The sewing classes continued for a number of years under the direction of a group of volunteer laywomen. The 1906 class had 56 students in attendance. See The Patrician (Jun 1908), 16.

The pastor's own literary bent no doubt spurred his attempt to revive the original aim of the Carroll Institute. Always an enthusiastic sponsor of the institute, he helped reorganize its literary society, improve its library, and renew interest in its night school. He supported these initiatives with a series of benefit lectures, such as the one he gave on "Macbeth and the Punishment of Crime" before a large, paying audience at the Columbia Theater in 1899. Thanks to his participation, the evenings of leactures and readings in the institute's library and its annual dinners enjoyed a brief vogue (although one might wonder how much the well-fed guests absorbed from lengthy after-dinner speeches like the one given in 1907 by Senator Albert Beveridge on church-state relations in France's Third Republic). While he lived Stafford never abandoned his attempts to elevate the interests of the institute, even though the overwhelming popularity of its gymnasium, minstrel shows, and amateur theatricals seemed more indicative of the future direction of what had once been a major literary society in Washington.[27]

Stafford's special interest in writing and literature led to the parish's sponsoring in 1904 a parish history prepared by a prominent journalist, Milton E. Smith. Stafford also found time to encourage the literary aspirations of young parishioners by reviewing the papers prepared by students of St. Vincent's Academy and meeting with them to discuss the finer points of grammar and rhetoric. These activities led to the establishment of a parish magazine, The Patrician. Advertised as a monthly, the journal in fact appeared about six times a year, far exceeding in scope and size what might be expected in parish publications. In addition to a calendar of events and detailed news about the activities of parish organizations and members of the congregation, it regularly featured essays and stories by parish students, inspirational poetry, and sermons and lectures by prominent clergymen. With Stafford and his successor retaining strict control of its content and contributing much of its copy, The Patrician continued publication until 1917.

It is tempting to smile at the earnestness of this exercise in literary uplift and parochial chit-chat. Yet even a cynical age must recognize that the magazine provided a comprehensive record of the manifold interests of a downtown parish. To see their work in print must have

27. Stafford's association with the institute was noted in the press. See, for example, Church News, 2 Nov 1895 and 25 Mar 1899, and the New Century, 5 Oct 1907. Senator Beveridge's appearance was described in the Star, 13 Feb 1907.

thrilled young authors and even encouraged some to further scholastic endeavor. The featured sermons and spiritual messages accurately reflected the wide variety of causes and the growing confidence of a religious group just beginning to assert itself. Unfortunately, the magazine also indulged in some heavy moralizing from time to time, decrying frequent attendance at movies or condemning the latest dance craze. It also reflected some of the worst of current social attitudes when it joined with Roosevelt and other civil leaders in criticizing the "constant agitation of the negro question." The subject should be dropped, it editorialized in 1906, because it only encouraged the black man "to believe that he owns the country."[28]

Whatever its faults and virtues, the magazine clearly demonstrates just how Stafford and his successor stimulated lay participation in the affairs of both church and city and showed by their example how their parishioners might move with confidence into the larger American society. In what might serve as a epitaph for "the gallant Dr. Stafford," a perceptive visitor commented on his wide-ranging interests and renown: "From the White House to the most distinguished *salons* or the most humble institutions, there does not exist in Washington a threshold over which one cannot enter as a friend, if only accompanied by the pastor of St. Patrick's."[29]

Epitaphs must have been far from parishioners' minds when thinking about their vigorous forty-seven-year old pastor, but in the summer of 1907 Stafford was suddenly hospitalized and later collapsed in Atlantic City where he had gone, so weak he could not walk, to recuperate. Victim of a diseased liver, he underwent an emergency operation at Providence Hospital, but in vain. His death on January 8, 1908, shocked the city. The funeral that followed was an interfaith celebration rare even today and truly extraordinary then. Presided over by Cardinal Gibbons and Archbishop Diomede Falconio, the apostolic delegate, the congregation included, in addition to a large contingent of federal and city officials, Washington's Episcopal bishop and other representatives of the city's Protestant clergy.[30]

In the weeks that followed, a group of prominent Protestants organized a memorial service for the popular priest at Chase Theater, the

28. *The Patrician* (Dec 1906), 6–7. See also, same publication, (Apr 1914), 8–9, and (Nov 1915), 13–14.

29. Klein, *In the Land of the Strenuous Life*, 268. Klein's stay at St. Patrick's resulted in an extensive summary (263–68) of Stafford's influence on the parish and city.

30. For a comprehensive account of the pastor's last illness and funeral, see the *New Century*, 11 Jan 1908, *Catholic Mirror*, 4 and 11 Jan 1908, and *The Patrician* (Mar 1908).

city's largest auditorium, where a crowd gathered on February 9 to hear pastors and rabbis, senators and commissioners speak about those characteristics that made Stafford so respected and loved. It was left to President Roosevelt to touch the source of this wide appeal and focus on what was a central theme of Stafford's brief pastorate. In a letter read to the audience, Roosevelt said that Stafford

illustrated in his life what we have a right to regard as one of the very strongest features of the American character, namely, the capacity to combine fervor of religious belief, fervor in the effort to strive for moral and spiritual betterment, with a wide and kindly tolerance of difference in individual convictions as to the form which conscientious adherence to religious belief may take.[31]

The congregation seemed devastated by its loss, and countless hours were spent discussing how best to memorialize its famous leader. An association was organized, and prominent city leaders pledged money and sought a suitable public site for a statue. But even before these plans foundered in the bureaucratic maze, the congregation had selected a far more appropriate project: it pledged the money and dedicated to his memory the massive marble pulpit he had designed shortly before his death.[32]

"That Theater on Tenth Street"[33]

Gibbons lost no time in selecting Stafford's successor, and on February 23, William T. Russell, the cardinal's long-time secretary and later rector of the Baltimore cathedral, became seventh pastor of St. Patrick's. Stafford's final plea, "Do what you can to keep St. Patrick's on the boom," was widely circulated, and if the selection of such a

31. Ltr., Roosevelt to D.C. Commissioner H. B. F. MacFarland, 6 Feb 1908, reproduced in *New Century*, 15 Feb 1908. For a list of the scores of sponsors of the memorial meeting, see same publication, 8 Feb 1908.

32. *New Century*, 2 May 1908. Stafford's death unleashed a spate of articles and sermons. Everything from the content of his will and the debates of the memorial committee to long essays on his contributions to the community and effect on the church in Washington appeared in the *New Century* during the next two years. See, for example, issues of 25 Jan and 30 May 1908 and 23 Jan and 17 Apr 1909. For a description of the pulpit, see chapter 14, below.

33. Several sources attribute this sarcastically meant but critically apt description of St. Patrick's during the early decades of the century to Father Valentine Schmidt, the tart-tongued pastor of St. Joseph's on Capitol Hill. See, for example, author's interview with Msgr. Arthur.

prominent official as Russell indicated the parish's importance, it also underscored Gibbons's determination to fulfill Stafford's dying wish.[34] Russell was no match for his predecessor's art and charisma, but he was a learned and cultivated man as well as an experienced executive with exceptional organizational ability.[35] Moreover, he possessed a missionary's burning spirit with a genuine desire to attract Washington's non-Catholics to the church and to lead his fellow Catholics to what he considered their rightful place in American society.

From the beginning he made it clear that he subscribed to Stafford's techniques for carrying out the parish's mission, and under his direction the grand ceremonies and events, which had become commonplace, now became even more magnificent, more crowded, and certainly more costly. Where Cardinal's Day had been an important occasion for Catholic Washington, it became under Russell a glittering social event that garnered national notice. The *Saturday Evening Post* described the luncheon that followed the ceremony in 1911 at which a hundred diplomats and government officials, including the British ambassador and "a fair smattering of major-generals and rear-admirals," honored the cardinal. The magazine went on to muse about how such a guest list, taken for granted at such an occasion in Washington, would be played up by the sophisticated New York press. Yet here, as a matter of course, it would seem, "big men" gathered at a parish rectory to greet a prince of the church and gave such good speeches "which, even in dinner-giving Washington, is not universally the case."[36]

The parish had in the past welcomed many foreign dignitaries, but never more frequently than under Russell. In 1908 St. Patrick's welcomed President Roosevelt along with other senior government officials and the diplomatic corps on behalf of the Austrian ambassador to a Mass commemorating the sixtieth year of Emperor Franz Joseph's reign. The *Star* passed on a theatrical moment during the proceedings when Cardinal Gibbons removed his biretta and bowed to Theodore

34. Stafford's remark was made just before his death to his assistant, Thomas E. McGuigan, and quoted in *The Patrician* (Apr 1917), 71.

35. While pastor at St. Jerome's in Hyattsville in 1894, Russell attended Catholic University where he earned the coveted licentiate in sacred theology. He also held two honorary doctorates. In 1908 Mount St. Mary's College awarded him a doctorate in laws and letters and St. Mary's Seminary a doctorate in divinity for his numerous books and articles.

36. *Saturday Evening Post*, 15 Feb 1911, as quoted in Fosselman, "A Downtown Parish," 224. See also Baltimore *Catholic Review*, 10 Jan 1915 and 20 Jan 1918.

Roosevelt as he left the altar.[37] (Eight years later many of the same people, along with President Woodrow Wilson, would gather at the
church to participate in a memorial service for the emperor.) Not content with honoring monarchs in absentia, Russell also arranged a reception for Queen Liliuokalani of Hawaii when that lately deposed
royal visited Washington. In 1910 the Pope's special representative,
Cardinal Vannutelli, received a glittering reception at St. Patrick's. The
crowds were so great that the Roman visitor agreed to bless the congregation from the rectory balcony, suitably draped for the occasion
in the papal banner surrounded by U.S. flags.[38]

During the later years of Russell's pastorate, St. Patrick's was continually bathed in ceremonial brilliance. By 1913, Forty Hours had become an occasion of "utmost splendor." The *New Century* described
with obvious approval the liturgical procession enhanced by the presence of children dressed like pages in a medieval court. On Easter Sunday in 1914 the apostolic delegate, Archbishop John Bonzano, presided
from his purple throne. That same year Russell received permission
for midnight Mass on Christmas, a rare event in those times, and by
1916, this ceremony, with its orchestra and special decorations all advertised in the press days before the event, caused so much interest
that tickets had to be distributed to control admittance.[39] This constant stream of ceremonies, special services, and distinguished visitors
produced the desired result. By 1916 St. Patrick's required six scheduled masses on Sundays while its popular evening prayer service
crowded the church every weekday—all in a parish that counted fewer
than two thousand Catholics within its boundaries. Once again, it
would seem, the whole city had become one parish.

Russell's most enduring contribution to church-state pageantry at
St. Patrick's was the Pan-American Mass. He claimed that the idea of
encouraging closer relations among representatives of the American
republics through a public act of thanksgiving struck him while reading Roosevelt's Thanksgiving Day proclamation in 1908. With the
help of John Barrett, secretary-general of the then Pan-American
Bureau, he won the newly elected William H. Taft's promise to participate, provided that all the Latin-American diplomats agreed to at-

37. *Star*, 2 Dec 1908.

38. *Star*, 30 Sep 1910. The deposed Hawaiian queen arrived in Washington on 29
Nov 1908, to petition the U.S. government for compensation. See *New York Times*, 30
Nov 1908.

39. Ltr., Russell to Gibbons, 5 Dec 1914, 114-O-16, Gibbons Papers, AAB. *New Century*, 11 Oct 1913, and Baltimore *Catholic Review*, 11 Apr 1914 and 23 Dec 1916.

tend.[40] Arrangements were successfully completed, and on Thanksgiving Day 1909, a solemn Mass was sung in the presence of Cardinal Gibbons, the apostolic delegate, representatives of the Latin republics and the President of the United States. The *Post* called the event a demonstration of religious toleration "unparalleled in the annals of religious functions in this country."[41]

At the luncheon that followed, Secretary of State Philander C. Knox suggested that the Mass be celebrated again the following Thanksgiving. (The Pan-American Mass would be repeated annually at St. Patrick's for almost six decades.) No embellishment would go untried in its staging. In 1909 Russell arranged for two choirs with organ and full orchestra to participate in a church ablaze with candles and spotlights, its columns and pews decorated with the flags of the Americas. Later masses featured a recessional march that somehow included in its measures the national anthems of all the Latin American nations plus the Star Spangled Banner![42] In 1915 a gigantic replica of the dove of peace was suspended above the main altar, and participants received a solid silver commemorative medal engraved with the *Santa Maria* on one side and the name of St. Patrick's pastor, never one to shy from celebrity, on the other. One enduring feature of the annual event: a rigid protocol rivaling that of the court of Louis XIV. The seating and ranking of diplomats caused innumerable problems for ushers and masters of ceremony schooled in the altogether more democratic ways of cardinals and presidents.[43]

The continued intimacy between St. Patrick's and the White House, together with the tendency for diplomats to regard the Pan-American Mass as an official function, did not go unnoticed in Protestant circles. When President Woodrow Wilson announced his intention to continue the tradition set by Taft, the clergy of several denomi-

40. "The First Pan-American Thanksgiving Day," *The Patrician* (Dec 1909), 9–24, is the most comprehensive contemporary source. See also *The New Century*, 27 Nov 1909. Later sources (see, for example, *Catholic Standard*, 18 Nov 1960 and 16 Nov 1962, and author's interview with Archbishop Hannan) credit Gibbons with conceiving the idea for the ceremony, but the unsigned article in *The Patrician*, probably written by Russell, includes an extract from Gibbons's speech that specifically gave credit to Russell.

41. *Post*, 26 Nov 1909.

42. Although the Baltimore *Catholic Review* (29 Nov 1913) reported the "The Pan-American March" was first performed in 1913, it was performed by Professor Gleotzer, its likely composer, and Jeanne Glennon in 1911. See *The Patrician* (Dec 1911), 5.

43. Protocol problems long endured. See author's interview with Archbishop Hannan, who supervised the Pan-American Mass in the 1960s.

nations held a series of protest meetings. The one organized by local Episcopalians at the Raleigh Hotel denounced the Thanksgiving celebration as an "effort by the Roman hierarchy to give the Roman mass the color of an official function." Russell was not one to turn the other cheek. Expressing sorrow that ministers of the gospel would object to a celebration dedicated to peace and good will, he denied that any responsible agent had claimed the event an official function. He wondered why critics should seek to dictate where the President might worship, "and try to prevent his enjoying the right of even the poorest citizen."[44]

Although Wilson attended the Mass in 1913, the criticism achieved its desired effect. That year marked the last appearance of a chief executive at a Pan-American Mass until 1967. Usually the United States was represented by the secretary of state, the chief justice, and other senior officials.

The dispute over the Pan-American Mass was just one more skirmish in an ongoing battle with elements of the Protestant clergy. Beginning with the so-called Evangelical Alliance in the 1880s and continued by the American Protective Association in later decades, respectable ministers openly appealed to old nativist fears with new attacks on the Catholic church. If the fire had not gone out of their arguments, their power to frighten what was once a largely immigrant congregation had certainly diminished. Now Catholics gave as readily as they got. In December 1887, for example, the pastor of St. Matthew's, Father Placide Chapelle, offered a spirited defense against attacks from the evangelicals, defending the Catholic church as "the truest and most powerful friend of what is best in civilization." For its part the *Catholic Mirror* sympathized with the evangelicals, who were just concluding their national conference in Washington. It was the goup's "impossible task," the paper editorialized "to harmonize the discordant elements of the various anti-Catholic sects."[45]

In Russell's day the Reverend Randolph H. McKim, rector of the nearby Epiphany Episcopal church, was among Catholicism's most articulate and implacable foes in Washington. Following the protest over Wilson's visit to St. Patrick's, he and Russell engaged in a locally celebrated debate that featured McKim's "Why I Am a Protestant" address and Russell's no less spirited rejoinder, "The Catholic Is the Most

44. Quotations from *New York Times*, 19 Nov 1913.
45. *Catholic Mirror* 17 Dec 1887. Father Chapelle's feisty rejoinder to Protestant critics was quoted in the *Star*, 12 Dec 1887.

PAN-AMERICAN MASS, 1911. President and Mrs. William Howard Taft escorted by the pastor, William T. Russell

Tolerant of American Citizens." With deep roots in Maryland society, Russell was famous for his authoritative account of the origins of Protestant–Catholic relations in his book, *Maryland, the Land of Sanctuary*. This fact, and his reputation for fierce put-downs, ensured a wide audience among the city's Catholics for his debate with McKim.[46]

The city was treated to a humorous if somewhat heavy-handed exchange between Russell and the rector of St. Thomas Protestant Episcopal Church in 1915. Some jester apparently sent the latter an invitation to St. Patrick's inquiry classes. His reply included the claim that he was a priest of the Catholic church which, in distinction to the Roman church, "has rightful jurisdiction in this country." He pressed the point, adding that, no matter its worldwide pretensions, the Roman church in England and America "is simply an Italian mission, an alien schism."

These words prompted a sarcastic rejoinder from Russell that did little to advance the cause of ecumenicism, but no doubt increased the doughty pastor's popularity with his congregation. He began by assuring the Anglican that, had he intended to cause a laugh, "he would have enjoyed the scene at St. Patrick's rectory when the rector read the letter to the clergy." Russell went on to lecture the recently naturalized Dr. C. Ernest Smith on the constitutional basis of religious liberty and poked gentle fun at one born under the English flag and into a denomination whose numbers in the United States "scarcely equal one-half the Catholic population of New York city." He chided Smith for calling native-born Catholics an alien class, but nevertheless took pleasure, he claimed, in learning of Smith's great respect for the Catholic Church "in those countries where it has rightful jurisdiction." In this, Russell concluded, "the rector of St. Thomas resembles the great men of all ages."[47]

Russell's confrontations with the Protestant clergy of Washington underscores an essential difference between him and his predecessor. Stafford possessed a true ecumenical spirit, a willngness to deal openly with non-Catholics in a mutual quest for truth and salvation. His lead-

46. The historian of Epiphany church noted that "toward the Roman Catholic Church McKim's words sometimes verged on the vitriolic." See Stetson Conn, *Washington's Epiphany: Church and Parish, 1842–1972* (Washington, 1976), 89. Russell's rejoinder, which appeared in the Baltimore *Catholic Review* beginning on 14 May 1914, was later reprinted under the title "Who Were the Founders of Religious Liberty in America?," copy in SPA.

47. Their exchange attracted press notice and was printed in full in *The Patrician* (Jan 1916), 11–12.

ership concentrated on breaking down the wall of the self-imposed ghetto where many Catholics lived philosophically secure but in many ways outside the mainstream of American intellectual life. The erudite Russell, on the other hand, was a proud leader of that ghetto church. With a self-assurance sometimes unwarranted, he rejoiced in the superiority of the Catholic position in all matters both theological and social. It followed that he felt constrained to challenge any slight; fiercely debate any difference of opinion; and base his highly praised evangelization on a strong dose of Catholic apologetics.[48]

The Missionary Spirit

Without gainsaying the often-stated purpose of the Pan-American Mass, it is obvious that that event and all the other elaborate ceremonies were used by Stafford and Russell to further their new goals for the city's downtown church. Such functions not only strengthened the loyalty of a congregation now drawn from all parts of the city, but also attracted national notice to the parish, thereby enhancing the prestige of the Catholic church in Washington. Yet if these externs came initially for the theater, as one disgruntled pastor put it in criticizing Russell's activities, they remained for more complicated reasons. Most important to Russell, the liturgical spectacle and enthusiastic city-wide congregation led naturally to the proselytizing that he considered the heart of the parish's mission.

The number of converts received at St. Patrick's during the nineteenth century attested to the importance always given evangelization in the parish. Priests like Dubuisson, O'Toole, and Stafford attracted great numbers of Washingtonians, both prominent members of society and humble laborers, to the church. In February 1907 Stafford organized a week-long lecture series for non-Catholics at St. Patrick's under the direction of the Paulist Fathers, which under his successor became an annual event. It was left to Father Russell to provide the greatest innovation in the parish's evangelization program when he succeeded in involving the laity directly in the work of Catholic outreach.

Russell's interest in evangelization and his determination to use parish resources to attract converts were not new. During his first pastorate, at St. Jerome's in Hyattsville in 1894, he had attracted attention

48. Spalding summarizes the philosophical underpinnings of the ghetto church in *Premier See*, 321–23.

by his work among the bedraggled poor and homeless members of Coxey's Army. That certainly peaceful group had marched to Washington to petition an unsympathetic government for social justice and jobs. Condemned by a public that saw in the movement a breakdown of law and order (the *Catholic Mirror* called it the "March of Cranks"), the hungry and dispirited men set up camp at nearby Bladensburg. There they encountered resistance from angry residents, including many St. Jerome's parishioners, who demanded their immediate eviction. Not so the young pastor. Russell organized a relief service to ensure that the men were fed and clothed, and he went among them to tell the Catholics that they were now part of his congregation. When he announced a mission for the men, some 250 of all faiths marched under the eyes of thirty sheriff's deputies to his little church.[49]

In subsequent years Russell sought permission to become a missionary, but was refused by Gibbons. Only after assignment to St. Patrick's, rich in human and material resources and located in the center of a capital ripe for evangelization, were his missionary instincts allowed full play. In the judgment of one expert, St. Patrick's then became the nation's best-organized parish for attracting converts, advertising its mission, and energizing its laity to participate in the work.[50]

To involve the laity in this enterprise, Russell formed the League of the Good Shepherd in 1908. The new organization imposed on its members a regimen of prayer, spiritual exercises, and religious instruction to prepare them to defend the faith by explaining the church's doctrines to non-Catholics, especially seeking the conversion of relatives and friends. Its members, all men, met on Sunday evenings to pray and hear lectures, such as the opening series during which Russell discoursed on the question "Is One Religion as Good as Another." Russell had no intention of limiting the parishioners to a passive role in what he conceived as a major effort directly linked to the church's universal missionary effort. During his audience with the Pope in July 1909, he spoke of the importance of lay involvement. The Pope approved the league and an arsenal of indulgences for participants. By 1913 more than a thousand men, including a substantial number of non-Catholic associate members and guests, had enrolled.[51]

49. *Catholic Mirror*, 31 Mar (source of quotation) and 4 Aug 1894. See also Walter Elliot, C.S.P., "An Apostolic Parish," *The Missionary* (Sep 1916), 481–87, for an extended account of Russell's work with members of Coxey's army.

50. Elliot, "An Apostolic Parish," 484.

51. The organization and work of the league received full coverage in the Catholic press, which is the source for the next few paragraphs. See, for example, *New Century,*

The league sponsored an annual mixed retreat (with a special section of the church reserved for non-Catholics) and a lecture series for non-Catholics that drew large audiences. The latter featured a "question box," in which league members and their non-Catholic friends would deposit questions on all sorts of subjects. The questions were answered by the pastor and other experts during well-attended meetings on the third Sunday of the month. The idea intrigued Cardinal Gibbons, who stayed in Washington especially to attend one of the early question box sessions in 1913. The league also built and supplied St. Patrick's pamphlet rack. Later a ubiquitous furnishing in churches, these libraries of popular essays sought to answer "almost every doubt or problem" for Catholics and "the non-Catholic seeker for Truth."[52] This evangelization generated an incredible amount of preaching. The *Catholic Review* faithfully recorded the many times Russell and two of his more eloquent assistants, James A. Smyth and John M. McNamara, along with scores of Paulists, Dominicans, and others spoke at league meetings. In April 1916, for example, nine hundred league members and one thousand guests gathered to hear Russell's adamant message on divorce. Calling the spreading problem a "loathsome leprosy," Russell concluded, "American as I am in every fiber of my being, I cannot but view with alarm and shame the divorce evil in our country."[53]

League work seemed to stimulate the parish's spiritual energies. In addition to the considerable increase in the number of converts, the priests were especially pleased to note more frequent reception of the sacraments among life-long Catholics, which they ascribed to attendance at league masses. Although similar groups sprang up in other parishes, Russell shied away from forming any kind of diocesan organization, and Washingtonians interested in such work tended to gravitate to St. Patrick's. There the league remained the principal lay organization for over a decade. During those years, attendance at weekly meetings averaged 350, with 900 men present at the monthly mass.

While the league pursued its mission of Christian outreach, the men of St. Patrick's were also participating in a series of activities designed to show their fellow citizens the growing power and importance of the church in American society. The mass parades and out-

7 and 14 Nov 1908, and 25 Sep 1909 and Baltimore *Catholic Review*, 15 and 19 Jan and 14 Oct 1916. For Russell's trip to Rome, see *Star*, 19 Jul 1909 and 24 Jan 1910 and *New Century*, 24 and 31 Jul 1909.

52. Baltimore *Catholic Review*, 19 Feb 1916.

53. Quoted in the Baltimore *Catholic Review*, 8 Apr 1916.

door rallies that characterized what has come to be called muscular Christianity would flower under Gibbons's flamboyant and combative successor, but they made their initial appearance in the years before World War I. Washington Catholics, like most of their fellow citizens, loved parades. Since the demise of the St. Patrick's Day parades around 1890, outdoor spectacles connected with the parish had been limited for the most part to abbreviated marches along Tenth Street by participants in special church ceremonies and May processions. All that changed early in the new century. Suddenly, it seemed, Catholicism was on the march.

In Washington the phenomenon began with the Holy Name parades. Originally founded to fight profanity, the society quickly grew into the largest organization for Catholic men in the diocese. (Because it was considered impractical to organize two major groups for its men, St. Patrick's merely affiliated its League of the Good Shepherd to the Holy Name organization and participated in its public functions.) The society sponsored the first of its local parades in 1910, when some 6,000 marchers, representing every parish in the region, swung up Pennsylvania Avenue past the White House. President Taft was on hand to review the various contingents as their bands blared out "Hail to the Chief." By 1912 the event had adopted the pattern familiar to coming generations of area Catholics. Contingents from parishes throughout the region, along with massed ranks of male religious from the houses of study associated with Catholic University, marched by divisions. (There was a separate division for black parishes.) The banners, flags, colorful religious habits, and music from a great number of bands all combined to make a lively spectacle, especially when they gathered at the conclusion for Benediction. In 1912 some 12,000 marchers and an estimated 20,000 spectators knelt together near the Washington Monument.

Other groups joined in these public displays of Catholic power. In 1911 Catholic war veterans and members of the semi-military organizations and beneficial societies sponsored a march that concluded with an audience numbering some 25,000, including President William Howard Taft, attending a so-called military field mass on the ellipse. The energetic Russell served as grand marshal of the event and spent long hours discussing logistics with an army of lay deputies. He was also the celebrant and took advantage of an occasion designed to honor the "patriotic dead" to assert that the presence of the Chief Executive demonstrated the government's sympathy with the work the church was doing on the nation's behalf. The experience gained from such extravaganzas stood Russell in good stead when in 1914 he was called upon to organize the participation of Washington parishes in a mammoth parade in Baltimore sponsored by the American Federation of Catholic Societies.[54]

The frequently stated purpose of these outdoor events, which would continue to grow in size and complexity in the next decades, was to demonstrate the God-centeredness of Catholic organizations as well as attract non-Catholics to the church. The parades would provide Cardinal Gibbons's successor with a bully pulpit to condemn the weak-kneed backsliders and extoll Catholic manhood. "No mollycoddles here," Archbishop Michael J. Curley would tell the crowd in 1922.[55] Just how such displays were supposed to support the serious work of evangelization is uncertain; it could even be asserted that such ostentatiousness was counterproductive as a method of Catholic outreach. In any event, the great rallies were hugely popular among the parishioners in Washington and actively encouraged by the clergy, who in the early years turned out en masse in their top hats and black coats to march with the faithful legions. Transcending the stated aims, the long lines of marchers also represented a group just beginning to free itself from the psychological restraints imposed by generations of nativist attacks and determined to show that it had become a power to be reckoned with in American society.

William Russell viewed his frequent negotiations with federal officials as a part of Catholic outreach. Of all St. Patrick's pastors, he had the most extensive dealings with the President and Congress on behalf of the worldwide interests of the church. During his years in Washington, international concern centered on the growing war in Europe and the revolution in Mexico, both of which had broad implications for the welfare of the church. Among the issues that deeply involved St. Patrick's pastor was the plight of the North American College in Rome during the revolutionary disturbances in Italy. Working through Secretary of State William Jennings Bryan, he succeeded in getting the American ambassador to place the college "publicly and officially under his protection." Later Russell won similar protection

54. The parades and rallies were fully covered in the press. See, for example, *Star*, 10 Nov 1910; the *New Century*, 27 May 1911 and 26 Oct 1912; and the Baltimore *Catholic Review*, 26 Sep 1914. Russell's remarks to President Taft are quoted in *The Patrician* (June 1911), 12–20.

55. See, for example, accounts in Baltimore *Catholic Review*, 14 Oct 1922 (source of quote), and 9 Jan and 20 Feb 1931.

for the Pope's delegate in Constantinople, who was working for Armenian relief.[56]

Russell also represented Gibbons in negotiations on behalf of persecuted Catholics in Mexico. In particular he asked the government's assistance in pressing the Constitutionalist party under Venustiano Carranza to guarantee the safety of the Mexican clergy and to protect church property. A flurry of consultations resulted in President Wilson's making a representation on the part of the church that achieved at least a temporary diminution of the persecution. In 1914 Carranza instructed his agent in Washington to assure Russell that the rights of the church would be honored.[57] During his last months in Washington, Russell continued to press the cause of the Mexican church as the revolution turned ever more anticlerical. In January 1917 he intervened on behalf of a Mexican bishop put on trial by the revolutionists. Reaching Secretary of State Robert Lansing at his home late at night, he won a promise from the Wilson administration to intervene. The next day he met with Senators Thomas J. Walsh and Joseph E. Ransdell, and, he reported to Gibbons, "We decided that they and others should go see Wilson tomorrow."[58]

Woodrow Wilson had reason to be grateful to St. Patrick's pastor, who had gone out of his way to extract the President from an embarrassing political situation. In April 1913 Russell had accompanied Cardinal Gibbons on his first visit to the Wilson White House. In subsequent weeks a story began circulating to the effect that the President had addressed the venerable cardinal as "Mr." Gibbons. Although apocryphal, the story refused to die and, seen as a terrible affront to the American church in some circles, began to excite considerable heat among Catholic voters. Finally in a widely quoted piece in the Baltimore *Catholic Review* in 1915, Russell tried to squelch the story. Denying that such a remark had been made in his hearing, he went on to say that Wilson would never "consciously do anything that might be considered as a lack of courtesy or consideration for any Catholic priest or prelate."[59] Nevertheless, the "Mr. Gibbons" story was widely

56. Ltrs., Russell to Gibbons, 15 May 1915, 115-Q-12 (source of the quote), and 17 May 1915, 115-R-6; Bryan to Russell, 15 May 1915, 115-R-1, and 17 May, 115-R-7; and Lansing to Russell, 14 Oct 1916, 117-M-9, and 26 Oct 1916, 117-N. All in Gibbons Papers, AAB. On the Roman riots, see Robert F. McNamara, *The American College in Rome, 1855–1955* (Rochester, New York: Christopher Press, 1956), 446–47.

57. Ellis, *Gibbons*, 2:207–9.

58. Ltr., Russell to Gibbons, 20 Jan 1917, 114-L-11, Gibbons Papers, AAB.

59. Baltimore *Catholic Review*, 6 Mar 1915. For a detailed account, see Ellis, *Gibbons*, 2:514–18.

circulated by the administration's foes during the 1916 presidential campaign. The cardinal, who was anxious to remain neutral during the election, merely called the story "foolish gossip," and, although Wilson dismissed it as preposterous, the Democrats were left only with Russell's article, which they distributed throughout the country to fight the rumor. It apparently helped defuse the politically explosive issue.

Throughout these years, St. Patrick's urbane pastor kept up an active social life among the movers and shakers of the city. Whether entertaining the likes of the speaker of the House of Representatives and influential congressmen at one of his well-known stag dinners at St. Patrick's rectory or accepting invitations to participate in civil and social functions involving the capital's intellectual elite, he set an example for his fellow Catholics as they, too, began to participate more fully in the social mainstream.[60] Intellectually formidable, Russell betrayed in his approach to the outside world a self-righteousness akin to that of Caffry and Walter. Notably lacking were the charm and easy accessibility characteristic of the truly ecumenical spirit of Matthews and Stafford.

During Russell's pastorate St. Patrick's was the scene of two meetings of the local Catholic clergy at which subjects of considerable interest to later Catholics were discussed. In February 1909 the regular quarterly gathering of the city's secular priests reviewed President Roosevelt's well-publicized views on birth control. A topic only recently introduced to public debate, birth control was branded by the President as a form of race suicide. The priests agreed with this sentiment and went on to condemn as immoral any attempt to limit the size of American families. They also stated that literature advertising birth control "should not be circulated or read."[61]

A year later the same group assembled in St. Patrick's church to take the oath against Modernism as required by Pope Pius X. The condemnation of Modernism was the outcome of a long dispute in the European church over attempts to reconcile traditional teachings with advances in scientific criticism. Unfortunately, Modernism was mistakenly associated by some with an earlier call by a group of American progressives led by Bishops Ireland, Keane, and O'Connor for adopt-

60. See, for example, account of a dinner at St. Patrick's for the editor of the *Dublin Review*, Wilfred Ward, that included among its guests Speaker of the House Champ Clark, Commissioner of Education Philander Claxton, and Senators Walsh and Ransdell in Baltimore *Catholic Review*, 20 Dec 1913.

61. Statement of Washington clergy as quoted in *Star*, 24 Feb 1909.

ing the American system of separation of church and state as a model for the universal church. Somehow when translated abroad their proposition became involved in the larger debate over Modernism, so that in 1899 Pope Leo XIII, siding with their opponents, condemned what became known as "Americanism." Just what was being condemned was not clear. This action and the more explicit condemnation of Modernism eight years later by Leo's successor had little direct effect on the life of American Catholics, although it ended speculation in Catholic intellectual circles for several decades and ushered in an era that emphasized church tradition and centralist authority.[62]

Considered in this context, the words chosen by Stafford in speaking to a parish group in 1892 could not have been a mere coincidence. "We must take the age as we find it, and not live in the past or the future," he said, adding,

There is no reason why we should not accept our age and glory in it, for with all its faults, it is great in its intense intellectual life, its desire for improvement, and its willingness to accept truth when seen. But to glory in our age, we must understand it; we must study it, examine it with unprejudiced eyes, and grasp as freely as we can its trend, use its language, and appreciate its aspirations. After that we will be prepared to direct it by pointing out the good and shunning the evil as only the possession of Catholic truth can enable us to do.[63]

Stafford followed this credo, and it would be a mistake not to recognize, in the parish's renewed openness toward its non-Catholic neighbors, its eagerness to participate in the church's social mission and its ardent defense of the separation of church and state the influence of men like Keane and Ireland at the parish level.

Parish Interests

Father Russell's work at St. Patrick's had not gone unnoticed by higher church authorities. In 1911 the Pope conferred on him the rank of domestic prelate with the title of right reverend monsignor, a rare distinction in those days. Few expected his advance to end there, as the press openly discussed his candidacy whenever a vacancy occurred in the hierarchy. Finally in December 1916 came the news that Russell

62. For a recent summary of the Modernism controversy and its effect on the American church, see R. Scott Appleby, *"Church and Age Unite!" The Modernist Impulse in American Catholicism* (Notre Dame: University of Notre Dame Press, 1992).

63. Address at the laying of the cornerstone of the Carroll Institute, 20 Jul 1892.

was to be the next bishop of Charleston, South Carolina.[64] Thanks in large measure to his dynamic leadership and sound management, the parish appeared in robust good health in both attendance and material resources at the time of his departure. In announcing the change in pastors, the *Star* reported that St. Patrick's was recognized as the richest Catholic parish in the United States. Although such an assertion amounted to little more than a wild guess, Russell openly referred to himself as the "wealthy pastor of St. Patrick's."[65]

A brief decline in revenue in 1914 had allowed Russell to demonstrate his fund-raising technique. He began by announcing that an increasing number of parishioners were neglecting pew and seat rents in favor of Sunday offering. Offertory collections were a notoriously unreliable source of support, he warned, and although St. Patrick's had never charged admission in the past as so many other churches did, it might be forced to reconsider if pew rents did not pick up. Actually Stafford had from time to time charged admission to special services to cover the cost of the music, although, as Russell was no doubt aware, admission fees were prohibited in the diocese. Without any specific reference to St. Patrick's or other local churches, the apostolic delegate had pointed out the church's universal ban on admission fees to the American hierarchy in 1911.[66] However sincere the pastor's threat in 1914, both pew rents and Sunday collections rose in subsequent years, providing sufficient funds for further improvements to the church.

Thanks to the generosity of its many extern parishioners and escalating income from its F Street property, St. Patrick's reached an unprecedented level of material prosperity by 1917. It had discharged all the debts associated with Stafford's construction program and made a substantial dent in the new loan contracted to pay for the addition of third-floor classrooms and a roof garden to the academy.[67] During this

64. Russell's consecration in Baltimore and the reception tendered him at Poli's theater in Washington were fully reported in the Washington papers. See, for example, *Star*, 15 and 19 Mar 1917. For an example of earlier rumors about Russell's assignments, see same paper, 1 Nov 1911. Russell was frequently mentioned as likely successor to Gibbons. See, for example, *Star*, 26 Mar 1921.

65. *Star*, 5 Dec 1916. Russell's comment was made as the new bishop of Charleston accepted a purse from his former parishioners. See *The Patrician* (Apr 1917), 49.

66. Russell's threat appeared in *The Patrician* (Mar 1914), 10–11. Stafford collected an admission fee on St. Patrick's Day; see *New Century*, 16 Mar 1907. The apostolic delegate's warning was carried by the *Star*, 14 Oct 1911.

67. The school addition cost $25,000. See ltr., Russell to Gibbons, 9 Feb 1912, 110-C-

period St. Patrick's led in contributions to diocesan causes, even top-
ping the sums collected in the Baltimore cathedral in 1917. In the previous year it contributed more than twice the sum collected at any
other church in the diocese to the annual Catholic University appeal,
always a favorite charity at St. Patrick's because of its affection for
Bishop Keane and the fact that its pastor was the president of the university's alumni.[68]

Like Stafford before him, Russell saw no virtue in frugality. During
his pastorate the parish spent large sums on embellishments. In 1910
it added a chancel organ and elaborately carved furnishings to the
sanctuary. In 1913 it remodelled the sacristy, installing parquet floors,
marble wainscoting, Flemish vestment cases, verde antique lamps and
new skylight—additions, noted one reporter with a gift for stating
the obvious, "that made the room elegant."[69] The following year
the church replaced the sanctuary floor with one of costly white
and green Vermont marble with Verdose marble trim and a much-
admired centerpiece, a large mosaic of a shamrock.

During this period the church also completed the installation of the
stained glass and designed a "dolorosa chapel" in the baptistry for
which the pastor commissioned a pieta and complementary wall
paintings. In 1915 the sodality donated a new statue of the Blessed Virgin. The congregation also sent to Italy for a marble statue of St.
Joseph, which they dedicated to the memory of Rose Russell, the pastor's recently deceased mother, a popular resident of the parish.
Among such donations as a "monsignor chair" for the sanctuary, altar
cards with illuminated texts, and pontifical vestment sets, the one that
stirred most comment (to judge by press coverage) was a gold and silver ciborium made from melted rings and other family jewelry donated by parishioners. Studded with some 350 jewels, the vessel was
valued at $12,000 (equivalent to $150,000 today). In response to those
who missed the chance to donate, Russell announced a second gold

---

6, Gibbons Papers, AAB. Gibbons's approval for the work concluded, "I hope you will
succeed in paying a good slice of the principal every year." See note, Gibbons to Russell, 1 May 1913, copy in SPA. Parish finances are difficult to trace during this period.
These figures are based on Fosselman's work in records no longer available.

68. The Baltimore *Catholic Review* published the results of the various diocesan collection drives which showed St. Patrick's leading all other churches in the amounts
collected in 1917. The Catholic University collection was sometimes treated specially
by Russell, who would send the money directly to the Cardinal. See, for example, ltr.,
Russell to Gibbons, 7 Dec 1916, 118-B-3, Gibbons Papers, AAB.

69. Quoted in the *New Century*, 25 Oct 1913.

drive, this time to make a thabor, the ornamental stand on which the monstrance was displayed.[70]

Clearly such aesthetic enterprises were never allowed to compete with traditional charities. With the pastor's encouragement, the numerous lay organizations, now including many nonresidents in their ranks, exhibited considerable robustness in assuming new obligations such as the Ladies Catholic Home Placing Bureau sponsored by the parish's Ladies of Charity. Forerunner of services performed by Catholic Charities in later years, the bureau worked throughout the city to systematize adoptions and develop a wider choice of institutions for the training and supervision of older Catholic orphans. While continuing the practical assistance to poor women and children that had always been their special responsibility, the women began to adopt some of the sophisticated techniques of modern social workers, as they carried out hospital inspections and home visitations. One of their particular concerns was the welfare of the residents of the Home for the Blind.

While the parish's St. Vincent de Paul Society and its women's auxiliary continued their traditional work, they also began to assume tasks now commonplace in urban American. Responding to a plea from the diocesan chancellor in 1910, the men's group sponsored a full-time chaplain for the city's correctional institutions.[71] In 1916 it opened The Good Samaritan House on Third Street as a shelter for the city's homeless. At about the same time the women's auxiliary began operations at Martha House, where it provided temporary accommodations for unemployed women or those whose wages left them in poverty.[72] The women also assumed a large part of the financial responsibility for the Nursery of the Holy Family, a day-care institution established by the Ursuline sisters in a rented building at Third and C Streets in 1916. As conceived by Monsignor Russell, who initiated the project, the nursery was meant to relieve the strain on the city's Catholic orphanages by providing working mothers an alternative to full institutional care for their children. The nursery remained

70. News about such gifts and additions were the stuff of weekly parish columns. See various issues of the *New Century* and Baltimore *Catholic Review*, 1910–1916.

71. The need for a full-time chaplain was discussed in ltr., Gavin to Russell, 19 Feb 1910, 108-B-7, Gibbons Papers, AAB.

72. Little is known about these charities, including how long they remained in operation. Both probably lasted through World War I. The Baltimore *Catholic Review*, 30 Dec 1916, and *The Patrician* (Jan 1917), 10, and (Apr 1917), 11, describe the purpose of the homeless shelters.

open long hours and provided children of the working poor between ages one and six with substantial meals and supervised play for five cents a day.

To support this relatively new concept in child care, the women organized the Ladies Auxiliary of the Holy Family Nursery that gathered members from across the city. Their annual dues, which, with additional assistance from benefit performances by the parish dramatic club and the modest tuition, covered operating costs. When the nursery moved to larger quarters on Fourth Street at the end of 1916, the parish donated $900 toward purchase of the new building; the rest was collected by the auxiliary. Five years later the parish acquired an adjoining property, enough to accommodate eighty children and, beginning in 1922, the primary classes from St. Patrick's Academy.[73]

Parish lay organizations continued to rely on old-fashioned money-raising methods. They collected annual dues from members, solicited personal contributions from individuals and local businesses, and sponsored fund-raising events like the annual Strawberry Festival and amateur theatricals. These entertainments continued to fill an important role in the parish's social life. The two-night homecoming festival sponsored by the Ladies of Charity in May 1916, for example, played to packed houses which watched a Knights of Columbus minstrel performance along with a patriotic panorama starring a member of the parish who sang "The Meaning of Uncle Sam" while colored spotlights played on the large American flag draped over her shoulders.[74] The always-popular dinner dances and euchre parties continued as regular parish events, not only realizing large sums for charity, but also demonstrating a considerable softening in the diocese's old prohibitions against such worldly entertainments.

The parish buildings were the scene of constant activity in those days, all centered around the devotional, educational, and charitable work of some twenty separate groups. With more than eight hundred members, the sodality was the largest in the city, its membership ex-

73. The Holy Family Nursery was described in *The Patrician* (Mar 1916), 13–14, and Wentz, *Inventory,* 18. Although the latter source implies that the parish purchased the properties on Fourth Street, tax records list the Ursuline sisters as owners of lots 808 and 809 in square 351 in 1923–24. By that date Archbishop Curley (read St. Patrick's) had also acquired ownership of the adjacent lot 807. Although the Ursuline and diocesan archives contain no record of these transactions, it is possible that some time after purchasing the properties, the parish transferred the convent and adjoining grounds to the sisters.

74. Baltimore *Catholic Review,* 13 May 1916.

ceeded only by that of the League of the Good Shepherd, which had come to be accepted as its male counterpart. The Children of Mary and the League of the Sacred Heart also attracted a large congregation for their special devotions. At the same time the church sponsored a well-organized Sunday school association whose forty teachers, both lay and religious, including a group of Holy Cross scholastics, presided over a student body that averaged 450 students. Three choirs flourished. So too did the Perpetual Adoration Society, Ushers Association, Sanctuary Society, Altar Boys Association, St. Patrick's Alumnae and Library Association, Propagation of the Faith, and Catholic Knights (a charitable society organized by Russell in 1909 for the parish's young men) as well as the St. Vincent de Paul Society, its Auxiliary Ladies of Charity, even the St. Patrick's String Orchestra and the Popular Science Association. All held their meetings, sponsored their special events, and fulfilled their special goals, hundreds of people from all parts of the city deeply involved in the spiritual and social life of the parish.[75]

In a day when such groups all looked to their spiritual directors for guidance, the number of priests needed to assist in the work of so many organizations and to officiate at church services had grown accordingly. In contrast to Father Stafford's two assistants, the staff had grown by 1911 to include five priests. One of their constant and most time-consuming tasks was hearing confessions, especially as Catholics from all over the city began to take advantage of the daily confession hours which Russell had instituted shortly after his arrival.

Later he started a weekly holy hour. The popularity of this devotion led to a regular evening prayer service that nearly filled the church. The pastor derived much pleasure from leading these simple exercises and always included one of his extemporaneous homilies. He loved to sing and took great delight in the sound of the boy's choir that accompanied the service, frequently augmenting its offering with a solo of his own. The long lines outside the confessionals, the constant stream of those "making a visit" during busy shopping trips, and the sight of so many people ending their day's business in prayer, would become hallmarks of St. Patrick's in succeeding generations. All this began with Russell in his last years as pastor. While the grand events at St. Patrick's continued to capture the headlines, the long-lasting influence

75. The activities of these various groups were chronicled in the pages of *The Patrician*, see various issues, 1909–17. The charitable work of the Catholic Knights, which had some 600 members in 1909, was outlined in the *Star*, 30 Nov 1909.

on the prayer life of thousands of Washington Catholics in the setting of these simple evening prayer services may in the end have been this eminent churchman's greatest contribution to religion in the capital.

Even with a seemingly limitless ability to attract the city's Catholics to St. Patrick's and stimulate their interest in its organizations, William Russell was not blind to the long-term threat posed by changing residential patterns. The decision to establish a second national parish—this one for Italian immigrants—within St. Patrick's boundaries during the last months of his pastorate showed not only how diocesan policy could exacerbate the parish's problems, but why development of a new role for the downtown church as pushed by Stafford and Russell was essential.

As early as 1904 the apostolic delegate had expressed concern about the treatment of the city's new Italian-speaking Catholics. In contrast to their nineteenth-century predecessors, who were now fully integrated into the city's Catholic community, these newcomers, mostly skilled masons and their families brought in to build Union Station and other public buildings, were frequently shunned by Catholic neighbors who had begun to exhibit many of the anti-foreign attitudes of their old nativist foes. Some of the immigrants reacted to their cultural isolation by answering the appeals of Protestant proselytizers. Finally in 1913 Cardinal Gibbons appointed Nicholas De Carlo, an Italian priest studying at Catholic University, to serve as pastor of the city's Italian-speaking community.[76] Under De Carlo the immigrants began to gather for Mass in a settlement house donated by the noted Washington philanthropist and founder of the Christ Child Society, Mary V. Merrick.

Father De Carlo immediately began planning a church for his estimated two thousand parishioners, apparently with Gibbons's approval. From the first he faced two obstacles: his congregation was widely scattered and the city's pastors all opposed the establishment of a national church in their parishes. St. Patrick's parishioners may well have shared some of the nativist sentiments, but their pastor's concern focused on the likelihood that yet another national church within his boundaries would further accelerate the already precipitous decline in parish population. Russell conceded that these new immigrants might be "led off by the Methodists" if they were denied a place to worship

76. Baltimore *Catholic Review*, 20 Dec 1913. See also *Star*, 15 Dec 1913. On national churches for Italians in the diocese see Spalding, *Premier See*, 275–76 and 296–97. On Irish-American opposition to the later immigrants see Olsen, *Catholic Immigrants in America*, 10–11.

in their own language. He agreed in 1914 to the establishment of a chapel for their use at the northeast edge of his parish. At the same time the cardinal accepted certain conditions. Holy Rosary must remain a succursal chapel of St. Patrick's (an ecclesiastical term that defined its subordinate status and the administrative rights of the pastor of St. Patrick's); admittance to its services must be strictly limited to Italians; and the whole arrangement must be understood by all to be temporary.[77] Under this agreement Holy Rosary Church was established in a house near Third and I Streets within St. Patrick's boundaries.

Neither Russell nor Gibbons seemed to appreciate the determination of Father De Carlo and his congregation. In May 1916 St. Patrick's pastor was surprised and angered to learn that Holy Rosary's congregation had purchased land at Third and F Street and was preparing to build a permanent church. That area bordered the only substantial residential section left in the parish. Moreover, Russell told Gibbons, it was near the site of St. Mary's, the other national church, which he branded as "a parasite of the parish, no longer used by the Germans to any extent, and doing all that can be done to draw away the English-speaking people."[78] His indignation barely controlled, Russell went on to explain how in a city that lacked any defined foreign enclaves or reason to expect further immigration, a national church was needed for fifteen years at most. The next generation would speak English and drift away to their local parishes, forcing the national church to entice other Catholics in the neighborhood in order to survive.

While deeming it "exceedingly unfair to injure St. Patrick's" by establishing another national church in its boundaries, Russell obviously appreciated the cardinal's dilemma. Holy Rosary had attracted the patronage of the apostolic delegate, who was exceedingly sympathetic to the aspirations of his compatriots, and Father De Carlo was never loath to appeal to that powerful protector. Russell offered a compromise. He would support a parish church for the Italians if it were located at the southeast corner of St. Patrick's territory near the Mall, which, he contended, was central to the scattered locations of the city's Italian population. Gibbons responded by ordering De Carlo to take no further steps in the purchase of land. It was probably good for

77. Ltrs., Russell to Rev. Eugene Connelly (assistant secretary to Cardinal Gibbons), n.d. (circa 10 Oct 1914), 144-H-10, and 14 Oct 1914, 114-H-7; Connelly to Russell, 13 Oct 1914, 114-H-5. All in Gibbons Papers, AAB.

78. Ltrs., Russell to Gibbons, 15 May 1916 (source of quotes) and Connelly to De Carlo, 17 May 1916, copies in Holy Rosary historical file, AAW.

the portly Russell's blood pressure that he was busy at work in Charleston when the cornerstone of Holy Rosary's permanent church on Third Street was blessed in 1919 with Gibbons presiding and the new pastor of St. Patrick's preaching the sermon.[79]

Actually, a manager as astute as Monsignor Russell very likely understood what his successor and Cardinal Gibbons would confirm in 1919: with the disappearance of the parish's resident population both inevitable and imminent, the presence of an additional national church was immaterial. Russell's anger and concern no doubt flowed from his conviction that a new rival would hasten the final state, but thanks to his efforts and those of the eloquent Stafford, St. Patrick's still retained a large and lively congregation even as its parish rolls continued to shrink. There was every reason to assume that the patterns developed during the last generation would continue, for in giving the old church its days of glory and triumph, the two pastors had also won for it the loyalty of thousands of Catholics throughout the city. St. Patrick's remained the most important Catholic church in Washington, approximately at its commercial and governmental center. As long as these twin conditions prevailed, its future appeared assured.

79. Baltimore *Catholic Review*, 9 Aug and 6 Sep 1919.

CHAPTER 10

A Church of Strangers

POPULATION CONSIDERATIONS no doubt prompted Monsignor Russell's unsuccessful fight over national churches, but there was little time for such matters in 1916, as everyone's attention started to focus on the question of peace or war. During his last months in the city, Russell watched President Wilson win a second term based on the slogan "He kept us out of war," even as American casualties, which began with the sinking of the *Lusitania* by a German submarine, sparked a national debate over military preparedness. That era also had its impassioned hawks and doves, but when Congress tripled the size of the reserve forces, young Washingtonians quickly filled the ranks of the city's expanded National Guard units.

In June 1916 Washington had staged a "Preparedness Day" parade in which organizations from around town marched up Pennsylvania Avenue behind President Wilson. Men, women, and children from St. Patrick's, each decked out in a green hat and carrying an American flag, formed a unit in the line of march behind the junior band of St. Mary's Industrial School and priests of the parish. Their colorful regalia provoked much spontaneous applause along the route and earned a great cheer when their band, passing the presidential reviewing stand, struck up "All Hail to St. Patrick."[1] Later commentators would note that much of Washington's enthusiasm that day was in support of the U.S. expeditionary force under General John J. "Blackjack" Pershing then chasing down Pancho Villa and the Mexican insurgents. Given the pastor's recent negotiations on behalf of the suffering Mexican church and the general antipathy of Irish-Americans toward Great Britain, it seems likely that the parish's conspicuous participation in the parade was less concerned with the war in Europe than with the American soldiers south of the border.

When the country finally joined in the war against Germany in April 1917, Washington once again turned to the task of creating a war machine. Overnight an army of government workers descended on the city to fill temporary office buildings that sprang up all around town. By fall the population had jumped some 25 percent to nearly 500,000, often augmented by some of the 130,000 soldiers stationed at nearby camps and training bases who spent their leave in town. The newcomers outstripped the city's ability to accommodate them and placed a tremendous burden on local institutions, including the churches. On a more personal level, some 19,000 Washingtonians, including 9,000 volunteers, served in uniform during the war. The number of parishioners in this group is not known. Since those eligible for induction could now be counted only in the scores, the honor roll was perforce a short one.

St. Patrick's in the World War I Era

In contrast to its ambiguous stand during the Civil War, the American church wholeheartedly supported the government in 1917. Led by Cardinals Gibbons and William H. O'Connell of Boston, many of the nation's bishops joined in pledging their loyalty to the American cause. Gibbons called on parishes in his diocese to sponsor talks on patriotism, and in response to a presidential proclamation, ordered special prayers recited during October 1917 for the success of the army and navy.[2] The aging cardinal threw himself into the war effort, visiting servicemen, blessing canteens operated by Catholic organizations, and attending war bond rallies. He promoted the National Catholic

---

1. *The Patrician* (Oct 1916), 12, and the Baltimore *Catholic Review,* 24 Jun 1916, offer colorful descriptions of the parade.

2. Baltimore *Catholic Review,* 27 Oct 1917. The hierarchy's statements about the war are discussed in the *Star,* 20 Apr and 13 May 1917.

War Council, a group organized at Catholic University in 1917 to coordinate the volunteer work performed by Catholic organizations in support of the war effort. At the President's request, Gibbons called for special days of prayer and fasting for peace. With his approval a special memorial Mass sponsored by representatives of the Slavic nations for the victims of the war in the Austro-Hungarian Empire was celebrated at St. Patrick's.[3]

It was left to Monsignor Cornelius F. Thomas, who became the eighth pastor two weeks after the United States entered the war, to lead St. Patrick's through the conflict and the troubling peace that followed. Although for many years associated with prestigious positions in Baltimore, including chancellor of the diocese and rector of the cathedral, Thomas was no stranger to Washington. His first assignment as a priest was as Father Walter's assistant at St. Patrick's, where he celebrated the first Mass in the new church. The new pastor must have reminded older parishioners of Walter, not only in the way he used a stern demeanor and sharp tongue to mask an essentially kindly nature, but also in his punctilious obedience to higher authority and his management of parish and diocesan affairs.

Thomas also clearly lacked his immediate predecessors' interest in the pomp that had surrounded the liturgy in the parish. Once, after enduring the rigid protocol that had grown up around the Pan-American Mass, for example, Thomas was called on by the archbishop to speak to the diplomats assembled at the interminable luncheon that followed. The weary pastor looked out over his guest-filled dining room and said, "Gentlemen, let's just say grace and get the hell out of here." On another occasion Thomas found himself kept awake late into the night by the considerable noise of the parish choir, orchestra, and organ rehearsing into the small hours for some liturgical event. The assembled forces in the choir loft were surprised to see a tall figure clad in bathrobe and night cap appear at the altar rail, shaking his fist up at them and calling on them to "stop the music, go home, and let people get some sleep."[4]

If Thomas displayed little enthusiasm for the faldcral, his years as chancellor and pastor of a major Baltimore parish left him well-equipped for the task of running St. Patrick's. During the war he

3. Baltimore *Catholic Review*, 25 May and 5 Jul 1918. See also, Philibert, *St. Matthew's*, 95. On Gibbons's role, see Spalding, *Premier See*, 315. For a comprehensive survey of the American church during the war, see John F. Piper, Jr., *The American Churches in World War I* (Athens: Ohio University Press, 1985).

4. Interviews, author with Msgr. Arthur and Mary Hope Stewart.

firmly supported parish organizations working among the troops. The sodality, for example, was just one of those groups that hosted socials in Carroll Hall for servicemen on leave. Others organized dances and shows for the non-commissioned officers from Ft. Meade or for local soldiers training at Camp Washington (now Ft. McNair) at Buzzard's Point. Parishioners also took their turn in sponsoring "Sunshine Days" at Walter Reed and the military hospital at Ft. Myer in nearby Arlington. At those times scores of St. Patrick's men and women showered patients with homemade desserts, magazines, and company.[5] Such pleasures might seem somewhat innocent for soldiers in wartime, but they were especially welcome now that the prohibitionists had finally won the day. Washington went dry in November 1917.

Taking their cue from Cardinal Gibbons, individual parishes supported the sale of war bonds, the so-called liberty loans. St. Patrick's sponsored a musical recital and liberty loan rally in Carroll Hall in early 1918 that realized a large sum for the war effort. In at least one area, however, the church refused to lend its support. When the particularly bitter cold weather of January 1918 left five thousand homes without heat and the city with less than one day's supply of coal, District Fuel Administrator Weaver ordered the closing of two-thirds of the city's churches. Monsignor Thomas countered by demanding that those Catholic churches that agreed to turn off their heat should be left open. Weaver refused, claiming that to allow any church to stay open, even if unheated, broke the spirit of the order.

Thomas appeared inclined to obey under protest, but Gibbons decided to fight. He asked Thomas to form a committee with the chancellor to deal with the government. By then the argument had escalated into a public debate, with charges exchanged among government officials and some of the more vocal clergy, including the pastor of St. Matthew's. In the end Thomas, working quietly with the authorities, arranged a compromise that authorized the allocation of enough fuel to heat all the churches six and one-half hours a week at times chosen by the pastors.[6]

The fact that some parishes used one furnace to heat both church and rectory made compliance difficult to enforce and allowed some pastors to defy the order. An early spring allowed church and state to back away from what might have become a serious confrontation.

5. Parish wartime activities were faithfully chronicled in the Catholic press. See, for example, Baltimore *Catholic Review*, 3 and 24 Nov 1917 and 2 Feb 1918.

6. Ltrs., Thomas to Gibbons, 16 Jan 1918, Gibbons Papers, and E. J. Connelly to Thomas, 25 Jan 1918, Nelligan Papers, both in AAB. See also *Star*, 27 Jan and 3 Feb 1918.

CORNELIUS F. THOMAS

Nevertheless, a similar issue arose in the fall when the overcrowded city suffered a virulent epidemic infection known as the Spanish influenza. More than 3,500 died in six weeks, and thousands of sick filled the hospitals. City services were disrupted, and troops had to be called in to help bury the dead. When the District Commissioners reacted in late September by ordering all churches closed, the archdiocese complied, banning all public masses, funerals, and outdoor services.

The ban continued for a month, eventually prompting Thomas to issue a public demand that the churches be reopened. Noting that other cities had defeated attempts to shut churches when authorities failed to impose similar bans on businesses, he charged that the order was now "unjustified, unnecessary, intolerable." He questioned the legality of the board's action, claiming that it worked "a grave curtailment of our rights as citizens and individuals" and, if unopposed, only invited governments to invade the church's rights on the slightest provocation. If the churches were not reopened by November 1 (four days hence), he would seek judicial action.[7] The churches reopened immediately.

Such disagreements did not in the least dampen the patriotic involvement of the city's Catholic organizations and individuals in the war effort. For their part, members of St. Patrick's congregation continued to purchase liberty bonds, entertain troops, care for the children of the war workers, knit sweaters, and join in those scores of other activities that constituted war on the home front.

The armistice that ended hostilities was celebrated in St. Patrick's on Thanksgiving Day in 1918 with the singing of the traditional *Te Deum,* and in the months that followed, the parish appeared to settle into its old role as a center of Catholic worship in Washington. Relieved of the restraints imposed by wartime austerities, the church entered the postwar era in a burst of liturgical splendor. It hosted a belated celebration of Cardinal Gibbons's golden anniversary as a bishop with a Mass that counted two cardinals, seventy other members of the American hierarchy, the apostolic delegate, and many government officials and business leaders in attendance. In April 1919 the parish commemorated its 125th birthday with great ceremony. Again the long procession of clergy, which included Gibbons and Bonzano, wended its familiar way from the rectory into a church filled with representatives of the government and diplomatic corps, with a crowd of old parishioners from all parts of the country. On Thanksgiving Day the Pan-American Mass, described by the *Star* as "the most brilliant of the twelve," counted both Secretary of State Lansing and General Pershing, the commander of the victorious American Expeditionary Force, among those attending.[8]

Throughout the postwar decades St. Patrick's continued to serve as a sort of pro-cathedral where liturgical occasions of national or citywide import were celebrated. In February 1922 government officials and representatives of foreign governments gathered for a solemn re-

7. Ltr., Thomas to Louis Brownlow (Chm, D.C. Commissioners), 27 Oct 1918, reproduced in *Star,* 28 Oct 1918.

8. These various ceremonies were given prominent press coverage. See, for example, *Star,* 28 Apr and 27 Nov 1919, and Baltimore *Catholic Review,* 3 May and 19 Oct 1919.

quiem for Pope Benedict XV. Two months later many of the same people, including all the parish priests in the city, returned to participate in a memorial service marking the first anniversary of Cardinal Gibbons's death. The following year Archbishop Bonzano celebrated a pontifical requiem for the victims of the great Japanese earthquake, again with the diplomatic corps in attendance.[9]

Although Monsignor Thomas took great pride in pointing out his family's Welsh heritage, he nevertheless faithfully organized the parish's traditional Irish celebrations. In September 1922 the Irish-American Union sponsored a Mass at St. Patrick's in memory of Michael Collins and Arthur Griffith, heroes in Ireland's struggle for independence. The city's St. Patrick's Day observance continued to center around the church named in his honor. The Mass in 1923 was especially interesting because it marked the first appearance of the new archbishop of Baltimore, the Irish-born Michael J. Curley, and the new apostolic delegate, Pietro Fumasoni-Biondi, at the patronal celebration.[10]

Like his predecessor, Archbishop Curley was a frequent participant in liturgical ceremonies at St. Patrick's, beginning with his official introduction to the city in January 1922 witnessed by a crowd of two thousand people.[11] This event proved to be the first of hundreds of times Curley visited the parish, which became his home in Washington. He remained especially faithful to the Pan-American and St. Patrick's Day celebrations, where his presence caused one noticeable change. The archbishop, it happened, suffered a severe allergic reaction to flowers, whose scent would send him off into fits of sneezing. When he was present the church had to depend on the ubiquitous fern as its botanical tribute.[12] During his early years as archbishop Curley decided to consolidate the confirmation of converts in a few churches. He designated St. Patrick's as the place where all white converts would receive the sacrament in Washington (black converts

9. Ltr., Curley to Thomas, 13 Sep 1923, 7-257, Curley Papers, AAB. See also *Star,* 25 Mar 1922, and Baltimore *Catholic Review,* 4 Feb and 1 Apr 1922.

10. *Star,* 15 Mar 1923. The Mass for the Irish heroes was described in the Baltimore *Catholic Review,* 23 Sep 1922.

11. Curley individually greeted all those who attended, including representatives of the diplomatic corps and the U.S. government. The crowd was said to be the largest assembled in the church to that time. See Baltimore *Catholic Review,* 14 Jan 1922.

12. Interview, author with Joseph T. Durkin, S.J., 18 Sep 1991. Father Durkin was ordained by Archbishop Curley and personally saw the havoc wrecked on an episcopal visit by the presence of a vase of flowers.

were confirmed separately at St. Cyprian's). In May 1923 he officiated in a St. Patrick's jammed to the doors with relatives and friends of the 359 adults and children confirmed that year.

The postwar period also saw the parish attempt to time its services to meet the needs of its extern congregation. In November 1919 it received permission to schedule mass at four o'clock on Sunday mornings for the convenience of the city's printers and others obliged to work early hours. Later it scheduled a weekday mass at noon during Lent so that those working in nearby offices and stores might better observe the season. The popularity of the noon mass prompted Monsignor Thomas to organize a Sunday noon mass, a rarity in those days. To disabuse those who assumed that mass celebrated at such a late hour would be a quick affair, Thomas himself inaugurated the service. He warned the congregation that they must take their Sunday obligation seriously and then went on to preach them an extra-lengthy sermon.[13]

The effort to schedule services to fit the needs of visitors, the frequent appearance of noteworthy preachers, and the exceptional beauty of the two choirs, offering both pure Gregorian chant and elaborate choral works, helped keep the church crowded. A nationally sponsored church census in 1923 reported that, at a time when the local Catholic population numbered 1,500, on average 3,000 people attended Sunday Mass at St. Patrick's. The large extern congregation also explained the crowds at the popular religious devotions sponsored by the parish. The American church was particularly attracted to St. Thérèse of Lisieux, and in May 1923 Archbishop Curley opened a tridiuum in her honor at St. Patrick's with a pontifical Mass. The parish installed a statue of the new saint, affectionately known as the Little Flower, and began a regular novena in her honor that attracted a large and faithful audience. Later St. Patrick's began a novena to Our Lady of Perpetual Help and built a shrine in the church to hold a copy of the widely venerated painting in the custody of the Redemptorists in Rome. A confraternity was organized and a special papal blessing with suitable indulgences bestowed on the thousands who came to participate in the popular novena.[14]

13. Interview, author with Archbishop Hannan. The new mass schedules were discussed in the Baltimore *Catholic Review,* 22 Nov 1919 and 25 Feb 1922.

14. The purpose for these popular devotions and description of the crowds who attended were well covered in the press. See, for example, clippings on file in the Washingtoniana Collection, DCPL. See also *Star,* 26 May 1923, and Baltimore *Catholic Review,* 31 Jan 1936.

Impressive evidence of loyal attendance notwithstanding, St. Patrick's actually faced in the postwar decades the beginning of a long, slow period of change in its extern population that was directly related to an ongoing transformation of the inner city. Viability as a parish in the canonical sense was clearly coming to an end, victim of a shift in residential patterns begun several generations before. Now its newly fashioned extern congregation, attracted to the church by elaborate and convenient services and proximity to the city's center, was already being threatened by the neighborhood's slow loss of commercial and social primacy.

The reasons for the transformation that continued to accelerate during the 1920s and 30s were as familiar as recent headlines. Racial tension, a product of social injustice and mutual suspicion growing out of the era of Jim Crow, reached a flash point on July 19, 1919, when reports of black crime and rumors of bolshevik infiltration—part of the "Red Scare" that was gripping the nation—galvanized roaming bands of white servicemen and local hooligans into assaults on black citizens. The melee continued to escalate on succeeding nights as armed African-Americans retaliated. Some of the worst fighting centered in southwest Washington and along Seventh Street just north of the parish's boundary. Only the presence of eight hundred soldiers and marines supporting local police kept the rioting bands from joining forces in the downtown business area. Peace was restored, but only after five days of mayhem that saw a number of citizens killed. For the most part, white Washington ignored the unmistakable warning. Even when the Ku Klux Klan staged a parade ending in a rally on the Monument grounds in 1925, none saw fit to object. In the years that followed, an isolated black community developed, surrounded by white suspicion and neglect and rigidly segregated with a color line carefully drawn through all the old neighborhoods to denote the boundaries of what had become a separate, secret city within the capital.[15]

Whites tended to blame black Washington for the rise in crime in the 1920s. In fact both races had their criminals, and if blacks were more often implicated in the increased number of street robberies and assaults that were beginning to frighten residents away from some areas of downtown, it was whites who were primarily engaged in the

15. Green's *Washington*, 2:260–72 and 325–36, and its companion volume, *The Secret City*, chapters 9 and 10, remain the primary accounts of emerging racial tensions during the interwar years.

flourishing bootlegging and other underworld activities that grew up in the postwar decades. Equally detrimental to the well-being of the area around St. Patrick's was the development along Ninth Street of what in Washington passed for a tenderloin district. Although the congregation had managed to survive the presence of brothels on E Street after the Civil War without undue concern, its more sensitive descendants were upset when forced to share the neighborhood with speakeasies and burlesque houses.

More important in the long run to the transformation of downtown was the building boom that began in the 1920s and the emergence of the automobile as Washington's major source of transportation. A few new professional buildings and commercial establishments sprang up in the old neighborhood immediately after the war, but they could not compete in size and number with the spate of commercial construction in other parts of town, especially with the massive government building that gave the city many of today's most popular monuments. The temporary wartime dormitories finally left the Union Station area, allowing restoration of the Columbus plaza. The Lincoln Memorial was dedicated, and the beautiful Memorial Bridge and nearby Potomac Park completed. Beginning in 1926 with Congress's decision to complete the scheme of office buildings that constituted the so-called Federal Triangle, the area just south of Pennsylvania Avenue became a hub of activity as government workers, later swollen in number by the needs of New Deal programs, provided the parish with an army of weekday visitors. Perhaps nothing symbolized the change in monumental Washington as much as the razing of the old Central Market on Pennsylvania Avenue. For generations the retail center of the city, the colorful emporium was replaced with the classical facade of the new National Archives in 1932.

It was during this period that the automobile began to assert its baleful influence on the center city. Washington's public transportation system had grown mightily since horsecars first appeared at St. Patrick's doors sixty years before with far-flung lines making movement from the outer reaches of the city and the newly developing suburbs relatively easy. Nevertheless by 1929 only one-third of those commuting to work or on private business used public transportation. Parking became a major problem as the ellipse was transformed into a vast parking lot and curb space went at a premium throughout downtown. Many Washingtonians, including parishioners at St. Patrick's, seemed to consider it their God-given right to park at the front door.

When denied that privilege on Tenth Street, some turned to neighborhood parishes instead. At the same time the automobile was proving a boon to suburbanites, who until then had found it easier to take public transportation into the center city than to get around their own sparsely settled communities. Where once it was easier for Catholics to hop a streetcar or bus in the outer wards of the city or suburbs to attend St. Patrick's, which stood at the transportation hub of the city, now it became just as easy to drive to one of the widely scattered churches in their own area.

A more subtle change in the F Street area, but one of immense import, was the gradual physical deterioration of the neighborhood that began after World War I. At first few seemed to notice that some of the prestigious professional firms were leaving for the increasingly fashionable Connecticut Avenue region. The loss of brokers and lawyers was only the beginning. Stores appealing to those looking for cheap goods and services began to proliferate around Seventh Street during the 1920s, the lower end of Ninth Street became increasingly unsavory, and a gradual physical deterioration of business establishments was noticeable.[16] The inevitable consequence of business relocations was still some decades away, temporarily postponed by the phenomenal popularity of the region during World War II. Moreover, the city's major department stores, theaters, and basic service companies remained firmly rooted along the F Street corridor, especially toward the western edge of the parish, keeping the area a busy, bustling place. Adding to the bustle, the region also boasted several of the city's most popular hotels, and its one exotic neighborhood, a six-block section of H Street whose colorful oriental stores and restaurants denoted Washington's Chinatown.

F Street itself remained a place of fine shops and theaters, and the deterioration of the neighborhood was not yet so advanced in 1930 to deter a group of investors from offering to lease St. Patrick's holdings in square 376. Reminiscent of discussions sixty years earlier, the arrangement would require razing of the church structures in favor of a large office building and theater. The parish would reproduce its buildings some blocks to the northeast while being guaranteed an annual income of $120,000. At the end of ninety-nine years the church would regain title to the land and improvements.[17] Faced with a de-

16. On the changing nature of F Street in the 1930s and its effect on the parish, see Fosselman in "A Downtown Parish," 229–39.

17. Ltr., Edwin Pilson to Thomas, 18 Mar 1930, SPA.

clining population and the long-range implications of a changing neighborhood, Monsignor Thomas did not allow sentiment to interfere with serious consideration of the offer. Yet even before he could broach the subject with the archbishop, his lawyer uncovered several impediments to the deal, including legal questions involving the old Caffry deed and residual problems concerning the alley in square 376.[18] No doubt most daunting to the pastor, the church would need to invest substantial sums to buy out the current F Street leases.[19] Whether it was these practical impediments or an overriding loyalty to the church's old neighborhood that made Thomas drop the matter, the question of moving St. Patrick's was again quietly shelved.

If the interest of the business community in the neighborhood seemed to fluctuate between the wars, the residential patterns showed no such tendency. Although a few scattered areas of middle-class housing, mostly multi-family rental units and a few sturdy single-family dwellings along the region's northern and eastern borders, would remain until after World War II, the neighborhood was being transformed into one of lower-income families, their large households crowded into deteriorating rental properties. The last new dwelling was built in the parish in 1929, and even before that date the conversion of larger residences into rooming houses, cheaper hotels, and tourist homes was under way. E. Robert Arthur, a new curate in 1938, recalled his surprise when making a sick call to find people living in low-ceiling, dirt-floored basement apartments within walking distance of the church.

For all practical purposes the transformation of the neighborhood in the inter-war years marked the end of a resident congregation. In 1938 the parish mailed a questionnaire to 1,000 homes (an estimated 4,000 dwellings were included within the parish boundaries). Some 750 of them came back marked "return to sender." A more detailed picture emerged from a door-to-door survey undertaken by the Mission Helpers of the Sacred Heart at about the same time. This group identified 1,522 people who called themselves Catholics. Of this number, 340 reported that they seldom or never went to church, more than 500 others attended nearby churches, principally St. Mary's and Holy

18. A routine survey in 1903 revealed that an alley designated in the original plat of the square and long considered closed ran through the church's property. Although the D.C. corporation counsel ruled that the commissioners had approved closing the alley in 1881, some legal ambiguities remained.

19. Ltrs., Henry W. Schon to Thomas, 24 Mar and 4 and 10 Apr 1930, SPA.

Rosary, while some 100 black Catholics regularly went to Holy Redeemer, established for black Catholics at Second and New York Avenue in 1922.[20]

These population trends were mirrored in the parish's school. As early as 1926 the pastor reported that just 47 of its 337 students lived in the parish. While the academy's high school division continued to attract students from all over the city, the elementary classes were more closely related to the parish population and competed for students with nearby St. Mary's. In the face of rapidly declining attendance, and to allow the Holy Cross sisters to concentrate on the popular business high school, Thomas arranged for the Ursulines to assume responsibility for the grade school. The kindergarten and first three grades joined the Holy Family nursery in the building on Fourth Street in 1922; the remaining grades followed in 1933.[21]

During the days of Stafford and Russell, the size and activities of the parish's various organizations had remained largely independent of the downward trend in resident population. As the nature of the extern population changed in the interwar years from those who considered themselves regular parishioners to casual visitors, the parish organizations rapidly declined. The highly regarded parish choir retained its loyal membership, but the other organizations faded away. The parish sodality might be taken as typical. Before World War I its 800 members, including those who worshipped at St. Patrick's but lived elsewhere, made it the largest such group in the city. By 1938 the sodality could count only 30 members, with perhaps a dozen in regular attendance for the weekly recitation of the Little Office of the Virgin Mary. Bowing to the inevitable, the pastor decided to abolish it. To forestall criticism from the city-wide Sodality Union, however, he retained the group on the list of parish organizations, although its meetings were not resumed after the 1938 summer recess.[22] The Holy Name Society was another case in point. The organization was a particular favorite of Archbishop Curley, who was forever pressing people desirous of founding new church-affiliated groups to join the Holy

20. Records of this and a census taken in 1951 are lost. Information is derived from the analysis of data captured in Fosselman's dissertation. The foundress of the Mission Helpers of the Sacred Heart, Mother M. Demetrias (Mary Frances Cunningham) was baptized at St. Patrick's in 1859.

21. The day nursary was discontinued in 1933. See, Wentz, *Inventory*, 18. For more on St. Patrick's schools, see chapter 13, below.

22. Interview, author with Msgr. Arthur, who was the sodality moderator at St. Patrick's in 1938.

Name instead.[23] St. Patrick's had earlier affiliated its popular League of the Good Shepherd to the Holy Name's national organization, but finally, because of the archbishop's interest, organized a parish Holy Name after World War I. The group claimed 500 members in 1922, yet by the time Father Thomas B. Dade became moderator twelve years later, it rarely attracted more than a dozen men to its meetings. This greatly complicated the young priest's job of mustering a marching unit for the Holy Name parades so fancied by the archbishop.

A Multiplicity of Responsibilities

St. Patrick's unique status as a church without a congregation freed its staff from many of the time-consuming tasks that fell to most parish priests. The duties assumed by Lawrence J. Shehan, who came newly ordained to St. Patrick's in 1923, might be considered typical for an assistant during the inter-war years: he celebrated daily mass, heard confessions on Saturday afternoon and evening and one weekday afternoon, and offered one or two masses with homily on Sunday. In addition he served as spiritual director of the parish's now greatly diminished St Vincent de Paul conference and taught religion to the orphans at St. Joseph's.[24] Even the task of providing for the crowds of visitors on Sundays and holy days was considerably relieved by the Holy Cross congregation, which continued to provide extra help.

Freedom from many regular chores did not signify a lessening of responsibilities. As Monsignor Arthur recalls, the priests of the parish merely traded the burden of organizing carnivals and the like for a full load of special assignments usually diocesan in nature. It is no exaggeration to assert that, before the creation of a separate archdiocese in Washington, the pastor and priests of St. Patrick's served as local surrogate for the Baltimore chancery, carrying on a parish tradition of involvement in tasks of city-wide interest.

The Pastor and the Chancery. Thomas once jokingly said that at one time or other he had held every job in the diocese except archbishop. While at St. Patrick's, he performed a host of special assignments that

23. See, for example, ltr., Curley to Thomas, 10 Mar 34, T-396, Curley Papers, AAB, in which he suggests that Irish-Americans looking to found yet another organization should turn to the Holy Name, "which would do them infinitely more good than any membership in the 'Knights of Equity,' and maybe they might change the name to the 'Knights of the New Deal.'"

24. Lawrence J. Shehan, *A Blessing of Years, The Memoirs of Lawrence Cardinal Shehan* (Notre Dame: University of Notre Dame Press, 1982), 76.

far exceeded the responsibilities of a typical pastor. For several years he retained supervision of the diocesan paper, the *Catholic Review,* which he had founded in 1913. Although Thomas eventually produced an informative journal, the paper was slow to gain popularity. In 1920 he complained to Gibbons: "I have put several thousands of dollars of my own good money in the paper, and the pastors will not cooperate." This outburst followed a run-in with the auxiliary bishop over the paper's coverage of local news, and soon Thomas, who had already given up personal management of the paper's daily operations, quietly abandoned his newspaper career.[25]

Since coming to Washington, Thomas had served as director of the boards of two orphanages and Mt. Olivet Cemetery and chairman of the city's theological conference. The latter was a quarterly gathering where the region's secular clergy listened to papers and discussed current topics like any group of scholars keeping abreast of developments in their profession. The conference had floundered of late, but with the more aggressive Thomas in charge, the meetings in St. Patrick's rectory became crowded and their discussions stimulating. Increasingly Gibbons used the conferences as a forum for diocesan business under Thomas's leadership.[26]

Gibbons also turned to Thomas to revitalize the work of the sodality in Washington. Typically the largest and most active spiritual group in Catholic parishes, the individual sodalities were loosely affiliated in a national organization, but lacked any local coordinating body to direct their charitable works. Working with Jesuit Father Edward F. Garesche, the national director of the Sodality Movement, Thomas set out to form an affiliation of local sodalities. In February 1918 he met with representatives from ten parishes in Carroll Hall, where they formed the Sodality Union of Washington, D.C., and elected an executive board (Miss Blanche Madigan of St. Patrick's served as the first president). Thomas was spiritual director of the union, which within a year numbered twenty-two individual sodalities in its ranks. Considerable sums were raised in those early years for the support of home and foreign missions before Archbishop Curley gave the women a special assignment in 1923. Presiding at a mass meeting

25. Ltrs., Chancellor [Nelligan] to Thomas, 12 May 1919; Thomas to Connelly [chancery official], 13 and 14 May 1919, and 24 Feb 1920 (source of quotation). All in Nelligan Papers, AAB.

26. See, for example, ltrs., Thomas to William Sticker [chancery official] 12 Jun 1917, and Sticker to Thomas 13 June 1917, Nelligan Papers, AAB. Ltr., Connelly to Thomas, 16 Dec 1917, 120-H-11, Gibbons Papers, AAB.

of the union in Carroll Hall, Curley asked the sodality to assume responsibility for building and maintaining diocesan schools in rural Maryland.[27]

Thomas could be forthright when advising his archbishops. In October 1919, for example, he told Gibbons that John M. McNamara, a popular assistant at St. Patrick's, should be appointed pastor of St. Gabriel's, the new parish in the Petworth region of the city. Although a more senior priest was angered at being passed over, Thomas was adamant. The man was temperamentally unsuited to starting a new parish, he bluntly warned Gibbons, nor would his appointment be well received by the rest of the local priests.[28] The same forceful expression of opinion was evident in Thomas's assessment of the bumptious chaplain at the D.C. jail. The man seemed to think that he owned the jail, Thomas reported, and because of his stubborn refusal to deal reasonably and politely with local officials, he should be dismissed.[29] So informed, the chaplain quickly mended his ways. In another case Gibbons sent Thomas to St. Stephen's to find a way "to bring the troubled parish together." Thomas proposed several practical steps to answer the congregation's complaints. When the pastor rejected these suggestions, claiming he could not break with custom, Thomas's no-holds-barred report prompted Gibbons to order a swift change in the way that the parish did business.[30]

If Thomas was blunt and forceful on diocesan matters, he was the soul of diplomacy when it came to dealing with the U.S. government for the cardinal. Like his predecessors, St. Patrick's pastor was often involved in negotiations with the State Department, especially in regard to the war and to President Wilson's attempt to win support for the League of Nations. Thomas was instrumental in Gibbons's decision to ignore a cablegram from the cardinal of Cologne, who was seeking support from the American church for German peace initiatives. The secretary of state was gratified that Gibbons had adopted the government's viewpoint in the matter, Thomas reported.[31] In July 1919 the State Department again asked Thomas to intercede with Gibbons,

27. Between 1923 and 1958 the Sodality Union was a major contributor to the establishment and maintenance of twelve schools in Southern Maryland. Thomas remained director until 1921.

28. Ltr., Thomas to Gibbons, 10 Oct 1919, 128-L-3, Gibbons Papers, AAB.

29. Ltrs., Gibbons to Thomas, 5 Dec 1919, 129-G-3, and Thomas to [Rev. Albert E.] Smith (the cardinal's secy), 13 Dec 1919, 129-H-7, both in Gibbons Papers, AAB.

30. Ltr., Thomas to Gibbons, 9 Mar (n.d., ca. 1920), 80-O-14, Gibbons Papers, AAB.

31. Ltr., Thomas to Gibbons, 7 Sep 1918, 123-B-6, Gibbons Papers, AAB.

this time for an endorsement of the League of Nations. Such an endorsement was needed to offset the opposition of some American bishops who objected that the proposed charter ignored the question of Irish self-determination. Thomas went to Baltimore to present the government's arguments. He later invited Gibbons to join a delegation visiting the White House, where they would endorse the League on the basis of a reservation that would address the Irish question. Gibbons did not attend, although Thomas was able to convey the President's thanks for the prelate's "hearty endorsement" of the league with the proposed change.[32]

Thomas also played an important role in the development of Catholic charity in Washington. This work was greatly in need of reform after World War I. Despite the efforts of Father Walter and others in earlier decades and much useful work by the individual St. Vincent de Paul conferences in the older parishes, charity remained largely unorganized, lacking in central direction, and thus dependent on hastily improvised programs to meet the increasingly complex problems of urban poverty. When he assumed direction of the city's St. Vincent de Paul council in 1917, Thomas complained that the meetings of the only city-wide organization of Catholic charities were so poorly attended that famous guest speakers often faced a sea of "empty benches." A year later the Catholic Home Bureau, the organization begun in St. Patrick's by the Ladies of Charity and carried on by the St. Vincent de Paul Society to place those coming out of the orphanages, was dissolved because of insufficient financial support. As late as 1921 half the city's parishes lacked a St. Vincent de Paul conference.[33]

Thomas began the slow work of building a professional charitable network in late 1919 when he induced the officers of the St. Vincent de Paul Society to create a central bureau, financed by the Particular Council, to undertake certain city-wide charities, including recruitment of Catholic social workers for the city's juvenile court. The prospect of an efficient metropolitan organization in turn prompted Archbishop Curley to order all parishes to contribute 5 percent of their pew rents and offertory collections to this central bureau. Finally in 1922 Curley hired Father John O'Grady to organize the Catholic Charities of the District of Columbia. Supported by a number of the capi-

32. Ltrs., Thomas to Gibbons, 23 Jul 1919, 127-L-1, and 28 Mar 1920, 131-U-9, and Gibbons to Thomas, 28 Mar 1920, same file. All in Gibbons Papers, AAB.

33. McColgan, A Century of Catholic Charity, 2:228 and 232; and Shehan, A Blessing of Years, 84–91. Unless otherwise indicated, the following paragraphs are based on these works. Msgr. Thomas's remark appeared in the Baltimore Catholic Review, 14 Jul 1917.

tal's business and professional leaders, Catholic Charities assumed the work of the central bureau, strengthening it with a staff of professionally trained social workers.

Thomas was clearly unsure of how best to deal with Michael Curley when that mercurial Irishman became archbishop. In conveying the complaints of his fellow pastors about O'Grady. Thomas opened his letter: "I may be getting in bad with your Grace, but here goes." The pastors especially objected to the new 5 percent tax, which they blamed on O'Grady. They complained that the powerful O'Grady was not even a member of the diocese. Curley's tart rejoinder revealed that he was not above shooting the messenger. He had full faith in O'Grady and had devised the new assessment policy himself, he informed Thomas. He went on to defend the choice of O'Grady (who was on the Catholic University faculty) for this important diocesan post. He politely yet forcefully suggested that the pastors, including Thomas, mind their own business and obey orders.[34]

Despite their rocky start, the pair quickly formed an effective team. Just weeks after the O'Grady incident, Curley appointed Thomas to a board to select the pastor of an important Baltimore parish. He also made Thomas chairman of an ecclesiastical survey of the Washington area empowered to review parish boundaries and determine the need for new parishes.[35] In 1923 Thomas's team recommended a parish for Takoma Park. He discussed the boundaries with Curley and reviewed the objections of Nativity's pastor, who complained that the new church would be too close. "It isn't," Thomas bluntly concluded. Later the group settled a dispute involving the pastor of Holy Name, who wanted to extend his southern boundary in the face of strong objections from Holy Comforter and St. Joseph's. Thomas rejected the proposal. Curley routinely approved the group's decisions, and after a year on the job Thomas felt easy enough to address Curley informally: "Let me butt in: could you not appoint a priest to establish a parish in Bethesda?"[36]

As Curley's confidence in St. Patrick's pastor grew, Thomas found himself assuming even more responsibilities. In 1923 he became a diocesan visitor, which required him to schedule inspections of the

34. Ltrs., Thomas to Curley, 17 Mar 1922, T-232, and Curley to Thomas, 18 Mar 1922, T-233, both in Curley Papers, AAB.

35. Ltrs., Nelligan to Thomas, 27 May and 1 Jun 1922, both in Nelligan Papers, AAB.

36. Ltrs., Thomas to Curley, 10 Apr 1923, T-240; 15 May 1923, T-247; and 8 Mar 1924 (source of quotation), T-269. All in Curley Papers, AAB.

area's parishes. He also became vicar to houses of religious women, leading to his involvement in all sorts of decisions about the hundreds of convents in the area. One such case sounds hopelessly outdated to modern ears. When the Medical Missionary Sisters told him that their work required the adoption of lay clothes, his only objection was that their skirts were not quite long enough.[37]

By 1924 the pastor of St. Patrick's had become for all practical purposes vicar general of Washington, for which the fair-minded Curley had secured his elevation to the rank of prothonotary apostolic, a rarely awarded papal honor that enabled the pastor to wear a bishop's miter and preside from a throne at pontifical ceremonies.[38] Curley even proposed that Thomas be made his second auxiliary. Bishop Owen B. Corrigan was a sickly man, and frequently when Curley travelled outside the diocese he would officially inform Thomas that in the event of Corrigan's death, Thomas was to be vicar and acting head of the Premier See. It was a disappointed archbishop who informed his friend of Rome's rejection on the grounds that two auxiliaries in a small diocese would be "altogether new"; that it might hurt Corrigan's feelings; and, probably hardest for Thomas to swallow, that the nominee was too old to serve under "so young and active an archbishop."[39]

"That looks like the end of a chapter," Curley told Thomas after what was actually only the last of a series of rejections. Gibbons had recommended Thomas twice for an episcopal post, the second time an occasion of considerable embarrassment when the press announced that Thomas was the new bishop of Savannah only to have the Vatican, after several months delay, select someone else.[40] The latest rejection on account of age probably explained Thomas's rueful reaction to the announcement in 1928 that Rome had selected his old protegé, John McNamara, as the new auxiliary. After telling Curley

37. Interview, author with Archbishop Hannan.

38. For a discussion of the many assignments Thomas undertook for the diocese and his considerable academic attainments, see articles by Albert E. Smith and John K. Cartwright on the occasion of Thomas's golden jubilee in the Baltimore Catholic Review, 23 Dec 1932.

39. Ltr., Curley to Thomas, 7 Jan 1924, T-263. For examples of Curley's appointing Thomas as vicar, vice Corrigan, see ltrs., Curley to Thomas, 18 Jun 1925, T-286, and 23 Jun 1927, T-311. All in Curley Papers, AAB.

40. Ellis, Gibbons, 2:442–43, and Shehan, A Blessing of Years, 81–83. The incident so embarrassed Thomas that he gave up his post as chancellor and rector of the cathedral.

that the choice was an excellent one, he added that it "imposes upon me the further obligation to live longer to bury him."[41]

Francis J. Hurney and the St. Patrick's Players. Father Hurney's assignment to St. Patrick's came after dangerous service as a wartime naval chaplain. Like the others, he celebrated Mass and heard the confessions expected of an assistant, but he also developed a unique mission among young Catholics in the city, first as chaplain of the local Catholic Actors' Guild and then as founder and director of the nationally known St. Patrick's Players. The guild, founded in New York in 1916 and popularly associated with St. Malachy's, the actors' church near Broadway, represented the church's belated effort to end centuries of suspicion and neglect of those in the entertainment profession. Hurney organized the guild's Washington chapter, tending to the spiritual welfare of the city's theaterfolk and members of the touring acting troupes that so often visited the capital. The schedule of services at St. Patrick's was prominently posted on the call boards of the National, Poli's, and the rest of the city's theaters, with the result that many actors and others associated with the entertainment business could be found in the congregation on Tenth Street. Hurney kept exceedingly odd hours as he tried to fit his spiritual counseling into the unorthodox schedules of his actor parishioners. In an era when live theater involved hundreds of Washingtonians, the tall, bespectacled priest was a familiar figure backstage.[42]

Hurney's work with professional entertainers and his own lifelong fascination with the stage convinced him that the theater offered a way to channel the enthusiasm and unrest that had seized the younger generation after the war. This and the belief that the church could exert a wholesome influence on the stage by promoting worthwhile drama and musical comedy prompted Hurney to begin an amateur theatrical troop for the city's youth. In nine seasons his St. Patrick's Players, employing hundreds of stage-struck Washington youth, produced many plays and musicals of professional calibre that attracted large paying audiences and press raves up and down the east coast.[43]

The considerable monies raised by the Players was used to support all sorts of worthy charities, including a number specially favored by one of the group's enthusiastic fans, the Baltimore archbishop. Curley

41. Ltr., Thomas to Curley, 2 Apr 1928, T-321, Nelligan Papers, AAB.

42. Hurney's association with the Catholic Actors Guild is described in the collection of letters and articles in the St. Patrick's Players Scrapbook, AAW.

43. For further a details about the plays and players, see chapter 14, below.

was especially supportive of the Players' elaborate Passion plays and was frequently found in attendance. In 1923 he thanked Hurney for a $2,743 check for the diocese's mission fund, receipts from a week's performance, adding, "The Passion Play was a glorious success and that is the principal part." The next year he praised the histrionic ability of the young performers and offered his "fullest approval for this presentation" along with the hope that "a great number of our people of the city, both Catholic and non-Catholic will avail themselves of the opportunity to witness the presentation."[44] On another occasion he assured Hurney that "you need no approval from me" for the plays. Buoyed by the success of its sacred drama, the group sought government support for establishing a permanent outdoor theater in Washington along the lines of the one at Oberammergau.[45]

Although the Passion plays won the archbishop's warm endorsement, the group's major stock in trade remained its popular musical reviews. Father Hurney was thoroughly enmeshed in the undertakings, often writing the skits and directing the reviews, and negotiating with the Broadway producers who frequently cooperated in what were in all essentials professional productions. Throughout his association with the musical theater he remained an ardent foe of censorship. Close cooperation between the church and the stage, he contended, would soften the demand for censorship and produce reforms from within the theater without recourse to social or legal restrictions.[46]

Although supported by his pastor and archbishop, such sentiments proved inadequate in the face of the concerted efforts of a small group of sanctimonious Grundyites. Their sense of propriety, offended by the sight of young Catholic actors dancing the Charleston and apparently cavorting under Catholic auspices, prompted a letter-writing campaign directed at the archbishop and the apostolic delegate. The American bishops' earlier dire warnings about dancing had gone largely ignored by Catholics of all ranks, and dances and card parties sponsored by parish organizations were commonplace across the

44. Ltr., Curley to Hurney, 7 May 1923, H-1711, Curley Papers, AAB; and Curley to Mrs. T. A. Donohue, 18 Mar 1924, copy in Players Scrapbook, AAW.

45. *Star*, 14 Mar 1924. For an example of the archbishop's public expression of gratitude for the performance and the money donated to charity, see the Washington *Times*, 5 Apr 1924. The Curley quotation is from ltr., Curley to Hurney, 24 Feb 1923, H-1706, Curley Papers, AAB.

46. Hurney's views on censorship were aired in a speech before the Catholic Actors' Guild and summarized in the *Star*, 6 May 1924.

country. As late as 1913 Cardinal Gibbons deftly avoided the apostolic delegate's question on the subject, even though his own Third Plenary Council had warned against church-sponsored dances.

Gibbons always seemed able to reinterpret, indefinitely postpone, or simply ignore Vatican directives when they clearly betrayed a misunderstanding of conditions in his diocese (as, for example, the directive forbidding nursing nuns from tending male patients). His successor apparently lacked the temperament and the skill to do the same. When, thanks to the apostolic delegate, the complaints finally reached Roman ears, the Sacred Consistorial Congregation acted. In October 1927 it instructed Curley to dissolve the Players within fifteen days. Reminding the archbishop of a Roman decree of 1912 that absolutely forbade priests from organizing, in any way encouraging, or even attending dances, including those for charity, the cardinal secretary noted that what made this offense "most unbearable" was the fact that a dramatic society had been organized by a priest in the city where the Pope's representative resided! By now under a full head of rhetorical steam, Cardinal Amleto Cicognani went on to tell the beleaguered archbishop "how sad the Holy Father was, when he was made aware, by the violation of a law of such importance with regard to protecting habits and morality, especially of youth." Not only the Players, but any other organization or group that was committing similar abuses, was to be dissolved.[47]

Curley had forthrightly ignored the earlier smear campaign because he was convinced that the musicals were harmless, the Passion plays inspirational, and the Players a solid benefit for needy causes. He continued to hold these sentiments, although he was fully aware that the 1912 decree had been violated in his diocese "and is being violated all over the Country," as he explained to a representative in Rome. Yet he saw no way to avoid a direct order. The Players were promptly disbanded, priests were told that they could no longer promote or attend parish dances, nor could dances sponsored by lay organizations be held on church property or advertised from the pulpit or in the *Catholic Review*.[48]

Curley mentioned that he had privately counseled his priests on the matter, but news of the Roman-ordered ban and the fact that it had

47. Ltr., Sacra Congregazione Concistoriale (No. 417) to Curley, 6 Oct 1927, Roman Letters, Curley Papers, AAB. The differing reactions of Gibbons and his successor to Roman decrees is mentioned in Spalding's *Premier See*, 313 and 342.

48. Ltrs., Curley to Msgr. Moses Kiley, 29 Dec 27, K-840, and 27 Jan 1928, K-841, Curley Papers, AAB.

been prompted by disgruntled lay persons was allowed to circulate freely in the Washington press.[49] A disappointed Hurney tried to resurrect the organization the following year, announcing that it would strictly conform to the decree against dancing. In 1928 the Players Guild, as the new group was called, experimented with radio plays and musicals without dancing, but nobody's heart seemed in it.

Before the Guild quietly disbanded, however, Father Hurney's group gave the archbishop a bad fright when the Washington *Times* ran an ad in May 1928 for a forthcoming performance that contained pictures of actors doing the Charleston! "What is the matter?" thundered the gun-shy Curley. The apostolic delegate had already complained about one Washington pastor advertising another dance, and a continuation of such things, Curley warned, "is going to prove so serious for you that it will knock the sight out of your eyes." Hurney hastened to explain that to save money (the group was performing without cost for the benefit of a poor Virginia parish), the paper had been supplied with a picture from an old performance. The offending ad had been withdrawn from later editions. Hurney knew that the resumption of dancing would be "gall and wormwood" to certain clerical parties, he explained to the archbishop, and "I would not allow even a finger to be wiggled by the performers for fear that snoopers would make a mountain out of it."[50] Thus one of the more popular programs of Catholic outreach ever undertaken at St. Patrick's ended without a finger wiggling.

If there was little Curley seemed capable of doing to save the Players, he soon showed his true feelings in the matter. In 1929 he appointed Hurney pastor of Immaculate Conception, promoting him to the prestigious job well ahead of his contemporaries. Hurney went on while at Immaculate Conception to launch the Catholic Radio Hour, another important and successful collaboration of the church with the world of entertainment. One further irony: just twelve years after the brouhaha over dancing, the *Star* announced that Father John K. Cartwright had been named honorary chairman of a committee in charge of a card party and dance at the Mayflower hotel for the benefit of the Catholic Radio Hour.[51]

49. See, for example, articles in the *Star,* 1 Nov 1927 and Washington *Times,* 24 Oct 1927.

50. Ltrs., Curley to Hurney, 19 May 1928, H-1721, and Hurney to Curley, same date, H-1722, both in Curley Papers, AAB.

51. *Star,* 28 Sep 1939.

Lawrence J. Shehan and Catholic Charities. Shehan had been moderator of the St. Vincent de Paul conference at St. Patrick's since 1923. Because of the rapidly dwindling resident congregation, only the pastor's
willingness to turn over all that was needed from the church's receipts
allowed him and his small group of dedicated laymen to continue distributing food, fuel, and rent to the neighborhood poor, acts that remained at the heart of the Vincentian philosophy of charity. The old
parish was an excellent place for Shehan to learn first hand something
of the complex nature of modern poverty. The economic boom and
bust cycle that characterized the roaring twenties had caused an
alarming increase in the number of poor, especially in a neighborhood
like F Street that was undergoing severe economic dislocation. Shehan
was ready for the job when Curley asked him in 1929 to serve as full-
time chief of operations for the new Catholic Charities.

Experience at St. Patrick's had convinced Shehan that the complexi-
ties of fund raising in an era of competing needs and diminishing assets called for greater cooperation among all the city's charitable organizations. The pitiful sight of proud workers reduced to selling apples
on the busy corners around St. Patrick's during the great Depression
might have produced unparalleled levels of generosity from worshipers, but, as Shehan noted, church revenues were among the first
to suffer in hard times. The idea of placing the main responsibility for
direct assistance on the local parish conferences, an acceptable approach in the 1920s, was in his eyes impractical and "doctrinaire" in
the 1930s.[52]

Director O'Grady, on the other hand, favored keeping the solicitation and distribution of money and supplies focused at the parish
level. He had managed to double the number of St. Vincent de Paul
conferences in Washington, and until the New Deal emergency programs brought relief in 1933, he continued to center the major work of
caring for the needs of the Catholic poor in individual parishes. True
to his philosophy, O'Grady also opposed cooperating with the city's
other charitable organizations in united fund-raising efforts.

These differing approaches led to a disagreement in Catholic Charities during which the lay board appealed over O'Grady's head to the
archbishop. Curley sided with the board and in 1938 asked Shehan to
assume the directorship, a post he would hold for the remainder of his
years at St. Patrick's. It was left to the new director to manage the
complicated financial negotiations that finally guaranteed that Catho-

52. Shehan, *A Blessing of Years,* 91.

lic Charities would receive a fair share of the city's charitable contributions through the Community Chest (forerunner of the United Way). If the move freed Shehan of the constant task of soliciting for funds, it also obliged him to spend many hours attending Community Chest functions and lending his considerable charm to the task of winning support among Catholics for that organization.[53]

Thomas Dade the Expediter. Father Dade was the first of three young priests assigned to St. Patrick's during the 1930s whose effective work in diocesan projects played a part in the smooth transition of Washington into an independent archdiocese. Dade's exceptional organizational talent, combined with an uncanny ability to win support from the city's business and professional leaders, gained him legendary status as an expediter and can-do activist. His name is indelibly linked to city-wide associations for the police and firemen, Catholic servicemen, and the youth of the city, all run from St. Patrick's rectory.

Dade's brother was a Baltimore policeman, and when the newly ordained priest arrived at St. Patrick's in the spring of 1934 he immediately noticed that Washington lacked an organization fostering the religious interests of Catholic police and firemen. After negotiating with the D.C. Commissioners and the police and fire chiefs, Dade organized the Catholic Police and Firemen's Society. On the first Sunday of December some four hundred of the city's finest stepped off behind the American Legion Band, the superintendent of police, Major Ernest Brown, and the Fire Department's Chief Engineer, Charles Schrom, to attend their first annual Mass at St. Patrick's. Local restaurateur Evan Sholl sponsored a communion breakfast for the group.[54] In succeeding years the parade and Mass were held on Mother's Day. The increasing crowds (which, with the addition of the U.S. Park Police and the Capitol and White House police, quickly came to average more than seven hundred participants) forced Dade to change the site of the breakfasts to the more commodious ballrooms of several of the city's major hotels. The society also inaugurated the police-firemen's smoker, a stag affair used by the Catholic officers to thank those colleagues who substituted for them on Mother's Day. By 1959 the Mass was attracting over eleven hundred police and firemen, providing, in-

53. See, for example, the account of Shehan's address to the Federal Community Chest, *Star,* 19 Mar 1941.

54. Baltimore *Catholic Review,* 7 Dec 1934. See also, Catholic Police and Firemen's Society, Washington, D.C., *Commemorative History* (Washington, 1974) and interview, author with Msgr. Dade, which are the source for these paragraphs.

cidentally, a useful avenue for scores of Catholic officers to return to the sacraments.[55]

Dade's work with the police and firemen served as a prelude to the more complex task of establishing the Catholic United Service Organization during World War II. America's first peacetime military draft had produced thousands of new soldiers by early 1941, and Archbishop Curley asked the St. Patrick's assistant to arrange some kind of entertainment for those flocking to Washington on leave from nearby training bases. Dade turned first to the movers and shakers who constituted the board of Catholic Charities. With their financial support and connections with the city government, along with the generosity of the Knights of Columbus (who donated the use of their building), Dade opened the local Catholic affiliate of the USO in August. It remained throughout the war a gathering place for thousands of servicemen and women.[56]

Dade arranged with the city's individual parishes to host one or two Sunday dinners at the club each year. Parishioners bought the food and served it to five hundred servicemen and women in shifts. In the midst of a wartime food shortage, the determined priest cajoled the city's wholesale grocers into opening their warehouses for the cause and somehow got nine dance bands (including some of the country's major military bands) to supply music for dances six days a week, including a three-band extravaganza every Sunday. Some eleven thousand young women, including four thousand in uniform, registered as hostesses for the dances, which attracted up to fifteen hundred visiting troops on weekend nights. One can only speculate how those who objected so strenuously to the St. Patrick's Players in 1927 reacted to the jitterbuggers at the Catholic USO. Underscoring the old truism that time solves all problems, the Vatican official who signed the order dissolving the Players, Archbishop Amleto Cicognani, was now the apostolic delegate and a benign witness as thousands of young Catholics danced the evening away under the watchful eye of a St. Patrick's priest.

55. The annual Mass received much attention in the press. See, for example, the *Star,* 29 Oct 1936 and 11 May 1959, and *Catholic Standard,* 11 May 1962. The event was canceled twice, in 1943 because of the war and 1971 because of the anti–Vietnam war demonstrations.

56. Theodore Hesburgh, *God, Country, Notre Dame* (New York: Doubleday, 1990), 38–40. Father Hesburgh, later president of Notre Dame, occasionally substituted for Dade as director of the USO club in Washington.

CATHOLIC POLICE AND FIREMEN. *Members of the society parade down F Street after their annual Mass at St. Patrick's.*

E. Robert Arthur and James E. Cowhig and the Tribunal. These priests, both graduates of the prestigious North American College in Rome, arrived at St. Patrick's in the late 1930s to be immediately involved in diocesan assignments. The code of canon law promulgated in 1918 required each diocese to organize an ecclesiastical court, the so-called tribunal, to render decisions on cases involving church law, for the most part disputes over the validity of Christian marriages. Archbishop Curley had asked St. Patrick's pastor to organize the tribunal in Washington and serve as its *officialis* or presiding judge. With an earned doctorate in divinity, Monsignor Thomas certainly qualified for the post; yet canon lawyers were a scarce commodity in the diocese, so a number of priests without special training, like Father Shehan, were pressed into service as tribunal officials. The appearance of two well-trained young priests must have seemed a heaven-sent opportunity to Curley, who needed to professionalize his court.

Father Cowhig arrived at St. Patrick's in 1939, a year after Arthur. He had studied canon law at the Gregorian University in Rome and already possessed his baccalaureate degree. In Father Arthur's case, the archbishop simply asked the new assistant to begin a course of study at Catholic University. Arthur had little choice, though after years of seminary training he was anxious to take up regular pastoral duties. In due course he obtained his licentiate degree and began a distinguished career on the tribunal that lasted more than fifty years. In 1938 Monsignor Thomas had asked the archbishop to relieve him of his duties as *officialis*. In the wake of new instructions from Rome the work had been greatly complicated, Thomas explained, "It told too much on my nerves to be learning new tricks."[57] After a brief interval, Shehan became both pastor and *officialis*. His successors Cowhig and later Arthur also served dual positions.

Arthur's experience as a law student incidentally illustrated an interesting facet of the archbishop's personality. Despite his legendary bluntness and fierce put-downs of erring subordinates, Curley harbored a fatherly interest and concern for the welfare of young priests. It was Curley who noticed on one of his frequent visits to St. Patrick's that Arthur's class schedule made him miss the main meal, which in Monsignor Thomas's rectory was served at midday. Curley ordered Arthur to forget the streetcar and use a taxi to get him home in time for dinner, and, very important for a new assistant, to send the bill for the special transportation to the archbishop.

At the Bustling Center

Underpinning the multiple assignments of the assistants at St. Patrick's was an efficiently operating parish under the no-nonsense control of its aging pastor. This orderliness was especially evident in Thomas's fiscal stewardship. In a gesture exceedingly novel in those years, he published the parish's financial statements in the *Catholic Review* during the mid-1930s. As in all things, Thomas was rigorously correct in these renderings, so much so that, unable to account for a one-dollar discrepancy in the 1934 balance sheet that totaled more than $78,000 in receipts, he conducted a special audit and included its results in the published report: "Due to a mistake on the part of the bookkeeper," who co-signed the report with him, "the Pastor's salary for December, 1934, was overdrawn one dollar ($1.00). This error will be rectified with the salary check for January, 1935, which will be drawn for ninety-nine dollars."[58]

These reports revealed a church that was fiscally healthy thanks to

57. Ltr., Thomas to Curley, 6 Oct 1938, Curley Papers, AAB.

58. "Financial Report of St. Patrick's Church Washington, D.C. for Year Ended December 31, 1934," reprinted in the Baltimore *Catholic Review*, 11 Jan 1935.

the receipts from its rental property, which accounted for approximately half its annual income. For the rest, the collections mirrored a declining population. Pew rents in the large church now brought in little more than $100 per month. On the other hand, the parish debt in 1937 stood at $10,000 (in the form of a loan from St. Joseph's Home), all that remained, Thomas noted with obvious pride, from the quarter million dollars owed at the time of his predecessor's departure.[59] When it was pointed out that funds were available to pay off the debt, Thomas refused, explaining that it was always good psychology to leave some debt on the books to stimulate contributions.

Thomas could not have been so sanguine about the annual tax of some $10,500 owed on the F Street property. Representing 20 percent of income, the tax was a particularly onerous burden in a parish with few parishioners and dwindling resources. Congress considered a proposal in 1941 to exempt such property, but the archbishop, who never faced the burden directly, adopted a surprisingly cavalier attitude. Although he drew the line at convents, he said, he believed that any of the church's income-producing property, even houses of study at the university, should be taxed. "I am not in favor of asking exemptions when we have no right to it," he airily informed St. Patrick's pastor.[60] In the end the bill to relieve Washington's churches failed to pass, leaving property taxes to claim an increasing share of parish income in later decades.

As the years passed the similarities between the educated, highly experienced Thomas and the generally unsophisticated Jacob Walter became more apparent. Reporters often referred to Thomas's abrupt style of writing and speaking— "epigrammatic" the *Catholic Review* called it. Indeed, like Walter, he always spoke his mind bluntly and forcibly to bishops and laymen alike. At the same time, those who knew him well appreciated the truth of Bishop Alfred Curtis's observation that Thomas showed a willingness to do from motives of kindness and generosity what others did only from a sense of duty and obligation.[61] He also resembled Walter in his attitude toward charity,

59. "Financial Report of St. Patrick's Church Washington, D.C. for Year Ended December 31, 1935," reprinted in Baltimore *Catholic Review,* 17 Jan 1936. See also 1936 statement, reprinted in *Catholic Review,* 15 Jan 1937.

60. Ltr., Curley to Shehan, 27 Nov 1941, S-1289, Curley Papers, AAB.

61. Quoted in Smith, *History of St. Patrick's Church,* 97. Bishop Curtis was the retired bishop of Wilmington, Delaware, who served as an auxiliary to Curley. For a assessment of Thomas's character and style in accord with Curtis's views, see interview, author with Arthur.

which during the Depression he had the opportunity to express on an unprecedented scale. Shehan referred to Thomas as a mainstay of the newly formed Catholic Charities.[62]

Archbishop Curley seemed especially fond of his senior pastor and obviously respected his ability, yet he was not above pulling the austere monsignor's leg on occasion. In 1938 Thomas took his only extended vacation to visit a niece in Hawaii. Overcome by the natural beauty of the islands, he impulsively promised Curley on his return that "if you'll settle $5,000 on me a year, I'll gladly retire to the Pacific." Curley, pretending to take the offer seriously, asked Thomas to put the offer in writing. A shaken pastor beat a hasty retreat, saying that at eighty years of age he was not yet quite ready for retirement.[63] On another occasion Curley began a letter to Thomas about the upcoming parish anniversary: "Whilst you are not yet one hundred and fifty years old." He wanted Thomas to be unstinting in his plans for the celebration, and to hold it in conjunction with the annual Pan-American Mass. "Let the younger men do the work under your supervision," he told the elderly pastor. Privately he had already asked Shehan to take charge of the event.[64]

In a simple letter of instruction concerning the disposition of his meager possessions after his death, Thomas told the archbishop that he had left no money for masses, because "I have said so many masses for deceased priests in this Archdiocese that I think the masses the survivors will say for me, will suffice." Such an assumption was justified. Thomas was, as Shehan noted, "especially beloved by the priests of the diocese," and his funeral in February 1941 attracted a singular gathering of priests as well as laity from both Washington and Baltimore to the church.[65]

Thomas's death came just months before America's entry into a world war that introduced a period of unparalleled activity at St. Patrick's. A large percentage of those drawn to the city because of the war seemed to find their way to the church, where great crowds attended every mass. One witness recalled the scene, especially on the eve of important holy days, with the aisles filled with long lines of penitents waiting their turn in the confessionals, thus making it difficult

62. In his *Blessing of Years,* 88, Cardinal Shehan reports on Thomas's "unbounded generosity" to Catholic Charities in the 1930s.

63. Interview, author with Msgr. Arthur.

64. Ltr., Curley to Thomas, 20 Jan 1939, Curley Papers, AAB.

65. As quoted in the Baltimore *Catholic Review,* 14 Feb 1941. Thomas's simple but affecting letter of instruction, dated 30 Jan 1924, is filed in the Necrology file, AAB.

to navigate into a pew.[66] With so many people demanding attention, the parish priests spent countless hours in church. As usual the Holy Cross fathers were there to help, and a young Father Theodore Hesburgh, who would later gain fame as the president of the University of Notre Dame, found himself so often at St. Patrick's that he later referred to it as his permanent parish assignment.[67]

Archbishop Curley, whose ardent anti-communism had made him a strong and vocal supporter of the isolationists before the war, was swiftly transformed by the Japanese attack on Pearl Harbor. He loudly urged members of the diocese to volunteer for defense-related jobs and supported the parishes in their war work, especially the USO, the Red Cross, and other organizations dealing with those in uniform.[68] Reporters could always count on Curley for a snappy quote. When a story circulated about women entering European churches bare-legged because of the stocking shortage, he was asked if such behavior would be permitted in his diocese. "I don't care if women come bare footed," the feisty prelate responded, and as for those metalworkers who complained that government rationing threatened their jobs as candlestick makers, the patriotic Curley pointed out that the churches could very well use empty bottles as candle holders.[69]

The archbishop's choice of Lawrence Shehan, who had been serving at St. Patrick's since 1923, to succeed Thomas as ninth pastor in February 1941 promised a smooth transition, and in fact there was little break in the policies that had evolved in the parish during the interwar years. Raised to the rank of monsignor in 1939 in recognition of his work with Catholic Charities, Shehan continued to direct that important organization throughout the war and to assume leadership of the tribunal as well. As for the rest, as he noted in his autobiography, the talented crew of assistants continued to pursue their special ministries, and with the help of the Holy Cross fathers they all managed to cope with the demands imposed by the wartime crowds.[70]

The war made the rectory a lively place, never more so than during the frequent gatherings of the Catholic military chaplains serving in

66. Interview, author with Msgr. Dade.

67. Hesburgh, *God, Country, Notre Dame,* 41.

68. Spalding, *Premier See,* 358–68. See also, Lou Jacquet, "The Way We Were," *Our Sunday Visitor* (1 Dec 1991), 10–12.

69. The quote is from an article in the *Star,* 12 Jul 1942. See also interview, author with Msgr. Arthur. Archbishop Francis Spellman, on the other hand, supported the candlestick makers in their demands.

70. Shehan, *A Blessing of Years,* 94–97.

PAN-AMERICAN MASS, 1943. *Pastor Lawrence J. Shehan escorting Vice-President and Mrs. Henry A. Wallace*

the Washington area. Father Dade had decided that these men, whose work often isolated them from any contact with fellow priests, needed a chance to recreate in clerical society. He organized regular get-togethers, where scores of uniformed priests exchanged news and enjoyed a buffet he somehow managed to produce despite wartime rationing. Meanwhile, all the priests, especially Father Hesburgh, pitched in to help Dade at the USO located just up the street.

The war years also witnessed several new initiatives of lasting importance in the parish. One involved the purely practical effort to complete the first large-scale renovation of the church interior since the turn of the century. The plastering and painting and replacement

of the organ with a modern three-manual instrument forced the congregation to maneuver around scaffolding for many months. Luckily,
Shehan reported to Curley, the inconvenience had not affected the
Sunday collections, which, thanks to the wartime visitors, had improved considerably over previous years.[71]

A second wartime initiative was far more significant, for it involved
the parish in the first tentative steps toward racial justice in the Washington church. Although black Catholics had continued to worship at
St. Patrick's through the decades, their post–Civil War numbers were
considerably reduced with the formation of black parishes, including
Holy Redeemer on nearby New York Avenue. Many of these Catholics
left to worship in all-black congregations, for, it must be said, St.
Patrick's had never seen fit to make them welcome by including them
in parish schools or organizations. By the time more enlightened policies began to prevail—the usually assertive Curley, for example, finally
got around to ordering the Sodality Union in Washington to admit
units from black parishes at the end of the war—St. Patrick's sodality,
like most other parish organizations, had disappeared along with its
resident population.

Wartime Washington remained a rigidly segregated city, where
most citizens of both races seemed to accept without protest the prevailing principle of separate but equal accommodation. In two areas,
however, St. Patrick's served as a harbinger of changes soon to occur
as part of the modern civil rights revolution. One involved the school,
which accepted its first black students in 1942. As so often when great
changes occur, this one began with one black family. New to the
neighborhood, the parents were unhappy with the black public
schools and applied for their children's admission to the parish grade
school. The Ursuline principal, Mother Baptista, accepted the black
students, even though the D.C. School Board responded to the news
with a letter of complaint. The parish ignored the government's objections at first, but upon receipt of a third query, Father Arthur finally
replied, assuring the board that St. Patrick's was merely following
church regulations. His assertion went unchallenged. Two years later
the oldest child in the family was ready for high school, and Arthur
discussed the integration of St. Patrick's Academy with its principal,
Sister Angels. As though rehearsing her arguments for the watchdogs
in the D.C. government, the principal told Arthur, "All I hear you say-

71. Ltr., Shehan to Curley, 30 Jul 1942, S-1308, Curley Papers, AAB. The renovations
actually began before the United States entered the war.

ing is that a graduate of the grade school is exercising her right to come to the academy."[72] Beginning with the experience of this one Catholic family, St. Patrick's launched its modern quest for racial justice.

During the war the parish also played host to the Catholic Interracial Council, which organized a Washington branch in 1944. This group of distinguished black and white Catholics, many of them educators and civil servants, sought through prayer and study to encourage a fuller acceptance of black Catholics. It also protested church segregation by staging a kind of sit-in once a month at selected city parishes. Some pastors openly discouraged the council from worshiping at their churches, and the group needed a place to hold its regular meetings. Shehan, who had already supervised the integration of Catholic Charities, stepped in and volunteered St. Patrick's. He attended the council's meetings in Carroll Hall and otherwise proved, as the head of the group put it, "a most helpful and valuable ally in our work."[73] Indicative of the long road ahead, the council's public meetings at St. Patrick's, which featured well-known speakers discussing interracial justice, failed to attract any but those already enlisted in the struggle. Still, when the group assembled periodically to attend Mass at St. Patrick's, the large integrated congregation must have closely mirrored the appearance of the congregation a century before.

The mighty crowds that filled the church during the war beguiled many into believing that it could continue indefinitely to depend on the support of "casuals," as pastors were wont to call those who used St. Patrick's as an inviting place to meet their spiritual obligations. Perhaps it could, but in peace as in war the church's viability remained closely related to the fortunes of the neighborhood, and although the war had masked the fact, those fortunes were beginning to ebb. The city's commercial center started shifting even before the war, a phenomenon that seemed likely to continue in the era of postwar prosperity. How the parish would retain the loyalty of the strangers that now filled its pews when the city was changing about them represented a postwar challenge, one key to the future of what was beginning to be called the downtown parish.

72. As quoted in interview, author with Msgr. Arthur.
73. John J. O'Connor, "A Man's a Man for A' That," *Interracial Review* (June 1947), 88. For an account of the often harsh reception afforded members of the council and the contrasting welcome they received at St. Patrick's, see Foley, "The Catholic Church and the Washington Negro," 156–58 and 224–25.

CHAPTER II

The Downtown Parish

HOURS AFTER news of Japan's surrender reached Washington on August 14, 1945, St. Patrick's pastor received a call from the apostolic delegate. Archbishop Cicognani wanted to commemorate the occasion with a *Te Deum*. Could Monsignor Shehan arrange the event for tomorrow? Having responded to a similar request when Germany surrendered in May, Shehan knew how to pass the word quickly to the area parishes and ready St. Patrick's musical and liturgical forces. To uphold the rectory's reputation, Father Dade cajoled his suppliers into providing a steak dinner for the delegate and visiting dignitaries. As they had so often during the war, crowds of worshipers streamed into the big church, this time to give thanks for the coming of peace.

The church had marked the end of many of the nation's wars with such ceremonies, but unlike earlier times, those who filled it in 1945 were not parishioners in the ordinary sense. By now St. Patrick's had become what Father Walter predicted was its destiny—a church of strangers. In distinction to other parishes, whose interests were largely defined by their residential neighborhoods, St. Patrick's now depended exclusively on a transient population. Its liturgical life was closely geared to the ebb and flow of the daily

tide of workers who crowded into the inner city each morning and de-
parted every night, leaving a largely deserted neighborhood.

In the days of Stafford and Russell, and continuing to a great extent
during the interwar years, the loss of residents did not affect the size of
St. Patrick's congregation. Before World War II, Catholics in the region tended to view the church as a local extension of the chancery
and the diocese's pro-cathedral. Such considerations acted as a powerful magnet for those who sought to worship at what they considered
the center of Catholic life in Washington.[1] With the war, and especially in light of St. Matthew's recent designation as cathedral, St.
Patrick's mission inevitably began to narrow. City-wide services like
the Te Deum in 1945 would soon move elsewhere, and the parish's loyal
extern congregation begin to disappear. Ironically, the shift in status
from an unofficial pro-cathedral to the city's downtown church of
convenience made St. Patrick's more than ever dependent on geography, its future closely linked to the survival of the neighborhood
around it. After so long at the center of things, the old mother church,
like old downtown Washington, faced an uncertain future.

Although all the elements that would influence the church's long-
term future fell into place during the postwar decades, those in charge
might be forgiven for failing to foresee what was coming. The sheer
size of the congregation, especially the throngs that gathered on holy
days and for daily mass or formed the long lines at the confessionals,
was an exciting thing to behold. A decline in the number of Sunday
worshipers could not be denied, but the priests were far too busy serving the needs of the thousands of weekday strangers to question the
future. When asked to nominate his successor in 1945, Shehan recommended John Cartwright, once an assistant at St. Patrick's and later
pastor of Immaculate Conception. Although Shehan knew that the
gifted Cartwright was being groomed to serve at the newly designated cathedral, he could truthfully assure Curley that "the pulpit at
St. Patrick's would be . . . probably the equal of, if not superior to, that
of St. Matthew's."[2] Shehan's opinion, hardly unique, was directly related to the continuing popularity of the old church, which seemed
destined to go on forever as every local Catholic's "other parish." In
fact great crowds would remain in evidence for another two decades,

1. The universality of this attitude was discussed in the author's interviews with
Abp. Hannan and Msgr. Arthur.
2. Shehan, A Blessing of Years, 97. Msgr. Dade agreed with this assessment in his interview with author.

which made the transformation, when it finally came, seem that much more sudden and complete.

Postwar Realities

Shehan's success at Catholic Charities made him a special favorite of both the apostolic delegate and the archbishop, yet when the appointment of a second auxiliary for the diocese was announced, St. Patrick's pastor seemed genuinely surprised by his selection. His consecration on December 12, 1945, marked the third time that ancient ceremony was enacted at St. Patrick's.[3] Father Cartwright was not destined for St. Patrick's; instead, the ailing archbishop accepted Shehan's second choice and appointed John Russell, pastor of St. Ursula's in Baltimore, to the post once held by his uncle, Bishop William Russell.

It was problematical from the start that Russell, who combined his uncle's enthusiasm for religious outreach programs with a warm, personal relationship with parishioners, would be satisfied presiding over an institution now devoted to the quotidian needs of commuters. From his arrival at St. Patrick's he bent his efforts toward revitalizing the sense of personal evangelization that had characterized the church in earlier generations. He quickly made himself known to a wide audience through his popular talks on the Catholic Radio Hour, which won an even larger audience when published in the press.[4] Russell continued Shehan's support for the Catholic Interracial Council while trying to breathe new life into the efforts of the Catholic street preachers in the public parks located in the parish. Since 1931 the Washington branch of the Catholic Evidence Guild had been training laymen and seminarians to explain church doctrine to people gathered in open-air forums like Franklin Park and Judiciary Square.[5] Although alien to

3. The others were Thomas O. Gorman, bishop of Sioux Falls, in 1896, and Johannes Gunnarsson, vicar-apostolic of Iceland, in 1943. Shehan's consecration was a hastily planned affair because the ill Curley was anxious to have an auxiliary in place in Baltimore. See Shehan, *A Blessing of Years,* 96–98, which also reveals Shehan's surprise at his selection. Dade ascribes Shehan's promotion to the intervention of the apostolic delegate, whose high regard was ignited when St. Patrick's pastor made a special point of welcoming Cicognani at Union Station when he first arrived in Washington. Curley showed his pleasure at Shehan's selection by donating $5,000 to cover the cost of the consecration and banquet and bestowing on Shehan one of his own pectoral crosses. See ltrs., Shehan to Curley, 24 and 26 Nov 1945, S-1332 and 1333, Curley Papers, AAB.

4. Russell's radio ministry is described in the Baltimore *Catholic Review,* 31 Oct 1947.

5. Members of the guild (its name was changed several times over the years) were

modern taste, sidewalk preaching was a popular pastime in Washington before and during World War II, and Russell remained in the forefront of those who considered it an effective way of spreading the gospel. For many years moderator of the Baltimore guild, he now assumed direction of the Washington group, and could be found regularly addressing passersby from a temporary rostrum in neighboring parks.

Evangelization ranked high among this pastoral priest's priorities, and in his short time at St. Patrick's he concentrated on conversions. Before the war Father Dade had tried to systemize this work by organizing annual classes, in which those interested in the church could progress through different levels of instruction leading to their reception as Catholics.[6] The numbers enrolled in these courses, which clearly presaged the system of instruction familiar in the post-Vatican II church, continued to grow during the war. Russell supported the idea, asking the congregation to submit names of unchurched friends and relatives and personally inviting hundreds of them to attend classes conducted by well-known preachers like Fulton J. Sheen and Ignatius Smith, then members of the Catholic University faculty. Sheen's efforts were especially well received and resulted in hundreds of Washingtonians joining the church during the next several years. Although some witnesses expressed skepticism about the classroom approach—deriding, for example, the fact that the moderator often had to plant questioners in the audience to stimulate discussion—inquiry classes in some form have remained ever since an important and popular method of evangelization at St. Patrick's.[7]

Nor did Russell ignore those already in the church. In December 1946, for example, he activated the Immaculate Heart of Mary Reparation Society at St. Patrick's. Founded by Agnes Mahan and Eliska deB. Dardis, the group was the first organized in Washington in response to the Fatima apparitions. It drew large crowds to the church on the first Saturday of the month, when each member spent an hour in prayer for the conversion of Russia.[8] In 1947 Russell inaugurated

licensed to preach by a board of clerical examiners appointed by the archbishop. For an account of their work, which reached its greatest popularity in the late 1930s, see Baltimore *Catholic Review*, 13 Dec 1935, and *Star*, 8 May 1939.

6. Shehan, *A Blessing of Years*, 95–96. See also, author's interview with Msgr. Dade.

7. Baltimore *Catholic Review*, 19 Mar and 15 Oct 1948. For a critical view of convert classes, see author's interview with Msgr. Joseph Teletchea. For a description of classes in the 1960s, see interview with Father Donald Brice.

8. The society remained a regular partner in the prayer life at St. Patrick's for years. See *Catholic Standard*, 4 Dec 1953.

classes in mental prayer that attracted hundreds of people desiring to learn something about this special form of religious expression. He also promoted widespread recitation of the daily rosary, beginning his crusade with a triduum of services conducted by Patrick Peyton, the well-known apostle of the rosary. Early after his installation as pastor he revived the parish's annual May procession, substituting students from the academy for the local children who had participated in years past.

Probably Russell's most popular and enduring initiative at the old downtown church was daily exposition of the Blessed Sacrament.[9] Firmly lodged in Catholic Washington's collective memory of those years were trips to department stores like Woodies and Landsburgh's, Reeve's Bakery and Velati's Candies, or Saturday afternoons at the Palace and the Earle theaters, to name just a few of the familiar downtown activities that always seemed to include a stop at St. Patrick's. There, genuflecting on both knees signified the special importance of a visit to this particular sanctuary.

Reminiscent of earlier parish programs involving the city's other churches was Father Dade's effort after the war to form a Catholic Youth Organization (CYO).[10] It began as a sports league in 1946. Dade formed a board of laymen under Leo Rover, the U.S. Attorney for the District of Columbia, as sponsor. No sportsman himself, Dade enlisted ten priest-athletes to manage the games and tournaments. He insisted that the referees and umpires be paid, thus ensuring a professional operation that shielded officials from the partisan demands of often over-enthusiastic parents and parish priests. The immediate success of the league won vital support from pastors, which in turn led to a broad new range of activities, including the popular CYO dances, that transformed the organization into the diocese's major program for Catholic youth.

Two problems faced by the CYO in its formative years revealed

9. Russell's various innovations were covered in the Catholic press. See, for example, Baltimore *Catholic Review*, 3 and 24 Oct 1947, and 15 and 22 Oct 1948. On the popularity and importance of the daily exposition of the Blessed Sacrament, see author's interview with George G. Pavloff.

10. The name CYO was not adopted until 1948, when Archbishop O'Boyle overruled an earlier decision by the Baltimore chancellor, who hoped to avoid association with the similarly named organization founded by the progressive auxiliary bishop of Chicago, Bernard Sheils. See author's interview with Msgr. Dade. The following account of the CYO is based on that interview and on Sister Virginia Hughes, ed., *Through His Eyes; A Memoir of Bishop Thomas Lyons* (Washington: Abbeyfeale Press, 1992), 10–11.

something about postwar Washington's social attitudes. Few complained at first, for example, when the group ignored the needs of female athletes, failing to develop programs for them in any way comparable to that offered boys. Thanks to the efforts of board members Monsignors Charles M. Cremona and Thomas W. Lyons, the latter a resident at St. Patrick's and later a popular auxiliary bishop, the organization eventually developed a full compliment of girls' programs. For his efforts Lyons earned the whimsical title of "Assistant High Commissioner of Junior High Girls' Basketball." Racial segregation proved a far more intractable problem. As the city's black parishes began to organize teams, simple justice demanded that the CYO defy local custom and integrate its games. Dade won agreement from a few parishes, though his board threatened to resign over the matter and most pastors, citing local attitudes, refused to cooperate. Until the integration of the Catholic schools later in the decade, most CYO activities quietly followed local custom.

Parish routine was rudely interrupted in December 1947 when the priests of St. Patrick's found themselves entertaining a permanent house guest in the person of the new archbishop of Washington, Patrick A. O'Boyle. The creation of a separate diocese in Washington had been debated off and on for almost a century, only to become inevitable with the nation's rise to world power status. In 1914 Cardinal Gibbons had reacted to a rumored division with considerable heat, suggesting to Rome that, should some special honor be deemed appropriate for the nation's capital, its name could simply be appended to the title of his archdiocese.[11] His successor at first countered renewed talk of division by denigrating Washington's importance to the church. "Heretofore," Curley pointed out, the nation's capital "has occupied in the Archdiocese of Baltimore the place of any small town within the limits of the Premier See." But Rome was not to be denied, and "with a gun to his head," as historian John Tracy Ellis put it, Curley reluctantly recommended that the "See of Baltimore be known hereafter as the Archdiocese of Baltimore-Washington."[12]

Rome considered such a compromise insufficient, and on July 22, 1939, a date meant to coincide with the capital's 150th anniversary, Pope Pius XII issued a bull announcing the formation of the Archdiocese of Washington. With a bow to the loyal Curley, the Pope added

11. Spalding, *Premier See*, 310.

12. Ltr., Curley to Cicognani, 6 Mar 1939, Roman Letters, Curley Papers, AAB. Ellis's comment on this letter was made in interview with author.

that "for the time being," the two distinct archdioceses would be united under one ordinary.[13] Although governed by one administration, the two cities would henceforth be canonically discrete entities, and, in an exception to the law that made holding two benefices in the church illicit, Michael Curley was named head of both the oldest and newest archdioceses in the United States. The papal bull also designated St. Matthew's Church as the cathedral seat of the archbishop in Washington.

The designation of a cathedral was of paramount interest to St. Patrick's which, because of its historical importance, size (both of its church and rectory), and central location, had always been considered the logical candidate for such distinction. Neither Gibbons nor Curley ever betrayed an inclination to break with their predecessors' habit of treating St. Patrick's as their special church in Washington. It may be assumed that the selection would have been different if made in the days of the bustling congregation and influential parish organizations created by the energetic Stafford and Russell. Certainly the rectory built in 1904 was designed as an archepiscopal residence, and even the positioning of the imposing Stafford pulpit at the epistle (right) side of the altar, as is customary in cathedrals, called attention to the expectations of both congregation and archbishop.[14]

Such speculation, however, overlooked the central importance of location in selecting the site for a cathedral, a point that the energetic pastors of St. Matthew's, Thomas Sim Lee and Edward L. Buckley, never ceased to trumpet. The aristocratic Lee always extolled the growing eminence of his parish's neighborhood and the fact that its boundaries encompassed the White House. Someday, Lee liked to tell his congregation as they were planning their new, monumental edifice on Rhode Island Avenue, the nation would have a Catholic president, and St. Matthew's must have a church worthy of such distinction. The apostolic delegate might well have discounted such exhortations, but he too was capable of reading the signs of continuing decline in the F Street area. When a disappointed Monsignor Thomas asked his old friend why he had chosen St. Matthew's, Archbishop Curley replied, "I was not consulted; I was informed."[15]

13. The full text of the 22 July 1939 papal letter is found in Roman Letters, 1939, Curley Papers, AAB.

14. The reasons enumerated in this and the following paragraphs for choosing St. Matthew's as the cathedral were suggested by Archbishop Hannan and Msgr. Arthur in their interviews with the author.

15. Quoted by Msgr. Arthur in his interview with author. See also Arthur's homily,

Although a reluctant Archbishop Curley finally took possession of the new See of Washington in a colorful ceremony at St. Matthew's on March 25, 1940, he continued to reside at St. Patrick's during his still-frequent visits to the capital. He kept a key to the side door on G Street, where he could slip in to use the archbishop's suite always kept ready for him.[16] The old warrior seemed to take special delight in the day-to-day minutiae of the busy downtown parish during the war. Although his eyesight was failing rapidly, he missed little that was going on. Once, for example, after observing the sexton during his daily rounds, he wrote Shehan a humorous report about that employee's solution to wartime shortages. He quickly extinguished votive candles soon after their donor's departure, thus providing for their reuse by subsequent visitors. The archbishop obviously saw more to laugh at than condemn in such prudence. On another occasion he returned to Shehan the usual stipend offered to the presiding official at the Pan-American Mass, with the comment that it was too late for him to change his old habit of refusing gifts for performing a bishop's job. In a gesture that would have gladdened the hearts of the old St. Patrick's congregation and its pastor, Jacob Walter, Curley frustrated plans for an elaborate celebration of his installation as archbishop of Washington in favor of hosting a party at the Little Sisters of the Poor. With cigar in hand and apostolic delegate in tow, an obviously contented prelate spent a happy afternoon with the old folks on H Street.[17]

The death of the long-ailing Curley in May 1947 set the stage for the de facto separation of the church in Washington from the Premier See, an event duly marked by the installation of the first resident archbishop at St. Matthew's the following January. Patrick O'Boyle's ap-

delivered at St. Patrick's on 25 Mar 1990, copy in SPA. Msgr. Teletchea (in interview with author) asserts that the apostolic delegate made the choice. The new St. Matthew's, an imposing church in the Italian style, was completed in 1913. It should be noted that over the years St. Matthew's had been granted equal recognition with St. Patrick's by the Baltimore archbishop. At the turn of the century Cardinal Gibbons, for example, granted both churches permanent rector status, thereby bestowing on their pastors special privileges in the diocese. In 1910, he designated both churches sites to obtain the Portiuncula Indulgence. (See *Star*, 27 Jul 1910).

16. Curley's continued use of St. Patrick's rectory is commented on in the Baltimore *Catholic Review*, 27 Jun 1948 and in Msgr. Dade's interview with author. For a full description of the ceremony at St. Matthew's, including Msgr. Thomas's part in the activities, see Philibert, *St. Matthew's*, 115–21.

17. Archbishop Curley deserves a modern biography. These stories are taken from the admirable summary of the archbishop's career in Spalding's *Premier See*, 325–85, especially 358–59. On the sexton and the votive lights, see ltr., Curley to Shehan, 19 Mar 1942, S-1303, Curley Papers, AAB.

pointment was different in several ways. Never before in the history of the American church had a Pope appointed a man to rule an archdiocese without his first serving as a bishop. In fact, the Scranton-born monsignor was never a pastor, rising instead through increasingly responsible positions in Catholic Charities and Catholic War Relief in his adopted New York archdiocese.

Of considerable importance to St. Patrick's, O'Boyle was also the nation's only ordinary who lacked a place to hang his hat. The cathedral rectory was too cramped to offer lodging, and the chancery in Baltimore, which had governed the church in Washington with limited knowledge of its geography or real estate, made no practical preparation for the inevitable arrival of an archbishop.[18] Like any other pastor eager to retain his independence, Russell might be forgiven any reluctance to take on such an important boarder. Nevertheless, he bowed to the logic of Father Arthur's observation that since it was inevitable that the new archbishop would take advantage of the episcopal accommodations at St. Patrick's until a permanent home could be found, the pastor might as well be credited with inviting him. In January 1948 Archbishop O'Boyle began his almost decade-long stay on Tenth Street.

The extent to which the archbishop's residency at St. Patrick's influenced the evolution of the new diocese has yet to be assessed, but it seems likely that O'Boyle's experience as a member of the "family," as he referred to those who lived together in the rectory, influenced the attitudes of a man new to the city and his role.[19] Several members of this family assumed important posts in the new diocese. Assistant James Cowhig became chancellor, while pastor Russell, who had already assumed direction of Catholic Charities, was also appointed a consultor, one of the archbishop's board of official advisors. The talented Robert Arthur, considered still too young to assume direction of the tribunal, was promoted to the post of vice-officialis, and Thomas Dade was the logical choice for director of Catholic Youth affairs.

Observers agree that at first the new archbishop turned most fre-

18. Archbishop Hannan reported that the chancery's understanding of Washington was so limited that when he was assigned to revalidate the boundaries of the Washington parishes he discovered Baltimore officials had drawn boundaries through apartment complexes, with the ludicrous result that the living room of one apartment belonged to St. Thomas the Apostle parish while the kitchen was counted elsewhere.

19. The following paragraphs on O'Boyle are based on interviews, author with Abp. Hannan; Msgrs. Arthur, Dade and Teletchea; and Sister Miriam André and Marie Julie, former principals of St. Patrick's Academy. It also quotes William S. Abel, ed., *Patrick Cardinal O'Boyle As His Friends Knew Him* (Washington, 1986).

quently to Baltimore for advice, principally to Monsignor Joseph Nelligan and the new archbishop, Francis Keough. Neither these men nor O'Boyle's old friends in New York were well versed in the particular needs of the new diocese or the qualifications of its personnel. As a result, some inappropriate appointments were made, as in the case of Chancellor Cowhig, whose Roman training seemed to inhibit his sense of collegiality and ability to indulge in the daily give and take essential in the chief of staff of a large organization. To the archbishop's credit, however, every diocesan official was also expected to perform parish work. In this way the development of a curial mentality among local church leaders was suppressed.

The desire to maintain some form of pastoral connection with area Catholics might explain O'Boyle's own extraordinarily long stay at St. Patrick's. Such living arrangements certainly entailed some sacrifice on the part of the archbishop, who was an especially light sleeper. Aware of this handicap, Monsignor Philip M. Hannan, who lived directly over O'Boyle's rooms, always remembered to remove his shoes before entering his bedroom. In those days the city sanitation department worked hard at keeping the old downtown clean, and the noise of their trucks during the night was a constant source of irritation to the archbishop, who frequently asked why the workers "just won't stop and let people get some sleep." When O'Boyle finally moved to the calm of Tenleytown in 1957, one wag at the chancery predicted that the boss would soon be complaining about the noise of grass growing. (After his first night in his new home on Warren Street, the archbishop reportedly told his secretary that he never realized how much noise birds made at night.)

O'Boyle was scrupulous at first about not interfering in parish operations, quietly saying Mass at a side altar and limiting his participation in public ceremonies to major feasts such as Christmas, Easter, and those special occasions always attended by his predecessors. Nonetheless, he was frequently in the church, chatting with members of the congregation and otherwise taking a lively interest in goings-on about the place. One of his favorite positions was near one of the church doors, which he would open for departing visitors with a friendly greeting or a longer conversation. Weary at hearing their incessant "thank-you, father," the academy's principal finally showed her students a picture of the archbishop to convince them that the smiling man in the simple black cassock who opened the church door for them might possibly deserve a slightly less breezy greeting. Yet O'Boyle was not one to place much emphasis on episcopal dignity. To the overawed domestic in St. Patrick's rectory who insisted on larding her conversation with "your excellency" this and "your excellency" that, the archbishop suggested, "Eleanor, why not say 'your excellency' when you bring me coffee at breakfast, and just let that once do for the day."

The archbishop quickly got to know the surrounding neighborhood during his daily evening walk. Usually in the company of one of the parish priests (as the youngest associate, Joseph Teletchea often got the job), O'Boyle learned first hand about the poverty that was beginning to grip the inner city despite the general postwar prosperity. It was his habit to carry a pocket full of quarters to pass out to panhandlers, but as the years passed he was dismayed to find their number multiplying to such an extent that he would run out of money before reaching home.[20]

His years at St. Patrick's not only gave the new archbishop his sole sustained parochial experience, but also seemed to strengthen his resolve to perform his job always in a way easily understandable and therefore acceptable to even the least sophisticated. To underscore this approach, he invented "Mrs. McGoosla," a mythical character meant to personify the loyal but undereducated and easily scandalized person he might well have encountered in his daily wanderings around the parish. Frequently his advisers would find themselves forced to defend their proposals by answering the question, "What's Mrs. McGoosla going to think about that?" Actually the sometimes blustering archbishop was a complex man. His often extremely traditionalist, and uncompromising approach to church affairs could be interrupted by a striking innovation, such as in the case of his celebrated push for racial equality. Yet because of Mrs. McGoosla's possible reaction, the man who fearlessly ordered the integration of the diocese's churches and schools years ahead of secular institutions also battled to make priests wear hats in the streets and cassocks in the office.[21]

O'Boyle once tried to comfort newcomer Teletchea, who was homesick for his old parish, by admitting his own homesickness, yet he appeared to enjoy his years at St. Patrick's. He sought to make the rectory a relaxed and amicable place, a difficult challenge at a time when some of his associates were at odds over how the parish and new diocese should function. The archbishop did his friendly best, es-

20. Several witnesses noted how O'Boyle became an easy mark for the professional beggars.

21. O'Boyle gave up his long battle over hats, he admitted, when visited by a hatless apostolic delegate, who explained that nobody in Rome wore hats anymore.

pecially at the dinner table, where he enjoyed needling and bantering with the "family" and guests. Yet as might be expected, no matter how sincerely O'Boyle resolved to tread lightly, nobody in the parish could remain indifferent to the extended presence of an archbishop in their midst.

He soon began making that presence felt in ways both humorous and telling. His bored reaction to the elaborate, lengthy Christmas Eve concert by the parish's celebrated choir was to send word to a surprised director that the group should sing "Jingle Bells." Actually, the archbishop had a tin ear, and Father Teletchea, who had a good voice, was drafted to teach him how to sing his part in the liturgy. O'Boyle also added a new note to the Pan-American Mass when, after listening to the lengthy speeches extolling all things Hispanic, he prefaced his own remarks by ad-libbing "All true. All true, but of course, as you know, the Irish are a pretty good group, too." St. Patrick's was a natural place for him to show his frank enjoyment of anything that concerned the land of his forebears, and it must have disconcerted the pastor when he learned that the archbishop had ordered a magnificent oriental rug removed from the sanctuary because it hid the great marble shamrock in the floor.

O'Boyle's presence made changes in personnel easy and inevitable. During his first months in the parish he came to understand Monsignor Russell's increasing frustration. A naturally gregarious man, Russell missed close-knit congregations and busy parish organizations, both now long gone from St. Patrick's. O'Boyle was also aware of the philosophical differences and increasing tension between Russell and Cowhig, and when in October 1948 the job of pastor at bustling Nativity parish came vacant, he offered it to Russell. In an unusual display of support for a pastor, O'Boyle presided at Russell's silver jubilee celebration at St. Patrick's and then personally introduced him to his new parishioners at Nativity.[22] At the same time the archbishop assigned Cowhig, soon to be invested with the rank of monsignor, to administer St. Patrick's.

Profile of a Downtown Parish

St. Patrick's would continue without a pastor for eight years while responsibility for its direction remained in the hands of administra-

22. *Star*, 22 Oct 1948 and 9 Jul 1958. After serving at Nativity for almost ten years, Russell was made the bishop of Charleston and later, bishop of Richmond. He was

tors, Monsignor Hannan succeeding Cowhig to the post in 1952.[23] Ostensibly the title administrator was employed because to name either man pastor would have meant jumping him ahead of many priests with far greater seniority. Yet when queried about the anomaly of long-serving administrators, O'Boyle bluntly explained that while he lived at St. Patrick's he considered himself pastor. Even though canonist Arthur later pointed out to O'Boyle that no one, not even an ordinary, could legally hold two positions simultaneously in the diocese, Hannan was nevertheless denied the title of pastor until the stubborn archbishop's departure from St. Patrick's in 1957.

Counting Hannan's later years as pastor, he and his predecessor would direct the affairs of the parish for a total of seventeen years. These years marked the end of a well-defined era in the life of both the neighborhood and the parish. The aging downtown commercial center was enjoying an autumnal burst of prosperity; St. Patrick's was seeing the last of the great crowds of worshipers in its pews. It was the end of a special period of innocence and pride that lingers vividly in the minds of the region's older inhabitants, none more so than its Catholic citizens.

The boundaries of the old parish were left unchanged when Archbishop O'Boyle reviewed the territorial claims of the diocese's churches in January 1949. Its eighty-one square blocks ran east and west between Third and Thirteenth Streets and north and south from L Street to Constitution Avenue. A census taken in 1951 identified 639 Catholics in this area, approximately five percent of its more than 12,000 residents.[24] Of that total, 158 admitted never or rarely attending church, while approximately 250 others, including members of 24 black families, worshiped regularly at neighboring parishes. Most local residents lived in apartments and rooming houses clinging along the northern border of the parish between Tenth and Thirteenth Streets

the third St. Patrick's pastor to be elevated to episcopal rank. For further analysis of the Russell-Cowhig differences, see author's interviews with Hannan, Dade, and Teletchea.

23. Unless otherwise noted, the following profile is based upon information provided in the author's interview with Father David J. Conway and those with Hannan, Dade, Arthur, Teletchea, Brice, George Pavloff, and Sisters Miriam André and Marie Julie.

24. This census, like the one also conducted by the Mission Helpers of the Sacred Heart in 1938, has been lost. What follows is based on the summary of the census in Fosselman's "A Downtown Parish," 232–39. Reaffirmation of the parish boundaries is found in ltr., Russell to Cowhig, 3 Jul 1948, and Archbishop of Washington Decree, 28 January 1949, both in St. Patrick's file, AAW.

near Massachusetts Avenue. The census counted 129 Catholic children of whom 37 attended Catholic elementary schools, most at St. Mary's on Fifth Street, to which they had transferred when St. Patrick's grade school closed in 1949. Two girls from the parish were included among the 280 students at the academy.[25]

Resident parishioners would just about disappear during the next fifteen years, yet these precise 1951 figures are useful in giving some indication of the true size of the church's postwar transient congregation. In 1952 St. Patrick's averaged nearly a thousand people at its four weekday masses, a number that almost doubled during Lent. Eyewitnesses confirm that the weekday masses, which during much of the period included one at 5:30 in the evening that saw the big church more than 75 percent full, maintained a sizable congregation throughout the 1960s.[26]

It required twenty-two masses to accommodate the twelve to fifteen thousand people who streamed in on holy days, Ash Wednesday, and All Souls Day. On one holy day in the mid-1950s a supply of 15,000 printed programs was exhausted well before the last mass. Once during that period a young police officer remonstrated with Hannan over how the hundreds of worshipers blocking the exits were in violation of the law. He demanded that Hannan "do something about it," only to retreat from the hopeless task himself when the pastor insisted that, as the representative of the law, he clear the aisles. Hannan was more concerned that the ushers, faced with huge numbers of worshipers, might act officiously, so he insisted on all the priests being present to help direct the crowds. Bishop Lyons left a vivid description of himself standing cassock-clad at the corner of Tenth and G Streets, directing swarms of worshipers surging across on the green light away from the packed church toward the school hall. Both Hannan and Lyons recalled the good spirits of the crowd and the windows of Woodward and Lothrop's across the street filled with employees marveling at the number of churchgoers. Although Lyons questioned the religious efficacy of the crowded, rushed masses, he too admitted the joy all seemed to experience in being part of a distinctive group making such a great public affirmation of their faith.[27]

25. These two pupils, Josephine Bertorelli and Mary Lou Mickson, were featured in the 1954 May Procession. See *Catholic Standard*, 7 May 1954.

26. The popular afternoon Mass apparently began as a featured part of the Marian Year celebration at St. Patrick's in 1954. See the *Star*, 26 Jan 1954.

27. Hughes, *Through His Eyes*, 16–17. See also author's interview with Archbishop Hannan.

EXTERN CONGREGATION. *Good Friday at St. Patrick's in the late 1950s*

The holy day crowds, the great lines at the confessionals, and the large attendance on weekdays were easily explained by the lingering vigor of the downtown commercial area and especially by the presence of so many government workers nearby. Sunday attendance was another matter, however, and was directly related to the parish's continuing ability to retain a loyal extern congregation. The church offered eight masses on Sundays, including two in the late afternoon. Eyewitnesses remember that throughout the postwar decades these masses continued to draw a respectable congregation, its size variously estimated at two to three thousand every week. Ushers would notice a steady decline in these impressive statistics by the mid-1960s, but the crowd remained sufficiently large to preclude any thought of reducing the number of masses.

Although no survey was taken, enough anecdotal information survives to provide some indication of the variety and nature of the Sunday congregation. The earlier masses, for example, attracted Catholics who worked on Sunday, including policemen, service workers who maintained the downtown offices and theaters, and those who were assigned weekend duty at nearby government agencies, especially the Federal Bureau of Investigation. Attorney General Robert F. Kennedy was frequently among these early attendees. Also to be found were members of Congress who would stop for Mass on their way to their Capitol offices. Speaker of the House John McCormick, who with his wife Harriet lived at the Washington Hotel on Fifteenth Street and considered St. Patrick's his parish, could be seen on Sunday mornings along with the likes of Congressmen Thomas "Tip" O'Neill and Hale Boggs. Such luminaries often rubbed shoulders with the many tourists who since the war had also helped swell the Sunday congregation. A common sight in the neighborhood on Sunday mornings was a Tenth Street clogged with buses from out of town waiting for their passengers to fulfill their religious obligation before setting off on the day's sight-seeing round.

Monsignor Hannan was especially sensitive to the needs of these parishioners, whose tight schedules, he warned his assistants, made a lengthy Mass and homily inappropriate. One of his new assistants ignored this warning, and when he began to preach at his first 7 a.m. mass was irritated when his congregation refused to sit down. In fact, they quietly remained standing until, defeated, he proceeded to recite the Creed. Remonstrating later with the pastor, he was surprised to find his boss siding with the rebels in the pews.

The later masses, especially the 9:45 high mass, which featured the music of the celebrated choir, drew many of the old externs, those former residents of the parish along with their now middle-aged children who continued to return regularly out of loyalty to the old church and a desire to worship in familiar surroundings with former neighbors. Some of these regulars were among the two hundred whose names were carried in the parish register well into the 1960s. They were joined each week by another large group of worshipers who, with no particular tie to the parish, faithfully attended St. Patrick's because it represented for them what a Catholic church should be: immense, serene, and gothic. The beauty of the clerestory windows bathed in the quiet Sunday morning light, the play of stained-glass colors on the massive pillars, and the sound of the majestic pipe organ exalted their sensitive spirits starved for such effects in suburban churches, which at that time were often makeshift affairs in school auditoriums. Such motives might well be condemned, yet they were deeply felt and strong enough to prompt a significant number of Catholics to find their way to St. Patrick's.

Those whose passports and green cards identified them as resident aliens constituted another notable segment of the Sunday congregation. Their presence must have especially appealed to the historically minded Hannan, who understood that, by serving as a refuge for newcomers to America, the parish was continuing a tradition as ancient as its foundation. Most noticeable in this group were survivors of the Hungarian uprising. Following the unsuccessful revolt against their Soviet oppressors in 1956, many Hungarians fled to America, and a sizable number made their homes in restored dwellings centered on G Place near the church. Unlike earlier newcomers, these eastern Europeans tended to be members of the aristocratic class, eager to maintain their language and traditions while learning English. For some time they had their own chaplain, whom Hannan invited to celebrate Mass regularly in Carroll Hall so that the group might enjoy sermons and prayers in their native tongue. In time these old freedom fighters were also much in evidence in the church, where Hungarian liturgy was featured on the third Sunday of the month and the Feast of St. Stephen, which was celebrated with due ceremony.[28]

Other eastern Europeans could be counted in the congregation. A prominent Czech patriot, Eduard Fusek, former head of the Catholic party in the Czech parliament, was a parishioner, and through his efforts many Czech immigrants frequented St. Patrick's, where special masses were always celebrated to mark their old country's national holidays. The parish also played host to the area's Ruthenian Catholics. The extraordinary beauty of their liturgy, in which everything is sung, attracted many Catholics interested in choral music to Carroll Hall. The hall also served as a sort of restaurant for the hungry worshipers, who lingered far into the day, socializing with their compatriots. In 1956 the archbishop authorized organization of a Ruthenian Rite parish, St. Gregory of Nyssa, and Bishop Hannan helped his guests find a church. It is interesting to note, given the problems his predecessors encountered with national parishes in their midst, that the site chosen for the Ruthenians was at some distance from St. Patrick's.

28. Ltr., Rev. Lazzlo Iranyi to Hannan, 17 Mar 1958. Hannan arranged English classes for the newcomers. See ltr., Hannan to Professor Charles Pulvavi, 18 Jul 1957. Both in SPA. See also, Joan Schampp, "A Heartfelt 'Deo Gratias' for Mass Sung in Latin," *Green Bay Register*, 14 Feb 1969.

Probably not since the early days of Father Matthews's church on F Street had St. Patrick's enjoyed such a heterogeneous congregation. Once again many of the city's Irish-born could be identified in the congregation. In a scene familiar to earlier generations, these mostly young working people (nannies, au pairs, laborers, and waiters) would gather at St. Patrick's for the late mass on Sunday, after which they had time to socialize with their fellow nationals, often prolonging the occasion at nearby Matt Kane's Bit of Ireland, the city's premier Irish pub.

The crowds that made St. Patrick's such a busy place during the week related to the fact that the neighborhood around the church had reached its apogee as the city's governmental, commercial, and theatrical center in the early 1960s. Cities, however, are constantly evolving entities, and by the mid-1960s the primacy of Washington's old downtown was being challenged on several fronts. The first suburban shopping centers, featuring branches of the city's well-known department stores, opened in Silver Spring and Wheaton and across the river at Seven Corners and Clarendon. Although the important retailers continued to attract discriminating shoppers to their F Street stores, competition from the suburbs as well as the growing popularity of shops along the lower Connecticut Avenue corridor signalled the retailers' imitation of the professionals in the slow drift away from downtown.

Even the theatrical landscape was changing. In 1963 the Capitol Theater, Washington's major vaudeville-movie palace, closed, presaging the fate of the other downtown theaters. The Capitol was of particular interest to St. Patrick's because the gallery of Washington's theatrical luminaries that adorned its lobby walls included a dramatic portrait of Father Stafford in appropriate Shakespearean pose.[29] The National, for decades Washington's major legitimate theater, found itself temporarily transformed into a second-rate movie house, victim of its management's insistence on excluding African-Americans. Meanwhile, the Kennedy Center was scheduled to open in 1971, an event that would just about complete the shift of Washington's night life, including its fine restaurants, away from downtown.

Washington was certainly no exception to the rule that governments never grow smaller, but during the 1960s the rapid development of federal office space in Foggy Bottom, the newly redeveloped South-

29. This picture, unfortunately lost, had long hung in the National Theater before being moved to the F Street movie house.

west, and across the river in Arlington meant that much of its postwar growth was outside the Federal Triangle. This change not only stimulated commercial centers outside the old business district, but taken in conjunction with other reasons for the sudden drop in the number of shoppers along F Street at the end of the 1960s, presaged a quieter future for the old neighborhood.

In most outward respects little had changed in the pleasant pre-war ambiance of downtown Washington. In an era when street crime was still largely limited to the occasional purse snatching, the region around the church was considered safe. Pedestrians peacefully strolled along F Street late into the evening, returning from a night at the theater or merely admiring the decorations in the store windows. Parents had no qualms about allowing their teenagers to commute to the academy on G Street. In fact, burglaries were still rare enough in the region to provoke a humorous report in the *Post* in 1962 when two desperados, trying to break into the rectory, were caught and held at bay by Monsignor Hannan and two assistants until the police arrived.[30] More worrisome, the church suffered its first break-in in 1964 when a thief smashed through one of the stained glass windows of the nave to rifle the poor boxes.

Far more common were the petty disturbances caused by the alcoholics who chose the church as a place to rest their weary bodies. One such guest awoke to find himself alone and locked in for the night. He tried to escape through a small window in the baptistry, only to become stuck in the aperture. Meanwhile the heat from the nearby votive candles roused his worst fears, and late night pedestrians were surprised to hear his frantic cry for help, "The Catholics have got me and are burning me alive."[31] If drunks were commonplace in downtown Washington, drug addicts were still in the future, although some hint of the scourge to come could be forecast from incidents in the 1960s when the parish was forced to summon the rescue squad (four times on one holy day) to treat recovering addicts suffering severe withdrawal symptoms.

The need for personal charity did not abate in the postwar decades, but the nature of that charity at St. Patrick's began to change. Some of the beggars Archbishop O'Boyle encountered on his evening walks obviously belonged to the brotherhood of professional panhandlers who aggressively demanded ever more help from priests and people.

30. *Post*, 30 Apr 1962.
31. Quoted by Sister Miriam André in interview with author.

At the same time the church served as a magnet for the genuinely destitute. Its proximity to the city's interstate bus terminals also produced a steady stream of stranded and penniless travellers temporarily down on their luck. For many years the rectory maintained a charge account at the Atlantic diner on Pennsylvania Avenue so that the priests could issue those in need a chit for a meal.[32] A similar arrangement was made with the nearby International Safeway. In a time before homelessness had become an overwhelming problem in the city, several priests kept a running account at some of the smaller transient hotels that still dotted the neighborhood to provide temporary lodging for the needy. Cases involving long-term aid for area residents were turned over to the parish's St. Vincent de Paul Society (by now reduced to half a dozen men) which investigated requests and dispensed assistance out of parish accounts. The rare funerals in the church were almost all small, charitable affairs arranged by the St. Vincent de Paul.

The increasing signs of poverty in the inner city were a sad commentary on the pretensions of America's affluent society, but even they paled in significance when compared with the city's enduring struggle with the baleful evidence of racial injustice. Despite some signs of progress—integration of the schools began after the Supreme Court's Brown v. Board of Education decision in 1954, and restaurants and places of entertainment opened their doors to black Washingtonians following the landmark decision involving Thompson's Restaurant in 1957—the civil rights revolution of the 1960s had little effect on the rigid residential segregation that continued to divide black and white Washington. Officially ignored, block busting, real estate covenants, and white flight continued, while tensions rose in the black community as the legitimate needs of its citizens went untended and its neighborhoods deteriorated. Meanwhile, local officials watched with righteous indignation events in Selma, Alabama, seemingly oblivious to injustices in their own neighborhoods and ready to be surprised when the whirlwind struck.

A Decade of Zealous Activity

The man appointed to guide the parish through this last period of downtown Washington's celebrity belonged to a family prominent in

32. In the 1960s the director of the local Salvation Army headquarters recalled that, when he had been in need years before, he ate at the Atlantic diner using St. Patrick's meal tickets.

both the city's business community and Catholic lay circles.[33] A graduate of St. John's High School, Philip Hannan was trained for the priesthood at the North American College in Rome and after ordination served as a wartime chaplain in a parachute regiment of the famed 82d Airborne Division. After demobilization he assumed a succession of key assignments in the new diocese, beginning with his appointment as vice-chancellor in 1948.

Like his predecessor Monsignor Thomas a half-century before, Hannan took on the task of establishing a diocesan newspaper. Ruefully noting that to get any Washington news in the *Catholic Review* "I would have to personally jump off the Washington monument," O'Boyle appointed Hannan the *Catholic Standard*'s first editor in 1951. A year later the archbishop, no longer able to ignore the mounting tensions associated with Monsignor Cowhig's management style at the chancery and at St. Patrick's, asked Hannan to assume both jobs.[34] Hannan was consecrated Washington's second auxiliary bishop in 1956 (Bishop John McNamara had stayed in the new diocese as O'Boyle's assistant).

By 1957 it had become obvious even to Patrick O'Boyle that two bishops were one too many in one rectory, even one as commodious as St. Patrick's. What finally convinced him to leave, he liked to explain, was his fear that when asked which bishop he had come to see, a visitor might reply, "The young one." Hearing of plans to buy a large home for him in the city's southern suburbs, O'Boyle claimed that "they're trying to get me out of town."[35] In June he finally relinquished the rectory suite that had served local ordinaries for more than half a century. At his departure he appointed Hannan, who had been administering the affairs of the parish for five years, eleventh pastor of St. Patrick's.

By then Bishop Hannan's definition of an appropriate ministry for the old downtown parish was fully formed. He had been especially

33. Hannan was only the second Washingtonian to lead St. Patrick's. Stafford was born in the city, but spent much of his early priesthood in Cleveland. Hannan's family was active in the affairs of St. Matthew's parish, his brother serving as model for one of the portraits in the great fresco that dominates the south wall of the cathedral.

34. Frequently criticized for his executive style, Cowhig developed into an able and popular leader as administrator and later pastor of St. Jerome's in Hyattsville. For an assessment of Cowhig's career in the diocese, see author's interview with Msg. Arthur. The O'Boyle quotation is taken from Abel, *Patrick Cardinal O'Boyle*, 19.

35. The first O'Boyle quotation is from Abel, *Patrick Cardinal O'Boyle*, 57; the second from Msgr. Teletchea's interview with the author.

BISHOP PHILIP M. HANNAN AND HOUSE GUEST. *The new pastor with Archibishop Patrick A. O'Boyle*

critical of the parish's loss in recent decades of leadership in diocesan affairs and in church-state relations as well as the failure of St. Patrick's to reach out to the city's non-Catholics in the spirit fostered by Pope John XXIII. In his dissatisfaction the dual-hatted young bishop did not always carefully distinguish between his role as chancellor and vicar of the diocese and his duties as pastor of a downtown parish. Still, it is obvious that he possessed a strong sense of history and, like several of his illustrious prewar predecessors, made a conscious effort to rejuvenate parish traditions, restore its historical role in community affairs, and develop a financial base to support extra-parochial interests. It was in his outgoing, open pursuit of these objectives that he came most closely to resemble his famous predecessor Denis Stafford.

Like Stafford, Hannan respected and encouraged the parish's emerging role as a spiritual refuge in the city center, where those with special needs might come for solace, encouraged by the anonymity afforded in the faceless crowds and the easy access to priests. More than one priest who served at St. Patrick's during those years used the analogy of a city monastery to explain the overwhelming numbers of confessions and special counseling that consumed so much of his time. Hannan particularly enjoyed the monastery analogy and sought to make those people with special spiritual needs feel welcome. Early on he made a point of standing at the church door, greeting those entering or leaving, and he encouraged his assistants to do the same—a kind of hands-on ministry quite novel in the pre-Vatican II church. Not since Stafford's time had a pastor shown such openness toward or collaborated so freely with those of differing beliefs. In the spirit of Pope John's open window to the world, his ecumenism was not expressed in the sometimes-strident apologetics used by William Russell and other leaders of the old ghetto church, nor even in the fervent pursuit of converts of more recent times, but, rather, in an atmosphere of mutual respect. Hannan, for example, was an active member of B'nai B'rith, an organization that worked to forge better relations between Christians and Jews, and he spoke frequently and hopefully on Christian unity before both Catholic and Protestant-sponsored audiences.[36]

After a boyhood spent listening to family stories about Catholic Washington, Hannan came to St. Patrick's with a strong sense of parish's role in the history of the city and the American church. He was aware, for example, of the then-largely-forgotten Mattingly cure in 1824, and when Judge Matthew McGuire unearthed the affidavits that supported the miraculous nature of the event, the new pastor reintroduced the novena to the Holy Name of Jesus that had formed the basis of Mattingly's supplications so long ago. The well-publicized service, with its special historical meaning for the parish, attracted hundreds to the church in 1959 and continues to this day as part of the parish's prayer life.

It was his strong respect for tradition that prompted Hannan to try to rejuvenate the celebration of St. Patrick's Day at the old church. The parish always enjoyed a special place among the area's Irish-Americans, a historical connection that the new pastor tried to underscore. In 1953 he had assembled the local hierarchy, along with the apostolic delegate and the Irish ambassador, to unveil a monument in front of the church commemorating the foundation of the first parish in the federal city by an Irish Dominican. With Gaelic aplomb, its

36. For one such Hannan address on Christian unity, see the *Star*, 13 Dec 1963.

plaque solved any lingering confusion over the parish's founding date by settling for "about 1792."[37] The 1960s marked the beginning of a strong revival of interest in Irish traditions and folklore. From the start Hannan took special care to make St. Patrick's the spiritual focus of this developing preoccupation. To ensure that March 17th remained a grand occasion, he procured a series of special guests and noteworthy preachers, along with luminaries of church and state to attend the annual celebration. With members of the Ancient Order of Hibernians alone filling half the church, the crowds were so great that tickets had to be issued for entrance. The Mass never failed to garner press notice, always with reference to the antiquity of the celebration in Washington and its connection to the church that bore St. Patrick's name.[38]

To all outward appearances the Pan-American Mass had changed little over the years. The crowds continued to attend—more than twelve hundred were present in 1959 to hear President Dwight D. Eisenhower's special greeting read to the diplomats on the occasion of the fiftieth anniversary of the affair. The secretary of state and chief justice of the Supreme Court were regularly present; in 1967 President Lyndon B. Johnson sat in the front pew, the first President to attend since Woodrow Wilson in 1913. In fact the Johnsons arrived early for Mass and appeared at an infrequently used entrance at the back of the rectory. A startled priest interrupted his task of emptying a trashbasket to guide the first family to their appointed position. The abundance of flowers and flags and music harkened back to the ceremony's prewar splendor, and the ushers, clad in rented cutaways, still directed the distinguished diplomats to their familiar places.[39]

Nevertheless, enthusiasm for the inter-American event had begun to flag by the 1960s. Some blamed the date, Thanksgiving Day, for the problem and sought to reschedule the Mass on Columbus Day. Oth-

37. Although somewhat rare on a historical marker, the "about" date is actually a reasonable assumption, given the fact that Father Caffry's 1794 request to the commissioners for land, the earliest surviving authentic record, mentions a congregation of Catholics which, presumably, had been in existence for some time.

38. Every March saw a spate of not always accurate articles about the church and the saint. On 17 Mar 1959, for example, the *Star* reported that the church, which it claimed was the first in the nation named for St. Patrick, was founded in 1790. On 17 Mar 1962 the same paper reported on the city's 170th St. Patrick's Day Mass, a ceremony it traced in an unbroken line to a celebration by Father Caffry in 1792. The *Catholic Standard* (in three successive issues beginning 11 Mar 1960) traced the history of St. Patrick's Day in Washington.

39. Hinkle, "St. Patrick's Church," 40-41. See also author's interview with Charles J. Patrak. Mr. Patrak has served as an usher at St. Patrick's since 1950.

ers, pointing out that the ceremony competed with demands on Latin American diplomts to attend functions at the United Nations in New York, wanted to broaden attendance by inviting representatives of other nations. Hannan worked hard to keep the ceremny going along the lines laid out by its organizers. He personally delivered invitations and continued to entertain the diplomats at an elaborate reception after Mass. Yet he was painfully aware of the inordinate time and stress caused by an occasion that often forced him to address the petty jealousies and bruised egos prevailing in the diplomatic community rather than concentrate on the spiritual aspects of the occasion.

More even than Stafford and William Russell, Hannan succeeded in establishing easy access to the White House and other government agencies. At first glance such efforts on the part of St. Patrick's pastor appears unnecessary, given the presence of a resident archbishop and fully staffed chancery. But O'Boyle was always diffident when it came to dealing with the government. A son of hard-working Irish raised far outside the Washington beltway, he tended to exaggerate the importance of senior officials and was genuinely concerned lest he be thought seeking the limelight or somehow breaking down the separation between church and state. As a well-placed native, Hannan suffered no such misconceptions about politicians or the cliff-dwellers, as Washington called its socially elite. Until his departure in 1965, St. Patrick's pastor continued to play a major role in the diocese's dealings with federal and city agencies and the town's economic and social elite.

Hannan's habit of greeting parishioners after Mass led to friendships with several influential congressmen. These politicians would make a point of attending the same Mass as Speaker McCormick, using the supposedly chance encounter to conduct a little unofficial business or engage in some special pleading in an impromptu caucus on the church steps. Hannan would often join the group, on occasion doing a little special pleading himself.[40] His relations with the national government became more complicated, however, when he assumed the entirely new role of unofficial adviser to the first Catholic president.

Hannan had become acquainted with John Kennedy some years before when the young Boston politician and other new congressmen were being pestered by a clerical gadfly from Baltimore who insisted

40. Friendships developed in these gatherings later enabled Hannan, for example, to win Speaker O'Neill's assistance in obtaining a large federal research grant for Catholic University's physics department.

on instructing them on the nation's Mexican policy. Hannan quickly put an end to the meddlesome friar's lectures, an act that sparked a friendship with Kennedy that gradually evolved into a relationship in which St. Patrick's pastor served as a sounding board for the church's views on matters of public policy. Such an arrangement, which continued after Kennedy entered the White House, suited presidential needs perfectly. To approach the archbishop with questions about Catholic attitudes might raise old fears about the separation of church and state and, should the President decide to ignore that official's advice, invite criticism from Catholic constituents. Advice from St. Patrick's pastor on the other hand, quietly sought and quietly given, could be accepted or ignored with impunity. Hannan would hear from the President himself or discuss Catholic attitudes on current events with a White House assistant, principally Ralph A. Dungan or Special Counsel Theodore C. Sorensen.

Although determined to deal with political leaders in the open manner adopted by several of his famous predecessors, Hannan remained sensitive to first amendment concerns. It was no coincidence that when the possibility of a Catholic occupying the White House was being hotly discussed in 1960, Hannan published an article in the *Catholic Standard* extolling Father William Matthews for his fruitful but always proper relations with government officials.[41] As pastor, Hannan seemed to emulate Matthews in his service to the city. He accepted appointment to the Federal City Council, a board formed to advise the National Park and Planning Commission and the Redevelopment Land Agency on urban renewal projects. Although he could not avert the ill-advised scheme to redevelop southwest Washington with its wholesale resettlement of the poor and its destruction of many beautiful buildings, Hannan was at least able to save St. Dominic Church from the developers and highway planners.

It was during the 1960s that Catholic Washington became swept up in the great civil rights revolution that was reaching its climax in the city and the nation. For many decades the so-called separate but equal doctrine ruled relations between the races in much of the country, including Catholic schools in the Archdiocese of Baltimore. Archbishop Curley supported the evangelization of African Americans, but when his effort to establish an integrated school in southern Maryland led to destruction of the building by angry whites, he became convinced that the diocese should continue racial policies developed under his

41. *Catholic Standard,* 16 Sep 1960.

predecessor. Fearing action on his part might inflame racial passions, he called it "the height of imprudence" for anyone to consider mingling blacks and whites in the same parish. His years in St. Augustine, Florida, also seemed to have convinced him that blacks prospered under white supervision and, in fact, did not want black priests.[42] By 1923 Washington had eight black parishes whose boundaries overlapped those of the white parishes. This separate jurisdictional grid closely aped the separate but equal pattern sanctioned by the secular government. The continuing witness of the Catholic Interracial Council was one bright ray of hope in an otherwise gloomy picture where most local Catholic institutions, including orphanages, old age homes, and schools—even Catholic University—generally excluded blacks.[43]

Segregation of Catholic institutions did not long survive the arrival of Patrick O'Boyle. In one of his first meetings with his consultors he announced his determination to integrate the diocese. Recognizing that sudden change would be hotly contested, especially in southern Maryland, where the tradition of segregation was centuries old, he agreed to a flexible timetable but demanded that planning begin immediately. In late 1949 he ordered the boundaries of the black parishes revised, limiting their pastor's jurisdiction to those black Catholics who lived within a "reasonable" distance of the church. Henceforth, all other black Catholics were expected to become full members of the parishes within whose boundaries they resided. His order did not end segregation overnight, as can be deduced from the gerrymandering of Holy Redeemer's boundaries in 1949.[44] It did, however, remove a major impediment to integration of the city's parishes and began a

42. Stephen J. Ochs, *Desegregating the Altar: The Josephites and the Struggle for Black Priests, 1871–1960* (Baton Rouge: Louisiana State University Press, 1990), 244–45, 312–13. (The Curley quotation is found on 242.) See also Foley, "The Catholic Church and the Washington Negro," 68. Historian John Tracy Ellis called the American church's racial policy its greatest failure. See author's interview with Ellis.

43. Catholic University admitted a black student to its school of nursing in 1936 and by 1939 had forty black students, all but nine in graduate schools. Blacks remained excluded from the university's nonacademic facilities before O'Boyle's arrival. See C. Joseph Nuesse, *The Catholic University of America: A Centennial History* (Washington: The Catholic University of America Press, 1990), 322 and 345. One further exception: the Little Sisters of the Poor cared for black Catholics, albeit in a separate wing of their institution. The dual parish structure and segregation of black Catholics is described in Foley, "The Catholic Church and the Washington Negro," 63–68, 156–58, and 231–55. Archbishop Hannan described the racial exclusion in parishes, particularly at St. Paul's and St. Matthew's in his interview with author.

44. Holy Redeemer boundary decree, 3 Oct 1949, laid out a parish that ranged across a jagged six-square mile section of central Washington. It was finally amended

gradual adjustment in the pattern of church-going among black Catholics.

The following year the archbishop began the far more difficult task of integrating schools, setting the diocese on the road to reform considerably ahead of the public schools. St. Patrick's pastor served as point man in this carefully orchestrated change, and Carroll Hall was the site of the volatile meetings O'Boyle held with the concerned parents in an attempt to defuse the situation. The archbishop pleaded for cooperation, reminding his flock of how their own forebears had once suffered discrimination and bluntly adding that discrimination was an evil the diocese must overcome. To those on the other hand who complained that progress was too slow, he said, "I'll take the segregation dishes off the table one at a time."[45]

Actually, the diocese's schools integrated with remarkable speed and with little untoward incident. Nor was the feat overlooked by the nation's leaders. When Chief Justice Earl Warren met the archbishop at the Pan-American Mass in 1953, the year before the court's historic Brown decision, he asked that they discuss the diocese's experience. Although O'Boyle failed to follow up on the invitation, he did agree to participate in a city-wide group working for racial justice. As first chairman of the Interreligious Committee on Race Relations he coordinated the work of local denominations in reviewing the effect of governmental programs on the city's civil rights initiatives. This post often thrust the archbishop, usually diffident in governmental matters, into the national limelight, forcing him to face the press from a White House rostrum. More pleasing to him were those times when the committee was quietly able to block legislation that would work further hardship on the city's minority poor, as in the case when it frustrated construction of the northern leg of the freeway until a suitable plan was worked out for relocation of people living in its path.[46]

Probably the most dramatic moment in the modern civil rights movement was the March on Washington For Jobs and Freedom in August 1963. St. Patrick's was represented by its pastor and several assistant priests and sisters who joined O'Boyle and Lawrence Shehan,

to conform with the archbishop's order on 3 February 1968. For copies of both decrees, see Holy Redeemer file, AAW.

45. O'Boyle summarized his ideas on the subject in a speech to the John Carroll Society. See Star, 29 Feb 1956. For a summary of diocese's desegregatation plan, see the author's interview with Archbishop Hannan. See also Abel, Patrick Cardinal O'Boyle, 8–11, which is also the source of the O'Boyle quotation.

46. Star, 17 Sep 1963.

now Baltimore's archbishop, and other Washington Catholics at the Lincoln Memorial after a day that began with a special Mass and breakfast at the parish. O'Boyle was scheduled to give the invocation at the event, but his participation remained in doubt almost to the last minute. Although he had been instrumental in changing the attitude of many of Washington's clergymen toward the march, he was dismayed to learn that one of the speakers planned to call for violence as an alternative solution to the nation's race problems. O'Boyle demanded that the offending passages be cut. Only when the march organizers finally agreed did the archbishop, a zealous law and order advocate, feel free to participate in the high purpose and exciting theater of the day. Just before Dr. Martin Luther King, Jr., began his memorable "I Have a Dream" address, Ralph Bunche, the distinguished United Nations official, leaned over to O'Boyle and said, "Now you're going to feel just a little like you are in a black Southern Baptist church."[47] It was a moment for the doughty prelate, who had fought hard for racial justice in Washington, to savor.

End of an Era

While St. Patrick's was engaged in these momentous events, the homely tasks involved in managing a large downtown church remained. The seventy-year-old building was experiencing structural problems. In 1952 engineers discovered that the weight of the marble furnishings had weakened the sanctuary floor, necessitating a time-consuming and costly shoring up of the foundations that began with the installation of a grid of supporting steel beams under the apse. Further investigation revealed that the floor of the nave, which the builders had laid over a masonry slab without excavating a full basement, was in an advanced state of decay. After first removing all the pews and furnishings, workers replaced the wood with a steel-reinforced concrete slab covered in green and white tile.

With structural problems solved, Hannan proceeded to concentrate on aesthetic ones. For some time he had been convinced that the main altar with its crenate spires, elaborate finials, and ornate statuary was more Victorian than gothic in spirit and, despite the fact that it had

47. As quoted by Hannan in his interview with the author. For a comprehensive survey of O'Boyle's racial policies, see Rory Conley, "'All One in Christ': The Church of Washington, Patrick Cardinal O'Boyle, and the Struggle for Racial Justice, 1948–1973" (Master's thesis, The Catholic University of America, 1993).

been designed by the church's architect, did not harmonize with the style of the building. After consulting his friend Philip Hubert Froh-man, architect of the Episcopal community's great gothic cathedral on Wisconsin Avenue, he decided to replace the altar's superstructure with a gothic reredos, something, he believed, that would add color and warmth to the sanctuary. Pastors know that one tampers with church furnishings at one's peril. Replacing a worn candleholder or moving a statue often sets off a storm of protest from self-appointed guardians of parish traditions. In this case, years of daily exposition of the Blessed Sacrament had led thousands of Catholics to regard St. Patrick's main altar as the central image of their religion in Washing-ton, and Hannan knew that the change would produce a storm of crit-icism. To avoid the crescendo of complaint likely to accompany piece-meal change, the pastor decided that the congregation's first sight of the new reredos should be the finished object in all its glory. He had the pieces assembled and installed practically overnight in time for Christmas Eve Mass in 1962. This tactic helped mute criticism and seemed to convert some of those initially hostile to the idea, but de-spite much praise for the addition, feelings ran deep. Thirty years after its installation, the gothic reredos retained its ardent detractors, who missed the lofty altar towers designed by Lawrence O'Connor seven decades before.[48] No such controversy attended the addition of stained-glass to the rose window in the church's west front in 1964.

Hannan's enthusiasm for improvements matched a determination to make the parish's valuable property better serve the needs of the Catholic community. The generosity of the transient congregation (the more than $2,000 collected on Sundays in Hannan's first years as pastor could be considered respectable in all but the city's most affluent parishes) coupled with the school's tuition receipts and the in-come from the F street property remained more than adequate to meet operating expenses and even allowed the pastor to donate money to pressing diocesan projects. In 1958, for example, the parish's financial health enabled him to write off the $275,000 that the diocese had borrowed from St. Patrick's earlier in the decade.

Future prospects, however, were not nearly so rosy. The F Street rents still grossed nearly $48,000 in 1963, but as one real estate expert pointed out, the gradual deterioration of the block's commercial at-

48. Archbishop Hannan discusses his reasons for the addition and attendant criti-cism in his interview with the author. See also *Catholic Standard,* 26 Dec 1962. The reredos is described in chapter 14, below.

tractiveness (manifested by several extended vacancies), the reluctance of merchants to commit to long-term lease agreements, and continually rising taxes all pointed to depressed earnings in the future. Hannan recommended that the parish reconsider an offer from a national retailer to build a new church complex on Ninth Street near the site of the new central library and Smithsonian gallery in exchange for the parish's holdings in square 376. Echoing arguments advanced nearly a century before, the realtor pointed out that the new site was somewhat removed from the area's commercial center and certainly superior to the aspect from Tenth Street with its "view of the Woodward and Lothrop's truck loading dock."[49] The pastor rejected the proposal. Respect for a Catholic presence on the site now stretching back over 170 years might have been dismissed by realtors as "the sentimental reasons," but sentiment prevailed. St. Patrick's would stay put.

At the same time Hannan saw nothing sacrosanct about the F Street property, and that same year he began exploring new uses for this major financial asset. After rejecting the proposal to move the church itself, he hired an architect to develop detailed plans for a ten-story, three-basement retail store/office building on the F Street lots. Times seemed propitious. The city, anxious to reverse business trends in the area, was ready to cooperate. In July 1963 the Knights of Columbus agreed to finance the project at reduced interest. Washington realtor Don Rosinski had already secured lease commitments from a group of retailers and business firms that would triple the church's annual income.

The effort went for nothing. Although O'Boyle knew and trusted Rosinski, he seemed overawed by the scale of the plan and frightened by the gloomy predictions of some advisors. The archbishop had always shown considerable foresight in the purchase of church property. Calling the newspapers' real estate advertisements his "Saturday bible," he prudently searched out land that could be obtained at reasonable prices in undeveloped suburban regions. When these later became the sites of new parishes, they represented a tremendous savings for the people of the archdiocese. Yet for a man with such foresight who had also dealt so skillfully with large sums of money in Catholic

49. Ltr., Carl G. Rosinski to Pastor of St. Patrick's, n.d., Operating Statement 921–914 F St. N.W., St. Patrick's file, AAW. The realtor unsuccessfully recommended that, to improve the commercial strength of its holdings, the parish buy the lot abutting its F Street property (the site of the old Washington Seminary donated to the Jesuits for their school by Father Matthews) for $135,000.

war relief, O'Boyle was strangely inhibited by the thought of committing major resources to a real estate enterprise in downtown Washington. He rejected Hannan's proposal, a decision that left the parish, its valuable property underdeveloped, facing an uncertain financial future.

This real estate project, like all of Philip Hannan's parish initiatives launched during his thirteen years at St. Patrick's, competed for his attention with his responsibilities as a diocesan official. Once he complained to the archbishop about the extent of these duties, only to be reminded that he need not perform them all at the same time. O'Boyle did try to lighten the load by appointing a new chancellor in 1962, but by then Hannan's duties as vicar general, a post he had assumed at the death of Bishop John McNamara in 1960, and his active participation in the sessions of the second Vatican Council left little time for St. Patrick's. As his pastorate neared its end, day-to-day direction of the parish fell increasingly to his principal assistant, Sylvester Hoffman.

Hoffman was a popular administrator who enjoyed the affection and esteem of priests and laity to an exceptional degree. Himself a late vocation, Hoffman showed a rare understanding of the daily concerns of his transient congregation. At the same time he was an extremely spiritual person, who fought a losing battle with cancer with quiet forebearance. Save for his affliction, he appeared likely to succeed Hannan when that prelate left in 1965 to become the archbishop of New Orleans. Instead Hoffman remained until his death the following February administrator of the downtown parish he had served for fourteen years.

It was left to Hoffman to complete the remodeling started by his predecessor. He installed air conditioning, repainted the interior for the first time since the war, and completed construction of a shrine in honor of the saints of the Americas in the north transept. For the most part, however, he concentrated on the spiritual needs of the downtown church's congregation of strangers. That congregation was as various as the one that gathered with Father Matthews a century and a half before. In 1820 government officials and the landed gentry arrived for Mass in carriages or on horseback often through a sea of mud; now congressmen and cliff-dwellers drew up in limousines. Then Irish workers walked from their humble homes in the shadow of the White House and the Capitol; now newcomers converged by public transit from all over a metropolitan region whose size would have staggered the imaginations of their predecessors. The church still attracted the powerful and prominent. Once in the mid-1960s an assistant priest was startled to encounter a stranger prowling the sacristy. He turned out to be a Secret Service agent preparing for an unexpected visit by President Johnson, who, like another President Johnson a century before, on occasion sought solace in St. Patrick's. O'Boyle once jokingly observed that the President had seen the inside of more of the city's Catholic churches than the archbishop.[50]

Increasingly, however, the church was attracting a large share of Runyonesque characters, whose presence reflected the growing numbers of displaced and lonely in downtown Washington. Despite the impersonality of the neighborhood, the priests became well acquainted with many in this varied congregation. They were made aware of the sometimes-dubious purpose of "Candle Mary's" visits, for example, when one of them finally caught her performing her trick of stealing money from the church's votive stands with the help of chewing gum on a taper. When he asked Hoffman what to do about it, the assistant was told to advise Mary to visit St. Matthew's, where the take was bound to be greater.[51] More than one priest found his attempt to deliver an inspiring homily frustrated as his congregation watched with rapt attention one of the church's denizens in her accustomed seat in a front pew repeatedly try to hang one of her several overcoats on an imaginary hook in a nearby marble pillar.

These were just two of the larcenous or simply confused and abandoned people who inhabited downtown Washington and found refuge in the church. Along with the students, shoppers, and government workers, they deserve to be counted as an element of the varied, colorful transient population that constituted St. Patrick's congregation in its eighteenth decade.

50. Author's interview with Sister Miriam André. Judging by the number of visits, President Johnson's favorite church in Washington was St. Dominic, where special arrangements were made for his frequent late-night visits.

51. Author's interview with Father Conway. The advice, jokingly given, must have been seriously taken, for Candle Mary was later caught at the Shrine of the Immaculate Conception after a considerable amount of money had been stolen from its great banks of votive stands.

CHAPTER 12

Redefinitions

THE ASSASSIN'S BULLET that struck down Dr. Martin Luther King, Jr., in April 1968 also unleashed a wave of urban violence that engulfed many of the nation's great cities. From their vantage point in the old neighborhood, the priests and sisters at St. Patrick's witnessed first-hand the arson and looting that raged in the capital for days, a riot that would change the face of downtown Washington forever. Occurring as it did during a period of intense national debate over the country's so-called wars on racism and poverty and coinciding with the civil disturbances associated with the conflict in Vietnam, the riot caused many people, both black and white, to abandon the city's old downtown even as it tested their assumptions about the inevitability of social progress. From the turmoil emerged an indifference on the part of large segments of the population to the plight of the inner city that threatened to wreck any plans for renewal.

For Catholics, this period of national turmoil also coincided with a time of confusion and agitation in the American church as many began to re-examine the nature of their beliefs and religious practices in the years following the second Vatican Council. Suddenly, the elaborate ritual and massive display of public devotion that had characterized St. Patrick's for six decades and had won for it a large and loyal extern congregation no longer seemed so central to Catholic life. For both church and state, nothing would ever be quite the same again in Washington.

A Friendly Occupation

Shortly after news of Dr. King's death reached the city on Thursday evening, April 4, the mood among the mourners gathering on upper Fourteenth Street turned ugly, and before the police could restore order later that night one rioter lay dead and some 150 stores in the region were looted.[1] With calm prevailing on Friday morning, the city's schools, stores, and offices all opened for business, but the calm proved illusory. By noon rioting had broken out again in many areas. Although they wanted to keep the children off the streets and away from the rioting, city authorities agreed they had no choice but to close the schools.

Sister Miriam André, the principal of St. Patrick's Academy, received no official notification of this decision, but after being warned of impending trouble by students recently released from Mackin High School, she acted quickly.[2] The girls were dismissed and arrangements made for escorting those who encountered any difficulty going home or who were too frightened to attempt the journey alone. Later several adults, including Father George Pavloff and William P. Harris, the school's highly esteemed maintenance engineer, drove students to the suburbs, only to face a hazardous return trip through riot-torn streets. Particularly hard hit on Friday afternoon were the business corridors along H Street, Northeast, and Fourteenth and Seventh Streets, Northwest. In an effort to stem the advance of the rioters down Seventh Street into the main retail area, police set up blockades at Mount Vernon Place near the old central library along the northern boundary of the parish.

Their efforts proved fruitless. By late afternoon roving gangs were making hit-and-run forays along F and G Streets, smashing windows and looting favored stores. The air was filled with the sound of auto-

1. Disturbances of one magnitude or another occurred in at least 125 American cities, including Baltimore, Chicago, Detroit, Cleveland, and eight other major urban areas. See Paul J. Scheips, "The Washington Riot of 1968" (unpublished manuscript, U.S. Army Center of Military History). Unless otherwise indicated, the following description of the King riot is based on this exhaustive study.

2. The following account of activities in the academy during the riot is based on author's interviews with Sisters Miriam André and Marie Julie and George Pavloff.

mobiles careening at high speed through the neighborhood as rioters eluded police. In time the overwhelmed officers gave up the chase in order to defend the fire fighters, who were converging from all over the region to work the two hundred major fires that were sending up great billows of smoke in many parts of the city. Among the hardest hit stores in the old downtown area were some along the 900 block of F Street, the Hecht Company at F and Seventh, and D. J. Kaufman's, the haberdasher at Tenth and Pennsylvania Avenue. Gaping holes replaced the smart, goods-filled windows of scores of retail establishments.[3] With the sound of breaking glass echoing around him, one of the passing rioters stopped to threaten Sister Miriam André with the promise that "we'll get you tonight." Determined to show no hint of fear, the principal replied with no little bravado: "You do, and you'll pay for it."

When government agencies and local businesses closed early, hordes of fearful commuters created a monumental traffic jam, further hindering officials trying to contain the mob. Finally at 4 p.m. President Johnson issued a formal proclamation calling on the rioters to cease and desist, thus fulfilling the final legal requirement before ordering federal troops into action against American citizens. Within the hour, units of the federalized District of Columbia National Guard were deploying from the Armory, and soldiers from nearby military bases in full combat gear began arriving in the city. Company D of the 3d U.S. Infantry, part of the famous "Old Guard" from Ft. Myer, assembled along Pennsylvania Avenue and immediately began sending out patrols north along the numbered streets between Sixth and Fifteenth Streets. Groups of soldiers, all armed with rifles, sheathed bayonets, riot batons, and tear gas grenades, marched along in front of St. Patrick's Church and rectory. During the night a battalion-size unit of military engineers from Ft. Belvoir set up headquarters in the federal building adjacent to the academy on G Street. The mayor placed the city under a strict curfew and banned the sale of gasoline and liquor. Before dawn, military units from as far away as Ft. Bragg, North Carolina, and ranging in size from small patrols accompanying local police units to 200-man companies deployed in battle formation, had spread all across the troubled region.[4]

3. Both the *Star* and *Post,* in their editions of 5 through 8 April 1968, provided vivid descriptions and photographs of the tumult and destruction in the neighborhood.

4. Based on the surviving official after-action reports, the unit headquartered next door to the academy has been identified as the 92d Engineer Battalion, one of the few units from Ft. Belvoir assigned to Task Force Washington. Before the riot was over,

From their lofty quarters in the academy, the sisters could see the flames rising against the darkened sky along Seventh Street and the farther reaches of the city. Although the acrid smoke penetrated the convent, they were reassured about their personal safety late that night by D.C. police detective Sam Wallace. In the morning they were surprised and further reassured to find the street in front of the school filled with soldiers. Some of the soldiers, anticipating the arrival of regular food that would end their use of the universally hated combat rations, had begun to set up a field kitchen. They welcomed the sisters' offer to provide coffee and open the school's soft drink and snack food machines. The sight of the hungry young soldiers prompted Sister Marie Julie to rush off to the International Safeway on Eleventh Street to buy food for their breakfast. Her purchases were so great that the store loaned her a shopping cart for the return trip. The sight of this diminutive but determined woman threading a food-filled cart through the broken glass and debris of G Street deserves inclusion in the city's collective memory of those days.

The Military District of Washington arranged with a number of public schools and private institutions for the use of cafeterias, gymnasiums, and locker rooms for the men. Without any formal agreement the academy opened its doors to the troops, who ate and showered in the school for four days. Once the army's food supplies finally arrived, they were routinely cooked and served in the school cafeteria. The nuns even found time to prepare Easter baskets for their special guests. With an uneasy calm prevailing by Palm Sunday morning, April 7, some of the soldiers wanted to attend Mass. Reluctant to appear in church with their military equipment, they prevailed on Sister Miriam André to store their guns, bayonets, and field packs in her office, which took on the appearance of a modest-sized armory. Later, when the army sent thanks to the sisters for their hospitality, along with money donated by the soldiers to pay for the food served them on the first day, news of the principal's extraordinary dealings with the men in uniform began circulating around the chancery, where Sister Miriam André became known as the "Queen of the Military."

By Sunday afternoon the army could concentrate on maintaining the hard-won peace that prevailed in most parts of town. Military units helped city authorities clear debris from the main traffic arteries and return essential services to the fire-devastated regions. Although

the White House committed 15,530 troops, including some 1,500 D.C. national guardsmen, to the capital region.

Woodward and Lothrop's was fire-bombed and many businesses in the neighborhood lay in ruins, neither the academy nor the rectory was ever in any immediate danger after Friday night. The riot, however, was both deadly and expensive. By the time Task Force Washington, the name given the federal forces in the city, withdrew on April 15, twelve people had been killed and some twelve hundred wounded (including 91 police, firemen, and soldiers). Federal officials estimated the cost of the riot at $27 million.

After the Riot

Not all the costs could be counted in dollars. Although parts of the city would bear visible scars of the riot for decades, everything was soon put right in the old downtown neighborhood. Most stores reopened, and the thousands of government workers continued to make the Federal Triangle and nearby streets a bustling, life-filled place on weekdays. "Business as usual," the papers were happy to report. Unnoticed, it seemed, was the subtle transformation that began to take place in the public's attitude toward the F and G Street shopping corridor in the months and years following the riot, a change no less real for all its measured pace, a wound to the area that has not yet healed.

At bottom was the public's new fear of the inner city, a fear fueled by the terrible sights of Washington in flames. In the aftermath of the riots, the loyalty of middle-class Washington, both black and white, to the old downtown began to evaporate, a change encouraged by steadily growing competition from suburban shopping centers. It had become easy and more attractive for many residents of Brookland and Petworth, for example, to head out to Silver Spring or Prince George's Plaza rather than downtown to shop. At the height of the riot, the *Star* quoted one anxious storekeeper talking about his G Street store: "I'm frightened, and I couldn't stand to go back."[5] Although most downtown entrepreneurs overcame the trauma of the riot and resumed business, they could not buck the changing trend in shopping habits. In the next few years increasing numbers of merchants followed their customers to the suburbs, to be replaced by businesses catering to those shopping for cheaper goods. Three major department stores would endure, but even they watched their suburban branches gain at the expense of downtown.

5. *Star,* 7 Apr 1968.

More than simple fear of the city and the lure of the suburbs and fancier parts of town was at work. Downtown Washington was no longer the attractive retail center of previous decades. The busy street cleaners who once disturbed Cardinal O'Boyle's sleep were losing the fight against the accumulated dirt and debris of a worn-out neighborhood. At the same time, the street people, who had routinely cadged the generous prelate's quarters in the 1950s, were by the end of the 1960s multiplying exponentially. The persistent panhandlers, drunks in urine-streaked doorways, petty thieves—all the sorry misery that stand witness to the collapse of the inner city in modern America— were transforming the center of the nation's capital. Adding to the noisomeness, Metro began wholesale excavation along G Street in late 1969. Popular reaction, although shortsighted, was predictable. The capital beltway, completed in 1964, now became the new main street of the metropolis. By the end of the decade it was common to hear natives of the city bragging that they had not been to downtown Washington in years.

At St. Patrick's the effect of this changing public attitude was also quite dramatic. Influenced by parents worried about the safety of their children, enrollment at the academy, which had totaled 325 in June 1968, dropped to 250 in September, a twenty-five percent decrease. This trend would continue at a slower pace until 1975, a low point in school population, when just 154 students enrolled. In the case of the church's congregation, the change was slower and more difficult to analyze. Attendance on weekdays, especially Ash Wednesday and holy days like the feast of the Immaculate Conception, remained high, thanks to the Catholics working in nearby government offices. The all-important Sunday externs, however, that large and diverse group of Catholics who gathered faithfully from all over the metropolitan area and for the last thirty years had constituted St. Patrick's congregation, rapidly melted away. Whereas in early 1968 more than two thousand worshipers might be counted in an average Sunday congregation, by early 1971 even three hundred would be considered a crowd. This represented an 85 percent decrease in thirty-six months. Monsignor Arthur noted that after his return to the parish in 1971 he could count an average of forty people in attendance at the earlier Sunday masses.[6]

Clearly the public's changing attitude toward the inner city was involved in this transformation in the size of St. Patrick's congregation.

6. For an extended discussion of the decline in the size of the congregation, see the author's interviews with Fathers Conway and Brice, George G. Pavloff, and Msgrs. R.

Immediately noticeable, for example, was a dramatic drop in the number of tourists and other casual transients at Sunday Mass. But the loss of such specialized visitors was by no means the only explanation. To an extent difficult to measure, the parish's experiences mirrored, albeit in a greatly magnified form, that of many parishes throughout the country, a decline in attendance that had nothing to do with changing urban conditions, but was more closely associated with the way the practice of Catholicism was evolving.

A major portion of the extern congregation that had endured into the late 1960s consisted of former residents of the old neighborhood who had remained loyal parishioners over the years. As one observer put it, "There were no youngsters in that crowd," and in fact by 1970 this population was rapidly being reduced by death and infirmity. Ironically, the few remaining Catholics resident within the parish boundaries, almost all black and very poor, preferred to attend Immaculate Conception, Holy Redeemer, or St. Mary's, which in most cases were more convenient to their homes. The externs, on the other hand, had always ignored convenience in the past. Some had travelled considerable distance out of loyalty to Bishop Hannan. His outgoing personality and gifts as a speaker had made him greatly admired by those old Washingtonians who considered the dynamic prelate from a well-known local family one of their own. His departure removed one of the principal reasons for their attendance, as did the changes in the church's musical program. As the result of necessary austerities, the large choir that had provided an accompaniment to their devotions, an element of the church's liturgy that was thrilling yet familiar and therefore comforting, disappeared.

Other small but noticeable elements of the congregation popularly associated with Bishop Hannan did not long survive his departure. The political refugees whom he had nurtured at the church left to begin their assimilation into American society. Many of the government employees and others who worked in the area's hotels and businesses on Sunday and who accounted for so many of those attending St. Patrick's early masses now took advantage of the liberalized schedules in their own parishes that included mass on Saturday evening. Few of the prominent government leaders were any longer in evidence. Speaker McCormick had moved away from the parish even before his

Joseph Dooley and E. Robert Arthur. These witnesses disagree on the rate of decline. Some remember a large drop-off even in the first weeks following the riot; others noticed no such dramatic change at first. All agreed, however, that the reduction was readily apparent by the end of 1968.

retirement in 1971, and the informal political caucuses on the steps of St. Patrick's so much enjoyed by Hannan were now a thing of the past.

Nor, it must be assumed, was St. Patrick's congregation immune to the tensions in the American church manifested in the dramatic change in church-going habits that occurred in the decade after the riot. In the years after Vatican II, attention focused initially on the significant reforms of the liturgy, which introduced the Mass prayers in English led by a celebrant facing the people. All of this, even the handshake of peace added to the Mass in 1970 (but not without an occasional and audible reaction from some unreconciled traditionalist), was peacefully accepted by most Catholics. In places like St. Patrick's, however, the timeless beauty of the Latin Mass sung by a famous choir had been a major attraction and would be sorely missed by those whose allegiance to the old church was rooted in such things. Those parishioners no doubt took cold comfort in the fact that the folk Mass never gained a foothold on Tenth Street. Their reaction to the brief Masses sung in English, jokingly dubbed "Lutheran masses" by some, can only be surmised.[7]

Because of its unique position as a church without a resident congregation, St. Patrick's never formed the parish councils and liturgical committees that made life in many parishes in those early days of experimentation with new organizations either bracing or boring but not infrequently controversial. It did, however, share with others a phenomenon noted elsewhere in the American church: as the numbers of those receiving communion rose, the lines at the confessionals dwindled.[8] The centrality of the sacrament of penance in the prayer life at St. Patrick's, manifested most noticeably in the great lines of penitents that snaked along the church aisles especially on the eve of important feasts, had been a hallmark of the parish for generations. Once-overwhelmed confessors now found themselves increasingly free of this arduous but heartening burden.

The lack of penitents seemed to be an outward sign of a deeper change that was occurring in the religious thinking of many Catholics. Called by some authorities a crisis of faith, it was treated by others as a sign of a growing spiritual maturity and understanding fostered by the highly publicized deliberations of the church fathers dur-

7. Interview, author with Michael Cordovana. For changes in the music program, see chapter 14, below.

8. Spalding, *Premier See,* 444. Spalding's summary of post-concilar events in the Baltimore archdiocese (433–67) touches on many factors also operating on the church in Washington.

ing the recent council. At any rate, one thing was undeniable: in the decade following the Vatican Council many issues became grist for the mill of controversy. Church leaders and an increasingly articulate laity and clergy debated the proper role of the church in the pursuit of racial justice and in the peace (anti–Vietnam War) movement. The crisis in religious vocations was scrutinized, as was the drift in Catholic schools, where the proportion of religious and lay teachers reversed in the decade ending in 1974. Yet all these discussions and viewpoints paled in the face of the storm that followed publication in July 1968 of Pope Paul VI's encyclical *Humanae Vitae,* which reaffirmed the church's traditional stand on contraception.

Humanae Vitae seemed to some to reverse a growing consensus among Catholics, most recently symbolized by the conclusions of a commission appointed by the Pope to study the issue. This papal pronouncement was publicly rejected by numerous priests and theologians. In Washington some thirty priests and teachers at the local Catholic universities and colleges, along with twenty priests of the archdiocese, staged a joint press conference at which they explained the reasons for their dissent. Similar disputes occurred elsewhere in the country and were resolved in various ways. In Washington, positions hardened, and after a considerable effort to reconcile the dissidents that included many personal meetings, Cardinal O'Boyle finally withdrew the faculties of some priests, including two who lived at St. Patrick's, Fathers George G. Pavloff, an associate pastor, and Joseph M. O'Connell, a resident who taught at Cathedral Latin school.[9] Eventually nineteen of the diocesan dissenters had their cases referred to the Congregation of the Clergy, which finally issued a verdict against them in 1971. The long-range implications of this controversy remain a matter of study and discussion a generation later.

The man fated to lead St. Patrick's through an era of change unprecedented in the twentieth century was Monsignor William H. Hoffman. A military chaplain in the Atlantic Fleet during World War II, Hoffman remained for many years a member of the naval reserve. He was pastor of Annunciation before being assigned to the downtown parish in March 1966, following Father Sylvester Hoffman's untimely death. At the age of sixty the new pastor still exhibited many of the traits of a military officer. In a time of increasing collegiality, he laid great stress on pastoral authority and the need to operate through

9. *Catholic Standard,* 3 Oct 1968. O'Boyle's role in the affair as well as his concern for his priests is outlined in Able, *Patrick Cardinal O'Boyle,* 7–8. To compare how the controversy played out in Baltimore, see Spalding, *Premier See,* 463.

the chain of command. He demanded firm obedience from himself no less than from his subordinates. He was, for example, extremely reluctant to leave Annunciation, he once told a subordinate, but when the cardinal pressed the request, he had finally saluted and said "Aye, aye, sir."[10] After a career marked by many changes of station, he came to treasure stability above all else. He envied some of his young associates because, he said, they had enjoyed greater continuity in assignments than he. To remind himself of his happy years in uniform, he had his naval clock installed in the rectory dining room, where it measured the day with the ringing of bells familiar to all who have been to sea.

Hoffman tried to chart a steady course for the parish during the unsettling period after the riot. St. Patrick's steadfastly pursued its evolving mission as a sacramental way station (as one of the priests termed it) in the heart of the city's business district. Changes in the liturgy that sometimes caused problems elsewhere sailed through at St. Patrick's without a hitch under a man who played by the book and felt comfortable with anything ordered by higher authority. Noticeably absent in his pastorate, however, was any overt attempt to duplicate Bishop Hannan's outreach to Catholics across Washington or to participate in any of the programs involving local residents that in the wake of the riot began to spring up in other churches in the neighborhood. Charitable programs remained unorganized; the associate priests continued to respond to individual appeals for help on an ad hoc basis.

Hoffman never deviated from his well-defined views of patriotism. The anti-war demonstrations increased in frequency and belligerence after 1967, and Catholic peace activists were among those burning draft cards and marching on the Pentagon. The trial of several Catholic priests as part of the so-called Catonsville Nine and other well-publicized convictions triggered an emotional reaction in Catholic circles where the proper role of the church in the highly controversial war was hotly debated. The demonstrations reached a peak when a quarter-million Americans, including some identifiable Catholic groups, staged a massive protest in Washington in November 1969. Father Geno Baroni, a local priest active in all sorts of social movements, organized logistical support for the Catholic peace marchers.[11] He

10. Interview, author with Father Brice. Unless otherwise noted the following account of the parish under Hoffman is based on interviews with Brice, Conway, Dooley, and Pavloff, all of whom served under Hoffman at St. Patrick's, and Msgr. Arthur.

11. Father, later Monsignor, Baroni once served as assistant secretary of Housing

arranged for a large contingent to be housed in St. Patrick's Academy. Learning early next morning after Mass that the school was filled with a rag-tail army of "peaceniks," Hoffman quickly went over and expelled his startled guests. Whether his ire was provoked by the presence of so many of those he considered disloyal or by what was obviously Baroni's failure to proceed through the proper chain of command is unknown.

There was no such ambiguity about Hoffman's views on the *Humanae Vitae* controversy. Although Father O'Connell left St. Patrick's in 1968, Pavloff stayed on until 1970, his future in the ministry clouded and his faculties as assistant pastor greatly curtailed. Father Pavloff was well liked by his co-workers at the tribunal and by his fellow teachers and the students at the academy, whom he served with particular distinction and understanding. One of his brother priests described him simply as "among the finest priests I have ever known." Hoffman might have shared these sentiments, but he was determined to maintain rigid discipline at St. Patrick's. He presided over a household where the issues of the day were subjected to heated discussion and opposition to any form of dissent was strongly expressed by some of the residents. Hoffman was not immune to the resulting tensions, which continued even after Pavloff's departure. In December 1970 he sought Cardinal O'Boyle's permission to retire, citing failing health as the reason. At the same time he made clear to his superior that his poor health had resulted from his continued frustration and unhappiness in trying to direct the parish through a time of such tumultuous change.

Hoffman's request was granted, and his early retirement led to the return of Monsignor Arthur to St. Patrick's as its thirteenth pastor in February 1971.[12] Like his predecessor, Arthur was reluctant to take the assignment. He had known St. Patrick's during its glory days as the crowded Catholic center of Washington, and he was convinced, he told Cardinal O'Boyle, that he would find reconciling current realities with his rich memories difficult and any attempt to alter the parish's new status ultimately frustrating. He eventually gave way, however,

---

and Urban Development in the Johnson administration, one of the few priests ever to serve in the federal executive branch.

12. In addition to his years on the diocesan tribunal, Arthur had, since leaving St. Patrick's in 1948, been pastor of Holy Redeemer, Kensington, where he built the church, and Amunciation in Northwest Washington. In 1970 the Pope bestowed on Arthur the rank of prothonotary apostolic, the same honor held by his old friend and pastor, Msgr. Thomas.

E. ROBERT ARTHUR

when the cardinal explained that someone who combined a realistic understanding of the old mother church's restricted future with a respect for its traditions was precisely what he wanted. O'Boyle had lived at St. Patrick's for nine years, and he had no illusions about bringing back the good old days. Nevertheless he approved the mission that was evolving in the downtown parish. He reminded Arthur that despite recent developments, St. Patrick's still commanded the resources to carry on its educational and charitable tasks as well as its liturgical traditions.[13] A further compliment to Arthur: O'Boyle confided that, despite old complaints about the noisy neighborhood, he hoped to live at St. Patrick's in his retirement and wanted to live with a pastor with whom he felt compatible.[14]

13. Interviews, author with Msgrs. Arthur and Michael Di Teccia Farina. Farina has been a resident at St. Patrick's since 1976. Unless otherwise indicated, the following paragraphs are based on these interviews.

14. In the end O'Boyle followed the wishes of others and remained on Warren Street in his retirement. He lived there for some years with Father Maurice Fox, later pastor of St. Patrick's.

Only when the new pastor reviewed the parish accounts did he discover just how overly-optimistic was O'Boyle's assessment. With the loss of its generous extern congregation, the parish had been relying almost exclusively on the income derived from its property on F Street. The leases on this property had been negotiated in less inflated times, and what little income they did produce was subject to ever-increasing taxes. Meanwhile, the school, largely self-supporting a decade before, had become an overwhelming burden as the number of lay teachers grew. During Arthur's first six years, the parish contributed $282,000 out of parish savings to cover ongoing school expenses.[15] Meanwhile, the need for capital repairs to the building and new equipment for the business courses could not be long postponed. The rectory and church also needed major renovation. Salaries of the support staff who worked in the church, rectory, and school had not kept pace with inflation, and simple justice demanded that they all immediately be given long-overdue raises. Under such assault, the parish's cash reserve, the product of Father Matthews's foresight in purchasing property and the generosity of parishioners from all over Washington, was fast disappearing.

It was time for some painful choices. Arthur started from the premise that other parish programs would be curtailed or outright sacrificed to keep the school open. The parish had been a major contributor to Catholic education for more than 150 years, and it seemed to him appropriate that this traditional mission be preserved above all else. Like Hannan before him, Arthur extolled the unique contribution made over the years by the academy's business curriculum, which, as he put it, had responded to the needs of the community by training thousands of young women with marketable skills while providing them a sound grounding in Catholic doctrine and values.[16] Arthur, more flexible than Hannan on this point, recognized that pre-college courses should be added to the curriculum despite the considerable added expense of more lay teachers. He supported a project initiated by the faculty in 1975 to re-evaluate the school's program of studies in light of criteria established by the Middle States Association and the changing mission for city schools devised by the diocesan board of education.[17]

Above all, Arthur understood that, with most other parish organiza-

15. Undated memo, "From Parish General Funds to School," SPA.

16. These reasons are spelled out in Arthur's "Subsidy Request 1976–1977 to the Archdiocese of Washington," 20 Nov 1975, SPA.

17. For discussion of the curriculum changes, see chapter 13.

tions and ministries gone, the academy had come to shoulder St. Patrick's tradition of service to the whole city. Having no children of its own to educate, the parish continued to subsidize this major diocesan outreach program. The student body reflected the racial and religious diversity of the capital: 52 percent black and 31 percent non-Catholic in 1971; 75 percent black, 12.7 percent Latino, 12.3 percent white, and 37.6 percent non-Catholic in 1981. Many of these children were from the often-neglected inner city, with a substantial number coming from single-parent and underprivileged families.

If such outreach continued to fulfill St. Patrick's traditional mission to the city, it also overwhelmed parish resources. A tuition increase to $500 in 1975 had strained many families to the limit, while a special appeal that year to the alumnae for extra support fell far short of its projected goal.[18] To cover the school's growing deficits, the parish postponed essential repairs. Arthur warned that even with expenditures pared to the bone, the parish's savings that had supported so many diocesan projects earlier in the twentieth century were about exhausted. After outlining these sobering facts to the director of education in 1976, he posed the rhetorical question: "How shall St. Patrick's Academy be funded?"[19]

Arthur had already demonstrated his willingness to sacrifice for the school when he gave up the church's music program, something especially dear to him. The choir had come on hard times in recent years, particularly after the death of its ebullient director, Salvatore Lupica, and the loss of many members in the wake of the riot. Arthur saw in a rejuvenated music program a means of attracting like-minded Catholics to the downtown church. Soon after his arrival he had contracted with Michael Cordovana, a professor in Catholic University's music department, to supply music for the principal Mass on Sunday and special ceremonies. In effect he got a small rent-a-choir of well-trained students and professional singers that enhanced the liturgy while providing the church with a curtailed music program but one with high artistic standards. Unfortunately, in an era of continuing inflation, the new arrangement could promise no substantial reduction in expenses. Even this retreat from extravagances of old lasted only four years be-

18. Arthur, "Subsidy Request 1976–1977 to the Archdiocese of Washington," 20 Nov 1975; unsigned, undated memo [prepared by academy officials in early 1975], "Two-Year Feasibility Study for the Continuance of Saint Patrick's Academy"; and ltr., Sister Marie Julie and Msgr. Arthur to Alumnae, 15 May 1975. All in SPA.

19. Memo, Arthur to Bishop Lyons, 30 Mar 1976, sub: St. Patrick's Academy, copy in SPA.

fore the ever-tightening economic noose forced the outright elimination of all music at the church in 1975.[20]

Despite the cardinal's reference to continuing parish traditions,
there was very little left of the diocesan gatherings and grand public
ceremonies that had filled the church and Carroll Hall in past decades.
The quarterly clergy conference, for example, which had been meeting at St. Patrick's since the days of Cardinal Gibbons, had transferred
to John Carroll High School. Marking the end of an era, the Pan-
American Mass, the occasion of some of the most prestigious gatherings of church and state in Washington, moved to the cathedral in
1974. The next year saw the end of another parish tradition, the annual
Mass of the Catholic Police and Firemen's Society.

Grown to almost three thousand members by 1969, the society had
continued to gather at St. Patrick's each Mother's Day.[21] In that year its
special connection with the parish was further strengthened when its
chaplain, Father R. Joseph Dooley, was assigned to St. Patrick's. By
then the position of chaplain had evolved into an important diocesan
ministry. Dooley worked almost full-time responding to emergency
calls and otherwise serving the needs of this special community. All
too often in an increasingly dangerous world, Dooley was summoned
to administer last rites to stricken police or firemen. In January 1969 in
the presence of Director J. Edgar Hoover and hundreds of members of
the F.B.I., he concelebrated a Mass to honor the memory of agents recently killed in the line of duty. This commemoration prompted the
society to organize an annual memorial Mass at the church to pay
tribute to fallen comrades. As a mark of his special respect for the
group, Archbishop William W. Baum presided over the society's 1973
Mass, his first official ceremony as archbishop.[22] Nevertheless, the traditional tie between the parish and the police and firemen also fell victim to the changes in the old downtown neighborhood. Since the beginning, the parade and communion breakfast had formed an important part of the annual event, and until 1971 suitable accommodations
for the gathering could be found in plentiful supply near the church.
Forced in subsequent years to move farther afield for a breakfast site

20. For some time an organist continued to support congregational singing at the
principal Sunday Mass, and Cordovana and his forces returned to perform on special
occasions. See chapter 14.

21. *Catholic Police and Firemen's Society Commemorative History* and the author's interview with Msgr. Dooley are the basis for the following paragraph.

22. Baum succeeded O'Boyle as archbishop of Washington in 1973. He was elevated
to the college of cardinals in 1976.

IRISH MUSIC. *Archbishop James A. Hickey performs during parish celebration of St. Patrick's Day, 1988.*

and with a parade no longer practical, the society moved from St. Patrick's in 1975, another link with the past broken.[23]

Only the celebration of St. Patrick's Day appeared to be sacrosanct. In recent decades the Irish prime minister was often in Washington for the occasion, and for several years in succession it was usual to find him and the Irish ambassador in attendance at Mass on Tenth Street. In 1972 the ceremony was presided over by William Cardinal Conway, primate of Ireland, on a day that also marked the modern revival of

23. The annual affair was moved to St. Aloysius in 1975 and the next year to Our Lady of Perpetual Help, where it continues today.

Washington's once-famous Irish parade.[24] In view of the many press-ing demands on the parish, Arthur had become increasingly con-cerned about the cost associated with this traditional affair, particu-larly the catered luncheon attended by a long list of notables. In 1974 he decided to cancel the celebration, only to be overruled by Arch-bishop Baum, who wanted it continued because, he believed, it was important for the archdiocese to maintain some of its old traditions. So amid the rising damp, the great clan continued to gather each year to mark the patronal feast in style. The commemoration in 1987 was particularly noteworthy when Helen Hayes, the famous actress whose association with the parish extended back to her youth in Washing-ton, served as lector at the Mass and later as grand marshal of the pa-rade down Constitution Avenue.[25] Appropriately enough perhaps, the annual celebration of St. Patrick's feast day has proved the most en-during event in the parish's two-hundred year history.

Such occasions provided a brief burst of activity in an otherwise quiet landscape. With a Sunday congregation in 1976 no larger than the group that gathered with Father Caffry in the little church on F Street in 1800, and increasingly hard-pressed to meet essential ex-penses, the harried pastor had little choice but to juggle priorities while awaiting some change in the fortunes of the parish and the neighborhood.

Searching for Resources

Such hopes were not so far-fetched, for the riot that had provoked an enduring change in the way many Washingtonians viewed the city's old downtown had also spurred the government's commitment to renewal in the inner city. The most visible sign of this renewal was the coming of Metro with its hub at Twelfth and G Streets. Spurred by the riots, the years of interminable planning and interstate negotiation suddenly ended and construction began in 1969, but it took another six years before the first five stations on the red line opened for riders. It was six years of intense confusion, described by a leading architec-tural critic as a "gibberish of construction that helps to give these blocks and the rest of downtown the ambience of a war zone after a

24. *Catholic Standard,* 16 Mar 1972.
25. *Catholic Standard,* 12 Mar 1987. Hayes was in town to serve as honorary chairper-son of the Irish Festival of St. Patrick, a five-day celebration of Irish culture sponsored by Paul VI Institute for the Arts.

devastating attack from the air."[26] Metro construction extended literally to the academy's front door, where test borings incidentally found sea shells at the thirty-foot level and running water at eighty feet, demonstrating that the old Tiber system was still very much alive and Father Caffry's old fishing creek had survived 150 years of urban development.[27]

By the time the sleek new trains began carrying passengers under G Street in March 1976, other forces for renewal were at work in the neighborhood. The Pennsylvania Avenue Development Corporation, created by Congress in 1972, had started to sponsor partnerships between government and private businesses to rebuild the avenue and other sites along the corridor between the White House and Capitol. The city's own Redevelopment Land Agency was planning similar projects in other parts of downtown, albeit with considerable less authority and financial resources at its disposal. These agencies, along with the National Capital Planning Commission and, after 1976, the city's own Office of Planning, were all focusing on the work of redevelopment at the city's commercial core.[28]

Despite such extensive government involvement, renewal of the old neighborhood depended ultimately on the state of the local economy, so progress occurred in fits and starts in a process that seemed interminable. Several structures of enduring beauty as well as architectural and historical interest—the neoclassical Patent Office (now housing two national art galleries) the old Pension Building, and even the imposing facades of the parish buildings at Tenth and G Streets were all to be included on lists of historic landmarks. Yet the predominant impression remained of a neighborhood of deteriorating buildings, empty stores, dirty streets, speculators' parking lots, and dismal retail strips. To a great extent this impression, which lingered into recent years, was abetted by the loss of familiar landmarks. Old businesses

26. Benjamin Forgey, "At Long Last the Phoenix May be Stirring," Star-News, 15 Apr 1974. This four-part series on downtown urban renewal appeared on four successive days.

27. Msgr. Dooley was present when the surprised engineers unearthed the evidence of the underground waterways that had done so much harm to construction in square 376 over the years. See his interview with author.

28. Ronald H. Adeiter, The Story of Metro (Glendale, CA: Interurban Press, 1985) and Smithsonian Institution, Worthy of the Nation: The History of Planning for the National Capital (Washington: Smithsonian Press, 1977) provide useful summaries of the development of Metro and role of the NPPC, RDLA, and other government organizations in the revitalization of downtown Washington.

continued to leave—Jelleff's Department Store, the International Safeway (the area's well-publicized grocery store) and historic Ebbitt's Grill, for example, all closed in the early 1970s. Ironically, those years also witnessed new construction that foretold a very different future. The cool, spare façade of the new central library at Ninth and G Streets, the city's only work by the internationally acclaimed architect Mies van der Rohe, was probably the most distinguished example of what would soon become scores of imposing new buildings rising in the old commercial corridor.

Even the streets themselves were undergoing transformation. Conceived as a means of attracting visitors and employers back to a downtown abandoned because of traffic congestion and fear of crime, the federal government's Redevelopment Land Agency's "Streets For People" program began by installing pedestrian malls in several blocks of F and G Streets. By 1977 the block in front of the academy had been transformed into an urban landscape of broad walkways with inviting benches, trees, and pools of water.[29] Somehow the agency's planners overlooked the fact that a chronically impoverished city must pay for the upkeep of these parks and that such inviting settings would also appeal to drug dealers and the area's street people, whose presence only added to the uneasiness of the very pedestrians they hoped to lure back to the region.

Revitalization of downtown took on new meaning after the passage of the Home Rule Act in December 1973. In the measured progress toward full political rights for Washingtonians, it had taken ninety-three years for the presidentially-appointed commission form of government to run its course. In 1967 President Johnson established a commissioner-council ruling body under Walter B. Washington, which served as an interim step to the elected mayor-city council government that took office in 1975 and brought the city to its current level of home rule. This imperfect measure of political independence brought radical change to the focus and process of local government, inserted a new and powerful voice in the debate over the renewal of the old downtown area, and created another proponent for the commercial revitalization of the city's retail hub.

Throughout its long history, St. Patrick's was often forced to accommodate to radical changes in the neighborhood, and the urban renewal that began in the mid-1970s once again promised to affect not

29. *Post,* 13 Oct 1974. See also RLA, "Streets for People, A Now and Then Publication About Activities Downtown," April 1977.

only the size of the congregation but the nature of the parish's mission. The government's oversight of urban renewal, however, also threatened the church's financial security and thus frustrated its efforts to accommodate to the challenge of a new downtown. All this was spelled out in 1982 when Monsignor Arthur testified before the city's Joint Committee on Landmarks for the National Capital. That group was considering a proposal to create a Downtown Historical District along the F Street and Seventh Street corridors which would include, along with Chinatown and the blocks around the nearby art galleries, the church's property. If the historical district was designated, restrictions on any changes to structures considered historically or architecturally significant could then be imposed by the city's Historical Review Board.[30] Such restrictions were immaterial in the case of the church, rectory, and school, which had already been designated historical landmarks, but might cause considerable difficulty in the case of the parish's property on F Street.

Arthur explained the church's dilemma. For many years, he told the committee, the property had provided a "necessary portion" of the money used to continue the parish's mission to the Washington community, and it was in the property's better utilization that "our hopes lie for the survival of St. Patrick's Academy."[31] He underscored the close link between the school and the parish's interest in preserving not just its buildings but also the services it offered to people in the downtown area. "Do not force us to sacrifice St. Patrick's Academy and perhaps more," he concluded, "in order to provide the city with a museum of late nineteenth-century low-rise commercial buildings." Despite these arguments and those advanced by local business leaders, the committee designated the two corridors a historic district and the District's historical preservation officer later nominated the region for inclusion in the National Register of Historic Places.[32]

In subsequent discussions church officials continued to spell out the

30. Debate over the designation was reflected in the local press. See, for example, the *Post*, 17 Mar 1982 and 25 Mar and 22 Sep 1984 and the *Catholic Standard*, 25 Mar 1982. The Historical Review Board was established by the D.C. Council in Mar 1979 to provide protection for historic landmarks and districts.

31. Arthur, Testimony before the Joint Committee on Landmarks For the National Capital, 16 Mar 1982, copy in SPA.

32. Through an administrative oversight, the preservation officer did not nominate the area for inclusion in the Register until September 1985, providing a loophole for several property owners to tear down buildings in the historic district. See *Post*, 22 Sep 1984.

need for high-rise development on F Street, leaving Arthur with the renewed hope that although any plans for the site would be subject to rigorous review, "our position is practically the same as it was before this Downtown Historic Area was created."[33] Such an upbeat assessment was welcome because, when the true extent of the school's financial problems became clear in the mid-1970s, Arthur had reopened discussion of redevelopment of the F Street property with business advisors familiar with local conditions.[34] The obvious model was the multi-story office building proposed by Hannan in the previous decade. Arthur considered and rejected several other options, including one that would have the parish rent space for the school in a new building which would span the block and include all of the academy but its legally protected facade. In 1982 he was close to agreement with a major developer for building a high-rise commercial structure on the site that would have assured the long-term financial security of the parish.

The agreement was especially desirable because of the pressing need to renovate the academy as part of the diocese's ongoing plans to consolidate inner-city schools. The planned merger of St. Cecilia's and St. Patrick's in the building on G Street, scheduled for the fall of 1986, called for the addition of more classrooms and other renovations costing more than $4.5 million.[35] This enormous expense could be assumed if the new F Street lease was consummated; without it, the merger would be impossible and the academy's future left in doubt. Because the proposed new school so closely matched the pastor's vision of the parish's continuing mission in the center city, it must have been especially disappointing to him to report in early 1983 that negotiations over the property had been canceled because of the continuing economic slowdown in Washington construction projects. Although he promised to explore other leasing possibilities, he confessed to the archbishop that meaningful negotiations depended on a return of business confidence, which his advisors predicted was several years away. Meanwhile the pastor remained optimistic that the property

33. Memo, Arthur to Hickey, 29 Mar 1984, copy in SPA.

34. Interview, author with Arthur, 2 Dec 1992. See also ltr., Richard W. Carr to Arthur, 23 Jan 1981. Carr, a member of the Oliver T. Carr Company, and George H. Beuchert, a Washington lawyer, were among the most prominent of a group that advised St. Patrick's pastor.

35. These renovation estimates included more than 28,000 square feet of new construction. See "St. Patrick's Church Summary of Development Costs," 27 Jul 1982, SPA. On merging St. Cecilia's and St. Patrick's academies, see chapter 13, below.

could eventually be developed to produce income sufficient "for the improvement of St. Patrick's Academy, maintenance of all parish buildings and liturgical and pastoral services which a downtown church must provide."[36] Although such determined confidence was admirable, it failed to halt the onrush of events that led to the archbishop's decision in October 1984 to close the academy and relocate the students in the more modern St. Cecilia's school building on Capitol Hill. When it became apparent that the move would be permanent, various proposals were advanced for the disposition of the building, including one made by Monsignor Michael Di Teccia Farina to use the building to house a Catholic cultural center that would support broad-based education programs with particular emphasis on the fine arts.[37] A disappointed Arthur reviewed the proposals for the archbishop, but in the end he seemed reluctant to endorse any of them, citing among other things the cost of renovation, legal complications, and the need to keep the parish's options open in regard to possible lease arrangements. He reported to Archbishop James A. Hickey that, he and his advisors agreed that, given the current glut of office space in the area, the parish should mark time, postponing its efforts to find increased support for its programs until 1987.[38] In later years the Farina proposal was accepted, and the Paul VI Institute for the Arts took up residence in the academy building.

Toward a New Parish Mission

Closing the academy reduced the terrible urgency about finances, but it was nevertheless a traumatic event that posed basic questions

36. Ltr., Arthur to Hickey, 4 May 1983; and Arthur, "Report on Proposed Development," 14 Jun 1983 (source of quotation), copies of both in SPA. The 1979–83 slowdown in commercial construction in Washington accounted for a 50 percent drop in building starts. See League of Women Voters, *Know the District of Columbia* (Washington: District of Columbia League of Women Voters Education Fund, 1986), 11.

37. Msgr. Michael Farina, "Proposal: St. Patrick's Academy A Catholic Cultural Center," n.d., att. to memo, Arthur to Hickey, 31 May 1985, sub: Current information regarding Academy building and F Street properties, copy in SPA.

38. Memo, Arthur to Hickey, 31 May 1985, sub: Current Information regarding Academy Building and F Street Properties, copy in SPA. Proposed uses for the building included a day-care center, a Catholic Charities center for senior citizens, and a convent. Several groups wanted to lease it for a school, including one group of parents galvanized into action by the closing of Immaculata.

Hickey succeeded Cardinal Baum as archbishop in June 1980. He was elevated to the college of cardinals in 1988.

about the parish's future. The departure of the students and their teachers severed a major link with the past and in a certain sense marked the end of the parish as that word was commonly understood in the American church. The term "church of strangers" now had specific application to the realities on Tenth Street. In discussing the parish's history and its current physical needs with a *Catholic Standard* reporter, Arthur revealed his own optimistic outlook. "I have no fears about the future of St. Patrick's," he commented. "It'll be here 200 years from now."[39] To a great extent that future depended on how the pastor and archbishop defined the church's mission. Judging by the past, the parish's future would remain closely linked to the evolution of the city's downtown neighborhood, but if education and charity were to remain the focus of that mission, how would they be adapted for a very different future?

In his last years as pastor, Arthur concentrated on getting the parish buildings in order. The need for major renovation could not be long postponed. Strapped for money in the early 1980s (at one point, Arthur reported, the parish had less than $2,000 in its bank account), he had settled for emergency repairs to the storm-damaged church roof, and in 1982 he found a painting contractor who would give the church's interior a quick facelift at a price the parish could then afford. Beginning in 1985, however, with the school subsidies at an end and new and more realistic leases in place on the F Street stores, the parish's bank accounts were rebuilt enough to allow him to initiate discussions with architects over the long-needed restoration of the parish's physical plant.

Arthur left before such plans could progress far. Although he would have been willing to remain beyond his seventy-fifth birthday, the customary retirement age, he told a reporter, he did not "regret acceding to the archbishop's wishes."[40] Those wishes were made clear when Hickey asked Arthur to assume the post of chaplain to the Little Sisters of the Poor. Hickey was anxious to appoint a senior priest sympathetic to the needs of the elderly. Arthur agreed with the policy of freeing young priests for parish work, and without fanfare he ended his twenty-six years service to St. Patrick's, a record exceeded only by the legendary Matthews and Walter. It had been his unenviable task for much of that time to cope with inexorable demands imposed on

39. *Catholic Standard,* 20 Nov 1986.
40. *Catholic Standard,* 8 Oct 1987.

the parish by changes in the neighborhood and the church. His single-minded effort to save the school failed, even as it manifested a determination born of a half-century's dedication to the mother church and its traditions.

In naming a successor for Arthur, Archbishop Hickey obviously thought about the need for redefining the mission of a parish whose history and location, he noted, "placed it in a position of pre-eminence within the archdiocese." The parish provided an unparalleled opportunity, he told the new pastor, Monsignor Maurice T. Fox, in April 1987, "for evangelization among the thousands of federal, district and private industry-based leaders and their staffs who work in the city of Washington."[41] "Morty" Fox, as he was known to hundreds of friends and associates in Washington's civic, business, and clerical circles, had abandoned a business career to become a priest. Since his ordination he had worked for years on the archbishop's staff, most recently as the director of communications. There he gained notice as organizer of the popular televised Mass for Shut-ins. He was also president of Catholic University's alumni, another job that sharpened his interest in the community and prepared him for bringing new emphasis to evangelization in the downtown parish.[42]

Fox wanted to use St. Martin's-in-the-Fields, the famous church in downtown London, as his model for the program he planned to launch at St. Patrick's.[43] The liturgy would continue to be celebrated as it had in the same neighborhood for almost two hundred years, but no longer would the priests worry over the size or constancy of their extern congregation. Instead Fox envisioned a new kind of evangelization that would develop a wider audience for the church's message through a program of prayer and study groups, lectures on theology and history, and concerts and other artistic events. As it had in past decades, the parish would adapt to changes in the neighborhood, which in the late 1980s was finally beginning to reemerge as a center of business, culture, and tourism. The scores of sleek new office buildings and condominiums that lined the nearby streets, the art galleries, both public and private, and the museums and theaters all indicated a new field for outreach.

41. Ltr., Hickey to Fox, 9 Apr 1987, AAW.

42. Fox's career was outlined, following his death on 22 August 1987, in a ltr., Hickey to Priests of Diocese, 24 Aug 1987, AAW, and in the *Catholic Standard,* 27 Aug 1987.

43. This brief summary of Fox's plans is based on interviews with two of his close friends, Michael Cordovana and Vincent Walter.

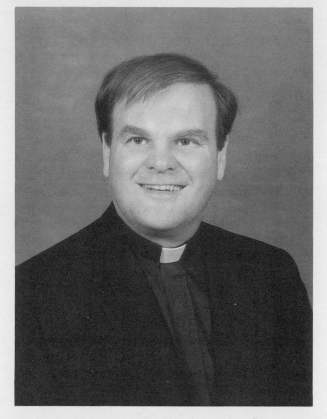

DONALD S. ESSEX

Tragically, Fox had just three months to work on his new initiatives for the parish before succumbing to a massive heart attack. A saddened Archbishop Hickey, underscoring his hope that St. Patrick's would continue to seek out new ways to reach the large crowds that were returning to downtown, turned to one of his young assistants, Father Donald S. Essex, who began his career as fifteenth pastor of St. Patrick's in October 1987. To Essex falls the task of leading the venerable parish into its third century of service to the church and the city.

St. Patrick's Academy

THE SCHOOL that opened on G street amid much ceremony in 1904 was merely the most recent manifestation of
St. Patrick's long-time sponsorship of education in the capital. Reminiscent of schools that figured prominently in
the congregation's earlier history, the academy was begun
as a pragmatic response to a pressing local need and rapidly came to assume responsibilities city-wide in scope.
The school survived eighty years, a relatively brief period
considering the venerable history of several other Catholic
schools in the city. Nonetheless, in that period, especially
in its final decades, it contributed in a special way to the
parish and the city it served.

This recent contribution was twofold. After World War
II the students, none residents in a parish that had watched
much of its local and extern congregation disappear, provided St. Patrick's with a sense of community and, in
effect, constituted its permanent congregation in an era of
profound change. Increasingly, the school became central
to parish activities, the chief responsibility of its priests,
and a continued source of vitality in an otherwise diminished institution. Small wonder that, to the end and despite considerable pragmatic evidence to the contrary, the
priests and faculty maintained that the academy was a

parochial institution and regretted the decision by higher authority to close its doors.[1]

While the parish was receiving a renewed sense of purpose and community from its school, it was providing a large group of young Washington women, including many non-Catholics, a specialized high school education. Always a hallmark of the parish's educational efforts, such outreach took on added significance in recent decades when St. Patrick's exhausted its financial resources to provide the essential prerequisites for meaningful employment or higher education otherwise difficult for many of its students to obtain, especially those from among the city's disadvantaged families.

Development of a Parish School

Such considerations would have seemed alien to a nineteenth-century congregation that, reflecting the concerns common in an immigrant-dominated church, gave less thought to secondary education than to what it saw as the increasing sectarianism of the public schools. A son of the old Maryland aristocracy and long-time member of the city's school board, Father Matthews was himself remarkably free of any anxiety about religious exercises in public institutions. In an era generally free from nativist strife, he promoted public schools as a means of educating the nation's new citizens and the children of Washington's working class. His interest in Catholic education focused instead on three institutions that provided quality education to the children of Washington's more affluent citizens: Georgetown College, Washington Seminary, and Visitation Convent. Despite its instant popularity and the fact that it prospered because of his administrative foresight, the day school attached to St. Vincent's orphanage always seemed an afterthought to Matthews.

St. Patrick's interest in parochial education quickened under Matthews's successors. In the wake of nativist uprisings, the bishops called for the establishment of free schools in each parish at their first plenary council in 1852, and shortly thereafter Father O'Toole started a small free (parochial) school in classrooms added to the parish rectory. This struggling institution conducted by lay teachers proved short-lived, as did its successor, a school with separate sections for tuition

1. Several who played principal roles in the school between 1965 and 1988 alluded to this sense of community. See the author's interviews with George Pavloff, Rev. James Meyers, Sisters Miriam André Williams and Eleanor Anne McCabe, and Msgr. Arthur.

and non-tuition students opened under the Christian Brothers in 1866 in a building erected by Father Walter adjoining Carroll Hall on G Street.

The failure of these institutions apparently caused little alarm. By then schools operated by the Sisters of Charity and the Sisters of the Holy Cross as part of the nearby St. Vincent's and St. Joseph's orphanages were popularly regarded as parish institutions, and apparently no one at St. Patrick's saw any need for new and expensive educational experiments. With two well-run Catholic schools just a stone's throw from their church, both dependent on St. Patrick's for students, the congregation ignored talk about "indispensible" parish schools at the second Plenary Council and concentrated instead on raising money for a new church and other pressing social needs. To the end of the century these two day schools satisfied the parish's educational requirements, despite the fact that both remained part of private institutions with a mission to the whole city, were operated by religious orders under independent charters, charged tuition, and ignored the needs of children beyond the elementary level.[2]

Although neither school was free, it is unclear just who paid for parish children. It seems likely that after 1879, when St. Vincent's School for Girls adopted the name St. Patrick's Female School at St. Vincent's and the boys school became St. Joseph's Male School of St. Patrick's Parish, the parish, always a major contributor to both orphanages, assumed some of the responsibility for tuition fees.[3] The Catholic Directory listed 200 pupils at St. Joseph's and 330 at St. Vincent's in 1882, figures that included the considerable number of resident orphans. It is unlikely that the combined enrollment of parish children in these schools ever exceeded 350.

The decision by the trustees of St. Vincent's to sell the orphanage's property to Woodward and Lothrop upset this comfortable arrange-

2. The changing status of these schools is discussed in Wentz, Inventory, 14–17.

3. Wentz, Inventory, p. 17, claims that St. Vincent's changed from a pay school to a parochial (free) school in 1879. The not always reliable Catholic Directories of the period record the name changes, but further confuse the issue by also listing a St. Patrick's Male School (in the 1879 edition), a Male Night School (1880), and a Holy Cross Academy with both male and female students (1896). It seems likely that the first two refer to classes sponsored by the Carroll Institute, although listing that enterprise under St. Patrick's is about accurate as including Holy Cross Academy among the parish's organizations. Adding to the impression of extraordinary educational activity, the Church News (4 Feb 1899) announced that a Mr. Ucker had been appointed superintendent of St. Patrick's schools.

ment. When the day school closed in December 1900, the girls transferred to St. Joseph's. Obviously a stop-gap measure, it seems strange that only after the sale did an ailing Father Gloyd—who was both president of St. Vincent's trustees and pastor of St. Patrick's—ask the Sisters of Charity to open a parochial school for girls.[4] When that community refused, Father Stafford, then administrator of St. Patrick's, successfully petitioned the Holy Cross sisters to staff a new St. Vincent's Academy that combined both elementary grades and high school commercial classes. The academy opened in September 1901 with one hundred female pupils in the parish building adjoining Carroll Hall.

The introduction of secondary school commercial courses immediately set the academy apart from other Catholic schools in Washington. With increasing numbers of women assuming clerical positions in government and private business, Stafford decided to follow the lead of the city's new public high schools by offering Catholic girls the opportunity in a parish setting to develop business skills along with the more conventional academic subjects, singing, and "plain and fancy sewing." Responsibility for teaching all these subjects fell to three sisters: the principal, Sister Eusebia Brown, was the only one who could be spared by the motherhouse in Indiana, while Sisters Redempta Maher and Veronica Dunn were loaned to the new enterprise by the superior of the local Holy Cross Academy. Sister Eusebia taught the high school business courses; the others divided responsibility for the grade school classes. Each in turn would serve as principal during the next twenty years. Before the first school year ended, poor health forced the departure of the first principal. Sister Eusebia's teaching duties were assumed by Sister M. Irmina Noonan, on loan from nearby St. Cecilia's Academy.

Typical of Stafford's *modus operandi,* the little school's first graduation exercise, in June 1902, included among the guests the secretary of the apostolic delegation as well as pastors and clergy from all over Washington. Distinguished prelates and Catholic educators like Bishops John Ireland of St. Paul and Thomas J. Shahan, rector of Catholic

4. *New Century,* 13 and 30 Jul 1901. See also [Rev. Joseph C. Eckert], "History of Saint Patrick's Academy 1901–1951," *Souvenir Book of the Golden Jubilee of the Sisters of the Holy Cross at Saint Patrick's Academy, Washington, D.C.,* 8. Unless otherwise indicated the following survey of the academy is based on this work; *Our Provinces* (Notre Dame: St. Mary's College, 1941), 195ff; Sister M. Campion Kuhn, "The Sisters Go East—And Stay," a paper prepared for the second Conference on the History of the Congregations of Holy Cross in the U.S.A.; and various issues of *The Patrician,* which devoted scores of articles to the academy.

University, were often invited to talk to the students. As in everything else initiated at St. Patrick's during his pastorate, the presence of these important guests underscored Stafford's effort to broaden his congregation's horizons. His frequent addresses at Carroll Institute and many of his patriotic orations conveyed his strong belief that Catholics should shed the limited ambitions of recent generations and take their place in the national mainstream. Both he and his successor were ardent proponents of Catholic education, as exemplified in their strong support of the new Catholic University, yet foremost in his thinking was what he considered the parish's obligation to encourage secondary education.

The new girl's school with its innovative commercial courses was a step in that direction, even if opportunities for St. Patrick's children continued severely restricted. In an era when high school diplomas were becoming increasingly important and even college training a middle-class ambition, the city could count four public high schools: Central, Eastern, Western, and Business, the latter serving pupils from all over the city. While Central High stressed academic courses, they all, follow.°ing the pattern set in the first city high school, founded in 1880, stressed vocational training (mapping, drawing, cooking, and commercial subjects).[5] The major alternative to these schools, which enrolled some 3,100 students, were the college preparatory schools run by the Jesuits and the Christian Brothers, the city's female academies, and the night school sponsored by the Carroll Institute. Those seeking similar instruction for their children in a parochial setting were left unsatisfied until Stafford came up with a new solution. St. Patrick's would operate a combined boys' and girls' parish school equipped to offer an education through twelve grades leading to diplomas in both academic and commercial subjects.

With Cardinal Gibbons's approval, Stafford moved the new girls' school in January 1904 to temporary quarters in the Carroll Institute's building, rented a residence for the sisters on K Street, and then demolished Carroll Hall and the two adjoining buildings to make room for what he exuberantly called "the handsomest school building in Washington." Reflecting the new realities, the school that opened in the imposing structure on G Street in September 1904 was called St.

5. Jean M. Pablo, "Washington and Its School System, 1900–1906," (Ph.D. dissertation: Georgetown University, 1973), 272–396. District high schools actually trace their foundation to 1876, when the first of two so-called advanced grammar schools began offering vocational training courses. McKinley Technical, a branch of Central High School for boys studying shop, opened in 1902.

Patrick's Academy. Its senior department constituted the first high school sponsored by a parish in the Archdiocese of Baltimore.[6]

Despite its imposing facade, this "handsomest" building was far from commodious. With a 95-foot frontage and a depth of 145 feet, it boasted separate entrances for boys and girls at its east and west ends. Stairways led directly to six large classrooms and adjoining cloak rooms on its two floors. The central entrance allowed public access to a school office and large auditorium. Designed as a center for both school and parish activities, the new Carroll Hall was built with seating for 1,000 people and a stage 36 feet deep with a 25-foot proscenium arch. A partial third floor constructed along the front of the building provided a residence for the sisters. These apartments and the school rooms below were strictly utilitarian, in contrast to the public areas, which were furnished with Flemish wainscotting, beamed ceilings, and ornate windows meant to harmonize with the gothic opulence of the church and rectory.

The addition of the male students from St. Joseph's day school, along with new registrations attracted by the publicity that always seemed to attend any Stafford initiative, meant that 325 students were crowded into the classrooms when the new school opened in September 1904. To handle the increase, two more sisters, three lay teachers, and Father Thomas E. McGuigan, the assistant pastor in charge of the school, joined the faculty. McGuigan taught Latin and James Hartnett began his long association with the school as professor of mathematics.

Reflecting the pastor's broad view of parochial education, the school differed considerably from other institutions operated by the Holy Cross sisters at the time. In addition to the usual narrow array of required academic subjects, the high school offered instruction in history (ancient, modern, French, English, and church history); geometry, physics, chemistry, and astronomy; logic and psychology; Latin, German, and French; and singing, drawing, and plain and fancy sewing. The commercial department provided typing, shorthand, bookkeeping, and business law. After one year of required courses, students were free to choose electives leading to separate diplomas granted by the academic and commercial departments. This rich mix of offerings prompted Stafford to tell parishioners in 1906, "We are giving you something very good at a very slight expense."[7]

6. Father Russell noted this fact in a article prepared for the Washington *Herald* and reprinted in *The Patrician* (Aug 1908), 17–18.

7. Quoted in *The Patrician* (Aug 1906). See also, same source (Sep 1906), *passim*.

Advanced pupils were expected to prepare and read papers on assigned subjects every month. Grades were announced weekly, and report cards issued quarterly. An article in the parish magazine hinted that these reports were not always producing the desired results. Warning that some pupils were hiding the cards from parents and that a "too indulgent mother" on occasion signed a card without attempting to redress problems indicated therein, *The Patrician* admonished parents to compare successive reports as a gauge of academic progress. In words that might give any errant pupil pause, it called on parents to "co-operate with the faculty" to remedy any problems.[8]

By 1908 school enrollment had risen slightly to 353 pupils. The faculty had eight religious and four lay teachers. The elementary division accounted for the majority of students; enrollment figures for 1909, for example, listed just 40 girls and 58 boys in the high school. Given the decline in parish population that began during this period, it appears likely that a least some of the new enrollment came from the extern congregation that Stafford and his successor, William Russell, were cultivating so assiduously. Although the building erected just five years before could not sustain any dramatic increase in students, there was no indication that either pastor ever gave thought to limiting the school's outreach. Readers of the parish magazine and the local Catholic press were treated to an unrelenting campaign extolling the academy's program and advertising for more students. To emphasize the new school's connection with the roots of Catholic education in Washington, the pastor routinely took to dating academy activities from the foundation of the school at St. Vincent's orphanage. (Thus graduation ceremonies in 1914 were billed as the "Ninetieth Annual Commencent.")

Russell's immediate reaction to the space crisis was to transfer the older boys to rented quarters in the Carroll Institute. There, beginning in 1908 just three blocks away, McGuigan and Hartwell, along with a group of instructors from Catholic University— all "laymen of culture and experience," *The Patrician* assured parents—taught courses leading to either academic or business diplomas, although special effort was being made, the magazine noted, to prepare the boys for college.[9] By 1912 three Xaverian brothers had been added to the faculty, and the pastor announced that members of that order

8. The Patrician (Mar-Apr 1908), 20.
9. *The Patrician* (Jul 1908), 21. The parish went to great pains to assure the parents that moving the boys from G Street would not somehow dilute their education. See, for example, same source (Sep 1908), 13, and *New Century,* 25 Jul and 12 Sep 1908.

would assume permanent responsibility for the older boys who, "following the usual custom" as the *New Century* put it, would continue to be segregated from the girls and taught by male teachers. Nevertheless, when the boys returned to the G Street building in 1913, lay teachers, not Xaverians, came with them. The reason for the Xaverians short stay was two-fold. The principal, Brother Bede, became increasingly annoyed with what he considered Father McGuigan's interference in the direction of the school, especially in disciplinary matters. At the same time, the limited number of pupils (fewer than sixty were enrolled) convinced the pastor that maintaining a separate boy's high school was financially untenable.[10]

The return to G Street was made possible by addition of a full third floor that doubled classroom space and added a 6,000-square-foot roof garden built over the reinforced ceiling of Carroll Hall. Russell was particularly proud of this unique feature. The *New Century* rhapsodized about "an area where tennis and baseball could be played in the clear air,"ignoring the realities of the games and the atmosphere in downtown Washington.[11]

Although the remodeling was paid for from parish funds, significant additions to the school's furnishings came from the academy's very active Alumnae and Library Association. Organized in 1906 at the instigation of Sister Veronica, the group sponsored card parties and dramatic entertainments to provide a library, science laboratory, and improvements to the building's grounds. The first organization of its kind to join the International Federation of Catholic Alumnae, the association went on in succeeding years to offer scholarships and underwrite the annual summer school fees of at least one faculty member.[12]

Ironically, the school's continued success, signified by increased enrollment and physical capacity, coincided with a retreat from Stafford's

10. Julian Ryan, *Men and Deeds, the Xaverian Brothers in America* (New York: Macmillan, 1930), 321–22. The *New Century* quote is from the edition of 21 Sep 1907. See also *Patrician* (Oct 1912), 11–12. On the segregation of the students by sex, see Kuhn, "The Sisters Go East," 48.

11. *New Century*, 27 Sep 1913. Actually, the 1913 construction program represented a second addition to the building. In 1909 the school was redecorated, new lighting was added, and several of the classrooms were enlarged. See *The Patrician* (Sep 1909), 5, and *New Century*, 4 Sep 1909.

12. The Alumnae became one of the parish's most enduring organizations. Its activities, including the election of officers, were frequently reported in the Catholic press. See for example, *New Century*, 6 Apr 1907, 2 Jan 1909, and 9 Apr 1910, and *The Patrician* (Apr 1909), 10, and (Dec 1909), 5. In recent years the association has contributed significant sums for the support of retired Sisters of the Holy Cross.

A classroom scene when boys attended St. Patrick's.

LEFT: *Kathryn C. Hannan, Marjorie Durham, Laura Hancock, Mae Sullivan, Margery Lucas, Lucille Gaskins, Dora Simpson, Margaret Weaver, Marie Easby Smith, Alice Lucas, Ella Corcoran, Anna May McCarthy and Catherine Sullivan.*

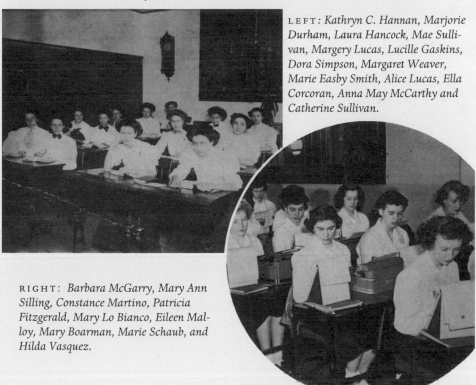

RIGHT: *Barbara McGarry, Mary Ann Silling, Constance Martino, Patricia Fitzgerald, Mary Lo Bianco, Eileen Malloy, Mary Boarman, Marie Schaub, and Hilda Vasquez.*

vision of educational choice. In 1913 the curriculum was redesigned and the high school division was transformed into a two-year commercial course. The reason for the reorganization appeared economic. The fact was that however much Stafford and Russell tried to kindle interest in college preparation courses, the city's private Catholic schools, despite their cost, remained more successful at attracting students with an academic bent. At the same time, the academy's full commercial curriculum (in distinction to the electives in typing and shorthand offered at some of the other Catholic schools) was attracting an increasing number of children from outside the parish. Just three years earlier the Washington pastors had advised Cardinal Gibbons that, with seven local Catholic schools offering academic preparation, more such institutions were unnecessary. St. Patrick's conversion to a purely commercial high school represented a belated acknowledgement of the wisdom of that assessment.[13]

It seems likely that the conversion to a two-year commercial course was gradual and provision was made for the graduation of those in the academic program. Certainly, the elimination of academic courses was rapidly followed by an increase in applications for the new commercial department and a precipitate drop in the number of boys in the commercial program. Enrollment in the revamped commercial course (soon expanded to a three-year program) rose steadily throughout the World War I era and soon accounted for most of the school's students. By 1922 the academy would admit 371 pupils after being forced to turn away sixty-five others for lack of space. By then the number of boys had fallen to less than forty percent of the total, most of them pupils in the diminishing grade school department.[14]

Meanwhile, Monsignor Russell followed Stafford's practice of providing the school with a steady stream of important visitors. Many of these were guests at the rectory next door, who, at the insistence of their host, frequently interrupted their business to lecture the children or attend school exercises. It was common to find the likes of Cardinal Michael Logue, the Irish primate, apostolic delegates Falconio and Bonzano, the rectors of Catholic University, especially Bishop Denis O'Connell, and various and sundry government officials and mem-

13. *Star*, 28 Apr 1910. The private Catholic schools included in the pastors' list were: Gongaza, St. John's, Georgetown Preparatory School, Holy Cross, St. Cecilia's, and Immaculata Preparatory School.

14. Owen B. Corrigan, *The Catholic Schools of the Archdiocese of Baltimore: A Study in Diocesan History* (Baltimore: Archdiocese of Baltimore, 1924), 195.

bers of Washington's diplomatic corps passing through the school's ornate reception hall. Cardinal Gibbons was a frequent guest at school functions, although the most important visitor of all might well have been overlooked in the melee of church-state leaders. Some thirty years before her enrollment in the calendar of saints, Mother Frances Xavier Cabrini visited the school and stayed for a few days with the sisters in their apartment on the third floor.

Reflecting the ardent patriotism of its founding pastors, the school went to great lengths to proclaim its Americanism. National holidays were observed with due ceremony. Special assemblies honored Washington and Lincoln on their birthdays in tableaux, speeches, and patriotic songs, while Arbor Day was spent planting trees. With his great interest in the state's history, Russell made sure that Maryland Day was suitably commemorated, pupils perforce becoming experts on events in the old colony. The school threw itself into the war effort in 1917. It was one of the first in the city to sponsor a junior Red Cross unit. Students knitted sweaters and other items for the servicemen and distributed magazines, scrapbooks, and religious articles at nearby military camps, turned over candy money to Belgium relief, and during the course of the war bought more than $3,000 worth of liberty bonds. When the influenza epidemic caused suspension of classes near the end of the war, the teachers turned to nursing the sick in the city's hospitals. After the war, parishioners took special pride in the fact that five students won prizes, including first place, in the *Star*'s patriotic essay contest with papers on "The Arms Conference and Its Significance."[15]

A Diocesan Mission

The dramatic increase in Washington's population during World War I only accelerated the flight of St. Patrick's parishioners. The effect of creeping commercialism was most readily noticeable in the changing grade school population. Even as scores of applicants were being turned away from the academy's commercial high school department for lack of space, the need for a grade school was ending. It was left to Monsignor Thomas to formulate a postwar education policy. In the course of the next several years the new policy would be made clear: St. Patrick's would continue its commitment to education

15. Baltimore *Catholic Review*, 15 Apr 1922. A detailed account of the academy's war work appeared in the *Review* on 22 Jun 1918. See also Kuhn, "The Sisters Go East," 48.

but limit itself to providing a commercial high school education for girls from all over Washington.

The change began in 1923, when the number of children in grades one through three was restricted to those who could be accommodated in a small suite of rooms on the academy's second floor. Three years later Thomas reached an agreement with the Ursuline sisters whereby that order assumed responsibility for the grade school in their day nursery on Fourth Street. The primary grades transferred in September 1922; the rest followed eleven years later in 1933. The last year the academy maintained a grade-school division, its graduating class numbered five boys and five girls.[16]

Two other decisions made in the same period completed the transformation of the school. "By order of Archbishop Curley," the pastor began his announcement in early 1926, boys were to be excluded from the high school.[17] No record of any such order survives. Given Thomas's position in the diocese and the fact that the change concerned a parish organization, it seems likely that the archbishop's name was invoked merely to lend an air of impersonality to what was an unpopular decision in some quarters. If Curley was actively involved, it was merely to formalize a change made inevitable by the recent decision to restrict the high school to a two-year commercial department. The last boy had graduated in 1919. The inefficiency of maintaining separate classes and teaching staff for the remaining few in a school still segregated by sex only hastened the move to an all-female student body. To ensure continuing access to Catholic high schools for children left in the parish, the pastor provided every male graduate of the grade school a scholarship to Gonzaga or St. John's. The girls were not offered a comparable choice, but were admitted without charge to the academy's business school.

The second major change occurred in 1927 when, in the process of reconstituting the four-year business course of Stafford's day, the school added a number of academic requirements to its business curriculum. Students were now required to study history and Spanish in addition to four years of English and typing, three years of shorthand, two of bookkeeping, and one course that combined commercial law and economics (business arithmetic).[18] In addition to these require-

16. Wentz, *Inventory*, 18. St. Patrick's Grammar School, as it was formally named in 1933, would continue under the care of the Ursulines until 1949. In its last year enrollment stood at 89. See *Catholic Review*, 22 Oct 1948.

17. Quoted in Eckert, "History of St. Patrick's Academy," 13.

18. Interviews, author with Mrs. Catherine Cleary Cordes and Mrs. Margaret Atchi-

ments, students also attended weekly religious instruction conducted by the priests of St. Patrick's. At more than a half-century remove, alumnae of those weekly sessions in the 1930s remember details of discussions with the urbane John Cartwright and youthful Lawrence Shehan who served as adjunct instructors. For the majority of pupils who now lived outside the parish, this weekly instruction constituted the principal association with St. Patrick's parish, except for First Friday Mass and confession. The May processions and parish activities such as the Children of Mary and the junior sodality that had depended on student participation in the past gradually disappeared along with the resident congregation.

The school gave all its students something of a musical education. The faculty included a full-time music teacher, and the ornate room to the left of the school's main entrance was designated the music department. Interested students received private lessons in piano and voice; for the rest, a student chorus trained diligently for its semi-annual public performances and graduations. Beginning in the early 1940s, a steady stream of professional singers, instrumentalists, and even a few student musicians introduced the academy to the world of opera and chamber music in regularly scheduled performances in Carroll Hall.[19]

Extracurricular activities concentrated on sports, journalism, and student government. Organized social affairs were rather rare in the 1930s. Proms, at least one of which was held in Carroll Hall in the 1920s, were canceled in the wake of a fatal automobile accident following a dance. The abrupt discontinuance of this popular activity appears directly related to the accident and not to the brouhaha over the Players and the Charleston. Nor is there evidence that the pastor's decidedly old-fashioned view (he once admonished a graduating class not to drag young men away from their studies by hurrying them off to dances) ever influenced school policy.[20] The proms resumed during the war when they and the many CYO dances of later years once again became social highlights of the school year.

The student's annual tuition fees totaled thirty dollars throughout

son Van Heuckeroth, class of 1933, and Miss Ruth Hellmuth, Mrs. Mary Grambo Wood, and Sister Marie Julie Shea, class of 1935. The paragraphs describing the school in the 1930s are based on these interviews.

19. See, for example, the *Shamrock* (Oct-Nov 1948) for a list of the music recitals scheduled for one fall season.

20. Thomas's speech to the graduating class of Calvert Hall was reprinted in the Baltimore *Catholic Review*, 16 Jun 1933.

most of the 1930s, a token sum by later standards, but perilously close to the limit many families could afford during the Depression. The academy's claim to distinction had little to do with the financial standing of its students. During this period several other parochial schools, like nearby Immaculate Conception and St. Paul's Academy, offered business courses as electives, but the fact that St. Patrick's was the only Catholic school that offered a complete four-year business program was a source of considerable pride for its students. The rigorous standards maintained by a well-trained faculty and manifested in a healthy attrition rate (the class of 1935, for example, started with seventy-three students and graduated just forty-four) was also a distinction that served as a magnet for potential employers. Government agencies and local commercial firms regularly recruited graduates, so much so that during the Depression other schools looked with envy on St. Patrick's as a place where "all the graduates seemed to win good jobs immediately."[21]

Although maintaining high standards required the cooperation of all the faculty, the comrehensiveness of the business curriculum and the discipline imposed on the students in the 1930s owed much to a series of extraordinary teachers and principals, especially to the formidable Sister Florian Daniels, who instilled a sense of purpose and no little apprehension in a generation of academy students. Yet the rigor of the four-year business course imposed by teachers like Sister Florian and Sister Ethel Dodd failed to impress professional evaluators, who considered the school's almost exclusive emphasis on commercial subjects reason to withhold regional accreditation. To answer their complaints, Sister Angels Everett, the school's wartime principal, added courses in geometry, French, and biology, a move which finally won the school its coveted affiliation with Catholic University in 1944.[22]

Renewed emphasis on academic content continued after the war. The academy brought in Sister Margaret Charles Boyle, one of the congregation's premier science teachers, to develop new science courses and assess the possibility of adding a science laboratory (a modern science lab proved prohibitively expensive). In 1949, however,

21. Interview, author with Mrs. Margaret Cleary Grambo, 5 January 1993. Mrs. Grambo was a graduate of Immaculate Conception Academy.

22. Sister Angels took this step on the advice of the her provincial, Mother M. Rose Elizabeth Havican. The math and language courses were introduced in the 1942 school year; the science course in 1943. Several of the commercial course would be restricted to third and fourth year students. See Minutes of the Council of the Eastern Province, 11 Oct 1942, p. 85, St. Mary's Archives, Notre Dame, IN.

yet another general assessment of the school's educational aims was undertaken, and after consultation with Holy Cross officials, school authorities decided that the academy's orientation as a commercial school should be retained and strengthened. Consequently, new commercial subjects were introduced and some of the recently instituted academic courses dropped.

Although this decision settled the question of the school's basic orientation, it did not end discussion about what constituted an appropriate combination of commercial and academic requirements.[23] Proponents of a stronger academic curriculum could enumerate several practical reasons for continuing the initiatives begun by Sister Angels in 1942. Rising aspirations among middle-class American Catholics meant that an increasing number of their daughters were entering college. Even students planning a business career wanted to keep their options open by graduating with the necessary college prerequisites as well as completing those courses that would ensure passing the civil service examination. The sisters themselves had a pragmatic reason for greater academic emphasis. St. Patrick's had proved a fruitful source of vocations for the Holy Cross Congregation; yet, because they lacked necessary academic courses, some of these postulants required further education before going on to the specialized training demanded by the congregation. Finally, those arguing for a broadened curriculum could point to a vague but growing perception in the postwar student body, one exacerbated by the attitudes of students in the academic high schools, that attendance at a four-year business school was somehow *déclassé*. Despite the undeniable popularity of the school, they reasoned, a lack of attention to academic courses would hurt the institution in the long run, not only with potential students but with accreditors.

Others saw no need for change. Bishop Hannan, for example, echoing those who had first revised the school's curriculum in 1913, stressed the fact that a four-year commercial school provided a unique service to the community and gave the academy a special "niche," as he called it, in the archdiocese's education system.[24] He defended the pure commercial curriculum by pointing to the popularity of the busi-

23. The following paragraphs on the curriculum are based on the author's interviews with Sisters Marie Julie Shea, Mary Louise Full, and Eleanor Anne McCabe, Archbishop Hannan, and Msgr. Michael D. Farina. "The Sisters Go East," 49–51, provides a brief outline of the revolving emphasis on commercial and academic studies during the postwar period.

24. Hannan's views were summarized in the *Catholic Standard*, 2 Apr 1970.

ness school, which by 1950 was operating at near physical capacity (the 330 pupils enrolled in 1962 marked a statistical high point).[25] Faced again with the need to turn applicants away, the academy had instituted entrance examinations in 1950. Furthermore, parents continued to show their eagerness to support a business school education for their daughters, paying tuition fees that had risen more than tenfold since Depression days. Although Hannan barred dunning parents for payments, the ample tuition receipts enabled the school to register a $10,000 surplus annually, which was applied to faculty salaries and some capital improvements.[26]

Particularly gratifying to Hannan was the fact that Washington employers continued to flock to the school for recruits. Pointing to what he called the "ridiculous" ease with which graduates secured well-paying jobs, he considered it his duty to lecture the students periodically on how such initial success could lend an entirely unrealistic perspective to their long-term future. Equally important, Hannan saw the business school attracting minority pupils in gratifying numbers, with African-Americans constituting some fifteen percent of the student body in 1968. "Be the best business school in the area," he told the principal in 1970. At his insistence and with the cooperation of the Holy Cross provincial, Mother Margaret Marie, no further effort was made to strengthen the academic curriculum.

Such weighty matters had little effect on the day-to-day activities of the students. The uniform of green blazers and skirts, white blouses, and beanies introduced in 1948 gratified that forceful minority of educators who pushed for uniforms as a way of suppressing social distinctions between the various economic classes and incidentally put St. Patrick's in line with some of the more socially prominent schools in the area. The school's budding musicians and actors were also winning greater recognition than their pre-war predecessors. The appearance of the academy's glee club in outdoor concerts during the Christmas season proved extremely popular with area shoppers and the thousands of Washingtonians who made their annual pilgrimage to

25. Between 1950 and the precipitous drop in 1968 in the wake of the riot following the assassination of Martin Luther King, enrollment hovered within ten percentage points of 300 pupils.

26. In the early 1960s the pastor established a separate school account, controlled by the principal, into which tuition fees were deposited. This account covered all expenses other than salaries and capital improvements. Any surplus was turned over to the parish, which applied it to salaries and improvements. See author's interview with Sister Miriam André, principal between 1962 and 1968.

view Woodie's famed Christmas windows.[27] A troupe of student players frequently performed skits in the children's wards of local hospitals. Financed through the archdiocese's Institute for the Arts and directed by Barbara Darowski, the program was intended to train students in the dramatic arts and in community service.

In 1962 the academy gained special notice when, at Bishop Hannan's insistence, it became the first area school to build an atomic fall-
out shelter. Following the advice of the city's civil defense director, Father George Pavloff partitioned off a section of the basement with its
eighteen-inch stone walls and fitted the space with hand-operated, fil-
tered air pumps, 200-gallon water tanks, portable toilets, and a two-
week supply of food. Reflecting a popular debate of the day, Pavloff assured a *Post* reporter that the shelter was designed to accommodate
the 340 students and staff of the academy, but "no one seeking admittance would be turned away as long as there was space."[28]

During the 1960s the school was a lively place well into the night.
For several years Catholic University rented space to conduct night
courses, and the C&P Telephone Company operated classes for employees seeking advancement. In 1966 Father Sylvester Hoffman committed the parish to supporting adult education classes for high school
dropouts organized by Father Joseph M. O'Connell, a resident at St.
Patrick's, and Sister M. Melathon of the Sisters Urban Center. Their
plan, endorsed by a group of area businesses, offered young people
stuck in low-paying service jobs an avenue to meaningful clerical employment. Such an ambitious undertaking required maximum effort
on the part of both teachers and pupils. Sister Miriam André, the academy principal, arranged the courses, and some of the school faculty
donated their evenings to teaching classes that ended with administration of the civil service examination. The courses continued for several years, although the average 25 percent absence rate made development of the necessary skills extremely difficult.[29]

Meanwhile, Carroll Hall, as it had for over a century, provided area
groups with a place to meet or practice the performing arts. One can
only muse on how Father Walter might have reacted to such lively
tenets as the Redskin cheerleaders practicing their high kicks or the
rehearsals of the Ford's Theater troupe's upcoming productions. One

27. These outdoor concerts received prominent press notice. See St. Patrick's file,
Washingtoniana collection, DCPL.

28. *Post*, 2 Jan 1962.

29. *Catholic Standard*, 17 Aug 1967, and author's interview with Sister Miriam André.

faculty member was certainly surprised by the excited director who gleefully informed her during rehearsals for "Godspell" that "we have finally found our new Jesus in New York."[30]

The generally placid tempo of daily life at the academy changed abruptly in 1968, a year that saw Washington racked with a major race riot, anti-war demonstrations, and an accelerating deterioration in the physical environment and civility of the old downtown neighborhood. All combined to change the perception of many parents, both black and white, about the safety and appropriateness of sending their daughters to an inner-city school. Parents in Prince George's County, in particular, were concerned about the long bus ride through parts of the city where the riot had taken a heavy toll, but all across the region memories were seared by pictures of the old neighborhood under assault. The result was dramatic: 260 girls enrolled in September, 1968, a twenty-five percent decrease since the previous spring. The trend continued over the next several years. The passionate crowds constantly protesting the Vietnam War at the nearby Selective Service building frightened some of the girls, as did the increased presence of street people. Boarded up stores and the noise and confusion attending construction of Metro's red line also did their part to swell the exodus. By 1975 enrollment was down to 154 students.

These losses and the corresponding loss in income from tuition coincided with the development of a series of new and unavoidable expenses. As in other Catholic schools, the number of lay teachers was rapidly growing. Although these dedicated people worked for less than their colleagues in the public schools, their salaries nevertheless represented a major new expense. At the same time, the advent of the heady new age of automatic data processing was making it increasingly expensive to offer meaningful business training. The school had electric typewriters and even an automated bookkeeping machine, but how to face the cost of personal computers, which would soon be an everyday necessity in the classroom? Added to these concerns, the last extensive remodeling of the school's interior had been completed with the installation of new lighting and sprinkler systems. Since then a number of pressing capital improvements had been postponed because of the lack of funds. After 1971 repairmen were routinely patching or making do when complete overhaul or replacement was needed.

30. The original "Jesus" had broken his leg. The author's interviews with Sisters Marie Julie, Miriam André, and Jovanna record their numerous shrewd and affectionate observations about life in the academy during the 1960s.

Many of the conditions leading to reduced enrollment figures were also responsible for the sharp downturn in the size of St. Patrick's extern congregation. As a result, parish revenues in the early 1970s were probably at their lowest ebb in the century. By imposing special austerities and postponing indefinitely necessary repairs to the church, Monsignor Arthur managed to divert funds to the school. Still the parish's slender resources continued to melt away. Although some diocesan subsidies were available, principally in the form of grants-in-aid to needy students, such help did little to alleviate the burden caused by too few students and an increasing number of families unable to meet tuition fees that now totaled some $600 annually.

While retaining the academy's goal of preparing students for what was then called "career girl society," the faculty of the 1960s and early 1970s introduced an innovation that would be used to advantage in later years to attract more pupils. As part of a concerted effort to provide valuable on-the-job experience, students were strongly encouraged to obtain part-time jobs, and class schedules were routinely adjusted to allow for what was a clear precurser of the later work-study program. The academy retained the usual array of extracurricular activities, but the glee club, basketball team, film club, and the rest all took second place to after-school jobs, with a lucky few winning employment in the school itself as receptionists, secretaries, and managers of the cafeteria. Operating under the reduced budgets of the early 1970s introduced an infectious "can do" spirit into the student body. Projects easily financed in more affluent schools were carefully discussed and prioritized at St. Patrick's. "We're just like a family," one student explained, "we can't have everything so we sit down and figure out what we can have."[31]

It was obvious that any improvement in the school's fortunes must begin with a reversal in enrollment trends. When Sister Mary Louise Full became principal in 1975 she launched a series of changes aimed at making the academy more competitive in a shrinking school-age market. She began with the curriculum.[32] Academic content had to be strengthened to meet minimum standards set by the city; furthermore, the lack of certain academic courses had become a drag on re-

31. As quoted in the *Catholic Standard*, 2 Apr 1970. This lengthy article by Maureen Limpert provides an illuminating report on life at the academy in post-riot Washington.

32. Kuhn, "The Sisters Go East," 51–52. See also, author's interviews with Sisters Mary Louis Full and Eleanore Anne McCabe. Unless otherwise indicated, the following pages are based on these sources.

cruitment among those looking for a full range of pre-college courses in addition to business training. Old decisions about curriculum content were abruptly reversed. Beginning in September 1975 the academy required students to take four years of English, three of social science, and courses in science and physical education in addition to the full array of business courses. Passing the civil service clerical examination and the federal proficiency typing test were also made prerequisites for graduation. In addition, the school offered electives in algebra and Spanish for those seeking college eligibility. As a sign of its commitment to stay in the forefront of modern business methods, the school somehow squeezed out the necessary funds to purchase two personal computers on which girls might be introduced to the newest office equipment.

In a further move designed to increase its appeal among those primarily interested in a clerical career, the school began a cooperative work-study program. Its full-time guidance counselor supervised arrangements whereby seniors along with some juniors could enter a contract with a local business firm or federal agency under which they would work twenty hours a week while continuing classes at the academy. Their performance, jointly evaluated by teachers and supervisors, earned them school credits as well as a substantial salary.[33] The work-study program proved extremely popular. As in earlier times, the school's reputation was enhanced by the performance of its students, and soon businesses were calling for more part-time workers. (In 1983 half the senior class enrolled in the program.) The recent changes were widely advertised when the school launched an aggressive recruitment campaign in the spring of 1976. Sister Mary Louise took full advantage of the annual "High School Night" that the diocesan education office sponsored to acquaint prospective students and their parents with the range of options offered in area schools. Both at these well-attended sessions and in talks at individual grade schools, she and her successor, Sister Eleanor Anne McCabe, extolled the advantages of an integrated business school education with its special mix of college preparatory courses. They also emphasized the advantage offered by a small school with a high teacher-to-pupil ratio. (With a full-time faculty of twenty and a student body of less than two hundred, St. Patrick's ranked among the best in the city.)

For some time, admission to high schools in the diocese involved

33. St. Patrick's Academy Press Release, n.d. (ca. 1980), The Cooperative Work Program," SPA.

a standard entrance examination, which graded all applicants, who listed their school preference in descending order. The academy began to appear on an increasing number of applications in the late 1970s, even if usually as someone's second or third choice. Sometimes a girl would enroll after being rejected by another school. Anxious parents would frequently plead with the school to accept a child whose poor grades and test scores made it unlikely that she would ever be eligible for a Catholic education. On occasion, the principal, after consultation with the grade school teachers and on the basis of personal assessment, would take a calculated risk and accept someone who had clearly not yet mastered the fundamentals of reading and mathematics. To help these students, the academy used remedial teachers, including one sister trained in such techniques who worked with the girls outside regular school hours and another provided on a part-time basis by the D.C. government.[34] In such ways, which would probably have been incomprehensible to parishioners a century earlier, St. Patrick's was continuing the outreach program that had so often animated its service to the Washington community.

The recruiting campaign paid off. Enrollment began a steady rise that produced 230 pupils in September 1980, a 33 percent increase in five years. It also meant a new and challenging kind of student body from a wide variety of socio-economic backgrounds. African-Americans had been enrolling at St. Patrick's in increasing numbers in the postwar decades and by 1968 constituted 25 percent of the student body. In succeeding years the percentage of minority students began to approach city averages, an achievement realized through a recruitment campaign that continued to appeal to students regardless of race and that eschewed any kind of quota system, despite at times not-too-subtle pressure to enforce one. By 1981 the student body was approximately 75 percent black and 12.7 percent Hispanic. The student profile of the early 1980s offered a startling contrast to the relatively homogeneous group that attended the academy just thirty years before. It was now one-third non-Catholic as increasing numbers of Washingtonians turned to parochial schools to educate their children. Approximately 25 percent of the 207 students, both black and white, came from middle-class suburban families; others commuted from the more affluent

34. Because of the special needs of some of its student population, the academy was eligible for participation in the ESAU program, including public support for remedial training in reading and math as well as English as a second language. The academy's own informal remedial reading program had been underway since the early 1970s.

SISTER ANN DONNELLY AND STUDENT

Washington neighborhoods, but many were from single-parent, inner city homes where the struggle against poverty and attendant social ills was unrelenting.[35]

The art of teaching such a varied group was obviously a special challenge. The exhilaration that came from producing so many self-disciplined, qualified graduates was balanced by all the difficulties encountered in any modern school. Discipline problems were frequent

35. Statistics from "Enrollment as of September 21, 1981," unsigned report in School file, SPA. These percentages remained relatively unchanged in succeeding years. See Kuhn, "The Sisters Go East," 51.

and far more complex than in the past, so much so that the principal was forced to reject the applications of several qualified and caring lay teachers whom she judged unable to cope. One problem more frequently encountered by schools in recent decades has been teen pregnancy. St. Patrick's policy was to allow unwed mothers to remain if they agreed to abide by school regulations. These allowed a work-at-home schedule, but demanded compliance with all assignments, passing all tests, and periodic meetings with guidance councilors. Principals came under some criticism for this policy, but they remained adamant, explaining that as members of a church opposed to abortion, the faculty should support these girls at this time in their lives.

The End of a Capital Institution

Unfortunately, the upswing in student enrollment proved temporary. St. Patrick's was caught up in changes that were affecting Catholic education in many parts of the country. The declining student population in the wake of the baby boom generation and the continuing dispersal of Catholic families into the far suburbs had left many dioceses with a surplus of classrooms in the inner city just as operating costs hit new highs. After a steady six-year rise in the number of students at St. Patrick's, the faculty watched all the gains melt away. By September 1984 enrollment stood at 156 pupils, two more than the low point a decade earlier. By then talk of school mergers and closings were flying about the capital.

Rumors started in 1975 when Cardinal Baum ordered a study of the diocese's secondary schools. Prepared by a board that included the superintendent of Catholic schools, the principals of all the high schools, and the director of the office of Black Catholics, the study discussed merger of Immaculate Conception, St. Cecilia's, St. Anthony's, and St. Patrick's. The schools involved invited concerned parents to express their views on what was a radical suggestion, considering that it involved the future of three parish-controlled institutions and one privately-run academy. Actually, the proposal generated little discussion around town, and the meeting for St. Patrick's parents was poorly attended. When the diocesan board of education heard testimony on the plan in January 1979, however, it encountered some criticism over certain hardships imposed on inner-city children if the combined school were located in Brookland.[36]

36. A summary of the testimony and the criticism of the new school's location was reported in the *Catholic Standard*, 18 Jan 1979.

Archbishop Hickey's decision, released in December 1982, partially addressed this concern. Beginning the next September, he announced, the female students of St. Anthony's High School would be merged with the student body of Immaculate Conception to form a new school, All Saints, at the St. Anthony's site in Northeast Washington. In September 1986, the student bodies of St. Cecilia's and St. Patrick's would be merged in a new school to be located in St. Patrick's building on G Street. This latter change, the archbishop added, was contingent upon the successful development of St. Patrick's F Street property and the renovation of the old school to be financed by that development.[37] Meanwhile Archbishop Hickey ordered a study of the long-range trends in Catholic secondary education in the city, commissioning an independent study of the situation by experts from Catholic University, who based their findings on considerable statistical information on family income, race, and religion supplied by the individual schools.

Before that study was completed, the Holy Cross sisters, pointing to the increasing financial burden involved in operating St. Cecilia's Academy, informed the diocese that they intended to close the school in June 1984. The diocese countered by proposing an immediate merger of St. Cecilia's with St. Patrick's, temporarily housed at the former location. Combining the two schools run by the same order just twenty blocks apart in the inner city had its obvious attraction, but the diocese's desire for an immediate change was opposed by the sisters, who feared the disruption that would occur when two institutions with different educational missions (St. Cecilia's had a straight academic curriculum) were merged without careful preparation. Instead, the order agreed to keep St. Cecilia's open for one more year while the diocese's ongoing study was finalized.

This deliberate and largely placid consolidation of the city's high schools was not to be. Shortly after the year of grace offered by the Holy Cross sisters began and before the archbishop could review the proposals being formulated by his commission, the Sisters of Providence, who owned Immaculata Preparatory School, dropped a bombshell on Catholic Washington. Without reference to the diocese's evolving consolidation plans and citing financial problems, they announced that their popular girl's school in Northwest Washington would close in June 1985. The news set off a storm of protest about

37. Archdiocese of Washington News Release, encl. to ltr., Hickey to Arthur, 14 Dec 1982, copy in SPA.

school closures accompanied by candlelight vigils and angry head-lines.[38] The ensuing turmoil prompted the archbishop to move quickly in the case of the Holy Cross schools. In October 1984 he called in the principals of St. Cecilia's and St. Patrick's and announced the merger of their schools into a new archdiocesan high school for girls combin-ing the full range of academic and commercial courses offered at the parent institutions.[39] The new school, called Holy Spirit, would tem-porarily be housed in St. Cecilia's recently remodeled building on East Capitol Street.

The archbishop asked the principals to break the news to the stu-dents before it was released to the press. After so much recent discus-sion about mergers, however, the decision came as no great surprise and generated none of the protests that greeted the announcement about Immaculata's closing just weeks before. The schools neverthe-less formed a committee of students, parents, and faculty members to address concerns about the merger, and approximately two-thirds of the St. Patrick's faculty prepared for transfer to the new institution along with their students.[40]

In retrospect, the greatest surprise may have been the speed with which the diocese abandoned its published intention to locate its in-ner-city high school at St. Patrick's. The centrality of the G Street building, so near the hub of the city's bus and metro lines, the church's historical connection with the roots of Catholic education in Washing-ton, and the fact that any school located on parish grounds would continue to receive parish support unavailable elsewhere all seemed to argue in favor of St. Patrick's. Such considerations, however, over-looked the fact that the diocese needed to act quickly in 1984, the modernized St. Cecilia's was ready for immediate occupancy, and plans for financing and refurbishing St. Patrick's, tied to commercial development and the vagaries of the Washington real estate market, had been suspended. Perhaps more to the point, after calling St. Patrick's business curriculum "a treasure the archdiocese should be careful to preserve," the archbishop's advisors recommended that the business courses be made co-educational and that government sup-port available for this special type education be solicited. To that end

38. See, for example, *Post* 9 Oct 1984.

39. In June 1985 the Holy Cross sisters reaffirmed an earlier agreement with the archdiocese that when the two schools operated by their congregation were merged, the consolidated school would become an archdiocesan school. See ltr., Sister Frances Bernard O'Connor to Hickey, 15 Jun 1985, AAW.

40. *Post,* 9 May 1985.

they pressed the archbishop to merge the all-male Mackin high school with the new Holy Spirit school, which, they concluded, should remain located at St. Cecilia's. Their study had concluded that this location was more appropriate for a co-ed school and less costly to purchase than any planned renovation of St. Patrick's.[41]

It quickly became apparent that what had been touted as a temporary measure was in reality a permanent move, and with heavy hearts and no little apprehension, the faculty and students of St. Patrick's Academy prepared to clean out the old building with its eighty-four years of accumulated memory and move on.

41. Ltr., John J. Convey, Project Director, to Hickey, 29 Jun 1984, AAW. Mackin never merged with Holy Spirit High School, which would remain in operation until June 1989, when yet another realignment sent its students and those at All Saints to John Carroll High School.

CHAPTER 14

The Arts at St. Patrick's

THROUGHOUT ITS HISTORY St. Patrick's has reflected the universal church's traditional promotion of art to intensify the appeal of the liturgy through the senses. The congregation adorned its church with beautiful objects and filled the air with beautiful sounds in the belief that art leads to a deeper appreciation of the sacred mysteries. This belief also partially explains the parish's support of the theater in later decades. Transcending the simple provision of wholesome entertainment while raising money for charity, St. Patrick's sponsored a series of elaborate sacred dramas seen by thousands. This ancient art form in the hands of gifted producers and actors became a practical catechetical tool helping audiences better understand their faith.

Although parish sponsorship of the arts had a spiritual purpose, the history of beautiful objects, music, and theater at St. Patrick's nevertheless mirrors to a great extent the aspirations and changing tastes of a congregation aware of its minority status yet seeking to express its identity in the capital. It also demonstrates the parish's belief that it stood at the center of Catholic life in Washington.

Lost Treasures

The struggle to organize a parish and build a suitable church apparently so occupied the energies and strained the purses of the first generation of Washington Catholics that little effort was spared for gathering artifacts that transcended the utilitarian.[1] Typical of the "meeting house" design characteristic in the Federal period, the 1809 church built by Father Matthews remained plain in the extreme. A simple maple altar and bare plaster walls reflected daylight entering through clear glass panes. A wood-burning stove set in the nave heated the building. If the church boasted chandeliers or statuary, they remained unnoticed by those who left descriptions of the interior. For years the pipes of the city's only organ, rising above the gallery, constituted the church's major decoration and distinction.

Over time several artifacts were donated to enhance the appearance of the church. All have been lost, so their artistic merit can only be approximated from often unreliable contemporary accounts. Nevertheless, given the wealth and station of the donors, it seems reasonable to surmise that the objects possessed value. Their careless treatment by subsequent generations and ultimate disappearance is lamentable.

The first donation of note was a hand-carved pulpit presented to the church in the 1820s by Senhor Robello, the Brazilian minister to Washington, in the name of his sovereign, Dom Pedro I. Robello imported a massive rough-hewn mahogany log from Brazil and contracted with the noted American craftsman Benjamin M. Belt to fabricate an imposing hexagonal pulpit with matching canopy. Its finely tooled and highly polished surface contained two large wrought-iron inscriptions on adjoining panels, one reading "I.H.S." superimposed with a silver cross; the other "P. I.," identifying the donor. Reportedly a fine example of early nineteenth-century American craftsmanship, the pulpit was later transferred to the new church on Tenth Street, where it was used until sometime after 1886.[2]

1. The following section on the visual arts at St. Patrick's is based in large part on the work of Kenneth Pribanic, whose detailed studies of the church's art and furnishings are on file in SPA.

2. *Catholic Mirror*, 5 Jun 1886. The Dom Pedro pulpit is also mentioned in the description of the 1809 church's interior by Anna M. Dorsey, "Recollections of Old St. Patrick's Church," *Sunday Morning Chronicle*, Sept 1873, and "Gonzaga College," *Woodstock Letters*, 19 (1890), 18. When Bishop Keane gave the parish a new pulpit sometime after 1886, Father Walter donated the Dom Pedro piece to St. Teresa's, the new parish in Anacostia. The present whereabouts of the pulpit is unknown.

Shortly after the installation of the pulpit, the French minister in Washington presented the parish with a painting from the royal collection of King Charles X.[3] The identity of the artist has been lost, but high praise from contemporary connoisseurs for the massive (twelve by eight feet) historical painting, "St. Louis Burying the Dead at Damietta," indicates the mixture of pride and piety generated by the royal gift. When the church was razed, the painting was restored in anticipation of its installation in the new building, yet as late as 1889 it remained, bereft of its great gilt frame, crowding the wall of the rectory parlor. Its final disposition is unknown, but the public announcement that the painting was too large to fit in the new church, perhaps true, also provided a diplomatic excuse for rejecting a work then unfashionable. That the notoriously frugal Jacob Walter had paid for its restoration might explain the painting's lengthy stay in his parlor.

Two other paintings of note were added to the 1809 church's furnishings in later years, both reportedly through the generosity of royal donors. One was a twelve-foot-high "Christ Carrying the Cross" installed behind the altar around 1835. Father Walter also had this painting restored after the old church closed, but it too must have been considered inappropriate for the new church, because in 1879 he donated it to St. Teresa's, where no record survives of its later history. Nor is there any trace of a third painting that hung in the old church, an eighteenth-century portrait entitled "Head of St. Paul." While it is unlikely that this canvas was ever installed in the new church, it remained in the parish's possession at least until 1889, when it was the subject of notice by the *Catholic Mirror,* which commented on the high monetary value of the piece.[4]

Long lost, the church's first known statue of St. Patrick has recently been rediscovered. A painted plaster work, carved in Munich, depicts the saint with a model of the new church in his hand. Its donor was described as "a rich New Yorker" and "one of Father Walter's Protestant friends." Initially considered for the new main altar, the statue was installed elsewhere in the sanctuary in April 1890.[5] Father Stafford was particularly fond of what now must be counted another lost trea-

3. Dorsey's "Recollections of Old St. Patrick's Church" mentions Louis XVIII as donor, but the chronology of the period and other evidence indicate that the *Catholic Mirror*'s attribution (27 Jul 1889) to Charles X was probably correct.

4. Both works were discussed in the *Catholic Mirror,* 1 Nov 1897 and 27 Jul 1889.

5. Nevertheless the statue received considerable press notice. See *Church News,* 30 Mar and 20 Apr 1890, and *Catholic Mirror,* 26 Apr 1890. The statue, in need of restoration, is currently on display in the Paul VI Institute.

sure of St. Patrick's, a painting of the Madonna and Child by the six-teenth-century Genoese artist Mazzolini. Gift of a private donor, the work was purchased in Spain, restored by a Washington craftsman, and hung in the new church in 1901 in a ceremony that featured a lecture by Stafford on the artist and his work. Stafford was so convinced of the artistic and financial value of the painting that he specifically willed it to Cardinal Gibbons for the congregation of St. Patrick's. Its present disposition is unknown.

A discussion of St. Patrick's lost treasures must include mention of the triple-canopied main altar designed by the church's architect, Lawrence O'Connor. Installed in 1896, the piece was executed in Vermont marble with green onyx plinths to support a mensa more than fifteen feet in length. Its superstructure contained two high relief panels depicting the gathering of manna in the desert and the sacrifice of Melchizedek, Old Testament prefigurements of the Kingship of Christ, and the Last Supper (which was portrayed in a third relief rendered in the base of the altar in the style of the famous da Vinci design).[6] Three spires surmounted three canopied niches of the altarpiece and rose more than twenty feet above the sanctuary floor. Early accounts of the church's interior regularly referred to the ethereal effect of the mixing of artificial electric light from within the spires and shimmering candlelight on the gothic structure.

The O'Connor reredos was replaced in 1962 with a towering flat reredos with gilded and polychromed statues of Irish saints set against backgrounds of gold and blue fabric with stencils. The life-size statues set in niches recessed into the flat and ornamented background recall English Gothic cathedral pieces like that at Winchester. This piece, ordered by Bishop Hannan after consultation with the noted architect Philip Hubert Froman, was the work of Robert Robbins.[7] Another altarpiece added to the church during the 1960s, a Pan American shrine commemorating the church's annual Pan American Mass, was dedicated to the memory of Father Sylvester Hoffman. The work of the Barcelona artist Enrique Monjo, the piece featured an over-sized representation of Our Lady Queen of the Americas superimposed above gessoed and polychromed reliefs of the saints and blessed of the New World. This was set in a diptych-type frame behind hinged, carved and

6. The subject and symbolism of the bas reliefs were discussed in *Church News,* 21 Sep 1895 and 21 Mar 1896. The base with the da Vinci relief is retained in today's altar.

7. A full description of the reredos, with illustration, appeared in the *Catholic Standard,* 26 Dec 1962.

AN AGE OF SPLENDOR. *Cardinal Gibbons and the apostolic delegate on flanking thrones in St. Patrick's sanctuary.*

gilded panels displaying the natural features and technological achievements of North and South America.[8]

Although of debatable artistic value, several other artifacts deserve mention in this catalogue because of the high esteem in which they were held in their day. The oldest was a large handmade hearth rug that for many decades covered the sanctuary floor of the old church. Worked in worsted by a local Washington craftsman, the rug was donated to the church in 1831.[9] Another greatly admired nineteenth-century work was the memorial commissioned by the congregation to honor Father Walter. Designed with a relief likeness of Walter in a central plaque flanked by niched statues of Saints Ambrose and Vincent de Paul, the work was executed in Vermont marble and Caen stone and exemplified the elaborate Victorian style of funereal art composition.[10]

Gone too is the widely praised sanctuary lamp originally installed at the time of the Eucharistic Congress of 1895. An out-sized fixture suspended from the sanctuary ceiling, the lamp featured a tier of genuflecting, life-like angels surrounding a glass cylinder and placed above a bulb of perforated and scroll work metal. Also removed from the sanctuary were carved Flemish oak thrones with pleated velvet canopies, the so-called monsignor chairs. The two chairs, one of which was donated by the congregation to honor Monsignor Russell's "zealous work" in the parish, were used by members of the hierarchy presiding at parish ceremonies.[11]

Lastly, any catalogue of lost treasures should mention the interior frescoing, dating from the 1890s, that completed the decorative scheme of the church architect. The principal features of this extensive plan for ceilings and walls were designed by A. D. Emmart after the Byzantine-style frescos in Notre Dame in Paris. The ceiling vaults of the sanctuary apse were ornamented with figures of blue, yellow, and gold aluminum. Similar designs in darker hues covered the ceiling vaults of the nave. The vault ribs, mouldings, and capitals of the great columns were all gilded with gold leaf. Perhaps the most significant

8. Archbishop O'Boyle officiated at the dedication ceremonies. For a full description of the altar piece and the ceremonies, see *Catholic Standard*, 2 Feb 1967.

9. Sarah E. Veddes, *Reminiscences of the District of Columbia or Washington City Seventy-nine Years Ago, 1830–1909* (St. Louis, 1909), 18. The donor was Mrs. Charles Hill.

10. The tablet was designed by C. F. Geier of Washington. See *Catholic News*, 5 May 1894. An illustrated description of the memorial is contained in Walter, *A Memorial Tribute*, 68–69.

11. The intricate carvings on the chairs are described in *The Patrician* (May 1912), 6.

component of the entire interior decorative plan was the tier of niches below the sanctuary clerestory windows. Twelve niches recessed nine inches into the apse walls contained oil paintings simulating mosaics of the apostles. Two additional niches, one at each end of the band of twelve, contained floral compositions. The impression of this architectural and artistic program must have been breathtaking on first observation. During a subsequent renovation the niches were sealed and a series of seven inscription-bearing colossal angels were painted on the panels. During still another interior refurbishing these angels were covered over.[12]

Church Furnishings

Most of the furnishings in St. Patrick's today can be traced to a thirty-year period before World War I and reflect what the pastors and congregation of that generation thought appropriate for the center of Catholic Washington. Of interest to the social historian, each addition was accompanied by a series of public announcements designed to acquaint the congregation with the uniqueness and value of the object and to attract donors for what were most often unfinanced additions. Readers were assured that each work was fabricated from the finest of materials or produced by Europe's foremost artists and craftsmen. The distinction of works designed and executed in European studios seemed of paramount importance to parishioners, as indeed it did to many Americans of that era. Taken as a whole, the additions to the church at the turn of the century accurately reflected the growing confidence of Catholics in Washington and their willingness to spend large sums to enhance the church.

Marble and Stone. The oldest surviving furnishings in the church, the side altars authorized by Father Walter in 1890, reflect a restrained approach to decoration in contrast to the ostentation that was to follow. Fabricated by Mullen and Sons of Baltimore, the structures of Italian and Tennessee marble were produced for the relatively modest sum of $1,100 each. The Blessed Virgin's altar, donated by the sodality from money raised at parish entertainments, featured gothic embellishments in Mexican marble; the Sacred Heart altar (later rededicated to St. Joseph) incorporated different colored marble columns to divide its gothic panels and featured a bronze monogram of the Sacred Heart in

12. The niches are being reintroduced in the bicentennial restoration of the sanctuary.

its center panel. The embossed brass tabernacle doors are particularly rich elements of the altarpieces.

Installation of the main altar in 1896 must have unleashed the parish's enthusiasm for high gothic decoration. The altar rail installed four years later was another rich gothic-inspired composition with petite multicolored marble columns supporting a continuous series of open arches on which a mantle of marble rested. Intricately detailed, brass-plated, cast and wrought bronze gates provided access to the sanctuary from the central aisle of the nave. The work of Washington sculptor James F. Early, the rail was set on marble risers. In a burst of hyperbole, the reporter for the *New Century* told his readers the finished altar rail would be counted as "perhaps the finest and most elaborate in the country."[13] The marble pulpit was also the work of Early. Installed in 1907 and later dedicated to Father Stafford, the pulpit follows a design provided by the popular pastor. The deep reliefs on its panels depict events in the life of St. Patrick and contain representations of Saints Paul and Chrysostom at the corners. The reading desk rests on the wings of an eagle, the symbol of the Evangelist John.[14]

In 1910 Father Russell authorized the renovation of the vestibule of the center entrance and the narrow enclosed space under the choir loft. A partition wall of wainscotting and glass was removed and the vestibule wainscotted with Skyros marble panels resting on a base of Tyros marble. New interior doors were added at each entrance, as was the Tennessee marble paving of the vestibule and narthex. The costly addition, the parish magazine explained, was necessitated by the constant overcrowding of the church, but, it went on to assure its readers, the addition both brightened the area and made it "a gem of beauty."[15] A marble floor was installed in the sanctuary in 1914. Composed of octagonal blocks of white and sylvan green Vermont marble with Verdusa marble borders, the floor had as its centerpiece the large shamrock mosaic that appealed so strongly to Cardinal O'Boyle in later years. In soliciting funds for the $2,400 addition, *The Patrician* promised parishioners that the marble would make the sanctuary "look much brighter . . . and appear even larger."[16]

13. *New Century,* 14 Jul 1900.

14. Many of pastor's prominent friends joined with parishioners in subscribing to the underwriting of a project whose total cost approached the then-astronomical figure of $10,000 ($150,000 today). The piece was dedicated to Stafford in November 1908. See *The Patrician* (Dec 1908), 8–9.

15. *The Patrician* (Oct 1910), 6.

16. *The Patrician* (Oct 1914), 17.

Statuary. The statues in the church all postdate the 1884 dedication of the edifice. The oldest work is the great crucifix executed by the Bavarian firm of Mayer & Company and installed in the church on Good Friday, 1909. The cast plaster corpus was modeled on a Spanish crucifix belonging to Father Russell. The cross itself was a tooled tree trunk with exposed bark, a style made familiar to generations of Catholics by the Redemptorist fathers, who would frequently open parish missions by carrying a large cross into the church. During his 1909 trip to Europe, Father Russell also commissioned the church's four holy water fonts. He personally selected the models for the genuflecting angels which, *The Patrician* stated, provided the church with "the real touch of Italian art."[17]

The parish's venerated representation of the Sorrowful Mother was installed in the baptistery on Good Friday, 1912. A plaster cast after a design by the Baltimore artist Edward Berge, the statue follows the typical outlines of this popular grouping, but with one noticeable difference. At the insistence of Father Russell, who lectured the artist at length on the matter, the focus of St. Patrick's pieta is not as is usually the case on the sorrowful mother, but on the dead Savior.[18] To underscore the reappointment of the baptistery as a Sorrowful Mother Chapel, the pastor commissioned Baltimore painter Gabrielle Clements to execute a series of wall paintings depicting a vision of Calvary after Christ had been taken down from the cross and laid in the arms of his mother.

The remaining statues, all of Carrara marble and all apparently commissioned in 1915, were the work of the Daprato Statuary Company of Pietrasanta and Chicago, at least two of them sculpted by Ferdinando Palla.[19] Although the pastor kept a knowing eye focused on the progress of the Italian artists, advising them on matters of design and execution, he warned parishioners in March 1916 that the war in Europe might extend delivery dates. Everyone must have been surprised that within a few months all five statues, traditional renditions of the Sacred Heart, the Blessed Virgin, and Saints Joseph, Patrick, and

17. *The Patrician* (Oct 1911), 12. The article was soliciting donations for the already-installed fonts. Another appeal was carried in the same source, (Jan 1912), 14–15.

18. Russell's role in the creation of this popular but artistically indifferent work is reported in the *Star,* 31 Mar 1912.

19. Unless otherwise indicated, information in these paragraphs is based on Kenneth Pribanic's "Study of the Statuary of St. Patrick's," 13 Jan 1993, SPA. The statues, all of a similar size, cost a modest $450 each ($5,088 in today's values).

Anthony, had arrived in Washington.[20] The statue of the Blessed Virgin, a copy of the Sistine Madonna, was blessed in May 1916 when the names of donors were ceremoniously deposited under the altar. The statue of St. Patrick, his right hand clasping a sea shell, a crosier in his left, was donated by the Sunday School's dramatic association using money raised from performances in Carroll Hall. Most excitement seemed to center on the St. Joseph statue donated by parishioners in memory of Rose Russell. Last to arrive, the statue was installed after Russell had been consecrated bishop of Charleston. He asked that in lieu of a gift, the parish add his name to that of his mother's on the statue's pedestal.[21]

Stained Glass. It was at Stafford's instigation that the congregation began to replace the church's tinted windows with costly leaded stained glass, a task largely finished before World War I by Monsignor Russell.[22] With the exception of the west rose over the choir loft, all were created by the Bavarian firm of Mayer & Company and were purchased before 1915. The various groups of windows were designed thematically. The seven in the sanctuary portray scenes in the life of St. Patrick; three of these windows are dedicated to former pastors. Three in the Virgin's chapel, three in the north transept, and the four of the north aisle all illustrate Marian themes. The windows on the church's south wall relate events in Christ's life. The remaining twenty windows of the nave clerestory feature various Old and New Testament personages, doctors of the church, and founders of religious orders. A baptistery window portraying the baptism of Jesus and the narthex window of the Good Shepherd were the two final windows of this campaign. The latter, a reproduction of Hoffman's popular painting, was a special favorite of generations of parishioners.

Although all from the same studio and time, these windows represent two schools of design. The larger windows of the aisles, transepts, and sanctuary are pictorial representations composed of sizable pieces

20. Russell's warning about delivery dates was carried in *The Patrician* (Mar 1916), 8.

21. *The Patrician* (Jun 1917), 10. Everyone in the parish must have donated to this statue. See same source (Jan 1916), 12.

22. Unless otherwise noted, the following paragraphs are based on Kenneth Pribanic's, *St. Patrick's in the City, a Tour* (Washington: 1989) and his later studies, copies in SPA. A detailed description of the windows installed by Stafford before 1904 are contained in Smith's *History of St. Patrick's* (inside rear cover, 1904 edition). Although *The Patrician* (June 1906) announced that Stafford was ordering clerestory windows depicting prophets, evangelists, and church doctors, the project was apparently shelved during his illness.

of colored and painted glass. The emphases on the characters
tured, their garments, and ancillary items like flowers and furn:
determine to a great extent the number and sizes of glass pieces.
These compositions incorporate large pieces of glass in a large field.
Strikingly different are the windows of the clerestory, which exhibit an
approach to the art utilizing a great number of smaller glass pieces
richer in tone and arranged in more intricate patterns. The difference
in styles is readily apparent: the larger ones are more romantic and im-
itative of canvas painting in their composition, while the smaller windows are more medieval in their jewel-like appearance.

The west rose was not installed until 1964. Executed in Dublin by
the artist John Hogan, the window is fifteen feet in diameter with 225
square feet of stained glass. At its center is a dove representing the Par-
aclete with tongues of fire extending to the apostles depicted in twelve
radiating panels. The Virgin and John the Baptist are also pictured in
this Pentecost window dedicated to the slain President, John Kennedy.[23]

Music at St. Patrick's

While the use of sacred music during St. Patrick's early years went
largely unrecorded, it seems safe to assume that *a capella* renditions of
familiar hymns and simple chant responses at the rare high Mass represented the total musical life of the parish. Formation of a choir apparently preceded dedication of the new church in 1809, a ceremony
that included Mass sung in the presence of two bishops, which must
have severely taxed the small congregation's musical resources. These
resources had recently been strengthened by the addition of a few
gifted musicians to the parish rolls when President Jefferson brought
to Washington two small groups of Italians—stone masons to decorate the Capitol and musicians for the U.S. Marine band. Some of
these newcomers, most notably the sons of Gaetano Carusi, brought,
in addition to their skill as instrumentalists, a familiarity with recent
European church music which could be placed at the service of the
congregation.

The pipe organ traditionally stands at the center of a church's music
program, and soon after the church's dedication the parish began soliciting in earnest for funds to purchase their own royal instrument. In

23. Completion was made possible by a substantial gift from Mr. and Mrs. John
Davis. See *Catholic Standard*, 7 Aug 1964.

March 1810, for example, the *National Intelligencer* announced that a collection would be taken up on St. Patrick's Day "which will be applied by the trustees toward purchasing an organ for the church."[24] Yet more than five years would pass before the church could celebrate the installation of the first organ in Washington.

This instrument had a curious history. The noted Washington physician and recent convert Dr. Thomas Miller told Father Matthews about the fate of the eighteenth-century, English-made organ that his mother once played in the family's Episcopal church (Cope Parish) in Westmoreland County, Virginia. The organ had been damaged during the War of 1812 when a British naval squadron under Admiral George Cockburn raided communities along the lower Potomac. The parish churches at Nominy and Yeocomico creeks (it is unclear which building contained the organ) were pillaged.[25] British troops typically carried metal molds in their field equipment, which they used to turn captured metal objects into musket balls. After some of the parish's organ pipes suffered this fate, the vestrymen dismantled the instrument and packed it away. Hearing Miller's tale, Matthews arranged to buy the old instrument, haul it to Washington, and after extensive repair, install it in the gallery of the new church.[26]

Bolstered by its *grand orgue,* as the parish liked to call their proud new possession, the choir became a regular fixture of the local musical scene. Its rendering of liturgical chants at the dedication of St. Matthew's in 1838, for example, earned respectful notice in a city paper.[27] By 1855 Vincent Masi, who combined the posts of organist and choir director, and his part-time assistant were paid a combined $200 for a nine-month season (through most of its life, St. Patrick's choir did not perform in the heat of Washington's summers). The bellowsman, who in the days before electric motors pumped air into the organ wind chest during services, received $20 a year for his strenuous

24. *National Intelligencer,* 14 Mar 1810.

25. William Meade, *Old Churches, Ministers, and Families of Virginia* (Philadelphia: Lippincott, 1857), 2:147–57.

26. Dorsey, "Recollections of Old St. Patrick's Church." The version of this event accepted by Smith (*A History of St. Patrick's*) and several others traces the organ to a church in Dumfries, Virginia, but this must be discounted, since the two Episcopal churches in Dumfries closed in 1752 and were in ruins by 1810. Some accounts describe the organ's transport to Washington by ox cart. Given the relative cheapness and speed of river transportation, it appears likely that any use of an ox cart was limited to the journey between the Washington Canal and F Street.

27. *National Intelligencer,* 24 Sep 1838.

work. For the first time the church's accounts for the year 1857 itemized a separate $180 "for expenses of choir." Whether this sum was used to pay salaries for soloists or to cover the cost of sheet music and other expenses was not indicated, although professional singers were by then commonplace in some parish choirs.

In 1857 the church acquired a new organist/director. Professor Caulfield (Americans seemed eager to bestow this title on all nineteenth-century organists) was hired at double the salary of his predecessor. This raise seems to have been related to the acquisition in that same year of a new organ for the church, deemed by one critic "one of the finest toned and most powerful in the city." Payment for the new organ included more than $1,500 allocated from regular parish funds over a three-year period, in addition to a substantial amount realized from the benefit concert at the Smithsonian that had proved such a serious source of contention between Archbishop Kenrick and the pastor. No doubt Father O'Toole had obtained the costly instrument with his "grand cathedral" in mind, for it was so large that, when jammed into the old St. Patrick's on F Street, its longest pipes almost touched the ceiling.[28]

Indicative of its considerable musical ambitions at the time, the choir performed a Mozart Mass at Georgetown College early on Easter morning, 1860, before crossing town to sing parts of Johan Hummel's elaborate E-flat Mass and "Gaudeamus" by the contemporary Austrian composer Anton Diabelli at St. Patrick's. The following Sunday it performed Haydn's "Theresien" Mass to mark the arrival of the church's new pastor, Jacob Walter.[29]

During the Civil War and extending into the early days of the congregation's exile in Carroll Hall after the old church was razed, the parish's musical forces were led by Professor Richter (organist) and Miss Margaret Murray (choir director), both well-known Washington musicians. Murray, in particular, was singled out for injecting a needed sense of discipline into performances and inspiring amateur musicians with what one reporter later called her thorough professionalism.[30] Richter and Murray organized the music performed at the laying of the new church's cornerstone in 1873.

28. "Statements of the Accounts of St. Patrick's Church. Washington, D.C.," 1854–1858, AAB. The quotation is from the *Catholic Mirror*, 18 Oct 1854. Several commentators noted the problem of fitting the new organ into the loft in old St. Patrick's. See, for example, *The Republican*, 26 Oct 1884, and *Catholic Mirror*, 18 Oct 1854.

29. *Star*, 9 and 16 April 1860.

30. Washington *Times*, 6 Dec 1903.

Notices surviving from this first half-century of organized musical activity at St. Patrick's indicate that in addition to bombastic marches and saccharine hymns by now-forgotten composers, the congregation regularly heard some of the finest Western church music. Works by Palestrina, Haydn, Handel, Mozart, Weber, and even contemporary masters like Rossini, Verdi, and Gounod were frequently included. Although no claims can be advanced concerning the competence of the singers, the fact that such compositions were regularly performed in a musically unsophisticated city not only offers a minor corrective to popular assumptions about the musical taste of a Catholic congregation during the Gilded Age, but also says something about the parish's role in the cultural life of the capital.

Father Walter greatly admired the polyphony of the Baroque masters. He asked the choir to perform works by Palestrina at the dedication of the new church but surrendered to the group's demand that they mark the occasion with a more elaborate offering. Yet even if his personal musical taste could not be faulted, Walter showed little interest in paying for a music program. The evidence suggests that he was one of those frugal pastors found in all ages who believe that raising a joyful noise to the Lord should be a free-will offering of the performers. Walter obviously disagreed with O'Toole's generosity to musicians. He admitted that the organist deserved compensation, but on his arrival he immediately reduced Professor Richter's wages, which in 1859 stood at a respectable $400, by 25 percent. Where O'Toole had paid $112 for "part of the choir paid for part of the year," there is no indication that, except for a brief period toward the end of his life, Walter ever paid soloists or choir directors, a fact that might explain the constant turnover in choir directors during his pastorate.[31]

In the late 1870s Miss M. Louisa Boone, a parishioner and local music teacher related to the family that erected the historic Boone chapel near Rosaryville, Maryland, succeeded Richter as organist. Boone appears to have been a most self-effacing artist. Although frequently called upon to combine the roles of organist and choir director during her twenty years at the church, she nevertheless would relinquish the more glamorous director's job from time to time when the church

31. "Receipts and Disbursements at St. Patrick's, Washington, D.C., from Nov 1/58 to Nov 1/59," AAB. Walter's first financial statement lists the organist's salary at $470, but that sum covered an eighteen-month period. In subsequent years the organist was paid $330, a figure increased substantially by the end of the war. See, for example, "Statements of the Accounts of St. Patrick's Church. Washington, D.C.," 1862 and 1866, both in AAB.

managed to attract some luminary for the post. In October 1884, for example, a nationally known organist and choir director, William Waldecker, directed a dedicatory concert that provided the congregation with its first view of the new church. One of the city's grand musical events that decade, the benefit performance for the building fund featured an array of organists, vocal soloists, and quartets, each doing a musical turn that, along with selections from the choir, ranged from choruses by Mozart and Handel to operatic overtures arranged for organ. In the excitement of the moment, the *Post* reporter claimed that St. Patrick's choir was "the best in the city." He went on to complain that the contralto soloist was sometimes "drowned out" by the choir, but lest the poor woman lose heart, concluded that "a few years training will strengthen and ripen what is now a beautiful voice."[32] Magnus Koechling, a prominent baritone soloist, led the choir during the first Mass in the new church, while W. H. Daniels directed the performances of Haydn's Imperial Mass at the formal dedication two months later.

In 1889 the indefatigable Louisa Boone organized a junior choir and a children's chorus that combined with the adult choir on major feasts. Yet even when these special occasions included appearances by well-known soloists such as Metropolitan Opera star Addie Randall, the choir apparently continued to exhibit all the weaknesses of the typical amateur group. Rarely able to muster more than twenty members at a time, its earnest array of sopranos greatly outnumbered the two tenors and four bases.[33] Even the parsimonious Walter must have come to realize that dedicated volunteers alone could not provide the parish with a music program commensurate with its status in Catholic Washington. Consequently his last years as pastor saw the inauguration of some changes leading to a more professional choir.

The transformation began with the appearance of Professor Mari-

32. Quoted in article attributed to the *Post*, 13 Oct 1884. The musical activities that accompanied the dedication of the new church are treated in length by the press, which listed the names of all choir members and the programs performed. See, for example, *The Republican*, 26 Oct 1884; *Catholic Mirror*, 4 Oct and 1 Nov 1884; and *Post*, 29 Dec 1884. Other choir directors during this period include L. E. Gannon and George Cecker. Boone's first name is a matter of conjecture. Over the decades the press also rendered it Lulu, Loulie, and Lulie. Parish music programs most frequently rendered it M. Louisa.

33. The Washington correspondent of the *Church News* was apparently much interested in the city's musical life and frequently reported on St. Patrick's choir and listed the names of its members. See, for example, notices on 16 Oct 1887, 21 Apr and 22 Dec 1889. See also *Catholic Mirror*, 24 Mar 1888.

ano Maina as guest soloist in January 1890. A prominent member of New York's opera world, Maina had come to Washington to open a "school of voice culture" at Ninth and H Streets. Within a month he was choir director. Maina was a natural showman as well as a fine singer. Less than a month on the job, he invited his friends, the opera stars Agostino and Pauline Montegriffo, to join him in a concert at the church and arranged for an appearance of the American prima donna Marie Decker with the choir. Such activities must have stimulated local interest, because membership in the choir increased dramatically. In announcing Maina's leave of absence in May 1890 to star in productions of "Martha" and "Faust" at the Grand Opera House in New York, the Church News concluded that the "wonderfully improved" choir now ranked among the city's very best.[34] The rejuvenated group presented Maina with a special leader's baton and in March 1891 sang a testimonial concert in his honor at the Lincoln Music Hall. A grateful Father Walter treated the choir to a supper catered by Harvey's Restaurant, inaugurating a tradition of annual dinners that was repeated for more than seventy years.

Perhaps temporarily carried away by the new celebrity of the parish's musical forces, Walter in an uncharacteristic gesture agreed to pay a regular salary, not only to its director, but to the quartet of soloists. He soon returned to his old ways, however; by August 1893 both Maina and the paid singers were gone, and the Church News announced that the choir, "which will be a volunteer one," would begin the fall season once again directed by Louisa Boone, who would continue as organist, "in which position she has given so much satisfaction for some years."[35]

The redefinition of the parish's mission that followed Father Walter's death in 1894 had an almost immediate effect on its music program. John Gloyd, and especially his dynamic young assistant and successor, Denis Stafford, realized that music played a central role in the liturgical ceremonies they considered so important for St. Patrick's. Of immediate concern was the challenge of producing a dignified but awesome musical setting for the opening ceremonies of the nation's first Eucharistic Congress scheduled for October 1895. They began by

34. Church News, 25 May 1890. See also, same paper, 26 Jan, 16 Feb, 2 Mar, and 13 Apr 1890.

35. Church News, 5 Aug 1893. The first regularly paid singers at St. Patrick's were: Blanche Mattingly, soprano; Mrs. J. Espata Daly, alto; T. Mulleady, tenor; and B. A. Ryan, bass. See same source, 2 Aug and 4 Oct 1890.

hiring L. Eugene French to direct the choir and a quartet of soloists, including two of those so unceremoniously dropped from the payroll the previous year. Louisa Boone remained as organist. The parish also formed a choir of thirty-five men and boys to sing in the sanctuary during high Mass and Sunday vesper services, even hiring instrumentalists to support these combined forces on special occasions such as their inaugural performance on St. Patrick's Day, 1895. Five months later, just eight weeks before the Eucharist Congress was to open, French suddenly resigned, leading Father Gloyd to rehire Professor Maina and appoint his wife contralto soloist.[36] On the eve of the opening of the congress, the choir sponsored a musicale and organ recital in the church, commanding fifty cents for general admission and the rather pricy fee of $1.00 for reserved seats.

This event was the last in a series of recitals that introduced the congregation to the full potential of its new pipe organ.[37] Designed and built by the well-known American craftsman Carl Barckhoff, the three-manual instrument, with 46 speaking stops, 8 couplers, 18 "automatic" connections, and 2,300 pipes, ranked among the city's largest. Its action, including that of the couplers, was mechanical, although a two-horse power motor operated the bellows. Its forty-one display pipes, ornamented in gold and colors to harmonize with the church's frescoes, stood above the twenty-foot-wide, quarter-sawn oak casework, which remains, a century later, the most visually prominent component of today's organ.[38]

At the time of the Eucharistic Congress the choir included forty-eight regular members, making it the largest such group in the city.[39] Without sacrificing its primary function in the church's liturgy, it once again had begun to play an important role in local musical circles, standing at the threshold of its greatest prominence. This transforma-

36. *Church News*, 20 Jul 1895. See also same source, 8 Sep 1894; 9 Feb and 16 Mar 1895; and 9 Jan 1898. Pauline Maina would retain her job for five years, although her frequent absences for maternity leave allowed the esteemed contralto Mary Grant to make her debut with the choir.

37. The dedicatory recitals featured the noted American organist, John Porter Lawrence. See *Church News*, 21 Sep 1895. The old organ was once more dismantled and moved to Carroll Hall. See same source, 10 Aug 1895.

38. *Church News*, 31 Aug 1895. The Barckhoff Church Organ Company of Mendelssohn, Pennsylvania, and Pomeroy, Ohio, ran a full-page ad in the 1904 edition of the *History of St. Patrick's* containing an illustration of the instrument as it appeared in 1895.

39. *Church News*, 21 Dec 1895.

tion was precipitated by a romance. In December 1898 Louisa Boone announced her resignation in anticipation of her forthcoming marriage to former director Eugene French. Her departure, and that of Maina a year later, left the way open for Armand Gumprecht to combine the positions of organist and choir director.

Gumprecht, who was also in charge of music at Georgetown University, was a first-rate artist, a pupil of Anton Bilse and S. B. Whitney of Boston. Under him the choir's repertoire enlarged dramatically, while the level of performance markedly improved with the addition of a group of highly talented soloists. Gumprecht's fondness for grandiose presentations and refulgent sound coincided perfectly with Stafford's ambitions for the church. As pastor, Stafford supported the director's efforts to recruit an orchestra of twenty-five musicians that regularly supplemented the choir on the increasing number of special occasions that filled the parish's calendar.[40] With these forces he performed large-scale renditions, not only of masterworks by Beethoven, Haydn, and Mozart, but also those by lesser-known and probably mercifully forgotten contemporaries Mercadante, Poniatowski, and Marzo. This penchant for works of brief notoriety was evident in 1904 when the choir's contribution to the dedication of the new school and rectory centered on the slender talents of English composer Sir Julius Benedict, whose lengthy oratorio, "Legend of St. Cecelia," was performed in the new Carroll Hall.[41] By 1907 the expense of such elaborate musical offerings had placed the parish in the canonically suspect position of charging admission for special services on St. Patrick's Day and during Holy Week!

Unfortunately, considering recent rulings by Pope Pius X concerning liturgical music, Gumprecht showed no comparable interest in chant or the more austere polyphony of earlier centuries. In 1903 the Pope issued a *motu proprio* that called for the elimination of female voices and modern harmonies from the liturgy and the reinstatement of Gregorian chant as the normative form in western church music. This decree, scheduled to go into effect in April 1909, imposed an impossible burden on the American church, where the European tradi-

---

40. *Washington Times,* 6 Dec 1903. Gumprecht's career at St. Patrick's was closely followed by the Washington correspondent of the *New Century.* See, for example, issues of 11 Jan 1902 and 30 Mar 1907. The parish's nine-piece string orchestra was also formed about this time, but while it performed at many parish functions, there is no record of its supporting the choir in church. See *The Patrician* (Apr 1909), 14.

41. *Star,* 21 Nov 1904.

tion of training boys in the choral arts was unknown and the expertise and money to support such an effort nonexistent. Cardinal Gibbons, a master of inactivity when the situation required, responded by noting that while some few churches were ready at once to follow the Pope's "advice" concerning female voices, in the majority of churches "some time must elapse before the full letter of the instructions can be carried out."[42] Meanwhile, he appointed a commission to propose a suitable diocesan response. He might have been divulging his own sentiments when he appointed Father William Russell, a singer of note and avid supporter of elaborate church music, to head the group.

As expected, the Russell commission was unable to propose a practical solution to the problem posed by the Roman directive. Its recommendations ignored the question of female voices and chant, concentrating instead on devising rules governing the types of music to be sung in church. It organized a review process to eliminate "modern" harmonies and the endless repetition of words and musical phrases that interrupted the flow of the sacred service. Other bishops generally followed Baltimore's lead. Citing differences between American and European music traditions, they did little in subsequent years to address the Pope's central demand, claiming that he had come to understand their problem and was not pressing for immediate change.[43]

What appeared a practical approach in the diocese at large was not necessarily the most prudent response at a church known far and wide for its elaborate musical programs and dwelling under the watchful eye of the Pope's delegate, a frequent visitor to its sanctuary. Father Russell's instinct leaned toward compromise. Soon after becoming pastor in 1908 he vowed that the parish choir, which he called "unsurpassed in the diocese," would continue its work unchanged.[44] At the same time and "in line with the movement for the reform of church music," he announced that St. Patrick's would organize a sanctuary choir of men and boys which would begin by replacing the mixed choir, as Gumprecht's forces came to be known, at benediction and vespers and would provide music during processionals and recessionals at high Mass. In less than a month, 80 boys and 20 men were training under "Professor" John O'Connor; they made their debut during Forty Hours devotions in October 1908. Substantial progress

42. As quoted in the Washington Post, 5 Mar 1904.

43. Spalding, Premier See, 312–13. The Star (10 Mar 1909) discussed the implications of the motu proprio and Russell's attempt to solve the problem it posed.

44. As quoted in the New Century, 27 Jun 1908.

under a second director, Henry T. Hall, was rewarded by an invitation from President Taft to perform at the White House on Easter Monday, 1909.[45]

Russell was unsatisfied with this achievement. The truth was his new sanctuary choir, while free of female voices, had not progressed much beyond saccharine hymns like the "Hark! Hark! My Soul" and "Send Down Thy Light" sung on Palm Sunday in 1909. What he really wanted was to establish a choir school at St. Patrick's that would teach Gregorian chant and support a male choir capable of performing the best of the church's musical heritage. To that end he hired R. Mills Silby, who was assistant choirmaster of London's Westminster Cathedral and a pupil of Richard Terry, one of England's foremost musicians. Silby had recently helped Terry launch what was widely regarded as a renaissance in Catholic polyphonic music in Britain. Upon his arrival at St. Patrick's in September 1909, he began testing and training boys between the ages of nine and thirteen from all over Washington, selecting a group of twenty-five boys and eight men.

The choir performed in public for the first time in October 1909 and became a regular feature of the parish's evening prayer service. It quickly began to acquire that characteristic and immensely satisfying timbre associated with the famed Westminster choristers, exciting favorable critical notice in Washington if not the whole-hearted understanding of a congregation raised on the rich harmonies of nineteenth-century choral music.[46] The singers were able to show off their new training during the first Pan-American Mass in November 1909 when they chanted the proper and sang Palestrina's 1530 "Veni Creator" while Gumprecht's choir, augmented by organ and orchestra, performed Beethoven's Mass in C.

This and other highly acclaimed performances of St. Patrick's musicians left the city unprepared for the Star's headline in June 1910 announcing the dismissal of Armand Gumprecht and three of the choir's principal soloists.[47] The pastor, who gave the musicians six month's

45. The Patrician, (Apr 1909), 8. The genesis of the choir and its first appearances were followed in the Catholic press. See, for example, New Century, 18 Jul and 19 Sep 1908 and The Patrician (Jul 1908), 20–21, and (Aug 1908), 16.

46. New Century, 25 Sep and 18 Dec 1909. For an extended analysis of the choir's sound, see undated review in the Washington Times, quoted in Fosselman's "A Downtown Parish," 225. The choir's work was exhaustively followed in The Patrician. See October 1909 (which listed the members of the original choir) and passim. Silby even found time to give a course of lectures on the "movement for the reform of church music" at Catholic University during his first months in Washington.

47. Star, 23 Jun 1910. See also similar summary in New Century, 2 Jul 1910.

THE SANCTUARY CHOIR, 1914. *R. Mills Silby (fourth row center) and his well-trained men and boys.*

notice, was unavailable for comment, the paper added, having left for an extended vacation in the Canadian wilderness immediately after mailing the dismissals. The *New Century* speculated that the firings presaged Silby's promotion to exclusive control over the parish's music program, an action, it claimed, that gave great satisfaction to local disciples of Gregorian music. The unopposed ascendancy of the mixed choir, in subsequent years under Jennie Glennon, effectively demolished such reasoning.[48] In fact Russell's reason for the mass firing remains a mystery, although it may well have been that St. Patrick's was proving too small for both Gumprecht and Silby, two highly trained

48. The date of Glennon's appointment in unknown. For some months after Gumprecht's departure Professor Gloetzner, who often assisted as organist, and Dr. Milton Boyce conducted the choir. See also, for example, *Bulletin of the Pan-American Union, 1911,* copy in Washingtoniana collection, DCPL, and *New Century,* 20 Dec 1911. Glennon, who was director at St. Matthew's, simply exchanged places with Boyce when St. Matthew's switched to an all-male choir. See interview, author with Everett Kinsman, 17 Dec 1992.

professionals with diametrically opposed views of church music styles. Glennon, also well trained, was a young local musician apparently quite willing to cooperate with Silby, whose star continued to rise throughout Russell's pastorate.

Another possible reason for Gumprecht's dismissal suggests itself in a strong editorial, almost certainly written by Russell, that appeared in *The Patrician* at the time. Branding the musical style in vogue in Catholic churches "garish and maudlin sentimentality," the author offered as examples renditions of the Gloria in waltz time, the popularity of light opera tunes "and even ragtime" in sacred services, with the use of organ stops more appropriate for the theater.[49] Gumprecht was certainly not guilty of such excesses, but his well-publicized dismissal, the timing of the editorial, and the increasing prominence given the sanctuary choir suggest that perhaps the ambitious pastor was not certain of Rome's continued indifference to the way the American church was responding to its *motu proprio*.

Russell remained a firm supporter of the boy's choir in his remaining years at St. Patrick's. He installed a so-called sanctuary or chancel organ and choir stalls for its use in the south transept in 1910, and in succeeding years helped Silby organize a summer training program at Chesapeake Beach, Maryland. There for several years the young musicians mixed lessons in chant with baseball and swimming at what the parish called "Camp Palestrina." Notice survives of successful performances by the group in Baltimore and elsewhere. The choir's local reputation was enhanced by frequent benefit concerts given throughout the city, such as one with the U.S. Marine Corps band in 1914 as well as its annual appearance in the Mayflower Hotel's Palm Court on Christmas Eve.[50] Silby remained choirmaster until after World War I, when he was succeeded by C. A. Benson, the group's long-time secretary and soloist. The sanctuary choir was finally disbanded by Monsignor Thomas as an austerity measure in 1930.

By then a considerably more experienced Jennie Glennon was fully in charge of the music program. Glennon was a skilled musician, who during her long directorship maintained high musical standards in performances of a limited repertoire centered on the French Roman-

49. *The Patrician* (Apr 1911), 9.

50. The new organ was dedicated during the women's retreat in October, 1910. See *The Patrician* (Oct 1910), 6. See also *New Century,* 13 Aug 1910, and Baltimore *Catholic Review,* 29 Jul and 5 Aug 1916. News of the choir's performances was frequently featured in the parish magazine, especially in various issues, 1914–1916.

tic school of the nineteenth century.[51] In 1915 the choir experimented briefly with chant for mixed voices and at least on one occasion chanted the simple responses during Sunday vespers. After the sanctuary choir was disbanded, Glennon organized a parish children's choir, which participated in a mass gathering of the city's Catholic choirs on Ascension Day, 1931.[52] Her main preoccupation, however, remained the great liturgical ceremonies that were so much a part of St. Patrick's parish life. For almost thirty years these many annual events were performed by the mixed choir (until 1930 with the assistance of the sanctuary choir) augmented by the organ and a large string orchestra complete with horns and harps.

If the artistic distinction of such large-scale musical efforts was uncertain, the theatrical effect was not, judging by the press reaction to the succession of Pan-American Masses and especially to the music program presented at the parish's 125th anniversary celebration in 1919. That occasion moved one witness to observe that "here the liturgy and chant of the Church are carried out with a completeness seldom found outside of Cathedrals."[53] Long forgotten, it seemed, was the central point of Pius X's exhortation. Archbishop Curley, frequently in the audience for these extravaganzas, once reminded the diocese of the "love and respect" all owed the Pope's pronouncements on church music and congratulated those parishes, obviously including St. Patrick's in this category, that had eliminated "objectionable" music from their programs.[54]

In 1932 the parish had the organ rebuilt. The Barckhoff organ was only thirty-seven years old, but, installed during the infancy of electricity, it lacked the electropneumatic action considered essential by later organists. Apologists could point to the urgent need for repairs, particularly where damage to leather couplings had caused leaks in the air reservoirs. In truth, changing musical taste and style dictate most organ renovations. In the 1930s, for example, it was fashionable to complain about the limitations imposed by the so-called tracker ac-

51. Interview, author with Mary Hope Stewart, 3 Jan 1992. Both Mrs. Stewart and her husband, Eugene, were involved with the Glennon choir.

52. Baltimore *Catholic Review,* 30 Oct 1915 and 10 Apr and 8 May 1931. Although the sanctuary choir traditionally sang vesper services, the mixed choir apparently sang on Sunday afternoons from time to time. See same source, 29 Sep 1917.

53. Rev. Michael J. Riordan, pastor of Immaculate Conception Church, Washington, as quoted in Baltimore *Catholic Review,* 3 May 1919.

54. Ltr., Curley to Rev. S. Leo Barley (liturgical music director), 11 Jun 31, as quoted in Baltimore *Catholic Review,* 12 Jun 1931.

tion of the old organs, just as fifty years later organists would decry the excesses of the modern electric instruments and seek to restore the purity of the older, mechanical action. In any event the 1932 renovation, which included installation of a new console and was done by the local firm of Lewis and Hitchcock for $10,000, retained approximately 50 percent of the original Barckhoff organ.[55]

An aging Jennie Glennon, her eyesight failing, finally relinquished her post in December 1941, and Monsignor Shehan appointed Eugene Stewart, a young musician with ties to the parish's music program, to replace her. Stewart was a musical *wunderkind*. As a pre-teenager he had studied under Glennon and served as organist at Holy Comforter. He continued to assist at St. Patrick's and, at the advanced age of fifteen, played the organ during the Pan-American Mass in 1924. Over Glennon's objections, Stewart later served as organist for the sanctuary choir before leaving to attend Baltimore's Peabody Conservatory.[56]

During the war Stewart had his pick of choir members from among the thousands of wartime residents in the Washington area. As usual the amateur group included a quartet of professional singers who received an ample $10 a week for their services. Stewart himself was paid $100 a month plus $5 for weddings and funerals. The professional musicians were expected to perform at the principal Mass on Sundays, holy days, and other special occasions as well as attend weekly rehearsals. Under Stewart the choir remained faithful to its long-cherished repertoire and the compositions with which it had become identified. Many Washingtonians, for example, made an annual pilgrimage to St. Patrick's Tre Ore (three hours) service on Good Friday to hear the choir sing Theodore Dubois's cantata, "The Seven Last Words of Christ," designed to accompany prayers and meditations offered by some eminent guest preacher.[57]

Stewart's taste in organ music ran to the full orchestral sound favored by the French masters of the late Romantic school, music that required an instrument of great expressive power. To this end he designed another series of major changes in the instrument after consultation with the acoustic architect Richard Whitelegg. Most of the in-

55. Interview, author with Jay Rader, 17 Dec 1992. For details of the renovation, see organ file, SPA.

56. Interview, author with Mary Hope Stewart. Eugene Stewart served as organist at Waugh Methodist Church for thirteen years before returning to St. Patrick's in 1941.

57. This popular work of the French composer was written in 1867 and apparently performed annually on Good Friday between 1908 and 1968.

novations occurred in the organ's swell division, where the addition of new reed stops added to the possible range of theatrical effects. As noted by the dean of Washington's music critics, Dr. Glenn Dillard Gunn, the reconstruction "wasted no time" on the ideals of the past, but added "so many orchestral voices that the whole range of modern organ literature is within the reach of the skilled performer." This second reconstruction of the organ, greatly complicated by wartime restrictions on the procurement of new parts, was executed by the M. P. Moeller Company of Hagerstown, Maryland.[58]

Stewart's inaugural recital on the new Moeller received high praise from Gunn and others, but such favorable notice did not protect him when Monsignor John Russell, a man with a considerably more utilitarian outlook on church music, became pastor. Although Russell respected Stewart's musicianship, he chafed at the director's perfectionism and unquestioned authority over things musical in the parish. Such an arrangement might have been acceptable to Monsignor Shehan, but Russell and Stewart came to disagree more and more sharply about the choir's role in the liturgy, and in 1948 Stewart lost his job. The post of organist was assumed by a series of well-known instrumentalists; Salvatore A. Lupica, the choir's gregarious tenor soloist, began his long service as director.[59]

At the beginning of the Lupica era the organist's chores were shared by Robert Twynham, then a student and later organist-choirmaster of the Baltimore's Mary Our Queen cathedral, and Everett Kinsman, who had assisted Stewart during the war and stayed on briefly to accompany the choir. William A. Maio filled in during the later part of 1949, and in December Monsignor Cowhig appointed Lawrence Sears to the post.[60] Sears, a well-known Washington recitalist and music critic, had strongly held musical views that frequently clashed with those of both Stewart and Lupica. Nevertheless he remained at St.

58. Stewart worked with the Moeller company on other organ projects, later designing two Moeller organs installed in St. Matthew's Cathedral. The Dunn review appeared in the Washington *Times Herald*, 17 Oct 1945.

59. Interviews, author with Msgr. Teletchea and Mary Hope Stewart. At Msgr. Arthur's recommendation, Msgr. Cartwright hired the recently dismissed Stewart to lead the cathedral choir. In a later review of Stewart's work at the cathedral, a critic called that choir "one of the city's best organized and trained." See *Star*, 1 Sep 1956.

60. Kinsman left St. Patrick's to become director of music at Sacred Heart and today serves in a similar capacity at Our Lady of Mercy. Maio was organist at a number of Washington's Catholic churches before his recent retirement. The following paragraphs are based on the author's interviews with Kinsman, William A. Maio, Jay Rader, and Mary Hope Stewart.

Patrick's for six years, during which time he designed a new organ console installed in the church by the Moeller Company in 1951. The principal alteration in the new console was a fourth manual, again an addition more closely related to the musician's ambitions than to practical necessity. If Sears hoped that the new fourth keyboard would lead eventually to the installation of more solo stops in the organ, he was disappointed. With the exception of chimes and a series of couplers, the fourth manual has remained silent for forty years.

Beginning in May 1955 Jean Phillips, a local pianist and organist, accompanied the choir. In addition to enhancing the liturgy, these talented musicians worked to keep St. Patrick's involved in Washington's musical life. Vocal recitals became a regular feature of the parish's calendar of events, while organ recitals became commonplace, not only those that featured the parish's own instrumentalists, but also artists from the city's other churches and such international stars as Pierre Cochereau, the organist at Notre Dame in Paris. Reminiscent of doings in Gumprecht's day, the individual choir soloists presented recitals, such as those in early 1955 featuring Lupica, contralto Claire Howard, and soprano June Barberis. As might be expected, the announcement that the popular Irish singers, the Four Lads, had interrupted their American tour to sing during Mass at St. Patrick's, sparked much local interest in the church's music program.[61]

Everything was on a more modest scale than in previous decades. Where once a full orchestra was on hand for special events, a string quartet was now employed. Although the choir retained its discipline and good sound, there was no noticeable expansion of repertoire. Familiar works of Dubois and Gounod continued to be performed regularly, with Mozart and Haydn Masses still used, although at times in severely truncated versions. Fauré's Requiem added to the reverence of Father Sylvester Hoffman's funeral obsequies in 1966, but except for an occasional performance of a motet by Igor Stravinsky, works by modern masters were unknown. As one choir member from that era summed up his experience: "We had great fun, made a good sound, but much of what we sang was second-rate."[62]

Since the 1920s most members of the choir had been drawn from the parish's large extern congregation. They came from all parts of the

61. *Catholic Standard*, 4 Feb and 22 Jul 1955 and 27 May 1956.
62. Interview, author with Vincent Walter, 4 Feb 1993. For a visitor's reaction to the choir's work at that time, see Joan Schampp, "A Heartfelt 'Deo Gratias'" for Mass Sung in Latin," *Green Bay Register*, 14 Feb 1969.

ST. PATRICK'S CHOIR, 1948, *with pastor John J. Russell (center), Fathers Arthur (left), and Dade (right), and director Salvatore Lupica (seated right with tie).*

metropolitan area, some travelling considerable distances to attend rehearsals and services. This era came to an end in the late 1960s, when Lupica's sudden death coincided with development of a new attitude toward the old downtown neighborhood. Like the congregation itself, the choir experienced a rapid drop in membership after 1968; when Monsignor Arthur arrived in 1971 he found the disintegration almost complete with the organist-director informing him of her intention to resign in the fall.

This crisis prompted Arthur to contract with Michael Cordovana, a professor in Catholic University's music department, to supply the church with a part-time choir, using some twenty-four university students to sing at the major Mass on Sunday before going off to provide similar services elsewhere. Especially appealing to the discerning, the professionalism of this well-trained group permitted it to take advantage of the church's lively acoustics to perform an exceptionally broad range of music. For the first time St. Patrick's rang with the sixteenth-century compositions of Heinrich Schutz as well as works of the modern master Olivier Messiaen. Yet even this satisfactory arrangement proved short-lived when the parish's continuing financial problems forced Arthur to choose between short-changing the school or abolishing the music program altogether. In 1975 he canceled the arrangement with Cordovana, who along with guest conductor Jack Ay still provided suitable music for St. Patrick's Day and other special occasions. For a time Joseph Darling accompanied congregational singing on Sundays, but then the music ceased altogether as the church entered a decade of silence.

The silence was broken in 1988 when St. Patrick's appointed Jay Rader as its first minister of music. Rader immediately took on the task of designing a program suited to the parish's changed circumstances, the requirements of the post-Vatican II liturgy, and the evolving musical tastes of American Catholics. He began by assembling a small group of professional musicians (eight to twelve singers, a cantor, and various instrumentalists for special feasts) capable of accompanying the liturgy in a wide variety of styles drawn from across the centuries. In association with Dr. Cyrilla Barr, a professor at Catholic University, the parish also began once more to sponsor public concerts by gifted choirs and soloists that attract audiences to the old church in keeping with its mission to the central city. With these modest but highly skilled forces, the parish begins its third century of sacred music in the capital.

Drama at St. Patrick's

The parish's identification with the dramatic arts is largely a twenti-eth-century phenomenon. The old church-sponsored dramatic clubs with their hastily produced, amateurish performances enjoyed consid-erable vogue in post–Civil War Washington, and it can be assumed that with their access to a large auditorium St. Patrick's various soci-eties joined in the lively entertainment. An 1895 notice mentions the girls of St. Vincent's appearing in a dramatic cantata, "The Little Gypsy," at Carroll Hall, and later that year members of Carroll Insti-tute, with major help from parishioners, inaugurating their popular minstrel shows. In 1896 the institute's dramatic club rented the Lafayette Square Opera House for a production of "David Garrick," which almost certainly counted many St. Patrick's parishioners in its cast.[63]

The genesis of what would become a major Washington amateur theatrical group can be traced to the productions of St. Patrick's Sun-day School Association in the early years of this century. Initial pro-ductions by the teachers adhered to the pattern set by other amateur groups, a one-time performance usually offered as an overture to a parish dance or euchre party. By 1907, however, the association had be-gun to sponsor more ambitious projects, including multi-performance productions of three-act comedies like "House of Too Much Trouble" and "Contrary Mary." There were as well popular reviews that fea-tured dramatic readings and solo performances by professional musi-cians from St. Patrick's choir accompanied by the parish's string or-chestra. In 1910, for example, the Sunday school teachers presented a musical review, "For One Night Only," written by Denis E. Connell and John O. Allen, both leading figures in local dramatic societies who would go on to play important roles in the St. Patrick's Players a decade later. Reviewing this duo's production of "House of Too Much Trouble," the parish magazine boasted that Connell and Allen were "known throughout the city for the best of amateur stage work."[64]

---

63. St. Patrick's sponsorship of amateur theatricals in the late nineteenth century were mentioned in the Catholic press. See, for example, *Church News,* 19 Oct 1895 and 15 Feb and 25 May 1896.

64. *The Patrician* (Feb 1907), 13. See also *New Century,* 2 Apr 1910. It is likely that Con-nell and Allen were founding members of the Association's theatrical club, which in-cluded fifteen regular members by 1910. For earlier notice of the association's activi-ties, see, for example, *The Patrician* (Apr 1909), 14, and (Dec 1909), 5, and *New Century,* 9 Feb 1907 and 1 May 1909.

Under the guidnace of these two gifted writers and producers, and especially influenced by Mrs. William Bognam, who directed many performances in the World War I era, the association's productions became better rehearsed, more elaborate, and money makers for local charities. The group was confident enough to take on plays by the popular priest-dramatist Hugh Benson and pre-World War I favorites like "The Tyrolian Queen" and "A Good Fellow." In 1911 Monsignor Russell became an active associate when he stepped in to direct a production of Benson's "A Mystery Play," a Nativity story with music supplied by the boys of the sanctuary choir.[65] By 1914 the association could charge fifty cents for adults and a quarter for children to see such plays as the comedy-farce "O Susannah!" A perennial group favorite was "My New Curate," which must have been seen at one time or another by every Catholic in Washington. With assistant pastor John McNamara serving as moderator, the association netted over $1,500 during the 1915–16 season for the Ursuline day care nursery, Martha House, the temporary shelter for unemployed women, as well as projects sponsored by the Ladies of Charity and St. Vincent de Paul Society.[66] Names of cast members from this era are mostly lost, with one notable exception: the young Washington singer, Kate Smith, appeared with the group around 1918.[67]

These various theatrical ventures probably never transcended the best work done by any of the city's more ambitious amateur groups. In an altogether different category, however, was the group's successor, the St. Patrick's Players. Organized in 1920, this extraordinary acting troupe is closely linked to the name of its founder, Francis J. Hurney. Father Hurney was convinced that serious amateur theater could be useful in channeling the postwar generation's love of music and dance into wholesome diversions and useful causes. Few things were more helpful, he once told a reporter, than "the enthusiasm aroused by amateur theatricals for encouraging young people to live the lives they should."[68] Along with the popular comedies and musical reviews,

65. *The Patrician* (Jan 12, 1912), 10–11.

66. *New Century*, 22 Dec 1911 and 1 Feb 1913 and Baltimore *Catholic Review*, 17 Jun and 30 Dec 1916. *The Patrician* often reviewed the plays, advertised coming attractions, and assessed the gate. See, for example, (Apr 1914), 7, and (Jan 1916), 7.

67. Father Hurney later introduced Smith to the New York impresarios, thus launching her national career. See *Catholic Standard*, 27 Feb 1986.

68. Detroit *Free Press*, 29 Aug 1926, copy in the St. Patrick's Players Press book, AAW. Unless otherwise noted, the following account of the Players is based on the hundreds of news clippings, handbills, reviews, and business communications concerning the Players collected in this valuable source.

Hurney also expected his actors to employ their developing dramatic abilities and sense of spectacle to reach large audiences with what he called "a practical and beautiful lesson in religion."[69] Beginning in its second year, the Players produced a religious drama each Lenten season, the so-called Passion play, that came to rival in concept if not in size or impact the famed productions at Oberammergau. These plays were attended by audiences in Washington and along the east coast numbering in the scores of thousands.

Hurney was well equipped to lead such a group. Closely connected with leaders of the American theater through his work with the Catholic Actor's Guild and a talented author, producer, and director in his own right, the young priest gathered together more than 300 young Washingtonians who served as actors, musicians, designers, and technicians. Hurney supervised all productions, selecting the plays and casts and writing many of the review skits, leaving Denis Connell and Edward O'Brien to direct the shows and supervise the casts. Connell and C. A. Benson, the director of the parish's sanctuary choir, also wrote several of the musicals. The group boasted a large backstage staff and a corps of set designers under Jean F. Hill, who supervised the staging, and technicians under Edward Duchesne, the lighting director. Elizabeth Bogan directed the all-female Players Orchestra, and Estelle Murray, a prominent local dance teacher, selected, trained, and directed the dancers. Father John Barrett, another parish assistant, was the group's business manager.

This latter position grew increasingly important as the Players evolved into a large, money-making operation. A nonprofit organization, the Players in their prime regularly realized more than $1,000 at each of fifty annual performances. Receipts from each opening night went to the parish; later earnings were turned over to a wide range of charities, such as the St. Vincent de Paul Society, Catholic orphanages, rural parishes and missions, international war relief, and, reflecting a special interest of its founder, the American Legion. Every production included one performance for disabled soldiers at Walter Reed and the veterans at Old Soldiers' Home. The group also toured. By the mid-1920s it was appearing on behalf of local sponsors, sometimes in large theaters in major cities between New York and Richmond, just as often on hastily-built stages in scores of parish auditoriums.

The Players' first season (1920–21) was limited to two musical reviews. In subsequent years it settled into a routine of three new pro-

69. Quoted in the Washington *Herald,* 21 Nov 1926.

ductions each season, a musical comedy in the fall, the Passion play during Lent, and a spring review. In its second season, the Players presented forty-two performances and collected $20,000 in receipts.[70] Typically, a production would play in Washington for a two-week run before going on the road, presenting a series of one- or two-night stands that featured not only current productions but sometimes reprieves of old hits. At first most Washington performances were mounted in Carroll Hall, but the popularity of the group and the need for larger stage accommodations, especially for the Passion plays, led to the regular engagement of local theaters like the National, Schubert-Belasco, and President.

New York producers followed the group closely, and were often on hand to review the shows. At times they arranged with Hurney to have the Players give some of their material a pre-Broadway tryout.[71] They frequently tried to lure the more talented performers away from Washington with tempting job offers. Estelle Murray, the dancer director, rejected an offer in 1923 to star in a musical comedy on Broadway, while a group of her colleagues, who managed to keep their government jobs while appearing in Washington vaudeville productions, turned down a $500-a-week offer to join the vaudeville circuit. Other stage-struck performers, however, went on to become professional actors. Foremost among these was Margaret Gorman, the first Miss America and star of the Players' "Leave it to Pierre" and "You Take It," who appeared on Broadway, as did Edna and Marie Bowman, Helen Ault, Rosemary Lynch, and others. Helen Hayes, who was a member of Father Hurney's theatrical group at Sacred Heart parish before World War I, remained closely associated with his work at St. Patrick's after launching her professional career in Ziegfeld's Follies.[72]

Much was made of the difficult tryouts undergone by prospective actors, whose admission depended on a winning performance in a vaudeville skit or a dramatic reading before an exacting panel of peers.

70. The group's activities were fully covered in the Baltimore *Catholic Review*. See, for example, 15 Jul 1922, 31 Jan and 7 Nov 1925, and 19 Nov 1926. Statistics on the 1921–22 season are from Washington *Times*, 17 Sep 1922.

71. The 1922 production of "Bonnie Prince Charlie," for example, used material from what would later be a Broadway hit, "Whirlwind of New York."

72. Hayes, then known as Helen Brown, appeared under Father Hurney's direction in several productions of the group established at Sacred Heart. When Hurney formed the Players in 1920, Hayes, already a professional performer, became a sponsor. Although several news accounts claim that Hayes performed with the Players, no record survives of her appearing in any production, nor did the late actress remember any such performance.

ST PATRICK'S PLAYERS *(left to right) Dorothy Heil, Clara Priddy, Helen Kearney, Mary Kane, Eleanor Giovanetti and Helen Sullivan.*

The musical review, easily adapted to the talents of Hurney's performers, formed the mainstay of the troupe's repertoire. Described by Hurney as "nothing more than a series of singing and dancing specialties broken up with an occasional humorous skit," the reviews nevertheless demanded the well-executed dance numbers, topical songs, and fast pacing of professional productions. Original reviews such as "A Broadway Prince," "Mistaken Mimi," and "Patter Review" provided audiences with shows that Hurney confessed "even the professional producers admit are pretty good."[73] He went on to stress that all Players' productions were "clean" and "suitable for every member of the family." Unlike his persistent critics, the priest obviously saw nothing to fear in performances of the latest dances that brought the Roaring Twenties to St. Patrick's.

73. Quoted in Washington *Herald,* 21 Nov 1926.

Although the musicals and reviews clearly excited the most attention among the New York producers and would eventually lead to the
group's disbandment, it was the annual Passion plays that attracted
the Players' largest and most influential audiences. These great religious spectacles were part of a movement spreading across postwar
America in imitation of the Oberammergau presentations. They enjoyed the strong support of the hierarchy and Catholic press. The
Catholic Review, for example, in commenting on Washington's first
Passion play, Gonzaga's presentation of Aurelio Palmieri's "On The
Slopes of Calvary" in 1918, proclaimed that since America could not
go to Oberammergau, Catholics needed to recreate its sacred drama
in the New World. Reflecting the views of many in the hierarchy, the
paper concluded that special blessings would accrue when every city
in the nation had its own Lenten passion play.[74]

These views neatly coincided with Hurney's own belief that the
Passion plays were an effective form of religious instruction and outreach. In that spirit the Players made a sacred drama the centerpiece
of each performance season. Beginning with a production in 1923 of
"On the Slopes of Calvary" that featured a cast of seventy-five actors
with the sanctuary choir singing an original score by its director, C. A.
Benson, the group went on to stage multiple productions of "The Upper Room," "The Holy City," "The Vision," and "Little Poor Man," a
drama based on the life of Francis of Assisi.[75] These later productions
were costly affairs using recent advances in scenery production and
costume design that stressed historical accuracy. Casts often included
more than two hundred performers and musicians. Before the troupe
was disbanded, its leaders were developing plans for a permanent outdoor amphitheater where these religious dramas might be performed
in a setting similar to European presentations.

The Players' fall from grace has already been told.[76] Other parishes,
most notably Sacred Heart, St. Aloysius, and St. Dominic in the early
decades and St. Paul's, St. Gabriel's, and Holy Trinity in more recent
times, have been closely associated with dramatic groups. For one
shining moment, however, St. Patrick's led the way in seeking better
understanding and a mutually beneficial relationship between the
church and the stage.

74. Baltimore *Catholic Review,* 9 Feb and 16 Mar 1918.
75. The Passion plays were also well covered in the Catholic press. See, for example, Baltimore *Catholic Review,* 29 Dec 1923, 29 Mar 1924, 28 Mar 1925, and 12 Mar 1926.
76. For an account of the Players' disbandment, see chapter 10, above.

Epilogue

CENTRAL TO THE HISTORY of St. Patrick's is the image of people at prayer. Consideration of institutional development, ecological change, and societal responsibilities aside, the essential truth of this story is that for two centuries many thousands of Washingtonians have knelt at this site, trusting in the promise of God's presence where two or more gather in his name. Worship creates the continuity that unites members of today's congregation with those who participated in the same ancient liturgies during the city's infancy. Worship is also that which nourishes hope for the future as a greatly changed parish embarks on its third century of service to the city and people of Washington.

Continuity was evident in the huge crowds gathered at St. Patrick's during Holy Week, 1993. Good Friday, for example, found the old edifice once again jammed to the doors, the variety of people in prayer evoking Lorenzo Johnson's image of the church in 1856:

here may be seen the genteel in appearance kneeling at the side of the day-laborer, who might have been born in other lands, and at the same time with persons of color, as if to say, "In the presence of God all distinctions are forgotten."[1]

Although outwardly transformed by late twentieth-century custom and costume, the same such people could be

1. *National Intelligencer*, 29 Apr 1856.

found in the pews on Good Friday, 1993. Members of the city's social elite along with business and government executives, men and women, white, black, and Hispanic, once again knelt beside Washington's clerks and laborers, its ubiquitous tourists and shoppers, immigrant newcomers, and streetpeople. In 1993 prayers were all recited in English, the choir numbered just four highly trained members, and in place of semi-operatic music of old, a cantor led the people in a simple Negro spiritual. Even so, the atmosphere remained uncannily like that described by Johnson almost a century and a half before— "the solemn stillness, the undivided directness of attention, the devout and earnest manner . . . the impressive sense of an awe-abiding presence."

The fact that few in this devout but motley congregation reside within parish boundaries, a reality predicted with considerable trepidation long ago by Jacob Walter, causes no special concern today. The congregation has clearly survived the crisis of recent decades. While no one expects a speedy return to the exciting postwar crowds that greeted Bishop Hannan in the 1950s, it is clear, as casual visitors turn into familiar faces, that once again a new congregation is forming.

As in the past, this most recent reversal in parish fortunes is closely linked to changes in the neighborhood surrounding it. Those at St. Patrick's on Good Friday walked out into one of Washington's beguiling spring days to be jostled on crowded sidewalks. True, many they met were tourists or government workers on lunch hour shopping runs; the same streets would see few pedestrians that night or on Sunday morning. Yet the upbeat atmosphere in the old downtown is undeniable. The crowded hotels, busy office buildings, and quickening commerce all promise new life for the region and a new challenge for St. Patrick's.

After so many decades of practical experience, the old church obviously fits comfortably into today's working definition of the parish as a faith community without boundaries. But with new definition comes new responsibility. St. Patrick's mission in its third century transcends the reality of the sacramental way station that emerged during World War II. As recently defined by Cardinal Hickey, that mission calls on the parish to evangelize the government and business leaders and their staffs working in the neighborhood, reach out in ecumenical and interfaith collaboration with other traditions, and help members of its community realize their baptismal identity in the Body of Christ.[2]

2. Ltr., Hickey to Essex, 11 Sep 1987, SPA.

Few things are totally new in any two-hundred-year-old institution—the cardinal's list little more than underscores what the priests and congregation on Tenth Street have been about for many decades. Yet if the parish's mission is timeless, the city it serves is constantly changing, a fact that promises for St. Patrick's a future no less challenging than the one faced by Father Caffry and his little congregation two centuries ago.

APPENDIX

Pastors and Administrators

Anthony Caffry	1794–1804
William Matthews	1804–1854
Timothy J. O'Toole	1854–1860
Jacob Ambrose Walter	1860–1894
John Gloyd	1894–1901
Denis J. Stafford	1901–1908
William T. Russell	1908–1917
Cornelius F. Thomas	1917–1941
Lawrence J. Shehan	1941–1945
John J. Russell	1945–1948
James E. Cowhig*	1948–1952
Philip M. Hannan	1952–1965
Sylvester M. Hoffman*	1965–1966
William H. Hoffman	1966–1971
R. Joseph Dooley*	1971
E. Robert Arthur	1971–1987
Michael diTeccia Farina*	1987
Maurice T. Fox	1987
Donald S. Essex	1987–

*Denotes parish administrator

Associate Pastors and Priests in Residence

Stephen L. Dubuisson, S.J.	1822–1825
Gabriel Richard	1823–1825
Jeremiah Keiley, S.J.	1826–1826
Peter Schreiber	1827–1831
Rev. Wainwright	1831
Timoleon (Jean) Figeac	1831–1836
Charles Constantine Pise	1832–1833
John Philip Donelan	1836–1841
Henry Myers	1841–1843
James B. Donelan	1843–1846
William D. Parsons	1846–1847
Thomas Patrick Foley	1847–1850
Michael Slattery	1849–1852
Hippolyte DeNeckere, S.J.	1850–1855
James A. Ward, S.J.	1850–1852
Timothy J. O'Toole	1852–1854
Alphonsus Charlier, S.J.	1853–1854
Francis E. Boyle	1854–1862
T. I. Stephen	1862
Patrick F. McCarthy	1863–1866
William Jordan	1865
John J. Keane	1866–1878
Henry Reardon	1868
Owen B. Corrigan	1873
Lodovac A. Morgan	1878–1880
J. B. A. Brouillet	1880
Rev. Quigly	1880–1881
Thomas Kervick	1881–1882
Cornelius F. Thomas	1882–1886
John T. Whelan	1886
Joseph F. McGee	1887–1899
Denis J. Stafford	1894–1901
Thomas S. Dolan	1899–1903
John Gaynor	1901–1903
Thomas E. McGuigan	1903–1917
William J. Carroll	1904–1914
James A. Smyth	1905–1920

Nicholas Jaselli	1910
John M. McNamara	1911–1920
Martin P. J. Egan	1914
John I. Barrett	1917
Francis J. Hurney	1920–1929
John J. Cartwright	1920–1933
Lawrence J. Shehan	1923–1941
John E. Graham	1930
Joseph D. Amon	1930–1933
Francis E. Montgomery	1932–1938
Francis J. Kelly	1933–1939
George F. Curtiss	1933–1934
Thomas B. Dade	1934–1950
E. Robert Arthur	1938–1948
James E. Cowhig	1939–1948
Stephen Hogan	1944–1949
Joseph C. Eckert	1948–1957
Joseph L. Teletchea	1948–1957
Leo J. Coady	1949
Patrick J. Nagle	1950–1958
Sylvester M. Hoffman	1952–1965
Milton A. Schellenberg	1957–1960
Thomas W. Lyons	1957–1961
Joseph J. Naughton	1958–1963
George G. Pavloff	1958–1970
Robert Ferguson	1960–1961
Francis J. Murphy	1961–1964
Joseph M. O'Connell	1962–1968
Donald P. Brice	1963–1966
David J. Conway	1964–1969
Armand F. LaVaute	1966
William F. Farrell	1966–1971
Henry J. Januszkiewicz	1968–1972
R. Joseph Dooley	1969–1977
Robert Barrett	1970
John Bellwoar, S.J.	1970–1975
Richard W. Burton	1970–1975
John J. Higgins	1971–1977
Michael diTeccia Farina	1976–

Frank Flaherty	1976
George Costabile	1976
Robert D. Duggan	1977–1980
Charles D. Gorman	1977–1985
James P. Meyers	1980–1986
Robert E. Cousins	1984–1987
P. Miguel Quinones	1986
Kevin T. Hart	1986–1990
Edward B. Pritchard	1987–
Peter J. Vaghi	1988–
G. Paul Herbert	1990–1992

(Sources suggest that Benedict J. Fenwick, John Smith, R. Duffy, George Fenwick, P. Walsh, and Bernard McGuire, all Jesuit fathers, also assisted at St. Patrick's for brief periods in the nineteenth century.)

Principals of St. Patrick's Academy

Sister M. Eusebia Brown	1901–1902
Sister M. Redempta Maher	1902–1909
Sister M. Veronica Dunn	1909–1920
Sister M. Angelita Zahn	1920–1922
Sister M. Reparata Gannon	1922–1923
Sister M. Angelita Zahn	1923–1927
Sister M. Agneze Simmons	1927–1933
Sister M. Ethel Dodd	1933–1935
Sister M. Florian Daniels	1935–1941
Sister M. Angels Everett	1941–1947
Sister M. Victoria Diehl	1947–1949
Sister M. Presentina Ryan	1949–1952
Sister Mary Justine Marr	1952–1955
Sister M. Agneze Simmons	1955–1956
Sister M. Jovanna Hanlon	1956–1962
Sister Miriam André Williams	1962–1968
Sister Marie Julie Shea	1968–1975
Sister Mary Louise Full	1975–1981
Sister Eleanor Anne McCabe	1981–1985

BIBLIOGRAPHY

Abbreviations

AAB	Archives of the Archdiocese of Baltimore
AAW	Archives of the Archdiocese of Washington
APF	Archives of the Propaganda Fide
Acta	*Acta Sacrae Congregationis*
Cong. Generali	*Scritture originali riferite nelle Congregazioni Generali*
Congressi	*Scritture riferite nei Congressi, America Centrale dal Canada all'Istmo di Panama*
Lettere	*Lettere e Decreti della Sacra Congregazione*
DCPL	Public Library of the District of Columbia (Washingtoniana Collection)
GUA	Georgetown University Archives
Hughes, *Documents*	Thomas Hughes. *History of the Society of Jesus in North America: Colonial and Federal.* 4 vols. London: Longmans, Green & Co., 1907–1917
JCP	Thomas O. Hanley, ed. *The John Carroll Papers.* 3 vols. (Notre Dame: University of Notre Dame Press, 1976)
LC	Library of Congress
NARA	National Archives and Records Administration
OR	*War of the Rebellion: A Compilation of Official Records of the Union and Confederate Armies* (Washington)
RCHS	*Records of the Columbia Historical Society*
SAB	Sulpician Archives, Baltimore
SPA	St. Patrick's Church Archives
WL	*Woodstock Letters*

Manuscript and Archival Materials

The Archives of the Archdiocese of Baltimore is the major source of primary materials on St. Patrick's parish. The papers of the archbishops from Carroll through Curley, the Parish Notitiae, the Nelligan Collection (separately organized files of chancellor Msgr. Joseph Nelligan), and the diocesan Necrology file contain scores of documents that help detail the evolution of the parish during its first 150 years. The parish historical files of the Archives of the Archdiocese of Washington, recently organized by Mr. Bernier, provide some items of interest about St. Patrick's and the two national churches within its boundaries. The parish archives, on the other hand, is a surprisingly modest collection, considering the antiquity of the institution, although its records relating to parish finances and real estate transactions remain the major source for this important subject. Copies of many of the documents cited in this study have recently been added to the St. Patrick's collection.

The Archives of the Propaganda Fide contains documents indispensible to an understanding of the role of William Matthews in the Philadelphia trustee dispute as well as the various efforts in the nineteenth century to make Washington a separate diocese. Most of the items concerning the American church in this extensive Vatican collection have been identified and microfilmed. A copy is on deposit in the Library of the University of Notre Dame. A comprehensive calendar of these documents was created by Finbar Kenneally, et al. See their *United States Documents in the Propaganda Fide Archives: A Calendar.* 7 vols. Washington: Academy of American Franciscan History, 1966–77. The Georgetown University Archives is the depository of the archives of the Maryland Province of the Society of Jesus, which includes correspondence between William Matthews and various Jesuits, the papers of Stephen Dubuisson and Anthony Kohlmann, and records of the Washington Seminary. Similarly, the Sulpician Archives of Baltimore contains numerous items of interest concerning the pastorate of William Matthews and his relations with diocesan officials.

Documents of importance to the history of Washington are scattered through several record depositories. A major source is the National Archives and Records Administration, which preserves several collections of primary material about the city of special importance to St. Patrick's history, including Records of the Commissioners for the District of Columbia, 1791–1802, RG 42; Petitions to the House of Rep-

resentatives, 1800–1860, RG 233; Petitions to the Senate, 1816–1878, RG
46. The District of Columbia's Office of the Recorder of Deeds maintains a record of all real estate transactions in Square 376 back to the
foundation of the city. The Historical Society of Washington, D.C., as
it is now called, possesses an important collection of maps and pictures along with a reference file on Washington institutions, including
St. Patrick's. Its publication, *Records of the Columbia Historical Society*, is
a major source of diaries, articles, and addresses pertaining to the history of the District. Items of exceptional interest to the parish are
listed individually under secondary materials, below. Finally, the
Washingtoniana Collection of the D.C. Public Library possesses, in
addition to a fine collection of secondary materials on the city's history, an extensive vertical file on many local institutions, including St.
Patrick's.

Interviews

Between July 1991 and February 1993 the author interviewed the following people about their special knowledge of the recent history of
St. Patrick's Church and Academy. A record of these interviews—in
the case of Archbishop Hannan, a full transcript—has been added to
the St. Patrick's archives.

Msgr. E. Robert Arthur
Rev. Donald Brice
Professor Michael Cordovana
Rev. David J. Conway
Mrs. Catherine Cleary Cordes
Msgr. Thomas B. Dade
Msgr. R. Joseph Dooley
Msgr. John Tracy Ellis
Msgr. Michael diTeccia Farina
Sister Mary Louise Full, C.S.C.
Mrs. Margaret Cleary Grambo
Sister Jovanna Hanlon, C.S.C.
Archbishop Philip M. Hannan
Miss Ruth Hellmuth
Mr. Everett Kinsman
Sister Eleanor Anne McCabe, C.S.C.
Rev. James P. Meyers
Mr. Charles J. Patrak

Mr. George G. Pavloff
Sister Marie Julie Shea, C.S.C.
Mrs. Mary Hope Stewart
Msgr. Joseph L. Teletchea
Mrs. Margaret Atchison Van Heuckeroth
Mr. Vincent Walter
Sister Miriam André Williams, C.S.C.
Mrs. Mary Grambo Woods

Newspapers and Bulletins

The author systematically screened the following Washington newspapers: *National Intelligencer; Evening Star* and *Sunday Star* (cited in notes as the *Star*); local Catholic papers, the *Church News* (1886–1900); *New Century* (1900–1904); and *Catholic Standard* (1951 to the present). Also screened were the *U.S. Catholic Magazine* (1840–1850); and two Baltimore papers, the *Catholic Mirror* (1850–1908); and *Baltimore Catholic Review* (later *Catholic Review* (1913–1950). Other newspapers consulted (all Washington papers): *Evening Express, Herald, Metropolitan, National Republican, Post, Times,* and *Times-Herald.* (A collection of articles about St. Patrick's from early Washington papers, especially the *National Republican,* is filed in the Toner Collection, LC.) *The Patrician,* the parish magazine published between 1907 and 1917, is of special importance to the social history of St. Patrick's in the early twentieth century. An almost complete run of this bulletin has been preserved in St. Patrick's archives.

Secondary Materials

Abell, William S. ed. *Patrick Cardinal O'Boyle as His Friends Knew Him.* Washington, 1986.

Ahern, Patrick H. *The Life of John Keane: Educator and Archbishop, 1839–1918.* Milwaukee: Bruce Publ., 1955.

Altenhofel, Jennifer L. "The Irish Century: A Story of Irish Immigrants and the Irish Comunity in the District of Columbia, 1850–1950." Paper submitted to D.C. Community Humanities Council, 1992.

_____. "Irish Women in Antebellum Washington: Their Lives and Labor." American University Research Seminar paper, 1992.

Appleby, R. Scott. *"Church and Age Unite!" The Modernist Impulse in American Catholicism.* Notre Dame: University of Notre Dame Press, 1992.

Anderson, George M. "Bernardine Wiget, S.J., and the St. Aloysius Civil War Hospital in Washington, D.C." *The Catholic Historical Review* 76 (Oct 1990): 734–64.

_____. "The Civil War Diary of John Abell Morgan, S.J., A Jesuit Scholastic of the Maryland Province." *Records of the American Catholic Historical Society of Philadelphia.* 101 (Fall 1990): 33–54.

Arnebeck, Bob. *Through A Fiery Trial: Building Washington, 1790–1800.* Lanham: Madison Books, 1991.

Barry, John P. "The Know-Nothing Party in the District of Columbia." Master's thesis, The Catholic University of America, 1933.

Billington, Ray A. *The Protestant Crusade, 1800–1860; A Study of the Origins of American Nativism.* New York: Macmillan, 1938.

Bland, Sister Joan. *Hibernian Crusade: The Story of the Catholic Total Abstinence Union of America.* Washington: The Catholic University of America Press, 1951.

Boehmer, Charles L. *History of St. Mary's Church of the Mother of God, Washington, D.C.* Washington, 1946.

Branson, Sister Serena. "Two Child-Care Institutions Administered by the Sisters of Charity in the District of Columbia." Master's thesis, The Catholic University of America, 1948.

Brislen, Sister M. Bernetta. "The Episcopacy of Leonard Neale, Second Archbishop of Baltimore." *Historical Records and Studies* 34 (1945): 20–III.

Brown, Letitia W. "Residence Patterns of Negroes in the District of Columbia, 1800–1860." *RCHS* 69–70 (1969–70): 66–79.

Bryan, Wilhelmus B. *A History of the National Capital.* 2 vols. New York: Macmillan, 1914–16.

Caemmerer, H. Paul. "Early Washington and Its Art," *RCHS* 48–49 (1946–1947): 209–25.

Carey, Patrick W. *People, Priests, and Prelates: Ecclesaistical Democracy and the Tensions of Trusteeism.* Notre Dame: University of Notre Dame Press, 1987.

Clark, Allen C. *Greenleaf and Law in the Federal City.* Washington: Roberts, 1901.

Connelly, James F. "The Visit of Archbishop Gaetano Bedini to the United States of America (June 1853–February 1854)." Doctoral dissertation, Pontifical Gregorian University, 1960.

Corrigan, Owen B. *The Catholic Schools of the Archdiocese of Baltimore: A Study in Diocesan History.* Baltimore, 1924.

Davis, Henry E. "Ninth and F Streets and Thereabouts." *RCHS* 5 (1902): 238–58.

De Carlo, Nicholas. *The Parish of the Holy Rosary in Washington, D.C.: Twenty-five Years of Mission Work, 1913–1938.* Washington, 1938.

Dolan, Jay P. *The American Catholic Experience: A History from Colonial Times to the Present.* New York: Doubleday, 1985.

_____. *Catholic Revivalism: The American Experience, 1830–1900.* Notre Dame: University of Notre Dame Press, 1978.

Dowling, Margaret B. "Development of the Catholic Church in the District of Columbia from Colonial times Until the Present." *RCHS* 15 (1912): 23–53.

Duhamel, James F. "Tiber Creek." *RCHS* 28 (1926): 203–28.

Durkin, Joseph T. *William Matthews: Priest and Citizen.* New York: Benziger Brothers, 1963.

Eckert, Joseph C. *Souvenir Book of the One Hundredth Anniversary St. Joseph's Home and School.* Washington, 1955.

Ellis, John Tracy. *Documents of American Catholic History.* Milwaukee: Bruce Publ., 1956.

————. *The Life of James Cardinal Gibbons, Archbishop of Baltimore, 1834–1921.* 2 vols. Milwaukee: Bruce Publ., 1952.

Fenning, H. *The Undoing of the Friars of Ireland.* Louvain: University of Louvain, 1972.

Fitzsimons, Raymund. *Garish Lights; The Public Reading Tours of Charles Dickens.* Philadelphia: J. B. Lippincott, 1970.

Foley, Albert S. "The Catholic Church and the Washington Negro." Ph.D. dissertation, University of North Carolina, 1950.

Fosselman, David H. "Transitions in the Development of a Downtown Parish: A Study of Adaptions to Ecological Change in St. Patrick's Parish, Washington, D.C." Ph.D. dissertation, The Catholic University of America, 1952.

Frye, Virginia. "St. Patrick's—First Catholic Church of the Federal City." *RCHS* 23 (1920): 26–51.

Gemmill, Jane W. *Notes on Washington, or Six Years at the National Capital.* Washington: Brentano Bros., 1883.

Gillard, John T. *The Catholic Church and the Negro.* Baltimore, 1928.

Gleason, Philip, ed. *Documentary Reports on Early American Catholicism.* New York: Arno Press, 1978.

"Gonzaga College." *Woodstock Letters* 18 (1889): 269–84, and 19 (1890): 3–22, 163–78.

Goode, James M. *Capital Losses.* Washington: Smithsonian Press, 1979.

Gordon, Martin K. "The Militia of the District of Columbia, 1790–1815." Ph.D. dissertation, George Washington University, 1975.

Green, Constance McLaughlin. *The Secret City: A History of Race Relations in the Nation's Capital.* Princeton: Princeton University Press, 1967.

————. *Washington A History of the Capital, 1800–1950.* 2 vols. Princeton: Princeton University Press, 1976.

Griffin, Martin I. J. "St. Patrick's Church, Washington." *American Catholic Historical Researches.* n. s. (1905): 64–65.

Guilday, Peter A. *The Life and Times of John Carroll: Archbishop of Baltimore, 1735–1815.* 2 vols. New York: Encyclopedia Press, 1922.

————. *The Life and Times of John England.* 2 vols. New York: America Press, 1927.

Hanley, Thomas O., ed. *The John Carroll Papers.* 3 vols. Notre Dame: University of Notre Dame Press, 1976

Hesburgh, Theodore. *God, Country, Notre Dame.* New York: Doubleday, 1990.

Hickey, Matthew E. "Irish Catholics in Washington Up to 1860." Master's thesis, The Catholic University of America, 1933.

Hines, Christian. *Early Recollections of Washington City.* Washington: 1866; repr. Junior League of Washington, 1981.

Hinkel, John V. "St. Patrick's: Mother Church of Washington." *RCHS* 57–58 (1960): 33–43.

Hughes, Sister Virginia, ed. *Through His Eyes: A Memoir of Bishop Thomas Lyons.* Washington: Abbeyfeale Press, 1991.

Hughes, Thomas. *History of the Society of Jesus in North America: Colonial and Federal.* 4 vols. London: Longmans, Green & Co., 1907–17.

Hunt, Gaillard, ed. *The First Forty Years of Washington Society, In the Family Letters of Margaret Bayard Smith.* New York: Frederick Ungar Pub., 1906.

Johnson, Lorenzo D. *The Churches and Pastors of Washington, D.C.* New York: Dodd, 1857.

Kelly, Joseph T. "Memories of a Lifetime in Washington." *RCHS* 31–32 (1930): 117–49.

Kenrick–Frenaye Correspondence, 1839–1852. Philadelphia: Wickersham Printing, 1920.

Kirk, Elsie K. *Music at the White House: A History of the American Spirit.* Urbana: University of Illinois Press, 1986.

Klein, Abbé Felix. *In the Land of the Strenuous Life.* Chicago: A. C. McClurg and Co., 1905.

Kuhn, Sister M. Campion. "The Sisters Go East—and Stay." Paper delivered at Congregation of the Sisters of the Holy Cross Annual Historical Conference, 1983.

Latrobe, Benjamin H. *The Journal of Latrobe, Being the Notes and Sketches of an Architect, Naturalist and Traveler in the United States from 1796 to 1820.* New York: Appleton & Co., 1905.

Lord, Walter. *The Dawn's Early Light.* New York: W. W. Norton, 1972.

McColgan, Daniel T. *A Century of Charity: The First One Hundred Years of St. Vincent de Paul in the United States.* 2 vols. Milwaukee: Bruce Publ., 1951.

McHale, Sister M. Loretta. "The Catholic Church in the District of Columbia, 1866–1938." Master's thesis, The Catholic University of America, 1938.

Maloney, Sister M. Xavier. "The Catholic Church in the District of Columbia (Earlier Period: 1790–1866)." Master's thesis, The Catholic University of America, 1938.

Marschall, John P. "Francis Patrick Kenrick, 1851–1863: The Baltimore Years." Ph.D. dissertation, The Catholic University of America, 1965.

Matthews, William. *A Collection of Affidavits and Certificates Relative to the Wonderful Cure of Mrs. Ann Mattingly.* Washington, 1824.

Meade, William. *Old Churches, Ministers, and Families of Virginia.* Philadelphia: Lippincott, 1857.

Metzger, Charles H. *Catholics and the American Revolution.* Chicago: Loyola University Press, 1962.

Misch, Edward J. "The American Bishops and the Negro from the Civil War to the Third Plenary Council of Baltimore (1865–1884)." Ph.D. dissertation, Pontifical Gregorian University, 1968.

Moore, W. G. "Notes of Colonel W. G. Moore, Private Secretary to President Johnson, 1866–1868." *American Historical Review* 19 (Oct 1913): 98–132.

Murtha, Ronin J. "The Life of the Most Reverend Ambrose Maréchal; Third Archbishop of Baltimore, 1768–1829." Ph.D. dissertation, The Catholic University of America, 1965.

Nevils, Coleman. *Miniatures of Georgetown, 1634 to 1934 Tercentennial Causeries.* Washington: Georgetown Press, 1935.

Ochs, Stephen J. *Desegregating the Altar: The Josephites and the Struggle for Black Priests, 1871–1960.* Baton Rouge: Louisiana State University Press, 1990.

O'Connor, John J. "A Man's A Man for A' That." *Interracial Review* (June 1947).

O'Grady, John. *Catholic Charities in the United States: History and Problems.* Washington: National Conference of Catholic Charities, 1930.

Olson, James S. *Catholic Immigrants in America.* Chicago: Nelson-Hall, 1987.

Osofsky, Gilbert. "Abolitionists, Irish Immigrants, and the Dilemma of Romantic Nationalism." *American Historical Review* 80 (Oct 1975): 889–912.

Pablo, Jean M. "Washington and Its School System, 1900–1906." Ph.D. dissertation, Georgetown University, 1973.

Philibert, Helene, Estelle, and Imogene. *Saint Matthew's of Washington, 1840–1940.* Baltimore: A. Hoen and Co., 1940.

Piper, John F. Jr. *The American Churches in World War I.* Athens: Ohio University Press, 1985.

Porter, Sarah H. *The Life and Times of Anne Royall.* Cedar Rapids: Torch Press Book Shop, 1909.

Pribanic, Kenneth. *St. Patrick's in the City, A Tour.* Washington, 1989.

Procter, John Clagett, ed. *Washington Past and Present: A History.* New York: Lewis History Publ., 1930.

Scheips, Paul J. "The Washington Riot of 1968." U.S. Army Center of Military History, 1992.

Seale, William. *President's House: A History.* Washington: White House Historical Association, 1986.

Shannon, Fred A. *The Organization and Administration of the Union Army, 1861–1865.* 2 vols. Cleveland: Arthur Clark, 1928.

Shaughnessy, Gerald. *Has the Immigrant Kept the Faith: A Study of Immigration and Catholic Growth in the United States, 1790–1920.* New York: Macmillan, 1925.

Shehan, Lawrence J. *A Blessing of Years: The Memoirs of Lawrence Cardinal Shehan.* Notre Dame: University of Notre Dame Press, 1982.

Smith, Kathryn S. *Port Town to Urban Neighborhood: The Georgetown Waterfront.* Dubuque: Kendall/Hunt, 1989.

Smith, Milton E. *A History of St. Patrick's Church.* Washington, 1933.

Spalding, Thomas W. *The Premier See: A History of the Archdiocese of Baltimore, 1789–1989.* Baltimore: The Johns Hopkins University Press, 1989.

———. *Martin John Spalding: American Churchman.* Washington: The Catholic University of America Press, 1973.

Sullivan, Eleanore C. *Georgetown Visitation Since 1799.* Baltimore: French-Bray, 1975.

Thornton, Mrs. William. "The Diary of Mrs. William Thornton." *RCHS* 10 (1907): 88–226.

Topham, Washington. "Northern Liberty Market." *RCHS* (1922): 43–66.

Veddes, Sarah E. *Reminiscences of the District of Columbia or Washington City Seventy-nine Years Ago, 1830–1909.* St. Louis: A. R. Fleming, 1909.

Walter, Jacob A. "The Surratt Case. A True Statement of Facts Concerning this Notable Case." *United States Catholic Historical Magazine* 3 (Dec 1890): 353–61.

Walter, Joseph M., ed. *A Memorial Tribute to Rev. J. A. Walter, Late Pastor of St. Patrick's Church, Washington, D.C.* Washington: Stormont and Jackson, 1895.

Warden, David B. *A Chronological and Statistical Description of the District of Columbia, the Seat of the General Government to the United States.* Paris: Smith, 1816.

Wentz, Charles H., ed. *Inventory of Records of St. Patrick's Church and School.* Washington: Library of Congress, 1941.

Weitzman, Louis G. *One Hundred Years of Catholic Charities in the District of Columbia.* Washington: The Catholic University of America, 1931.

Wilson, J. Ormond. "Eighty Years of the Public Schools of Washington—1805 to 1885." *RCHS* 1 (1895): 3–232.

Yeager, Sister M. Hildegarde. "The Life of James Roosevelt Bayley, First Bishop of Newark and Eighth Archbishop of Baltimore, 1814–1877." Ph.D. dissertation, The Catholic University of America, 1947.

Young, James S. *The Washington Community 1800–1828.* New York: Columbia University Press, 1966.

A Parish for the Federal City: St. Patrick's in Washington, 1794–1994 was designed and composed in Monotype Dante by Kachergis Book Design of Pittsboro, North Carolina. It was printed on 60 lb. Glatfelter Smooth and bound by Braun-Brumfield, Inc. of Ann Arbor, Michigan.